# Families in Rural America: Stress, Adaptation and Revitalization

edited
by
Ramona Marotz-Baden
Charles B. Hennon
Timothy H. Brubaker

National Council on Family Relations,
St. Paul, Minnesota, 1988

*For information address:*

National Council on Family Relations
1910 W. County Road B #147
St. Paul, MN 55113
612/633-6933

Printed in the United States of America

International Standard Book Number 0-916174-21-2

**Acknowledgement**
Original quilt design created by Jean Humenansky of the Country Peddler Quilt Shop in St. Paul, Minnesota.

FIRST PRINTING

HQ
535
.F315
1988

# Table of Contents

# Acknowledgements

A large crew contributed to the completion of this project. We would like to express appreciation to a number of individuals who helped to "steer this vessel into port!" The National Council on Family Relations' support has been enormous. Mary Jo Czaplewski has devoted numerous hours to this project and her leadership is appreciated. Hamilton McCubbin (Past-President), Graham Spanier (President), and Charles Figley (Publications Chair) have provided guidance and encouragement throughout the development of this book.

Since many of the chapters in this book were originally published as a special issue of *Family Relations*, gratitude is extended to the persons who diligently reviewed numerous manuscripts. These reviewers include Craig M. Allen, Karen Altergott, Margaret Arcus, DeeVon Bailey, Kenneth Barber, Pauline Boss, Fred Bozett, Gregory Brock, Ellie Brubaker, Jane Cardea, Charles L. Cole, Marilyn Coleman, John Crosby, Paula Dail, Christann Dean, Mary Dellmann-Jenkins, Peggye Dilworth-Anderson, Bill Doherty, Cheryl Evans, C. R. Figley, Mark Fine, Judy Fischer, Lawrence Ganong, Catherine Gillis, Karen P. Goebel, Gary L. Hansen, Shirley Hanson, Judy Hooper, Robert Hughes, Robert W. Jackson, Carl Jantzen, Cynthia Johnson, Jim Johnson, Anthony Jurich, Norah Keating, Patricia K. Knaub, Robert Larzeiere, Joseph T. Lawton, Bob Lewis, Rebecca P. Lovingood, Carol MacKinnon, Michael J. Martin, Hamilton McCubbin, Patrick McKenry, Joyce Mercier, Cynthia Meyer, Patricia Nelson, Jeanette K. Newhouse, Sharon Nichols, Rosalie Huisinga Norem, Dennis Orthner, Angie Parsons, Gary Peterson, Phyllis Pirner, William Reid, Karen A. Roberto, Bryan Robinson, Mark Roosa, Paul C. Rosenblatt, Candyce S. Russell, Sonya Salamon, Jean Pearson Scott, Stephen Small, Susan Steinmetz, Mary Stephenson, Gary Strauss, Patricia Voydanoff, James Walters, Lynda Walters, Randy R. Weigel, Emily S. Wiggins, Stephan M. Wilson, and Britton Wood. Each of these individuals provided excellent reviews of the manuscripts submitted for the special issue on rural families.

Robin Heltzel, Samantha Inskeep and Justine Kennedy from the Family and Child Studies Center at Miami University provided assistance at the copy editing and proofreading stages. Their attention to detail is recognized. Mary Tharp provided immeasurable assistance in the project. She was deeply involved at every stage and, without her "beyond the call of duty" help, the end would not have been realized. Special gratitude is extended to Agnes for her meticulous attention to numbers. Thanks to all the crew, we're done!

Ramona Marotz-Baden
Charles B. Hennon
Timothy H. Brubaker

# Foreword

The Nelson family was in trouble. They remember the event of two years past as if it just occurred . . . a second ago. The county sheriff knocked on the door of their Wisconsin home to foreclose on the property they had received from their parents, and their parents before them. As soon as the Federal Land Bank bought their 120-acre farm in Rhinelander, Mrs. Nelson, 33 years old took on the challenge of sewing children's clothes to sell at fairs and craft shows, turning her long-time hobby into a profession. Initially, the money she earned put food on the table and a little spending money in the hands of her two young children, ages 9 and 10, both boys. Eventually, after a year of searching, Mr. Nelson got on his feet and became fully employed, but Mrs. Nelson's income still pays for the family's car insurance and helps with those unexpected expenses.

There are similar real and touching stories across rural North America, where farmers frustrated by the years of sharply fluctuating income are turning to their families, their communities, and within themselves to find ways to cope with the unstable economic condition and to create a life for themselves in rural North America.

The picture is not all bleak! Families have been quite creative, seizing crises such as this to build a new and maybe even better life. They have also been part of an emerging entrepreneurship, creating small businesses mostly built around traditional home economics activities of cooking, sewing, and other traditional skills taught in 4-H clubs. In a recent article, the *New York Times* reported on several noteworthy success stories:

- In Iowa three women started using other farm women to finish jogging suits. Today their company, Bordeaux Inc. has emerged as one of the Midwest's largest farm-based enterprises with an annual gross sales of about 3 million dollars;

- In Nebraska a woman started an enterprise called Sweeter Measures, a mail-order company that makes clothing for large-size women. Today she employs six local women and estimates her gross sales for 1987 at $100,000.

- In another Nebraska town, a woman started making and selling wood-and-fabric home decorations on her farm five years ago. Today her company, Betsy Bobbins Inc., has 40 employees and grosses about 1 million dollars in sales to gift and department stores.

Families do suffer and experience extreme hardships—the threat to or actual loss of part of themselves and their self worth. Suicides, while infrequent, do occur even in those families that their friends would have judged to be indestructible. But not all families fall apart in the face of such crises. Some families such as those in Iowa and Nebraska see the crises as windows of opportunity and muster the skills to make something out of nothing.

How farm and rural families respond to crises varies from family to family and situation to situation. But there are common threads, common experiences, feelings, and reactions which can be described, documented, and shared with others. This anthology is about these common threads and experiences in farm and rural families. It is about the hardships families may experience, the coping strategies they may employ, and the economic and social consequences of an unstable economic situation—on the internal workings of the family unit. This book is also about strengths in families and how they cultivate, motivate, and inspire from within and among others, the ability to press forward, even to recover. This book is about resources to support families in crises and what can be done to help them through these difficult times; it is about families in need and with a special feeling about the quality of life in rural America.

Guided by theory and research but with an appropriate emphasis upon how families can be helped, counseled, and educated to survive and endure, the editors have compiled a coherent collection of scholarly work to shed light upon the plight of rural families. Predictably, this book offers a unique and insightful perspective to the trials and tribulations of this special group of families who invested in rural America.

Hamilton I. McCubbin
University of Wisconsin–Madison
Charles R. Figley
Purdue University

# Rural Families: Characteristics and Conceptualization

## Charles B. Hennon and Timothy H. Brubaker*

The investigation of rural families is an important but, at times, neglected focus of family scholars' research and teaching. During the 1980's several volumes have been devoted to the study of rural society (Coward & Lee, 1985; Coward & Smith, 1983; Dillman & Hobbs, 1982). Yet, there still are a number of issues which have not been fully addressed in the study of rural families. For example, how do rural (non-farm and farm) families deal with economic stressors? How have rural families adapted to the recent changes in rural America? What action can be taken to strengthen rural family life?

A bias against scholarly work on farm families has been noted by Rosenblatt, Nevaldine, and Titus (1978). Two reasons cited for this bias are that only a small proportion of the population engage in agricultural production, and the differences between farm and nonfarm families tend to be small in the United States. However, Rosenblatt et al. argued that farm families differ from other families in some theoretically important ways. This bias against studying farm families has prevented scholars the opportunity to understand interaction in all families. While it has been asserted that rural families do not differ greatly from urban families (Schumm & Bollman, 1981), the lim-ited theoretical and empirical work on rural families may obscure the differences. Thus, continued study of rural families is necessary.

Recently, there appears to be an increase in interest in rural families by family scholars (Hennon & Marotz-Baden, 1987). This increased focus, partially due to the "farm crisis" but perhaps partially stimulated by the reverse migration trend (that is, from urban to rural areas; Clifford, Heaton, Voss, & Fuguitt, 1985; Fuguitt, 1985; Fuguitt & Tordella, 1980; Longino, Wiseman, Biggar, & Flynn, 1984; Wardwell, 1982) has resulted in the publication of a number of books on a variety of family topics. These books have addressed general trends in rural society (Dillman & Hobbs, 1982), the delivery of family services (Coward & Smith, 1983), the aged in rural society (Coward & Lee, 1985), and rural family patterns (Coward & Smith, 1981).

A number of research and applied articles on rural families can now be found in professional journals. For example, attention has been given to the stress experienced by rural families and their members (Berkowitz & Perkins, 1985; Heffernan & Heffernan, 1986; Olson & Schellenberg, 1986; Rosenblatt & Keller, 1983), how to provide effective therapy and other interventions in rural areas (Bagarozzi, 1982; Blundall, 1986; Jackson, 1983; Jurich, Smith, & Polson, 1983), and how to reach rural families with family life education efforts (Crawford, 1986; Edmondson et al., 1985; Hennon & Peterson, 1981). Often a comparative approach has been taken, comparing rural with urban families (Bokemeier, Sachs, & Keith, 1983;

*Charles B. Hennon, Professor and Chair, Department of Home Economics and Consumer Sciences, and Associate Director, Family and Child Studies Center, Miami University, Oxford, Ohio 45056. Timothy H. Brubaker, Professor, Department of Home Economics and Consumer Sciences, and Director, Family and Child Studies Center, Miami University, Oxford, Ohio 45056.

Marotz-Baden & Colvin, 1986), or using rural-urban place of residence as an important variable (Gerner & Zick, 1983). Other scholars have focused on important family phenomena, and have investigated rural families in depth or have drawn rural/urban comparisons.

In addition to differences and similarities noted concerning family interactions, differences in demographic indices (such as the proportion of the population that is elderly, Clifford, Heaton, Voss, & Fuguitt, 1985) have been noted. Racial, ethnic, and subcultural variations have been documented (Christopherson, 1979; Hawkes, Kutner, Wells, Christopherson, & Almirol, 1981; Peterson, Stivers, & Peters, 1986; Salamon, 1987; Savells, 1985/1986), as well as issues related to migrant farm workers (Smith & Coward, 1981).

These examples are not all inclusive of the topics of interest to researchers or practitioners in the rural families arena nor are the citations intended to be exhaustive. A review of current periodicals will show the diversity of topics currently being investigated, the reemergence of rural families as target populations, or rurality as an important research variable.

This recent interest in rural families or rurality raises two questions. First, are rural families really different from urban families? If comparative studies are not done, it is easy to assume that rural families are different in theoretically important ways from other families. Studies that investigate some aspect of rural families, without corresponding investigations of urban families, would seem to be making this implicit assumption. While it is important to know how farm families manage stress, it is also important to know if this differs in any meaningful way from how other families respond to stressors. Investigation of rural families can help specify, clarify, and provide data for customized intervention programs, while comparative studies can help generalize, build theory, and provide a broader database.

One approach to answering the first question of differences is to first provide baseline demographic data. The next section of this chapter provides census data on selected characteristics of families in the United States showing some structural commonalities and differences among farm, rural, and urban families. Some attention is also given to possible differences in values and familism. Other chapters in this book provide reviews of other key rural-urban differences and commonalities.

The second question arising from the study of rural families is defining what, exactly, is a rural family? Or perhaps more importantly, what is it about rural residence or family rurality that makes it an important variable? Place of residence is often considered an important independent variable (e.g., Gerner & Zick, 1983), although occasionally some aspect of rurality is considered. Rural-urban is often treated as a dichotomous variable. Sometimes rural-urban is noted as a continuum. However, analysis may be conducted as if the variable was dichotomous rather than continuous, thus treating families as "rural" or "urban" rather than examining degree of rurality or urbanism.

One approach to answering this second set of questions is the development of a widely accepted definition of rural, or family rurality, that is theoretically and empirically useful. The last section of this chapter will review this definition dilemma and lay the groundwork for the development of a multidimensional conceptualization of family rurality-urbanity.

## Some Selected Characteristics of Farm, Rural, and Urban Families

Major differences may not exist between rural and urban family dynamics (Schumm & Bollman, 1981). Some (e.g., Burchinal, 1964; Hennon & Marotz-Baden, 1987) have suggested that there has been and will continue to be a convergence of rural and urban values and lifestyles. However, there are some persistent demographic characteristics, family structure variables, ecological factors, and life chances that characterize rural life. This section will describe some commonalities and differences among farm, rural, and urban families.

*General Characteristics:* The United States Bureau of the Census (1982) defines urban and rural as type-of-area concepts rather than specific areas outlined on maps. The urban population comprises all persons living in urbanized areas and in places of 2,500 or more inhabitants outside of urbanized areas; the rural population consists of everyone else. A rural classification does not necessarily imply farm residence or a sparsely settled area since a small town is rural as long as it is outside an urbanized area, and has fewer than 2,500 inhabitants. An urbanized area is defined as a population concentration of at least 50,000 inhabitants, generally consisting of a central city and the surrounding, closely settled, contiguous territory (suburbs).

According to the 1980 census (U.S. Bureau of the Census, 1983: Table 72) there were 59,491,167 persons living in rural areas. This was 26.3% of the 226,545,805 total persons in the United States. Of the total rural inhabitants, 7,034,378 (11.8%) lived in places with a population of 1,000–2,500; the other 52,456,789 (88.2%) lived in other rural areas. The number living on rural farms was 5,617,903; 9.4% of all rural persons or 2.5% of the total U.S. population. The median age of rural persons in 1980 was 30.2 years (35.8 years for farm residents). This compared to 30.0 years for urban residents (U.S. Bureau of the Census, 1983: Table 98). Of the total rural population, 18,447,649 or 31% were under 18 years of age. Of this group 84.0% lived with two parents. Persons under 18 totaled 1,602,806 or 28.5% of persons on farms; 92.8% lived with two parents. Comparative percentages for urban areas were 27.1% and 73.7% (U.S. Bureau of the Census, 1983: Table 100).

*Rural Racial and Ethnic Groupings:* Although primarily white, the rural population is composed of several other racial or ethnic groupings. In 1980 (U.S. Bureau of the Census, 1983: Table 74) whites made up the vast majority of rural inhabitants (54,086,986; 90.9%) followed by Blacks (3,898,504; 6.6%) and American Indians (671,933; 1.1%). Other groupings and their proportion of the rural population were: Japanese (60,097; 0.1%), Filipino (59,308; 0.1%), Hawaiian (30,538; .05%), Asian Indian (30,138; .05%), Eskimo (28,888; .05%), Korean (25,256; .04%), Chinese (24,630; .04%), Vietnamese (11,607; .02%), Aleut (6,440; .01%), Guamanian (2,560; .004%), Samoan (1,600; .003%), other Asian and Pacific Islanders (9,902; .02%), and others (542,780; 0.9%).

*Family Composition and Employment:* The total number of rural families in 1980 was 16,184,466, of which 1,618,992 or 10% were farm families. Rural families represented 27.3% (and the subset of farm families equalled 2.7%), of all families in the United States. In rural areas in 1980 there were 14,360,688 married couple families. This was 88.7% of all rural families, which compared to 80.5% of all urban families. Female householders with no husband present totaled 8,205,279 in 1980. Of this total 1,359,735, or 16.6%, were rural, representing 8.4% of all rural families; 57,621 were farm families representing 3.6% of all farm families. In urban areas female householders with no husband present comprised 15.9% of all families. Of the female headed families in rural areas, 55.5% had children under 18 and 17.0% had children under six. The comparative statistics for urban areas were 61.0% and 21.5%. In 1980, approximately 1% of all rural families and 3% of all urban families were female headed, no husband present, and with own children under the age of six (U.S. Bureau of the Census, 1983: Table 100).

The marital histories of ever-married persons age 15-54 years (rural population = 23,290,652 or 27.7%; urban = 61,416,481 or 72.3%) showed some slight rural-urban differences in 1980. In rural areas, 78.1% of this group had never been widowed or divorced compared to 73.4% in urban areas. About 3.0% of both the rural and urban persons in this grouping had been widowed, and approximately 19.4% of rural versus 24.0% of urban persons in this grouping had been divorced. Within the rural population of ever married persons age 15-54 years, 1,999,980 (8.5%) lived on farms. Of this group, 86% had never been widowed or divorced while approximately 2.0% had been widowed and 11.5% divorced (U.S. Bureau of the Census, 1983: Table 100).

Rural dual-employed families total 5,513,621 in 1980. This was 38.4% of all (14,360,688) rural married couple families. Urban dual-employed couples totaled 14,682,316 which was 42.4% of all urban married couple families. Of all married couple families in the U.S., 41.2% were dual employed families in 1980. Of all married couple families, 30.0% were dual-employed families living in urban areas, while 11.3% were dual-employed families living in rural areas. Fifty percent of rural female householders with no husband present were employed compared to 56.3% of their urban counterparts. A total of 534,959 rural families had unemployed husbands in 1980. This was 3.7% of all rural married couple families. A total of 1,012,160 urban families had unemployed husbands in the same year. This was 2.9% of all urban married couple families. Both husbands and wives were unemployed in 45,432 rural married couple families 1980. This was less than 1% of all rural married couple families. An additional 260,580 (.02%) rural families had unemployed husbands and wives not in the labor force (U.S. Bureau of the Census, 1983: Table 100).

In 1983, the unemployment rates (U.S. Bureau of Labor Statistics, 1985: Table 10) for men, 20 years of age and over, were 10.7 in central cities, 7.6 in suburbs, 9.9 for non-farm residents, and 3.2 for farm residents. The comparative statistics for women were 9.0, 7.0, 9.1, and 4.3. Wide differences were recorded by race and Hispanic origin. For whites the unemployment rates were 8.5 in central cities, 7.7 in suburbs, 9.7 for non-farm residents, and 3.9 for farm residents. For Blacks, the rates were respectively 21.2, 16.3, 19.1, and 14.6. The comparative statistics for those of Hispanic origin were 13.1, 13.0, 17.4, and not ascertained due to the small number living on farms. However, for 1982 this unemployment rate was 18.8.

*Travel Time to Work:* Workers in both rural and urban areas reported about the same travel time to work. Rural workers had a mean travel time of 22.4 minutes vis-à-vis 21.5 minutes for urban workers. Of those traveling 45 or more minutes, rural workers had a mean of 60.4 minutes and urban workers a mean of 59.4 minutes (U.S. Bureau of the Census, 1983: Table 101).

*Characteristics of older persons:* The number of persons aged 60 and over in rural areas in 1980 was 9,175,047. This was 15.4% of the rural population. The same age group made up approximately the same percent of the urban population. Persons 75 years of age or older, often considered to be the elderly most at risk, total 2,365,642 or 4.0% of the rural population, about the same as in urban areas. Of the older rural residents, 1,066,781 lived on farms. This was 11.6% of the rural population aged 60 or older. Four percent of farm residents were aged 75 years or older. This was 3.8% of the total rural population (U.S. Bureau of the Census, 1983: Table 98).

Of the 4,131,978 rural persons aged 65 to 74 years, 3,174,214 or 78.6% lived in families. Of this group 11.7% had 1979 incomes below the poverty level. In this same age group 837,712 (20.3%) lived alone, and

34.6% percent were below the poverty level. Homes for the aged were the residence of 45,025 or 1.1% of this rural age group. Of the 11,458,130 urban persons aged 65 to 74 years, 8,010,305 or 69.9% lived in families. Of this group 5.8% had 1979 incomes below the poverty level. A total of 2,912,341 (25.4%) urban persons in this age group lived alone, and 23.3% were below the poverty level. Those in homes for the aged totaled 193,937 or 1.7% of this urban age group (U.S. Bureau of the Census, 1983: Table 98).

Further differences between rural and urban areas in the elderly's living arrangements and percent living in poverty were found among the group of persons aged 75 years and over. In rural areas, 1,380,707 or 58.4% lived in families compared to 3,867,870 or 51.3% in urban areas. While 15.6% of this age group living in families in rural areas were below the poverty level, only 7.2% of the comparative urban group were below the poverty level. Living alone were 747,252 (31.6%) rural persons aged 75 years or older. Of this group, 42.7% were living in poverty. Comparative urban figures and percentages were 2,569,234 (34.1%) with 28.1% living below the poverty level. Homes for the aged contained 178,390 rural residents aged 75 years and over. This represented 7.5% of this age group in rural areas. In urban areas, 815,606 (10.8%) persons aged 75 years and over lived in homes for the aged (U.S. Bureau of the Census, 1983: Table 98).

Nonmetropolitan areas experienced a net growth of 106,935 in their elderly (aged 65 years and above) populations between 1975 and 1980 (Golant, 1987). This is in spite of the fact that 21% of the mobile rural elderly population, or 4.2% of the total rural elderly population, moved to metropolitan areas. The moving patterns of the elderly did not differ from the 45 to 64 age group, but did differ from the under-45 age group. This might suggest preferences for rural or urban living do not change dramatically from late middle to older age. Golant (1987, p. 538) concluded, as did Longino (1980) who studied 1975–1980 migration, that the shifts of the elderly people "hardly [represent] a strong current of migration away from the great centers of commerce and industry." The net effects on rural areas of this migration between urban and rural places by the elderly was thus small in terms of numbers. However, the social-psychological impacts, changes in service demands, economic repercussions, and political climate changes are not necessarily known, and may be greater in selected locations.

*Value Systems and Familism:* Rural families and individuals may differ from urban counterparts in terms of their value systems and related attitudes (England, Gibbons, & Johnson, 1979; Fischer, 1975; Glenn & Hill, 1977). Some evidence has suggested that rural individuals are more conservative and value family and community interaction. Urban individuals are reported to be less conservative and to value economic and cultural aspects of community life. Rural men and women are also believed to have more traditional gender role ideologies (Bescher-Donnelly & Smith, 1981; Hennon & Photiadis, 1979). A study by England, Gibbons, and Johnson (1979) suggested that a rural environment (as defined by population density and percent of labor force employed in agriculture) resulted in a greater importance for kindness, physical development, honesty, religion, self-control, intellectualism, social skills, status, and creativity. However, mining appeared to be related only to honesty, self-control, and creativity, and the additional value of independence. These results supported Warner's (1974) contention of value diversity *within* rural environments. The work of Heller and Quesanda (1977) found empirical support for regional differences among rural families in degree of familism, or the maintenance of kin-group cohesiveness through use of rights and obligations pertaining to members of a given kin network. Their work suggested two distinct forms of rural familism in the United States: extended kin-oriented and primary kin-oriented.

## A Multidimensional Conceptualization of Rurality-Urbanity

Any serious consideration of rural families, or families in rural settings, raises the question of what constitutes a rural area or a rural family. The difficulty of defining rurality has been discussed by many authors and a clear definition has eluded scholars for some time (Heller & Quesanda, 1977). This dilemma has been addressed in a variety of ways. One easy but conceptually imprecise way is to assert that we all know what a rural

area is and we all know what an urban area is when we see them. The debate is thus on the boundaries of these areas. When does urban become rural? One study (Christopherson, 1979) suggested that rural was "something of which everyone has a reasonably accurate concept, but which can be defined in a variety of ways" (page 65). This study then operationalized rural as implying a community of less than one-half the size of the census criterion of 2,500 inhabitants, outdoor privies and relative lack of indoor plumbing, poor housing, unpaved roads, lack of sewers, and few recreational facilities or social services.

The United States Bureau of the Census has defined the urban population to include everyone living in an urbanized area or in a place of 2,500 or more people. The rural population thus includes everyone living elsewhere. An urbanized area comprises an incorporated place and densely settled surrounding areas that together have a population of 50,000 or more people (Clifford, Heaton, Voss, & Fuguitt, 1985). However if communities, open country, or unincorporated areas with a population of 2,500 or less are in close proximity to a large metropolitan area, are economically dependent upon the larger urban center, and are suburban-like in many of their characteristics, they are still defined as rural. This definition also excludes from the rural category many small towns (e.g., 5,000 to 10,000 population) that are important business, economic, and social centers for rural residents (Coward, 1983).

Another distinction has been suggested—metropolitan or nonmetropolitan (Coward, 1983). Metropolitan residents are those living in a Standard Metropolitan Statistical Area (SMSA) in which there is at least one city of 50,000 or more. The area is comprised of all contiguous counties socially and economically integrated with the urbanized area. Nonmetropolitan residents are all those living in counties not meeting the above criteria. The problems with the dichotomy are that many towns of approximately 40,000 have lost their rural flavor and are really small cities, and some communities that are rather rural and a good distance from the urbanized area are included in the SMSA simply because some counties are rather large (Coward, 1983).

As Coward (1983) so aptly noted, the use of a dichotomous approach has dulled appreciation of residence as a continuum. The extremities are significantly different; it is the multitude of small towns, villages, and cities that are less different and thus less easy to categorize. The use of a dichotomous approach has also implied that there is homogeneity within categories, which of course is not true. Their use has also implied that rural America has not kept pace with urban America. Heller and Quesanda (1977) suggested that attending to regional differences may allay some of the confusion in studies of rurality.

What is needed is a more complex conceptualization that recognizes the multidimensionality of what many researchers and practitioners have in mind when they consider rural families. This section will lay the theoretical groundwork for a multidimensional conceptualization of family rurality-urbanity that can be measured on a continuum. This conceptualization considers place of residence, but recognizes other factors that also give definition to family rurality-urbanity. This conceptualization starts with the premise that just because a family lives in open country, in a small town, or on a farm, does not necessarily mean that its values, world view, economic dependency, or lifestyle reflect rurality. This conceptualization accepts the fact that there is wide diversity between geographic locations and families living in these locations; for example, non-urbanized New England is not necessarily like non-urbanized Iowa or non-urbanized West Virginia. It also accepts the fact that there is diversity among families living within rural New England, just like there is diversity among those living on farms and in villages in Iowa and the hollows of West Virginia. This conceptualization recognizes that the critical dimensions of family rurality-urbanity includes more than just geographic location and population density.

Some variables set the physical and socioeconomic context. These variables include population size of the community, population density, and an economic base dependent upon the land (agricultural, mining, lumbering, or in some cases fishing), or based upon one or few industries. Other variables might include distance from an urban center, transportation access to an urban center, and the amount of community and social services, or at least easy access to them. Another important consideration may be access to and use of contemporary technology.

These variables, while they help define rural or urban, are neither necessary nor sufficient in capturing the spirit of family rurality-urbanity. It is suggested here that family rurality-urbanity is more than just where a family lives. Families living in urban areas may reflect rurality in values, world view, and many behaviors. Recent migrants to urban areas may typify this idea. Families and/or individuals living in rural areas may be urban in many ways, such as concern with financial markets, urban politics, social services, and urban fashions and trends. Examples might include recently retired couples moving to rural areas, young professionals, and youth aspiring to a different lifestyle.

It is suggested that a conceptualization of family rurality-urbanity needs to consider attitudes, value sets, behavioral patterns, and world views of families. While these may be conditioned by place of residence or origin, it is assumed here that there is no one-to-one correspondence. It is also suggested that there could be much diversity relative to these variables among families and individuals living in the same or similar regions.

From the above discussion, it is suggested that there are three components to what is to be captured by the concept of family rurality-urbanity. The first is a dimension determined by physical and socioeconomic criteria. These criteria set the context for determining the degree of rural or urban. This dimension is a continuum, and communities (and consequently families) can be located along this continuum based upon such characteristics as population size, population density, distance to urbanized centers, economic base, type of housing, and land use. Other important variables would be ease of transportation access to urbanized centers or communities with larger populations, and number of retail outlets, social services, and recreational opportunities.

Another, perhaps more subjective characteristic, is the community's orientation. Is it oriented toward an urbanized area (itself possibly), or toward a more rural area? For example, a community of 2,000 which is located 40 miles from a city of 500,000, which is connected through mass transit and/or super highways, and serves as a "bedroom community" for the large city is probably not rural in its orientation. On the other end of this orientation continuum would be a community of 2,000 located 100 miles from a larger community of 35,000 and which serves as the business, recreational, and residential center for families whose members are primarily employed in mining. This community's orientation would most likely be rural.

This first continuum then sets the *physical/socioeconomic* context or environment for measuring and/or defining whether a community is rural or urban (with rural as the left end point and urban as the right end point on the continuum). As mentioned earlier, there is no general agreement as to what constitutes rural or urban in this domain; the extremities are more easily defined than at the midpoints. However, by adopting multimeasures of this domain, the combination of scores could produce an index which would enable the placement of a community along this continuum.

The second component to the concept of family rurality-urbanity is a dimension determined by access to and use of *technology*. While the physical/socioeconomic continuum may be conceptualized as a horizontal dimension, the technological dimension can be visualized as a vertical axis. The end points of the continuum may be labeled as high (the upper end point) and low (the lower end point). The intent of this continuum is to place communities (and/or families) relative to their knowledge and use of technologies such as communication, medical and health developments, data and word processing, and industrial innovations. Some communities have more access to technologies and the latest developments than others. Families within these communities are consequently effected. On a more micro level, families have differentiated access to and/or use of technologies (e.g., microwaves, computers, satellite dishes, video recorders, drugs, agricultural production advances).

While not making the assumption that more is necessarily better, the upper end of this continuum would seem to be qualitatively as well as quantitatively different from the low end. Quality of life, or at least lifestyle, consequences would seem to be related to where a community and/or family fell along this continuum. For example, a family with easy access to lifesaving medical and health technology would seem to have different life chances than a family without this access. A farm family that uses the latest in agricultural technologies is different than one that does not. As an illustration, consider the family on a large incorporated farm in Indiana with its Amish neighbors, or a substance farm family in the Ozarks. Multimeasures of technology would be required to develop an index for this domain. Some might be community level measures, while others would be more micro or family level measures (for example, community availability versus individual family use of technology).

While the first two components establish the horizontal and vertical dimensions of the social space composing the family rurality-urbanity concept, the third component gives depth to the concept. The third component is the *meaning* domain [this is somewhat akin to Kantor and Lehr's (1975) concept], and is a more subjective and a family systems level component than the first two discussed. The meaning domain provides the cognitive and behavioral pathways to accessing if a family is more urbanized or ruralized, as traditionally defined, in its self-definition. The end points on this continuum are urbanized (in the foreground) and ruralized (in the background). This dimension taps the world view, values, attitudes, customs, rituals, and other behaviors. Certain patterns can be considered to be more traditionally urban (e.g., cosmopolitan in nature) while others can be considered more traditionally rural (e.g., self-worth defined through ownership of land).

This meaning domain is also similar to family paradigm as discussed by Reiss and Oliveri (1980). They note that the family's mode of conceptualizing its position in the world, during times of noncrisis, is in the background as a gentle coordinator of family affairs. During crisis the mode of conceptualization becomes more conspicuous. The family can be reorganized and new organization brought to its typical mode of construing events and the environment. This new system of constructs can be a point around which the family organizes. The force and pervasiveness of the construct system comes from its continuing role in providing family coherence. Reiss and Oliveri (1980) defined family paradigm as "that new idea or approach, born in crisis, which serves as a background and orienting idea or perspective to the family's problem solving and daily life. A family paradigm serves as a stable disposition for orientation whenever the family must actively construe a new situation" (p. 435). These underlying shared beliefs cannot easily be reported by the family. Often they must be inferred by observation.

A variety of variables would need to be measured in order to determine placement of families along the meaning continuum. Some examples of factors within the meaning domain would include self-worth defined through attachments to land, valuing family and community integration, valuing economic and cultural aspects of the community, orientation toward time and its use, definitions of self-sufficiency/interdependency, and valuing intellectualism, creativity, and honesty.

The combination of these three dimensions—physical/socioeconomic, technology, meaning—provides a metaphor of a three dimensional social space that captures the notion of family rurality/urbanity. While this is a theoretical concept, it is suggested here that it's components can be measured and a summary score developed to place families empirically within the matrix. The scores would be at least at the ordinal level of measurement and would allow use of a continuum rather than a dichotomy for research and intervention purposes.

It is important that the components of the concept of family rurality-urbanity not carry a negative connotation. The end points of the continuum listed above do not imply positive or negative; they simply imply a difference in degree along one of many theoretically important dimensions that appear to shape lifestyles and various resulting consequences. The empirical question is whether combining measures of the various dimensions is possible, and if this results in a useful index of family rurality to urbanity.

This chapter has only laid the theoretical groundwork to this conceptualization. Developing valid and reliable measures of these dimensions would appear to be a prudent next step, as well as determining how to combine them in theoretically meaningful ways to obtain an overall score that can be used to measure the degree of family rurality-urbanity. The "best" predictors among these dimensions could also be determined to achieve a more parsimonious instrument.

This index could then be used to disaggregate families from similar geographic regions (as well as aggregate families from dissimilar areas) along the family rurality-urbanity continuum. Research can determine if this is an important continuum and/or variable that helps better explain and predict family dynamics, behaviors, and consequences. Use of this conceptualization might allow more specificity and analytical insight.

## Summary

This chapter is threefold in its purpose. First, to indicate the importance of rural families, or at least rural-urban place of residence, as a research topic and/or variable. Second, this chapter provides some baseline demographic data on farm, rural, and urban families (as defined by the U.S. Bureau of the Census). Third, this chapter provides the theoretical groundwork for the development of a multidimensional conceptualization of the family rurality-urbanity continuum. It is suggested that this conceptualization will allow better explanation and prediction of family phenomena and lead to better theory building and intervention strategies.

REFERENCES

Bagarozzi, D. (1982). The family therapists role in treating families in rural communities: A general systems approach. *Journal of Marital and Family Therapy,* **8,** 51–57.

Berkowitz, A., & Perkins, H. (1985). Correlates of psychosomatic stress symptoms among farm women: A research note on farm and family functioning. *Journal of Human Stress,* **11,** 76–81.

Bescher-Donnelly, L., & Smith, L. (1981). The changing roles and status of rural women. In R. Coward & W. Smith, Jr. (Eds.), *The family in rural society* (pp. 167–185). Boulder, CO: Westview Press.

Blundall, J. (1986). The initial response from a community mental health center. *Human Services in the Rural Environment,* **10,** 30–31.

Bokemeier, J., Sachs, S., & Keith, V. (1983). Labor force participation of metropolitan, nonmetropolitan and farm women: A comparative study. *Rural Sociology,* **48,** 515–539.

Burchinal, L. (1964). The rural family of the future. In J. Copp (Ed.), *Our changing rural society: Perspectives and trends.* Ames, IA: Iowa State University Press.

Christopherson, V. (1979). Implications for strengthening family life: Rural Black families. In N. Stinnett, B. Chesser, & J. Defrain (Eds.), *Building family strengths: Blueprints for action* (pp. 63–72). Lincoln, NE: University of Nebraska.

Clifford, W., Heaton, T., Voss, P., & Fuguitt, G. (1985). The rural elderly in demographic perspective. In R. Coward & G. Lee (Eds.), *The elderly in rural society* (pp. 25–55). New York: Springer.

Coward, R. (1983). Serving families in contemporary rural America: Definitions, importance, and future. In R. Coward & W. Smith, Jr. (Eds.), *Family services: Issues and opportunities in contemporary rural America* (pp. 3–25). Lincoln, NE: University of Nebraska Press.

Coward, R., & Lee, G. (Eds.). (1985). *The elderly in rural society.* New York: Springer.

Coward, R., & Smith, W., Jr. (Eds.). (1981). *The family in rural society.* Boulder, CO: Westview Press.

Coward, R., & Smith, W., Jr. (Eds.). (1983). *Family services: Issues and opportunities in contemporary rural America.* Lincoln, NE: University of Nebraska Press.

Crawford, C. (1986). Response to the rural crisis: Missouri Cooperative Extension Service. *Human Services in the Rural Environment,* 10, 33–35.

Dillman, D., & Hobbs, D. (Eds.). (1982). *Rural society in the United States: Issues for the 1980's.* Boulder, CO: Westview Press.

Edmondson, J., Meyers-Wallis, J., Cudaback, D., Nuttall, P., Bower, D., Nelson, P., Martin, D., & Lingren, H. (1985). How effective are family life education programs? In R. Williams, H. Lingren, G. Rowe, S. Van Zandt, P. Lee, & N. Stinnett (Eds.), *Family strengths 6: Enhancement of interaction* (pp. 291–306). Lincoln, NE: Center for Family Strengths, University of Nebraska-Lincoln.

England, J., Gibbons, W., & Johnson, B. (1979). The impact of rural environment on values. *Rural Sociology,* 44, 119–136.

Fischer, C. (1975). The effect of urban life on traditional values. *Social Forces,* 53, 420–432.

Fuguitt, G. (1985). The nonmetropolitan turnaround. *American Review of Sociology,* 11, 259–280.

Fuguitt, G., & Tordella, S. (1980). Elderly net migration: The new trend of nonmetropolitan population change. *Research on Aging,* 2, 191–204.

Gerner, J., & Zick, C. (1983). Time allocation decisions in two-parent families. *Home Economics Research Journal,* 12, 145–158.

Glenn, N., & Hill, L., Jr. (1977). Rural-urban differences in attitudes and behavior in the United States. *Annals of the American Academy,* 429, 36–50.

Golant, S. (1987). Residential moves by elderly persons to U.S. central cities, suburbs, and rural areas. *Journal of Gerontology,* 42, 534–539.

Hawkes, G., Kutner, N., Wells, M., Christopherson, V., & Almirol, E. (1981). Families in cultural islands. In R. Coward & W. Smith, Jr. (Eds.), *The family in rural society* (pp. 87–126). Boulder, CO: Westview Press.

Heffernan, W., & Heffernan, J. (1986). Impact of the farm crisis on rural families and communities. *The Rural Sociologist,* 6, 160–170.

Heller, P., & Quesanda, G. (1977). Rural familism: An interregional analysis. *Rural Sociology,* 42, 220–240.

Hennon, C., & Marotz-Baden, R. (1987). From the guest co-editors. *Family Relations,* 36, 355–357.

Hennon, C., & Peterson, B. (1981). An evaluation of a family life education delivery system for young families. *Family Relations,* 30, 387–394.

Hennon, C., & Photiadis, J. (1979). The rural Appalachian low-income male: Changing role in a changing family. *The Family Coordinator,* 28, 608–615.

Jackson, R. (1983). Delivering services to families in rural America: An analysis of the logistics and uniqueness. In R. Coward & W. Smith, Jr. (Eds.), *Family services: Issues and opportunities in contemporary rural America* (pp. 69–86). Lincoln, NE: University of Nebraska Press.

Jurich, A., Smith, W., Jr., & Polson, C. (1983). Families and social problems: Uncovering reality in rural America. In R. Coward & W. Smith, Jr. (Eds.), *Family services: Issues and opportunities in contemporary rural America* (pp. 41–66). Lincoln, NE: University of Nebraska Press.

Kantor, D., & Lehr, W. (1975). *Inside the family: Toward a theory of family process.* San Francisco: Jossey-Bass.

Longino, C. (1980). Residential relocation of older people: Metropolitan and nonmetropolitan. *Research on Aging,* 2, 205–216.

Longino, C., Jr., Wiseman, R., Biggar, J., & Flynn, C. (1984). Aged metropolitan-nonmetropolitan migration streams over three census decades. *Journal of Gerontology,* 39, 721–729.

Marotz-Baden, R., & Colvin, P. (1986). Coping strategies: A rural-urban comparison. *Family Relations,* 35, 281–288.

Olson, K., & Schellenberg, R. (1986). Farm stressors. *American Journal of Community Psychology,* 14, 555–569.

Peterson, G., Stivers, M., & Peters, D. (1986). Family versus nonfamily significant others for the career decisions of low-income youth. *Family Relations,* 35, 417–425.

Reiss, D. & Oliveri, M. (1980). Family paradigm and family coping: A proposal for linking the family's intrinsic adaptive capacities to its responses to stress. *Family Relations,* 29, 431–444.

Rosenblatt, P., & Keller, L. (1983). Economic vulnerability and economic stress in farm couples. *Family Relations,* 32, 567–573.

Rosenblatt, P., Nevaldine, A., & Titus, S. (1978). Farm families: Relation of significant attributes of farming to family interaction. *International Journal of Sociology of the Family,* 8, 89–99.

Salamon, S. (1987). Ethnic determinants of farm community character. In M. Chibnik (Ed.), *Farm work and fieldwork: Anthropological perspectives on American agriculture* (pp. 167–188). Ithaca, NY: Cornell University Press.

Savells, J. (1985/1986). Survival and social change among the Amish in five communities. *Lifestyles: A Journal of Changing Patterns,* 8, 85–103.

Schumm, W., & Bollman, S. (1981). Interpersonal processes in rural families. In R. Coward & W. Smith, Jr. (Eds.), *The family in rural society* (pp. 129–146). Boulder, CO: Westview Press.

Smith, W., & Coward, R. (1981). The family in rural society: Images of the future. In R. Coward & W. Smith, Jr. (Eds.), *The family in rural society* (pp. 221–229). Boulder, CO: Westview Press.

United States Bureau of the Census. (1982). *1980 census of population and housing: User's guide* (PHC 80–R1–B). Washington, DC: U.S. Government Printing Office.

United States Bureau of the Census (1983). *1980 census of population, volume 1, characteristics* (PC 80–1–C1). Washington, DC: U.S. Government Printing Office.

United States Bureau of Labor Statistics. (1985). *Handbook of labor statistics* (Bulletin 2217). Washington, DC: U.S. Government Printing Office.

Wardwell, J. (1982). The reversal of nonmetropolitan migration loss. In D. Dillman & D. Hobbs (Eds.), *Rural society in the U.S.: Issues for the 1980s* (pp. 23–33). Boulder, CO: Westview Press.

Warner, K. (1974). Rural society in a post-industrial age. *Rural Sociology,* 34, 306–318.

# The History of Recent Farm Legislation: Implications for Farm Families*

Linda F. Little, Francine P. Proulx, Julia Marlowe, and Patricia K. Knaub**

In order to understand what is happening to contemporary farm families, one must examine the changing structure of agriculture (Haney, 1982). The current economic crisis of many farmers[1] is hardly the first time major financial difficulties have been faced by this segment of American society. In fact, United States agricultural policy stems from the very creation of our country when colonials revolted against England's excessive taxation and control of agricultural exports (Rasmussen, 1985).

This chapter reviews from a historical perspective current major agricultural and financial legislation affecting today's farmer. First, it demonstrates that legislation was created in response to domestic social and economic conditions of the United States.

Secondly, it illuminates the impact of world economic conditions in recent years. The irrevocable inclusion of the American farm economy into the global macroeconomy in the 1970s will illustrate the complexity of the farm issue. Farm legislation in isolation cannot provide all the support necessary to improve the farmer's economic condition. Thirdly, the philosophical shift in emphasis of farm legislation from welfare of the farm family in the 1930s, to the commercialization of the farm in the 1970s, and to today's market orientation will be explored. Finally, it is argued that if family scientists are to understand what is happening to farm families today, the implications of the historical economic context within which these families are living must be examined.

Major legislation in the early 1900s began with the *Country Life Commission* appointed by President Theodore Roosevelt in 1908. As a result, over the next 10 years laws were passed that created better conditions for rural America. In 1914 the *Smith-Lever Act* created the Cooperative Extension Service, and in 1916 the *Federal Farm Loan Act* set up the structure for the Farm Credit System. However, it was not until the 1930s that the Federal Government instituted major farm programs which are the forerunners of those that exist today.

## History of Modern Farm Legislation

Much of the present farm legislation originated from policy developed during the

*Funds were made available for this project by the United States Department of Agriculture S-191 Research Project, Farm Wife's External Employment, Family Economic Productivity and Family Functioning, and the Virginia Agricultural Experiment Station. Special acknowledgement is extended to Dr. Wayne Rasmussen, Chief, USDA Agricultural History Branch, for validating the accuracy of this chapter's content.

**Linda F. Little is Associate Professor and Program Director of the Department of Family and Child Development, Virginia Polytechnic Institute and State University's Northern Virginia Graduate Center, 2990 Telestar Court, Falls Church, VA 22042. Francine P. Proulx is a graduate student in Marriage and Family Therapy at Virginia Polytechnic Institute and State University's Northern Virginia Graduate Center, 2990 Telestar Court, Falls Church, VA 22042. Julia Marlowe is Adjunct Assistant Professor of Family Economics at Virginia Polytechnic Institute and State University, Blacksburg, VA 24061. Patricia K. Knaub is Associate Professor, Department of Human Development and the Family, University of Nebraska-Lincoln, 104E Leverton Hall, Lincoln, NE 68583-0809.

Reprinted from *Family Relations*, 1987, **36**, 402–406.

1930s as part of the government's effort to struggle out of the Great Depression. The *Agricultural Adjustment Act of 1933* introduced the "first major price support" (Bowers, Rasmussen, & Baker, 1984, p. iv), a minimum price for a particular crop guaranteed by the government. This legislation also instituted a voluntary acreage reduction program decreasing the number of acres planted to meet market requirements. Intended to be a temporary measure for the 1930s agricultural emergency, this Act's provisions with modification are still in force (Rasmussen, 1985).

During the 1930s attention was also given to the unique characteristics of farming. These included natural disasters, irregular cash flow conditions, the need for loan terms longer than 90 days, and other conditions not present in the nonfarm credit market. Legislation was passed to resolve this credit gap for farmers creating government-sponsored credit agencies which made insured, guaranteed, and direct loans to farmers. Most significant were the creation of the *Resettlement Administration* (later to become the Farmers Home Administration), the *Commodity Credit Corporation,* and the *Farm Credit Administration* to oversee the Farm Credit System. Their major functions are discussed below.

The *Farmers Home Administration* (FmHA) is the "lead federal agency for providing financial and technical assistance to qualified farmers and rural communities who cannot find other sources of financing on terms or conditions they can meet" (Meekhof, 1984, p. 8). In addition to being the major lending source of last resort, FmHA administers farm and rural related programs and services through its county offices around the country.

The *Commodity Credit Corporation* (CCC) strengthens the farmer's income with nonrecourse loans using the commodity as collateral. When prices are high and profit is anticipated, farmers sell their commodities and pay off the loans. When prices are low, loss is avoided by forfeiting the commodity to the government as payment of the loans. The major attraction of CCC loans until the mid-1970s was an interest rate approximately 50% lower than other funding sources.

The *Farm Credit Administration* oversees all the financial operations making up the Farm Credit System. The Farm Credit System was initially created "to provide a

sound, reliable, and permanent credit source under all economic conditions to all regions and to all eligible producers and agriculture-related activities" (Meekhof, 1984, p. 19). In 1916 Federal Land Banks and Federal Land Bank Associations were created, followed in 1923 by the creation of Federal Intermediate Credit Banks. The system further expanded with the establishment in 1933 of Production Credit Associations and the Farm Credit Administration. These financial institutions are farmer-owned cooperatives in which the borrower buys stock. As discussed later, by 1985 this plan of a stable credit source had been undermined.

These programs continued to be modified, and new legislation was written in the 1940s and 1950s. However, the context of today's farm economic problems can be traced to a shift in the underlying premise of the policies begun in the 1930s (Meekhof, 1984). With the Depression of the 1930s, the policy thrust was in reestablishing economic stability through farm ownership, rather than farm tenancy, with a strong emphasis on the social welfare of the farm family. During the 1960s, there was a gradual policy change from the family focus of farming towards commercialization of the farm. This took place "in the midst of a technological revolution that was decreasing the number of farmers while greatly augmenting the productivity of those remaining on the land" (Bowers et al., 1984, p. 23).

## The Growth of the 1970s: Setting the Stage for the Farmers' Fall in the 1980s

### Legislation

The legislation of the 1970s, through expanded credit and government support, solidified the promotion of the commercialization of farming. With the rising value of land, farm families' major asset and collateral, many borrowed as never before to expand and meet growing global needs. When land values plummeted in the 1980s, farmers who had mortgaged assets to facilitate commercial expansion found themselves in severe financial difficulty. This, in turn, increased the stress on farm families.

A conducive financial environment for commercialization of farming was created by the *Farm Credit Act of 1971.* This legislation expanded the credit capability and flexibility of the farmer in a number of ways. Probably most significant was the increase in the percentage of appraised real estate value, from 65% to 85%, which could be used as collateral with Federal Land Banks. The *Rural Development Act of 1973* complemented this ability to borrow more funds with an increase from $35,000 to $50,000 in day-to-day farm operating loan ceilings. This Act also initiated federal loan guarantees for farm credit to commercial funding sources.

The shift in emphasis from family farming to commercial farming was confirmed with the *Agriculture and Consumer Protection Act of 1973*. This legislation "emphasized expanded production to meet world demand" (Bowers et al., 1984, p. v). Target prices, or set prices designated by legislation for particular crops, were introduced with this Act. Also initiated were deficiency payments, also called income supports, supplementing existing price supports. These government deficiency payments are made to farmers when market prices or price supports (guaranteed minimum prices) fall below target prices. It also lowered the maximum ceiling of government payments to farmers from $55,000 per crop to $20,000 per crop on certain commodities.

Prior to the introduction of target prices, projected government price supports were based on a parity formula. In very simplified terms, the government paid the farmer an amount per volume unit (i.e., bushel) with the same purchase power as in past years. In other words, if the government paid $2.50 for a bushel in one year and inflation had lowered the value of the dollar by 10%, the government would pay the farmer $2.75 a bushel the next year. The 1973 Act, with its 4-year life span, designated 1976 and 1977 target prices based on 1975 prices. These figures were based on the assumption of an increasing export market with high prices. However, the 1975 world recession prompted by the first oil crisis deflated prices. But in 1976, inflation returned. Thus, deficiency payments to farmers in 1976 and 1977 were low because the target price was tied to the low 1975 prices while market prices were again on the rise.

## Tax Policies

In addition to farm legislation, tax policies had an effect on farm management in the 1970s. Four specific policies that encouraged business investment in general will be discussed: investment tax credit, interest deductibility, corporate taxes, and estate taxes based on farm value.

In 1971 the investment tax credit, "a dollar-for-dollar reduction in tax liability" (Hrubovcak & LeBlanc, 1985, p. 9), was reinstituted into law. This credit favored short-lived assets (equipment), exclusive of land and, therefore, "a greater amount of benefit from the credit" (Hrubovcak & LeBlanc, 1985, p. 10). In other words, when farmers bought equipment with 3-year life spans, they could deduct one third of the cost from the amount of tax owed in the 3 successive tax years until 100% of the cost was deducted. "Nearly 20 percent of net investment in agricultural equipment during the period of 1956-78 is attributed to tax policy" (Hrubovcak & LeBlanc, 1985, p. 12). Investment tax credit is recognized as "probably the most effective tool in stimulating investment" (Hrubovcak & LeBlanc, 1985, p. 12).

The existing tax policy of interest deductibility also added an incentive for business-oriented farmers. They could expand by acquiring more land regardless of the level of interest rates. The interest deduction on income taxes lowered one's tax bracket and made long-term investment through credit an attractive alternative.

At the same time, corporate tax rates were lower than individual rates which resulted in 110% increase in corporate farms between 1974 and 1982 (Durst & Fromang-Milon, 1985). The incorporation of the family farm necessitates thinking of the farm as a legal business entity rather than a kinship operation. The rules and hierarchy, now formalized by state and federal law, become impersonal, binding, and relatively fixed and are no longer the result of the family's interaction. Salamon and Markan (1984) found that this long-term strategy for short-term goals of tax benefit can create intergenerational conflict, particularly on the issue of inheritance.

Another incentive to expansion was introduced by the *Tax Reform Act of 1976*. Until this time farm land's value for estate tax purposes was based on the highest and best use principle (the potential for residential or commercial development). The 1976 Act eliminated such evaluation when certain conditions were met, allowing the land to be assessed for estate tax purposes as a farm. The result decreased estate values by as much as $750,000 and, therefore, lowered the estate tax assessment (Grabowski, 1984). This estate tax revision was critically important to many surviving spouses, particularly farm wives, for they then could continue operation of their farms even as land values increased.

Thus, all four of these policies meant that farm families would be less affected by large debts due to the tax advantages existing in the 1970s. As a result, many became heavily indebted.

## The Macroeconomy and Resulting Legislation

In the early 1970s, rising global inflation, population growth—urban growth in particular—(McDonald, 1983; Paarlberg, Webb, Morey, & Sharples, 1984), and increasing affluence expanded the world market. In response, the American farmer expanded production by increasing the total agricultural export rate by 25% (Bowers et al., 1984). Increased production meant investing in more land. Coupled with mounting domestic inflation, the resultant demand for farm land created a scarcity driving real estate values to all-time highs. In turn, farmers' inflated assets augmented their borrowing ability to continue expansion.

The growth of American agricultural participation in the world's economy was not without costs. World events would begin to play an increasingly important part in the life of the American farm family. At the same time that domestic policies provided incentives for farm production expansion, the international community adopted a floating monetary exchange rate which added instability to export income. Rather than being fixed to a particular exchange standard, monetary exchange rates became dependent on both political and economic variables in individual countries, affecting their ability to purchase American products.

The first oil crisis of 1973-74 brought on a world recession in 1975 which slowed down exports, created surplus crops at home, and forced down prices. By 1977, the total net farm income had fallen 42% below its 1973 high (Bowers et al., 1984). To offset this dramatic decline, the *Food and Agriculture Act of 1977* increased price and income supports and established farmer-owned grain reserves with the government paying storage costs. Acreage allotments, the designation of how much a farmer could plant of any one crop, were reestablished to limit production. On a graduated scale, government payment (the amount of money the farmer would be compensated by the government) on certain crops was increased from $20,000 to $50,000.

The 1977 Act, however, did not do enough for financially troubled farmers. Thus, the *Emergency Assistance Act of 1978* provided a $4 billion emergency loan program and a moratorium on Farmers Home Administration foreclosures (Bowers et al., 1984). In one year's time, these loans would equal 40% of the total farm debt because of the numbers of farm families participating and the extent of their financial needs.

Also in 1978 the *Agricultural Credit Act* made emergency funds available with a $400,000 ceiling per farm for current and financed farm expenses, excluding farm expansion. Family corporations, cooperatives, and partnerships were added to the farm loan eligibility list, further demonstrating the shift towards farm commercialization. The Act also set a 5% interest rate on disaster emergency loans. While these pieces of legislation were meant to bolster farmers' financial stability, they (in some cases) created a false sense of security instead, as disaster loans and favorable interest rates were soon eliminated.

Farm families traditionally conservative in financial matters began the decade of the 1970s with a vision of farm expansion and increased profitability. Favorable credit, tax, and agricultural policies, together with the growing export market, encouraged borrowing against land holdings. By mid decade, however, when the export market did not continue to expand with high prices as anticipated and surplus crops depressed domestic prices, many farm families faced staggering debts. Those families who had held to traditional "pay as you go" values and resisted incentives to enlarge operations and commercialize farming ended the decade in solvency. Unfortunately, by the winter of 1978-79, many others faced losing much more than a business enterprise. Farm family stress was at a peak.

## Legislation in the 1980s

From 1980 to 1985, the overall economic situation declined significantly for many farmers. Farm assets fell $53.8 billion, and liabilities increased $45 billion (Johnson, Baum, & Prescott, 1985). In constant dollars, net farm income decreased (Bowers et al., 1984). Land values began falling in 1982 and continued to fall through the mid-1980s. From 1982 to 1986, land values fell more than 27%. Export income reached an all-time high in 1981, then sharply declined resulting in decreased farm income. Each of these factors had a profound impact on farm families.

In 1980, the *Agricultural Credit Adjustment Act* was extended. Emergency funds were made available to farmers to circumvent loan foreclosures and to invest in current production, but no longer at the favored or reduced interest rate. With the commercial interest rate beginning to soar and the existing high inflation, farmers' operating costs rose correspondingly. The *Federal Credit Act* amendments increased from 85% to 97%, the amount of appraised land value which could be used for collateral with Federal Land Banks. Thus, farmers were allowed to borrow more in 1980. However, those farmers who did found themselves in serious financial trouble when economic conditions worsened. The *Federal Crop Insurance Act of 1980* increased government payments on covered crops but also eliminated most of the government disaster payments to farmers.

Intended to create a more competitive financial market, the *Financial Deregulation and Monetary Control Acts of 1980 and 1982* were enacted. In so doing, farm credit was removed from the local monetary market and tied to the total, national financial market. Many small commercial banks in rural areas were unable to compete in the national market and suffered financially which, in turn, hurt their clients—many of them farmers (Reid, 1986). The decline in land values (the loan collateral) further decreased the banks' security for existing and new loans. Another dramatic and immediate effect of deregulation was the removal of interest rate controls, thus allowing rates to skyrocket and making credit more expensive.

In 1981 the drafting of new farm legislation was complicated by the serious concern for the mounting federal deficit. During the 1980 political campaign, farmers were more sensitive to balancing the federal budget than any other group of voters (Sigelman, 1983). Paradoxically, farmers were simultaneously pressuring for more government support to offset their income losses.

In addition to a poor harvest in 1981, prices of many subsidized crops fell. These factors, coupled with government payments of a maximum of $50,000 to individual farmers, were not enough for some farmers to recoup their investments. *The Agriculture and Food Act of 1981* removed the link between target prices and inflation. However, since high inflation did not continue, market prices fell below target prices, resulting in a higher total of government expense than anticipated.

Favorable weather helped produce record harvests in 1982. Nevertheless, the strong American dollar abroad, at unprecedented high levels not seen since 1973 (Shane & Stallings, 1984), and the continuing worldwide recession brought the first decline in American exports since the mid-1970s. Crops produced for export but not sold to foreign countries caused a domestic surplus which further reduced prices.

Loan delinquencies increased dramatically in 1982 as land values continued to decline. Since income was lower than anticipated and land had been mortgaged beyond its current worth, even farm sales could not help many farmers meet their total loan obligations. In an effort to supplement farm income, more farm family members sought off-farm employment. In 1982, 60% of the farm family income came from nonfarm sources (Manchester, 1985). In 1983, a payment-in-kind (PIK) program was instituted to encourage farmers to reduce production and thereby reduce government surplus. If a farmer did not produce a crop, the government paid the farmer with the stored surplus commodity which the farmer could then sell. Unexpected high participation resulted in retiring a record 82 million farm acres (Bowers et al., 1984). Farmers who did not participate suffered greatly during the 1983 drought, the worst since the Depression (Bowers et al., 1984). With government cost for farm programs so high, the *Agricultural Programs Adjustment Act of 1984* froze target prices to reduce government expense.

There were good harvests in 1985, but with the continuing strong dollar abroad and the slow global recession recovery, prices had declined to 1979 levels. Thus, farm income again decreased. In January 1985, over 370,000 American farms were reported to be in serious to severe financial stress. Three percent, or approximately 51,000, were technically insolvent with over 100% debt/asset ratios; 7.3%, or 123,000 farms, had over 70% debt/asset ratios; and 11.6%, or approximately 197,000 farms, were highly leveraged with a debt/asset ratio of between 40-70% (Johnson et al., 1985). In September 1985, the Farm Credit System, carrying one third of the United States agricultural debt (Sinclair, 1985), reported delinquencies on $3.5 billion worth of loans (Berry, 1985). The resulting consequence was its first net operating loss in more than 50 years. In December 1985, Congress passed legislation strengthening the Farm Credit Administration and provided an avenue for emergency federal aid to keep the system solvent. Also in December 1985, Congress passed a 5-year Farm Bill calling for a gradual lowering of price supports while maintaining income supports and continued acreage controls to limit production. A new conservation program, in which farmers must participate to be eligible for price and income supports, was also enacted. Some farmers may have been saved from insolvency, but it was not a cure for those already in serious financial difficulty.

## The Outlook for the Rest of the 1980s

For many farmers, the second half of this decade was begun without much promise. Many farm families were in serious financial difficulty because they had borrowed heavily, paid high interest rates, suffered severe droughts, received decreased farm crop prices, faced a shrinking world market for their exports, and been caught in a political battle to reduce federal deficits. Decreased land values have given them less leverage in the financial market. Their ability to borrow and, thus, their ability to finance present production and pay interest on past debts have been severely limited.

Predictions for the near future include: a continuing decrease in the total number of farms; a gradual decline in the economic well-being of farm families; increased dependency on off-farm employment (Scholl, 1986); greater reliance on current cash flow as well as collateral financing (Reid, 1986); an increase in farm land leasing; fewer commercial services offered in farming communities (Sinclair, 1986); and with lower com-

munity tax bases, the reduction of local and governmental services.

While 80% of farm families are currently functioning within an acceptable debt limit, many foreseen and unforeseen factors could affect this status. Unrelieved financial stress, decreasing government support, the precarious condition of the Farm Credit System, the uncertainty created by the 1985 legislation and the 1986 income tax reform, as well as another severe drought in 1986, bode a dismal future for the farm economy during the remainder of the 1980s.

## Implications for Family Professionals Working with Farm Families

Prior to even attempting work with farm families, specialists need to understand recent farm legislation, tax policies, and events in the macroeconomy that helped shape the current functioning of farm families. It is equally important that professionals supply a *systemic* frame of reference to farm families. Such a conceptualization of farm families' present economic situation suggests that financial functioning has far-reaching ramifications. Economic stressors in family systems where the boundary between work and family remains diffuse could trigger symptom eruption in any or all aspects of family life. Economic stress could precipitate disruption in family roles, rules, the division of labor, parenting capabilities, children's functioning, and family interaction with the larger community. Inability to finance farm operations could facilitate a chain of events that emerges in an effort to cope (i.e., external employment of the adults—additional demands for time management efficacy—role sharing and reallocation). This increases the demands for new behavior and, thus, the level of stress that is experienced by the farm family.

Farm families who have experienced severe disruptions as a result of financial stress need to have the "stress fallout" (i.e., individual depression, marital discord) that co-exists with such experiences normalized. In other words, farm families need to be assured that their responses, which may feel crazy or unique to them, are normal and sane responses to external stressors. For example, farm families who blame themselves for earlier financial decisions, now proven unwise, need to be helped in seeing that there were indeed support and encouragement for those decisions at that time.

Farm families experiencing life disruptions need education about the normal grief process (Friedman, 1980). While many farm families have not lost their lands, many did lose a way of life and a tradition that, in many cases, had existed for multiple generations. Again, professionals can aid in normalizing their experiences by encouraging families to permit themselves to grieve and by validating the emotions that are triggered.

Equally, education on the process of change is vital (Terkelsen, 1980). Farm families need to understand that after a shock has been experienced and prior to reaching a new level of functioning, destabilization, feelings of vulnerability, and trial and error learning are natural processes. In working with individual farm families, professionals could profit from compiling a recent history of farm functioning and an analysis of how that pattern differs from previous performances. Changes that have been made by family members in order to cope with economic hardship and the concomitant implications for other family members need to be chronicled. Evaluation of the number and magnitude of changes made could provide a rough index of current family stress with targeted areas for intervention identified.

Farm families need encouragement, advocacy, and exposure to successful role models who are willing to share their coping and farm management strategies in community settings. Educational programs on a variety of coping strategies (stress management, time management, financial management, career planning, decision making, and communication skills) are indicated for some families who are experiencing manageable levels of stress. Many extension offices and local churches have begun such programs. Remedial and crisis intervention programs designed for the specific needs and cultural values of farm families are being expanded to encompass rural areas and intensified in areas where they previously existed.

Farm families have long valued self-sufficiency while holding institutionally based support services in low esteem (Camasso & Moore, 1985). Considering farm families' recent history with "expert advice," it is reasonable to assume that trust of family professionals could be at an un-precedented low level. Much work needs to be done to establish and maintain beneficial working relationships. An imminent task of family specialists who work with farm families is the dissemination of information regarding intervention strategies, both preventive and remedial, that have a positive impact on family functioning.

## END NOTE

1. The term "farmer" is used throughout this chapter in reference to the family system involved in the farming process. It is not gender specific.

## REFERENCES

Berry, J. M. (1985, October 24). Farm bank losses high. *The Washington Post,* p. E-1.

Bowers, D. E., Rasmussen, W. D., & Baker, G. L. (1984). *History of agricultural price-support and adjustment programs, 1933-1984* (Agriculture Information Bulletin No. 485). Washington, DC: U.S. Government Printing Office.

Camasso, M. J., & Moore, D. E. (1985). Rurality and the residualist social welfare response. *Rural Sociology,* **50,** 397-408.

Durst, R., & Fromang-Milon, A. (Eds.). (1985). *Agricultural outlook special reprint: Tax reform* (1985-460-938:20010-EMS). Washington, DC: U.S. Government Printing Office.

Friedman, E. H. (1980). Systems and ceremonies: A family view of rites of passage. In E. A. Carter & M. McGoldrick (Eds.), *The family life cycle: A framework for family therapy* (pp. 429-460). New York: Gardner Press, Inc.

Grabowski, T. R. (1984, March). Special-use valuation helps plan your farm estate. *Farm Wife News,* pp. 26-27.

Haney, W. G. (1982). Women. In D. S. Dillman & D. J. Hobbs (Eds.), *Rural society in the U.S.: Issues for the 1980's* (pp. 124-136). Boulder, Colorado: Westview Press.

Hrubovcak, J., & LeBlanc, M. (1985). *Tax policy and agricultural investment* (USDA Technical Bulletin No. 1699). Washington, DC: U.S. Government Printing Office.

Johnson, J., Baum, K., & Prescott, R. (1985). *Financial characteristics of U.S. farms, January 1985* (Agricultural Information Bulletin No. 495). Washington, DC: U.S. Government Printing Office.

Manchester, A. C. (1985). *Agriculture's links with U.S. and world economics.* (Agriculture Information Bulletin No. 496). Washington, DC: U.S. Government Printing Office.

McDonald, T. (Ed.). (1983). *High value agricultural exports: U.S. opportunities in the 1980's* (Foreign Agriculture Information Bulletin No. 188). Washington, DC: U.S. Government Printing Office.

Meekhof, R. (1984). *Federal credit programs for agriculture, background for 1985 farm legislation* (Agricultural Information Bulletin 483). Washington, DC: U.S. Government Printing Office.

Paarlberg, P. L., Webb, A. J., Morey, A., & Sharples, J. A. (1984). *Impacts of policy on U.S. agricultural trade* (USDA Staff Report No. AGES840802). Washington, DC: U.S. Government Printing Office.

Rasmussen, W. D. (1985). Historical overview of U.S. agricultural policies and programs. In K. C. Clayton & R. Bridge (Eds.), *Agricultural-food policies review: Commodity program perspectives* (Agricultural Economic Report No. 530, pp. 3-8). Washington, DC: U.S. Government Printing Office.

Reid, T. (1986, June 3). Pressure building on rural bank. *The Washington Post,* p. A-11.

Salamon, S., & Markan, K. K. (1984). Incorporation and the family farm. *Journal of Marriage and the Family,* **46,** 167-178.

Scholl, K. K. (1986). Farm families: Economic outlook for 1986. *Family Economics Review,* **2,** 10-16.

Shane, M. D., & Stallings, D. (1984). *Financial constraints to trade and growth: The world debt crisis and its aftermath* (Foreign

Agricultural Economic Report No. 211). Washington, DC: U.S. Government Printing Office.

Sigelman, L. (1983). Politics, economics, and the American farmer: The case of 1980. *Rural Sociology, 48,* 367–385.

Sinclair, W. (1985, November 20). Farm credit rescue outlined. *The Washington Post,* p. A-7.

Sinclair, W. (1986, June 3). Many quit farming as credit crisis dims hope. *The Washington Post,* pp. A-1, A-11.

Terkelsen, K. G. (1980). Toward a theory of the family life cycle. In E. A. Carter & M. McGoldrick (Eds.), *The family life cycle: A framework for family therapy* (pp. 21–52). New York: Gardner Press, Inc.

# PART II: STRESS

Rural families have been experiencing a number of changes within the past decade. The economics of farming have been altered and subsequently, nonfarm, rural families are affected. Some marital and family relationships have been strengthened by the different rural milieu. Others have experienced difficulties within their marriages and families. Chapters in this section address stress experienced by rural couples and their families.

The initial set of chapters focuses on the stress within marriages. Two of the chapters examine farm couples and one reports data from a sample on rural nonfarm couples. Rosalie Norem and Joan Blundall describe marital disruption of 12 persons who were attempting to deal with the difficulties of economic crisis within their marriages. The indepth interviews suggest that stress may be a result of threats to the farm family lifestyle, confused role relationships, intergenerational issues, community factors, concerns for children, and financial issues related to separation and divorce. A multi-system model for intervention is developed to assist family therapists, family life educators and family policy-makers.

The relationship between financial stress, well-being, and family life satisfaction of farm husbands and wives are examined by Stephen Duncan, Robert Volk and Robert Lewis. Data are gathered from a sample of 299 farm husbands and 352 farm wives. The findings support Hill's A-B-C-X Model of Family Stress which views the perception of stressor events and resources available for coping with stressful events. Implications for intervention are presented.

Mari Wilhelm and Carl Ridley explore the effects of unemployment on stress in 44 rural nonfarm couples. Issues related to financial management, arguments about finances, and coping resources are considered. The findings suggest that, especially for wives, increases in financial arguments are more predictive of stress than actual changes in financial management. For both husbands and wives, avoidance coping was predictive of stress and mediated the relationship between financial arguments and stress.

The final set of chapters in this section address stress within rural families. Karen Davis-Brown and Sonya Salamon combine farm management types with the family stress model developed by McCubbin and Patterson to present a framework for understanding farm families in crisis. In so doing, the chapter integrates family stress theory and empirical research on farm families. Based on this integration, an assessment instrument for farm crisis counselors is presented.

Lilly Walker and James Walker focus on the prevalence of stress symptoms in 808 farm men and women. Occupational stressors associated with high stress levels are identified and suggestions for family life education are presented.

Norah Keating, Brenda Munro and Mary-anne Doherty consider stress within farm marriages and the importance of psychological and social resources and demands in dealing with the stress. The sample included 753 men and women representing 414 farm units. The findings suggest that resources may be more important than demands in understanding stress. A number of suggestions for reducing stress are reported.

Ramona Marotz-Baden examines the normative and non-normative stressors in a sample of 94 urban and 83 rural couples. Differences between urban and rural couples and their implications for family professionals are discussed.

The chapters in this section indicate that rural, farm as well as nonfarm, families have experienced a number of stressors. Some families have the resources to deal with the stress, others do not. These chapters identify some of the factors related to stress in rural families.

# Farm Families and Marital Disruption During a Time of Crisis

**Rosalie Huisinga Norem and Joan Blundall***

The marriage might have had a chance, a possibility, if we hadn't been on the farm. But it's all he ever wanted to do. It's still what he wants to do. I'm not a risk taker and in farming you have to be. He really got burned out. I helped as much as I could. I realize now I could have done more, but then he never told me anything; he never said I'm worried. I had no idea how troubled he was about the economy—and then things really got bad and the blaming started, all the bitterness. There were times I would say "Don't you wish you had married someone who could do more." And his folks would say things like "I don't know what's wrong with kids today, they don't know what hard times are." If we had stayed together on the farm—I don't think—I still do not believe our marriage is the reason he left. I think it was a convenient thing to blame it on, I mean, I think it was because he could not stand to sit there and watch that. How could he watch his empire fall?

The above statement describes the situation of a 43-year-old farm woman whose husband of 20 years left her and her three children with the responsibility of planting, cultivating and harvesting the crops on their 200-acre farm. He lives nearby but does not participate in the farm operation or decision-making about the farm they own together. Her struggle to understand what happened to her marriage, family and way of life is typical of the stories told by the 12 persons interviewed for the study reported in this chapter. This is a descriptive study with a focus on the process these persons found themselves involved in as they tried to sort through the mire of relationship and economic issues which disrupted their lives.

There are many reasons for trying to more fully understand the unique aspects of family life for rural people engaged in agricultural production as a primary economic activity. The study was designed, as an exploratory study based on in-depth interviews, to respond to questions identified by helping professionals faced with an increase in the number of farm families requesting agency services during a period of escalating farm crisis. These professionals realized that in order to respond more effectively to certain aspects of the divorce process for farm families, they had to understand that process more fully.

## Theoretical Perspectives

Three general areas of literature about the family provide relevant theoretical perspectives for this study. These areas are rural families, family stress, and marital disruption and divorce. There is considerable overlap between the family stress literature and the other two areas but little, if any, among all three. Studies which focus on rural families and stress provide guidance for identifying stressors which may have par-

*Rosalie Huisinga Norem is Associate Professor of Family Environment, Iowa State University, Ames, IA 50010 and Joan Blundall is affiliated with the Northwest Iowa Mental Health Center, Spencer, IA 51301.

ticular importance for rural families (Berkowitz & Hedlund, 1979; Coward & Jackson, 1983; Hedlund & Berkowitz, 1979; Light, 1985; Poole, 1981; Rogers & Salamon, 1983; Russell, Griffin, Flinchbaugh, Martin & Atilano, 1985; Weigel, Weigel & Blundall, 1987). For example, Hedlund and Berkowitz (1979) in their study of social-psychological stress in farm families, develop a classification schema of stressor categories including the marital relationship, intergenerational relationships, sibling rivalry and the wife's role. They also include a category of non-familial stressors. Hedlund and Berkowitz focus on communication and decision-making style as important stress mediating characteristics of the family system. The importance of non-familial stressors is also supported by other work such as the discussion of environmental stress by Coward and Jackson (1983) who challenge the popular images of rural life as tranquil and undisturbed. They point out the complexities of community and environmental stressors experienced by rural families such as the economic conditions and relative isolation.

The literature on rural families also provides a perspective on the values attached to farm life, including a strong orientation to "farming as a way of life" (Coward & Jackson, 1983; Light, 1985; Weigel et al., 1987). Families have held and farmed the land for generations in many cases. Farming is part of their tradition, the present, and their dreams and aspirations for future generations. Relationships are formed and maintained within the context of this way of life (Schumm & Bollman, 1981). Disruption of those relationships also occurs within the same context, and the context must be examined in building an understanding of the relationship process. Alexis Walker (1985, p. 833) points out the importance of "descriptive data that consider differential characteristics of persons and families in, and contexts of, stressful situations." The present study seeks to incorporate a focus on both the differential characteristics of farm families and the context which farm life creates for them.

The family stress literature supports use of a contextual approach by helping us understand the importance of values as part of the resources a family has available to modify the effect of stressors on their system (Boss, 1987; Hill, 1958; McCubbin & Patterson, 1983a). Of particular relevance are concepts of the definition of stressors and family organization. The study of family stress and crisis also provides an understanding of aspects of family stress which may be different or similar for families depending on whether change occurs as a transition or catastrophe (Figley, 1983; McCubbin & Patterson, 1983b). For farm families experiencing the trauma of marital disruption in the midst of a wide-spread farm crisis, elements of each are evident. It is also important to understand the effects of the pileup of stress occurring for these families (McCubbin, Joy, Cauble, Comeau, Patterson, & Needle, 1980). Stressors from various sources affect not only the interpersonal relationships, but economic well-being and overall life style. This complexity of interpersonal and financial stressors makes it desirable to study stressor pile-up and stress response within the context of various levels of systems. As Walker (1985, p. 833) points out, "The interdependence of the levels of the social system necessitates knowledge of the individuals, marriages, families, social networks, communities and societies under stress."

Marital disruption and divorce research raises the issue of whether divorce is a stressor event in the family or a process which occurs as a family moves from a nuclear family situation into a new structure. The first perspective promotes studies which focus on divorce adjustment (Albrecht, 1980; Chiriboga & Cutler, 1977; Green & Sporakowski, 1983; Menaghan & Lieberman, 1987; Plummer & Koch-Harrem, 1986). The second perspective promotes studies which focus on divorce as a stressful process which alters family relationships but does not end them (Ahrons, 1979; Price-Bonham & Balswick, 1980). The present study draws on the latter perspective which views divorce as a process and tries to identify aspects of that process which are unique for farm families.

An interview guide was developed for the present study incorporating ideas from the literature on rural families, family stress, and marital disruption and divorce. Four general content themes are included: (1) commitment to farming as a way of life, (2) role congruence, (3) intergenerational relations and (4) extra-familial stressors. These themes provide an overall framework within which issues related to communication and decision-making may be addressed, and within which other concerns not identified in advance of the interviews may be raised. The themes are a modification of Hedlund and Berkowitz's (1979) classification schema of stressor categories for farm families, expanded to include the concept of non-familial stressors from Coward and Johnson's work (1983) and to assess the influence of attitudes and values related to a farming life style. Hedlund and Berkowitz's stressor categories of the marital relationship and the wife's role are combined into one theme called role congruence. However, their category of sibling rivalry is not a focus for the present study.

The data from the interviews are discussed in the following sections, using the four content themes as an organizing structure. In addition, parenting concerns and the issue of financial concerns and settlements as a consequence of divorce are discussed. Finally, based on the interviews completed for this study, a multi-systems model for planning intervention is presented.

## Methodology

The interviewers were trained family therapists. When the interviews were arranged and at the beginning of each interview, it was explained to the respondent that the purpose of the interview was to learn more about farmers and the farm crisis. The interviews lasted about 1½ hours each and took place in the respondent's home. Audio tapes of the interviews were transcribed and provided the data base for the present study. The ages ranged from 27 to 58 years for respondents and from 28 to 61 years for their spouses.

The interviews reported here were completed during the late spring and summer of 1985. Twelve persons, 8 women and 4 men, who were separated from their respective spouses and at some point in the legal divorce process were interviewed. The sample was identified from among clients of a rural mental health center who had originally contacted the center with a presenting problem associated with the farm crisis and/or marital disruption. The respondents had been married at least 5 years with the range of length of marriage being 5–22 years. Six of the persons interviewed had been married 19 years or more. All respondents and their (ex)spouses have at least a high school education with several having undergraduate

and graduate degrees. All respondents have at least one child.

It is difficult to generalize about the economic status of the persons who participated in this study because almost all of them were in a state of flux. They were not sure what was going to happen to them in terms of their own financial situation or in terms of their farm operation. Several of them had lost land, were negotiating a financial settlement or were unable to finalize a divorce settlement because of the farm crisis. They had been or are involved in both cropping and livestock systems. Land holdings ranged from 40–600 acres owned and total acres in the farm operation, including leased land, range from 80–825 acres. Eight of the farm operations involve some type of intergenerational tie. Four of the intergenerational family farm ties are with the wife's family and 4 are with the husband's family.

## Commitment to Farming

This section focuses on the first context theme for the interviews, farming as a family life style. Most of the persons interviewed for this study came from family farms. All of them grew up in farm communities. They share basic values that farming is more than an economic activity, it is a way of life, based on beliefs about living on the land and working the land and what that means in terms of family patterns and relationships. Life plans tend to be sketched in terms of continuity rather than change. For example, building a farm enterprise is often seen as a multi-generational effort. Sacrifices are made today with the assumption that "the farm" will be part of the family legacy for generations to come. Young couples often choose farming not only as an occupational alternative but as a life style they wish to preserve for themselves and their own children, thereby continuing a pattern established by their parents and grandparents.

All of the respondents in this study were struggling with the agricultural life style in their marriage. Quotes could be extracted from each of the interviews to illustrate this theme. One man talked about the isolation factor being an issue for his wife. He reported that she perceived him as being so ingrained with the idea of what a farm wife should be that it was impossible for him to change. He believes she felt constraints related to educational and professional opportunities because of their distance from an urban area and the amount of time she was expected to be at home on the farm. Yet he described them both as having started out with the dream of being on the farm to raise their kids. Another man felt his wife married him because she needed somebody to operate the family farm. One 53 year old divorced woman described her frustration with her ex-husband's unwillingness to supplement the farm income because of his ideas about what it meant to be on the farm:

> I wanted to be a partner, when we were 27 years old and I thought we could get jobs and pay for the land, but his attitude was that the land would take care of us.

The desire to own at least part of the land they farmed was also an important issue for many of the marriages in this study. Buying land did not seem to have been a point of conflict but it often exacerbated financial strains for the couples. The following quotes from two women are good examples:

> Remember that 6 months when land went from $4,000 to $2,000 an acre? Well, we were one of the last ones to buy at the top—it was so dumb—but he was so anxious to have his own land, his own farm. I think that's very important to farmers . . . all he wanted to do was to drive on that piece of land and say "Hey, I own it." I'm not saying that was the problem between us . . . but it was the icing on the cake, the economy was the icing on the cake. (Woman, age 31, husband rented 200 acres.)

> Yeah, you know, we wanted a place of our own, some people might call that greedy, it's only an 80. We wanted a place of our own . . . and the banker came along and said "I've got this 80 and you can buy it," so we bought it, no down payment. "We'll back you all the way," he said, you know, and then 18 months later we had to have co-signers. (Woman, age 35, husband's family owned 300 acres.)

The latter couple experienced a foreclosure by the bank and subsequently lost their land and other farm assets. The former couple was forced to renegotiate their contract with a private seller. As a result, they felt they had not lived up to their financial obligations to the seller. This feeling was heightened when the seller verbally attacked them in their attorney's office.

The interview excerpts included here do not suggest that a farm life style promotes marital disruption, nor does it imply that farming presents only negative stressors for a marriage relationship. The respondents do help in understanding how integral their life style is to their marital relationships and their perceptions of themselves as individuals. For this reason, as stated earlier, understanding marital disruption among farm families requires an examination of the disruption process within the context of farm life.

## Role Congruence

Role congruence focuses directly on the marital relationships of the persons interviewed for this study. When they talked about their expectations and experiences related to husband and wife roles in their marriages, a pattern of confusion and dissatisfaction emerged. Transcripts of the interviews reveal a strong general orientation to the idea of a traditional division of labor, with the husband being primarily responsible for the farm operation and the wife being primarily responsible for the home and family. Most of the wives participated in "outside" work, but it was perceived as "helping out" rather than being part of their role. The husbands were described as not participating very much in "inside" work and this was generally not seen as part of their responsibility. One man talked about his annoyance with being expected to help with tasks like carrying trash out of the basement on rainy days, just because he couldn't be outside doing his work. This general role definition is consistent regardless of whether the interviewee is male or female and whether he or she is describing self or his/her (ex)spouse.

Confusion and dissatisfaction surface as the roles in these marriages are explored in detail related to day-to-day living. As Berkowitz and Hedlund (1979, p. 48) stated, "In farm families husband-wife role definitions take on added significance due to the fusion of economic and social roles which results from operating a family business localized around the home in relative geographical isolation." The marriages described by persons interviewed are good examples of relationships which experience marital stress due to an inability to reach a congruent definition of those economic and social roles. The following quotes describe distress experienced in these marriages.

> (He expected) everything, the garden, canning, the house to be perfect . . . it was never a joint situation. I never participated in decisions, it was always his decisions, even the carpeting, the refrigerator. (Woman, age 52, divorced.)

> On the farm I was helping him in the fields, I plowed, I disced, I brought all the food out to the fields, the lunches, you know, side by side. I really loved it. I thought this is just beautiful. He was dominating me. I was like a doormat, his possession. I didn't even know we had lost all that money, that really bothered me, he did all the buying and everything. (Divorced woman, age 47, had owned 240 acres with husband.)

> One 37-year-old man whose wife owned the farm said: We always sat down and discussed everything. Now I wonder if I was ever part of the farm.

This man also talks about how his wife would be working out in the field and, when she saw her parents' car arriving, she would run to the house so they would not know she spent so much time with the farm operation. For this couple there was an incongruence between how roles "should" be defined, according to their expectations and the definitions prescribed by their extended families and the community, and how the roles were operationally defined on a day to day basis.

The last quote above is the only situation described in the 12 interviews where both husband and wife participated in the majority of decision-making aspects of the farm. Other relationships did not fit with a picture of farm families where a husband and wife operate in a decision-making partnership. Instead, interviews portray systems in which decisions tend to be made by one spouse, often in cooperation with extended family members. Several of the respondents talked about difficulties in communication in their marriages, especially about decision-

making and the farm crisis situation. In several situations, communication breakdowns eroded the role patterns which had evolved in the marriage, leaving the respondent with a feeling of isolation and despair in a situation which forced him/her to try to pick up the pieces. Some examples are given in the following quotes:

> I had such a deep depression, I wanted to kill myself. That was the economy was starting to go downhill and I was feeling to blame . . . he went out and talked with other women for consolation to help him with the farm crisis and he fell in love. (Divorced woman, age 47, also quoted earlier.)

> But he pulled away and I pulled away. I think back now and I didn't really say that but I felt I don't care if you hurt anymore. I'm hurting too. . . . But he was never there for me. . . . He would be so tense he would just start shaking. (Woman, age 28, operated 600 acre grain and animal production system with her ex-husband.)

Role relationship issues were major stressors for both husbands and wives. Generally, the pattern was the husband being the predominant decision-maker, whether or not the wife preferred that pattern. Incongruence occurred when a lack of flexibility in roles prevented adaptation to the changing family and economic situation and it was not possible to renegotiate role definitions accordingly.

## Intergenerational Relations

Families described in these interviews were not only experiencing marital disruption but, often because of the farm crisis in their communities, they were experiencing severe disturbance in their intergenerational relationships. As Rogers and Salamon (1983) point out in their discussion of core concerns of family farmers, "Family farmers are apt to live in relatively stable communities composed of families who are linked to the land and who strive for or have achieved intergenerational continuity in the family/land relationship" (p. 535).

The above statement is helpful in understanding issues related to intergenerational relations which surfaced from transcripts of the 12 interviews. This was sometimes exemplified by conflicts about continued or heightened economic dependency on extended family and sometimes by feelings of failing to uphold family values related to farming as a way of life. Some had a feeling of pressure being brought to bear on the part of extended family members because of the marital disruption or the farm crisis. The following quotes illustrate this point:

> I did not talk to her (my mother-in-law) for years. She blamed me for everything that happened. (42-year-old woman.)

> His brother-in-law and sister came to my house and said, "How can you do this to him (my husband), he worked 20 years at this." (Woman, 47, who was negotiating a divorce settlement.)

> We both (my husband and I) felt like we killed my dad. We didn't, you know and I know that, and I came to grips with it a lot faster than he did. (Woman, age 38, had gone through bankruptcy before separating from husband.)

Involvement of extended family in the major economic activity of a couple can be a source of difficulty in a marriage, whether or not a farm crisis is a factor. The following quotes are illustrative:

> Her input on farming decisions was none. I was in partnership with my father and my uncle. She was not involved in the operation of the farm, which is basically a tradition in the family. It has been a point of pride, we didn't need women to run the tractors. (Divorced man, age 36, in family partnership.)

> Yes, I was in the middle. What I found out years later . . . he kind of used me to say, (to his family) well (respondent's name) wanted to do that. (Woman, divorced, age 37, husband farmed 250 acres inherited from his family.)

A family farm often means more than a nuclear family. Extended family(ies) were involved in the farm operations of 10 of the persons in the present study, either financially, in a major decision-making capacity and/or on a day-to-day operational basis. Intergenerational issues added to the stress pile-up of persons in this study in various ways. Relationships were affected by financial and interpersonal conflicts and expectations.

## Extra-familial Stressors

The fourth content theme, the impact of extra-familial stressors, is of particular importance for the families whose experiences provide the basis for the present study. The study was done at a point in time when many farm communities were in a state of economic crisis. Some banks and businesses were closing, farm mortgages were being foreclosed, many farmers were experiencing bankruptcies, and the future of farming as a life style was uncertain at best (DeWitt, 1986; Lasley, 1986). Mental illness, relationship problems and suicides were on an increase in farm populations as evidenced by calls to rural hotlines and demands on mental health centers (DeWitt, 1986; Des Moines Register, December 8, 1986). Community resources were being strained as the demand for services increased and federal funding for these services was being cut. As stated in the section above on theoretical perspectives, the context of marital disruption for the families in this study is the community and society at large (Walker, 1985).

All of the families lived in communities which had been hard hit by the current economic farm crisis. Even if they themselves were not among those in deep financial trouble, they knew friends and/or other family members who were. They were painfully aware of the effects of the situation on their community as a whole. The impact of these extra-familial stressors on the marriage relationships was very evident from the interviews, as illustrated by the following quotes:

> We weren't in danger of going down the tubes. We could have made the payments, but you never know, but everyone else was, it was getting tighter and tighter. (Woman, age 31, husband rented 200 acres.)

> I'd like to say the farm crisis (hurt our relationship). We had our own financial troubles. We bought the farm 7 years ago when things were starting down. We started the process of blaming each other, for the financial situation and other things. (Man, age 39, farmed 300 acres.)

Not only is the general community situation an important factor but the interaction with persons from the community and the perception of the reaction of these persons to one's own situation are sources of conflict and distress. These extra-familial stressors are evident from the following quotes:

> My old friends all left me. They felt I took part of my husband's dream away. My husband's farm . . . it is just like the man owns it, it's the man's world and you goofed it up. That really hurt me. (Woman, age 47, quoted earlier.)

> His dad was talking around town and telling people, you know, how this was the end, this last year. How do you face people when you know that is happening? (Woman, 38, bankruptcy case quoted earlier.)

The interview excerpts in this section focus on the community as a context within which stressors occur. It is important to recognize that this community context also provided a base of social *support* for persons in this study.

## Parenting Concerns

One of the strengths of research using an in-depth interview methodology is the possibility for themes to evolve from the interviews which were not a part of the original interview structure. Two additional themes were identified in the present study. The first was parenting concerns. Undoubtedly, there are many aspects of parent-child relationships in families which are critical to understanding their situations, but from the interviews discussed here, only a few aspects can be highlighted. These concerns could be included in a discussion of family roles and intergenerational relationships, but it is felt that they are important enough to be discussed separately.

One specific issue which was identified from several of the interviews is the involvement of children in the "farming as a way of life" orientation of these families and what this means as the divorce process occurs. For example, one woman describes her children choosing to stay on the farm rather than perceiving their choice being related to which parent they wanted to live with as custodial parent.

> Well, at first the kids were going to stay at the farm house. They were going to stay on that farm no matter who got it. . . . The boy stayed to work with the

stock, and now the stock have all been sold. (42-year-old woman who had just separated from her husband and moved to town.)

Another woman talked about the problems involved in making sure her son was able to go out to the farm every day to participate in doing chores and caring for horses even though he lived with her in town. She saw this as an important part of his life and as being worth the difficulties involved in the continuity of his involvement on the farm. One man talked about how he and his wife felt it was good for their children to spend a good portion of their time "on the farm," as a separate consideration from time with each parent. In other words, parents in this study have a concern for maintaining the farming life style for their children. This is expressed as a separate, though related, issue from child custody.

## Financial Statement Issues

In studying the transcripts of the interviews, several points related to the financial settlement as part of the divorce became apparent. This is the second theme emerging from the interviews. Elements from each of the previously presented themes are apparent here as well. First, several couples were unable to complete a settlement because of the farm crisis situation. An example of this is from one of the men (age 32) interviewed:

> Basically our money was invested in 40 acres of land, the family corporation, which was liquid enough for me to buy her share, but the land is becoming a negative cash flow and the corporation isn't interested in buying . . . that has continued to be a problem for her, the unliquid nature of the land.

Second, the divorce settlement may become even more complicated than usual as a result of family land ownership issues. The previous quote illustrates this second point also. When there was intergenerational land ownership and/or farm operation it involved either the husband's *or* the wife's family. In several situations, the spouse whose family of origin did not own the land was basically left with no settlement. This was true for two of the men who had farmed land belonging to their wife's family.

Third, for some couples, the financial

struggle to maintain the farming operation continued for both spouses even though they were ending the marriage. One 28-year-old wife described her situation as follows:

> And even though the divorce is filed, I had to sign on a new loan to get the crops in or he couldn't have gotten the seed and the fertilizer, I mean, I couldn't turn him down on that, but I resent it.

## Summary

Reviewing the interview transcripts from the present study provides insight into the situations of a small sample of members of the farm population who are experiencing marital disruption during a time of economic crisis in their communities. The interviews reveal a high level of stress pile-up related to threats to a farm family life style. Confused role relationships, intergenerational issues and issues related to divorce financial settlements were also discussed by several respondents. The content themes used to organize the data provide a structure for presenting material from the interviews, but it is also apparent that the themes are inter-related. For example, relationship problems and financial concerns cannot be neatly compartmentalized into mutually-exclusive categories. The stressors occurring in the lives of the respondents involve a complex interaction among a variety of systems at various levels. In the following section a model is introduced to illustrate that interaction.

## A Multi-Systems Model for Planning Intervention

The initial stimulus for the present study was to provide a basis for a clearer understanding of divorce and farm families for helping professionals working with those families. The interviews clearly illustrate the importance of being aware of various systems influencing the lives of rural families. The model in Figure 1 illustrates some of the interactions among the levels of systems comprising the societal context for the families described in this study. The systems included in the model become progressively micro-level (moving down the model from top to bottom). Policy actions affecting the more macro-level national and state economic systems are somewhat removed from the day-to-day life of farm families, but those actions do have an eventual impact on families and marital relationships. Because the family farm is an economic system, it is involved in linkages with more macro-level systems. Farm family relationship systems become a part of these linkages because of the lack of clearly defined boundaries between the family and the farm.

Following the model, several generalizations from the current research are presented below and discussed. Each generalization includes reference letters which relate to the model, identifying interactions between various systems and systems levels which may be influencing the marital relationship. The final section of this paper discusses implications for intervention based on the following generalizations:

1. The economic instability of the past few years has had a widespread impact on the communities of farm couples (A).
2. The influence of the macro-economic situation on the community at large strongly affects the policies and practices of financial institutions in the community (B). In the extreme, this may include the failure of the community's financial institutions.
3. The impact of economic instability on the community creates ripples which may disturb the family farm system (C,D) and the marital relationship of the farm couple (F,G) in diverse ways. This may include strained, severed, or lost relationships with financial institutions, increased demand for community services, business decline and/or failure, and disruptive impact on community institutions such as churches and schools.
4. The dependency of both the family farm and the farm family on the financial institutions in their community creates a situation which may lead to a sense of lack of control over their own economic security and well-being (G,D,H). This is evident when mortgages are foreclosed, operating loans are unavailable, and land values drop.
5. The people of the community within which the couple lives, while a potential source of support, can also add to the distress experienced within a

*Figure 1:* Multi-level systems model of marital distress in farm families. Letters indicate points of potential negative impact on the marital relationship. Order is for ease of presentation and does not reflect order of importance.

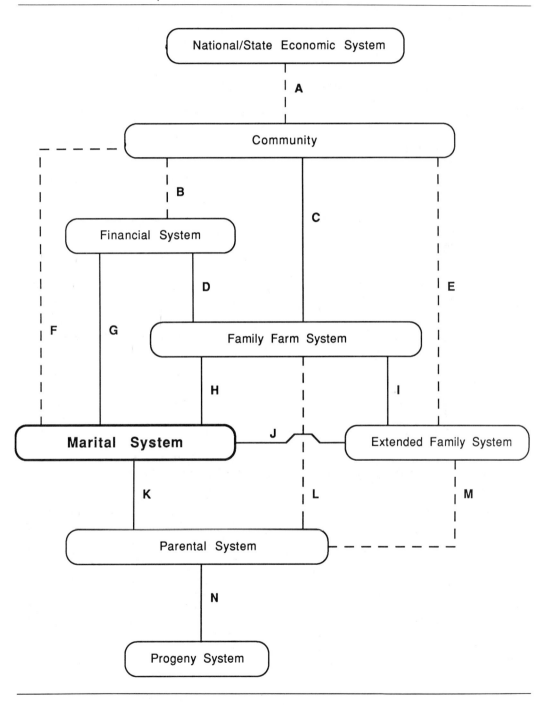

marriage and during the divorce process (F).

6. The family farm system and the marital system are integrally related for the persons we interviewed, and yet they are separate systems, each with its own boundaries. However, the farm couples described in this study did not seem to be able to maintain these boundaries, especially during a period of disruption (H). This becomes a particularly complex issue when the marital system and the extended family system make up the family farm system (J,I,H).

7. The influence of the marital system on the parental system is an important component in understanding the differences between the two (K). The parental system, of course, is in direct interaction with the progeny, or child, system of the family (N). Parenting roles are affected by marital disruption, interference from extended family members, and the family farm's crisis situation (K,M,L on N).

8. The involvement of extended family in the major economic activity of a couple may also foster difficulties in separating concerns related to the farm and extended family systems (H,I,J). The involvement of extended family in the farm operation may carry over into interaction with the parental system (I,M). The extended family linkages to the community, which may impinge on the community's perception of the farm couple, may be another factor in a feeling of helplessness (E,J).

## Implications for Intervention

The model and generalizations presented here suggest several implications for intervention. One of the goals of intervention in a crisis is to do an assessment of the client's situation in order to help him/her focus more clearly on what can be changed in order to bring some relief as quickly as possible. Assessment for farm families should be based on an awareness of the complexity of systems at the various levels involved. This includes an awareness that relationship systems and family farm systems share various interface points, and that focusing on these systems may involve

helping a client clarify which issues relate to which system. For instance, there were several examples from the interviews when an individual felt blamed for problems related to the farm or to extended family, or to the larger community, over which he or she actually had little control. The blaming which occurred made it very difficult to examine more specific relationship issues which were a part of the marital disruption process. Intervention which does not acknowledge the multi-level systems involvement may hinder the client's progress toward implementing problem-solving behaviors.

Intervention also seeks to facilitate the client's access to support from various sources within his/her existing network and to help identify new sources of support if necessary. A multi-level systems approach can help identify those linkages which can provide support. However, these interviews also alert the clinician to the fact that networks may be sources of distress as well as support. It may be unrealistic to expect a client to turn to friends and/or family who are perceived as making negative judgments about the client's situation. This seems self-evident but can be overlooked if there is a lack of awareness of the various systems linkages involved. Some of these linkages may be unique because of involvement in farming and what farming means in the community.

Another related factor is the reluctance of many farm people to admit they are having difficulties, based on a tradition that people keep their problems to themselves except in times of death, natural disaster or serious illness. Clients may feel they have failed because somehow they were not able to live up to the expectation that if you work hard and make good decisions, you will succeed on the farm. They may also perceive decisions made with the advice of community support sources (such as a financial institution or cooperative extension) as being disastrous decisions. This perception may make it difficult for them to trust other sources of support in a time of crisis. Exploring various systems linkages can assist clients in realistically examining past experiences and assessing existing alternatives for support.

The model presented here may also provide ideas for preventive intervention programs. Information, opportunities for group discussion, training materials and support groups are just a few examples of opportunities for including a multi-level systems approach.

## Implications for Future Research and Policy

This study supports the idea that for farm families the divorce process may include elements which have not been addressed in past research. Studies of divorce have not explored differences between farm and non-farm families. Studies of rural families have focused to some extent on marital relationships and relationship satisfaction but not on divorce. The present exploratory study needs to be expanded to include more couples and include both partners in the relationships studied. The argument is not that none of the aspects included in the study of farm families and divorce are relevant for non-farm families, or vice versa, but that the farm segment of the population does have special issues and stressors which affect the marital relationship.

Obviously, there are many marriages which are not disrupted as a result of the farm crisis. It is important to do comparative research with farm couples who are experiencing similar situations in terms of the farm crisis, but whose marriages are not disrupted and are perhaps strengthened because of their experience.

Policy makers must be aware of the potential impact of economic policy on farm families. Policy related to the provision of community services should be evaluated in context of the overall community situation and not with the assumption that service providers will somehow take up any slack. The situation in many farm communities at present is such that a segment of the population which has traditionally not demanded mental health services is making heavy demands on those services. It is clear that relationships are also at high risk during such a crisis. Policy makers need to find ways to include risk management components in service delivery systems.

REFERENCES

Ahrons, C. R. (1979). The binuclear family: Two households, one family. *Alternative Lifestyles*, **2**, 499–515.

Albrecht, S. L. (1980). Reactions and adjustments to divorce: Differences in the experiences of males and females. *Family Relations*, **29**, 59–68.
Berkowitz, A. D., & Hedlund, D. E. (1979, April). Psychological stress and role congruence in farm families. *Cornell Journal of Social Relations*, pp. 47–68.
Boss, Pauline. (1987). Family stress. In Marvin B. Sussman & Suzanne K. Steinmentz (Eds.), *Handbook of marriage and the family* (pp. 695–723). New York: Plenum Press.
Chiriboga, D. A., & Cutler, L. (1977). Stress response among divorcing men and women. *Journal of Divorce*, **1**(2), 95–106.
Coward, R. T., & Jackson, R. W. (1983). Environmental stress: The rural family. In H. I. McCubbin & C. R. Figley (Eds.), *Stress and the Family, Vol. 1: Coping with normal transitions* (pp. 188–200). New York: Brunner/Mazel.
Des Moines Register. (1986, December 8). *Des Moines Register*.
DeWitt, J. (*1986 Iowa Farm Survey*). Iowa State Extension Service and Iowa Crop Livestock Reporting Service.
Figley, C. R. (1983). Catastrophes: An overview of family reactions. In C. R. Figley & H. I. McCubbin (Eds.), *Stress and the family, Vol. 2: Coping with catastrophe* (pp. 3–20). New York: Brunner/Mazel.
Green, R. G., & Sporakowski, M. J. (1983). The dynamics of divorce: Marital quality, alternative attractions and external pressures. *Journal of Divorce*, **7**(2), 77–88.
Hedlund, D., & Berkowitz, A. (1979). The incidence of social-psychological stress in farm families. *International Journal of Sociology of the Family*, **9**, 233–243.
Hill, R. (1958). Generic features of families under stress. *Social Casework*, **48**, 139–150.
Lasley, P. (1986). *1986 Statistical Profile of Iowa*. Iowa State Extension Service and Iowa Development Commission.
Light, H. K. (1985, June). *How strong is your family: Perceptions of farm men and farm women*. Paper presented at the American Home Economics Association Annual Meeting and Exposition, Fargo, ND.
McCubbin, H. I., Joy, C. B., Cauble, A. E., Comeau, J. K., Patterson, J. M., & Needle, R. H. (1980). Family stress and coping: A decade review. *Journal of Marriage and the Family*, **42**, 125–141.
McCubbin, H. I., & Patterson, J. M. (1983a). The family stress process: A double ABCX model of adjustment and adaptation. In H. McCubbin, M. Sussman, & J. Patterson (Eds.), *Social stress and the family: Advances and developments in family stress theory and research* (pp. 7–37). New York: Haworth Press.
McCubbin, H. I., & Patterson, J. M. (1983b). Family transition: Adaptation to stress. In H. I. McCubbin & C. R. Figley (Eds.), *Stress and the family, Vol. 1: Coping with normative transitions* (pp. 5–25). New York: Brunner/Mazel.
Menaghan, E. G., & Lieberman, M. A. (1986). Changes in depression following divorce: A panel study. *Journal of Marriage and the Family*, **48**, 319–328.
Plummer, L. P., & Koch-Hattem, A. (1986). Family stress and adjustment to divorce. *Family Relations*, **35**, 523–529.
Poole, D. L. (1981). Family farms and effect of farm expansion on the quality of marital and family life. *Human Organization*, winter, 344–349.
Price-Bonham, S., & Balswick, J. O. (1980). The noninstitutions: Divorce, desertion and remarriage. *Journal of Marriage and the Family*, **42**, 959–972.
Rogers, S. C., & Salamon, S. (1983, October). Inheritance and social organization among family farmers. *American Ethnologist*, pp. 529–550.
Russell, C. S., Griffin, C. L., Flinchbaugh, C. S., Martin, M. J., Atilano, R. B. (1985). Coping strategies associated with intergenerational transfer of the family farm. *Rural Sociology*, **50**(3), 361–376.
Schumm, W. R., & Bollman, S. R. (1981). Interpersonal processes in rural families. In R. T. Coward & W. M. Smith, Jr. (Eds.), *The family in rural society* (pp. 129–246). Boulder, CO: Westview Press.
Walker, A. J. (1985). Reconceptualizing family stress. *Journal of Marriage and the Family*, **47**, 827–838.
Weigel, R. R., Weigel, D. J., & Blundall, J. (1987). Stress, coping and satisfaction: Generational differences in farm families. *Family Relations*, **36**, 45–48.

# The Influence of Financial Stressors Upon Farm Husbands and Wives' Well-Being and Family Life Satisfaction*

Stephen F. Duncan, Robert J. Volk and Robert A. Lewis**

Economic strains continue to be a source of stress for American farmers. For example, one-third of medium to large-sized farms have a debt-to-asset ratio that spells financial stress (Bosc, 1985; Melichar, 1984). According to a 1985 report by the U.S. Department of Agriculture, one-third of family farms with annual sales of $40,000-500,000 had some financial difficulty; 20% had a negative cash flow and high debt load and 10% had too little cash flow to maintain their loans. The painful irony of the "farm crisis" was noted in a recent issue of *U.S. News and World Report:* "A farm worth $500,000 will earn an average of $10,000 a year—$40,000 less than that amount would draw if put in a bank" (Sheets, 1985:48). Undoubtedly, these financial strains experienced by farmers eventually will have serious, negative impacts upon farmers' feelings about themselves and their family life.

## Review of the Literature

Generally speaking, there has been a serious lack of systematic research on farm family life (Poole, 1981). However, there are a few studies which provide clues to the major influence of financial conditions on farmers' well-being and satisfaction with their family life. For instance, Poole (1981) found that *economic status*, based on the ratio of net family income to satisfaction with income was positively associated with marital and family satisfaction. Although farm women were not included in the major portion of the study, findings from a small sample of wives indicated high agreement with their husbands.

A somewhat different picture appears, when one considers the influences of *economic difficulties.* For example, the decline of family farming, defined as decreases in the size and income generated by a family farm operation, has been found to be associated with lower quality of life scores among farmers (Gilles, Hirschi, Campbell, & Heffernan, 1984). However, these data were not recent; they were gathered between 1950 to 1970.

Economic distress, defined as "dissatisfaction ... at one's economic situation" (Rosenblatt & Keller, 1983:568), has been correlated with spousal blaming in farm marriages. The practice of blaming one's partner for financial problems is undoubtedly associated with lower marital satisfaction; however, such a relationship was not investigated by these researchers. Interestingly, actual economic loss due to lower prices for farm goods, high indebtedness and other factors was not correlated with spousal blaming either. This finding reinforces the idea that the *perception* of the loss is more

*This study was conducted as part of the AES Regional Research Project, NC-164, *Stress, Coping, and Adaptation in the Middle Years of the Family Life Cycle.* It was funded through The United States Department of Agriculture and administered by the Cooperative State Research Service for six years.

**Stephen F. Duncan and Robert J. Volk are doctoral candidates in the Department of Child Development and Family Studies, Purdue University. Robert A. Lewis is Professor, Department of Child Development and Family Studies, Purdue University. All authors may be contacted at the Family Research Institute, 525 Russell St., West Lafayette, IN 47906.

important than the loss itself in predicting stress (Rosenblatt & Keller, 1983).

Farm life has a unique potential for developing economic stress. For example, farmers typically carry a high capital investment and a substantial debt load to keep their operations solvent (Rosenblatt & Anderson, 1981). In addition, the amount of capital investment necessary to operate the farm continues to rise (Coward & Jackson, 1983). When farm income does not at least increase proportionately, family tensions may increase, negatively influencing farmers' feelings about their life and their satisfaction with family life.

Given the potentially stressful lifestyles of many farm families, including farmers' frequent dissatisfactions with their farm income, it is surprising to read that some farmers are just as likely to evaluate their overall life, family life, and marriage as positively as those of other occupations (Marans, Dillman & Keller, 1980). However, it seems likely that, just as farmers differ about how hard they may be hit by financial difficulties (Rosenblatt & Keller, 1983), these differences in financial conditions are probably related to different levels of personal well-being and satisfaction with family life. In sum, little attention has been paid to possible differences among farm husbands and wives.

## The ABCX Model of Stress

There are a number of theoretical models available for examining the effects of stress on families. One theoretical explanation for viewing the impact of financial conditions upon families is the ABCX Model advanced by Hill (1949, 1958) and extended by Burr (1973). Another more recent model is the Double ABCX Model of McCubbin (McCubbin and Patterson, 1983). Boss (1987:709) has also added a new construct, boundary ambiguity, to take into account situations where "family members are uncertain in their perception of who is in or out of the family." Any of these models could help to explain the impact of financial conditions on families; we have chosen the Hill/Burr model because of its parsimony.

In Hill's ABCX Model the following three factors are posited: "A" (the stressor or change-producing event) which interacts with "B" (the family's crisis-meeting resources or vulnerability to stress), and with "C" (the family's definition of the seriousness of the changes). These three factors produce "X" (the crisis). "The second and third determinants—family resources and definitions of the event—lie within the family itself and must be seen in terms of the family's structures and values. The hardship of the event, which goes to make up the first determinant, lies outside the family and is an attribute of the event itself" (Hill, 1958:141). From this perspective, the specific interaction of a) the *stressors* (i.e. economic losses), b) the *perceptions* that the husband and wife have of the seriousness of the change(s), and c) the *resources* available to them (material and nonmaterial) determine the amount of crisis experienced by the family members. In effect, this study considers the influence that the financial stressors and the actual and perceived financial resources of farm wives and husbands have on farmers' well-being and family life satisfaction.

## Hypotheses

The purpose of this study was to examine the relationships between financial conditions as well as family life satisfaction and personal well-being of the farmer husbands and wives in nine central states. Therefore, based on earlier research and on our theoretical perspective, we hypothesized that:

(1) Income will be positively related to well-being and family life satisfaction for farm husbands and wives.

(2) Income adequacy will be positively associated with well-being and family life satisfaction for farm husbands and farm wives.

(3) Farm husbands and wives who report a negative change in their income over the last three years will score lower on well-being and family life satisfaction than those who report no change or positive change.

(4) Farm husbands and wives reporting a worsening financial condition will score lower on well-being and family life satisfaction than those reporting a stable or improving financial condition.

## Methods
### The Sample

Data for this study were collected for the Agricultural Experiment Station regional project, NC-164, titled "Stress, Coping, and Adaptation in the Middle Years of the Family Life Cycle." The basic sampling unit was intact families in the middle years, where wives were between 35 to 64 years of age. The sample was selected by a commercial direct mail marketing company by a systematic sampling of 100 urban, 100 rural/nonfarm and 100 rural/farm families in each of nine central states (Indiana, Iowa, Kansas, Kentucky, Louisiana, Michigan, Minnesota, Missouri, and Nebraska). The data for this study were collected by questionnaires from both husbands and wives in March, 1983. Each couple had to have had at least one child who was still living at home. The response rates, which varied from 30 to 50 percent in each of the nine states, were considered adequate in light of the 28-page length of the questionnaire. The total number of returned questionnaires was approximately 1900 cases.

Selection of the farm subsample was based on whether either the husband or wife met each of the following criteria: a) they lived in a community of less than 2,500 persons and outside a SMSA (Standard Metropolitan Statistical Area or urban area); b) their home was on more than one acre of land; c) they lived on a farm; and d) their farm produced $1,000.00 or more in sales of crops, livestock, or other farm products during the preceding year. These criteria allowed for the inclusion of farmers who reported a profit and those who reported a "negative net income."

The subsample selection procedures yielded a total of 299 husbands and 352 wives. The sample included predominantly high school-educated, white, middle-aged, Protestant individuals with three children. They earned between $30,000-$40,000 per year. Other demographic characteristics are given in Table 1.

## The Measures

*Independent Measures.* Financial condition was assessed using four single-item indicators. An objective measure of financial condition was obtained by asking participants to indicate their gross family income

Table 1.
*Demographic Characteristics of the Sample*

| Demographics | Husbands | Wives[a] |
|---|---|---|
| Sample Size: | 299 | 352 |
| Age: | | |
| Mean | 50.0 | 46.6 |
| Standard Deviation | 8.0 | 7.3 |
| Range | 35 to 72 | 36 to 66 |
| Education in years: | | |
| Mean | 12.4 | 12.9 |
| Standard Deviation | 2.6 | 2.0 |
| Range | 6 to 20 | 7 to 20 |
| Number of Children: | | |
| Mean | 3.3 | 3.4 |
| Standard Deviation | 1.4 | 1.4 |
| Range | 1 to 7 | 1 to 7 |
| Family Income: | | |
| Mean | 39,755 | 32,670 |
| Standard Deviation | 39,230 | 28,077 |
| Range | 1,000 to 300,000 | 1,000 to 239,000 |
| Religion: | | |
| Catholic | 35 (12%) | 45 (13%) |
| Protestant | 230 (80%) | 271 (78%) |
| Jewish | 11 (4%) | 17 (5%) |
| Nondenominational | 8 (3%) | 6 (2%) |
| Agnostic/Atheistic | 4 (1%) | 2 (1%) |
| Other | 1 (0%) | 2 (1%) |
| Race: | | |
| Black | 5 (2%) | 4 (1%) |
| Native American | 1 (0%) | 2 (1%) |
| White | 285 (98%) | 341 (98%) |
| Other | 1 (0%) | 0 (0%) |

[a]Of the total sample, data were available from 289 husband and wife pairs.

for 1982. Gross family income averaged $39,755 for husbands and $32,670 for wives. (Additional descriptives for income are offered in Table 1.) A second objective measure was the degree of change in income over the last three years. Possible responses included: a) decreased more than 25%; b) decreased 5% to 25%; c) changed less than 5%; d) increased 5% to 25%; e) increased more than 25%; and f) fluctuated up and down. The frequencies of responses for each of these categories are given in Table 2. Because of the small number of husbands and wives reporting an increase of more than 25% in income, this category was collapsed with the "increased 5% to 25%" category. In addition, it was decided not to include in the analyses those farmers responding "fluctuated," because the degree and direction of change in income experienced by these farmers was not clear.

Two subjective measures of financial condition were also used. The first asked participants to evaluate their overall financial condition for the last three years. There were five possible responses: "much worse," "worse," "same," "better," or "much better." The frequencies of responses for each of these categories are given in Table 2. As with changes in income, it was decided to collapse the two upper categories—"better" and "much better." For a second subjective measure of financial condition, (income adequacy), participants were asked to evaluate the degree to which their income was enough to live on at the time of the survey. Categories for this item included "can't buy necessities," "can meet necessities only," "can afford some of the things we want but not all we want," "can afford about everything we want," and "can afford everything we want and have some left over." Data from this item were normally distributed and treated as a continuous variable. The mean for both husbands and wives was 2.8 with a standard deviation of .95.

*Dependent Measures.* Overall evaluations of one's sense of well-being were assessed using the Index of Well-Being developed by Campbell, Converse and Rogers (1976). The index contains eight semantic differential items, each a measure of how the participant feels about his/her life, and a single Likert-scale item addressing satisfaction with life as a whole. Scores were a weighted sum of the individual items. Internal consistency analyses of the index

Table 2.
*Frequencies for Change in Income and Evaluation of Financial Condition Over the Last Three Years*

| Change in Income | Husbands | Wives |
|---|---|---|
| Decreased > 25% | 64 (21%) | 59 (19%) |
| Decreased 5% to 25% | 59 (20%) | 53 (17%) |
| Changed < 5% | 49 (16%) | 53 (17%) |
| Increased 5 % to 25% | 60 (20%) | 65 (21%) |
| Increased > 25% | 13 (4%) | 8 (3%) |
| Fluctuated | 55 (19%) | 69 (23%) |

| Evaluation of Financial Condition | Husbands | Wives |
|---|---|---|
| Much Worse | 44 (14%) | 39 (12%) |
| Worse | 95 (31%) | 101 (31%) |
| Same | 105 (35%) | 115 (36%) |
| Better | 51 (17%) | 54 (17%) |
| Much Better | 8 (3%) | 12 (4%) |

yielded an alpha of .95 for wives and .94 for husbands. The range of score for husbands was 1.72 to 6.85, with a mean of 5.17 and a standard deviation of 1.15. The range of scores for wives was 1.99 to 6.85, with a mean of 5.12 and a standard deviation of 1.33. As these descriptive statistics suggest, the distributions were negatively skewed with most farmers experiencing higher well-being.

Satisfaction with family life was assessed using the Kansas Family Life Satisfaction Scale, or KFLSS (Schumm, McCollum, Bugaighis, Jurich, & Bollman, 1986). The four-item scale assesses the individual's satisfaction with family life as a whole, the relationships one has with his or her spouse and children, and the relationships children have with each other. Scoring involved summing the items. Alpha values for the scale were .88 for wives and .93 for husbands. Scores for the KFLSS ranged from 4 to 28 and were negatively skewed for both husbands and wives. The mean for husbands was 22.7 with a standard deviation of 5.12; the mean for wives was 22.5 with a standard deviation of 4.52.

## Data Analysis

The distribution of scores for both husbands and wives were negatively skewed on the Index of Well-Being and the KFLSS, and positively skewed for income. Square root transformations were performed on the well-being and family life satisfaction variables, and base 10 logarithmic transformations were performed on the income variable. Following these transformations, group comparisons were performed for the evaluation of financial condition and change in income variables on the dependent measures using One-Way ANOVA contrasts. Pearson product-moment correlations were performed to test the association of income adequacy and income with the two dependent measures.

## Results

*Total Family Income.* We hypothesized that income would be positively associated with well-being and family life satisfaction. As seen in Table 3, no support was found for this hypothesis. For husbands and wives, total family income (the variable *income* in Table 3) was not correlated with either well-being or family life satisfaction.

*Income Adequacy.* We hypothesized that income adequacy would be positively related to well-being and family life satisfaction. As shown in Table 3, partial support was found for this hypothesis. Income adequacy was positively associated with well-being for husbands and wives, with a somewhat stronger correlation for the farm wives. Family life satisfaction was not associated with income adequacy for either husbands or wives.

*Changes in Income.* We hypothesized that farm husbands and wives who reported a negative change in their income would score lower on well-being and family life satisfaction. Partial support was found for this hypothesis, as seen in Table 4. Wives who reported a decrease in income over the last three years scored significantly lower on well-being compared to those who reported an increase or change of less than 5%.

Table 3.
*Pearson Product-Moment Correlations of Well-Being and Family Life Satisfaction with Income and Income Adequacy*

| Income Variables | Well-Being | | Family Life Satisfaction | |
|---|---|---|---|---|
| | Husbands | Wives | Husbands | Wives |
| Income | .11 | .04 | .00 | .01 |
| | (216)[a] | (201) | (214) | (200) |
| Income Adequacy | .15* | .22** | -.02 | .06 |
| | (287) | (310) | (289) | (315) |

[a]The number of cases for each correlation is given in parentheses.
*$p < .01$.
**$p < .001$.

Changes in income did not differentiate between farm husbands on well-being. Finally, changes in income had no differential effect on family life satisfaction for either husbands or wives.

*Evaluation of Financial Condition.* We hypothesized that farm husbands and wives reporting less favorable evaluations of their financial condition would score lower on well-being and family life satisfaction. Table 5 offers partial support for this hypothesis. Wives who evaluated their financial condition as much worse or worse scored lower on well-being as compared to those who reported evaluations of the same or better financial condition. The findings for husbands' well-being were inconsistent, with no difference between evaluations of much worse and better and a significant difference between worse or much worse and same or better. Again, family life satisfaction was not differentially associated with evaluations of financial condition for either husbands of wives.

Table 4.
*T-Values from Comparisons of Changes in Income on Well-Being and Family Life Satisfaction*

| Change in Income Comparisons | Well-Being | | Family Life Satisfaction | |
|---|---|---|---|---|
| | Husbands | Wives | Husbands | Wives |
| Decreased > 25% versus Increased > 5% | -1.28 | -1.68* | 1.40 | -.29 |
| Decreased > 5% versus Changed < 5% or Increased > 5% | .61 | -1.72* | .06 | .35 |

*$p < .05$.

Table 5.
T-*Values from Comparisons of Evaluation of Financial Condition on Well-Being and Family Life Satisfaction*

| Evaluation of Financial Condition | Well-Being | | Family Life Satisfaction | |
| --- | --- | --- | --- | --- |
| | Husbands | Wives | Husbands | Wives |
| Much Worse versus Better | −1.10 | −2.24** | 1.03 | −.55 |
| Much Worse or Worse versus Same or Better | −1.99* | −2.53** | −.39 | −.90 |

*p < .05.
**p < .01.

## Discussion

From our analyses, it is apparent that satisfaction with family life does not vary with potentially stressful financial conditions regardless of how they are measured. Total family income had no significant effect on well-being for either farm husbands or wives. However, husbands and wives' well-being did vary positively with perceptions of income adequacy. Wives' well-being varied positively with changes in income and overall evaluation of financial condition; husbands' well-being varied to a lesser degree with overall evaluation of financial condition. Thus, subjective aspects of financial conditions appeared more strongly related to well-being among husbands and wives. This finding lends support to the Hill/Burr model of family stress which states that the amount of crisis is not determined by the stressor event alone but by the perception of the stressor. Secondly, financial stress appears more strongly related to wives' versus husbands' well-being.

Why do financial stressors influence farmers' well-being but not their satisfaction with family life? It is not surprising that adequacy of income is positively related to well-being in that the quality of one's life is related to one's economic condition (Campbell, Converse, and Rogers, 1976). In addition, farming is more than just an occupation to farmers; it is a way of life connected to their cultural and family heritage. Thus, symbolically and literally, they stand to lose a great deal more than just a job when farming does not financially pay off. It is possible that the reason that family life satisfaction was not affected by financial stressors may be related to the nonmaterial resources farm families have at their disposal. For example, Stinnett (1979) remarked that rural families have "internal strengths" that they call upon

in times of crisis. Farm husbands and wives provide each other with social support which acts as a stress-buffering mechanism in times of difficulty (Berkowitz & Perkins, 1985; Husaini, Neff, Newbrough, & Moore, 1982). Resources such as these may lessen the impact of financial stressors on farm family life.

Why would the relationship between financial stressors and well-being be somewhat stronger for wives than husbands? We suspect that farm wives more often play a financial manager role in their family than farm husbands. In addition, farm wives often share a large commitment to the family farm business (Berkowitz & Perkins, 1984). Thus, we would expect the impact of financial strains to be greatest for the one who deals most with day-to-day farm family economic needs.

Since this study provides evidence of decreased well-being among farmers (especially wives) who report greater financial sressors, what steps should we take to assist farmers? A number of helpful interventions could be used. Before interventions are suggested, though, we must first be aware that farmers place a high value on independence and self-sufficiency (Targ, 1981; Willits, Bealer, & Crider, 1982) which may lead to a reluctance to ask for help, even when needed. We assume that in most cases these values are functional and important to farmers. Thus, before we advocate certain interventions, we must first ask ourselves: does the program/policy help farmers to maintain their independence and self-sufficiency? An individual's well-being is enhanced when s/he behaves in a manner consistent with his/her values (Christensen, 1969). Therefore, when interventions direct farmers away from their core values, unless these values are dysfunctional to their growth as individuals and within relationships (Aponte, 1985), they ultimately cannot enhance farmers' well-being.

## Implications

Based on this framework, what potential interventions seem most likely to enhance farmers' well-being? One approach is to intervene at the source of the stress. That is, increase farm income to the point where farm husbands and wives perceive it as adequate. While government programs can be attempted, they do farmers little service, in terms of well-being, unless they help them to become more self-sufficient and independent. Government assistance, if not used in this manner, may create a false illusion of prosperity and makes farmers even more dependent on external sources for financial maintenance. This is contrary to their basic values. Thus, in the long run, this may be more costly and detrimental to farmers than the current financial stressors. One example of an intervention which might encourage self-sufficiency and independence would be short-term financial assistance, with incentives for farm and professional growth (which could lead to increased cash flow) and payback clauses to encourage individual accountability.

A second approach is the enhancement of resources for coping with financial stress through existing agencies which serve farmers. Increased competition in the marketplace and a growing sophistication in farm technology requires that today's farmers be highly skilled in financial matters. Noting that perceptions of income adequacy are more important than actual income, farmers could benefit from services that help them better use existing economic resources. Agencies such as the Cooperative Extension Service could provide (if not already offered) seminars in financial management and planning skills with a "Self-Sufficiency Farming" theme.

However, there is evidence that farmers rely heavily on internal resources in coping with change (Marotz-Baden & Colvin, 1986; ICFR Newsletter, 1986). Most of the farmers in this research more often used spiritual resources, family and friends to a lesser extent, and community resources least of all. This concurs with the findings in our 1985 study of Indiana farmers. It suggests that resources to assist farmers should be available where they are most likely to use them,

(i.e., the church). It also suggests interventions which aid in the development of internally-based coping strategies. For example, the clergy, with the indirect assistance of other mental health professionals, could encourage farm husbands and wives in the development of faith, courage, and persistence. The development of resources such as these may assist farmers in putting today's challenges in the broader context of the natural oppositions and challenges which are a part of everyday farm life, and encourage hope for the future.

## REFERENCES

Aponte, H. J. (1985). The negotiation of values in therapy. *Family Process, 24,* 323-338.

Berkowitz, A. D., & Perkins, H. W. (1984). Stress among farm women: Work and family as interacting systems. *Journal of Marriage and the Family, 46,* 161-166.

Bosc, M. (1985, November 18). Family life takes beating in farm crisis. *U.S. News and World Report,* p. 62.

Boss, P. (1987). Family stress: Perception and context. In M. B. Sussman & S. Steinmetz (Eds.), *Handbook on marriage and the family* (pp. 695-723). New York: Plenum.

Burr, W. R. (1973). *Theory construction and the sociology of the family.* New York: John Wiley and Sons.

Campbell, A., Converse, P. E., & Rogers, W. L. (1976). *The quality of American life.* New York: Russell Sage Foundation.

Christensen, H. T. (1969). Normative theory derived from cross-cultural family research. *Journal of Marriage and the Family, 31,* 209-222.

Coward, R. T., & Jackson, R. W. (1983). Environmental stress: The rural family. In H. I. McCubbin & C. R. Figley (Eds.), *Stress and the family, Vol. I: Coping with normative transitions* (pp. 188-200). New York: Brunner/Mazel.

Gilles, J. L., Hirschi, D., Campbell, R., & Heffernan, W. D. (1984). *Agricultural change and quality of life in three land resource regions.* Paper presented at the annual meeting of the Rural Sociological Society, Columbia, MO.

Hill, R. (1949). *Families under stress.* New York: Harper.

Hill, R. (1958). Generic features of families under stress. *Social Casework, 49*(2), 139-150.

Husaini, B. A., Neff, J. A., Newbrough, J. R., & Moore, M. C. (1982). The stress-buffering role of social support and personal competence among the rural married. *Journal of Community Psychology, 10,* 409-426.

Indiana Council on Family Relations (ICFR) Newsletter. (1986). West Lafayette, IN: Purdue University.

Marans, R. W., Dillman, D. A., & Keller, J. (1980). *Perceptions of life quality in rural America: An analysis of survey data from four studies.* Ann Arbor, MI: Institute for Social Research.

Marotz-Baden, R., & Colvin, P. L. (1986). Coping strategies: A rural-urban comparison. *Family Relations, 35,* 281-288.

McCubbin, H. I., & Patterson, J. M. (1983). The family stress process: The double ABCX model of adjustment and adaptation. In H. I. McCubbin, M. B. Sussman, & J. M. Patterson (Eds.), *Social stress and the family* (pp. 7-37). New York: Haworth Press.

Melichar, E. (1984). A financial perspective on agriculture. *Federal Reserve Bulletin, 70,* 1-13.

Poole, D. L. (1981). Family farms and the effects of farm expansion on the quality of marital and family life. *Human Organization, 40,* 344-349.

Rosenblatt, P. C., & Anderson, R. M. (1981). Interaction in farm families: Tension and stress. In R. T. Coward and W. M. Smith, Jr. (Eds.), *The family in rural society* (pp. 147-166). Boulder, CO: Westview Press.

Rosenblatt, P. C., & Keller, L. O. (1983). Economic vulnerability and economic stress in farm families. *Family Relations, 32,* 567-573.

Schumm, W. R., McCollum, E. E., Bugaighis, M. A., Jurich, A. P., & Bollman, S. R. (1986). Characteristics of the Kansas family life satisfaction scale in a regional sample. *Psychological Reports,* **58**, 975-980.

Sheets, K. R. (1985, February 4). America's farmers down the tubes? *U.S. News and World Report,* pp. 47-49.

Stinnett, N. (1979). In search of strong families. In N. Stinnett, B. Chesser, and J. DeFrain (Eds.), *Building family strengths: Blueprint for action* (pp. 23-30). Lincoln, NE: University of Nebraska Press.

Targ, D. B. (1981). Middle age in rural America: Adapting to change. In R. T. Coward and W. M. Smith, Jr. (Eds), *The family in rural society,* (pp. 187-198). Boulder, CO: Westview Press.

Walters, C. M., & McKenry, P. C. (1985). Predictors of life satisfaction among rural and urban employed mothers: A research note. *Journal of Marriage and the Family,* **47**, 1067-1071.

Willits, F. K., Bealer, R. C., & Crider, D. M. (1982). Persistence of rural/urban differences. In D. A. Dillman & D. J. Hobbs (Eds.), *Rural society in the U.S.: Issues for the 1980's* (pp. 69-76). Boulder, CO: Westview Press.

# Stress and Unemployment in Rural Nonfarm Couples: A Study of Hardships and Coping Resources*

**Mari S. Wilhelm and Carl A. Ridley\*\***

cent economic trends have resulted in a special concern for individuals and families coping with economic uncertainties unique to rural life. The thrust of this attention has been directed toward rural families faced with potential for actual loss of their primary source of family income, the family farm (Rosenblatt & Keller, 1983). Less attention has been directed toward the economic problems of rural nonfarm families. Many of these families have been living and working in small rural towns with few employment opportunities. Major shutdowns of mines and industries which form the economic base of these rural towns have resulted in large numbers of rural unemployed.

One hardship which appears common to all unemployed is loss of income. The most obvious changes which occur when a family loses income due to unemployment of a family member are finding new ways of bringing money into the household (e.g., taking on odd jobs, having other family members start work) and making changes in financial man-

agement (Caplovitz, 1979; Cavan & Ranck, 1938; Elder, 1974; Moen, 1979; Voydanoff, 1983). In rural areas, finding other ways of bringing money into the household is limited; and thus unemployed families may be forced to take a more serious look at changes in money management.

Research has demonstrated that unemployment and the hardships which accompany reduced income contribute to the overall stress felt by individual family members during unemployment (Guadagno, 1983; Liem, Atkinson, & Liem, 1982; Rosenblatt & Keller, 1983; Zvonkovic, Crouter, & Huston, 1983). Families and individual family members vary in the extent to which they experience stress or are otherwise affected by the hardships which occur due to the unemployment of the family's primary breadwinner (Cavan & Ranck, 1938; Liem et al., 1982; Voydanoff, 1984).

Little research is available, however, to provide professionals (e.g., counselors and educators), who are frequently asked to assist the unemployed individual and his/her family, with an understanding of the relationships between hardships experienced during unemployment and individual stress. Additionally, little research is available concerning the ability of various coping resources to mediate the relationship between hardships and stress. The findings of this study should enhance the ability of professionals in working with families who are experiencing unemployment.

*This research was supported by Arizona Research Station Project #174509-R-07-64 and is part of the Agriculture Experiment Station Project W167: Coping With Stress: Adaptation of Nonmetropolitan Families to Socioeconomic Changes.
**Mari S. Wilhelm is Assistant Professor and Carl A. Ridley is Professor in the School of Family and Consumer Resources at the University of Arizona, Tucson, AZ 85721.

Reprinted from *Family Relations*, 1988, **37**, 50-54.

## Framework and Previous Research

In order to explore adaptability to stress, Hill's ABCX model of stress recovery was identified as one of the most frequently used and useful frameworks for guiding stress research (Crossman & Edmonson, 1985; McCubbin et al., 1980; Plummer & Koch-Hatten, 1986). The model was used in the context of this research to facilitate the identification of variables to be studied and the relationship of those variables to each other. No attempt was made to test the complete model.

The ABCX model consists of four components, three of which are used to develop the framework used in this study of rural couples: "A" represents the stressor event and/or hardships resulting from the stressor; "B" represents management of the stress through coping resources; and "X" represents the resulting level of crisis. The "C" component, which is not used in the framework of this study, represents perception of the severity of the stressor by the family and/or family members. A specific description of variables of interest in this study follows.

## The Stressor Event and Accompanying Hardships

Stress is not viewed as inherent to a particular event (e.g., unemployment); rather, it results from the various hardships created by the event (Burr, 1973; Hill, 1949; McCubbin et al., 1980). Hardships associated with the stressor event are usually difficult to identify. Researchers frequently ignore hardships or integrate them into a stress recovery model as a coping response rather than the hardship which results because of the stressor event (McCubbin et al., 1980).

The stressor event in this research was the unemployment of the primary breadwinner of families living in a rural nonfarm community. Based on prior unemployment research, the hardships identified as important to the present study were increases in financial management behaviors and increases in financial arguments. Both were identified from previous research as changes which frequently occur due to unemployment (Caplovitz, 1979; Cavan & Ranck, 1938; Elder, 1974; Voydanoff, 1983).

## Coping Resources

According to the ABCX model of stress recovery, the availability and utilization of various coping resources (e.g., personal resources, coping abilities) could mediate the relationship between the stressor event (or hardships of the stressor event) and the potential for crisis. In the study reported here, the focus was on assessing the importance of personal and coping resources as mediators of stress.

*Personal Resources.* The personal resources important to stress recovery can include objective financial situation, good physical health, education to facilitate problem solving, and emotional well-being (McCubbin et al., 1980). Research has suggested that the availability of financial resources, such as savings and unemployment compensation, reduces the detrimental effects of unemployment (Thomas, McCabe & Berry, 1980; Voydanoff, 1983). Objective financial situation, as indicated by a measure of net worth, was used in the present research as a personal resource capable of mediating the relationship between the hardships of unemployment and stress.

*Coping Abilities.* The second category of coping resources addressed in this study is coping abilities. Ability to confront and resolve problems is a coping resource which reflects the level of family organization. When measured at the onset of a stressor event (pre-crisis), it can help to identify the family's immediate responses to a stressor event (McCubbin et al., 1980). Previous studies of unemployed families reported that those individuals and families who were able to think through a greater number of alternative solutions to their economic problems were better able to respond positively to unemployment (Elder, 1974). Additionally, studies have reported that the ability of family members to be emotionally available for each other during stressful events contributed to positive outcomes (Elder, 1974; Voydanoff, 1984). Conflict management and general coping strategies were used as indicators of coping ability resources.

## Crisis Outcome

*Stress.* For purposes of the present research, level of stress is the "X" factor, the indicator of crisis. The framework suggests that hardships of unemployment will create disequilibrium within the family and thus a feeling of stress for family members. The extent to which coping resources of family members are available should influence the relationship between hardships and stress. In this research stress was viewed from husbands' and wives' perceptions of their feelings on control over their lives.

### Hypothesis of the Study

The purpose of the present investigation was twofold. First was to examine the influence of changes in financial management and increases in financial arguments on individual levels of stress reported by husbands and wives *immediately* following the layoff of the family's primary breadwinner. Second was to examine the ability of coping resources to mediate those relationships. Specifically, the hypothesis tested for husbands and wives separately was:

The relationship between hardships (financial management behaviors, increase in financial arguments) and stress will be reduced as coping resources (net worth, couple conflict management, coping abilities) are available.

## Method

### Sample

The participants of this study were from a small mining town in Arizona. This particular town was selected due to shutdown of the copper mine which was the town's primary employer. In order to represent the population of the town at the time of the shutdown, the total sample for this study is made up of those couples who remained in the town and those who moved within 3 months following the shutdown.

In order to select those couples remaining in the town, telephone numbers were randomly selected from the telephone directory. Based on a random start, every tenth phone number was called to determine willingness of the couples to participate. This procedure was continued until a total sample of 25 couples experiencing unemployment was found. Husbands and wives (22 couples) from this group participated in a 1½-hour interview. Each husband and wife also completed an extensive questionnaire. Only questionnaire data were used in this analysis.

In order to select those participants who had moved, letters were sent to all names (not already surveyed) listed in the telephone directory. The letter asked for indication of having moved and willingness to volunteer in the study. Twenty-four couples qualified as movers and volunteered to participate. Twenty-two couples actually completed and returned the questionnaires. The resulting 88 participants comprised approximately 4.5% of the population of the town at the time of the shutdown.

As seen in Table 1, the 88 participants of this study were primarily in their early 30s and were of Anglo ethnic background. The 88 participants were comprised of 44 husband and wife couples. Over 60% of the husbands and wives were in their first marriage, and they had been married to their present spouse an average of just over 11 years. Families had an average of just over four members. Greater than 80% of the sample had at least a high school education, with over half having some college or trade school. Previous to the shutdown most families had one member, primarily the husband, working outside the home.

Table 1.
*Sample Description*

|  | Wives (N = 44) | Husbands (N = 44) |
|---|---|---|
| Percentage of Sample: |  |  |
| Presently in first marriage | 68 | 71 |
| With high school education | 91 | 82 |
| With post high school education | 74 | 57 |
| White/Anglo | 89 | 89 |
| Hispanic | 11 | 11 |
| Sample Average for: |  |  |
| Age | 34.6 | 33 |
| Length of present marriage | 11.2 years | 11.1 years |
| Family size | 4.3 | 4.4 |
| Number working before layoff | 1.3 | 1.2 |

## Instruments

*Hardships—Increases in Financial Arguments.* Participants were asked to indicate whether there had been an increase, decrease, or no change in nine money-focused conflicts between themselves and their spouse. The conflicts included such items as arguing over money and blaming spouse for money problems. A total score was created by counting the number of times the participant indicated an increase versus a decrease or no change in one of the money-focused conflicts.

*Hardships—Increases in Financial Management Behaviors.* Participants were given a list of 26 financial management behaviors and were asked to indicate whether these activities had decreased, stayed the same, or increased in frequency since unemployment. Based on a factor analysis six financial management factors were identified. Those factors included increased borrowing or credit use (credit), planning for major expenditures (spend), keeping closer tabs on check writing and bill paying (check), increasing saving behavior and checking the ability to pay one's bills (save), keeping more detailed records of income and expenses (record), and budgeting for daily expenses (budget). Six "increases in financial management" behaviors were then computed by counting the number of behaviors in each factor which had increased since the onset of unemployment.

*Coping Resources—Net Worth.* Participants were asked on the questionnaire to indicate the total dollar amount of their savings and investments and the total dollar amount of their debt. A measure of net worth was calculated by subtracting the amount of debt from the amount of savings and investments. Thus, the measure of net worth in this study is a reflection of the amount of savings relative to the amount of debt.

*Coping Resources—Couple Conflict Inventory.* The measure of interpersonal conflict management styles was obtained by asking respondents to complete one of the five scales (perceptions of their own conflict management styles) in the Conflict Inventory developed by Margolin (1980). The scale (21 items) yields three scores: problem solving, withdrawal, and aggression.

*Coping Resources—Coping Abilities.* A measure of coping ability was obtained by asking participants to indicate the extent to which they used 32 coping strategies previously identified by Moos (1983). No use of a particular strategy was coded zero; using a strategy once or twice received a score of one; using a strategy sometimes received a score of two; and using a strategy fairly often received a score of three. Three categories of coping strategies were identified following the recommendation of Moos. Those categories based on face validity included cognitive, avoidance, and active behavioral coping.

*Crisis Outcome—Perceived Stress.* Perceived stress is the dependent variable of interest in the present study and served as an indicator of the impact of unemployment on husbands and wives. The measure used was the Perceived Stress Scale (PSS) developed by Cohen, Kamarck, and Mermelstein (1983). Respondents were asked to indicate on a 5-point Likert-type scale from never to very often how frequently they had experienced a total of 14 feelings within the last month. The items included such feelings as being angered with things outside of one's control and being upset from unexpected happenings. Typically, a total stress score is computed by summing the responses to all 14 items. This procedure was followed here.

## Results

Analyses were performed separately for the group of husbands and for the group of wives. Results of the analysis for husbands are reported in Table 2. Results of the analyses for wives are reported in Table 3.

Stepwise, hierarchial multiple regression was the statistical method used in this research. This analysis allowed the researchers to look at the relationship of hardships, coping resources, and stress in a series of steps. Multiple regression also allowed the researchers to control the order in which variables were studied.

The first step was to explore the relationship of the various indicators of hardships to level of stress. The results of these analyses are reported in each table (husbands and wives) as Model 1. Hardships were allowed to enter the model according to the strength of their relationship to stress. Hardships were no longer allowed to enter the model if the strength of their relationship to stress fell below an F value of 1.0. The standardized beta coefficients in Model 1 provide information about the importance of

Table 2.
*Standardized Beta Coefficients from the Hierarchal, Stepwise Multiple Regression of Husbands' Perceived Stress onto Hardships of Unemployment and Coping Resources (N = 44)*

| | Model 1 (Hardships Only) | Model 2 (Hardships and Net Worth) | Model 3 (Hardships, Net Worth, and Avoidance Coping) | Model 4 (Complete Model) |
|---|---|---|---|---|
| Hardships | | | | |
| Save | −.31 | −.33 | −.22 | −.18 |
| Financial Arguments | .22 | .21 | .08 | .11 |
| Coping Resources | | | | |
| Net Worth | | −.36* | −.34* | −.41* |
| Avoidance Coping | | | .33** | .42** |
| Withdrawal Behavior | | | | −.23 |
| Adjusted $R^2$ | .04 | .15 | .22 | .24 |
| Significance of Model | .20 | .05 | .02 | .02 |

*$p < .05$.
**$p < .058$.

a specific hardship in predicting stress relative to other hardships in the model.

The second step was to allow coping resources to enter the analysis. Again, coping resources were allowed to enter according to the strength of their relationship to stress while controlling for the hardships that were previously allowed to enter. Coping resources were no longer allowed to enter the analysis if the strength of their relationship to stress fell below an F value of 1.0. The standardized beta coefficients in Models 2 through 4 for husbands (Table 2) and Model 2 and Model 3 (Table 3) for wives give information concerning the importance of coping resources in predicting stress relative to hardships and other coping resources which are already in the model. Change in the standardized beta coefficients of the hardships as each coping resource is added to the analysis gives information concerning an interaction between that coping resource and a particular hardship in predicting stress.

As indicated in Table 2, only two hardships had a strong enough relationship to stress to enter Model 1 at the first step of analysis for husbands. Increased attempts at saving were associated with less stress. Increases in financial arguments were associated with higher levels of reported stress. Together, the hardships contributed to 4% of the variance in the level of stress. The model, as a whole, was not a significant predictor of stress.

By moving across Table 2 to Model 4, the reader can see that three coping re-

sources were allowed to enter the complete model. Net worth, as a personal resource, and withdrawal behavior, as a conflict management strategy, were associated with less stress. Avoidance coping, as a coping resource, was associated with more stress. Net worth was the only significant contributor ($p = < .05$); however, avoidance coping approached significance ($p = < .058$). The coping resources contributed an additional 20% to the variance, resulting in a model of hardships and coping resources which accounted for 24% of the variance in stress.

The interaction of hardships and coping resources was observed through changes in the standardized beta coefficients at each step in the analysis. No change is noted in the coefficients of the hardships upon the addition of net worth to the model. The addition of avoidance coping resulted in lowered coefficients for both saving and financial argument hardships. The addition of withdrawal behaviors further decreased the coefficient for saving and slightly increased the coefficient for financial arguments.

Results of the multiple regression analysis for wives are reported in Table 3. Hardships were more predictive of stress for wives than for husbands. Planning for expenditures (spend) and increases in financial arguments were associated with more stress; increased saving behavior was associated with less stress. Increase in financial arguments, however, was the only hardship which was a significant ($p = < .01$) contrib-

Table 3.
*Standardized Beta Coefficients from the Hierarchal, Stepwise Multiple Regression of Wives' Perceived Stress onto Hardships of Unemployment and Coping Resources (N = 44)*

| | Model 1 (Hardships Only) | Model 2 (Hardships and Avoidance Coping) | Model 3 (Complete Model) |
|---|---|---|---|
| **Hardships** | | | |
| Financial Arguments | .50* | .40* | .41* |
| Save | −.35 | −.32 | −.35 |
| Spend | .18 | .21 | .17 |
| **Coping Resources** | | | |
| Avoidance Coping | | .31** | .29** |
| Net Worth | | | −.19 |
| Adjusted $R^2$ | .23 | .31 | .32 |
| Significance of Model | .02 | .007 | .008 |

*$p < .01$.
**$p < .05$.

utor to Model 1. Together, the hardships created a significant model which accounted for 23% of the variance in stress.

Moving across Table 3 to Model 3, the reader can see that two coping resources were allowed to enter the complete model. Avoidance coping, as a coping resource, was significantly ($p = < .05$) associated with more stress. Net worth, as a personal resource, was associated with less stress; but the relationship was not significant. The coping resources contributed an additional 9% to the variance, resulting in a model of hardships and coping resources which accounted for 32% of the variance in stress.

Interaction of hardships and coping resources was again observed through changes in the standardized beta coefficients at each step in the analysis. Inclusion of avoidance coping (Model 2) resulted in a reduced beta coefficient for financial arguments but only a slight increase for increases in saving and planning for expenditures (spend). The inclusion of net worth (Model 3) does not appear to influence the relationship between the hardships and stress.

The findings of this study only partially supported the stated hypothesis. It was hypothesized that coping resources would mediate the relationship between hardships and stress. Avoidance coping was the only resource that significantly contributed to an overall model predicting stress and significantly mediating the relationship between hardships and stress. Avoidance coping reduced the impact of financial arguments and saving on stress of husbands. Avoidance coping reduced the relationship between financial arguments and stress for the wives.

## Discussion and Conclusions

While for this sample it was the husband who was unemployed, it was the wife whose stress level appeared to be most affected by changes in financial management. Past research suggested that it is, in fact, the wives who tend to make the day-to-day financial decisions of the household (Ferber & Lee, 1974). Their findings suggested that changes in the management of those tasks during unemployment have considerable impact on the wives.

Increased arguments with her husband over finances were the greatest contributor to the wife's stress, suggesting that the husband was either "interfering" in the day-to-day financial management or was complaining about the manner in which the wife handled those tasks. Either way, conflict over finances appeared to contribute to stress, especially for the wife.

In working with couples, therefore, it would appear that changes per se are not the problem; but rather, the problem lies in the interaction with the spouse concerning those changes. It would be wise for counselors and educators to do more than merely inform clients of a means to make ends meet. Clients would most likely benefit from assistance in constructive problem solving and conflict management.

The only coping strategy which surfaced as an important predictor of stress was avoidance coping. More avoidance was associated with more stress. Avoidance coping also appeared to mediate the relationship between hardships, especially the hardship of increased financial arguments, and stress.

Avoidance behaviors consisted of keeping feelings to self, refusing to believe it happened, and eating, drinking, and smoking to relieve tension. Obviously several of these behaviors would lead to less interaction with one's spouse and at least initially result in a lessened impact of financial arguments on stress.

On the surface this may appear constructive; however, the reader must recognize that avoidance coping also reduced the positive impact of saving on level of stress for husbands. Families may be better served in the long run if individuals develop appropriate skills in conflict management and problem solving.

In summary, conclusions drawn from the data suggest that professionals can provide constructive assistance to unemployed clients by:

1. Providing constructive information concerning changes that can be made in financial management. Findings of this study suggested that these changes do not necessarily increase stress. Well-known recommendations such as planning for spending, paying bills on time, and keeping adequate records appear appropriate during unemployment. Special attention to the family's ability to contribute to savings, no matter how little, may contribute to less stress of family members as indicated by the negative relationship of saving to stress for couples in this study.

2. Along with information concerning financial management, discuss with clients ways to identify their financial goals and how to share those goals with their spouse. Focusing on goals is contrary to avoidance in some ways, similar in others. Goal setting is confronting the situation but symbolic that all is not lost and that there is life after unemployment.

In addition, most financial counselors stress the importance of identifying goals in making appropriate financial decisions. Unclear goals and differences in goals be-

tween family members are frequently sources of conflict (Paolucci, Hall, & Axinn, 1977).

3. Providing clients with ways in which to handle conflict with their spouse would be especially beneficial for the wives. The improvement of communication is a frequent goal of counselors and educators. Financial management could be incorporated as the "topic" into any strategy for communication training.

## REFERENCES

Burr, W. (1973). *Theory construction and the sociology of the family.* New York: John Wiley and Sons.

Caplovitz, D. (1979). *Making ends meet.* Beverly Hills, CA: Sage Publications.

Cavan, R., & Ranck, K. (1938). *The family and the great depression.* Chicago: University of Chicago Press.

Cohen, S., Kamarck, T., & Mermelstein, R. (1983). A global measure of perceived stress. *Journal of Health and Social Behavior,* **24,** 385–396.

Crossman, S., & Edmondson, J. (1985). Personal and family resources supportive of displaced homemakers' financial adjustment. *Family Relations,* **34,** 465–474.

Elder, G., Jr. (1974). *Children of the great depression.* Chicago: University of Chicago Press.

Ferber, R., & Lee, L. C. (1974). Husband-wife influence in family purchasing behavior. *Journal of Consumer Research,* **1,** 43–49.

Guadagno, M. (1983). Economic stress: Family financial management. In H. I. McCubbin & C. R. Figley (Eds.), *Stress and the family: Coping with normative transitions.* (pp. 201-217). New York: Brunner/Mazel, Inc.

Hill, R. (1949). *Families under stress.* New York: Harper and Row.

Liem, R., Atkinson, T., & Liem, J. (1982). *The work and unemployment project: Personal and family effects of job loss.* Paper presented at the National Conference on Social Stress, University of New Hampshire, Durham.

Margolin, G. (1980). *The conflict inventory.* Unpublished manuscript, University of Southern California, Los Angeles.

McCubbin, H., Joy, C., Cauble, A., Comeau, J., Patterson, J., & Needle, R. (1980). Family stress and coping: A decade review. *Journal of Marriage and the Family,* **42,** 855–871.

Moen, P. (1979). Family impacts of the 1975 recession. *Journal of Marriage and the Family,* **41,** 561–572.

Moos, R. (1983). *Health and daily living form manual.* Palo Alto, CA: Stanford University, Stanford Research Institute.

Paolucci, B., Hall, O. A., & Axinn, N. (1977). *Family decision making: An ecosystem approach.* New York: John Wiley & Sons.

Plummer, L., & Koch-Hatten, A. (1986). Family stress and adjustment to divorce. *Family Relations,* **35,** 523–529.

Rosenblatt, P., & Keller, L. (1983). Economic vulnerability and economic stress in farm couples. *Family Relations,* **32,** 567–573.

Thomas, L., McCabe, E., & Berry, J. (1980). Unemployment and family stress: A reassessment. *Family Relations,* **29,** 517–524.

Voydanoff, P. (1983). Unemployment: Family strategies for adaptation. In C. R. Figley & H. I. McCubbin (Eds.), *Stress and the family: Coping with catastrophe* (pp. 90-102). New York: Brunner/Mazel, Inc.

Voydanoff, P. (1984). Economic distress and families. *Journal of Family Issues,* **5,** 273–288.

Zvonkovic, A. M., Crouter, A., & Huston, T. L. (1983, October). *For richer or poorer: The effects of income change on marital interaction and satisfaction.* Paper presented at the meeting of the National Council on Family Relations, St. Paul, MN.

# Farm Families in Crisis: An Application of Stress Theory to Farm Family Research*

**Karen Davis-Brown and Sonya Salamon****

Counseling and self-help programs for farm families suffering from the current agricultural crisis challenge our understanding of how family stress research can be applied to the needs of this specific population (North Central Regional Center for Rural Development, 1986). Recent critics have noted that classic stress theory isolates individuals and families from their larger social and cultural contexts, leaving important gaps which diminish its applicability to concrete situations (Auerswald, 1981; Mostwin, 1980; Reiss & Oliveri, 1983; Spiegel, 1982; Walker, 1985). This lack of specificity has hindered many counseling programs when generic solutions for relief do not account for the unique stressors experienced by and within families involved in agriculture.

Farm crisis counselors need a brief and simple but accurate instrument to assist in assessing the stressors, capabilities, and definitions specific to the family seeking help. In this chapter, the McCubbin and Patterson Double ABCX model (1983) provides a conceptual framework permitting the ex-

amination of stressors common to farm families and unique to different management types within the agricultural population (Salamon, 1985). Drawing on this application of stress theory to empirical findings, the Farm Family Assessment Instrument is presented for use by farm crisis counselors who need to evaluate the causes and determine potential strategies for dealing with farm family stress.

## Stress and the Farm Family

The ABCX family stress model developed by Hill (1949) and elaborated by McCubbin and Patterson (1983) delineates stressor events (designated "aA" in the model) which interact with a family's unique capabilities for avoiding crisis ("bB") and definitions of themselves and their experiences ("cC") to produce a response to the stressor that either minimizes or maximizes the potential for family crisis ("xX"). Thus, stress arises when an event demands more resources than a family is capable of immediately mustering, thereby threatening established and shared familial definitions and requiring adjustment or adaptation to avert disruption, disorganization, or dysfunction. According to the model, crisis occurs when the family is unable to adjust or adapt to the stressor in a manner which achieves a new balance and restores stability. Family crisis is not to be confused with the agricultural crisis, which in this schema is an element of the stressor event, or "aA."

Farm families possess a characteristic affiliation and structure, termed by Bennett (1982) "the agrifamily system," that is a potential source of stress. The primary dis-

*This chapter draws on research funded through cooperative agreements with the Economic Research Service, U.S. Department of Agriculture. The authors wish to thank Catherine A. Surra, Robert Hughes, Jr., and Elizabeth Slusser of Lutheran Social Services for their valuable input.

**Karen Davis-Brown is a Research Associate, Division of Human Development and Family Ecology, University of Illinois at Urbana-Champaign, IL 61801. Sonya Salamon is a Professor, Division of Human Development and Family Ecology, University of Illinois at Urbana-Champaign, IL 61801.

Reprinted from *Family Relations,* 1987, **36,** 368–373.

tinction between farm and nonfarm families is that, among farmers, familial and economic roles are combined; workers are both proprietors and closely related family members so that personal and family needs compete with enterprise needs. Other characteristics typical of farm families that may contribute to stress include the close working relationships among family members, often of several generations; the need to make important business decisions involving large amounts of capital on a daily basis; and dependence upon variable, unpredictable factors such as weather and markets for financial viability (Rosenblatt & Anderson, 1981).

Such distinctive characteristics may also foster family capabilities for minimizing crisis and new definitions of stressors and their effects. In turn, these capabilities and definitions can facilitate adaptation to change. When a stressor is perceived as a serious threat to common agricultural goals, combined familial and economic roles and close intergenerational working relationships potentially enable cooperation, sacrifice, and the exchange of advice, ideas, and skills. Daily decision making and dealing with the unpredictable can provide experience valuable for dealing with the loss of an operation.

Within the farm population, the basis for family and enterprise decision making differs, depending upon a family's perception of its relationship to land; commitment to continuing agriculture as a family occupation; obligations to past and future generations, particularly to children; and the value placed on cooperating with family members to achieve group goals (Kohl, 1976; Salamon, 1984). Many differences among farm families are related to where they fall on a yeoman-entrepreneur farming style continuum developed by Salamon (1985). The central contrast between these two ideal types is their respective agricultural goals. The yeoman's goal is continuity—to pass on the family farm and farming as a trade to at least one member of the next generation. The entrepreneur's principle goal, however, is optimizing profit—to run an efficient, productive, money-making business. Salamon found these divergent goals to be manifested in different operating strategies, farm organization, family characteristics, and community structures, as shown in Table 1. The differing familial goals and characteristics delineated

by the Salamon typology, when combined with the McCubbin and Patterson model, provide a framework for understanding the divergent needs and responses of farm families currently facing the loss of an operation.

## Farming Types and Family Stress

When a family is unable to attain desired goals because of an event which threatens their established relationships and structure, stress is increased. Whether the frustrated goals are utilitarian, derived from network or reference group, or based on intrapersonal standards, has important implications for individual and family responses to the stressor event. Threats to personal or reference group goals often cause more stress than those originating from purely utilitarian concerns (Janis & Mann, 1977; McCubbin & Patterson, 1983).

Regardless of farming types, farm families currently share a common stressor event—the potential or actual loss of the family enterprise due to the current agricultural crisis. Assets, labor, and financial capital are types of resources common to all farm families, as are definitions of farming, farm management, land and livestock ownership, and intergenerational obligation. Table 2 shows the characteristic differences between yeoman and entrepreneurial farming types, categorized according to response to the stressor and by family capabilities and definitions.

As described above, yeoman agricultural goals derive primarily from identity and family concerns, whereas entrepreneurial farming goals are predominantly utilitarian. As seen in Table 2, yeoman and entrepreneurial families differ dramatically in how capabilities are utilized and values defined. Yeoman family support and commitment to agricultural persistence contrast sharply with entrepreneurial independence and business orientation. Thus, responses of the two types to farm failure will differ significantly, with a greater potential for stress existing among yeomen than among entrepreneurs. The determining factor in how, and how well, farmers cope with farm loss is largely determined by how families of either type utilize capabilities and adapt their definitions to changed circumstances.

The following sections explicate Table 2 by elaborating the divergent yeoman and en-

Table 1.
*Different Farm Family Goals and Their Consequences*

| YEOMAN FAMILIES | ENTREPRENEUR FAMILIES |
|---|---|
| **FARM GOALS** | |
| Continuity of a viable farm and producing a family farmer | Manage a well-run business that produces profits |
| **Management Strategy** | |
| Expansion limited to family capabilities | Ambitious expansion limited by available capital |
| **Family Characteristics** | |
| Intergenerational cooperation<br><br>Parents assume responsibility for setting up son/heir, and intergenerational transfers<br><br>Family members, including non-farmers live in community | Intergenerational competition<br><br>Each generation must establish itself, and heirs responsible for intergenerational transfers<br><br>Many family members leave farming and the community |
| **Local Implications** | |
| Close-knit social networks<br><br>Strong attachment to church and village<br><br>Substantial commitment to community stability | Loose-knit social networks<br><br>Weak attachment to local church and village<br><br>Commitment lacking for community persistence |

trepreneurial experience of farm loss and the contrasting family capabilities and definitions available to the two groups in dealing with the stressor. Quotes are used throughout to illuminate contrasting farm family characteristics. These data derive from fieldwork conducted by Davis-Brown from January to October 1985 while residing in a north-central Illinois agricultural county (Salamon & Davis-Brown, 1986) and exemplify findings from over a decade of research by Salamon.

## The Stressor Event

As noted above, divergent reactions to actual or impending farm failure result from the yeoman goal of family agricultural continuity contrasted with the entrepreneurial goal of personal success. For yeomen, losing the family operation (Table 2, aA) results in familial as well as financial stress. This was evident for one farmer who lamented the financial problems caused by his attachment to family land: "... When (my cousin) decided to sell it I just felt like I had to buy it, since it had been in the family for so long and it's where we live .... It was probably a mistake, with prices the way they were. It's awful feeling like you're married to a piece of land." For an entrepreneur, however, farm failure focuses more on the financial loss of the individual operator. One entrepreneurial

Table 2.
*The ABCX Model Applied to Yeoman and Entrepreneur Farming Family Types[a]*

| STRESSORS (aA): Farm failure, impending or actual | | |
|---|---|---|
| | FOR YEOMAN: | FOR ENTREPRENEUR: |
| Perception of Stressor | threat to identity, family enterprise continuity | individual fiancial loss, failure |
| **FAMILY CAPABILITIES (bB): Agricultural resources** | | |
| | FOR YEOMAN: | FOR ENTREPRENEUR: |
| Assets (land, live-stock, equipment) | family commitment to enterprise persistence | willingness to sell to survive |
| Labor | reliable kin network involvement | independence from kin network |
| Financial capital | access to extended family resources | latest management practices, preferences for nonkin sources |
| **FAMILY DEFINITIONS (cC): Values placed on farming, land ownership, and intergenerational obligation** | | |
| | FOR YEOMAN: | FOR ENTREPRENEUR: |
| Farming | a way of life | a business |
| Farm management | enterprise takes priority over personal and household needs | personal and household demands take priority over farm |
| Land and livestock ownership | family heirloom | assets an income source |
| Intergenerational obligation | responsible to past genera-tions and future heirs | responsibility narrowly focused on family of procreation |

[a]Adapted from H. McCubbin and J. Patterson, "The Family Stress Process: The Double ABCX Model" in H. McCubbin, M. Sussman, and J. Patterson (Eds.), *Social Stress and the Family,* 1983. New York: Haworth Press.

farmer expressed his farming philosophy, declaring: "I figure you've got a 50–50 chance to succeed .... It's better to be a 'has been' than a 'never was.' "

Because, for the yeoman, the stress of individual financial failure is compounded by the frustration of internal and family-derived goals, greater demands are placed on family capabilities (Table 2, bB) and a greater challenge made to its accepted definitions (Table 2, cC) than is the case for entrepreneurial counterparts. A yeoman farmer perceived leaving farming as losing a value system: "I don't think it's farming itself as much as the values that go with farming—the church, the family, personal relationships ... When people move to the city it's more difficult ... There's a rootlessness and an isolation. ... "

## Family Capabilities and Definitions

Yeoman and entrepreneurial farm families have differing capabilities and definitions (Table 2, bB and cC) that aid in coping with farm loss. Among yeomen, an extended kin network is an important re-

source and primary focus. Therefore, yeomen rely heavily on the extended family for help in a stressful situation; contributions of money, labor, in-kind donations, and moral support are expected. One yeoman farmer echoed typical sentiments when he affirmed, "That's the nice thing about working for family .... You're in it together, you help each other."

Entrepreneurial independence from family and relative lack of identity investment in land and farming may also be potential resources. Entrepreneurial operators are likely to be comfortable with making decisions and assuming personal responsibility and may, therefore, be better able to deal with stress when extended family cannot, or will not, become involved. An entrepreneur, taking financial difficulties in stride, commented that he entered farming because " ... My dad was old, it was the easy thing to do. I could've gone into anything else .... Sometimes, I think maybe I should have."

Yeoman risk-aversive financial strategies include assumed family cooperation and the priority of enterprise needs over those of the individual or household. Because of these traditional strategies, it was less likely that members of this farming type overextended their financial resources during the inflationary 1970s, the cause of present severe financial problems for many operators (Barlett, 1984; Salamon & Davis-Brown, 1986). A typical yeoman attitude toward financial priorities was expressed by a farmer's recitation of the adage, "A barn will pay for a house but a house won't pay for a barn." For yeomen who did overextend, the emphasis these families place on land as a trust and on farming as an occupation makes them more susceptible to family crisis than entrepreneurs, who view farming as a business and land as an income source.

The obligation to past, present, and future generations felt by the yeoman compounds the stress engendered by financial problems. The yeoman commitment to extended family is typified by one operator's concern with preserving family land: "We just feel like we're taking care of that land for . . . all those generations who farmed it before we did. We're concerned that the land won't be as good for the next generation." When an entrepreneur's operation is threatened, in contrast, the major obligation perceived is that of economic support for the immediate family; extended family and farm are less important than the nuclear household. Reflected an entrepreneurial farmer with a high debt-asset ratio: "I've spent a lot of money . . . . But, I've given my kids a lot of things, I don't regret that. I'm broke now but I gave my kids something."

The same farming type, yeoman or entrepreneur, is commonly shared by members of a nuclear family (Davis-Brown, Salamon, & Surra, 1987). However, a farm operator and other family members may have different farming styles, evolved from life course experiences (education, for example) that add to intrafamily stress. The most frequently encountered conflict is a young member of a yeoman family advocating more entrepreneurial management practices than an elder. Other problems occur when a more entrepreneurial nonfarm member is landlord to yeoman farming kin, or when a woman landowner is more yeomanlike than her husband (Fink, 1986) or other kin tenants.

Most farm families fall somewhere between the ideal yeoman and entrepreneur types, experiencing both financial and relational stress when faced with the loss of an operation. However, assessing whether a

family tends toward the yeoman or entrepreneur helps counselor and client determine whether counseling should focus primarily on financial, personal, or interpersonal stress. For the entrepreneurial farmer, who perceives agriculture as a business, moving into another business can be a relatively easy adjustment; the main stressor is financial, or utilitarian. When farming is perceived as an intergenerational trust, as it is by yeomen, utilitarian stressors compound with personal and social, making family crisis more likely. The family's farming type then serves to guide exploration of capabilities for dealing with crisis due to farm loss and identification of shared definitions that will help or hinder adaptation to an altered financial and personal situation.

## Community Characteristics as Family Resources

Just as yeoman commitment to family and farming, and entrepreneurial commitment to self and profitability, can either ease or contribute to farm family stress, communities where yeomen or entrepreneurs dominate offer different resources and obstacles to families experiencing farm loss. A stronger connectedness within yeoman agricultural communities (Bott, 1971; Rogers & Salamon, 1983; Salamon, 1987) is manifested in close-knit social networks, active voluntary organizations, neighborly cooperation, and community solidarity (Salamon, 1985). Such characteristics make it more likely that members of yeoman communities are more willing and able to offer support and services to families who have lost or are losing their farms. Yeoman operators agreed that, as one stated: "There are some things more important than the almighty dollar . . . It's not worth ruining relationships or causing problems with other people just to get a little richer."

In yeoman communities, even if many families are in economic jeopardy, a tradition of mutual support and community commitment often translates into the forming of formal or informal support groups based upon existing social networks that help deal with crisis. For example, churches in predominantly yeoman communities are an important source for developing formal programs and informal assistance, and many denominations have become publicly involved in farm crisis issues at the local, regional, and national levels. A Mennonite farmer explained: "I don't believe that the answer to the farm crisis is purely economical. . . . It's a spiritual issue, ultimately, not just Mennonite. It's religious but there are Methodists and Catholics who feel the same way."

Correspondingly, the dominant agricultural focus and identity of a yeoman community make adjustment to a future off the land potentially more difficult for a family who loses the farm. The struggle to deal with guilt over the potential betrayal of family trust may be hampered by implicit judgment or self-comparison to neighbors and acquaintances with whom one interacts on a daily basis. One yeoman described his concern over responsibility to his extended family when his father died: "I had my mother and my sister and my own family to worry about. . . . I had the whole family to be responsible for."

This close identification with agriculture, family, and home community can also make it emotionally difficult for yeoman operators and their families to out-migrate, even when the move is dictated by employment needs. One yeoman farmer explained that in his community, ties to the local support network persist beyond the exodus from agriculture: "As operators got bigger and needed more land, more and more had to move into town. A lot of people live here and work in (an urban area over an hour's drive away)."

Entrepreneurial agricultural villages, in contrast, are characterized by loose-knit social networks, little cooperation either among households or under the auspices of voluntary organizations, and detachment from other community residents (Salamon, 1987). Village infrastructure and identity are likely to have eroded over the past few decades (Fink, 1986), leaving few institutions, including churches, that can offer interpersonal or financial support. In entrepreneurial communities having many financially suffering farm families, the few support sources that existed prior to the farm crisis may disintegrate, and the characteristic competitive and self-oriented philosophy results in exclusive concern for personal economic survival. The entrepreneurial emphasis on individuality over the relational aspects of farming may lead to the minimizing or ignoring of both the existence and effects of family stress, exacerbating further the potential for crisis.

Because entrepreneurial communities are less cohesive, do not provide a strong source of attachment and identity, and accepted out-migration to nonagricultural occupations prior to the farm crisis, troubled operators from these communities should find it less difficult to leave home and take up nonfarm employment. An entrepreneur bragged that, "If I had gone into shoes I'd have 15 stores by now," and joked about his approaching retirement with no regret about leaving the farm: "(My son) will take over as soon as I make enough money to retire to the golf course."

## Intervention with Families Facing Farm Failure

Determining the social context and worldview of a distressed farm family is a critical first step in helping them cope with the actual or impending loss of an operation (D'Zurilla & Goldfried, 1971; Egan, 1986; Searight & Openlander, 1984; Wadsworth & Ford, 1983). The Farm Family Assessment Instrument is presented below to aid the counselor or other helping agent in assessing whether farm family members are more yeomanlike or entrepreneurial in the capabilities and definitions possessed for dealing with this shared stressor.

Arranged in a grid format, the Farm Family Assessment Instrument explores client perceptions of self, major concerns, long-range objectives, and potential resources. These perceptions are further differentiated across the various life roles of a respondent. (Some family member may not consider themselves farmers; for these, the farmer category is better dropped from subsequent queries). The questions which comprise the Instrument are:

1. How would you describe yourself, as: (a) an individual? (b) a family member? (c) a farmer? (d) a community member?
2. What are your major concerns, as: (a) an individual? (b) a family member? (c) a farmer? (d) a community member?
3. What would you like to accomplish in the next 5 years, as: (a) an individual? (b) a family member? (c) a farmer? (d) a community member?
4. What material and social resources can you draw upon to help you cope with your concerns (listed in #2) and

accomplish your objectives (in #3), as: (a) an individual? (b) a family member? (c) a farmer? (d) a community member?

This Farm Family Assessment Instrument has yet to be tested for validity or reliability; therefore Figures 1 and 2 typify hypothetical yeoman and entrepreneur responses. Obviously, counselees will not reply with the exact phrases shown, and few are likely to be a pure example of either ideal type. However, these typical responses delineate two major factors which summarize the different causes of stress for yeomen versus entrepreneurs: (a) whether losing the farm causes more stress in the financial sphere or for personal identity; and (b) degree of family and community network embeddedness.

Most troubled farm families suffer both financial and relational stress, but differ in the extent to which one is the predominant cause for potential crisis. Particularly when the counseling relationship is short-term,

the helping agent will want to focus on one of these family stress factors to make the most progress in the short time available. If stress is primarily financially related, the counselor's response is more effectively directed toward that concern; if primarily intra- and interpersonal, those areas should be the counselor's focus. If a client and family possess high network connectedness, this can be an additional source of stress and/or assistance; if an operator and his family are only loosely connected to their social networks, the result may be isolation or independence from burdensome expectations, but capabilities for dealing with stress are much more likely to come from within.

Utilization of the Farm Family Assessment Instrument delineated in Figures 1 and 2 should help the counselor: (a) focus on the major factors of where the stress is located and degree of network embeddness, as well as other sources of stress; (b) determine the family's capabilities and how shared definitions about farming and social network help or hinder problem resolution; and (c) clarify

*Figure 1:* Sample Grid of Yeoman Farm Family Assessment Instrument Responses

| INSTRUMENT QUESTION | AN INDIVIDUAL? | A FAMILY MEMBER? | A FARMER? | A COMMUNITY MEMBER? |
|---|---|---|---|---|
| 1. HOW WOULD YOU DESCRIBE YOURSELF, AS . . . | cooperative, rather than competitive | from a long line of farmers | conservative | close with neighbors, friends |
| | slow to change time-tested ways | responsible to family for actions | steward of land, operation | involved in local groups, causes |
| 2. WHAT ARE YOUR MAIN CONCERNS, AS . . . | loss of identity as farmer | children not able to farm | loss of operation | opinions of others |
| | guilt over failure | loss of way of life | no commitment by successor | forced to leave to find work |
| 3. WHAT WOULD YOU LIKE TO ACCOMPLISH IN THE NEXT 5 YEARS, AS . . . | regain identity | regain family operation | get back into farming | pay debts |
| | regain self-respect | plan next generation's succession | able to buy land | stay in home community |
| 4. WHAT MATERIAL AND SOCIAL RESOURCES CAN YOU DRAW UPON TO COPE WITH YOUR CONCERNS AND ACCOMPLISH YOUR OBJECTIVES, AS . . . | a team-worker | shared commitment to family operation | willing to defer household needs for enterprise | moral support |
| | commitment to agriculture | in-kind, financial assistance | advice, experience of past generations | shared equipment, labor, services |

Figure 2: Sample Grid of Entrepreneur Farm Family Assessment Instrument Responses

| INSTRUMENT QUESTION | AN INDIVIDUAL? | A FAMILY MEMBER? | A FARMER? | A COMMUNITY MEMBER? |
|---|---|---|---|---|
| 1. HOW WOULD YOU DESCRIBE YOURSELF, AS . . . | competitive | independent | business-man | detached |
|  | risk-taker | self-reliant | up-to-date | selective involvement based on personal preference |
| 2. WHAT ARE YOUR MAIN CONCERNS, AS . . . | personal failure | maintaining standard of living | loss of investment | being beat out by someone else |
|  | dependence on others | finding employment | loss of income source | being beholden to creditors |
| 3. WHAT WOULD YOU LIKE TO ACCOMPLISH IN THE NEXT 5 YEARS, AS . . . | regain independence | provide for wife, children | able to expand | move on to better financial opportunities |
|  | get a new start | plan children's education | have a decent income | show others comeback |
| 4. WHAT MATERIAL AND SOCIAL RESOURCES CAN YOU DRAW UPON TO COPE WITH YOUR CONCERNS AND ACCOMPLISH YOUR OBJECTIVES, AS . . . | personal education, skills, abilities | income from wife's job | willing-ness to leverage | refinance debt with local lenders |
|  | farming not only desirable occupation | independence, self-reliance of children | advice, guidance of agents, experts | contacts to help find off-farm employment |

the client or clients' aspirations for farm and family. Because all family members may not share the same farming type, a counselor should separately assess each family member involved in the farm operation and be alert to differences and the compound problems caused by discrepancies in family farming goals.

While this Instrument bears testing "on the front lines," it fills the void for a counseling tool specific to farm families and is adaptable to a variety of contexts. Among the settings in which the interview might be useful are workshops or support groups. In these situations, the questionnaire can be completed by the participant and then used by leaders as a basis for guided discussion. This Instrument also provides a valuable foundation for subsequent telephone or face-to-face counseling by clergy, social workers, nonprofessional volunteers, peer counselors, or trained therapists.

Intended for use during the preliminary portion of a one-time meeting or the first in a series of sessions, the Instrument was developed for use particularly by helping agents not trained as counselors. The Instrument's logical progression helps clarify, for client and counselor, the former's definitions of self (Question 1), the specific stressors he or she is facing (Question 2), goals for remedying the stressful situation (Question 3), and capabilities for achieving those remedies (Question 4). These responses allow the determination of a client's farming orientation. Specific answers obtained, combined with background knowledge about the yeoman-entrepreneur continuum, provide the basis for subsequent discussions and counselor input into client decision making.

## Discussion

This chapter has a twofold purpose: first, to integrate family stress theory with empirical farm family research and, second, using the integration of theory and empirical findings, to produce a practical assessment instrument for use by farm crisis counselors.

Programs addressing families affected by the farm crisis have concentrated on providing financial counseling, often neglecting the crisis experienced by a family faced with losing a farming operation. Other programs have dealt with intra- and interpersonal stress, applying generic concepts and models to farm families without regard for their unique stressors, capabilities, and definitions. Social service agencies, religious and financial institutions, mental health professionals, and lawmakers, at all levels, must become more knowledgeable regarding the critical ways in which farm and nonfarm families differ and concerning the significant differences existing within the farming population. If farm families are to be truly helped to cope with financial, personal, and social loss, a better understanding of their specific needs and strengths must inform the programs and legislation designed to assist them.

The synthesis of stress and farm family literature and the Farm Family Assessment Instrument presented above are contributions to this educational effort. The Instrument is designed to assist crisis counselors at the local level to quickly and effectively assess the stressors, capabilities, and definitions, and from these factors the farming type of a client family. Such an assessment will better assist farm families in coping with stress, thereby averting more severe crisis.

## REFERENCES

Auerswald, E. H. (1981). Interdisciplinary versus ecological approach. In G. D. Erickson & T. P. Hogan (Eds.), *Family therapy: An introduction to theory and technique* (pp. 404–413). Monterey, CA: Brooks/Cole Publishing Company.

Barlett, P. F. (1984). Microeconomics of debt, drought, and default in South Georgia. *American Journal of Agricultural Economics, 66*, 836–843.

Bennett, J. W. (1982). *Of time and the enterprise.* Minneapolis, MN: University of Minnesota Press.

Bott, E. (1971). *Family and social network* (2nd ed.). New York: Free Press.

Davis-Brown, K., Salamon, S., & Surra, C. (1987). Economic and social factors in mate selection: An ethnographic analysis of an agricultural community. *Journal of Marriage and the Family, 49*, 41–55.

D'Zurilla, T. J., & Goldfried, M. R. (1971). Problem solving and behavior modification. *Journal of Abnormal Psychology, 78*, 107–126.

Egan, G. (1986). *The skilled helper: A systematic approach to effective helping* (3rd ed.). Monterey, CA: Brooks/Cole Publishing Company.

Fink, D. (1986). *Open Country, Iowa: Rural women, tradition and change.* New York: State University of New York Press.

Hill, R. (1949). *Families under stress.* New York: Harper and Row.

Janis, I. L., & Mann, L. (1977). *Decision making: A psychological analysis of conflict, choice and commitment.* New York: Free Press.

Kohl, S. (1976). *Working together.* Toronto: Holt, Rinehart & Winston of Canada.

McCubbin, H. I., & Patterson, J. M. (1983). The family stress process: The double ABCX model of adjustment and adaptation. In H. I. McCubbin, M. B. Sussman, & J. M. Patterson (Eds.), *Social stress and the family: Advances and developments in family stress theory and research* (pp. 7–37). New York: Haworth Press.

Mostwin, D. (1980). *Social dimensions of family treatment.* Washington, DC: National Association of Social Workers.

North Central Regional Center for Rural Development. (1986). *Farm crisis response: Extension and research activities in the North Central Region.* Ames, IA: Iowa State University.

Reiss, D., & Oliveri, M. E. (1983). Family stress as community frame. In H. I. McCubbin, M. B. Sussman, & J. M. Patterson (Eds.), *Social stress and the family: Advances and developments in family stress theory and research* (pp. 61–83). New York: Haworth Press.

Rogers, S. C., & Salamon, S. (1983). Inheritance and social organization among family farmers. *American Ethnologist, 10*, 529–550.

Rosenblatt, P. C., & Anderson, R. M. (1981). Interaction in farm families: Tension and stress. In R. T. Coward & W. M. Smith, Jr. (Eds.), *The family in rural society* (pp. 147–166). Boulder, CO: Westview Press.

Salamon, S. (1984). Ethnic origin as explanation for local land ownership patterns. In H. Schwarzweller (Ed.), *Focus on agriculture: Research in rural sociology and development. Vol. 1: Focus on agriculture* (pp. 161–186). Greenwich, CT: JAI Press.

Salamon, S. (1985). Ethnic communities and the structure of agriculture. *Rural Sociology, 50*, 323–340.

Salamon, S. (1987). Ethnic determinants of farm community character. In M. Chibnik (Ed.), *Farm work and fieldwork: Anthropological perspectives on American agriculture* (pp. 167–188). Ithaca, NY: Cornell University Press.

Salamon, S., & Davis-Brown, K. (1986). Middle-range farmers persisting through the agricultural crisis. *Rural Sociology, 51*, 503–512.

Searight, H. R., & Openlander, P. (1984). Systemic therapy: A new brief intervention model. *Personnel and Guidance Journal, 62*, 387–391.

Spiegel, J. (1982). An ecological model of ethnic families. In M. McGoldrick, J. K. Pearce, & J. Giordano (Eds.), *Ethnicity and family therapy* (pp. 31–51). New York: Guilford Press.

Wadsworth, M., & Ford, D. H. (1983). Assessment of personal goal hierarchies. *Journal of Counseling Psychology, 30*, 514–526.

Walker, A. J. (1985). Reconceptualizing family stress. *Journal of Marriage and the Family, 47*, 827–837.

# Stressors and Symptoms Predictive of Distress in Farmers*

**Lilly Schubert Walker and James L. Walker***

Until recently, the public image of farming was one of a tranquil and idyllic life style viewed as considerably less stressful than urban living. The reality of life on the farm has probably never corresponded with this popular stereotype, and the discrepancy may now be even more pronounced due to the current economic crisis facing North American agriculture.

In a study of 130 occupations, the National Institute for Occupational Safety and Health ranked farming among the 10 most stressful occupations (Smith, Colligan, & Hurrel, 1977). Although farmers and professionals working with farm families are beginning to address the subject of farm stress, there is only a relatively limited empirical literature on the topic of stress in farm families. [See Hedlund & Berkowitz (1978) for a review.]

Most current definitions of stress (Lazarus & Folkman, 1984; Pervin, 1968; Taylor, 1986) emphasize the relationship between the individual and the environment. These theories emphasize that stress is a consequence of a person's appraisal of whether one's personal resources are sufficient to meet the demands of the environment. In other words, stress is a person's subjective reaction to an appraisal of environmental demands (i.e., stressors). Stress is conceptualized as the process of appraising events (i.e., stressors) and reacting with personal distress (i.e., stress) in the absence of appropriate coping strategies. The model used in the present chapter views physiological, emotional, cognitive, or behavioral changes (i.e., symptoms) as consequences of personal stress. Symptoms are thus viewed as a product of, rather than a precursor to, stress.

Farming is a complex and demanding business with numerous pressures which can generate stress. Rosenblatt and Anderson (1981) identified a number of farm stressors including multigenerational family members working together on a common enterprise; wide seasonal variations in work requirements; an irregular, unpredictable income, substantial financial investment and risk; and the relative isolation of farm families from support systems and services.

Jevne (1979) suggested that an increasing incidence of farming-related stress is associated with radical changes in the farming life style as farming evolved from a largely physical occupation into one that requires a wide range of intellectual capabilities. Marotz-Baden and Colvin (1986) reported that rural families face a different mix of stressors than urban families. Rural families were found to report greater financial and business strains, while urban residents reported intrafamily strains as their major stressors.

In a recent study of farm stressors, farmers' reactions to those stressors (i.e., stress), and the consequences of this stress

*This research was supported by Grant #7223 from the Manitoba Health Research Council.

**Lilly Schubert Walker and James L. Walker are both Associate Professors of Psychology, Brandon University, Brandon, Manitoba, Canada R7A 6A9. They currently are on leave as Visiting Professors, Department of Psychology, University of Manitoba, Winnipeg, Manitoba, Canada R3T 2N2.

Reprinted from *Family Relations*, 1987, **36**, 374–378.

(i.e., symptoms), Walker and Walker (1987b) found the major farm stressors were economic factors, work overload, and relationship issues. For men, the best predictors of stress included time pressures, financial issues, government policies, personal illness at peak times, weather, social isolation, work overload, and pressures in keeping up with new technology and products. For women, the top predictors of total stress included financial concerns, government policies, time pressures, problems in operating agreements with relatives, not enough time to spend with spouse, death of a friend, media distortions of the farm situation, and work overload.

A number of researchers have suggested that a major component of the economic pressure of modern farming is contributed by the restricted and irregular cash flow associated with farming, the large capital investment, and financial risk necessary to maintain a modern farming operation (Keating, Doherty, & Munroe, 1986; Kohl, 1971; Rosenblatt & Anderson, 1981; Walker, Walker, & MacLennan, 1986; Walker & Walker, 1987b).

Stress levels have been found to differ as a function of the type of farming operation (Walker & Walker, 1987b). Farmers in mixed operations (grain and livestock) showed higher stress levels than grain farmers. In the same study, younger farmers were also found to show significantly higher stress scores than older farmers, presumably because of the higher financial pressures and debt loads carried by younger farmers. Higher stress levels in younger farmers may also be related to feelings of powerlessness from living on a multigenerational farm and having less control over the farm situation. Farmers working off the farm in addition to their regular work were also found to have higher stress scores compared to those farmers not working off-farm. Work demands and overload may be related to these differences. In this context, Walker and Walker (1987b) reported a comparison between farmers and senior level executives showing that 89% of the farmers reported work overload as a significant source of stress, while only 51% of the executives reported workload as a significant stressor. In the Walker and Walker study, fall and spring were overwhelmingly reported as the most stressful seasons in farming. It is during these seasons, of course, when work overload is most common.

Walker and Walker (in press) also reported a high incidence of self-reported cognitive, social, and physical symptoms commonly associated with chronic stress. Comparing farm families to urban families, farmers reported significantly higher incidences of loss of temper, back pain, behavior problems in children, forgetfulness, fatigue, headaches, marriage problems, sleep disruptions, and frequent illnesses. The best discriminator between farmers and nonfarmers was frequent loss of temper. Stress symptoms among farmers were also found to differ as a function of the type of farm operation. Farmers in mixed operations and dairy farmers showed higher stress symptom scores than grain farmers. Younger farmers showed higher symptom levels than older farmers, and farmers working both on and off the farm had more symptoms than farmers not employed off the farm.

A number of studies have addressed the issue of stress in farm women. Farm women report significantly higher stress scores than farm men (Capener & Berkowitz, 1976; Hedlund & Berkowitz, 1979; Walker et al., 1986; Walker & Walker, 1987b). The concept of role overload, too many job responsibilities to complete in too little time, has been proposed as a major source of stress for women. Work overload may also be related to the many different and conflicting roles of farm women who report that their multiple roles often produce feelings of anxiety and confusion as they strive to bridge the worlds of family, farm work, and community involvement (Walker et al., 1986). In support of the role overload hypothesis, Walker and Walker (1987b) found that among 60 farm stressors, three items related to the concept of role overload (balancing work and family responsibilities, not enough help from spouse, and working on the farm as well as managing the house and family) predicted 38% of the variance in stress symptom scores among farm women. Capener and Berkowitz (1976) and Hedlund and Berkowitz (1979) reported that one third of the farm women in their sample experienced role dependent stress. Further evidence supporting the role of overload in generating stress was provided by Walker and Walker (1987b) who found that both stress and symptom levels were significantly higher in women working off-farm in addition to their farm duties as compared to farm women not working off-farm. Stress and symptom levels were also found to be higher in women actively involved in the operation of the farm business as compared to those farm women not involved in the farm business.

A potential buffer to the stress women experience as a result of role overload was identified by Berkowitz and Perkins (1984), who reported that a key factor in reducing stress for farm women was the husband's support of his wife's roles and duties. This finding suggests that workload may interact with presence or absence of spousal support in determining level of stress.

The literature on farm stress suggests that farming is considerably less idyllic than commonly pictured, that farmers share some stressors which are common to all occupations as well as having a number of stressors which are specific to farming, and that farm families are showing a high incidence of stress-related symptoms.

The purpose of the present chapter is to: (a) provide empirical information of the prevalence of stress symptoms among farmers, (b) to identify the occupational stressors of farming which are most closely associated with high symptom levels, and (c) to determine which individual symptoms are most predictive of overall high levels of symptoms among farmers. These empirical findings can be beneficially applied in clinical work with farm families in the identification of individuals at risk due to chronic farm stress and can be used in planning stress management workshops for farm families.

## Method

### Subjects

Subjects were 808 men and women involved in farming as their principal occupation. Data were collected between January and May 1986 and were drawn from three sources: participants at farm management workshops sponsored by the Departments of Agriculture in Manitoba, Saskatchewan, and Alberta; volunteers from 40 Farm Business Groups throughout Manitoba; and volunteers secured at the Royal Manitoba Winter Fair.

There were 470 male and 338 female respondents who ranged in age from 18 to 73 years with a mean age of 38.4 years. The sample contained a larger proportion of younger farmers as compared to the ages of Canadian farmers (Ministry of Supply and Services Canada, 1982a). In the sample 23.7% were between the ages of 20–29 compared to 10.9% of Canadian farmers, 31.3%

were between 30–39 years versus 21.2% nationally, 22.4% were between 40–49 years compared to 23.6% nationally, and 15.6% were between 50–59 years versus 24.9% nationally. Eighty-seven percent of the sample were married.

The proportions of different types of farm operations represented in the sample were comparable to the breakdown of types of Manitoba farms provided by Statistics Canada (Ministry of Supply and Services Canada, 1982b). Grain farmers composed 29.5% of the sample compared to 23% of Manitoba farmers, 62.5% of the sample reported being engaged in mixed operation farming compared to 67.7% of Manitoba farmers, and 8% of the current sample were dairy farmers versus 6.8% of Manitoba farmers. The percentage of respondents holding an extra job off the farm was 36.8% which is comparable to national statistics of 41% of Canadian farmers reporting off-farm employment (Ministry of Supply and Services Canada, 1982a); 33.3% of the men reported off-farm employment and 41.1% of the women reported working off the farm.

The mean number of children reported by respondents was 2.57 (range = 0–9), the mean number of children still living at home was 1.73 (0–8), the mean number of years the farm had been in the family was 43.1 years, and a mean of 15.87 years was reported for the number of years operating the farm. Ten percent of the respondents had completed elementary school, 49% had completed high school, 24% had attended university or college, and 17% had earned a post-secondary degree. Comparable statistics for Canadian farmers for these demographic characteristics were unavailable.

### Measures

Using the conceptual framework described earlier which defines "stress," "stressors," and "symptoms," the occurrence of stressors was measured with the Farming Stress Inventory (FSI), a self-report measure of stressors commonly associated with farming and farm life. The 60 FSI items were derived from interviews with farm men and women who identified personal stressors associated with family farming. Twenty-seven of the FSI items described situations common to farming, and 33 items reflected pressures found in most occupations. Frequency of occurrence of stressors was measured on a 5-point Likert scale with end points labeled "almost never" and "almost always." Respondents were instructed to leave an item blank if the stressor was never experienced. Total frequency of occurrence scores on the inventory could thus range from 0–300.

The FSI is in the preliminary stages of development as an instrument to measure the occurrence of farm-related stressors and perceived stress in response to these stressors. Initial findings indicate that the instrument reflects satisfactory levels of reliability and validity. The internal consistency alpha reliability coefficient of the scale is 0.95, and it has been found to have a 2-week test-retest reliability coefficient of .91 (N = 45). The FSI has been found to correlate significantly ($r$ = .27) with scores on the Beck Depression Inventory; a stepwise discriminant analysis using FSI subscale scores has been found to correctly classify 77.5% of respondents into depressed or nondepressed groups; and a stepwise multiple regression using FSI subscale scores as independent variables yielded a multiple $R$ of .38 in predicting Beck Depression Inventory scores (Walker & Walker, 1986). Recent work with the FSI indicates that it shows an $r$ = .45 (N = 91) when correlated with Trait Anxiety scores as measured by the State-Trait Inventory (Spielberger, Gorsuch, & Lushene, 1970). A stepwise multiple regression using the FSI subscale scores to predict Trait Anxiety yielded a multiple $R$ of .51.

Respondents were also asked to respond to 19 items measuring the frequency of 19 commonly cited stress symptoms. These items were adapted from the Hopkins Symptom Checklist (Derogatis, Lipman, Rickels, Chlenhuth, & Covi, 1974) and the Health Problems Checklist (Schinka, 1984). They included increase in drinking, increase in smoking, weight gain/loss, change in health, trouble relaxing, nightmares, chronically tired, sleep disruptions, getting sick often, headaches, forgetfulness, trouble concentrating, frequent colds, increase in arguments, behavior problems in children, marriage problems, back pain, losing temper, and avoiding decisions. Responses for frequency of symptom occurrence were recorded on a 5-point Likert scale with anchor points of "almost never" and "almost always." Respondents who had never experienced the symptom left the item blank, so scores could range from 0–95.

## Data Analyses

Data were analyzed using $t$-tests and stepwise multiple regressions with BMDP programs (Dixon, Brown, Engelman, Frane, & Jennrich, 1979). Persons for whom data were missing were excluded from the relevant analyses, and the number of subjects and

Table 1.
*Means and Standard Deviations For Stress Symptom Items*

| Item | Males | | | Females | | | Total | |
|---|---|---|---|---|---|---|---|---|
| | M | SD | N | M | SD | N | M | SD |
| Increase in drinking | 1.26 | 0.84 | 473 | 1.28 | 0.90 | 338 | 1.27 | 0.87 |
| Increase in smoking | 1.27 | 0.97 | 473 | 1.34 | 1.10 | 338 | 1.29 | 1.03 |
| Weight gain or loss | 1.61 | 1.06 | 473 | 2.33 | 1.49 | 338 | 1.91 | 1.31 |
| Change in health | 1.58 | 1.00 | 473 | 1.94 | 1.12 | 338 | 1.73 | 1.07 |
| Trouble relaxing | 2.41 | 1.39 | 473 | 2.71 | 1.38 | 338 | 2.53 | 1.39 |
| Nightmares | 1.23 | 0.87 | 479 | 1.36 | 0.93 | 338 | 1.28 | 0.89 |
| Feeling chronically tired | 2.38 | 1.33 | 479 | 2.76 | 1.40 | 338 | 2.54 | 1.37 |
| Sleep disruptions | 1.98 | 1.26 | 479 | 2.31 | 1.40 | 338 | 2.11 | 1.33 |
| Getting sick often | 1.31 | 0.84 | 479 | 1.45 | 0.93 | 338 | 1.37 | 0.88 |
| Frequent headaches | 1.59 | 1.08 | 473 | 1.99 | 1.34 | 337 | 1.75 | 1.21 |
| Forgetting things | 2.48 | 1.32 | 473 | 2.49 | 1.36 | 337 | 2.48 | 1.33 |
| Trouble concentrating | 2.27 | 1.22 | 473 | 2.31 | 1.32 | 337 | 2.28 | 1.26 |
| Frequent colds | 1.61 | 1.05 | 473 | 1.48 | 0.92 | 337 | 1.55 | 0.99 |
| Increase in arguments with spouse or children | 1.64 | 1.09 | 471 | 2.17 | 1.24 | 335 | 1.86 | 1.18 |
| Problems with children | 1.52 | 1.06 | 471 | 1.90 | 1.25 | 335 | 1.68 | 1.16 |
| Marriage problems | 1.22 | 0.93 | 471 | 1.47 | 1.02 | 335 | 1.32 | 0.98 |
| Back pain | 2.07 | 1.37 | 470 | 2.18 | 1.42 | 332 | 2.11 | 1.39 |
| Losing temper | 2.32 | 1.23 | 470 | 2.67 | 1.31 | 332 | 2.46 | 1.28 |
| Avoiding decisions | 1.93 | 1.12 | 470 | 2.06 | 1.22 | 332 | 1.98 | 1.17 |
| TOTAL | 34.03 | 11.30 | 470 | 38.46 | 12.38 | 332 | 35.87 | 11.96 |

Table 2.
*Percentiles of the Total Symptom Scale Scores for Farmers*

| | | Raw Scores | |
| | | Men | Women |
|---|---|---|---|
| Quartile I | (0–24 percentile) | 0–26 | 0–28 |
| Quartile II | (25–49 percentile) | 27–31 | 29–36 |
| Quartile III | (50–74 percentile) | 32–39 | 37–45 |
| Quartile IV | (75–100 percentile) | 40–83 | 46–80 |

degrees of freedom thus vary somewhat for various analyses.

## Results

The 19-item symptom scale showed a high level of internal consistency (coefficient alpha = 0.88). Means and standard deviations for each item and the total score are presented in Table 1. Females showed a statistically significant higher mean score than males, $t(673) = 5.16$, $p < .001$. The obtained range of total symptom scores for females was 9–80 and the males showed a range of 3–83.

Percentile norms for the total symptom scores are presented in Table 2 for the 802 farm men and women with complete data on the symptom scale. Practitioners wishing to administer the 19-item scale to farm families may find these data useful in judging how individual client scores compare with quartile norms for the sample of farmers participating in the present research.

The relative importance of various symptoms in predicting the total symptom scores was assessed by conducting two stepwise regressions. The best predictors of overall symptoms for both men and women were trouble concentrating, sleep disruptions, change in health, and increase in arguments. For men, back pain was one of the top five predictors of total symptoms, while for women losing temper was a major predictor. For both men and women, the five symptoms isolated in the analyses accounted for 85% of the variance of the total symptom scores. The results are presented in Table 3.

In order to identify which stressors are most predictive of symptoms among farm men and women, stepwise regressions using the frequency of occurrence of the stressor to predict the total symptom scores were conducted. The results of these analyses for each sex are presented in Tables 4 and 5. The best predictor of symptoms for both men and women was "problems in balancing work and family responsibilities." For men the major stressors were generally work related and included issues related to financial concerns, geographical isolation, farm labor resource needs, and concern about the future of the farm. Women's stressors included a greater diversity of work, family, and political issues. Stressful events most predictive of symptoms for farm women included conflict with spouse, time pressures, political issues, government regulations, financial worries, and geographic or personal isolation. Over half of these stressors were events which were specific to farming.

Table 3.
*Stepwise Multiple Regression Analysis Predicting Symptom Scores in Men and Women[a]*

| Men | | | | Women | | | |
|---|---|---|---|---|---|---|---|
| Variable | R | R² | | Variable | R | R² |
|---|---|---|---|---|---|---|---|
| Trouble concentrating | .66 | .43 | | Trouble concentrating | .70 | .49 |
| Sleep disruptions | .79 | .63 | | Sleep disruptions | .81 | .67 |
| Change in health | .86 | .75 | | Increase in arguments with | | |
| Increase in arguments with | | | |    spouse or children | .87 | .75 |
|    spouse or children | .90 | .81 | | Change in health | .90 | .81 |
| Back pain | .92 | .85 | | Losing temper | .92 | .85 |

[a]At each step, minimum acceptable $F$ to enter = 4.0, minimum acceptable tolerance = 0.01.

Table 4.
*Stepwise Multiple Regression of Stressors Predicting Total Symptom Scores for Men*

| Variable | R | R² | Increase in R² |
|---|---|---|---|
| Problems in balancing work and family responsibilities | .48 | .23 | .23 |
| Personal illness during planting or harvesting | .61 | .37 | .14 |
| Conflict with spouse over spending priorities | .68 | .47 | .09 |
| No farm help or loss of help when needed | .71 | .51 | .04 |
| Worrying about keeping the farm in the family | .73 | .54 | .03 |
| Death of a friend | .74 | .55 | .02 |
| Farming-related accident | .75 | .57 | .01 |
| Having to travel long distances for service | .76 | .58 | .01 |
| Surface rights negotiations | .77 | .57 | .01 |
| Machinery breakdown at a critical time | .77 | .59 | .01 |

Table 5.
*Stepwise Multiple Regression of Stressors Predicting Total Symptom Scores for Women*

| Variable | R | R² | Increase in R² |
|---|---|---|---|
| Problems in balancing work and family responsibilities | .48 | .22 | .22 |
| Conflict with spouse over spending priorities | .57 | .33 | .10 |
| Pressures in having too much to do in too little time | .62 | .38 | .05 |
| Government cheap food policies | .65 | .42 | .03 |
| Major decisions being made without my knowledge or input | .68 | .46 | .03 |
| Death of a friend | .69 | .47 | .02 |
| Worry about owing money | .70 | .49 | .02 |
| Feeling isolated on the farm | .71 | .51 | .02 |
| Need to learn and adjust to new government regulations/policies | .72 | .52 | .01 |
| Concerns about the continued financial viability of the farm | .73 | .53 | .01 |

# Discussion and Implications

The findings reported here suggest that farmers are experiencing a variety of occupational stressors and are showing numerous symptoms. Family practitioners working in either therapeutic-remedial or in educational-preventative settings may find these data useful in designing appropriate intervention strategies.

The relationships identified in the present research between individual symptom items and total scores on a longer inventory of somatic and cognitive symptoms may provide a useful diagnostic screening technique for practitioners. For both farm men and women, frequency of occurrence of only three symptoms was able to account for 75% of the variance of scores on the longer symptom inventory, and inclusion of five of the symptom items accounted for 85% of the total variance in scores. When farm clients report trouble concentrating, sleep disruptions, increase in family conflict, changes in health, back pain, or loss of temper, the practitioner should be alerted to the possibility that the client is experiencing high levels of personal distress and further assessment of the extent of the stress and client coping capabilities may be advisable.

In cases where clients report the occurrence of symptoms most closely associated with high overall symptom levels, it may be desirable to administer the longer symptom inventory. The norms presented from the 808 farm men and women studied in the present research may be useful in this regard, allowing the practitioner to compare the client symptom score to quartile norms from other farmers. Clients showing symptom scores in the upper quartiles may benefit from stress management intervention techniques.

The present research also identified the occupational stressors of farm life which are most predictive of distress levels. This information may be of practical use in the assessment of client stress levels and in the identification of particular stressors requiring innovative or enhanced coping strategies. In this regard, it is interesting to note that many studies of farm stress have used general or nonspecific measures of life stress which do not tap the occupationally specific stressors associated with farming. Over half of the stressors identified in the present study as being predictive of distress levels were situations specifically associated with farm life.

This finding raises the possibility that researchers and practitioners who assess stress levels among farm families using instruments such as general life event inventories may be missing important sources of variance which reflect the major stressors associated with a farming life style.

Besides their potential usefulness in an assessment framework, the data from the present research may be useful in the design of stress management programs for farm families. Design of such programming might pay particular attention to a consideration of suitable coping strategies for those stressors found to be most closely related to overall distress levels. An examination of the stressors identified in Tables 4 and 5, for example, would suggest that stress management programming for farm families might include a consideration of coping strategies which enhance ability to balance the complex roles demanded of farm men and women, present conflict resolution strategies, investigate work sharing possibilities, explore possibilities for the development of supportive and nurturing social networks, consider strategies for cooperative decision making and problem solving, and explore coping skills related to time management and management of worry.

Stress management programs for farm families (Walker & Walker, 1987a) should not only relate directly to the issues most closely associated with overall stress levels among farmers, but should also consider enhancing coping strategies already accepted and used by rural people. In this context, Marotz-Baden and Colvin (1986) have observed that rural families use coping strategies more frequently than urban families and that the internal strategy of reframing is used most frequently, followed by seeking spiritual support, acquiring social support, passive appraisal, and finally, mobilizing the family to acquire and seek help. These findings supplement the present research by suggesting ways in which coping strategies which already have a familiarity to farm families might be applied to management of the stressors identified in the present chapter. For example, since farm families' top preferences for coping with stress are reframing and spiritual support, practitioners should provide illustrations of how these strategies can each be used to cope with the same issue, such as intraper-

sonal conflict, isolation, time pressures, or illness. It might also be useful to explore the reasons why rural clients do not use seeking help as a coping strategy. The information on rural coping strategies might also be beneficially applied to program delivery. Since farm families make frequent use of seeking spiritual support as a coping strategy, educational efforts might enhance this already existing coping preference by using church networks to co-sponsor or organize stress management programs which, because of their relationship to the church, might reach farm families who do not participate in human service workshops delivered by agricultural organizations or rural mental health clinics.

In summary, this chapter presents practitioners with information about the occupationally specific stressors that produce symptoms among farmers and provides suggestions for topics in the design of relevant stress management programming for farm families.

REFERENCES

Berkowitz, A. D., & Perkins, H. W. (1984). Stress among farm women: Work and family as interacting systems. *Journal of Marriage and the Family, 46*, 161–166.

Capener, H. C., & Berkowitz, A. D. (1976). The farm family: A unique organization. *Food and Life Science Quarterly, 9*(3), 8–11.

Derogatis, L. R., Lipman, R. S., Rickels, K., Chlenhuth, E. H., & Covi, L. (1974). The Hopkins symptom checklist (HSCL): A self-report symptom inventory. *Behavioral Science, 19*, 1–15.

Dixon, W. J., Brown, M. B., Engelman, L., Frane, J. W., & Jennrich, R. I. (1979). *Biomedical computer programs: P-series*. Berkeley: University of California Press.

Hedlund, D., & Berkowitz, A. D. (1978). *Farm family research in perspective: 1965–1977* (Rural Sociology Bulletin 79). New York: Cornell University, Department of Agricultural Economics.

Hedlund, D., & Berkowitz, A. D. (1979). The incidence of social psychological stress in farm families. *International Journal of Sociology of the Family, 2*, 233–245.

Jevne, J. (1979). *Women of unifarm report: Stresses in the family farm unit*. Hussar, Alberta: Unifarm.

Keating, N., Doherty, M., & Munroe, B. (1986). The stress of farm debt. *Agriculture and Forestry Bulletin, 9*(2), 23–25.

Kohl, S. (1971). The family in a post-frontier society. In K. Ishwanran (Ed.), *The Canadian family* (pp. 79–93). Toronto: Holt, Rinehart & Winston.

Lazarus, R. S., & Folkman, S. (1984). Stress appraisal and coping. New York: Springer.

Marotz-Baden, R., & Colvin, P. L. (1986). Coping strategies: Rural-urban comparison. *Family Relations, 35*, 281–288.

Ministry of Supply and Services Canada. (1982a). *1981 census of Canada: Agriculture, Canada* (Publication No. CS 96–901). Ottawa, Ontario: Government of Canada.

Ministry of Supply and Services Canada. (1982b). *1981 census of Canada: Agriculture, Manitoba* (Publication No. CS 96–908). Ottawa, Ontario: Government of Canada.

Pervin, L. A. (1968). Performance and satisfaction as a function of individual-environment fit. *Psychological Bulletin, 69*, 56–68.

Rosenblatt, P. C., & Anderson, R. M. (1981). Interaction in farm families: Tension and stress. In R. T. Coward & W. M. Smith (Eds.), *The family in rural society* (pp. 147–166). Boulder, CO: Westview Press.

Schinka, J. A. (1984). *Health problems checklist.* (Available from Psychological Assessment Resources, P.O. Box 98, Odessa, FL 33556.)

Smith, M. J., Colligan, M. J., & Hurrel, J. J. (1977, November). *A review of N.I.O.S.H. psychological stress research.* Paper presented at a conference on job stress. University of Southern California, Los Angeles.

Spielberger, C. D., Gorsuch, R. L., & Lushene, R. E. (1970). *Manual for the State-Trait Anxiety Inventory.* Palo Alto, CA: Consulting Psychologists.

Taylor, S. E. (1986). *Health psychology.* New York: Random House.

Walker, J. L., & Walker, L. J. S. (1986). *Occupational stress and depression among farmers.* Manuscript submitted for publication.

Walker, J. L., & Walker, L. J. S. (1987a). *The human harvest: Changing farm stress to family success.* Winnipeg: Manitoba Agriculture.

Walker, J. L., & Walker, L. J. S. (in press). Self-reported stress symptoms in farmers. *Journal of Clinical Psychology.*

Walker, J. L., Walker, L. J. S., & MacLennan, P. M. (1986). An informal look at farm stress. *Psychological Reports, 59,* 427–430.

Walker, L. J. S., & Walker, J. L. (1987b, March). *Individual differences in occupational stress and stress symptoms among farmers.* Paper presented at Conference on Applications of Individual Differences in Stress and Health Psychology, Winnipeg, Manitoba.

# 8

# Psychosomatic Stress Among Farm Men and Women*

**Norah Keating, Brenda Munro, and Maryanne Doherty****

The difficult economic milieu for North American farms has lead to concern about the viability of the farming industry and the personal costs of being in farming. The increasing number of farm bankruptcies, high debt loads and low commodity prices have focussed the attention of many researchers on financial and work load demands of farming (Walker, Walker, & MacLennan, 1986). Others have been interested in the resources that rural families have which might reduce the impact of such demands (Marotz-Baden & Colvin, 1986). Practitioners concerned about the outcomes of the farm crisis have developed programs to help farm families manage stress (Fetsch, no date). Most often these inquiries have emphasized one aspect (demands, resources or outcomes) of the stress equation.

Although concepts differ from one definition to the next, stress is most often seen as having at least three elements: demands or stressors, capabilities or resources, and a set of outcome symptoms or imbalance in functioning. McCubbin and Patterson (1982) use the term stressor to describe those variables which have the potential to cause stress. In the case of farm families, high debt loads, long work days, and ongoing conflicting demands of several work roles have such potential. Outcomes are mediated by capabilities or resources of which personal and social resources have been seen as especially important (Perlin & Schooler, 1978). Social resources are networks of people who are a potential source of crucial support; family, friends, fellow workers, neighbors, and voluntary associations. Psychological resources are the personality characteristics that people use to deal with threats from the environment. One such personal resource is mastery, the extent to which individuals regard life to be under their control as opposed to being ruled by fate (Perlin & Schooler, 1978; Walker et al., 1986).

The definition of the outcome or stress used here is from Berkowitz (1984). Stress is defined as a set of physical or mental reactions to anything that places demands upon a person which exceed his or her ability to cope. Operationally defined, stress includes such things as nervousness, sleep disturbances and headaches. The purpose of this analysis is to determine the relative importance of demands and resources in determining stress levels of a group of farm women and men.

## Literature Review

There are many demands in the life of the farm family that have the potential to cause stress. Some are transitory (an injury, a bad crop year, machinery breakdown). Others are more enduring (patterns of work and long-term financial issues). The latter

*The authors gratefully acknowledge the Agricultural Research Council of Alberta, Farming for the Future, which funded the research on which this chapter is based.

**Norah Keating is a professor and Brenda Munro is an assistant professor in the Department of Family Studies, University of Alberta, Edmonton, Alberta, T6G 2H1. Maryanne Doherty is a curriculum development coordinator, Department of Education, Government of Alberta, Edmonton, Alberta 75K 0L2.

stressors were chosen for examination in this study because of their centrality to the lives of farm families and the theoretical importance of long-term stressors in causing stress/health problems.

## Demands

Farm men and women often have several work roles including farm and off-farm employment for men, and household, farm and off-farm employment for women (Keating, 1987). Many have very long work days, especially during busy seasons of seeding and harvesting. Within this work milieu is the potential for two kinds of role difficulties: role overload and role conflict.

*Role overload.* Too many requirements of a job with too little time to fulfill them (Sieber, 1974), is one type of work related stressor. Although long work hours are part of the everyday life of farmers, there is no direct evidence that the number of work hours per se is stress producing. Rather, work induced stress seems likely to vary for men and women, depending upon the type of work done and the status associated with the specific job (Sieber, 1974).

If farm men see their dominant identities as those of farmers (Symes & Marsden, 1981), then being actively engaged in farm work may actually keep stress levels low. In contrast, off-farm work may be seen by the farm man as an indication of his lack of success at the farm enterprise (Lyson, 1985; Wilkening, 1981). It seems likely that for men, farm work hours may keep stress low, but off-farm work hours may be related to high stress.

Some researchers have argued that the identities of farm women are less focussed than those of the farm men (Symes & Marsden, 1981) so that women may feel fragmentation of their lives between home, family, farm, and community. Others imply that women's public identities are focussed on homemaking but fragmentation is evident in the work they perform (Kohl & Bennett, 1982; Scholl, 1982).

It is not clear whether either household or farm work hours are related to stress in farm women. It seems likely that a heavy work load in the farm role that is unrecognized might well cause stress reactions. However, at least one study of women on dairy farms found home and farm task loads to be unrelated to stress (Berkowitz & Perkins, 1984).

Similarly, the research on farm women's employment is equivocal on the issue of the relation between employment work load and stress. Bescher-Donnelly and Smith (1981) suggest that rural women have a traditional (sic. negative) attitude toward employment outside the home. Others argue that off-farm employment for women may reduce stress by giving them more power in the farm business through their economic contributions (Coughenour & Swanson, 1983). The predictions in this study was that, for men, off-farm work hours would be related to stress; while for women, farm work hours would be related to stress.

*Role conflict.* Stryker and Macke (1978) describe three elements of role conflict: structural (caused by the simultaneous occupancy of conflicting structural positions), interactionist (disagreement on the content or performance of roles, and personal (between a person's internalized view of self and external role demands).

Many role conflicts experienced by farm men are structural conflicts between off-farm work and farm work. Off-farm work is generally done to support the farm operation and may symbolize hours away from real work, which is farm work (Wilkening, 1981). There has been little research done on interactionist or personal aspects of role conflict of farm men. The farm work role may be sufficiently clear in its definition by farm men and by the farming community at large, that farmers experience relatively little such conflict. In contrast, the diversity and complexity of tasks involved in the farm role make it likely that many farmers would find their own efforts in some way deficient in comparison with the ideal. Since work is so central in the lives of farmers, role conflict seems likely to be related to stress.

There has been more research on structural role conflict of farm women than men, perhaps due to the assumption that they have more potential for such conflict because they are likely to have more roles which are less clearly defined. Hedlund and Berkowitz (1979) found that farm women had conflicts over the demands of household and farm roles. Others (Stryker & Macke, 1978), have suggested that farm women with off-farm jobs have a greater potential for role conflict than urban women because their off-farm work is added to household and farm work.

In a study of 126 New York dairy farm wives, Berkowitz and Perkins (1985) found that stress was related to interactionist conflict. Farm women who were able to reach agreement with their husbands about their farm roles were less likely to report stress-related health symptoms than their counterparts who disagreed with their husbands about farm roles. Since farm women have many diverse work roles which are difficult to reconcile, their role conflict may be related to stress. The prediction in this study was that role conflict would be related to stress for both men and women although the sources of role conflict might differ between them.

*Debt load.* Some researchers have argued that economic factors such as high debt load may be the most important predictors of stress (Ireland, 1981; Marotz-Baden & Colvin, 1986; Walker et al., 1986). Although debt load is likely to be related to stress levels for both men and women, its relative importance is unclear. In a study of stress associated with farm related events, Weigel (1981) found that family and individual events, such as divorce or personal illness, were rated as more stressful than financial events, such as high debt load. Weigel's work suggests that debt load may be less central than other predictors of stress.

*Business adequacy.* The major relationship between financial situation and stress for farm families may lie in the assessment of farming as a way to make a living. In a study of economic vulnerability of farm couples, Rosenblatt and Keller (1983) argue that the feelings the couples had about their losses may be more significant than the actual amount of the loss. The willingness to see farming as a good way to make a living may help reduce stress more for men than for women. In a study of farm families in Wisconsin, Wilkening (1981) found that farm women tended to see farming more as a way of life than as a profit making business, while the reverse was true for men. This willingness to focus more on lifestyle may provide a buffer from stress for farm women.

## Resources

*Mastery.* Despite information on the impact of life events on stress, there has always been enough variance among people in similar situations to raise questions about other possible moderators of stress. Several authors (Lefcourt, 1983; Perlin & Schooler, 1978; Wheaton, 1980), argue that the perception of control over one's life is one such moderator, particularly in situations where individuals actually have a fair amount of discretion or freedom of movement. As independent business people, farmers are their own bosses. Yet while some farmers feel a strong sense of control over their destinies, others have little sense of mastery.

Several authors have argued that the high mastery people have low stress both because they view the world as controllable and because of the way in which they deal with the world. High mastery people are more ready to defer gratification and more likely to prefer delayed, larger goals to immediate, smaller ones (Lefcourt, 1983). They are also more likely to assume that their efforts will have some effect and are therefore more likely to persist in working toward those goals (Wheaton, 1980). However, under extreme conditions or with a persistent stressor, the relationship between mastery and stress may change (Lefcourt, 1981). For example, high mastery people might feel very stressed under conditions of high debt load since they think they should be able to control their debt. Low mastery people could blame someone else or fate and experience little stress.

Life events such as debt load and work hours may not be as important as mastery in predicting stress levels of farmers. Weigel (1981) in a study of Iowa farm men and women, states: "If the farmer feels generally self-confident and expects to solve a problem successfully, the stress will not be as severe, even if it is a difficult problem" (p. 3). In a study of stress levels of Manitoba farm women and men, Walker et al. (1986) found that both women and men perceived little control over farm stressors. Based on this small amount of information, it seems likely that mastery is a predictor of stress for both women and men.

*Support from spouse.* Because of the interdependence between the work and family lives of farm couples, support from spouse has been considered one of the most important social resources for farmers (Berkowitz & Perkins, 1984). Jensen (1982) argues that since the farm wife is not part of the decision-making team, she is starved for attention and left with the need to feel worthwhile. Jensen suggests that general emotional support from spouse should help reduce the stress inherent in this situation. Others agree. In a study of New York State dairy farm wives, Berkowitz and Perkins (1984) found that farm women who felt supported by their husbands were less likely to report stress-related health symptoms than their counterparts who felt unsupported.

There are few studies of the importance of spouse support in reducing stress levels for rural men. However, in a study of urban couples, Burke and Weir (1977) found that those individuals who were most satisfied with the help they received from their spouses in coping with their tensions, reported experiencing less stress in their lives. The relationships between stress and satisfaction with spouses' help were strongest for men.

The review suggests that the high stress farm man works long hours at his off-farm job, experiences role conflict, has a high debt load, sees farming as a poor way to make a living, has little sense of mastery over his life and feels little support from his wife in dealing with his tensions. The high stress farm woman works long hours in the farm operation, experiences role conflict, has a high debt load, has little sense of mastery over her life and feels little support from her husband in dealing with her tensions or farm work.

## Methodology

### The Sample

Grain growers make up the majority of farmers in the province of Alberta. Since grain farms differ substantially from other farm operations in their methods and size of operation, the population for this study consisted of Alberta farm owner-operators who, in the 1981 census, reported at least 51% of their farm income from grain. The sample of 3000 units was drawn by Statistics Canada. To ensure representation from all areas of the province, the sample was stratified according to the eight crop districts designated by Alberta Agriculture. To ensure anonymity, questionnaires were mailed from the offices of Statistics Canada and completed questionnaires were returned directly

to the authors. Data for the study were collected in 1984/85.

### Research Instrument

The questionnaire consisted of three sections. In the first section the farm owner was asked to complete information on legal and financial aspects of the unit, debt load and stress related to debt. The other two sections of the questionnaire were identical, with one form for the male and one for the female. On these, farm men and women were asked to give details of their work activities, work conflicts and personal stress.

### Sample Size and Description

Questionnaires were completed by 753 people representing 414 farm units, a response rate of approximately 20 percent. The men in these units ranged in age from 22 to 79 years with an average age of 46. Women were somewhat younger with a range in age from 21 to 76 with an average age of 43. This is similar to the age profile of Alberta farm owners (primarily men) who in 1981 averaged 46 years. Most of the men and women were married although a substantial minority (13%) of the men were without a partner. They had an average of three children, with a range from 0 to 12. A larger proportion of men (89.4%) than women (66.9%) was raised on a farm. Farms ranged in size from 20 to 4700 acres owned with an average of 707. Most were owned by an individual (male) or jointly owned by a husband and wife. Stress scores ranged from 1 to 4 for both men and women, with a possible range from 1 to 5. The mean stress score for men was 2.0 and 2.1 for women. A lower score indicates lower stress.

## Data Analysis

Wheaton (1980) argues for a stress model in which both stressors and coping resources have separate and additive impacts on stress. Each additional unit of stressor adds to the chances of developing a disorder; each additional unit of coping resources subtracts from the chances of developing a disorder. Therefore, stress is a matter of adding the effects of stressors and the counteracting effects of coping resources. The decision to use this model was based on the rather meager amount of information available on the relative importance of stressors and resources in explaining stress. Two analyses were run to address this question. First, stepwise multiple regression analyses were run to test the relative importance of stressors and resources described in the literature review. Separate analyses were run for men and for women based on the question of whether their sources of stress differed. Second, Sheffes were conducted in an attempt to understand why debt load was not significantly associated with stress. Since the latter were post hoc analyses, the rationale is presented in the results section.

## Dependent Variable

*Stress.* The measure of stress in this study is an adaptation of a 22-item scale developed by Lagner (1962) as an indicator of impairment in life functioning due to common types of psychiatric symptoms. Berkowitz and Perkins (1984) adapted the scale by choosing eight questions that provided the highest predictive ability for measurement of mental health. Scores on each question were added to produce one measure of stress. The Berkowitz and Perkins adaptation was used in this study. In conducting validity and reliability work on the Lagner scale, Wheaton (1980) concluded that the Lagner index is strongly related to the chances of having a current psychiatric diagnosis. Wheaton also conducted a factor analysis which showed that mastery and stress are separate constructs.

## Independent Variables

*Role overload.* Role overload was measured by total yearly hours spent in each of farm, off-farm and household work.

*Role conflict.* The role conflict measure was adapted from the Berkowitz and Perkins (1984) measure of role conflict and included structural, interactionist and personal elements of conflict. The measure used in this study included conflict over home, farm, and off-farm employment as well as conflict over meeting expectations of self and others. Questions were how often they were bothered by the particular conflict on a Likert scale from 1 (never troubled) to 5 (always troubled). Since not all people had all roles, a mean was taken as the role conflict score. A high score indicated high role conflict.

*Debt load.* Debt load is a ratio of debt to gross sales of agricultural products.

*Business adequacy.* This measure was the response to the question, "How satisfied are you with farming as a way to make a living?" Responses were on a five-point scale from very dissatisfied to very satisfied. A high score indicated high satisfaction.

*Spouse support.* This measure was also adapted from Berkowitz and Perkins (1984) whose measure was of wife's satisfaction with husband's support regarding her farm and household work. The measures for both men and women included six items:

—satisfaction with spouse's support for your farm work, household work and off-farm work
—satisfaction with spouse's contribution to farm and to household work
—satisfaction with support from spouse in coping with your tensions

*Mastery.* This measure is a 7-item scale developed by Perlin and Schooler (1978) to measure psychological resources. A high score indicated high mastery.

## Results

### Correlates of Stress

*Men.* Table 1 shows the results of the multiple regression analysis with stress as the dependent variable. Mastery, hours of off-farm employment, role conflict, and satis-

Table 1.
*Results of Multiple Regression Analysis for Men and Stress*

| Independent Variables | $R^2$ | Beta | t |
|---|---|---|---|
| Mastery | .124 | −.251 | −2.765* |
| Hours of off-farm employment | .075 | −.349 | −3.935* |
| Role conflict | .054 | .210 | 2.238* |
| Satisfaction with farming as a way to make a living | .032 | −.185 | −2.057* |
| Cumulative    $R^2$ = .285    F = 9.642    $p < .001$ | | | |

*$p < .05$.

Table 2.
*Results of Multiple Regression Analysis for Women and Stress*

| Independent Variables | $R^2$ | Beta | $t$ |
|---|---|---|---|
| Mastery | .132 | −.270 | −2.718* |
| Satisfaction with husband's support for your farm work | .079 | −.265 | −2.752* |
| Role conflict | .040 | .209 | 2.111* |
| Cumulative $R^2$ = .251 F = 9.269 p < .001 | | | |

*$p$ < .05.

faction with farming as a way to make a living were significantly related to stress. The high-stress farm man has a low sense of control over his life, works few hours at his off-farm job, feels conflict over competing demands with his work roles, and is dissatisfied with farming as a way to make a living.

*Women.* Table 2 shows the results of the multiple regression analysis with stress as the dependent variable. Mastery, satisfaction with husband's support for wife's farm work, and role conflict were significantly related to stress. The high stress farm woman has a low sense of control over her life, is dissatisfied with the amount of recognition she receives from her husband for her farm work, and feels conflict over competing demands with her work roles.

## Post Hoc Analyses

Despite indications from the popular media that debt is the major predictor of stress, debt rate was not significantly associated with stress for either farm men or farm women. This may be because of an interaction between mastery and stress. High mastery may be an asset when problems are solvable, but may not be when problems cannot be solved. In a situation of high debt load, the high mastery people might have higher stress than the low mastery people. If found, this relationship might account for the lack of relationship between debt load and stress. To test this hypothesis, men and women were divided into high and low mastery and high and low debt rate based on means for men and women on each of these variables. Separate Sheffes for men and women were run to determine group differences on stress.

*Men.* Table 3 shows the mean stress levels for men with different combinations of mastery and debt load. The group comparisons did not provide support for the hypothesis of a relationship between high

Table 3.
*Mean Stress Levels by Mastery by Debt Rate for Men*

| | | Mastery | |
|---|---|---|---|
| | | Low | High |
| Debt load | Low | x̄ = 2.07 | x̄ = 1.76 |
| | | Group 1 | Group 3 |
| | High | x̄ = 2.16 | x̄ = 1.79 |
| | | Group 2 | Group 4 |

Significant Sheffe differences
between groups 1 and 3
1 and 4
2 and 3
2 and 4

mastery and high debt rate in regard to stress. In general, high mastery men have low levels of stress regardless of their debt rate.

*Women.* Table 4 shows the mean stress levels for women with different combinations of mastery and debt load. As with men, Sheffe comparisons for women did not provide support for a hypothesized relationship between high mastery and high debt rate in regards to stress. In general, high mastery women have lower levels of stress regardless of their debt rate.

Table 4.
*Mean Stress Levels by Mastery by Debt Rate for Women*

| | | Mastery | |
|---|---|---|---|
| | | Low | High |
| Debt Rate | Low | x̄ = 2.22 | x̄ = 1.96 |
| | | Group 1 | Group 3 |
| | High | x̄ = 2.27 | x̄ = 1.86 |
| | | Group 2 | Group 4 |

Significant Sheffe differences
between groups 1 and 4
2 and 4
2 and 3

## Discussion

The findings provide support for the argument that stress outcomes are a result of a combination of stressors and resources. For these farmers, resources accounted for more of the variance in stress than did stressors themselves, although men and women differ somewhat in the stressors and resources affecting their stress levels.

### Resources

Mastery was the most important predictor of stress for both men and women. High stress farmers felt that their fate and consequently their livelihood were out of their control. This finding supports the contention of many people that perception of control is a significant determinant of how people respond to aversive events in their environment.

Such stressors are part of the lives of farm men and women. Yet mastery is an asset even in situations that are difficult to solve. The analysis of the interaction between mastery and debt load showed that high mastery men and women have lower stress levels than low mastery men and women, even under conditions of high debt load. Thus, a sense of control over one's fate appears to be the best, single predictor of low stress levels for both men and women.

The only significant social support predictor of stress was that of husband's support for women's farm work. Although most women in the study did farm work, women are not considered to be farmers. They are dependent for recognition upon the people who know about their work, notably their husbands. This finding supports that of Berkowitz and Perkins (1984) who found that husband support is an important coping mechanism for farm women. Spouse support was not a predictor of stress for men. This may be because men's identities are so clearly focussed on farm work and there is general community support for their farm role.

### Demands

Of the stressors examined, the most important for men was hours of off-farm employment, with fewer off-farm hours associated with high stress. This negative relationship makes it seem unlikely that role overload is causing stress. Rather, as discussed earlier, having an off-farm job may be an indicator to the farm man of his lack of success at the farm operation. Working a relatively few number of hours at an off-farm job may be the worst possible situation. The farm man is reminded of his inability to be a success at full-time farming and yet he earns a low income at that job because he is working only a few hours. The man who is working full-time at his off-farm job may not have his identity so tied to the farm and has greater advantage from his off-farm income.

Although it was expected that farm women would suffer from role overload because of their many work roles, women's work hours were not related to stress. A strong work ethic in which work is valued and a strong attachment to the land may be one reason why long work days and irregular hours do not result in stress symptoms.

Although work loads did not affect stress levels, role conflict was a predictor of stress for both men and women. Since the measure of role conflict included a combination of structural, interactionist and personal elements, it was not possible to determine which of these was most important for men and women. However, sources of role conflict may be different from men and women.

For men, conflict is likely to come primarily from competition of off-farm work role, farm work and from not meeting personal standards regarding the success of the farm operation. On individual items from the role conflict scale, men scored highest on worry about neglecting farm duties. For women, conflict often comes from feelings of not meeting expectations of either themselves or others. Women felt that their lack of knowledge and skill about the farm operation prevented them from being more involved in farm work.

Contrary to expectations, debt load was not a significant predictor of stress. This may be in part because those whose debt loads were so high that they lost their farms were not part of this study. It may also be because debt has different meanings for different people. For some, the way of life is worth the costs.

In contrast, the assessment of farming as a good way to make a living was associated with lower levels of stress for men. This personal evaluation of the adequacy of their income was more important than any of the actual income variables. Some farm men are discouraged about farming as a way to make a living while others appeared more accepting.

In sum, high mastery provides the best buffer against stress for both farm men and women. For women, the additional resource of husband's support for her farm work was also important. Of the stressors measured, role conflict was important for both, although probably for different reasons. Low hours of off-farm employment and evaluation of farming as a poor way to make a living were associated with stress for farm men.

## Reducing Stress Levels: Increasing Mastery

Results of this study have shown the importance of personal and social resources in determining stress. They have also shown that although some sources of stress for farm men and women are similar, some are quite different. These findings have implications for ways in which farm families might reduce their stress levels and rural practitioners might help them in that endeavor. Three areas of intervention are in increasing mastery, reducing role conflict, and using social resources.

The importance of mastery in explaining stress suggests that mastery is a basic concept which affects the meaning a person attaches to an event. If the high mastery person sees life as controllable, then that person may see most life events as less catastrophic than the low mastery person. Farmers and those who work with farmers can help build a sense of mastery through increasing their knowledge, changing their perspective about stressors, and taking action.

*Increasing knowledge.* Extension specialists and others need to be able to give farmers accurate, up-to-date information regarding the economic climate in which they operate. Information on changes in taxation legislation, commodity prices, incorporation, and marketing provide a basis on which to make sound decisions. In addition, many farm families might benefit from skills in using that information through courses in better decision making, goal setting, and time management.

Knowledge about sources of stress can also provide information on ways to reduce stress. Farm men might learn to assess the advantages and disadvantages of a part-time job since taking that job might be stressful.

Farm women might learn more about the farm operation since lack of knowledge adds to their role conflict. Differences between farm men and women in sources of stress need to be acknowledged. Although farm men and women have interdependent lives, different role responsibilities and attitudes toward those roles may account for some of the differences in factors which are associated with stress. While lack of support may be stressful for women, feeling unsuccessful as a farmer is stressful for men.

*Changing ones perspective.* Stress resistent families are solution oriented, not catastrophe oriented. Berkowitz (1984) has some practical suggestions for farmers who want to work toward the goal of seeing problems as solvable. These include taking time to relax and put aside worries; thinking positively and not catastrophising about stressors; and concentrating on what you can accomplish rather than on what is out of your hands. Farmers need to confront the very things that make it difficult for them to change their perspective (McGhee, no date). These include: (a) Clinging to a fatalistic orientation even when it appears change would be positive; (b) Competing for bigger and better farm size, when more prudent practices might be less stressful ("The Farmer's Maschismo"); (c) Experiencing pressure from the next older generation who managed during tough times and wonder why the younger generation cannot cope; and (d) Valuing silence and stoicism when in a high stress occupation.

*Taking action.* Action can be taken on a personal level to confront these problems. It can also be taken at a community level through the provision of sound farm business management programs to help farm men keep up to date and to help farm women acquire greater skills. Communities or local governments might also investigate the feasibility of developing a corps of persons with proven managerial abilities, such as semi-retired farmers and new agricultural diploma graduates who would be available for holiday relief, advice on problems, or emergency situations.

## Reducing Role Conflict

Acknowledgement of women's contribution to farm work has begun to be more publicly acknowledged in such things as divorce settlements. A more positive acknowledgement would be from spouses to one another. One of the stressors experienced by both men and women is role conflict. Work by Boss (1986) implies that part of this conflict comes from rigid conceptions held by farmers of what it means to be a real man or woman. If a man comes from a tradition that says a successful farm man doesn't have to work off the farm and has a wife who does not have to work, he is going to experience great stress when she does go to work or when both of them do. In this situation the farm man may see himself as a personal failure as a farmer and as an inadequate man because he cannot support his wife and family.

According to Boss, one big challenge is to bring about an attitudinal change regarding work and success, in order to help ease stress in farm families. Berkowitz (1984) would concur. He says that the stress resistant family is one which is flexible in its roles; flexible so that people can help one another when needed and that more than one person knows how to do any task. Developing more flexible roles could have the added advantage of encouraging members of farm families to talk more about what they do and what they like to do. It might help minimize situations discussed previously in which one partner feels she is doing a great deal of work and the other partner does not recognize her contribution.

## Using Social Resources

Spouses can be very supportive to one another, but often that support needs to be more open and explicit. Berkowitz (1984) recommends that couples make an effort to communicate openly and share responsibility and decision making.

Support can also come from other people, both friends and professionals. Friends are a resource when people take the time to keep in contact and when they are willing to discuss problems with them. A network of people who understand because they are in a similar situation can be one of the best buffers against stress. Taking time off to spend with friends can be time well spent.

However, the presence of a group of family and friends may not be enough to buffer people against stress. Lefcourt (1983) and others suggest that there may be a relationship between the ways in which people use their social resources and the personal resource of mastery. He argues that low mastery people do not use their social contacts effectively to diminish the impact of stressors, even though they often have more social contacts. If this is the case, the low mastery person may have difficulty turning to spouse, friends or professionals for help in reducing his stress.

Professionals working with rural people can also be more effective resources for farm men and women if they can listen and respond sympathetically to families who are stressed. The results of a study in Ontario (McGhee, no date) show that this does not always happen. When asked about their contact with professionals, farm men and women cited problems of lack of understanding by those professionals. Physicians, when consulted about stress related illness, suggested taking a vacation, although many farmers cannot afford to get away and are unable to find temporary help. Loan officers at banks frowned on vacations if debt load was high. Staff at rural mental health centers had little understanding of rural life and its problems. Hazards were created when mood-altering drugs, especially tranquilizers, were prescribed because most farmers and their spouses operate heavy equipment and/or look after large animals. Knowledge about stressors in the lives of farmers can help professionals respond more appropriately to farmers' needs.

There is much more work to be done to discover all of the sources of stress of farm men and women. There are many other life events that might be stressors: personal and family problems, developmental changes, and differences in types of farm operations. Similarly there are many possible resources to these farmers, such as supportive networks of friends or extended kin. Other psychological resources, such as personality traits or religious faith, may also help determine who will experience most stress.

REFERENCES

Berkowitz, A. D. (1984). *Coping with stress on the farm.* Paper presented at the Annual Finger Lakes Grape Growers Convention, Keuka Park, New York.

Berkowitz, A. D., & Perkins, H. W. (1984). Stress among farm women: Work and family as interacting systems. *Journal of Marriage and the Family,* **46**, 161–166.

Berkowitz, A. D., & Perkins, H. W. (1985). Correlates of psychosomatic stress symptoms among farm women: A research note on farm and family functioning. *Journal of Human Stress,* **11**(2), 76–81.

Bescher-Donnelly, L., & Whitener Smith, L. (1981). The changing roles and status of rural women. In R. T. Coward & W. M. Smith (Eds.), *The family in rural society* (pp. 167-185). Boulder, CO: Westview Press.

Boss, P. (1986). Farm family displacement and stress. In *Increasing understanding of public problems and policies—1985* (pp. 61-78). Oak Brook, IL: Farm Foundation.

Burke, R. J., & Weir, T. (1977). Marital helping relationships: The moderators between stress and well-being. *Journal of Psychology, 95,* 121-130.

Coughenour, C. M., & Swanson, L. (1983). Work statuses and occupations of men and women in farm families and the structure of farms. *Rural Sociology, 48,* 23-43.

Fetsch, R. (no date). *Stress management for couples.* Lexington: University of Kentucky, College of Agriculture, Cooperative Extension Service.

Hedlund, D., & Berkowitz, A. D. (1979). The incidence of social-psychological stress in farm families. *International Journal of Sociology of the Family, 2,* 233-243.

Ireland, G. (1981). *The psychological effects of financial stress on farm families.* A brief presented to the Ontario Federation of Agriculture Task Force on the Financial Crisis. Hanover, Ontario, 1-6.

Jensen, L. (1982). Stress in the farm family unit. *Resources for Feminist Research, 11*(1), 11-12.

Keating, N. (1987). Reducing stress of farm men and women. *Family Relations, 36,* 358-363.

Kohl, S. B., & Bennett, J. W. (1982). The agri family household. In J. W. Bennett (Ed.), *Of time and the enterprise: North American family farm management in a context of resource marginality* (pp. 148-171). Minneapolis: University of Minnesota Press.

Lagner, T. S. (1962). A twenty-two item screening score of psychiatric symptoms indicating impairment. *Journal of Health and Human Behavior, 3,* 269-276.

Lefcourt, H. M. (1983). *Research with the locus of control construct* (Vol. 2). New York: Academic Press, Inc.

Lefcourt, H. M. (1981). *Research with the locus of control construct* (Vol. 1). New York: Academic Press, Inc.

Lyson, T. A. (1985). Husband and wife work roles and the organization and operation of family farms. *Journal of Marriage and the Family, 47,* 759-764.

Marotz-Baden, R., & Colvin, P. (1986). Coping strategies: A rural-urban comparison. *Family Relations, 35,* 281-288.

McCubbin, H. I., & Patterson, J. M. (1982). Family adaptation to crisis. In H. I. McCubbin, M. E. Cauble & J. M. Patterson (Eds.), *Family stress, coping and social support* (pp. 26-47). Springfield, IL: Charles Thomas.

McGhee, M. (no date). *Women in rural life, the changing scene.* Ministry of Agriculture and Food, Ontario.

Perlin, L. I., & Schooler, C. (1978). The structure of coping. *Journal of Health and Social Behavior, 19,* 2-21.

Rosenblatt, P. C., & Keller, L. O. (1983). Economic vulnerability and economic distress in farm couples. *Family Relations, 32,* 567-573.

Scholl, K. (1982). Household and farm task participation of women. *Family Economics Review, 3,* 3-9.

Sieber, S. D. (1974). Toward a theory of role accumulation. *American Sociological Review, 39,* 567-578.

Stryker, S., & Macke, A. S. (1978). Status inconsistency and role conflict. *Annual Review of Sociology, 4,* 57-90.

Symes, D. G., & Marsden, T. K. (1981). Complementary roles and asymmetrical lives. *Sociologia Ruralis, 23,* 229-241.

Walker, J., Walker, L., & MacLennan, P. (1986). An informal look at farm stress. *Psychological Reports, 59,* 427-430.

Weigel, R. (1981). *Stress on the farm.* Pamphlet available from Alberta Agriculture, Edmonton, Alberta. #884-00-19.

Wheaton, B. (1980). The sociogenesis of psychological disorder: An attributional theory. *Journal of Health and Social Behavior, 21,* 11-124.

Wilkening, E. A. (1981). Farm families and family farming. In R. T. Coward & W. M. Smith (Eds.), *The family in rural society* (pp. 27-37). Boulder, CO: Westview Press.

# Stressors: A Rural-Urban Comparison*

Ramona Marotz-Baden**

Until recently, country living has been depicted as being simple, pure, wholesome, slow-paced, and free from pressures and tensions. Articles on stress and stress management in popular farm magazines (e.g., Braun, 1981; Tevis, 1980, 1982) and cooperative extension publications (e.g., Fetsch, 1984; Hennon & Harder, 1982; Weigel, 1981a, 1981b) developed for farm families in the early 1980s are good indicators, however, that farm and ranch families do not lead stress-free lives.

In the 1970s and early 1980s, a number of factors coalesced, producing a difficult economic situation for many farmers and ranchers. The OPEC oil embargo in the 1970s and the subsequent rise in oil prices raised the price of fuel, fertilizer, pesticides, herbicides, and other materials. Interest rates rose sharply in the late 1970s and early 1980s. Foreign markets dwindled due to embargoes on grain shipments to Communist countries and increased agricultural production in other countries. Bumper crops further contributed to commodity surpluses driving prices down (e.g., Carson, 1986; Montana Crop & Livestock Reporter, 1982). Beginning in 1983, devaluation of agricultural land reduced the equity against which farmers could borrow (Farm Land Values Fall, 1985). Although precise figures on the proportion of farm families in financial trouble do not exist, all farm and ranch families have been impacted (Agricultural and Rural Economics Division, 1986; Schotsch, 1985).

Until recently, researchers focused on the effects of a single stressor on the family (e.g., Hill, 1949; LeMasters, 1957). Now research on the effects of numerous stressors over a short period is more common (e.g., Holmes & Rahe, 1967; McCubbin, Cauble, & Patterson, 1982). Although a single event may be of significant magnitude to induce a crisis, the number of events or demands to which a family or individual is trying to adjust at the same time may be the real determinant of how well a family or person handles a crisis-provoking event. Researchers hypothesize that the number of stressors encountered in a brief time, such as a year, are directly correlated with the probability of illness, accident, or disruption of the family unit (e.g., Holmes & Masuda, 1974; Coddington, 1972; Patterson & McCubbin, 1983).

According to McCubbin and Patterson's (1981) Double ABCX Model, stressors (change-inducing events) are additive. Stressor "pileup" consists of prior and current stressors to which the family has not fully adapted. A stressor can be either a normative or non-normative life event affecting the family unit at a particular time, producing change in the family system. When the family faces a new stressor, members may become aware of unresolved tensions. Demands for change from prior stressors may be sapping family members' time, energy, and other resources. While stressor events occur at discrete points in time, non-resolved stressor events resulting in tension may not be as easy to identify and, therefore, more difficult with which to cope. A family's ability to adjust satisfactorily to new stressors depends in large part on the pileup of stressors being faced, available re-

*This research was supported by Montana Agricultural Experiment Station grant number MONB00266.

**Ramona Marotz-Baden, Professor, Department of Health and Human Development, Montana State University, Bozeman, MT 59717.

sources, and family coping strategies (Mc-Cubbin & Patterson, 1981).

Although there is agreement that families face normative and non-normative stressors over the course of the family life cycle, little attention has been focused on determining the kinds and amount of stressors "normal" families face. The exception is Olson and McCubbin's research. They found:

(a) the relative persistence of stressors and strains over the family cycle; (b) the major pile up of stressors and strains occurring at the Adolescent ... and Launching stages of the family cycle; (c) discernible drop in demands (stressors and strains) at the Empty Nest ... and the Retired Couple ... stages of the family cycle; and (d) differences between husbands and wives in their assessment of the number of "demands" the family unit struggles with (Olson & McCubbin, 1983:121).

Their research provides baseline data on predominantly white rural and urban, middle-income families across the life cycle. Additional research delineating differences in stressors between populations could detect groups experiencing high levels of pile up who, therefore, are at risk for illness, accidents, and poor job performance. Such data would be extremely relevant for counselors, extension agents, mental health and other professionals, and policymakers interested in prevention and/or intervention.

The exploratory research reported below was designed to address this issue by comparing the amounts (pileup) and types of stressors faced by samples from two different populations, rural farm families and urban families, which, until recently, were believed to have different stress levels. Although farming has been documented as stressful (e.g., Hedlund & Berkowitz, 1979; Marotz-Baden, 1986; Olson & Schellenberg, 1986; Rosenblatt & Keller, 1983), it is not known if farm families face more or fewer stressors than families in other locations.

People living in different environments have different life styles (Tallman & Marotz, 1970). Farming and ranching differ from most occupations because of the agricultural tasks and their rural outdoor setting. While it is thought that normative stressors, i.e., those associated with normal life cycle changes such as the birth of a baby, wed-dings, and deaths, would not differ by residence location, certain non-normative stressors might be more common in one setting than in the other. Therefore, two hypotheses were tested: (1) that there would be no difference in the level or pileup of stressors faced by rural and urban families; and (2) that certain kinds of stressors would be more prevalent in rural families than in urban families and vice versa.

# Methodology

## The Sample

The rural sample was randomly selected from a list of names of farm and ranch families compiled from county extension agent lists of Montana families who obtained their incomes primarily from farming and ranching. The urban sample was randomly selected from names of husbands and wives in the phone directories of Great Falls and Billings, both of which have SMSA populations in excess of 80,000.[1] A questionnaire was mailed separately to 300 urban husbands and their wives and 300 rural husbands and their wives. The response rate from the initial mailing and two follow-up mailings was 70%. One hundred seven urban husbands, 111 urban wives, 89 rural husbands and 113 rural wives completed the questionnaire.

Mean education of the 94 urban husbands was 14.2 years; of the 83 rural husbands, 13.6 years; of the 94 urban wives, 14.1 years; and of the 83 rural wives, 13.8 years. These differences in education were not statistically significant. Rural respondents had significantly more children. The mean number of children living at home was 1.83 for rural husbands and wives and 1.36 for urban husbands and wives. Because a printing error in the questionnaire invalidated an age comparison, stage in the life cycle was compared.[2] The urban respondents were fairly evenly distributed across the life cycle. There were, however, significantly more rural couples in the adolescent stage than in any other life cycle stage. Since the average age of Montana farmers and ranchers in 1978 was 49.6 (U.S. Bureau of the Census, 1978) and the sample was randomly drawn in 1982, the larger proportion of couples with adolescents may be an accurate reflection of the Montana farm/ranch population.

Table 1.
*Employment Status by Residence Location and Gender (Percentages)[a]*

| | Husbands | | | | Wives | | | |
|---|---|---|---|---|---|---|---|---|
| | Urban (*n* = 94) | | Rural (*n* = 94) | | Urban (*n* = 83) | | Rural (*n* = 83) | |
| | f | % | f | % | f | % | f | % |
| Employed Full Time | 71 | 76 | 84 | 90 | 38 | 46 | 15 | 18 |
| Employed Part Time | 7 | 7 | 4 | 4 | 16 | 19 | 11 | 13 |
| Unemployed | 5 | 5 | — | — | 3 | 3 | 1 | 1 |
| Retired | 11 | 12 | 6 | 6* | 5 | 6 | 5 | 6 |
| Full-Time Homemakers | — | — | — | — | 21 | 25 | 51 | 62** |

[a]Percentages may not add up to 100 due to rounding error.
*Chi square = 10.12; df = 4; $p < .05$.
**Chi square = 25.58; df = 4; $p < .001$.

The occupational differences in employment status reported in Table 1 were statistically significant by place of residence for each gender. As was expected, most rural husbands were employed full time on the farm/ranch and some urban husbands were out of work. Also, as expected, fewer farm/ranch wives had off-farm jobs, probably because of the traditional involvement of many women in the work of the farm/ranch (e.g., Rosenfeld, 1985), the lack of job opportunities in small towns, and the large distances from towns that some Montana farm families live, especially in the eastern part of the state.

## Stressors

Stressors (life events) were measured by FILE, Family Inventory of Life Events and Changes (McCubbin, Patterson, & Wilson, 1982). Families often face several life events or stressors simultaneously, and FILE scores provide an index of potential vulnerability as a result of stressor pileup. Mullan (1983) argues that life event scales may not be reliable or valid because of inaccurate and selective recall. This may be the case but there was no reason to suspect that either set of couples would be more susceptible to these concerns. Therefore, FILE appears to be an appropriate measure for comparisons of life events between the urban and the rural samples.

FILE's 171 self-report items tap normative and non-normative life events and changes families may have experienced during the past 12 months. However, because children were not included in this study, the stressors these parents report may not include those of their children. A subset of 34 items records events experienced prior to the last year which generally require longer adaptation or which generate prolonged strain because they are chronic. Viewing the family as a system, couple scores were obtained using McCubbin, Patterson, and Wilson's (1982) technique of assigning a score of one to each of the 171 items if *either* of the couple reported the event as occurring. If both reported it, the couple still received a score of one. McCubbin et al., report the overall reliability of the scale as .81, with subscale scores varying from .30 to .73, based on Chronbach's Alpha.

On the basis of factor analysis, McCubbin, Patterson, and Wilson grouped the 171 FILE items into nine subscales: Intra-family strains, marital strains, pregnancy and child bearing strains, finance and business strains, work-family transitions and strains, illness and family care strains, losses, transitions in and out of the family, and legal violations strains. These conceptual groupings were used as the measures of the different types of stressors. Couple scores on items in each of the subscales were summed for each subscale and then summed overall to obtain total couple scores.

## Results

### Stressor Pile-Up: Total Recent and Past Family Life Changes

A one-way analysis of variance was used to compare the mean stressor scores of the rural and urban samples. Table 2 presents these mean scores by residence. The Total Recent Family Life Changes score consists of the sum of the 171 FILE items which respondents said occurred within 12 months

Table 2.
*Mean Scores of Family Life Changes by Residence and ANOVA Results*[a,b]

| Family Life Changes | Rural Means (n = 83) | Urban Means (n = 94) | Effects of Residence F |
|---|---|---|---|
| Total Recent Family Life Changes | 11.93 | 14.35 | 5.01* |
| Total Past Family Life Changes | 5.13 | 6.88 | 7.70** |
| Subscales | | | |
| Financial and Business Strains | 4.16 | 3.34 | 6.21** |
| Intra-Family Strains | 3.72 | 4.54 | 2.70 |
| Work-Family Transitions and Strains | 1.54 | 3.07 | 28.52*** |
| Illness and Family Care Strains | 0.94 | 1.00 | 0.10 |
| Transitions In and Out | 0.57 | 0.69 | 0.69 |
| Losses | 0.59 | 0.67 | 0.34 |
| Marital Strains | 0.18 | 0.54 | 14.51*** |
| Pregnancy Strains | 0.12 | 0.29 | 4.46* |
| Family Legal Violations | 0.11 | 0.20 | 1.82 |

[a]Means have been rounded to the nearest hundredth of a percent.
[b]df for Residence = 1, for error = 175.
*$p < .05$.
**$p < .01$.
***$p < .001$.

prior to the interview. The urban couples had statistically significantly higher mean scores (14.35) than the rural respondents (11.93). Urban couples also had significantly higher Total Past Family Life Changes mean scores (6.88) than rural couples (5.13). The latter score consisted of the stressors the respondents reported as occurring prior to the last 12 months. The greater pileup of past and recent stressors reported by the urban sample did not support the hypothesis of no difference in stressor pileup between the two samples as measured by FILE. Although FILE attempts to represent the range of normative and non-normative stressors families experience across the life cycle, undoubtedly there are some that are not represented.

## Types of Stressors

The second hypothesis, that certain kinds of stressors would be more prevalent in one location than another, was tested by comparing mean scores on the nine subscales of FILE. Each subscale represents a different type of stressor encountered within the 12 months prior to the interview. The subscales are presented in Table 2 in an approximation of the extent to which the type of stressors measured by the subscales contributed to the Total Family Life Change score. Since the subscales are composed of different numbers of items, this ranking is only a general ordering. In the following

analysis of each subscale, if 25% or more of either group of couples reported experiencing the stressor measured by a subscale item or if there was a statistically significant difference by residence on any subscale item, the individual item is discussed.

*Financial and Business Strains.* This 12-item subscale reflects strain on the family money supply due to investments or increased expenditures. Rural couples reported experiencing significantly more of these stressors than urban couples.

There were no differences by residence in the first three items of the subscale. A majority (68% rural and 77% urban) of all couples reported "increased strain on family money for food, clothing, energy, and home care." Over a quarter of the couples reported "increased strain on family money for children's education," and almost half reported that "a member purchased a car or other major item."

Significantly more rural than urban couples, however, reported large changes in their financial status. Fifteen percent more rural (54%) than urban (39%) couples "took out a loan or refinanced to cover increased expenses." Three times as many rural (74%) as urban (25%) couples "noted changes in conditions (economics, political, weather) which hurt the family business, and 63% more rural (88%) than urban (25%) couples reported a "change in agricultural market, stock market, or land values which hurt family investment and/or income." Significantly more rural (14%) than urban (4%) couples also reported that "a member started a new business." On the other hand, three times as many urban (27%) as rural (8%) couples increased their financial debt by over-use of credit cards, and 21% more urban (52%) than rural (31%) couples reported "increased strain on family money for medical and dental expenses."

All but two of the items of this subscale checked by at least 25% of the urban or rural respondents reflect negative financial stressors. Starting a new business and purchasing a new car or other major item are usually viewed as positive stressors unless they are unplanned expenses. Regardless of whether a stressor is positive or negative, however, it still requires adaptation.

*Intra-Family Strains.* This 17-item subscale measures the hardships of parenting and increased tension and strain between family members. The item analysis of this subscale revealed that the most frequently reported stressors in the last year for all respondents were "an increase in the number of tasks or chores which do not get done" (55% urban, 61% rural), "an increase in the number of problems or issues which don't get resolved" (52% urban, 31% rural), and "an increase in the number of activities in which their children are involved" (45% urban, 57% rural).

Although there were no residence differences in the overall subscale means, there were residence differences on some of the items. Significantly more urban (51%) than rural (26%) couples reported an "increase in the husband's time away from home" and also "an increase in the wife's time away from the family" (41% vs 22%). This may reflect an increase in job-related activities, especially on the part of the wife, to cope with the high inflation rate (9.8%) at the time of the study in 1982.[3] Significantly more urban (49%) than rural (16%) couples reported that a family member "appears to have an emotional problem" or "depends on alcohol and drugs" (18% urban vs 7% rural).

Family conflict was evident in both locations. Twenty-nine percent of the rural and 17 percent of the urban couples noted "increased conflict with in-laws or relatives" and 31 percent of the urban and 28 percent of the rural couples reported an "increase in conflict between parents and children." These differences were not statistically significant. Significantly more urban (37%) than rural (21%) couples, however, reported an increase in conflict between husband and wife, and significantly more rural (17%) than urban (7%) couples noted "increased difficulty in managing teenage child(ren)." The latter was probably due to the greater proportion of rural families with teenagers.

*Work-family Transitions and Strains.* This 10-item subscale measures job changes by family members. Table 2 shows that significantly more urban than rural couples reported such changes. There was also greater variation among the urban couples according to the standard deviations (2.02 vs. 1.76) of the means.

The item analysis yielded significantly more urban (47%) than rural (27%) couples reporting "a family member changed to a new job/career." Accompanying this, or perhaps preceding these job changes, was a greater incidence of urban (27%) than rural (11%) couples reporting a "decrease in satisfaction with job/career." Similarly, more urban (22%) than rural (7%) couples reported that "a member was promoted at work or given more responsibility." More urban (33%) than rural (5%) couples reported that a "member lost or quit a job," "a member started or returned to work" (35% vs 20%), and "a member stopped work for an extended period (laid off, leave of absence, strike) (25% vs 10%). These differences are hardly surprising since the greater majority of the rural husbands were self-employed and more urban than rural wives were employed full or part time.

There were two significant differences in the items of this subscale to which less than 25 percent of either sample responded. Significantly more urban (10%) than rural (3%) couples reported "a member retired from work." Also, significantly more urban (22%) than rural (7%) couples reported that "a child/adolescent changed to a new school." Despite the typographical error invalidating the age question, it was thought that the urban sample was younger on average than the urban sample because more urban respondents were in childbearing stages of the life cycle. Most of the urban respondents, however, were employees who may have had mandatory retirement at a certain age. Self-employed farmers have more choice over the timing of their retirement. The higher numbers of urban children changing to new schools may simply reflect differences in school structure. Urban areas often have elementary, middle, junior high, and high schools while rural areas usually have elementary (often including 7th and 8th grade) and high schools.

Almost 80% of the stressors measured by FILE that the respondents experienced in the 12 months prior to the study were represented by the first three subscales. As can be seen in Table 2, the means on the remaining six subscales were not very high. Statistically significant differences appeared on only two of the six, Marital Strains, and Pregnancy Strains.

*Marital Strains.* This 4-item subscale reflects sources of tension in the marital role arising from separation and sexual issues. The mean summary scores show strong residential differences, with urban respondents reporting significantly more marital stress

than rural respondents. Again, a comparison of standard deviations revealed greater variation among the urban couples (0.77 vs. 0.42).

The only subscale item with more than 25 percent of the couples in any group responding was "increased difficulty with sexual relationships between husband and wife." Significantly more of the urban (39%) than than rural (16%) couples reported this. In addition, significantly more urban (6%) than rural (0%) couples reported that their spouse had an affair in the past year. These data provided some insight into the symptoms of the marriages of some of the urban couples. Clearly, they were experiencing more marital strain as measured by these items than were the rural couples.

*Pregnancy Strains.* This four-item

Table 3.
*Mean Couple Summary Stress and Transition Scores by Residence and Life-Cycle Stage*[a]

| Type of Strain | Stage in Life Cycle | | | | |
|---|---|---|---|---|---|
| | No Kids | Preschool | Elementary | Adolescent | Retired |
| Total Recent Life Changes | | | | | |
| Urban | 14.54 | 16.05 | 14.69 | 15.06 | 8.91 |
| Rural | 8.61 | 11.69 | 13.89 | 14.11 | 7.14** |
| Total Past Life Changes | | | | | |
| Urban | 6.79 | 5.31 | 10.13 | 5.94 | 7.00* |
| Rural | 4.06 | 4.77 | 4.67 | 5.83 | 5.57 |
| Subscales | | | | | |
| Finance and Business | | | | | |
| Urban | 3.64 | 3.86 | 3.13 | 3.47 | 1.64* |
| Rural | 3.50 | 3.85 | 4.44 | 4.94 | 2.00** |
| Intra Family | | | | | |
| Urban | 3.93 | 5.32 | 5.44 | 5.18 | 2.27* |
| Rural | 3.09 | 4.23 | 6.67 | 4.28 | 2.45*** |
| Work-Family | | | | | |
| Urban | 3.14 | 3.50 | 3.69 | 3.06 | 1.18** |
| Rural | .61 | 1.92 | 1.56 | 1.92 | 1.29 |
| Illness and Family Care | | | | | |
| Urban | 1.21 | 1.09 | .56 | .71 | 1.36 |
| Rural | 1.72 | .69 | .44 | .81 | .71* |
| Transition "in and out" | | | | | |
| Urban | .86 | .50 | .38 | 1.12 | .46 |
| Rural | .67 | .08 | .00 | .94 | .00*** |
| Losses | | | | | |
| Urban | .71 | .64 | .56 | .41 | 1.18 |
| Rural | .61 | .31 | .56 | .72 | .43 |
| Marital | | | | | |
| Urban | .75 | .36 | .44 | .59 | .45 |
| Rural | .06 | .15 | .22 | .22 | .29 |
| Pregnancy | | | | | |
| Urban | .07 | .68 | .31 | .12 | .27** |
| Rural | .11 | .46 | .00 | .06 | .00*** |
| Legal Violations | | | | | |
| Urban | .21 | .09 | .19 | .41 | .09 |
| Rural | .06 | .00 | .00 | .22 | .00** |

[a]Means have been rounded to the nearest hundred.
*$p \leq .05$.
**$p \leq .01$.
***$p \leq .001$.

subscale taps pregnancy difficulties as well as adjustment to a new family member. The mean summary score of this subscale indicates that pregnancy related stressors were not very prevalent. Significantly more urban than rural couples reported them, however, and there was more variation in the urban sample according to standard deviation scores (0.63 vs. 0.36). This is not surprising since more urban couples were in childbearing, life cycle stages.

*Summary and Additional Analysis.* The second hypothesis that certain kinds of stressors would be more prevalent in rural families than in urban families and vice versa was supported. Rural couples reported significantly more economic stressors while urban couples reported significantly more work/family marital and pregnancy stressors.

The rationale behind this hypothesis is that non-normative stressors vary with type of work and residential setting while normative stressors do not. Normative stressors, however, might be more numerous in certain life cycle stages. To test this, one-way analysis of variance was used to ascertain differences in stressor pileup in life cycle stage as measured by the Total Recent and Past Life Change scores and each of the subscale scores. Table 3 presents these data.

There were a number of significant differences. To ascertain if the perceived differences were in fact real differences, a BMDV statistical program was used to compute t-values for contrasts in group means on those scores for which there were statistically significant differences by life cycle stage as noted in Table 3. There was a general pattern, especially in the rural sample, of fewer stressors in the retired stage of the life cycle. Retired rural couples had significantly lower mean Total Recent Life Changes scores, and retired urban couples had significantly lower mean Total Past Life Changes scores than couples in the other life cycle stages. Retired couples in both locations reported significantly fewer finance and business, intrafamily, and (for urban couples only) work/family strains. This is probably due to smaller household size, less focus with work, and fewer financial demands. There were significant differences on particular subscales by couples in other stages in the life cycle. Retired couples, however, were the only group with significant differences on more than one subscale.

Thus far, attention has been focused on the family as a system with the stress scores being a composite of the husband's and wife's score. Since different stressors were reported by the husbands and wives in Olson and McCubbin's study (1983) which used FILE as the stressor measure, the life event scores of the rural and urban husbands and wives were compared. An analysis of the mean summary scores of the nine subscales of FILE using an analysis of variance revealed no significant findings by gender. However, there was a difference in the Total Past Family Life Changes mean score. Both rural and urban wives reported significantly more prior stressors than did their husbands. Perhaps their memories were better or perhaps they have not worked through the changes required by these stressors as well as have their husbands.

## Discussion and Implications

Contrary to the null hypothesis, the urban couples reported facing significantly more stressors in the 12 months prior to the study than did the rural couples. The hypothesis that certain kinds of stressors would be more prevalent in one location than the other, however, was supported. Rural couples reported significantly more economic stressors, and urban couples reported significantly more work/family, marital, and pregnancy stressors.

Financial strains were the most commonly cited stressors in Olson and McCubbin's (1983) study followed by intra-family and work-family strains. With the exceptions of a lack of gender differences and no significant increase in stressors for families in the adolescent life cycle stage, the findings in the two studies are consistent.

The finding that stressor pileup was less for the rural sample than for the urban sample seems odd given the farm crises that the media have been portraying for the past several years (e.g., Dentzer et al., 1985; Sheets et al., 1985). One of the hazards inherent in survey research is the potential biasing of a sample by nonrespondents. Would farmers and ranchers facing large pileups of stressors be less likely to respond to a mailed questionnaire than urban couples facing large pileups of stressors? Unfortunately, it was not possible to answer this question.

It is also possible that FILE was not an adequate measure of the kinds of stressors these rural couples faced. The underlying assumption of the second hypothesis was that people with different life styles would face somewhat different non-normative stressors. FILE is a measure of typical stressors. Therefore, occupationally related stressors, such as a serious outbreak of disease in livestock or a worker's strike, were not measured. Since this study was begun, certain stressors have been documented as being more common to agriculture than to other rural or urban occupations (e.g., Tevis, 1982; Weigel, 1981b; Walker, Walker, & MacLennan, 1986). Researchers and practitioners should take occupationally related stressors into account. Once such stressors have been identified, programs can be designed to help the target population improve their coping strategies and/or reduce their stress. Researchers should also include occupationally related stressors when studying stress.

FILE appears to be somewhat biased as a measure of more general normative and non-normative stressors. It became evident as these data were being analyzed that the Work-Family Transitions and Strains subscale did not include as many stressors for the self-employed (most men in the rural sample) as it did for employees (most men in the urban sample). If this bias were corrected, it is possible that the rural/urban differences in this subscale and in the Total Life Change sum scores would have been smaller.

The pileup of economic stressors reported by the urban couples is consistent with the findings noted by Olson and Schellenberg (1986) in their literature review article of farm stressors, i.e., that financial stressors appear more intense and are more prevalent than other kind of stressors. Yet some writers (e.g., Easterbrook, 1985; Watts, 1986) claim that most farm families are at least moderately financially well off. More comparative studies are required to ascertain if, indeed, farmers face more economic stressors than owners of other small businesses such as gas stations or restaurants, for instance. While many farm and ranch families attempting to cope with serious economic stressors will benefit from financial planning, counseling, legal, and other kinds of services, families involved in other kinds of family-owned businesses may also benefit from such services.

Given the press coverage of farm stress, it is important to keep in mind that the urban families in this study reported significantly more stressors than the rural families. Their higher marital and pregnancy stressor scores, for example, suggest that a number of these families might benefit from marriage counseling. Their higher work/family strains would also indicate some demand for services which would help them adapt to work-related stressors. Marotz-Baden and Colvin (1986) found that, while urban and rural couples used the same coping strategies, urban couples did not appear to be using them as effectively. Programs to improve skills related to coping, as well as stress management workshops and other services designed to address specific concerns of urban families, could help them reduce their stress levels.

## END NOTES

1. Mountain Bell estimated at the time of the survey that 80% of the household phones in these areas were listed in both husband's and wife's name. Such a high proportion of dual listing may be unique to Montana. Newcomers from out of state and certain types of professionals, i.e., physicians, were less likely to dual list (private communique, 1981).

2. The life cycle was divided into five stages on the basis of age of youngest child: no children (pre and post childbearing), preschool, elementary, junior and senior high school, and retired (no children). Because of the printing error in the age question, it was not possible to distinguish between pre and post childbearing couples.

3. Although the average annual inflation rate was 8% to 9% from 1973 through 1982, it varied from year to year as well as from month to month in a particular year. U.S. Bureau of the Census, 1983.

## REFERENCES

Agricultural and Rural Economics Division (1986). Public policies for displaced farmers and their families. Unpublished report, Economic Research Service, United States Department of Agriculture, Washington, DC.

Braun, D. (1981, March). Smoke-signals when farming and marriage clash. Farm Journal, pp. 32-33.

Carson, C. (1986). The trouble with farming. In Paul L. Poirot (Ed.), The farm problem (pp. 13-24). Irvington-on-Hudson, NY: The Foundation for Economic Education, Inc.

Coddington, D. R. (1972). The significance of life events as etiologic factors in diseases of children II. A study of a normal population. Journal of Psychosomatic Research, 16, 205-213.

Dentzer, S., McCormick, J., Thomas, R., Weathers, D., Abramson, P., Shapiro, D., & Wang, P. (1985, February 19). Bitter Harvest. Newsweek, pp. 52-59.

Easterbrook, G. (1985, July). Making sense of agriculture. The Atlantic, 256(1), 63-80.

Farm Land Values Fall. (1985, June 7). Bozeman Daily Chronicle, p. 3.

Fetsch, R. J. (1984. *Stress series: Farming—A stressful occupation; Stress symptoms; Stress management for farmers; Stress management for couples; When generations farm together;* and *Farm stress management plan.* (Cooperative Extension Service leaflets 283, 284, 285, 286, 287, 288). Lexington, KY: University of Kentucky College of Agriculture.

Hedlund, D., & Berkowitz, A. (1979). The incidence of social-psychological stress in farm families. *International Journal of Sociology of the Family, 9,* 233-243.

Hennon, C., & Harder, K. (1982). *Managing farm stress.* University of Wisconsin—Extension Bulletin B2744-1. Department of Agricultural Journalism, University of Wisconsin-Madison.

Hill, R. (1949). *Families under stress.* New York: Harper and Row.

Holmes, T., & Masuda, M. (1974). Life change and illness susceptibility. In B. S. Dohrenwend and B. P. Dohrenwend (Eds.), *Stressful life events: Their nature and effects* (pp. 45-72). New York: John Wiley.

Holmes, T. H., & Rahe, R. H. (1967). The social readjustment rating scale. *Journal of Psychosomatic Research, 11,* 213-218.

LeMasters, E. E. (1957). Parenthood as crisis. *Marriage and Family Living, 19,* 252-255.

Marotz-Baden, R. (1986, November). Two-generation politics: Transferring the family farm. Paper presented at the annual meeting of the National Council on Family Relations, Dearborn, MI.

Marotz-Baden, R., & Colvin, P. L. (1986). Coping Strategies: A rural-urban comparison. *Family Relations, 35,* 281-288.

McCubbin, H. I., Cauble, A. E., & Patterson, J. (Eds.) (1982). Family adaptation to crisis. *Family Stress, Coping and Social Support.* Springfield, IL: Charles C. Thomas.

McCubbin, H. I., & Patterson, J. (1981). *Systematic assessment of family stress, resources and coping,* pp. 9-18. St. Paul, MN: University of Minnesota.

McCubbin, H. I., Patterson, J., & Wilson, L. (1982). FILE—Family inventory of life events and changes. In D. Olson, H. I. McCubbin, H. Barnes, A. Larson, M. Muxen, & M. Wilson (Eds.), *Family Inventories* (pp. 69-89). St. Paul, MN: Family Social Science, University of Minnesota.

*Montana Crop and Livestock Reporter* (1982, November). Montana Crop and Livestock Reporting Service, Helena, MT.

Mullan, J. (1983, October). *The mis-meaning of life events in family stress theory and research.* Paper presented at the preconference theory and research methodology workshop. National Council on Family Relations annual meeting, St. Paul, MN.

Olson, D., & McCubbin, J. I. (1983). *Families: What makes them work.* Beverly Hills: Sage Publications.

Olson, K. R., & Schellenberg, R. P. (1986). Farm stressors. *American Journal of Community Psychology, 14,* 555-568.

Patterson, J., & McCubbin, H. (1983, April). The impact of family life events and changes on health of the chronically ill child. *Family Relations, 32,* 255-265.

Rosenblatt, P. C., & Keller, L. O. (1983). Economic vulnerability and economic stress in couples. *Family Relations, 32,* 1-18.

Rosenfeld, R. (1985). *Farm women.* Chapel Hill: The University of North Carolina Press.

Schotsch, L. (1985, March). Who will farm in five years? *Farm Journal,* pp. 13-15.

Sheets, K. R., Shapiro, J. P., Barr, R., & Sheler, J. L. (1985, March 11). Farmers up in arms. *U.S. News,* pp. 22-25.

Tallman, I., & Marotz, R. (1970). Life-style differences among urban and suburban blue-collar families. *Social Forces, 48,* 334-348.

Tevis, C. (1980, October). Stress. *Successful Farming,* pp. 20-21.

Tevis, C. (1982, February). Stress. *Successful Farming,* pp. 27-42.

U.S. Bureau of the Census. (1978). Census of agriculture. U.S. Department of Commerce. Volume I State and County Data, Part 2b, Montana AC78-A-26. Government Printing Office, p. 3.

Walker, J., Walker, L. S., & MacLennan, P. (1986). An informal look at farm stress. *Psychological Reports, 59,* 427-430.

Watts, M. (1986). Analyzing financial health and liquidation. Staff paper No. 86-5. Staff papers in economics. Agricultural Economics and Economics Department, Montana State University, Bozeman, MT.

Weigel, R. R. (1981a, March). *Stress on the farm* series. Cooperative Extension Service, Iowa State University, Ames, IA 50011. PM-988-a-d.

Weigel, R. R. (1981b). *Stress on the farm—An overview* (pamphlet). Ames: Cooperative Extension Service at Iowa State University.

# PART III: ADAPTATION

Rural families experience various levels of stress and have differing resources with which to deal with stress. The adaptations of rural families provide information about how families deal with changing environments. Adaptations within marriages, households, parent relationships, kin interactions, later life families, other family and health situations are considered in this section.

Four chapters focus on adaptations in marriages. Lorraine Dorfman and Alex Heckert explore the division of household tasks, decision-making patterns and leisure activities among a sample of 149 retired rural couples. The findings suggest that egalitarianism may increase after retirement. Janet Bokemeier and Richard Maurer focus on the relationship of conjugal labor involvement and marital quality among a sample of 770 nonmetropolitan households. Although their findings indicate that there are different types of conjugal labor involvement, patterns of conjugal labor involvement are not associated with marital quality. Raymond Coward, Stephen Cutler and Frederick Schmidt examine residential differences in marital status and household type of elderly. Differences between rural and urban elders are discussed and implications for caregiving are noted. A qualitative analysis of data from a sample of couples who have experienced income loss is reported by Anisa Zvonkovic, Tom Guss and Linda Ladd. The data are organized around five issues including interpretation of the situation, personal resources, health and stress, marital relationships and family and social support. Strategies for working with underemployed families are presented.

Two chapters address the use of time within the household. Jane Meiners and Geraldine Olson examined the issue of time allotments to household, paid, and unpaid work in a sample of farm, rural nonfarm and urban women. In a qualitative study, Betty Beach examines the allocation of work time in fifteen rural home-working families. These chapters provide information about the ways in which rural families use their time.

Four chapters examine issues related to parenting across the life cycle. Carol Mertensmeyer and Marilyn Coleman analyze the correlates of inter-role conflict among young rural and urban parents. Pauline Boss, Debra Pearce-McCall and Jan Greenberg compare the adaptations of seventy rural and urban parents to an adolescent leaving home. Ramon Marotz-Baden and Deane Cowan consider the mothers-in-law and daughters-in-law relationship. Joyce Mercier, Lori Paulson and Earl Morris examine the differences in the quality of the parent-child relationship between rural and urban parents.

The next four chapters compare rural and urban interactions in later life. Gary Lee's study examines the degree to which rural and urban older persons are embedded in a social network. Jean Scott and Karen Roberto focus on exchanges of assistance and social activities with children and friends of 180 urban older persons and 145 rural older persons. Vira Kivett explores adult sons' involvement in the support network of older rural men. The activities of unmarried older persons are considered by Pat Keith and André Nauta. These chapters provide information about the support networks of rural older persons.

The ways in which families adapt to the changing rural environments are examined in two chapters. Sara Wright and Paul Rosenblatt report data on isolation, farm loss and the reasons why neighbors may not be supportive of these farm families. Randy and Daniel Weigel identify stressors and coping strategies within two-generation farm families.

Health issues of rural families is discussed in the chapters by Clarann Weinart and Kathleen Long, and Janette Newhouse and William McAuley. The health care needs and services in a rural setting are reported by Weinart and Long. Newhouse and McAuley examine the informal in-home care of 1,196 rural older persons.

# Egalitarianism in Retired Rural Couples: Household Tasks, Decision Making, and Leisure Activities*

**Lorraine T. Dorfman and D. Alex Heckert\*\***

With the exception of a recent study by Dorfman, Hill, Kohout, and Heckert (1986), there has been no research focused on retired rural couples. Yet, the percentage of couples who are elderly and retired in rural areas is substantial. One of every four persons age 65 and older resides in rural areas, either in small towns of 2,500 or less or on farms (U.S. Department of Commerce, 1983), and a higher proportion of those rural elderly are married than are their urban counterparts (Sotomayor, 1981). Recent literature indicates that life style differences persist between urban and rural elderly subpopulations despite diminishing urban/rural differences (Coward & Smith, 1982; Lee & Lassey, 1980). It can be expected that some of these life style differences are reflected in the retirement experience.

The purpose of this study was to investigate conjugal role organization in retired rural couples. Although there are conflicting findings, research provides some support for the theoretical position that role integration increases and gender differentiation decreases among later life couples (Brubaker, 1985a). A number of investigators have reported a decrease in gender-differentiated role behavior after retirement in urban couples (Kerckhoff, 1966; Lipman, 1961; Model, 1981). There is, however, no empirical data on this question focused on retired rural couples, and there is no theoretical justification for direct extrapolation from data on retired urban couples to questions involving retired rural couples. The present study investigated three major aspects of the conjugal relationship that are often affected by retirement in urban settings: division of household tasks, decision-making patterns, and leisure activities shared by the couple. It is hoped that the study will provide useful information concerning conjugal role organization for family life educators, counselors, extension workers, and other practitioners who work with rural adults and their families, and will contribute to policies and programs that will more effectively serve the rural subpopulation.

## Nonrural Data

With regard to division of household tasks, a number of studies with a nonrural focus have reported that couples engage in more sharing of household tasks after retirement, with husbands increasing their level of participation (Brubaker, 1985b; Dressler, 1973; Kerckhoff, 1966; Lipman, 1961; Model, 1981). The husband's participation in household tasks, however, may be primarily in

*This research was supported by National Institute on Aging Contract NO-1-AG-0-2106, "Establishment of Populations for Epidemiologic Studies of the Elderly." The authors wish to thank Carol Mertens and Mary Willie-Sutton for their valuable suggestions.

**Lorraine T. Dorfman is Associate Professor, Department of Home Economics, University of Iowa, Iowa City, IA 52242. D. Alex Heckert is Research Associate III, Center for Health Services Research, Memphis State University, Memphis, TN 38152.

Reprinted from *Family Relations*, 1988, **37**, 73-78.

such traditional, "masculine" tasks as mowing the lawn, household repairs, or car maintenance (Ballweg, 1967; Keith & Brubaker, 1979). Some nonrural studies suggest that newly shared control of household responsibilities may be unwelcome in retirement, especially for wives (Aldous, 1978; Fengler, 1975; Heyman, 1970). Other nonrural research, however, shows that most couples continue preretirement patterns of division of household tasks, which are often traditional and gender-differentiated (Keating & Cole, 1980; Keith & Brubaker, 1979; Szinovacz, 1980).

Little information exists regarding decision-making patterns in retired couples. Nonrural research has indicated that changes in decision making due to loss of the occupational role may be resented by the spouse, especially by the wife (Fengler, 1975). Dressler's (1973) nonrural study, however, found no significant change in the way couples made decisions after retirement. A Boston study (Sheldon, McEwan, & Ryser, 1975) found that the majority of couples said they made most decisions jointly during retirement. Agreement on decision making was associated with life satisfaction of both spouses, especially husbands, in that study.

Retirement may also affect the more expressive aspects of the conjugal relationship, including amount of time the couple spends together and the leisure activities they share. Nearly three fourths of the couples in Dressler's (1973) sample reported an increase in time spent together after retirement. Fengler (1975) found that wives who were optimistic about their husbands' retirement stressed companionship and activities shared with their spouse, whereas wives who were pessimistic about their husbands' retirement did not stress companionship or activities shared with their spouse. Lipman (1961) reported an increase in recreational activities shared by the couple after retirement. Moreover, he found that increase in joint recreational activities was positively related to morale in retired men.

## Rural Data and Hypotheses Under Investigation

Information on the aspects of the conjugal relationship discussed above is almost nonexistent for retired rural couples. Findings for retired nonrural couples cannot be directly extrapolated to retired rural couples since family patterns are not necessarily the same for the two groups. Therefore, it is important to do research directly on rural couples.

With respect to division of household tasks, rural couples in general appear to show more marital role segregation than do urban couples (Lee & Cassidy, 1985). Rural wives have been reported to espouse more traditional norms and play more traditional roles than do urban wives (Flora & Johnson, 1978; Powers, Keith, & Goudy, 1979; Rosenblatt & Anderson, 1981; Schumm & Bollman, 1981; Youmans, 1973). Flora and Johnson (1978) suggest that rural life may be more attractive than urban life to women with traditional viewpoints. Moreover, they suggest that rural women may not be socialized to think of themselves in any but traditional ways. One study (Brubaker & Hennon, 1982) found a traditional division of household responsibility even among dual-retired, mainly nonurban wives; however, those wives expected a more egalitarian division of household tasks. Based on these studies, it was hypothesized in the present study that rural wives would spend more time in household tasks after retirement than would their husbands, and that level of household role segregation would not decrease after retirement.

With respect to marital decision making, rural couples have often been stereotyped as traditional, with the husband dominant in decision making. Recent research, however, suggests that behavioral differences between urban and rural authority structures are quite small and that a pattern of decision making is emerging among rural couples similar to that found among nonrural couples with respect to egalitarianism (Dorfman & Hill, 1986; Lee & Cassidy, 1985; Schumm & Bollman, 1981). On the basis of this literature, it was therefore hypothesized that rural couples would make most decisions jointly rather than individually during retirement.

Finally, with regard to leisure activities shared by the retired couple, "too much togetherness" has been identified as a potential problem among rural, especially farm couples (Dorfman & Hill, 1986; Rosenblatt & Anderson, 1981). There also may be relatively fewer opportunities for leisure-time pursuits in rural areas than in urban areas (Kivett, 1985) even if shared leisure activities are satisfying to retired couples (Dorfman et al., 1986). It was therefore hypothesized that the number of leisure activities shared by rural couples would not increase significantly after retirement.

## Method

### Sample

Respondents were all married couples ($n = 149$ couples) for whom data were available in the retirement substudy of an 8-year epidemiological investigation of persons age 65 and older in two rural counties in Iowa (Dorfman, Kohout, & Heckert, 1985; Dorfman et al., 1986). A stratified random sample was drawn for the retirement study from a cohort of over 4,000 people who are participating in the larger epidemiological investigation. The sample was stratified by nonfarm vs. farm residence and by sex. Interviews were completed with 54 dual-retired couples and 95 husband retired/housewife couples, representing a response rate of 85%. Housewives were defined as women who had not been in the labor force for at least 10 years immediately prior to their husbands' retirement. No spouses were currently employed. Length of retirement ranged from 6 months to 10 years. The mean age of husbands was 71.9 years and of wives 69.3 years, with a range of 66-90 years for husbands and 41-87 years for wives. The majority (53%) of husbands had been engaged in farming, with nonfarm managers and administrators (16%) and professional and technical workers (14%) being the next most highly represented categories. The most frequent occupational category for wives was professional and technical workers, especially nurses, health technicians, and teachers (37%), followed by food service workers and clerical workers (25% each). Median household income was $12,500 in 1982. Data were collected in home interviews lasting approximately 45 minutes. Husbands and wives were interviewed simultaneously but separately.

### Measures

Division of household tasks was assessed by asking respondents, "Before you retired, how many hours per week on the average did you and your spouse spend doing the following chores?" and "How many hours per week on the average do you and your spouse now spend doing the following

chores?" Five different kinds of household tasks were listed: washing dishes, grocery shopping, preparing meals, cleaning, and laundry. Past research has suggested that retirement may particularly affect participation in those "inside" household tasks due to the increased presence of the husband in the home (Aldous, 1978; Fengler, 1975; Kerckhoff, 1966; Lipman, 1961). In order to derive information beyond the basic measures, an index of household role segregation was constructed by summing the difference between number of hours per week spent by husband and wife in the five household tasks. Item analysis indicated that the internal consistency for the index of household role segregation, as measured by Cronbach's Alpha, was .64 for husbands and .80 for wives. The difference between those Alpha coefficients was not statistically significant.

Conjugal decision making was examined in four areas: finances, trips, running the household, and entertainment. The assessment of both preretirement and current decision making was made using questions similar to those used for household tasks. An index of joint decision making was constructed by summing the proportion of decisions made jointly by the couple in the four specific decision-making areas. Cronbach's Alpha for the index of joint decision making was .75 for husbands and .73 for wives.

Leisure activities shared by the couple (e.g., church activities, gardening, taking trips, attending movies or sports events) were summed over 18 different areas to derive a global measure of number of leisure activities shared by the couple. Respondents were asked to recall this information for the preretirement period as well as currently.

### Data Analysis

Pre- and postretirement levels of participation in household tasks, decision making, and leisure activities shared by the couple were examined for the entire sample of husbands and wives in order to provide global information on conjugal role organization that would be useful to practitioners. Because the design of the survey is cross sectional, questions about preretirement activities could be addressed only indirectly through retrospective data.

Z-tests for paired observations with large samples were used to test for dif-

Table 1.
*Division of Household Tasks Reported by Rural Husbands and Wives: Pre- and Postretirement*

| | Preretirement Division of Household Tasks | | | | Postretirement Division of Household Tasks | | | |
| | | Self | Spouse | | | Self | Spouse | |
| | $n$ | $\overline{X}$ | $\overline{X}$ | $Z$ | $n$ | $\overline{X}$ | $\overline{X}$ | $Z$ |
|---|---|---|---|---|---|---|---|---|
| **Husband's Report** | | | | | | | | |
| Number of hours per week spent in: | | | | | | | | |
| washing dishes | 129 | 1.91 | 7.06 | -9.91** | 132 | 2.89 | 5.67 | -6.18** |
| grocery shopping | 135 | 1.07 | 1.94 | -6.08** | 136 | 1.43 | 1.95 | -3.83** |
| meal preparation | 124 | 1.83 | 11.65 | -11.73** | 126 | 2.62 | 10.07 | -9.46** |
| housecleaning | 123 | 1.07 | 7.00 | -10.04** | 124 | 1.52 | 6.54 | -7.27** |
| laundry | 124 | 0.31 | 3.02 | -10.74** | 127 | 0.42 | 2.70 | -9.30** |
| Index of household role segregation | $n = 116$ | $\overline{X} = 28.83$ | | | | $\overline{X} = 22.78$ | | $Z = 5.45**$ |
| **Wife's Report** | | | | | | | | |
| Number of hours per week spent in: | | | | | | | | |
| washing dishes | 139 | 5.96 | 3.06 | 4.27** | 143 | 4.74 | 3.27 | 3.10* |
| grocery shopping | 140 | 1.56 | 0.99 | 3.73** | 143 | 1.49 | 1.27 | 1.75 |
| meal preparation | 138 | 9.00 | 3.59 | 5.73** | 141 | 8.81 | 3.49 | 6.48** |
| housecleaning | 140 | 5.13 | 2.09 | 5.33** | 144 | 4.52 | 2.22 | 4.97** |
| laundry | 139 | 2.45 | 0.90 | 5.52** | 143 | 2.09 | 0.80 | 5.69** |
| Index of household role segregation | $n = 134$ | $\overline{X} = 27.89$ | | | | $\overline{X} = 21.65$ | | $Z = 6.65**$ |

*$p \leq .01$.
**$p \leq .001$.

ferences between husbands' and wives' level of participation in household tasks and in decision making both prior to and in retirement (Downie & Heath, 1959). Z-tests were also used to test for differences between pre- and postretirement levels of participation in household tasks, decision making, and shared leisure activities. Since reports of husbands and wives may differ on the same activities (Larson, 1974; Safilios-Rothschild, 1969; Thompson & Walker, 1982; Troll, Miller, & Atchley, 1979), both the husband's and the wife's reports were included in every analysis. Z-tests were also used to test for significant differences between husband's and wife's reports of the same activities.

## Results

### Division of Household Tasks

Table 1 shows a consistent, traditional pattern of division of household tasks both prior to and in retirement: Both rural husbands and rural wives reported that the wife spent more hours per week in household tasks than did the husband. The index of household role segregation, however, showed a significant decrease in overall level of household role segregation after retirement, reported by both husbands and wives (see Table 1). One possible explanation for the finding of decreased household role segregation after retirement is that husbands may be compensating for their lost

work role by participating in household roles (Lipman, 1961). Another possibility is that the couples may want to share more household tasks in order to spend more time together during retirement.

Whereas the data in Table 1 compare self reports of the division of household labor between husbands and wives, Table 2 compares pre- and postretirement levels of participation in household tasks reported by rural husbands and wives. The means shown in Table 2 differ slightly from those shown in Table 1. Table 1 includes only those cases where the respondent reported data for both self and spouse, while Table 2 shows data for self only. Husbands said they spent more hours per week in all five household tasks after retirement than they did prior to retirement. Wives, however, said the husbands spent more hours per week only in grocery shopping after retirement. Both husbands and wives said that the wife spent fewer hours per week in three of the five household tasks after retirement. Husbands reported wives spending less time in dishwashing, laundry, and meal preparation while wives reported themselves as spending less time in dishwashing, laundry and housecleaning.

Husbands' and wives' reports sometimes differ. Differential perceptions between spouses, it has been noted, are an aspect of family reality (Larson, 1974; Thompson & Walker, 1982). Z-tests were used to test for significant differences between husband's and wife's reports. Signifi-

Table 2.
*Mean Level of Participation in Household Tasks Reported by Rural Husbands and Wives, Indicating Changes Between Pre- and Post-retirement*

| | Participation of Husband in Household Tasks | | | | Participation of Wife in Household Tasks | | | |
| | | Pre-retirement | Post-retirement | | | Pre-retirement | Post-retirement | |
| | n | $\overline{X}$ | $\overline{X}$ | Z | n | $\overline{X}$ | $\overline{X}$ | Z |
|---|---|---|---|---|---|---|---|---|
| **Husband's Report** | | | | | | | | |
| Number of hours per week spent in: | | | | | | | | |
| washing dishes | 140 | 1.79 | 2.79 | -4.20*** | 131 | 6.98 | 5.66 | 3.96*** |
| grocery shopping | 141 | 1.04 | 1.39 | -3.16** | 135 | 1.94 | 1.96 | -0.14 |
| meal preparation | 139 | 1.67 | 2.38 | -3.28*** | 124 | 11.64 | 9.97 | 4.54*** |
| housecleaning | 137 | 0.98 | 1.42 | -3.44*** | 123 | 6.99 | 6.52 | 0.90 |
| laundry | 137 | 0.28 | 0.40 | -3.12** | 125 | 2.98 | 2.64 | 2.94** |
| **Wife's Report** | | | | | | | | |
| Number of hours per week spent in: | | | | | | | | |
| washing dishes | 143 | 2.98 | 3.27 | -1.04 | 139 | 5.96 | 4.80 | 3.57*** |
| grocery shopping | 142 | 0.97 | 1.24 | -3.49*** | 140 | 1.56 | 1.51 | 0.66 |
| meal preparation | 143 | 3.46 | 3.44 | 0.08 | 138 | 9.00 | 8.92 | 0.24 |
| housecleaning | 144 | 2.03 | 2.22 | -1.11 | 140 | 5.13 | 4.64 | 2.10* |
| laundry | 144 | 0.87 | 0.80 | 0.94 | 139 | 2.45 | 2.13 | 3.36*** |

*$p \leq .05$.
**$p \leq .01$.
***$p \leq .001$.

cant differences were found between spouses' reports of participation in four household tasks prior to retirement and in three household tasks during retirement. Although not given in the tables, all of these significant differences showed the same general effect: Both rural husbands and rural wives reported that their spouse spent more time in household tasks than the spouse reported spending. It is possible that these husbands and wives assume that their spouse is doing more household work than the spouse himself or herself reports doing because they are in general maritally satisfied. Yogev and Brett (1985) have found this relationship in a recent study of nonretired spouses.

## Decision Making

As shown in Table 3, both rural husbands and rural wives said that the husband made more decisions about finances and that the wife made more decisions about running the household both prior to and in retirement. Husbands also reported that the wife made more decisions about entertainment prior to and in retirement, whereas wives reported that the husband made more decisions about trips during retirement. Z-tests (data not shown) demonstrated that there were few significant differences between husband's and wife's reports: Spouses' reports differed in no more than one decision-making area either prior to or in

Table 3.
*Mean Percentage of Individual Decision Making Reported by Rural Husbands and Wives: Pre- and Postretirement*

| | Preretirement Decision Making | | | | Postretirement Decision Making | | | |
| | | By Self | By Spouse | | | By Self | By Spouse | |
| | n | $\overline{X}$ | $\overline{X}$ | Z | n | $\overline{X}$ | $\overline{X}$ | Z |
|---|---|---|---|---|---|---|---|---|
| **Husband's Report** | | | | | | | | |
| Percentage of decisions made about: | | | | | | | | |
| finances | 145 | 29.83 | 18.34 | 4.12** | 145 | 24.38 | 18.31 | 2.47* |
| trips | 145 | 15.41 | 16.14 | -0.38 | 144 | 13.47 | 17.08 | -1.90 |
| running the household | 145 | 11.69 | 69.21 | -15.54** | 145 | 14.10 | 62.31 | -11.94** |
| entertainment | 145 | 16.60 | 28.07 | -4.05** | 145 | 16.90 | 28.17 | -3.78** |
| **Wife's Report** | | | | | | | | |
| Percentage of decisions made about: | | | | | | | | |
| finances | 144 | 18.20 | 32.46 | -4.71** | 144 | 18.02 | 28.26 | -3.47** |
| trips | 144 | 16.70 | 21.77 | -1.52 | 144 | 15.03 | 21.28 | -1.98* |
| running the household | 142 | 54.68 | 18.77 | 8.26** | 145 | 48.86 | 19.34 | 6.86** |
| entertainment | 143 | 28.08 | 22.06 | 1.78 | 145 | 27.13 | 21.77 | 1.66 |

*$p \leq .05$.
**$p \leq .001$.

Table 4.
*Mean Percentage of Joint Decision Making Reported by Rural Husbands and Wives: Pre- and Postretirement*

| | n | Preretirement Joint Decision Making $\bar{X}$ | Postretirement Joint Decision Making $\bar{X}$ | Z |
|---|---|---|---|---|
| **Husband's Report** | | | | |
| Percentage of decisions made jointly about: | | | | |
| finances | 145 | 51.83 | 56.90 | -2.39* |
| trips | 144 | 65.45 | 65.28 | 0.09 |
| running the household | 145 | 19.10 | 23.59 | -2.73** |
| entertainment | 145 | 55.33 | 54.93 | 0.29 |
| Index of joint decision making | n = 143 | $\bar{X}$ = 47.96 | $\bar{X}$ = 50.24 | Z = -1.72 |
| **Wife's Report** | | | | |
| Percentage of decisions made jointly about: | | | | |
| finances | 144 | 49.34 | 53.72 | -2.26* |
| trips | 143 | 60.56 | 62.03 | -0.85 |
| running the household | 142 | 26.97 | 31.41 | -2.52* |
| entertainment | 143 | 49.69 | 50.42 | -0.54 |
| Index of joint decision making | n = 143 | $\bar{X}$ = 46.76 | $\bar{X}$ = 49.60 | Z = -2.46* |

*$p \leq .05$.
**$p \leq .01$.

retirement. Thus, husbands and wives did not disagree for the most part in their perceptions of self and other decision making.

Table 4 shows proportion of decisions made jointly by the couple prior to retirement and in retirement. Both rural husbands and rural wives reported that more than half of the decisions in all decision-making areas except running the household were made jointly during retirement. Both spouses also reported a significant increase in proportion of decisions made jointly about finances and about running the household after retirement. Z-test results (not shown) indicated that husband's and wife's reports did not differ significantly with respect to joint decision making in any of the four decision-making areas. The index of joint decision making based on wives' reports (Table 4) showed a significant increase in overall level after retirement. The index of joint decision making based on husbands' reports also showed an increase in overall level, just failing statistical significance ($p < .087$). It is possible that the finding of increased joint decision making after retirement may be related to the husbands' loss of earning power and occupational status. Husbands may be compensating for this loss by becoming more involved in decisions about the home (Fengler, 1975). Alternatively, it may be that the couples are spending more time together after retirement and thus have more opportunity to share the decisions of everyday life.

## Shared Leisure Activities

Rural husbands and wives both reported nearly 10 shared leisure activities both prior

to retirement and in retirement (data not shown). The number of shared leisure activities did not change significantly after retirement, as reported by either spouse.

## Summary and Implications

The overall findings of this study show a movement toward more role integration and less gender differentiation among rural couples after retirement. This finding has a number of implications for family life educators, counselors, extension workers, and other practitioners who work with rural adults and their families, as well as for program development in rural areas.

First, and most importantly, the finding of increased egalitarianism in rural couples after retirement challenges the stereotype of the traditional rural couple (Lee & Cassidy, 1985; Schumm & Bollman, 1981). Although the wives in this rural sample spent more time performing household tasks than did their husbands both prior to and in retirement, the overall level of household role segregation decreased significantly after retirement. Likewise, joint decision making increased significantly after retirement, especially with regard to finances and running the household. The majority of decisions in all but one decision-making area (running the household) were made jointly by the couple during retirement. It is hoped that the findings on increased egalitarianism in retired rural couples will help practitioners and program planners become more aware of the reality of retired rural marriages so that programs developed in rural areas will be based on fact rather than on intuition. Many commonly held myths about the rural elderly are not supported by empirical research (Coward & Kerckhoff, 1978). It is important for practitioners to recognize that there are a variety of relationships among retired rural couples.

Family life educators, preretirement educators, and extension workers can then incorporate the findings on egalitarianism after retirement into information offered in workshops and other educational programs that are designed to assist in the transition to retirement. Information on changes in life style and spousal roles after retirement, as well as on finances and health, is helpful in the transition to retirement (Siegel & Rives, 1978). Rural preretirees can be told what to expect in retirement, so that they will be better prepared for what actually happens during retirement. It is very important that such preretirement programs include both husbands and wives, since retirement is a "family affair." Other practitioners, including marriage and family counselors, clergymen, and other mental health professionals, can also provide information to rural couples about what to expect in retirement.

The finding of increased egalitarianism after retirement could be incorporated in written materials such as newsletters and in mass media presentations aimed at informing large audiences of rural adults about the retirement experience. In rural areas, extension workers have a special opportunity to develop the kind of media presentations and written materials that can help people become better informed about retirement.

Finally, since it was found that rural couples participated in a substantial number of shared leisure activities during retirement, and since shared leisure activities are an important source of satisfaction for rural couples (Dorfman et al., 1986), it might be helpful if YMCA's, senior centers, churches, and extension programs in rural areas offered more joint activities for retired couples. These joint activities should be balanced, however, with the opportunity to pursue individual activities, in order to avoid the problem of "too much togetherness" (Dorfman & Hill, 1986; Rosenblatt & Anderson, 1981). A community-based information line could be used to give information about joint and individual activities that are currently going on in the community.

Little information exists at present on retired rural couples; therefore, it is important that the results of this study be replicated in other rural locations in order to test their generalizability. Future research should also investigate the discrepancies between spouses' reports regarding division of household tasks that were found in this study. It would be useful to know, for instance, if retired people who are more maritally satisfied assume that their spouse is doing more household tasks than the spouse reports doing. Such relationships have been found among certain subsets of non-retired spouses (Yogev & Brett, 1985). The present data did not allow for an examination of such relationships.[1] Future research might provide more detailed information on subgroups of retired rural couples by examining socioeconomic status, length of retirement, farm/nonfarm residence, and whether or not the wife was employed before retirement. In addition, linkages among the different aspects of the conjugal relationship might be explored.

Today, one of every four elders lives in rural areas, either in small towns of 2,500 or less or on farms. Relatively little is known about these rural elders. A great deal more research is needed to determine the extent to which rural elders differ from their urban counterparts. As Willitts, Bealer, and Crider (1982) have recently pointed out, failure to recognize urban/rural differences can lead to policies that are relevant only to the dominant urban society or to policies that cannot be adequately implemented in sparsely populated areas.

### END NOTE

1. The Office of Management and Budget classified measures of marital satisfaction as too sensitive for inclusion in the study; therefore, no measures of marital satisfaction were used in this study.

### REFERENCES

Aldous, J. (1978). *Family careers: Developmental change in families.* New York: John Wiley & Sons.

Ballweg, J. A. (1967). Resolution of conjugal role adjustment after retirement. *Journal of Marriage and the Family,* **29,** 277-281.

Brubaker, T. H. (1985a). *Later life families.* Beverly Hills, CA: Sage Publications.

Brubaker, T. H. (1985b). Responsibility for household tasks: A look at golden anniversary couples aged 75 years and older. In W. A. Peterson & J. Quadagno (Eds.), *Social bonds in later life* (pp. 27-36). Beverly Hills, CA: Sage Publications.

Brubaker, T. H., & Hennon, C. B. (1982). Responsibility for household tasks: Comparing dual-earner and dual-retired marriages. In M. Szinovacz (Ed.), *Women's retirement* (pp. 205-219). Beverly Hills, CA: Sage Publications.

Coward, R. T., & Kerckhoff, R. K. (1978). *The rural elderly: Program planning guidelines.* Ames, IA: North Central Regional Center for Rural Development.

Coward, R. T., & Smith, W. M., Jr. (1982). Families in rural society. In D. A. Dillman & D. J. Hobbs (Eds.), *Rural society in the U.S.: Issues for the 1980's* (pp. 77-84). Boulder, CO: Westview Press.

Dorfman, L. T., & Hill, E. A. (1986). Rural housewives and retirement: Joint decision-making matters. *Family Relations, 35*, 507-514.

Dorfman, L. T., Hill, E. A., Kohout, F. J., & Heckert, D. A. (1986, November). *Rural couples and retirement: Conjugal role organization, social networks, and satisfaction.* Paper presented at the 39th Annual Scientific Meeting of the Gerontological Society of America, Chicago, IL.

Dorfman, L. T., Kohout, F. J., & Heckert, D. A. (1985). Retirement satisfaction in the rural elderly. *Research on Aging, 7*, 577-599.

Downie, N. M., & Heath, R. W. (1959). *Basic statistical methods.* New York: Harper.

Dressler, D. (1973). Life adjustment of retired couples. *International Journal of Aging and Human Development, 4*, 335-349.

Fengler, A. P. (1975). Attitudinal orientations of wives toward their husbands' retirement. *International Journal of Aging and Human Development, 6*, 139-152.

Flora, C. B., & Johnson, S. (1978). Discarding the disstaff: New roles for rural women. In T. R. Ford (Ed.), *Rural U.S.A.: Persistence and change* (pp. 168-181). Ames, IA: Iowa State University Press.

Heyman, D. K. (1970). Does a wife retire? *The Geron-tologist, 10*, 54-56.

Keating, N., & Cole, P. (1980). What do I do with him 24 hours a day? Changes in the housewife role after retirement. *The Gerontologist, 20*, 84-89.

Keith, P. M., & Brubaker, T. H. (1979). Male household roles in later life: A look at masculinity and marital relationships. *The Family Coordinator, 28*, 497-502.

Kerckhoff, A. C. (1966). Family patterns and morale in retirement. In I. H. Simpson & J. C. McKinney (Eds.), *Social aspects of aging* (pp. 173-192). Durham, NC: Duke University Press.

Kivett, V. R. (1985). Aging in rural society: Non-kin community relations and participation. In R. T. Coward & G. R. Lee (Eds.), *The elderly in rural society* (pp. 171-191). New York: Springer Publishing Co.

Larson, L. E. (1974). System and subsystem perception of family roles. *Journal of Marriage and the Family, 36*, 123-138.

Lee, G. R., & Cassidy, M. L. (1985). Family and kin relations of the rural elderly. In R. T. Coward & G. R. Lee (Eds.), *The elderly in rural society* (pp. 151-169). New York: Springer Publishing Co.

Lee, G. R., & Lassey, M. (1980). Rural-urban differences among the elderly: Economic, social and subjective factors. *Journal of Social Issues, 36*, 62-74.

Lipman, A. (1961). Role conceptions of couples in retirement. *Journal of Gerontology, 16*, 267-271.

Model, S. (1981). Housework by husbands. *Journal of Family Issues, 2*, 225-237.

Powers, E. A., Keith, P., & Goudy, W. J. (1979). Family relationships and friendships among the rural aged. In T. O. Byerts, S. C. Howell, & L. A. Pastalan (Eds.), *Environmental context of aging* (pp. 80-101). New York: Garland STPM Press.

Rosenblatt, P. C., & Anderson, R. M. (1981). Interaction in farm families: Tension and stress. In R. T. Coward & W. M. Smith, Jr. (Eds.), *The family in rural society* (pp. 147-166). Boulder, CO: Westview Press.

Safilios-Rothschild, C. (1969). Family sociology or wives' family sociology: A cross-cultural examination of decision-making. *Journal of Marriage and the Family, 31*, 290-301.

Schumm, W. R., & Bollman, S. R. (1981). Interpersonal processes in rural families. In R. T. Coward & W. M. Smith, Jr. (Eds.), *The family in rural society* (pp. 129-145). Boulder, CO: Westview Press.

Sheldon, A., McEwan, P. J., & Ryser, C. P. (1975). *Retirement patterns and predictions.* Rockville, MD: National Institute of Mental Health.

Siegel, S. R., & Rives, J. M. (1978). Characteristics of existing and planned preretirement programs. *Aging and Work, 2*, 93-99.

Sotomayor, M. (1981). The rural elderly. In P. K. H. Kim & C. P. Wilson (Eds.), *Toward mental health of the rural elderly* (pp. 31-51). Washington: University Press of America.

Szinovacz, M. (1980). Female retirement: Effects on spousal roles and marital adjustment. *Journal of Family Issues, 1*, 423-438.

Thompson, L., & Walker, A. J. (1982). The dyad as the unit of analysis: Conceptual and methodological issues. *Journal of Marriage and the Family, 44*, 889-900.

Troll, L., Miller, S., & Atchley, R. (1979). *Families in later life.* Belmont, CA: Wadsworth Publishing Co.

U.S. Department of Commerce, Bureau of the Census. (1983). *1980 census of population, general population characteristics, U.S. summary.* Washington, DC: U.S. Government Printing Office.

Willits, F. K., Bealer, R. C., & Crider, D. M. (1982). Persistence of rural/urban differences. In D. A. Dillman & D. J. Hobbs (Eds.), *Rural society in the U.S.: Issues for the 1980's* (pp. 69-76). Boulder, CO: Westview Press.

Yogev, S., & Brett, J. (1985). Perceptions of the division of housework and child care and marital satisfaction. *Journal of Marriage and the Family, 47*, 609-618.

Youmans, E. G. (1973). Perspectives on the older American in a rural setting. In J. G. Cull & R. E. Hardy (Eds.), *The neglected older American* (pp. 65-85). Springfield, IL: Charles C. Thomas.

# Marital Quality and Conjugal Labor Involvement of Rural Couples*

**Janet Bokemeier and Richard Maurer\*\***

The implications of different work and family arrangements for marriages are receiving considerable attention in current research. Most studies focus on wife's labor force participation and the impact of wife's/mother's employment on marital and family quality. Less often is husband's employment status varied or is any other dimension of work status examined. This study adopts a more comprehensive research approach. Data from both husbands and wives are used to identify the alternative patterns of conjugal labor involvement, to describe the personal, family, and social characteristics associated with different types of involvement, and then to compare the marital quality of these couples with different patterns of conjugal labor involvement.

*Conjugal labor involvement* refers to the intensity of labor force participation by a married couple and considers the employment statuses of spouses and the number of jobs held by each spouse. Conjugal labor involvement patterns include couples in which neither spouse is employed, traditional couples (one employed head of household), dual-worker couples (both spouses are employed), and multiple jobholder couples (one or both spouses hold two or more jobs). Conjugal labor involvement takes into account both extreme employment patterns as well as male and female labor force participation.

This study departs from traditional approaches in its focus on couples. The decisions that lead to a particular work and family strategy reflect the interests, preferences, and opportunities open to both the husband and wife. Furthermore, by including the work status of both husband and wife, more alternative strategies that couples may choose are identified. Also avoided is the pitfall of assuming that the work role of either the husband or wife is more critical for marital quality. Finally, such considerations will lead to comparisons among couples based on who is involved in market work and how many jobs they hold. Thus, single and dual-worker patterns are considered in addition to the number of jobs held by the couple.

Previous research has neglected the relationship of work and marital quality of rural/nonmetropolitan couples. The impact of work on marital quality is important to consider because nonmetropolitan households, especially farm households, are experiencing significant changes in marital, family, and work arrangements (Berkowitz & Perkins, 1984; Bokemeier, Sachs, & Keith, 1983; Lyson, 1985). An increasing number of women and men are employed off the farm. Nonmetropolitan workers face employment

*Portions of this chapter were presented at the 1983 Annual Meeting of the Rural Sociological Society in Lexington, Kentucky. The authors gratefully acknowledge the comments and technical assistance of Bruce Gage. Research was supported by the Agricultural Experiment Station, University of Kentucky (Project 830 and 839).

**Janet Bokemeier is Associate Professor and Richard Maurer is Associate Extension Professor in the Department of Sociology, University of Kentucky, S-205 Agricultural Science Center North, Lexington, KY 40546-0091.

Reprinted from *Family Relations*, 1987, **36**, 417–424.

problems because of limited job opportunities and job training (Bokemeier et al., 1983). Thus, the strains of current economic conditions make the negotiation of work/family roles critical in rural family situations (Coward & Smith, 1982). Farm families are most often examined, especially in the mass media, but the economic problems in agriculture spill over to rural areas in general and affect nonfarm families as well.

This study of conjugal labor involvement patterns and their associations with marital quality has both applied and theoretical importance. Family practitioners, working with rural families as they respond to the changing rural economic situation and family farm crises, are interested in the range of alternative employment patterns adopted by rural couples. The consequences for marital quality of rural couples' choices about who works should be considered in counseling with rural couples. Practitioners may wonder whether the social acceptance of different conjugal labor involvement patterns found among urban couples (Ross, Mirowsky, & Huber, 1983) is found also among rural couples. This study highlights the importance of working with the couple as well as with the individual family member. Rural sociologists argue that the family unit is the basic unit of family economic decision making. For example, although one spouse may not be involved in farm labor, his or her income derived from off-farm work is an important contribution to the farm operation and represents an important strategy for economic survival of the family farm (Barlett, 1984; Lyson, 1985).

The results of this study will be of interest to family educators, especially those who work with rural families. Economic conditions and employment patterns have been changing rapidly in rural areas, as evidenced recently in terms of "farm crisis" and related effects on rural industries. Rural couples must work out appropriate arrangements in terms of employment patterns and work schedules, household tasks, child care alternatives, transportation, and preferences for employment as well as life style. The goal of this research is to help provide some indication of how such factors are related to marital quality among rural couples, so that couples can begin to determine as completely as possible their own situation and the alternatives available to them.

These research issues and the rural economic situation make the study of marital quality and conjugal labor involvement of rural couples important. This chapter studies the extent to which conjugal labor involvement is related to marital quality among rural couples, both farm and nonfarm. Two general research problems are addressed. First, what are the personal, family, and social characteristics of couples with different conjugal labor involvement? Second, how is conjugal labor involvement related to marital quality? In the next section, past research is reviewed in two general areas—multiple jobholding patterns and the relationship of employment and marital quality. Based on this review, two competing explanations for the relationship of conjugal labor involvement and marital quality are examined.

## Multiple Jobholding

Recent research on farm families has documented their dependence on off-farm income. Over 80% of family income is from off-farm sources for 45.5% of farm families (Rosenfeld, 1985). Part-time farmers are multiple jobholders in that they are farm operators who hold regular jobs off the farm. In this research, it was found that many rural nonfarm couples were also multiple jobholders. However, little research has focused on issues related to multiple jobholders. Multiple jobholders are persons who are employed and either (a) are wage or salary workers with two or more employers, (b) are both self-employed and hold wage or salary jobs (e.g., part-time farmer or farm women and men who indicate an average of 30 hours or more per week on the farm and who have an off-farm job), or (c) are unpaid family workers in their primary jobs and hold secondary wage or salary jobs (Brown, 1978). Moonlighting, in this chapter, refers to multiple jobholding by a worker.

The national rate of multiple jobholding has been at about 5% since 1969 (Sekscenski, 1980). With the growing trend toward fuller female labor force participation, a decline in the incidence of moonlighting was expected (Alper & Morlock, 1982) because it was assumed more wives were taking jobs instead of their husbands taking a second job. Instead the rate of multiple jobholding has been stable because there is a growing proportion of women holding more than one job. In 1979 women accounted for 30% of all multiple jobholders compared to 16.5% in 1969 (Sekscenski, 1980). Single women were more likely than married women to hold multiple jobs, while married men were more likely than single men to moonlight. For this study, it is important to note that certain occupations and industries—public administration, agriculture, education, entertainment, and recreations—are more conducive to moonlighting. These occupations and industries are characterized by flexible work schedules, seasonal opportunities, and worker autonomy.

Explanations of why workers hold multiple jobs have emphasized either relative deprivation and life-cycle squeeze or economic factors. Wilensky (1963) proposed that multiple jobholders tend to be men "caught in a life-cycle squeeze" with many dependents and fewer resources than required to meet their aspirations. This squeeze is particularly likely to occur during the family child-rearing years when the primary wage earner is initiating his or her career and is at a low point in earning capacity. Wilensky also argued that multiple jobholders tended to have unusual control of their work schedules and possessed the relevant skills and information necessary to acquire another job.

In contrast, Miller (1972) found no evidence of relative deprivation among moonlighters. Although moonlighters tended to have more young children, the majority of moonlighters had moderately well-paid primary jobs and gave reasons other than financial need for moonlighting. Thus, as Alper and Morlock (1982) argue, the conjugal decision for the husband to moonlight rather than the wife to enter the labor force is influenced by the relative productivity of the wife in both market and nonmarket work. Family life-cycle situation and relative income potential, as well as sex role attitudes of wives and their husbands toward female employment, are important factors in making employment decisions.

For this study, a statewide sample of couples living in nonmetropolitan areas in Kentucky was selected. A fairly high rate of moonlighting in nonmetropolitan areas was expected because the agriculture industry is conducive to second jobs, the population is not well-off economically, and there is a high proportion of married couple households (American Demographics, 1983).

## Employment and Marital Quality

In the absence of a theory to explain the impact of various conjugal labor involvement patterns on marital quality, two competing theories of the impact of wives' employment on marital quality will be used. One approach, the status competition model (reviewed in D'Amico, 1983; see also Parsons & Bales, 1955; Pleck, 1977), suggests that if both husband and wife are career-oriented, the results will be marital stress, disruptive competition, role conflict, and instability.

Evidence in support of the status competition model is found in early qualitative studies of dual-career families. More specifically, some studies found that reorganization of family roles and the conflicts between dual-career patterns and societal expectations led to marital stress (Holmstrom, 1972; Rapaport & Rapaport, 1976). Other studies found that husbands in dual-earner households tended to be less content with marriage, work, and life in general than men in traditional, single-earner marriages. Discontentment resulted from loss of an active support system and an increased pressure to participate in household tasks conventionally done by wives in addition to change in the balance of power in decision making (Burke & Weir, 1976; Martin, Berry, & Jacobsen, 1975; Stanley, Hunt, & Hunt, 1986). Nevertheless, in general, women in dual-earner households remain responsible for domestic tasks and child care and are more likely to accommodate their husbands' careers than vice versa (Aldous, 1982; Berk, 1985).

An alternative theoretical explanation, the status enhancement approach, argues that the family, as a decision-making unit, will select a pattern of labor market involvement that will improve its status (Oppenheimer, 1982). As a unit, the family maximizes its rewards by placing workers in the market depending on the perceived values of relative costs and benefits associated with market work (Becker, 1965). Therefore, the wife's ability to enhance family status by labor force participation improves marital stability and personal satisfaction. This model does not imply that wives' employment will necessarily be associated with higher levels of marital quality. For certain couples, marginal, if any, economic advantage is derived from the wife's/mother's employment. For example, women who are in low salary occupations, who face high child care expenses, and whose husbands are in high salary occupations, may experience little economic gain for their hours of market labor. The status of such couples is more likely to be enhanced by the husband's moonlighting than by the wife's gainful employment. The decisions on conjugal employment require couples to consider potential income, age, number of children, and education. Thus, conjugal labor involvement will be either positively associated with marital quality or not associated at all.

With a status enhancement model, the issues of role conflict and stress are interpreted differently. Rather than an undesirable state, stressors from dual-worker life styles are thought of as "contingencies" of family life that couples either resolve or accommodate (Kingston & Nock, 1985) or as situations that couples perceive as unavoidable or preferable to the stressors in the single-earner life style (Bebbington, 1973). Furthermore, certain conditions (e.g., husband's involvement in household tasks, reduced fertility, androgynous sex role concepts) exist that aid couples in handling stressors and may even promote a positive evaluation of stress (Meeks, Arnkoff, Glass, & Notarius, 1985; Rapaport & Rapaport, 1976; Ross et al., 1983).

Likewise, role homophyly theory, another example of the status enhancement approach, states that "similarity of roles builds marital solidarity" (Simpson & England, 1982). When husbands and wives have comparable roles in economic and household maintenance, they share a common social outlook and a greater mutual appreciation which leads to fuller communication and companionship within the marriage. Furthermore, the resource balance associated with role congruity leads to more equitable division-of-labor and decision-making patterns.

Ross et al. (1983) argue that the greater participation of women in market work has stimulated more positive attitudes regarding wives' employment and has led to a shift from complementary marriages to parallel marriages in which spouses perform similar tasks on an equitable, mutually acceptable basis. In the transition from complementary to parallel marriages, the deleterious impact of wives' market work is explained by the preferences of husbands and wives for alternative work patterns and the husband's participation in household tasks. This premise is consistent with the persistent finding that similarity between spouses' sex role attitudes is associated with greater marital satisfaction (Cooper, Chassin, & Zeiss, 1985; Thomas, Albrecht, & White, 1984).

The role of preferences for various employment and household work patterns may direct the decision-making process. The greater the congruency of preference for work patterns and the actual behavior, then the higher the level of marital quality. Thus, the status enhancement model suggests that couples rationally select an employment pattern that best suits their needs, preferences, and potential. Consequently, the marital quality of couples in various conjugal labor involvement arrangements would not differ significantly.

In summary, two competing hypotheses are tested. If couples seek to achieve a level of labor involvement that maximizes their social and economic status, then marital quality will not be explained by conjugal labor involvement. If a status competition model holds true, then couples with dual workers or one worker with multiple jobs will report different levels of marital quality in terms of tension, communication, and sociability than single-worker, single-job couples.

## Procedures

### Sample

The data were collected in 1981 by a state-wide mail survey of Kentucky adults who lived in nonmetropolitan (non-SMSA) counties. Respondents were selected from lists of registered voters. Using the total design method (Dillman, 1978), two questionnaires were sent to each household, one for a male adult and one for a female adult to complete. Three follow-up mailings were conducted to reach the final response rate. The overall sample size was 2,818, which represents a response rate of 61% for the total sample. The subsample of 777 couples used for this analysis includes those households where responses were received from both the wife and husband and from households where the husband and wife were both between 18 and 65 years old.

Descriptive statistics are presented to give a general description of the sample. The wives and husbands in the couple subsample have an average age of 41.7 years and typically have slightly more than a high school education and a family income in the $15,000 to $20,000 per year category. Nineteen percent of the couples live on a farm. Twenty-seven percent of the couples have children 5 years of age or younger, while 81% have school-age children (6-18 years) at home.

## Measurement

Conjugal labor involvement is measured by the number of workers and the number of jobs held by a married couple. The values of conjugal labor involvement are: (a) neither spouse is employed, (b) one worker (traditional), (c) one worker who moonlights, (d) dual-worker couple, (e) dual-worker couple with at least one spouse who moonlights.

Marital quality is measured by a 23-item index in which respondents are asked to indicate how often they disagree on selected issues or participate in certain activities as a couple. The marital quality scale was developed for use in a mail survey of the general population by modifying and integrating the Marital Adjustment Balance Scale (Orden & Bradburn, 1968) and the Dyadic Adjustment Scale (Spanier, 1976). For this study a marital quality score was derived by summing the responses to each Likert-type item and dividing it by the number of items. Respondents who left over eight items blank were considered to be missing cases. A Cronbach alpha test for reliability generated an alpha value of .89. For further analyses, the scale was divided into subscales for three dimensions of marital quality: tension, communication, and sociability. Cronbach alpha values for the subscales ranged from .837 to .905.

Sex role orientation is measured by a 7-item Likert scale in which respondents were asked their level of agreement with each statement. The scale score is the sum of responses divided by the number of items. A lower scale score value indicates a more traditional orientation. A Cronbach alpha test of reliability generated an alpha of .67. Sex role orientation difference of couples is indicated by the absolute difference of husband and wife scores. Related to sex role orientation is personal background experience with an employed mother. Respondents were asked if their mothers worked outside the home when they were growing up. Responses were: (1) no; (2) yes, part-time

for less than 5 years; (3) yes, part-time for at least 5 years; (4) yes, full-time for less than 5 years; and (5) yes, full-time for at least 5 years.

Husbands' involvement in household tasks was measured by the degree to which husbands were involved in seven tasks which could be considered the traditional responsibility of the wife. Responses to each task were rated on a scale of 1 to 5, where 1 is the wife always performs the task and 5 is the husband always performs the task. By totaling the seven tasks, the range of scores for husbands' involvement is 7 to 35.

Other independent variables included: age—self-reported years; education—nine categories from (1) never attended school through (9) a graduate degree; place of residence—six categories from (1) farm through (6) a town of over 50,00; personal income, annual income during the previous year, was measured by nine categories from (1) less than $5,000 through (9) $50,000 or more. Personal income for individuals who are not currently employed may be derived from non-salary sources such as rent of tobacco allotments, disability pay, Social Security, or sale of home-produced items. Also, since employment refers to the time of the survey, annual personal income may be from jobs held previously that year. Children living at home were measured with two dummy variables. One variable indicated whether any child under 6 years of age lived at home, and the other measured whether any child aged 6 or older lived at home. Number of voluntary organizations of which one is a member was included as a measure of community involvement. Farm employment was considered as a dummy variable, with 1 as farm employment and 0 as nonfarm employment.

Two different statistical techniques are utilized for analyses of the data. Discriminant analysis is used to determine which of the independent variables are most useful in describing differences among the conjugal labor involvement categories. Multiple regression analysis with dummy variables is used to examine the effect of conjugal labor involvement upon marital quality while controlling for other independent variables which might affect the relationship between conjugal labor involvement and marital quality.

## Findings

The frequency distribution for this sam-

Table 1.
*Frequencies for Conjugal Labor Involvement (N = 777 Couples)*

| Conjugal Labor Involvement Type | Relative Percentage (N) | Spouses' Employment Status | Relative Percentage |
|---|---|---|---|
| Both not employed | 9.7 (75) | | |
| One worker (traditional) | 38.1 (296) | Husband employed | 83.1 |
| | | Wife employed | 17.9 |
| One-worker moonlighter | 8.0 (62) | Husband moonlights | 93.5 |
| | | Wife moonlights | 6.5 |
| Dual worker | 31.5 (245) | | |
| Dual worker with at least one moonlighter | 12.7 (99) | Husband moonlights | 68.7[a] |
| | | Wife moonlights | 47.5 |

[a]Percents do not total 100% because in 15 couples both spouses moonlight.

Table 2.
*Subgroup Means for Discriminant Analysis of Conjugal Labor Involvement Groups (N = 777 Couples)*

| | Both Unemployed (1) | 1 Spouse Has 1 Job (2) | 1 Spouse Has 2 Jobs (3) | Both Work 1 Job Each (4) | Both Work and 1 or Both Have 2 Jobs (5) | F |
|---|---|---|---|---|---|---|
| Male's sex role orientation | 6.97 | 7.71 | 7.98 | 9.57 | 9.31 | 16.15* |
| Female's sex role orientation | 7.39 | 8.32 | 8.58 | 10.23 | 9.94 | 16.56* |
| Male's personal income | 2.84 | 3.93 | 4.20 | 3.77 | 4.11 | 6.06* |
| Female's personal income | 0.45 | 0.53 | 0.42 | 2.05 | 1.95 | 117.00* |
| Male's organization membership | 1.11 | 1.81 | 1.79 | 1.60 | 2.27 | 4.12* |
| Female's organization membership | 0.72 | 1.37 | 1.16 | 1.51 | 2.01 | 8.02* |
| Male's age | 52.53 | 44.41 | 41.39 | 40.15 | 41.65 | 18.22* |
| Female's age | 49.21 | 41.14 | 38.77 | 37.18 | 38.11 | 17.85* |
| Male's education | 4.05 | 4.99 | 5.16 | 5.29 | 5.83 | 12.07* |
| Female's education | 4.34 | 4.91 | 5.08 | 5.54 | 5.90 | 19.74* |
| Husband's house hold tasks | 15.25 | 14.47 | 13.84 | 15.33 | 14.12 | 3.60* |
| Younger children | 0.09 | 0.28 | 1.02 | 0.74 | 0.92 | 2.38* |
| Older children | 0.56 | 0.85 | 1.02 | 0.74 | 0.92 | 2.38* |
| Female's mother worked | 1.38 | 1.60 | 1.66 | 1.75 | 1.61 | 2.89* |
| Male's mother worked | 1.36 | 1.42 | 1.62 | 1.56 | 1.56 | 2.05* |
| Farm/nonfarm employment | 0.09 | 0.13 | 0.47 | 0.13 | 0.45 | 25.91* |
| Place of residence by size | 2.32 | 2.43 | 1.82 | 2.61 | 2.03 | 7.35* |

*$p < .05$.

ple of nonmetropolitan working age adults provides an interesting picture of conjugal labor involvement in rural areas (Table 1). The prevalence of dual-worker couples is evident in that dual-worker couples (44.3%) are nearly as common as one-worker couples (46.1%). Couples in which neither spouse is currently employed account for 9.7% of the households. These include spouses who are unemployed, students, retired, disabled and/or homemakers.

The most common conjugal labor involvement pattern is one worker with one job, which accounts for 38.1% of the couples. Among these single-provider couples, 83.1% of the employed workers are men. The dual-worker couple labor involve-

ment pattern, with each spouse having one job, is also quite prevalent, with nearly one-third of all couples falling into this category.

The increasing proportion of dual-worker couples has not replaced the moonlighting labor involvement patterns. The prevalence of moonlighting is higher in this sample than in reported national averages. One-worker, two-jobs couples account for 8.0% of the sample; 10.8% of the couples are dual-worker couples with one multiple jobholder; and an additional 1.9% of the couples are dual-workers with both spouses holding multiple jobs. For the remainder of the analyses, dual-worker couples with either one or both spouses moonlighting will be treated as one group.

Table 2 shows the subgroup means and Table 3 shows results of discriminant analysis of conjugal labor involvement groups. The subgroup means of personal, marital, and family characteristics were all significantly different between conjugal labor involvement types. The single-worker and dual-worker couples differ from each other in that dual-worker couples have more egalitarian sex role orientations (reflecting a positive attitude toward women working outside the home) and are younger, with higher educational levels. Couples with a moonlighting worker tend to have more formal education, more children, and husbands who perform fewer household tasks. As expected, living on farms and working in agricultural occupations and industries are also associated with moonlighting.

The 20 demographic characteristics of families were examined using stepwise discriminant analysis. Twelve variables significantly entered into the three statistically significant discriminant functions (see Table 3). The results suggest that a couple's level of labor involvement can be differentiated based on 12 demographic variables. That is, in combination these 12 variables can best discriminate between the conjugal labor involvement groups. Examination of the group centroids (also called the group mean) shows that *function 1* differentiates groups by number of workers. That is, labor involvement groups without a provider or with one provider have negative centroids and groups with dual workers have positive centroids. *Function 2* discriminates groups by the number of jobs that a couple holds. *Function 3* appears to differentiate those couples who are overemployed (more than two jobs) and underemployed (no jobs) from those who have more traditional employment patterns.

The standardized discriminant coefficients are interpreted similarly to a standardized regression coefficient in that the size of the coefficient indicates the relative importance of the variable to the discriminant analysis of the groups. The factors that are

Table 3.
*Stepwise Discriminant Analysis of Conjugal Labor Involvement Groups (N = 777 Couples)*

| | Standardized Discriminant Coefficients | | |
|---|---|---|---|
| | Function 1 | Function 2 | Function 3 |
| Male's personal income | .068 | .176 | -.453 |
| Female's personal income | .911 | -.236 | .233 |
| Female's organization membership | .028 | .014 | -.161 |
| Male's age | -.025 | .091 | .416 |
| Female's age | -.333 | -.126 | .370 |
| Male's education | .196 | .397 | .102 |
| Husband's household tasks | -.110 | -.247 | .052 |
| Younger children | -.104 | .237 | .045 |
| Older children | .026 | .208 | .002 |
| Male's mother worked | .017 | .096 | .199 |
| Farm/nonfarm employment | .253 | .707 | .332 |
| Place of residence | .100 | -.208 | -.203 |
| Eigenvalue | .735 | .210 | .057 |
| Lambda* | .441 | .766 | .926 |
| Canonical correlation | .651 | .416 | .233 |
| Chi-square | 627.60 | 204.90 | 58.72 |
| P | .0001 | .0001 | .001 |

Group Centroids

| | Both Unemployed (1) | 1 Spouse Has 1 Job (2) | 1 Spouse Has 2 Jobs (3) | Both Work 1 Job Each (4) | Both Work and 1 or Both Have 2 Jobs (5) |
|---|---|---|---|---|---|
| Function 1: Number of workers | -1.199** | -0.683 | -0.502 | 0.894 | 1.052 |
| Function 2: Moonlighters | -0.542 | 0.0015 | 1.020 | -0.372 | 0.648 |
| Function 3: Extreme labor patterns | -0.582 | -0.192 | 0.027 | -0.062 | 0.268 |

*The larger the lambda, the less discriminating power is present for that function.
**Those categories which are underlined are significantly different, on that function, from those categories which are not underlined.

most important in differentiating groups by number of workers (*function 1*) are wife's personal income, wife's age, husband's education, and employment in farm occupations. Dual-worker couples are characterized by younger wives with higher personal income and by more highly educated husbands. Sex role orientation is not a significant discriminant; its effects may be accounted for by income and education.

The factors with the greatest discriminating ability in *function 2* that differentiate moonlighters from other couples are farm/nonfarm employment, husband's education, number and age of children, husband's level of household work, wife's income, and size of the place of residence. Moonlighter couples in which one or both spouses have multiple jobs tend to have younger children, husbands with higher levels of education, and wives with lower income. Husbands tend to report doing fewer household tasks. The farm/nonfarm employment and place of residence suggest that moonlighting is more characteristic of those workers living in farm or open country areas and who are either in farming or an agricultural occupation or industry.

These findings in part support Wilensky's (1963) theory that one's occupation is an important determinant of multiple job-holding. That is, employment in agriculture appears to be conducive to multiple jobholding. The income factors are more tricky to interpret as they reflect income from both primary and secondary jobs. The finding of a wife's lower income, yet a husband's higher income among moonlighters, suggests that the couple sees a relative economic advantage to the husband's moonlighting.

*Function 3* identifies discriminating variables that maximize the differences between groups of workers who are underemployed and overemployed and those who are traditional one-worker, one-job couples. Couples in extreme labor involvement patterns tend to be older, to have husbands with lower incomes, and to have wives with higher incomes. These couples are more likely to live on farms and to have jobs in agricultural occupations and industries.

The three discriminant functions are all statistically significant at the .001 level. However, function 1, number of workers, clearly has the strongest discriminating ability, accounting for 73.5% of the variance explained by the discriminant analysis.

Function 2, moonlighters, accounts for 21% of the explained variation and the third function, extreme labor patterns, accounts for 5.7%.

To validate the predictive ability of the discriminant functions, a classification matrix is created which gives each case a group score based on the discriminant analysis and, then, compares the computed group assignment to the actual score. Based on these significant independent variables, this discriminant analysis of conjugal labor involvement correctly classified 49.8% of the couples in labor involvement groups. The discriminant functions performed better than what would be found at the proportional chance level of 27.6%. Therefore, the ability to differentiate between the five groups is greatly enhanced by knowledge of these independent variables.

The next step in the analyses was to determine if conjugal labor involvement was significantly related to marital quality when other factors were controlled. The conjugal labor involvement categories were treated as a series of dummy variables in a regression analysis with each of the marital quality measures. (Couples with neither spouse employed are not included as a variable but rather are represented by the constant.) Other variables included in the regression, which are control variables for the relationship between conjugal labor involvement and marital quality, are wife's education, husband's age, wife's sex role orientation, difference in husband's and wife's sex role orientation score, small children at home, and farm status.

Only a few differences are present between the conjugal labor involvement categories in relation to the marital quality variables; the magnitude of this relationship is quite small. Those couples with one moonlighter, with dual workers, and with dual workers with at least one spouse who moonlights have significantly higher tension levels than do couples in which neither spouse works. Also, dual-worker couples with at least one spouse who moonlights report significantly higher sociability scores than do couples with neither spouse employed. However, when the other independent variables are included (controlled for) in the analysis, the differences between the conjugal labor involvement categories disappear. Significant effects are accounted for by other independent variables. Couples whose

Table 4.
*Regression Analyses of Conjugal Labor Involvement Type and Selected Personal, Marital, and Family Characteristics on Marital Quality*

| | Marital Quality | | | | | |
| | Tension | | Sociability | | Communication | |
| | Model 1 b | Model 2 b | Model 1 b | Model 2 b | Model 1 b | Model 2 b |
|---|---|---|---|---|---|---|
| One worker | -1.01 | -.52 | .28 | .21 | -.14 | -.31 |
| One moonlights | -2.32* | -1.45 | .15 | .06 | -.41 | -.43 |
| Dual worker | -2.06* | -1.10 | .17 | .06 | -.02 | -.12 |
| Dual-worker moonlighter | -1.95* | -1.04 | .55* | .45 | -.12 | -.05 |
| Wife's education | | .20 | | .00 | | .03 |
| Husband's age | | .07** | | -.01 | | -.02 |
| Wife's sex role orientation | | -.20** | | .00 | | -.10** |
| Sex role difference | | -.25** | | -.03 | | -.13** |
| Small children at home | | -.62 | | -.07 | | -.24 |
| Farm status | | -.01 | | .05 | | -.30 |
| Constant | 47.48** | 45.71** | 5.58** | 6.03** | 18.57** | 20.65** |
| F | 2.39* | 5.89** | 1.83 | 1.11 | .25 | 2.77** |
| $R^2$ | .01 | .07** | .01 | .01 | .00 | .03 |
| $R^2$ Change | | .06** | | .00 | | .03** |

*$p < .05.$
**$p < .01.$

husband's and wife's sex role orientation scores differ greatly and couples in which the wife has a more egalitarian sex role orientation have higher levels of tension. In addition, couples with older husbands have lower tension levels. Lower levels of communication are also present among couples with greater differences in sex role orientation scores and with a more egalitarian sex role orientation of the wife. Once again, however, the magnitudes of the relationships are relatively small, as are the R-squares for the regression analyses.

The lack of effect of the conjugal labor involvement variable in the regression analyses provides support for the status enhancement model. Since there is little or no difference in the marital quality of couples with different labor involvement when controlling for other variables, it appears employment status and number of jobs that couples have are not significantly associated with tension, communication, and sociability levels. It appears that farm couples' marriages are also not adversely affected by increased involvement in the labor force.

## Summary and Conclusion

The purpose of this study is to describe the conjugal labor involvement of rural couples and to assess the relationship between labor involvement and marital quality.

The level of female employment among rural couples was found to be similar to urban families. Clearly couples' employment statuses differ on more dimensions than wives' employment. A substantial proportion of these married couples who are 18 to 65 years of age did not have an employed spouse at the time of the survey. This group, currently not employed, tends to be neglected in most research on employment and marital quality. Also, there is a significant proportion of couples in which one or both spouses moonlight. Thus, when the work situations of both wife and husband are considered, many married couples either have no jobs or more than two jobs.

These variations in conjugal labor involvement represent distinct patterns for integrating work and family roles and are associated with unique family needs and characteristics. Couples with certain family compositions, personal and family characteristics, and employment opportunities are found in alternative patterns of conjugal labor involvement. The profiles of multiple jobholders, single-earner families, and dual-earner families in this study suggest, as Miller (1972) found, that moonlighters tend to have younger children and are more highly educated (a factor which enhances their employment opportunities) than other couples. They do not, however, differ in community involvement. In fact, moonlighters are somewhat more social than other families. Furthermore, the finding of a higher prevalence of agricultural jobs and farm residence among couples with multiple jobholders when income level is controlled suggests that occupations with more flexible schedules promote this employment pattern. Thus, relative job opportunities and income potential of spouses are key determinants of the particular employment strategies that couples will adopt. The dual-earner couples reported a higher average level of husbands' participation in household tasks than moonlighters. This suggests that couples are adopting a strategy whereby if the husband has multiple jobs, then the wife assumes more household and child care responsibilities. Dual-earner families have husbands who are more likely to assume greater household responsibility. In summary, personal characteristics of both the wife and the husband, as well as family life course characteristics, distinguished between conjugal labor involvement groups.

However, couples' adoption of distinctive patterns of employment is not associated with significant differences in marital quality as indicated by levels of tension, sociability, and communication. This finding rather convincingly supports the status enhancement theory of family employment behavior. Likewise, after reviewing a decade of studies, Smith (1985) found that, in studies of wife's employment status and marital adjustment, no differences were found in 79% of the comparisons. Factors other than employment status are more important for understanding differences in marital quality. For example, sex role orientation and, particularly, similarity of husband's and wife's sex role orientation scores, were more strongly related with marital quality than with employment status. Thus, once couples select an employment strategy that fits their particular situation, if the employment demands conform to the couple's sex role orientations at that time *and* as wife and husband they are in agreement as to the appropriateness of this employment, then marital quality is not affected. It is interesting that sex role orientations are not important discriminators of labor involvement types when other characteristics are considered. Perhaps, individuals adjust their sex role concepts to be in harmony with their personal employment experiences and, thus, avoid dissonance in their life styles. In con-

clusion, couples adapt to various conjugal labor involvement patterns. Role stressors and overloads are viewed as a feature in their alternative life styles. Thus, as suggested, the stressors are contingencies in marriages that couples learn to accommodate.

This study has implications for family life education and counseling. To promote marital quality, a stronger emphasis on identification and choice of appropriate patterns of conjugal labor involvement for rural couples is recommended. Rural couples may be interested in the various patterns adopted to take advantages of employment opportunities in rural areas and to meet family needs. Rural life styles are often stereotyped as or assumed to be rather homogeneous. This study has highlighted the flexibility and range of choices open to rural families.

Certain principles need to be considered by educators in developing programs. First, this study has established the importance of working with couples, that is both husbands and wives, in assessing alternative employment patterns. Factors that couples may need to take into account in assessing employment opportunities are potential income, number of children, education, division of household tasks, and sex role orientation. Second, these results suggest that increases in level of conjugal labor involvement among rural and especially farm families in response to the current economic crises in rural areas may not necessarily result in marital discord. Assumptions that wife's employment or multiple jobholding will result in lower marital quality are unwarranted. Rather, differences between spouses in sex role orientation appear to be more detrimental for marital quality than employment issues. Programs which aid couples in considering the costs and benefits associated with alternative strategies will provide them with an opportunity to negotiate an arrangement that is compatible with their sex role orientation and preferences for division of household work.

Rural communities may have limited employment opportunities and community services necessary for couples to realize their preferred labor involvement patterns. Rural family educators may need to provide information to rural community and industrial leaders on options that would promote greater employment flexibility in rural communities such as child care, after school programs, job training, job sharing, and flextime. These programs are important for couples who are adapting to the contingencies associated with employment patterns that involve multiple jobs and dual-worker arrangements.

Rural life styles are often stereotyped as or assumed to be rather homogeneous. This study has highlighted the flexibility and range of choices of employment patterns open to rural families. Increases in level of conjugal labor involvement among rural and especially farm families in response to the current economic crises in rural areas may not result in marital discord. Future research on these issues needs to take into account other dimensions of labor involvement such as number of hours worked, career orientation, and other work experiences such as commuting, work scheduling, and job tenure. Taking all of these factors into account using the couple as the unit of analysis should also provide useful information for family educators working with these important issues.

## REFERENCES

Aldous, J. (1982). *Two paychecks: Life in dual-earner families.* Beverly Hills, CA: Sage Publications.

Alper, N. O., & Morlock, M. J. (1982). Moonlighting husband or working wife: An economic analyses. *Journal of Family Issues, 3,* 181–198.

American Demographics. (1983). How they rank: 1980 Census results ranked for states, metropolitan areas, and cities of 50,000 or more. *American Demographics, 5,* 30–43.

Barlett, P. F. (1984). Microdynamics of debt, drought, and default in south Georgia. *American Journal of Agricultural Economics, 66,* 836–843.

Bebbington, A. C. (1973). The function of stress in the establishment of the dual-career family. *Journal of Marriage and the Family, 35,* 530–539.

Becker, G. S. (1965). A theory of the allocation of time. *Economics Journal, 75,* 493–517.

Berk, S. F. (1985). *The gender factory: The apportionment of work in American households.* New York: Plenum Press.

Berkowitz, A. D., & Perkins, H. W. (1984). Stress among farm women: Work and family as interacting systems. *Journal of Marriage and the Family, 46,* 161–166.

Bokemeier, J. L., Sachs, C., & Keith, V. (1983). Labor force participation of metropolitan, nonmetropolitan, and farm women: A comparative study. *Rural Sociology, 48,* 315–323.

Brown, S. C. (1978). Moonlighting increased sharply in 1977, particularly among women. *Monthly Labor Review, 101,* 27–30.

Burke, R. M., & Weir, R. (1976). Relationships of wives' employment status to employment status of husband, wife, and pair satisfaction and performance. *Journal of Marriage and the Family, 38,* 279–287.

Cooper, K., Chassin, L., & Zeiss, A. (1985). The relation of sex-role self-concept and sex-role attitudes to the marital satisfaction and personal adjustment of dual-worker couples with preschool children. *Sex Roles, 12,* 227–242.

Coward, R. T., & Smith, W. M. (1982). Families in rural society. In D. A. Dillman & D. J. Hobbs (Eds.), *Rural society in the U.S.: Issues for the 1980s* (pp. 77–84). Boulder, CO: Westview Press.

D'Amico, R. (1983). Status maintenance or status competition? Wife's relative wages as a determinant of labor supply and marital instability. *Social Forces, 61,* 1186–1205.

Dillman, D. A. (1978). *Mail and telephone surveys: The total design method.* New York: Wiley.

Holmstrom, L. L. (1972). *The two-career family.* Cambridge, MA: Schenkman.

Kingston, P. W., & Nock, S. L. (1985). Consequences of the family work day. *Journal of Marriage and the Family, 47,* 619–629.

Lyson, T. A. (1985). Husband and wife work roles and the organization and operation of family farms. *Journal of Marriage and the Family, 47,* 759–764.

Martin, T., Berry, K., & Jacobsen, R. (1975). The impact of dual-career marriages on female professional careers: An empirical test of a Parsonian hypotheses. *Journal of Marriage and the Family, 37,* 734–742.

Meeks, S., Arnkoff, D. B., Glass, C. R., & Notarius, C. I. (1985). Wives' employment status, hassles, communication, and relational efficacy: Intra- versus extra-relationship factors and marital adjustment. *Family Relations, 34,* 249–255.

Miller, G. W. (1972). The extent, characteristics and effects of multi-jobholding in South Central Kansas. *Rocky Mountain Social Science Journal, 9,* 19–25.

Oppenheimer, V. K. (1982). *Work and the family: A study in social demography.* New York: Academic Press.

Orden, S., & Bradburn, N. M. (1968). Dimensions of marriage happiness. *American Journal of Sociology, 73,* 715–731.

Parsons, T., & Bales, R. F. (1955). *Family, socialization and interaction process.* Glencoe, IL: The Free Press.

Pleck, J. (1977). The work-family role system. *Social Problems, 24,* 417–427.

Rapaport, R., & Rapaport, R. (1976). *Dual-career families reexamined.* New York: Harper.

Rosenfeld, R. A. (1985). *Farm women: Work, farm, and family in the United States.* Chapel Hill: University of North Carolina Press.

Ross, C. E., Mirowsky, J., & Huber, J. (1983). Dividing work, sharing work, and in-between: Marriage patterns and depression. *American Sociological Review, 48,* 809–823.

Sekscenski, E. S. (1980). Women's share of moonlighting nearly doubles during 1969-1979. *Monthly Labor Review, 103,* 36–39.

Simpson, I. H., & England, P. (1982). Conjugal work roles and marital solidarity. In J. Aldous (Ed.), *Two paychecks: Life in dual-earner families* (pp. 147–171). Beverly Hills, CA: Sage Publications.

Smith, D. S. (1985). Wife employment and marital adjustment: A cumulation of results. *Family Relations, 34,* 483–490.

Spanier, G. (1976). Measuring dyadic adjustment. *Journal of Marriage and the Family, 38,* 15–28.

Stanley, S. C., Hunt, J. G., & Hunt, L. L. (1986). The relative deprivation of husbands in dual-earner households. *Journal of Family Issues, 7,* 3–20.

Thomas, S., Albrecht, R., & White, P. (1984). Determinants of marital quality in dual-career couples. *Family Relations, 33,* 513–521.

Wilensky, H. L. (1963). Moonlighter: A product of relative deprecation. *Industrial Relations, 3,* 105–124.

# Residential Differences in Marital Status and Household Type Among the Elderly*

Raymond T. Coward, Stephen J. Cutler and Frederick E. Schmidt**

Despite the rapid growth of formal services for the aged in the United States, research in social gerontology has repeatedly demonstrated the large and continued critical role of *families* in maintaining the quality of life of elders (Branch and Jette, 1983; Cantor, 1979; Coward, 1987a; Litwak, 1985; Stephens and Christianson, 1986; Stoller and Earl, 1983; Stone, Cafferata, and Sangl, 1986). Because of the prominence and importance of the long term care provided by families, considerable effort has been directed at describing the structure and functions of the family networks surrounding elders and illuminating the interpersonal dynamics of their exchanges (Hooyman, 1983; Sauer and Coward, 1985; Litwak, 1985).

For many elders, the "first line of defense" in responding to their escalating needs are those individuals with whom they reside—referred to as intra-household caregivers by Brody (1985). Thus, conspicuous within the general research theme of family gerontology has been a concentrated effort to understand better those factors that are associated with, and predictive of, different household configurations (Soldo and Myllyluoma, 1983). Such research has demonstrated, for example, that the composition of the household in which an elder lives is significantly associated with the help-seeking behaviors which they manifest—altering both the pattern of aid received from the informal network of family and friends (Coward, 1987a) as well as the utilization of services from the formal network (Stoller and Earl, 1983).

Currently, evidence indicates that the household composition of elders varies significantly by both characteristics of the person under study (e.g., age and gender) as well as the environment in which they live (e.g., *residential* location). For example, there is evidence that suggests that marital status, a major determinant of household composition, is associated with both age and gender. Whereas 83.0 percent of males and 54.8 percent of females age 65-69 years of age (the "young-old") were married, among the "oldest old" (85 years of age or greater) only 48.4 percent of the males and 8.4 percent of the females were married (Rosenwaike, 1985; see also U.S. Senate Special Committee on Aging, 1985, Table 2). At the same time, other researchers have demonstrated that marital status varies significantly by residence. Whereas 52.0 percent of persons aged 65 years and over in metropolitan communities were married, 73.3 percent of the nonmetropolitan farm elderly were married and 56.1 percent of the nonmetropolitan nonfarm elderly were married (Clifford, Heaton, Voss and Fuguitt, 1985). What is less well understood, however, is how these micro and macro variables *interact* to influence such factors as

*Support for this research was provided under a grant from the National Institute on Aging (#AG06125). The authors want to acknowledge and express appreciation for the work and support provided by staff of the research project: Sarah Gilmore, Thomas Arnold and William Robb.

**Raymond T. Coward is a Professor and Director, UVM Social Work Program, and Research Professor in the Center for Rural Studies, 452 Waterman, The University of Vermont, Burlington, VT 05405. Stephen J. Cutler is the Bishop Robert F. Joyce Distinguished University Professor of Gerontology, Department of Sociology, The University of Vermont, Burlington, VT 05405. Frederick E. Schmidt is the Director, Center for Rural Studies and Associate Professor of Sociology, Hills Building, The University of Vermont, Burlington, VT 05405.

household composition or marital status. Research to date, for example, has not examined the distribution of marital status simultaneously by age, gender *and* residence. Such analyses, when completed, would permit gerontologists and family sociologists to begin to untangle the differential effects of these multiple factors (Coward and Cutler, in press).

When research *has* attempted to focus on the interactions between residence and other personal descriptors, it has typically been characterized by two deficiencies (Stone, Cafferata, and Sangl, 1986). First, important variables (like residence and age) have often been aggregated into large categories, frequently dichotomies (e.g., rural/urban, metropolitan/nonmetropolitan, or elderly/nonelderly), which have served to obscure some of the more specific covariation that exists. Second, relatively few studies have had sample sizes sufficiently large so as to permit the examination of the simultaneous interaction of major factors. As a consequence, our understanding of the precise association between residence and other major socio-demographic characteristics (such as age, gender and household composition) is both unclear and incomplete.

Thus, there are two primary objectives of the research reported below. First, we examine the relationships between age, gender and residence and two measures of the availability of intra-household sources of support—marital status and household type. Moreover, for the age and residence variables we employ a multi-category classification system that avoids the problems associated with dichotomous definitions of these variables. Second, we perform these analyses within the context of a data set that is sufficiently large so as to permit analysis of the simultaneous effects of these factors and that is also nationally representative (so that our findings are not limited to a particular local or regional area).

## Methods

In the work reported below, a concern for the comprehensive understanding of the impact on elders of household form and type of residence led us to select the one percent Public Use Microdata Sample (PUMS), File C, as the basic data source (see Note 1). Extracted from the 1980 Census of Population and Housing, the PUMS contain individual level responses which allow users to retabulate information to their own specifications. Each microdata file is a stratified random sample of the population, actually a subsample of the full sample (19.4% of all households) that received and completed the census long-form questionnaires.

Our basic interest in residential differences in the composition of the households of elders led to the following design decisions. From the total sample in PUMS, File C, we included the person-level records for all *individuals* 65 years of age and older (N = 239,329), exclusive of those living in any type of group quarters. In addition, we included the person-level records for all individuals under 65 years of age living in a household with an elder (N = 117,787). Finally, at the household level, our data include information on 184,024 *households* in which one or more elders reside (Note 2).

## Variable Definitions

Five variables were used in the analysis—three independent variables (age, gender and residence) and two dependent variables (marital status and household type). The definitions of these variables were taken from technical documents prepared by the U.S. Bureau of the Census (1983) and are briefly described below.

Age is measured in several ways on the Census questionnaire. Both "age at last birthday" and the write-in entries of month and year of birth are requested. From these questions, a specific single year age is assigned to each respondent. We aggregated the sample into three age categories: (1) respondents 65 to 74 years or the "young-old" (63.6% of the sample or 152,278 persons); (2) those 75 to 84 years or the "moderately-old" (29.5% or 70,648); and (3) the "old-old," persons over the age of 85 years (6.9% or 16,403).

Gender was the second independent variable. In the Census, gender is ascertained on a complete count basis. In this sample of elders, 41.0 percent were males (98,181) and 59.0 percent were females (141,148).

The final independent variable was residence. The residential categories available on the PUMS, File C, are a variation of the traditional rural/urban dichotomy. As defined by the Census Bureau, the urban population includes all persons living in either an urbanized area or in places of 2,500 or more inhabitants outside an urbanized area. The rural population consists of everyone else.

On the PUMS, File C, the urban category can be divided into three parts:

1. Central Cities: Generally, the largest incorporated place in an urbanized area. While a total urbanized area must have at least 50,000 residents, there is no minimum size for central cities. These cities, however, are the center of a population concentration. In the sample selected for this research, 31.4 percent of the elders lived in central cities or a total of 75,036 persons.
2. Urban Fringe: That part of an urbanized area outside a central city—commonly referred to as the suburbs (67,017 elders or 28.0%).
3. Urban, Outside Urbanized Areas: These are places that are not located within the boundaries of an urbanized area but that have a population of more than 2,500 residents (35,209 or 14.7%).

The remaining elders in the sample (25.9% or 62,067 persons) lived in rural environments or, more specifically, in places that were outside an urbanized area and that had fewer than 2,500 inhabitants. We were able to divide this category further into rural farm and rural nonfarm persons (a distinction earlier work had led us to conclude was significant, see Coward and Cutler, in press). The rural farm category was comprised of individuals living in a rural area and with *household* income of $1,000 or more from the sale of crops, livestock or other farm products during the preceding calendar year. In this subsample, there were 6,992 such elders (2.9% of the total sample of elders or 11.3% of the rural elders). The remaining rural elders (55,075) were placed in the rural nonfarm category (28% of the total sample and 88.7% of all the elders living in rural areas).

The first dependent variable, marital status was divided into four categories. The first category was "*now married*, except separated." This category contained the majority of elders in the sample (54.3% or 130,016 elders) and was made up of persons whose current marriage had not ended through widowhood, divorce or separation (regardless of previous marital history). The next category was comprised of *widows and widowers* who had not remarried (84,339 persons or 35.2%). Because of the small numbers of *divorced* or *separated* elders (3.9% and 1.1%, respectively), we created one category that included both persons who were legally divorced and had not remarried as well as persons legally separated or otherwise absent from their spouse because of marital discord (a total of 11,994 elders or 5.0%). Finally, the *single* category included all persons who had never been married (12,980 persons or 5.4% of the sample).

The second dependent variable, household type, is an indicator of the composition of the persons occupying a housing unit. In general, there are two types—family households and nonfamily households. Family households are comprised of two or more persons who are related by birth, marriage, or adoption, and who live together as one household. A family household may also include nonrelatives living with a family. In contrast, nonfamily households consist of a person living alone or of a householder living with only unrelated individuals.

By combining questions on sex and relationship, family households can be further divided into three categories: (1) married couple family households (see Note 3): a family in which the householder and his/her spouse are enumerated as members of the same household (137,835 persons or 57.6% of the total sample); (2) male householder, no wife present (6,543 elders or 2.7%); and (3) female householder, no husband present (20,222 elders or 8.4%).

The nonfamily households can also be subdivided. For the elderly, the vast majority of persons living in nonfamily households are living alone. As a consequence, in the presentation of results, we have shown this subdivision. In this sample, 74,729 persons (31.2% of the total sample) lived in nonfamily households. The vast majority (94.3%) of those in nonfamily households were living alone (70,480 or 29.4% of the total sample). The second part of this category includes elders living with an unrelated person (4,249 elders or 1.8% of the total sample).

## Results

In this section, the findings on residence differences in marital status and household type are presented. Our discussion at this point will be largely descriptive. Interpretations and explanations of the results, as well as possible implications, will be considered in the concluding section. First, the bivariate relationships between residence and the two dependent variables, marital status and household composition, are examined. Then, multivariate analyses are performed to determine the simultaneous effects of age, gender and residence on the dependent variables.

## Residence and Marital Status

Data in Table 1 indicate some pronounced differences in the marital status of persons 65 years of age and older by residence. The highest percentage of married elders (nearly 7 out of 10) is found among persons in the rural farm category. In contrast, less than half (47.8%) of those living in central cities are currently married. Diversity within rural and urban areas is also apparent. While 69.7 percent of rural farm elders are married, only 59.3 percent of persons residing in rural nonfarm areas are married. Among elders living in urban fringe areas, 56.4 percent are married, but only 47.8 percent of those residing in central cities are.

Clear residence differences are evident among those who are widowed. The highest percentage (38.1%) of persons 65 years of age and older who are widowed occurs

among individuals living in central cities, and the lowest percentage (22.6%) is seen for persons living on rural farms. In contrast to the married category, differences in the prevalence of widowhood among types of urban areas are less pronounced, but there is still a substantial difference between the rural farm and rural nonfarm categories.

While the prevalence is considerably lower, the pattern of differences for those who are divorced or separated parallels the findings for persons who are widowed: the highest prevalence is seen in central cities and the lowest is on rural farms. The other three residence categories are similar, although elders residing in rural nonfarm areas are more than twice as likely to be divorced or separated as their rural farm counterparts.

As was the case for the divorced and separated, only a small minority of older persons are single and never married. Again, the highest percentage (7.2%) occurs among central city residents. Here, however, the lowest percentage (4.3%) is seen for persons living in rural nonfarm areas, and interestingly the percentage of rural farm elders who are single is closer to the central city residents than to the other residence categories.

## Residence and Household Type

The findings for household type reveal clearly that the majority of all elders live in a family household of some kind (see Table 1).

Table 1.
Marital Status and Household Type by Residence: U.S. Population, 65 Years of Age and Older, 1980, by Percentages[a,b]

| | Residence | | | | |
|---|---|---|---|---|---|
| | Central City | Urban Fringe | Other Urban | Rural Nonfarm | Rural Farm |
| Marital Status: | | | | | |
| Married | 47.8 | 56.4 | 53.4 | 59.3 | 69.7 |
| Widowed | 38.1 | 34.6 | 37.1 | 32.6 | 22.6 |
| Divorced/Separated | 6.9 | 4.4 | 4.6 | 3.9 | 1.6 |
| Single | 7.2 | 4.6 | 4.9 | 4.3 | 6.0 |
| Household Type: | | | | | |
| Family households (total) | 64.0 | 71.8 | 64.9 | 72.3 | 82.8 |
| Married couple family household | 50.5 | 61.2 | 55.1 | 62.6 | 72.4 |
| Family household with male householder, no wife present | 3.1 | 2.5 | 2.0 | 2.7 | 5.3 |
| Family household with female householder, no husband present | 10.4 | 8.1 | 7.8 | 7.0 | 5.1 |
| Nonfamily households (total) | 36.0 | 28.2 | 35.1 | 27.7 | 17.2 |
| Living alone | 33.6 | 26.5 | 33.7 | 26.5 | 16.5 |
| (n) | (75,036) | (67,017) | (35,209) | (55,075) | (6,992) |

[a]Source: U.S. Bureau of the Census, Public-Use Microdata Sample, File C.
[b]Percentages may not add to 100 due to rounding.

There are differences among the residence categories, but it is worth emphasizing that nearly 2 in 3 individuals living in central cities and more than 4 in 5 older persons on rural farms resided in family households in 1980.

Married couple family households were the most prevalent type of family household where elders were found (Note 3). Older persons in this specific type of household setting constitute a majority in all residence categories, although the percentages range from a high of 72.4 percent on rural farms to a low of 50.5 percent in central cities. Again, there are substantial differences within the urban and rural categories. Among all urban residents, elders residing in urban fringe areas are most likely to be found in a married couple family household setting, while rural farm residents are more likely to be living in such a household than those in rural nonfarm areas.

The least prevalent household form among older persons is the family household with a male householder, but with no wife present (e.g., an older widower living with children). Although the percentages of this type of household are small for all residence categories, it did occur with relatively greater frequency in rural farm areas and is found least often in other urban areas.

Family households with a female householder and no husband present (e.g., an older widow living with an adult daughter or an older woman living with a sibling) are somewhat more prevalent in all residence categories except rural farm, although only a small minority of elders lives in such households. When they do occur, the major difference is between central cities and rural farms with the percentage of elders in these households being twice as high in the former as in the latter.

Beyond married couple family households, the second most frequently observed type of household in which elders reside is the nonfamily household. As the data in Table 1 clearly demonstrate, most older persons living in nonfamily households are living alone in one person households. Slightly more than 1 in 3 older persons living in central cities and in other urban areas are in nonfamily households, percentages which are twice as high as for older persons living on rural farms. Elders residing in urban fringe and in rural nonfarm areas occupy an intermediate position.

## Multivariate Analysis

The findings in Table 1 point to a number of important residence differences in marital status and household type among the population 65 years of age and older. Often, the largest differences are those for central city vs. rural farm residents. It is important to note, however, that there are other differences which distinguish elders living in these areas, differences which may yield further insights into the residential variation in marital status and in household type seen in Table 1.

For example, we have examined the age distributions of persons 65 years of age and older within each of the five residential categories. These results show that the rural farm population tends to be the youngest and the central city population the oldest. Thus, the highest percentage of the "young-old" (i.e., 65-74 years of age) is found in the rural farm category, while the highest percentage of the "oldest-old" (i.e., 85 years of age and older) is seen among central city residents. Given these age differences and the strong association of age with the sex ratio, it is not surprising that there are also residence differences in sex composition. The highest percentages of older women are found in the urban categories and the lowest in the rural. At the extremes, only 38.3 percent of central city elderly residents are males, while a *majority* (51.6%) of rural farm elders are males (Note 4).

In view of these compositional differences in age and gender by residence, we have reanalyzed the data in Table 1 in somewhat greater detail. Table 2 presents the relationships between marital status and residence by gender and age. Similarly, the data in Table 3 show the results of the analysis of residence differences in household type, again with controls for gender and age. Although our principal focus will be on variation by residence, brief mention will also be made of important gender and age effects.

## Multivariate Comparisons of Marital Status

To begin, the data in Table 2 show, at every age and within every residence category, that females are less likely than males to be married and are more likely to be widowed. Interestingly, there is a higher per-

Table 2.
Marital Status by Residence, Age, and Sex: U.S. Population, 65 Years of Age and Older, 1980, by Percentages[a,b]

| | Males | | | | | Females | | | | |
|---|---|---|---|---|---|---|---|---|---|---|
| | Married | Widowed | Divorced/Separated | Single | (n) | Married | Widowed | Divorced/Separated | Single | (n) |
| **65-74:** | | | | | | | | | | |
| Central city | 75.8 | 10.7 | 7.4 | 6.2 | (18,969) | 42.2 | 41.1 | 8.9 | 7.9 | (27,457) |
| Urban fringe | 84.0 | 8.6 | 4.0 | 3.4 | (18,837) | 50.4 | 38.2 | 6.1 | 5.4 | (24,727) |
| Other urban | 83.2 | 8.2 | 4.5 | 4.1 | (9,102) | 47.7 | 41.2 | 6.0 | 5.2 | (12,671) |
| Rural nonfarm | 82.2 | 8.5 | 4.9 | 4.5 | (16,723) | 55.2 | 37.3 | 4.0 | 3.6 | (19,041) |
| Rural farm | 85.0 | 4.9 | 2.2 | 7.9 | (2,527) | 70.6 | 24.2 | 1.3 | 3.8 | (2,224) |
| **75-84:** | | | | | | | | | | |
| Central city | 67.7 | 21.3 | 5.1 | 5.9 | (8,076) | 21.5 | 65.3 | 5.2 | 8.0 | (15,042) |
| Urban fringe | 74.4 | 19.5 | 3.0 | 3.2 | (7,076) | 26.0 | 65.1 | 3.2 | 5.8 | (12,100) |
| Other urban | 73.3 | 19.5 | 3.3 | 4.0 | (3,868) | 24.5 | 65.7 | 4.0 | 5.9 | (7,082) |
| Rural nonfarm | 72.3 | 19.5 | 3.6 | 4.7 | (6,609) | 29.6 | 63.3 | 2.4 | 4.7 | (8,979) |
| Rural farm | 73.3 | 17.1 | 1.5 | 8.2 | (894) | 40.1 | 53.8 | 1.4 | 4.7 | (922) |
| **85+:** | | | | | | | | | | |
| Central city | 51.9 | 39.9 | 3.6 | 4.7 | (1,720) | 8.6 | 80.6 | 3.0 | 7.9 | (3,772) |
| Urban fringe | 56.6 | 37.5 | 2.7 | 3.3 | (1,395) | 11.1 | 81.2 | 2.6 | 5.2 | (2,882) |
| Other urban | 54.5 | 40.0 | 1.7 | 3.9 | (832) | 9.6 | 82.5 | 2.0 | 6.1 | (1,654) |
| Rural nonfarm | 53.0 | 39.6 | 2.6 | 4.9 | (1,369) | 11.6 | 81.7 | 1.9 | 4.9 | (2,354) |
| Rural farm | 54.4 | 38.0 | 2.2 | 5.4 | (184) | 12.9 | 81.7 | .4 | 5.0 | (241) |

aSource: U.S. Bureau of the Census, Public-Use Microdata Sample, File C.
bPercentages may not add to 100 due to rounding.

centage of women than men who are single at all ages in the three urban categories, but there is no difference between rural nonfarm men and women in the percentage single at ages 75-84 years and 85 years and older. For those living on rural farms, the pattern observed for urban areas reverses itself, with males being more likely than females to be single.

Within residence categories and without exception, as age increases the percentages of both males and females who are married decline and the percentages who are widowed increase. The relative frequency of being divorced or separated also varies consistently with age, declining for both men and women within each residence category.

Several important patterns emerge when we turn to the residence differences in marital status reported in Table 2. Among males, central city residents are the least likely to be married at all ages. However, in contrast to the results reported in Table 1, where a substantially higher percentage of rural farm residents were married, the differences between rural farm males and males living in urban fringe, other urban, and rural nonfarm areas are minimal. Among males, in other words, the controls for age and gender reduce considerably the clear marital "advantage" of persons living on farms which was apparent in Table 1. Furthermore, among males 85 years of age and older, residence differences in general become far less pronounced.

It is among females, on the other hand, where the original residence differences in percent married persist, although here there appears to be clear evidence of a "specification" effect with age. Among all age groups, women living in central cities are the least likely to be married and women living on rural farms are the most likely to be married. These differences in being married are most apparent among female elders 65-74 years of age (where there is a 28.4% difference between women residing in central cities and on rural farms); the difference is still substantial (18.6%), but less so, among women 75-84 years of age, and it is much reduced (4.3%) among women 85 and older. A similar weakening of the differences with age is seen for rural farm and rural nonfarm residents. Thus, among men and to an even greater extent among women, increasing age acts to exert a levelling influence on residence variation in being married.

Not surprisingly, roughly the same pattern is observed among the widowed. Among men at ages 65-74 years and 75-84 years, central city residents are most likely to be widowed and rural farm residents are the least likely; among women, rural farm residents are the least likely to be widowed, although females living in central cities do not differ appreciably from women living in urban fringe, other urban, and rural nonfarm areas. Also at these ages, residents of rural nonfarm areas are more nearly similar in the percentage widowed to residents of urban fringe and other urban areas than they are to rural farm residents. By ages 85 and older, however, the residence differences nearly disappear.

For all but 85 years and older males, there are persistent residence differences among the divorced and separated, with those living in central cities having the highest percentage and those living on rural farms the lowest.

Finally, among single elders, there are interesting variations on the pattern of residence differences seen in Table 1. For males, the highest percentages of older single persons are found among the rural farm residents and the lowest occur among residents of urban fringe areas. In contrast, single women are most likely to be found in central cities and are generally least likely to reside in the two rural areas.

## Household Type

Regarding the data on household type presented in Table 3, we again begin with a brief consideration of age and gender differences. Among males and for all residence categories, with increasing age there are declines in the percentages living in family households. Among women, however, decreasing percentages occur between 65-74 years and 75-84 years which (except for the other urban category) are then followed by increasing percentages living in family households at ages 85 years and older.

For the specific types of family households and for all residence categories and both genders, the prevalence of married couple family households decreases with age; the prevalence of family households with male householders, no wife present, increases; and the prevalence of family households with a female householder, no husband present also increases with age.

Among males, the percentages of nonfamily households and households composed of males living alone increase with age in all residence categories. For females, however, the prevalence of nonfamily households and of living alone increases with age to 75-84, but then either decreases at ages 85 years and older (central cities, urban fringe areas) or remains relatively constant.

In terms of gender differences, for all residence categories and at all ages, the results of Table 3 indicate that males are more likely than females to be in family households in general, to be in married couple family households, and to be in family households with a male householder and no wife present. Women, in contrast, are consistently more likely to be residing in family households with a female householder and no husband present, in nonfamily households in general and, specifically, living alone.

Returning to the main focus of the discussion, important residence differences are apparent among the several household types considered in Table 3. With but one exception (males 85 years and older), elders living on rural farms are most likely to be found in family households, although the differences between rural farm and other categories are more pronounced among women than among men. For males at all ages, the percentages living in family households are lowest for central city residents, but for females 75-84 and 85+ years of age, living in a family household is least common among residents in the other urban category.

The pronounced residence differences in the prevalence of married couple households seen in Table 1 are much reduced at all ages among males, and the rural farm/nonfarm difference nearly disappears. For women, residence differences in living in married couple family households persist at all ages, but with increasing age there is a notable decrease in the magnitude of central city/rural farm and rural farm/nonfarm differences. For example, there is a 14.5 percent difference in the percentages of rural farm and rural nonfarm women ages 65-74 who live in married couple households; at ages 75-84, the difference is 11 percent; and at ages 85+, the difference is reduced to 7.5 percent.

At all ages, it is rural farm males who are most likely to be living in family households with a male householder, no wife present,

Table 3.
Household Type by Residence, Age, and Sex: U.S. Population, 65 Years of Age and Older, 1980, by Percentages[a,b]

| | Household Type | | | | | | |
| | Family Households (Total) | Married Couple Family Household | Family Household with Male Householder, No Wife Present | Family Household with Female Householder, No Husband Present | Nonfamily Households (Total) | Living Alone | (n) |
|---|---|---|---|---|---|---|---|
| **Males, 65-74:** | | | | | | | |
| Central city | 82.0 | 75.5 | 4.2 | 2.3 | 18.0 | 15.3 | (18,969) |
| Urban fringe | 88.7 | 84.5 | 2.8 | 1.4 | 11.3 | 9.9 | (18,837) |
| Other urban | 87.1 | 83.1 | 2.6 | 1.4 | 12.9 | 11.7 | (9,102) |
| Rural nonfarm | 87.0 | 82.5 | 3.1 | 1.4 | 13.0 | 11.9 | (16,723) |
| Rural farm | 91.3 | 85.2 | 5.2 | .9 | 8.7 | 8.2 | (2,527) |
| **Females: 65-74:** | | | | | | | |
| Central city | 59.8 | 44.4 | 1.8 | 13.6 | 40.2 | 37.9 | (27,457) |
| Urban fringe | 66.3 | 54.5 | 1.5 | 10.3 | 33.7 | 32.0 | (24,727) |
| Other urban | 59.9 | 48.8 | 1.1 | 10.0 | 40.2 | 38.8 | (12,671) |
| Rural nonfarm | 68.6 | 57.5 | 1.3 | 9.6 | 31.5 | 30.3 | (19,041) |
| Rural farm | 81.8 | 72.0 | 2.5 | 7.3 | 18.2 | 17.4 | (2,224) |
| **Males, 75-84:** | | | | | | | |
| Central city | 76.0 | 68.3 | 4.9 | 2.8 | 24.1 | 21.7 | (8,076) |
| Urban fringe | 82.8 | 76.4 | 4.1 | 2.3 | 17.2 | 15.6 | (7,076) |
| Other urban | 78.9 | 74.1 | 3.3 | 1.5 | 21.1 | 19.8 | (3,868) |
| Rural nonfarm | 80.3 | 74.1 | 4.6 | 1.6 | 19.7 | 18.5 | (6,609) |
| Rural farm | 83.5 | 73.9 | 8.7 | .9 | 16.4 | 15.8 | (894) |
| **Females, 75-84:** | | | | | | | |
| Central city | 45.3 | 27.0 | 2.4 | 15.9 | 54.7 | 52.0 | (15,042) |
| Urban fringe | 53.1 | 36.0 | 2.4 | 14.7 | 46.9 | 44.8 | (12,100) |
| Other urban | 42.8 | 28.3 | 1.5 | 13.0 | 57.2 | 55.5 | (7,082) |
| Rural nonfarm | 52.1 | 36.8 | 2.3 | 13.0 | 47.9 | 46.7 | (8,979) |
| Rural farm | 66.4 | 47.8 | 7.2 | 11.4 | 33.6 | 32.3 | (922) |
| **Males, 85 +:** | | | | | | | |
| Central city | 69.2 | 55.9 | 8.1 | 5.2 | 30.9 | 28.7 | (1,720) |
| Urban fringe | 77.9 | 64.7 | 8.0 | 5.2 | 22.2 | 19.8 | (1,395) |
| Other urban | 67.5 | 57.7 | 5.8 | 4.0 | 32.6 | 30.4 | (832) |
| Rural nonfarm | 73.3 | 61.8 | 7.7 | 4.3 | 26.2 | 24.8 | (1,369) |
| Rural farm | 77.2 | 63.6 | 11.4 | 2.2 | 22.8 | 22.3 | (184) |
| **Females: 85 +:** | | | | | | | |
| Central city | 49.7 | 21.6 | 3.1 | 25.0 | 50.3 | 47.2 | (3,772) |
| Urban fringe | 57.9 | 33.2 | 3.4 | 21.3 | 42.1 | 39.7 | (2,882) |
| Other urban | 41.4 | 19.5 | 2.2 | 19.7 | 58.6 | 56.8 | (1,654) |
| Rural nonfarm | 53.3 | 29.4 | 3.3 | 20.6 | 46.6 | 45.2 | (2,354) |
| Rural farm | 67.6 | 36.9 | 7.5 | 23.2 | 32.4 | 31.1 | (241) |

[a]Source: U.S. Bureau of the Census, Public-Use Microdata Sample, File C.
[b]Percentages may not add to 100 due to rounding.

and they are the least likely to be residing in a family household with a female householder and no husband present. Rural farm females are consistently more likely than residents of other areas to be living in a family household with a male householder and no wife present. For women, the pattern for family households with a female householder and no husband present is one in which the highest percentage is seen among central city residents and the lowest (except for ages 85 +) among persons living on rural farms.

There are persistent differences between rural farm and nonfarm areas, at all ages, in the percentages living in nonfamily households and living alone, although the differences are greater for women than for men. In each age group, rural farm women are least likely to be living in these types of households, as we saw in Table 1, and women living in other urban areas tend to be the most likely, especially among those 85 years and older. Among males, the picture is less clear and no residential category emerges consistently across all ages as having the highest or lowest percentage of elders living in nonfamily households in general or living alone in particular.

## Discussion

In this concluding section, we want to "step back" from the specific data and attempt to capture some of the significant differences, and their implications, that have emerged from the analyses. In doing so, we hope to emphasize the importance of residence as a factor in understanding the life circumstances of elders while also attempting to disentangle its effects from that of other factors with which it co-varies.

### Greater Residential Differences Among Women

The data in Tables 2 and 3 demonstrate greater residential variability in the two dependent variables, marital status and household composition, among women. For example, the percentage differences in those male elders who are married in the "young-old" category (ages 65-74) do not begin to approximate the magnitude of the differences found among women of the same age group.

Although this residential discrepancy in marital status among the elderly has been commented on before (Clifford, Heaton, Voss and Fuguitt, 1985; Coward, 1987b), the analysis here provides two additional insights. First, the largest differences can be attributed specifically to older farm women. Older rural nonfarm women are noticeably similar, although still different, in the patterns of their marital status to women in the other residential categories (particularly the urban fringe and other urban categories and to a lesser extent the women in central cities). Except in the oldest age category (85 years plus), it is the patterns of the older farm women who are out-of-step with their peers.

A second new insight offered by these data involves the diminished interaction of gender and residence as age increases (the next section on the levelling effect of age will deal more specifically with this observation). As a consequence of these two new insights, therefore, we are more able to specify that the residential differences in marital status among the elderly are attributable, in large part, to differences among women 65-74 years of age who are living on farms.

The distinctive marital status pattern of farm women may be, in part, however, an artifact of the Census definition of rural farm which is *not* strictly a residential classification but, rather, one that includes occupational and income dimensions as well (see the specific definition of rural farm presented in the Methods section). As a consequence, some rural women may lose their "farm" designation when, at the death of their spouse, the farming operation is turned-over to adult children who reside in a different household. Under those circumstances, the elderly women may no longer have direct household income from the sale of farm products. Such women may not physically move from the farm, but may now be classified as rural nonfarm.

Others have suggested a migrational difference, speculating that farm widows have "traditionally moved from farms to nearby villages and small towns at the time of the death of their spouse" (Clifford, Heaton, Voss and Fuguitt, 1985, p. 31). But there is little empirical, and no longitudinal, evidence that documents this contention.

Finally, for perspective we must remind ourselves that *farm* residents are the clear minority in rural areas (representing just 11.3% of the *rural* residents in the PUMS data). As a consequence, although the residential differences remain noteworthy between nonfarm women and women living in other residential categories (i.e., central cities, urban fringe and other urban), the magnitude of such differences, even at the younger age categories, are markedly smaller.

## The Levelling Effect of Age

The data presented above indicate a levelling off of residential differences as age increased, to the point that there were only marginal differences between residential categories for those 85 years and over. For example, whereas there was a 28.4 percent difference in the proportion of rural farm women, compared to central city women, aged 65-74 years, who were married, this difference had been reduced to 18.6 percent among women 75-84 years, and to 4.3 percent for those women over the age of 85 years. Similar levelling with age was evident among men (although, of course, to begin with their differences were smaller).

The levelling effect of age among the "old-old" has been identified in the investigation of other phenomena. For example, Havlik and Suzman (1987) have reported data that indicated a rapid decline in the proportional difference between male and female death rates, from all causes, as age increased—the smallest differences being in the over 85 years of age category. There may be a kind of "survivor" effect in operation—i.e., those characteristics that contribute to an individual living to this "old-old" category may be such as to transcend other variables that are more powerful, and differentially distributed, in younger age categories.

## U-Shaped Curve of Family Households for Women

The data in Table 3 reflect a slight U-shaped nature to the pattern of women living in family households as age increases. For example, among central city women, 59.8 percent of those aged 65-74 years were living in family households, 45.4 percent between the ages of 75-84 years, and 49.7 percent over the age of 85 years. Similar patterns were found in three of the remaining four residential categories.

This rise in the proportion of "old-old" women living in family households may reflect a number of widows moving in with

married relatives—primarily adult children (see Note 3). With respect to residential differences, the rural farm women remained the highest proportion living in family households across all three age categories and demonstrated the smallest "rise" (1.8%) at the old-old age category (with the exception of the women in the other urban category where no U-shaped pattern was apparent). In contrast, the two urban categories that demonstrated the U-shaped curve, central cities and urban fringe, had considerably higher increases between 75-84 years and over 85 years of age (9.7% and 9.0%, respectively). If this rise in the upper age category is due in large part to the movement of unmarried elders into the homes of their married relatives, then there does appear to be a difference in the prevalence of this pattern across residential categories.

## Differences Within Residential Categories

When looking for household compositional differences *between* residential categories, we must be careful not to obscure the large differences that exist among settings that are relatively proximate on the residential continuum. Perhaps the most striking example of this observation is the large farm/nonfarm difference reflected in these data, but it is not the only one that exists. In many instances, the household composition patterns of central city residents stand apart from their contiguous urban counterparts. Indeed, in general terms the marital status and household type variations could be characterized into three aggregates: central city and rural farm residents anchoring the extremes and the other three residential categories (urban fringe, other urban and rural nonfarm) "clustered" in the middle.

Consider the following differences, and their consistency, between the two extremes:

- Central city residents had: (1) the smallest percentage of elders who were still married and the largest percentage that were widowed; (2) the largest percentage that were divorced/separated or who had never married; (3) the smallest proportion living in family households; and (4) the largest percentage living alone.
- Rural farm residents, in contrast, had: (1) the highest percentage of elders

that still had a living marital partner and the lowest percentage widowed; (2) the smallest percentage who had divorced or separated; (3) the highest proportion living in family households; and (4) the lowest percentage living alone.

In all of these contrasts, the other three residential categories fell somewhere in between these extremes—although not always in a neatly arrayed pattern along an urban to rural continuum.

## Single Men and Women by Residence

The data in Table 2 indicate a "flip-flop" of the distribution of single men and women by residence. Among women, higher proportions of single, never-married are found in central cities with declining amounts across all other residential locations with the smallest percentages being in the two rural categories. Among men, just the opposite was true. Rural farm men had the highest proportions of single, never-married men. This significant gender by residence interaction is completely masked in the bivariate analysis presented in Table 1 and illustrates, once again, the importance of multivariate analytical frameworks to disentangle the differential effects of several variables.

## The Availability of Intra-Household Caregivers

By examining marital status and household type we had hoped to uncover, indirectly, information about residential differences in the availability of intra-household caregivers. We understand that the availability of another person in the household does not guarantee that that person will be willing, or able, to provide aid when needed. Moreover, we are fully aware of the breadth and magnitude of aid that comes from family members who do not reside in the household (Coward, 1987a). Nevertheless, there is evidence to indicate that there is a high probability that family members who share the household with needy elders will not only be providing help (Soldo and Myllyluoma, 1983), but that they will be providing, on the average, more help and to a more disabled person than those family caregivers living outside the home (Cantor, 1979; Hess and Soldo, 1985). It is as if, when possible, the

people with whom you live are the "first line of defense" in meeting your needs.

There did seem to be a pattern of residential differences that would seem to place some elders at an advantage. Rural elders, particularly women and those living on farms, seemed to have a distinctly higher probability of living in a family household than did their counterparts from central cities and a slight advantage in this regard over residents of the other two urban categories. This advantage declined sharply with age to the point that among those 85 years of age and older the residential differences were minimal. This greater probability of residing in a family household was, for the most part, a function of the greater availability of marital partners among elderly rural women.

The analysis reported above provides further evidence of the important residential differences that occur in the family life of elders. These data confirm the need to continue to examine and explore residential differences in the life circumstances of elderly persons. Simultaneously, however, the multivariate approach that was employed illustrates the importance of attempts to ascertain the effects of residence above and beyond other factors with which it co-varies. Without such an approach, social gerontologists and family sociologists will be limited in their ability to understand the unique effects of residential environments on the aging family.

### END NOTES

1. File C of the PUMS was selected, rather than File A or B, because of the closer fit between the available residential categories and our research interests. For further information about the differences between these files and about the characteristics and limitations of the PUMS in general, see U.S. Bureau of the Census (1983).

2. The reader should keep the distinction between persons and households as units of analysis firmly in view. The data on marital status reported later are for *persons* 65 years of age and older. The data on the household type in which an elder resides are at the *household* level. Thus, an elder living in a "married couple, family household" could be married and living with a spouse *or* be widowed and living in the household of a married child. To take another example, an older person living in a "family household with female householder, no husband present" could be a widowed homeowner with one or more of her children residing in her house or a widowed elder living in the home of an unmarried daughter.

3. In Table 1, it should be noted that the percentages of older persons residing in married couple family households are consistently higher across residence categories than the corresponding percentages of married elders. In the total sample, 7.7 percent of elders living in married couple family households are themselves unmarried. Of these, the largest group (82.8%) is

widowed, 9.1 percent are divorced or separated, and 8.1 percent are single. The reason for the discrepancy, therefore, appears to be due largely to the presence of widowed elders in the households of married relatives, principally children and siblings.

4. Because of space limitations, the tables upon which this information is based have not been included in this presentation. However, they are available upon request from any of the authors.

## REFERENCES

Branch, L., & Jette, A. (1983). Elders' use of informal long-term care assistance. *The Gerontologist, 23*, 51-56.

Brody, E. M. (1985). Parent care as a normative family stress. *The Gerontologist, 25*, 19-29.

Cantor, M. (1979). Neighbors and friends: An overlooked resource in the informal support system. *Research on Aging, 1*, 434-463.

Clifford, W. B., Heaton, T. B., Voss, P. R., & Fuguitt, G. V. (1985). The rural elderly in demographic perspective. In R. T. Coward & G. R. Lee (Eds.), *The elderly in rural society* (pp. 25-55). New York: Springer.

Coward, R. T. (1987a). Factors associated with the configuration of the helping networks of noninstitutionalized elders. *Journal of Gerontological Social Work, 10*, 113-132.

Coward, R. T. (1987b). Poverty and aging in Rural America. *Human Services in the Rural Environment, 10*, 41-47.

Coward, R. T., & Cutler, S. J. (in press). The concept of a continuum of residence: Comparing activities of daily living among the elderly. *The Journal of Rural Studies*.

Havlik, R. J., & Suzman, R. (1987). Health status: Mortality. In *Vital and health statistics: Health statistics of older persons, United States, 1986*. Washington, DC: National Center for Health Statistics, Public Health Service, U.S. Department of Health and Human Services, Series 3, No. 25.

Hess, B., & Soldo, B. (1985). Husband and wife networks. In W. J. Sauer & R. T. Coward (Eds.), *Social support networks and the care of the elderly: Theory, research and practice* (pp. 67-92). New York: Springer.

Hooyman, N. (1983). Social support networks in services to the elderly. In J. Whittaker & J. Garbarino (Eds.), *Social support networks: Informal helping in the human services* (pp. 134-164). New York: Aldine.

Litwak, E. (1985). *Helping the elderly: The complementary roles of informal networks and formal systems*. New York: Guilford Press.

Rosenwaike, I. (1985). A demographic portrait of the oldest old. *Milbank Memorial Fund Quarterly: Health and Society, 63*, 187-205.

Sauer, W. J., & Coward, R. T. (Eds.). (1985). *Social support networks and the care of the elderly: Theory, research and practice*. New York: Springer.

Soldo, B. J., & Myllyluoma, J. (1983). Caregivers who live with dependent elderly. *The Gerontologist, 23*, 605-618.

Stephens, S. A., & Christianson, J. B. (1986). *Informal care of the elderly*. Lexington, MA: Lexington Books.

Stoller, E. P., & Earl, L. L. (1983). Help with activities of everyday life: Source of support for the noninstitutionalized elderly. *The Gerontologist, 23*, 64-70.

Stone, R., Cafferata, G. L., & Sangl, J. (1986). *Caregivers of the frail elderly: A national profile*. Paper presented at the American Society on Aging, San Francisco, CA.

U.S. Bureau of the Census. (1983). *Census of Population and Housing, 1980: Public-Use Microdata Samples Technical Documentation*. Washington: U.S. Bureau of the Census.

U.S. Senate Special Committee on Aging. (1985). *How older Americans live: An analysis of census data* (Serial No. 99-D). Washington, DC: U.S. Government Printing Office.

# 13

# Making the Most of Job Loss: Individual and Marital Features of Underemployment*

Anisa M. Zvonkovic, Tom Guss, and Linda Ladd**

nderemployment has become a common experience for many families throughout the United States. This phenomenon may be especially problematic in rural areas, because estimates indicate that close to 50% of employable people in rural areas are underemployed (Clogg, 1979), and because the closing of any single plant or company can have very dramatic effects on small communities (Gordus, Jarley, & Ferman, 1981; Leff & Haft, 1983; Mick, 1975). Rather than focusing on job status (employed or unemployed), this chapter considers the burden of the working poor, people who are employed at lower salaries than they had previously earned. Changes in work hours and income have been shown to affect the worker physically and psychologically (Kasl & Cobb, 1977; Root, 1977). This chapter concentrates on how adjustment to underemployment can be influenced by the marital relationship. Spouses can be a source of support for workers undergoing financial strains, but they can also experience stress and feelings of failure or blame.

In order to understand how families facing income loss may be helped, an exploratory study was conducted examining the ways in which underemployment affected the lives of married couples. Particular attention was given to comparing families who seemed to maintain good relationships despite the challenges of curtailed income with families whose relationships had appeared to suffer. By observing characteristics of couples who had adjusted well, this study aimed to identify areas to strengthen more troubled couples. The study used a strategy involving qualitative data and a content analysis of study participants' remarks in this first effort to understand how couples cope with underemployment. Beyond describing different individual and family reactions to underemployment, the authors wished in the end to draw implications for marital counseling and other interventions.

## How Changes in Work and Income Impact on Individuals and Marriages

The experience of being underemployed and of having faced periods of unemployment in the past may be a stressor for individuals and families. Strains may be felt on

*Research for this chapter was supported by a grant from the Oregon State University Agriculture Experiment Station, Regional Project W-167: Coping With Socioeconomic Change, and funding from the Department of Human Development and Family Studies, Oregon State University, Corvallis, OR 97331. The authors thank June Henton for assistance.

**Anisa M. Zvonkovic is an Assistant Professor and Tom Guss and Linda Ladd are doctoral students, Department of Human Development and Family Studies, Oregon State University, Corvallis, OR 97331.

Reprinted from *Family Relations*, 1988, **37**, 56-61.

an individual level, within families, and in the social context of the couple. Underemployed men may feel powerless to control happenings in the past, present, and future (Komarovsky, 1940; Liker & Elder, 1983). Other family members will experience their own reactions and may express criticism and blame (Liem, 1982; Rubin, 1976). When husbands are unemployed, both spouses have reported trouble with communication and increased conflict (Liem & Liem, 1979). The experience of underemployment may increase previous family difficulties or may by itself lead to dissatisfying and unstable relationships (Lewis & Spanier, 1979; Patterson, 1982; Voydanoff, 1984).

Literature from the Great Depression indicates that family relationships were not always harmed by income drops (Angell, 1936; Bakke, 1933; Cavan & Ranck, 1938; Elder, 1974; Komarovsky, 1940). Some factors which seem to impact on how people adjust to underemployment include longstanding attitudes that they bring to the underemployment situation (Kanter, 1977; Larson, 1984; Pleck, 1984) and attributional factors that relate to how they view their economic circumstances (Hill, 1949; Moen, Kain, & Elder, 1983). Both sorts of factors may be profoundly affected by individuals' flexibility and by previous life experiences. The community in which the underemployed person is embedded may also impact on the family's ability to face their new circumstances. A community with strong social ties, with resources available to allow for pooling of property, may support families emotionally and materially (Elder, 1974; Garbarino & Sherman, 1980; Jahoda, Lazarsfeld, & Zeisel, 1971).

## The Problem of Underemployment in Rural Communities

Underemployment has been defined in different ways, such as involuntary income loss, employment at a job below an individual's skills, or changes in jobs toward ones of less earnings and skill levels (Berg, Freedman, & Freedman, 1978; Clogg, 1979; Glyde, 1977; Gordon, 1972; Schiller, 1984; Sullivan, 1978). Economists have determined that the underemployment rate is higher in agricultural communities than in urban areas (Clogg, 1979; Sullivan, 1978). Because underemployment is, in a sense, a phenomenon

that springs from the job opportunities in a given community, it is necessary to consider the specific attributes of the community in order to understand the options and adjustments of underemployed people. In rural communities, if families wish to remain in the community, they often find little alternative to underemployment. Families often reject relocation due to ties to friends and kin (Jahoda et al., 1971). Often families are reluctant to leave their homes or experience difficulty selling homes (Burke, 1985; Ferguson, Horwood, & Beatrais, 1981; Gordus et al., 1981). In today's agricultural situation, farm and ranch owners often are employed outside the operation, albeit with low earnings, in order to bring money into the farm (Doherty & Munro, 1986; Rathge & Mammen, 1985).

The problems of such workers, as well as individuals in small towns, often are not considered in reports of America's economic well-being. Attention is given instead to shifts in the unemployment rate. If the rate is high, people commonly expect individuals and families to undergo difficulties. By the same token, people have come to regard America's economy as healthy and families' financial situations to be comfortable if the unemployment rate is low. Thus, labor market statistics emphasize work status (Moen, 1980) and ignore underemployment and the situation of people who are employed but financially strained (Burris, 1983; Levitan & Taggert, 1974). The purpose of this exploratory study was to examine how a group of individuals and their spouses adjusted to income loss. Underemployment of husbands, the principal breadwinners, was defined as a situation in which husbands had experienced a period of unemployment and were now working for a reduced wage from what they had made during their earlier employment experience. The study hoped to learn how individuals could better cope with their experiences by allowing them to describe how the phenomenon of underemployment had affected them as individuals, marital partners, and members of their communities.

## Method

### Sample

Twenty respondents, husbands and wives from 10 couples, participated in qualitative interviews in the summer of 1985.

The sample was drawn from two predominantly rural counties in the Pacific Northwest, each having a population of approximately 75,000. Major industries in the counties are agriculture, wood products, and manufacturing. In each county, the largest city is home to less than 30,000 people. A land grant university is situated in one county; the other contains a community college. The sample was generated by contacting a local community agency whose mission was to retrain persons who had been unemployed.

The sample was chosen with the goal of maximizing variability in experience. All men in the sample had been unemployed and were now working for a reduced wage. The other criterion for inclusion was that the men be married. With the exception of race (all respondents were white), the couples were diverse. Men and women were represented who had been married for less than one year and others had been married as long as 29 years (mean = 12.3 years). The ages of the couples ranged from 24 to 62. Seven couples had children who ranged in age from less than one year to over 30 years old.

The educational experiences of this sample were centered on high school completion with one or two community college courses taken at a later date. The men were generally better educated than their wives. While the majority of men had been involved in the lumber industry in some form, most had entered new service areas such as janitorial work, gardening, fishing, and farming. Table 1 presents the employment experiences of the sample, including the previous work and present work of husbands. Two wives did not work by choice. Of those wives who did work outside the home, only two identified themselves as having a career. The remaining wives worked in order to help the family meet financial needs and looked forward to cutting back or quitting when their husbands found the right jobs.

## Procedure

Each couple was contacted by one member of the research team. Couples who agreed to be interviewed were given a $20 payment. The partners were interviewed by interviewers of the same gender. Interviews lasted about 1½ hours each. The interviews were taped and later transcribed.

The qualitative interview consisted of a series of 52 open-ended questions. These questions were generated from an examination of the literature on unemployment and underemployment and from the clinical counseling experience of one of the interviewers. Coverage of many aspects of a person's life was attempted; partners spoke about the individual adjustment to their financial circumstances, about the impact

Table 1.
*Occupation and Employment of Sample*

| Couple | Prior Work | Husband Present Work | Wife Work Status Unchanged |
|---|---|---|---|
| 01 | production millwright | millwright (relocated, less salary) | not employed by choice |
| 02 | equipment operator | part-time ranch hand | head cashier and bookkeeper |
| 03 | procurement officer | painter | nurse's aide |
| 04 | worker in furniture factory | part-time farmer and odd jobs | baby-sits in own home |
| 05 | mill worker | mill worker (relocated, less salary) | mill worker |
| 06 | designer and artist for company | self-employed designer and artist | veterinarian's assistant |
| 07 | production worker, lead man | fisherman (forklift operator) | sales: bakery department in grocery store |
| 08 | union construction laborer | mill worker | not employed by choice |
| 09 | mill worker | self-employed gardener paper route | manages rental property, cleans houses |
| 10 | mill worker | part-time custodian | baby-sits in own home |

on marital and family life, and about their social contacts.

Transcripts of the interviews averaged about 25 pages in length per partner. A scoring system was devised by the investigators to categorize the information as to how it pertained to individual, marital, and social adjustment. Characteristics of respondents were chosen to be analyzed and scored according to a content analysis procedure. If more than five respondents mentioned a characteristic of themselves as individuals, of their marriages, or of their social contacts, then this characteristic was used to analyze all transcripts. Each characteristic was treated like an item in a questionnaire. Therefore, the content analysis procedure relied on the themes and relevant characteristics expressed by study participants during the interviews (Budd, Thorp, & Donohew, 1967; Kerlinger, 1973; Krippendorff, 1980).

Interview comments were content analyzed separately by two trained raters. The coding consisted of a bivariate rating of whether each characteristic was present or absent for each respondent. Characteristics were coded in such a way that high scores reflected good adjustment. The entire transcript was considered in the evaluation of each characteristic. This was done because respondents often mentioned, for example, an illness or stress disorder during a part of the interview addressing another issue. An advantage of content analysis is that the data analysis is not restricted by the categories that the investigator has predetermined (Budd et al., 1967).

Once the interview items had been analyzed by both raters, reliability could be assessed by the agreement between coders. For husband respondents, from 71-88% of responses were coded the same without discussion; after coders discussed the ratings, 91-100% of responses reached agreement. For example, the exact name of a job skill or presence of a factor as a social support or not as a support were often clarified after discussion. For wife respondents, the comparable percentages were 67-90% outright agreement and 94-100% agreement after discussion.

After characteristics had been coded, the data needed to be further reduced into groups of constructs which shared a logical commonality (Krippendorff, 1980). Characteristics were examined in terms of whether they related to the individuals themselves, their marriages, or their social contacts. A total of five thematic features were derived: (a) the marital relationship, (b) interpretation of the situation, (c) health and stress, (d) personal resources, and (e) family and social supports. Table 2 presents sample items that were included in each feature. Three of the features (interpretation of the situation, health and stress, and personal resources) relate to the resources and coping of the individual. Interpretation of the situation concerns the meaning the underemployment experience had for each respondent; it is similar to the "definition of the situation" construct of Hill's (1949, 1958) ABCX model. The area of health and stress concerned physical complaints expressed by respondents. Personal resources considered the job skills and educational background possessed by individuals. The marital relationship feature related to the quality of the adjustments to the challenge of underemployment that respondents had made in their marriages; it included the areas of marital satisfaction, communication, decision making, conflict, and cohesion. The fifth feature concerned family and social supports; the extent to which individuals had supportive contact with their family members and others in their community was considered in this feature.

## Results

To begin to address the question of how the marital relationship relates to other features of underemployment, each individual's score on the marital relationship feature was totalled and compared with scores on the other four features. Scores on the marital relationship ranged from 0-16. The mode was 10; 10 was also the median. In these analyses, the scores divided at 8, the arithmetic mean (where there was also a natural break). Individuals who scored below 8 were low in marital relationship features, and those who scored above 8 were high. Thirteen individuals were high in the marital feature; seven were low.

The group of 13 individuals who scored high on the marital feature saw their financial difficulties as a challenge. In this group, husbands described their wives as their best friends. Wives expressed a loyalty and belief in their husbands' skills and motivation to overcome the situation. This group of respondents is labelled the maritally chal-

Table 2.
*Five Features of Underemployed Families: Sample Items*

Interpretation of the Situation
1. Husband's feelings concerning the unemployment period
2. Whom the husband blamed for the job loss
3. How strong the interviewers perceived the husband's work motivation to be
4. Regrets of the husband or wife concerning job loss

Marital Relationship
1. How the couple communicates on topics they identified during the interview
2. What adjustments the couple has made to accommodate for the job loss, such as time spent together
3. If the couple or either partner budgets monthly income
4. How satisfied the couple perceives themselves to be, as well as how well they problem solve together

Health and Stress
1. The individual's self-reported health both before and after the job loss
2. How active the individual reports himself/herself to be in searching for another job
3. What outlets the individual has successfully maintained, such as hunting or going to the movies, which help the individual cope with stress
4. What kinds and amounts of residual stress are present in the marriage

Personal Resources
1. The number and type of jobs that person has held
2. The number and diversity of skills that person describes himself/herself as having
3. What educational experience that person has accomplished, both formal and self-taught
4. How aware the interviewers perceive the individual to be concerning alternatives in the job market

Family and Social Support
1. Changes in couple's relationships to friends: in frequency of activities, type of activities, feelings about friends
2. Changes in church attendance or membership in organizations
3. Help received from relatives; help given to relatives
4. Changes in relationships with relatives

lenged group. They did feel the strains of financial losses but reported being satisfied with their problem-solving abilities and with their marriages in general. These partners were highly cohesive. Satisfaction with decision making and communication was evident among all challenged couples.

In contrast, respondents with low scores on the marital feature (N = 7) fell into the maritally troubled group. Often these couples faced many other problems at the same time they were struggling with underemployment. People whose transcripts revealed multiple problems did spend time with their spouses but reported little satisfaction with their communication. Husbands did not reflect an understanding of their wives' feelings; wives seemed supportive only in a general sense. These couples did not use problem-solving skills in their decision making; instead, they were either waiting for something to happen or were reaching frantically for unrealistic solutions.

Chi-square statistics were computed examining individuals who scored high or low on marital features by their scores on the other features (all broken at the arithmetic mean in two categories, high or low) (Bruning & Kintz, 1977). Chi-square statistics were used rather than comparing means on the features due to the small N of the study. The standard deviations for each feature were very large, precluding suggestive differences in the means from reaching statistical significance. The mean scores on each feature and the standard deviations are listed in Table 3.

By chi-square statistics, breaking the

Table 3.
*Mean Scores on the Four Features of Underemployment by the Marital Relationship Feature*

|  | Interpretation of Situation | Family and Social Support | Health and Stress | Personal Resources |
|---|---|---|---|---|
| Mean for Challenged Group ($N = 13$) | 11.81 | 10.85 | 17.08 | 11.64 |
| Mean for Troubled Group ($N = 7$) | 7.43 | 6.57 | 12.43 | 11.07 |
| Standard Deviation | 8.77 | 6.88 | 7.50 | 7.69 |

scores on each feature into high and low, scores on the marital feature were compared to scores on the other features. Interpretation of the situation ($\chi^2 = 6.31$, $p$     .01), family and social support ($\chi^2 = 9.4$, $p$     .01), and health and stress ($\chi^2 = 4.4$, $p$     .05) were related to the marital feature. High and low personal resources were not related to whether a person was maritally challenged or troubled ($\chi^2 = .04$, $p$     .1). The phi values, an estimate of the association between the marital feature and the other features, reflect the same general pattern: Interpretation, family, and health were associated with the marital feature ($\phi = .56, .69, .47$, respectively), resources were not ($\phi = .04$).

Results indicate that individuals who report that their marriage relationships are doing well also indicate that they have good cognitive adjustment or interpretation of the job loss (e.g., resisted blaming the partner, felt the spouse has strong motivation to get another job). People who report good marriage relationships described fewer health problems than the maritally troubled group. Finally, for this sample, satisfying marital relationships were associated with supportive contact with family and friends. The feature having to do with job skills of respondents was not related to happiness in marriages. This lack of an association suggests that mere possession of many skills may not be related to the individual's ability to use them to change their financial situation, or to use them in effective marital problem solving. These data are cross-sectional and exploratory. Directions for future research include using the characteristics derived from the content analysis as a questionnaire or assessment tool, seeing if the characteristics factor into the features used in this study and possibly replicating the present results. Later, longitudinal work may illuminate how the features of underemployment are related. The way that the different features of underemployment are experi-

enced by respondents is portrayed in this next section in respondents' own words.

## Discussion: In Respondents' Own Words

The transcripts of the interviews themselves were used to explain the results of the chi-square analysis. First, the relationship of the amount of personal resources or skills to the couples' adjustment is considered. Most of the men in the sample had experienced a variety of previous jobs and had amassed an impressive list of job skills. For example, one individual listed skills of painting, mechanics, millwright (which he considered his trade), production work, supervision, car renovation, carpentry, electronics, computer programming, engineering, and chemistry. Another husband had creative skills in commercial art and design and had performed in a variety of jobs in this area, including owning his own business. Although this worker had a great many skills and a great deal of experience, he had health problems, felt emotionally stressed, and had considered divorce. Doubtless the amount of resources from which a person can draw may potentially increase the chances for reemployment, but the existence of skills has no straightforward link to adjustment.

The participants regarded contact with family and friends as a boon to their adjustment in some cases. For one father, the son provided encouragement. Both parents saw the financial crisis as allowing the father-son relationship to grow closer.

> "I've turned a lot on my son. He's only 6 years old ... He keeps me going. He helped me do some sanding on the table that I have in the bedroom ... When I'm thinking down, I think of him because he gives me a little initiative."

The wife, who was working, concurred with her husband's perspective and saw an added benefit to the father-son companionship at home.

> "He gets along really good when he's taking care of our son, for the last 2 weeks he was with him quite a bit and I would go to work and come home and . . . they'd be vacuuming, dusting . . . he does laundry and dishes . . . and now he understands how much there is to do."

Outside of the nuclear family, the couples reported little tangible aid from family in dealing with their stresses, unlike the useful role of network support reported in the literature (Elder, 1974; Jahoda et al., 1971). One couple received gifts from the wife's father, which caused considerable friction between the couple. The husband saw the aid as an insult:

> "At least when you give something to someone, it should be done so that a guy can feel good about it. It doesn't have to be with the idea that I'm not supporting her . . . I am, the best I can."

The wife reframed the support as gifts, and regarded the help as positive: "We're fortunate, my Dad helps. He's not going to let us starve . . . But he doesn't give us everything either, he helps out." She mentioned gifts of money and a VCR as examples. The way aid is given and received seems to affect whether gifts are viewed as a help to the family or as a point of conflict.

Contact and support from friends can be a help or a problem, depending on whether individuals feel shamed about their finances (Elder, 1974) and whether the social network is able to be supportive (Garbarino & Sherman, 1980). Only two couples reported extensive networks of mutually supportive friends. Other couples became isolated from friends or neighbors, either intentionally or incidentally, as leisure activities changed due to lack of money. One couple recognized that contact with people in their same predicament could be a drain: "You have to be around positive people. You can't be around negative people and expect to keep your own mood up" (husband). This couple, according to the wife, had adopted a strategy of keeping active in social life, in some form of work, in community life.

Most respondents experienced only minor health problems such as overeating, smoking too much, sleeping too much or too little, and feeling aches and pains.

Sometimes body aches were quite severe since many men were working at physical jobs and may have been aging or out of shape. Lack of health insurance was a problem noted by investigators and often recognized by families. If wives were employed full-time, their husbands were typically included in the health plan. If not, in more than half of the sample, families did not take out medical insurance. The cost was prohibitive. Often, husbands and wives were hoping they would not need the service. For several couples, an illness could potentially devastate the family's fragile position. One husband had a serious heart condition, yet was working at a physical job while taking night classes. Families seemed aware of the risks but could see little alternative.

Underemployed men often recalled their job loss as a time when they felt angry, hurt, and depressed. Some men still had such feelings, marking them as at risk for mental and physical health problems (Kasl & Cobb, 1977; Komarovsky, 1940; Liker & Elder, 1983; Root, 1977). Men whose marriage relationships were a source of support achieved a productive perspective on the situation, often perceiving something positive about it, perhaps changing their self-concept.

> "I probably have more of a desire to succeed than I've ever had. I've never had such a bulldoggish attitude as I do right now. I'd literally run over the top of the president of the company if that's what it took to make it go. I've never had that attitude before. Maybe it's being scared half to death and being unemployed or maybe it's just now that I'm older."

Some men regarded the job loss as giving them an opportunity they would not have exploited before. Many men talked about the high wages they had been making (some made more than $30,000 a year) as disincentives to career retraining.

> "I think in some ways it's probably been a blessing really . . . It's given me the opportunity to realize things, like going to school, looking into other careers, that I probably would never know if that place hadn't folded. I'd probably still be there. There are probably a lot of opportunities I wouldn't have looked into if it hadn't happened."

Challenged men may have blamed themselves, the company, or the economy for the cause of their situation. They recognized that some events are outside the control of any one person. But they accepted responsibility for what they could influence and control as they looked to change their economic misfortune.

Adaptive interpretation of the situation was associated with good marriage relationships. The couples who were able to achieve strong relationships often had survived a critical period in their marriage when acute tension from unresolved feelings and issues had surged. For two couples, an all-night session cleared the air. It was a time of crisis when the possibility of ending the relationship was high. Whether or not such a crisis occurred, challenged couples clarified personal direction, reestablished trust, improved communication, and redefined their relationships. Working through marital relationship problems, utilizing effective communication to deal with the loss of resources, was important (Lewis & Spanier, 1979). Some couples are so endangered by marital issues that underemployment is simply the final straw; marital therapy would be the most advantageous treatment for them. For couples who are not near the breaking point, an analysis of their coping strategies can help them identify areas of strength and areas that need work. The procedure used in the present study allowed individuals to explain in their own words how changes had occurred in their lives.

## Implications

The burden of underemployment cuts across many areas of family life. Respondents in this study expressed needs on three levels: individual, to evaluate resources and feelings about job changes; relational, to improve marital and family relationships, enabling them to be a source of strength for the underemployed; and ecological, to increase the family's ties to the community. Also, the economic consequences of underemployment might be ameliorated by concentration on strategies the family, and particularly the underemployed man, could use to change the current financial situation and to plan for the future.

The challenge in creating programs for rural underemployed families is in recognizing their ecological niche. The American rural population is more diverse than ever before. In addition to families who have always lived in the community, rural areas are increasingly inhabited by individuals from cities (Coward & Smith, 1984). These new rural dwellers have developed and used certain skills and qualities in their careers (e.g., financial management, flexibility, communication skills). Skills commonly found in traditional rural families include autonomy, ability to tailor and extend available assets, and dedication to privacy and family life (Coward & Smith, 1984).

The growing diversity of the rural population means that each family who may be faced with income loss possesses strength which could be shared for the benefit of others in the community. Using rural families in similar economic circumstances as resources and as trainers for each other enables them to exchange information and services. A program which allows people to explore their skills and abilities, a "life skills review," would be useful for encouraging workers and their spouses to recognize skills they have, including those developed through hobbies and in community college courses. Perhaps skills have been forgotten or have gotten "rusty." The variety of skills in any particular group could spark ideas for bartering and exchange of skills and resources. For example, one of the couples in this study had survived 5 years of hard times by exchanges of services. The strategy of sharing skills would take advantage of the natural helpers in the community (D'Augelli & Ehrlich, 1982), could help to integrate new members into the community, and might be more congruent with the pride and concern with autonomy evident among rural dwellers.

Financially, underemployed families operate on a much reduced budget. Few couples in the sample had prepared for their period of unemployment despite awareness that the layoff was coming. There is a need for financial management advice, evaluation of budget strengths and weaknesses, and career counseling beyond what is available for the unemployed person. Too often, in this sample, people did not consider their total skill package when looking for jobs, instead targeting their efforts to jobs much like their previous work. The intention would be to match their skills from the life skills review with areas of available jobs, and to encourage development of new skills through retraining and career counseling while the person is working at some job. The underemployed person, having found a job, commonly stops looking for ways to improve the financial situation. A frequent result is that the new job also goes under, and the underemployed person has not benefitted from the experience. Working on financial and ecological aspects of family living should provide underemployed people with renewed enthusiasm and skills to combat their employment predicament.

A program concerned with the effects of underemployment would be incomplete without some attention to family life. Because the rural underemployed are susceptible to stress, depression, and isolation, the marital relationship can be an important source of strength. The couples in this study who viewed underemployment as a challenge exhibited a sense of friendship and reported open communication. These characteristics were not easy to achieve when finances were strained. Couples should be encouraged to plan leisure activities and to consciously attend to time management. They can better manage their time and maintain enjoyable, active, even uplifting leisure activities that are inexpensive.

Most of the couples in this study reported no changes in marital power or decision making, perhaps reflecting the stability of marital patterns and the resistance to change on the part of the population. Nevertheless, a marriage relationship which is flexible enough to allow for changes in the wife's role and changes in the husband's role would be most adaptive in economic hard times. Wives may be employed, at least part-time, and husbands may be found at home more. In this situation, it would be beneficial if both spouses could participate in income-earning activities, in household maintenance work, and in child care.

Spending more time with family has been mentioned by the respondents, and in the literature, as a positive by-product to job loss (Elder, 1974; Komarovsky, 1940; Liem & Liem, 1979). When marital communication is open and family roles are relatively free of strain, when couples can interact positively with social supports and with their communities, then they can be in better positions to grow out of the underemployment experience. Changes in the country's economy away from production and certain industries are bound to produce underemployment for many people, at least for a temporary period. The challenge for researchers, family life educators, and public policy-makers is to explore and develop ways that families can make the most of changes in jobs and income.

## REFERENCES

Angell, R. C. (1936). *The family encounters the Depression.* New York: Charles Scribner's Sons.

Bakke, E. W. (1933). *The unemployed man: A social study.* London: Nisbet and Company, Ltd.

Berg, I., Freedman, M., & Freedman, M. (1978). *Managers and work reform: A limited engagement.* New York: Free Press.

Bruning, J. L., & Kintz, B. L. (1977). *Computational handbook of statistics.* Palo Alto, CA: Scott, Foresman and Company.

Budd, R. W., Thorp, R. K., & Donohew, L. (1967). *Content analysis of communication.* New York: Macmillan.

Burke, R. J. (1985). Consequences of not working sixteen months after a plant closing. *Industrial Relations, 40,* 162–169.

Burris, B. (1983). *No room at the top: Underemployment and alienation in the corporation.* New York: Praeger Press.

Cavan, R., & Ranck, K. H. (1938). *The family and the Depres sion.* Freeport, NY: Books for Libraries Press.

Clogg, C. C. (1979). *Measuring underemployment: Demographic indicators for the United States.* New York: Academic Press.

Coward, R., & Smith, W. (Eds.). (1984). *The family in rural society.* Boulder, CO: Westview Press.

D'Augelli, A., & Ehrlich, R. (1982). Evaluation of a community-based system for training natural helpers: II. Effects on informal helping activities. *American Journal of Community Psychology, 10,* 447–456.

Doherty, M., & Munro, B. (1986). *Work patterns of farm families.* Paper presented at the annual meeting of the National Council on Family Relations, Dearborn, MI.

Elder, G. H., Jr. (1974). *Children of the Great Depression.* Chicago: University of Chicago Press.

Ferguson, D. M., Horwood, L. J., & Beatrais, A. L. (1981). The measurement of family material well-being. *Journal of Marriage and the Family, 43,* 715–725.

Garbarino, J., & Sherman, D. (1980). High-risk families and high-risk neighborhoods. *Child Development, 51,* 188–198.

Glyde, G. P. (1977). Underemployment: Definition and causes. *Journal of Economic Issues, 11,* 245–260.

Gordon, D. M. (1972). *Theories of poverty and underemployment.* Lexington, MA: D. C. Heath and Company.

Gordus, J., Jarley, P., & Ferman, L. (1981). *Plant closings and economic dislocation.* Kalamazoo, MI: W. E. Upjohn Institute for Employment Research.

Hill, R. (1949). *Families in stress.* New York: Harper and Row.

Hill, R. (1958). Generic features of families under stress. *Social Casework, 49,* 139–150.

Jahoda, M., Lazarsfeld, P. F., & Zeisel, H. (1971). *Marienthal: The sociology of an unemployed community.* Chicago: Aldine-Atherton.

Kanter, R. (1977). *Work and the family in the United States: A critical review and agenda for research and policy.* New York: Russell Sage Foundation.

Kasl, S. V., & Cobb, S. (1977). *Termination: The consequences of job loss.* Cincinnati, OH: U.S. Department of Health, Education, and Welfare, Public Health Service.

Kerlinger, F. (1973). *Foundations of behavioral research.* New York: Holt, Rinehart & Winston.

Komarovsky, M. (1940). *The unemployed man and his family.* New York: Dryden.

Krippendorff, K. (1980). *Content analysis.* Beverly Hills, CA: Sage Publications.

Larson, J. H. (1984). The effect of husbands' unemployment on marital and family relations in blue-collar families. *Family Relations, 33,* 503–511.

Leff, W., & Haft, M. G. (1983). *Time without work: People who are not working tell their stories.* Boston: South End Press.

Levitan, S. A., & Taggart, R. (1974). *Employment and earnings inadequacy: A new social indicator.* Baltimore: The Johns Hopkins University Press.

Lewis, R. A., & Spanier, G. B. (1979). Theorizing about the quality and stability of marriage. In W. Burr (Ed.), *Contemporary theories about the family, Vol. 1* (pp. 268–294). New York: Free Press.

Liem, R. (1982). Unemployment and mental health implications for human service policy. In F. Redburn & T. Buss (Eds.), *Public policy for distressed communities* (pp. 201–257). Lexington, MA: D. C. Heath.

Liem, R., & Liem, J. H. (1979). Relations among social class, life events and mental illness: A comment on findings and methods. In B. S. Dohrenwend & B. P. Dohrenwend (Eds.), *Stressful life events and their contexts* (pp. 347–379). New Brunswick, NJ: Rutgers University Press.

Liker, J. L. & Elder, G. H., Jr. (1983). Economic hardship and marital relations in the 1930's. *American Sociological Review,* **48,** 343–359.

Mick, S. S. (1975). Social and personal costs of plant shutdowns. *Industrial Relations,* **14,** 203–207.

Moen, P. (1980). *Work-family linkages: Problems, payoffs and policy implications.* Paper presented at the annual meeting of the Society for the Study of Social Problems. New York: Department of Human Development and Family Studies, Cornell University.

Moen, P., Kain, E., & Elder, G. H., Jr. (1983). Economic condition and family life: Contemporary and historical perspectives. In R. Nelson & F. Skidmore (Eds.), *American families and the economy* (pp. 213–253). Washington, DC: National Academy Press.

Patterson, G. R. (1982). *Coercive family processes: A social learning approach.* Eugene, OR: Castalia Publishing Company.

Pleck, J. (1984). Work-family roles system. In P. Voydanoff (Ed.), *Work and family: Changing roles of men and women* (pp. 8–19). Palo Alto, CA: Mayfield Publishing Company.

Rathge, R., & Mammen, S. (1985). *Shifts in farm women's labor force patterns and their off-farm earnings.* Paper presented at the annual meeting of the National Council on Family Relations, Dallas, TX.

Root, K. (1977). *Perspectives for communities and organizations on plant closings and job dislocations.* Ames, IA: North Central Regional Center for Rural Development.

Rubin, L. (1976). *Worlds of pain.* New York: Basic Books.

Schiller, B. (1984). *The economics of poverty and discrimination.* Englewood Cliffs, NJ: Prentice-Hall.

Sullivan, T. A. (1978). *Marginal workers, marginal jobs: The underutilization of American workers.* Austin, TX: University of Texas Press.

Voydanoff, P. (1984). *Work and family: Changing roles of men and women.* Palo Alto, CA: Mayfield Publishing Company.

# Household, Paid, and Unpaid Work Time of Farm Women*

Jane E. Meiners and Geraldine I. Olson**

Across the United States the family farm enterprise has a large number of economic, environmental, and political pressures affecting its survival. The objective of this study is to examine the roles farm women play as part of the family farm enterprise. Of particular interest are work roles. Household work is the traditional primary work responsibility of farm women, yet household work allocations are affected by participation in paid (off-farm) work and unpaid (farm) work. In this triad of work roles, it is also important to consider how women's unpaid (farm) work is affected by paid (off-farm) work.

## History and Background

Patterns of *household work* include the total time spent on household work, the apportionment of time among various household work activities, and the times of day when household work is performed. Patterns of household work also vary according to the season of the year, the availability of other workers, and the standards that set the level

for a job well done. These household work patterns exist in every household, but the special nature of the farm household may result in a unique household work pattern.

Food preparation, house cleaning and maintenance, clothing care and construction, child care, shopping, and management are engaged in by all family members. However, women, whether farm or nonfarm, perform the bulk of this work (Fox & Nickols, 1983; Manning, 1968; Nickols & Metzen, 1978; Robinson, 1982). The amount of time women spend in household work has been remarkably stable. In studies from 1929 to the present, the household work hours of married nonemployed women have been estimated to range between 52 and 56 hours per week (Hefferan, 1982; Manning, 1968; Olson, 1982; Vanek, 1974; Wilson, 1929).

Women who live on farms are increasing their participation in *paid work* (off-farm). While the employment levels of nonfarm women have doubled in the last 50 years, the labor force participation rates for farm women have quadrupled (Scholl, 1983). In 1983, 46% of farm women were part of the labor force, while the rate for nonfarm women was 52% (Banks & Mills, 1984). Women's off-farm jobs tend to be in nonagricultural occupations, while the opposite is true for farm men.

The off-farm work patterns of farm husbands and wives influence each other. The effects of age, education, health, number of children, and other factors on off-farm work patterns are different for families where both husband and wife work off-farm,

*This research was supported by Oregon Agricultural Experiment Station and NE-113 Regional Research Project. Technical paper No. 8214.

**Jane E. Meiners is Assistant Professor, Department of Family Resource Management, College of Home Economics, Oregon State University, Corvallis, OR 97331. Geraldine I. Olson is Associate Professor and Department Head, Department of Family Resource Management, College of Home Economics, Oregon State University, Corvallis, OR 97331.

Reprinted from *Family Relations*, 1987, **36**, 407–411.

compared to families where only one spouse is employed off-farm (Huffman & Lange, 1985). A 1980 study of American farm women reports that if the husband is not employed off-farm, the wife is also less likely to be employed off-farm. If only one member of the farm is employed off-farm, it is twice as likely to be the husband. These differences are thought to be due to the differential in wages for men and women (Jones & Rosenfeld, 1981).

Because of growing interest in the emerging role of women on United States farms, attempts are being made to measure the participation of women in *unpaid work* (on-farm). In these studies, women are asked whether certain tasks are ever, never, or occasionally their responsibility (Boulding, 1980; Goetting, Fogle, & Howland, 1982; Jones & Rosenfeld, 1981; Nickols, 1980; Wilkening & Bharadwaj, 1966). There is agreement that the tasks most consistently assigned to women are taking care of a vegetable garden, farm bookkeeping, and running farm errands. In every study at least some women report field work, livestock care, equipment repair, building maintenance, crop or livestock transport, and supervisory or management activity.

Farm women believe that their participation in the farm work is of such a nature as to qualify them as one of the main operators of the farm (Jones & Rosenfeld, 1981). The majority of women report that help would have to be hired to replace them if they were incapacitated from farm work (Nickols, 1980). They believe they could run the operation, with hired help, if something were to happen to their husbands.

Particular attention is being directed to the interaction of household, paid, and unpaid work patterns of families. Of interest here are the interactions of household and paid (off-farm) work, household and unpaid (farm) work, and unpaid (farm) work and paid (off-farm) work. In research on nonfarm populations, it is well established that women reduce their time spent in household work in response to employment (Hall & Schroeder, 1970; Hefferan, 1982; Olson, 1982; Robinson, 1982; Vanek, 1974; Walker & Woods, 1976). The husbands and children of nonfarm women do not increase their household work if the wife/mother is employed outside the home (Fox & Nickols, 1983; Geerken & Gove, 1983; Walker, 1970). The household work of nonfarm men also responds negatively to in-

creased hours in their own employment (Abdel-Ghany & Nickols, 1983; Walker & Woods, 1976). Comparable analysis is not available for farm families.

There is anecdotal information about the ability of farm women to move flexibly between farm and household work (Nickols, 1980). However, the trade-offs between hours spent in farm and household work have not been studied.

There is no agreement on how farm work responds to off-farm work. While some studies indicate that employment off-farm reduces hours spent in farm work (Beaulieu & Molnar, 1985; Young & Caday, 1979), there is also evidence that engaging in both increases the total work load ("Women's Roles," 1982). Doing analysis with the same data base, Jones and Rosenfeld (1981) report that employed women were less involved in farm tasks, while Scholl (1983) indicates that employed women engage in the same amount of farm work as nonemployed women. There is agreement that when husbands take off-farm work, wives increase their farm hours (Boulding, 1980; Gasson, 1981; Jones-Webb & Nickols, 1984). There is also evidence that the marginal productivity of women's farm work hours can be considered equal to that of their off-farm wage (Huffman, 1976).

## Objectives

The objective of this research is to learn how farm women currently spend their time. Of particular interest is how farm women, in contrast to rural nonfarm women and urban women, apportion their time among the various household work activities. Also of interest is how women's household work time is influenced by time in paid and unpaid work and other factors, and how unpaid work is influenced by paid work and other factors.

## Methodology

The data for this research came from the Northeast Regional Research Project, *An Interstate Comparison of Urban/Rural Families' Time Use* (NE-113). Eleven states participated in the project: California, Connecticut, Louisiana, New York, North Carolina, Oklahoma, Oregon, Texas, Utah, Virginia, and Wisconsin. Each state used the same sample design in order to compare the results from one state to another (Sanik, 1979).

The design was a stratified random sample of two-parent, two-child families within rural and urban areas. Selecting only two-parent, two-child families helped to hold family composition constant so that other variables that affect time use could be examined more fully. Based on age of children, families were selected from each of five age strata: a younger child under the age of one, age one, ages 2 to 5, ages 6 to 11, and ages 12 to 17.

The urban sample in each state (n = 105) was drawn from a city of 100,000 or more and/or the places surrounding the city that had populations of 2,500 or more. The rural sample in each state (n = 105) was drawn from towns of less than 1,500 and farms and open country (including nonfarm residences). The total sample thus consists of 2,100 families, of which half are urban and the other half are rural (*Family Time Use,* 1981).

The farm population was identified by occupation. In this study, a farm woman either declared herself to be in a farming occupation *or* was married to a man who declared a farming occupation.

The instrument for the study was made up of two parts, a time diary and a questionnaire booklet. The diary was designed to allow each family member's time use to be recorded in 5-minute segments for a 24-hour period. Eighteen predetermined categories of time use were listed in the diary instrument. The 18 categories included 8 household production activities, 2 categories for care of family members, unpaid work, paid work, school activities, 2 categories of personal care, social and recreational activities, organizational participation, and other. Two days time use were recorded. For the first day, this time was recorded by the interviewer from the homemaker's recall of the previous day. On the second day the homemaker kept the time diary for all the members of the family who were over the age of six. For the present analysis the data from both days were combined and an average determined. The sample was selected in such a way that all days of the week in all seasons of the year were equally represented.

The amount of time spent per week in household work activities, unpaid work, paid work, school activities, organizational participation, personal care of self, social activities, and eating was determined as follows: The minutes spent in the activity for both days were added together. This sum was then divided by 2 to get a daily average. This average was then multiplied by 7 (days in a week). This estimate of number of minutes spent per week in the activity was then converted to hours per week.

In order to generalize from the sample to the population, the sample data were weighted to reflect the true proportions of various types of families in the population. The weights were derived from population figures in the 1970 census. They took into account the urban and rural population of each state relative to the total 11-state population for two-parent two-child families (3,173,947). Within the urban and rural samples for each state, there was a separate weight for each age strata. (See *Family Time Use,* 1981, for more information concerning the study.)

## Results

The typical farm woman in the sample was about 33 years old, had several years of education beyond high school, and was a full-time homemaker. She worked an average of 48.5 hours per week in the household, while rural nonfarm and urban women worked about 46 hours per week. These hours included women who reported no household work. The total number of hours of household work replicated previous research (Hefferan, 1982; Manning, 1968; Olson, 1982; Vanek, 1974).

The most time-consuming household task was food preparation and dishwashing. This activity accounted for about 31% (14.9 hours per week) of the farm woman's household work time, compared to 29% (13.2 hours per week) for rural nonfarm and 28% (12.9 hours per week) for urban women. Farm, rural nonfarm, and urban women allocated about 22% of household work time to housecleaning and maintenance of the home, yard, cars, and pets, and about 20% of their time to physical and nonphysical care of family members. This "child care" time was divided evenly between physical activities such as bathing and feeding and nonphysical activities such as talking and listening to children.

Other household work activities accounted for lesser proportions of women's work time. Twelve percent was accounted for by laundry and sewing activities and 13% by shopping. Management represented the smallest proportion of household work time, a little over 4% in all three groups. Management may have been underrepresented because it was often carried on in conjunction with other activities (Walker & Woods, 1976).

One-way analysis of variance and Scheffe's test were used to test for significant differences between the groups (farm, rural nonfarm, urban) in time women allot to household work. There were no significant differences among the three groups of women in the amount of time spent in any category of household work. In 1929, Wilson found no evidence to indicate that the household work patterns of farm women were unique compared to rural nonfarm or urban women. Fifty years later, the present study documents the continued consistency of household work patterns for farm, rural nonfarm, and urban women.

## Time in Unpaid and Paid Work and Other Activities

Unpaid work was "work or service done either as a volunteer or as an unpaid worker for relatives, friends, family business or farm, social, civic, or community organizations" (Family Time Use, 1981, p. 86). Farm women spent a mean of 5.38 hours per week in unpaid work (the range was 0 to 72 hours per week); rural nonfarm women spent a mean of 3.05 hours and urban women a mean of 3.01 hours (F = 2.834, p = .059). Farm women spent more time in unpaid work than did urban or rual nonfarm women (Scheffe p < .10). Although the data do not permit a definitive answer, it is possible that farm women allocated more time to unpaid work because of the opportunity to do farm work.

Farm women worked an average of 8.4 hours per week for pay; this activity represented 5% of their total work week. Ten per-

cent of the farm women were engaged in paid work as farm laborers. Rural nonfarm women worked for pay about 15 hours per week and urban women 11.5 hours. The differences in paid work time among the three groups were significant at the .01 level (F = 6.170). Rural women's hours were significantly higher than urban women's (Scheffe p < .05), but farm women were not significantly lower in their hours of paid work.

In other activities, farm women reported that they devoted 5.43 hours per week to organizational participation, compared to 3.23 for rural nonfarm and 2.37 for urban (F = 10.770, p = .001) women. Farm women's time was significantly higher than both rural and urban women, and rural women spent more time in organizational activities than did urban women (Scheffe p < .05). Social and recreational activity took up a large proportion of every woman's week: almost 18% of the week's time for urban women, 17% for rural nonfarm women, and about 16% for farm women.

Because personal care of self included sleep, more than one third of women's weekly hours were consumed in personal care. Differences in time in social and personal care activity among the three groups of women were not significant. Time spent eating significantly varied across the three groups (F = 8.220, p = .001). The mean of 8.65 hours spent by urban women in eating was significantly higher (Scheffe p < .05) than the 7.78 mean hours rural nonfarm women spent eating. Farm women's eating time (8 hours) was not significantly different from the other groups.

## Regression Analysis

Regression analysis was used to deter-

Table 1.
*Multiple Stepwise Regression of Selected Variables on Hours Spent in Household Work by Farm Women (n = 50)[a]*

| Independent Variables | Estimated Beta | Standardized E | F | Significance Level | $R^2$[b] |
|---|---|---|---|---|---|
| Hours in paid work | −.49 | .12 | 15.60 | .000 | .240 |
| Hours in unpaid work | −.47 | .29 | 2.66 | .110 | .306 |
| Income | −.13 | .11 | 1.52 | .225 | .347 |
| Age of the younger child | −.66 | .31 | 4.48 | .040 | .369 |
| Age of woman | .09 | .05 | 3.30 | .076 | .414 |
| Education | .03 | .15 | .03 | .864 | .414 |

[a]Weighted.
[b]Adjusted $R^2$ = .333.

mine whether certain variables could explain variation in time spent in household and unpaid work. The dependent variables were time used in household work and time used in unpaid (farm) work. Separate regression equations were run for farm, rural nonfarm, and urban women.

For each dependent variable, the independent variables tested were: (a) paid work time, (b) family income, (c) age, (d) education level, and (e) age of the younger child. Unpaid work was an additional independent variable when household work was the dependent variable; likewise household work served as an independent variable when unpaid work was the dependent variable. The independent variables were chosen because they had demonstrated predictive power in other research (Nickols & Metzen, 1978; Walker & Woods, 1976). The stepwise multiple regression procedure contained in Statistical Package for the Social Sciences (SPSS) was used for this analysis (Nie, Hull, Jenkins, Steinbrenner, & Bent, 1975).

The results of the regression analysis for the dependent variable "time used in household work by farm women" are presented in Table 1. The variable was derived by summing the hours women spent in all categories of household work. About 33% of the variation in household work time was explained by the six independent variables (F = 5.07, p = .001). The women's hours in paid employment accounted for most of the explained variation. This finding was consistent with other studies of household work of urban women (Hall & Schroeder, 1970; Nickols & Metzen, 1978; Walker & Woods, 1976); it appears to be applicable for farm women as well. Interpretation of the Beta value revealed that for every hour the woman allocated to paid employment, she allocated about half an hour less to household work.

Hours in unpaid work in the family farm or business added another 7% to explained variance. However, the Beta value for unpaid work was not significant; thus, it cannot be estimated from this analysis how farm women might adjust their household work time in response to time in unpaid work.

The six independent variables explained about 36% of the variance in both rural nonfarm (F = 44.767, p = .001) and urban (F = 150.538, p = .001) women's total household work time (Tables 2 and 3). As with farm women, hours in paid work accounted for most of the explanation of the variance. For every hour rural nonfarm and urban women

Table 2.
*Multiple Stepwise Regression of Selected Variables on Hours Spent in Household Work by Rural Nonfarm Women (n = 389)[a]*

| Independent Variables | Estimated Beta | Standardized E | F | Significance Level | $R^2$[b] |
|---|---|---|---|---|---|
| Hours in paid work | −.52 | .04 | 169.53 | .000 | .361 |
| Hours in unpaid work | −.42 | .11 | 14.66 | .000 | .347 |
| Age of the younger child | −.27 | .10 | 7.78 | .006 | .364 |
| Income | −.12 | .07 | 3.07 | .081 | .368 |
| Education | .03 | .07 | .26 | .607 | .369 |

[a]Weighted.
[b]Adjusted $R^2$ = .361.

Table 3.
*Multiple Stepwise Regression of Selected Variables on Hours Spent in Household Work by Urban Nonfarm Women (n = 1,534)[a]*

| Independent Variables | Estimated Beta | Standardized E | F | Significance Level | $R^2$[b] |
|---|---|---|---|---|---|
| Hours in paid work | −.49 | .02 | 585.60 | .000 | .275 |
| Age of the younger child | −.60 | .05 | 124.76 | .000 | .343 |
| Hours in unpaid work | −.36 | .06 | 41.63 | .000 | .357 |
| Age of woman | .05 | .01 | 24.55 | .000 | .366 |
| Income | −.12 | .34 | 13.46 | .000 | .372 |
| Education | .01 | .03 | .13 | .718 | .372 |

[a]Weighted.
[b]Adjusted $R^2$ = .369.

allotted to unpaid work, rural nonfarm women reduced their household work by 25 minutes and urban women reduced household work by 22 minutes.

When the unpaid work of farm women was the dependent variable in the regression equation, neither hours of paid employment nor household work affected the variation (Table 4). Because the Betas were not significant, neither paid employment nor household work are related to a consistent increase or decrease in the hours allotted to unpaid work.

In contrast, rural nonfarm women appear to have varied their unpaid work hours in response to both paid and household work demands (Table 5). For every hour these women spent in paid work, they reduced unpaid work by 6 minutes; for every hour they spent in household work, they reduced unpaid work by 5 minutes. However, it is important to note that rural nonfarm women reduced household work time in response to paid and unpaid work by many more minutes than they were willing to reduce unpaid work time in response to paid and household work time (Table 2). Half an hour of household work was "given up" for an hour of paid work and 25 minutes of housework for an hour of

unpaid work. In contrast, unpaid work was reduced by only 6 and 5 minutes respectively for every hour spent in paid work and household work. In general, the level of explained variation of unpaid work accounted for by the six independent variables was low (adjusted $R^2 = .060$, F = 5.093, p = .001). The results for urban women (not shown) were similar to those for rural nonfarm women.

## Implications

Household work appears to be a demanding set of tasks that require about the same amount of time regardless of urban, rural, or farm residence. Although it may seem that the farm household work load is a heavy one, it may actually be the unresponsiveness of unpaid (farm) work to other work demands that creates a unique situation for farm women.

This research demonstrates that farm women use more time for unpaid work (some of which presumably is farm work) than do rural nonfarm or urban women. Furthermore, regression analysis indicates that while urban and rural women reduce their household work by approximately 20 minutes for each hour that they spend in unpaid work, the

Table 4.
*Multiple Stepwise Regression of Selected Variables on Hours Spent in Unpaid Work by Farm Women (n = 50)*[a]

| Independent Variables | Estimated Beta | Standardized E | F | Significance Level | $R^2$[b] |
|---|---|---|---|---|---|
| Hours in household work | −.12 | .08 | 2.66 | .110 | .057 |
| Hours in paid work | −.10 | .07 | 1.79 | .188 | .088 |
| Education | .07 | .07 | .97 | .330 | .106 |
| Age of the younger child | .06 | .17 | .15 | .705 | .125 |
| Income | .03 | .05 | .35 | .558 | .130 |
| Age of woman | .01 | .03 | .19 | .662 | .134 |

[a]Weighted.
[b]Adjusted $R^2 = .013$.

Table 5.
*Multiple Stepwise Regression of Selected Variables on Hours Spent in Unpaid Work by Rural Nonfarm Women (n = 389)*[a]

| Independent Variables | Estimated Beta | Standardized E | F | Significance Level | $R^2$[b] |
|---|---|---|---|---|---|
| Hours in paid work | −.10 | .02 | 22.37 | .000 | .017 |
| Hours in household work | −.09 | .02 | 14.62 | .000 | .062 |
| Age of the younger child | .09 | .06 | 2.17 | .141 | .073 |
| Education | .02 | .03 | .46 | .498 | .074 |
| Income | −.01 | .03 | .09 | .763 | .074 |
| Age of woman | .003 | .01 | .08 | .781 | .074 |

[a]Weighted.
[b]Adjusted $R^2 = .060$.

household work time of farm women is not directionally influenced by their unpaid work. Nor do farm women reduce unpaid work in response to paid work, as do both rural nonfarm and urban women.

Farm women do reduce their household work time in response to paid work (as do rural nonfarm and urban women). It therefore appears that, for farm women, choosing to spend time in paid work is balanced by reductions in the household work load, but choosing to spend time in unpaid (farm) work may be an addition to the total work load. It also seems that household work responds more flexibly to demands for paid and unpaid time, rather than vice versa.

It is not clear why farm women are willing to reduce their household work time in response to paid work, but not in response to unpaid work. If unpaid farm work is engaged in irrespective of household work and/or paid work, it may be due to the pressing demand for labor contributions on the farms and ranches where the women engage in farm work. Perhaps farm work is perceived as an immediate demand (hungry calves must be fed "now"), while household tasks are perceived as work that can be put off for later. The cost/price squeeze of some farming enterprises may demand the labor inputs of family members, in addition to the members' involvement in other productive activities.

Future research should investigate how the financial status of the farm/ranch enterprise affects the woman's level of participation in farm work. Do women contribute more farm hours when the enterprise is financially stressed? Do women substitute for hired labor in such situations? Or, in the face of financial stress, do women decrease farm hours and increase off-farm work hours in order to contribute dollars rather than direct labor to the enterprise? How do men's and women's work activities and hours interrelate? Rural labor outmigration, declining birth rates, and the supply of paid employment should also be examined for their effect on the unpaid farm work hours of farm women.

Because unpaid work may be underrepresented in this sample, due to a lower than expected number of interviews for the farm sample during the May-August period, future research should carefully measure the season variable. Another important refinement would be to separate unpaid farm work from other forms of unpaid work, such as community volunteer work.

The importance of unpaid and paid work in the household work regression equations emphasizes the interdependence of the household and market sphere. Although one's farm or nonfarm residence does not seem to affect time spent in household work, labor force participation is related to a reduction of household work time. How such reduction occurs is partly explained in other research; reductions appear to be evenly spaced throughout the categories of household work (Walker & Woods, 1976).

A subject for further investigation is whether household production is reduced by substituting market equivalents (eating out, professional laundry, etc.), or by changing the goals and/or standards of family members, or some of both. Since farm families are more likely to be geographically separated from some of the market substitutions for production, their reductions in household work time are more likely to be changes in family standards and goals. When the farm woman spends her morning working in town as a bookkeeper, the trade-offs may be an unbaked apple pie, an unpatched pair of blue jeans, or a story not read to the 3-year-old. These trade-offs would affect the farm family's decision to concentrate efforts in household production, off-farm employment, or farm production. Measures of family awareness of the trade-offs would contribute to decision-making theory.

The results of this research have implications for organizations and governmental agencies that plan programs for farm audiences. It is critical for such groups to recognize the wide variation in level of participation in farm enterprises by farm women. Many women in this sample report no time spent in unpaid family farm work. Yet others report spending 40 hours or more per week. Acknowledgement of this variation can help avoid stereotypes about women's level of work.

Women's contributions to farm enterprises could be increased by efforts to provide farm and financial management information geared especially to women. The value of women's labor to the farm enterprise could be greater than the benefits of off-farm employment. This could occur when outside work opportunities are constrained by her education, skills, and the job market.

The similarity of farm, rural nonfarm,

and urban women's household work roles suggests that professionals may use existing urban data as the basis for calculating the dollar value of farm women's household work. This information is suitable for use in liability suits involving the loss of farm women's household services, but further research is required before recommendations can be made regarding the value of the unpaid farm work of farm women. The authors are engaged in a follow-up study which measures labor contributions of husbands and wives to farm enterprise activities. The study should shed light on time spent in specific farm activities by both husbands and wives and the family's goals for participating in both on and off-farm work.

## REFERENCES

Abdel-Ghany, M., & Nickols, S. Y. (1983). Husband/wife differentials in household work time: The case of dual-earner families. *Home Economics Research Journal, 12*, 159–167.

Banks, V. J., & Mills, K. M. (1984). *Farm population of the United States: 1983* (Current Population Reports, Series P-27, No. 57). Washington, DC: Bureau of the Census.

Beaulieu, L. J., & Molnar, J. J. (1985). Community change and the farm sector: Impacts of rural development on agriculture. *The Rural Sociologist, 5*, 15–22.

Boulding, E. (1980). The labor of U.S. farm women: A knowledge gap. *Sociology of Work and Occupations, 7*, 261–290.

*Family time use: An eleven-state urban/rural comparison.* (1981). (Bulletin VPI-2). Blacksburg, VA: Virginia Tech, Extension Distributions.

Fox, K. D., & Nickols, S. Y. (1983). The time crunch: Wife's employment and family work. *Journal of Family Issues, 4*, 61–82.

Gasson, R. (1981). Roles of women on farms: A pilot study in England and Wales. *Journal of Agriculture Economics, 32*, 11–20.

Geerken, M., & Gove, W. R. (1983). *At home and at work: The family's allocation of labor.* Beverly Hills, CA: Sage Publications.

Goetting, M., Fogle, V. F., & Howland, S. S. (1982). *The farm and ranch wife's economic contribution to the agricultural business* (Bulletin No. 1275). Bozeman: Montana State University, Cooperative Extension Service.

Hall, F. T., & Schroeder, M. (1970). Effects of family and housing characteristics on time spent on household tasks. *Journal of Home Economics, 62*, 23–29.

Hefferan, C. (1982). Workload of married women. *Family Economics Review*, No. 3, pp. 10–15.

Huffman, W. E. (1976). The value of the productive time of farm wives: Iowa, North Carolina, and Oklahoma. *American Journal of Agricultural Economics, 58*, 836–841.

Huffman, W. E., & Lange, M. D. (1985, February). *Off-farm work decisions of husbands and wives: Joint decision making.* Paper presented at Agricultural Conference Days, Corvallis, OR.

Jones, C., & Rosenfeld, R. A. (1981). *American farm women: Findings from a national survey.* Chicago: National Opinion Research Center.

Jones-Webb, J., & Nickols, S. Y. (1984, May/June). Programming for modern farm women. *Journal of Extension*, pp. 16–22.

Manning, S. L. (1968). *Time use in household tasks by Indiana families* (Bulletin No. 837). West Lafayette, IN: Purdue University Agricultural Experiment Station.

Nickols, S. Y. (1980, October). *Women on the farm: Economic roles and life satisfaction.* Paper presented at the annual conference of the Southcentral Women's Studies Association, Arlington, TX.

Nickols, S Y., & Metzen, E. J. (1978). Housework time of husband and wife. *Home Economics Research Journal, 7*, 85–97.

Nie, N. H., Hull, C. H., Jenkins, J. G., Steinbrenner, R., & Bent, D. H. (1975). *Statistical package for the social sciences* (2nd ed.). New York: McGraw-Hill.

Olson, G. I. (1982). The effect of homemakers employment level and age level of the youngest child on time use in two-parent, two-child families. *Proceedings of the 22nd Annual Western Regional Home Management-Family Economics Educators Conference*, pp. 96–99, Portland, OR.

Robinson, J. P. (1982). Of time, dual careers, and household productivity. *Family Economics Review*, No. 3, pp. 26–30.

Sanik, M. M. (1979). A two-fold comparison of time spent in household work in two-parent, two-child households: Urban New York State in 1967-68 and 1977; urban-rural New York-Oregon in 1977 (Doctoral dissertation, Cornell University, 1979). *Dissertation Abstracts International, 39*, 5334B-5335B.

Scholl, K. K. (1983). Farm women's triad of roles. *Family Economics Review*, No. 1, pp. 10–15.

Vanek, J. (1974). Time spent in housework. *The Scientific American, 11*, 116–120.

Walker, K. (1970, June). Time used by husbands for household work. *Family Economics Review*, pp. 8–11.

Walker, K. E., & Woods, M. E. (1976). *Time use: A measure of household production of family goods and services.* Washington, DC: American Home Economics Association, Center for the Family.

Wilkening, E. A., & Bharadwaj, L. K. (1966). *Aspirations, work roles, and decision making patterns of farm husbands and wives in Wisconsin.* Wisconsin Agriculture Experiment Station Bulletin 266.

Wilson, M. (1929). *Use of time by Oregon farm homemakers.* Oregon Agriculture Experiment Station Bulletin 256.

Women's roles in North American farms (1982, July). Conference sponsored by the Equity Policy Center, Racine, WI. In *Women and Food Information Network Newsletter* (1983, December/January), No. 7, pp. 1–3. (Available from Office of International Agriculture, University of Arizona, Tucson, AZ.)

Young, J. A., & Caday, P. (1979). *Small scale farming: A portrait from Polk County, Oregon* (Paper No. 2). Corvallis, OR: Western Rural Development Center.

# 15

# Time Use in Rural Home-Working Families

Betty A. Beach*

Time is a precious commodity to working parents. Time pressures emerge repeatedly as stressors in fulfilling work and family responsibilities, whether in large scale surveys (General Mills, 1981) or in smaller interview studies (Kamerman, 1980). Consequently, many studies, recognizing "time" as a key ingredient in work/family relations, have focused on some aspect of time use: general studies of time allocation to work and household duties, effects of work schedules on families (e.g., Staines & Pleck, 1983), or impacts of work-schedule innovation on family life (Bohen & Viveros-Long, 1981). Implicit in most of these articles is the use of time as a finite tool of analysis, readily quantifiable and a scarce resource to be allocated. Staines and Pleck (1983) summarize the principal threads of time research as related to family life, noting that "the common denominator of time and its use becomes a way of linking work and family roles both theoretically and empirically" (p. 5). Accordingly, "work time" stands as a metaphor for nonfamily time, whether the subject of investigation is shift work, work schedules, or the allocation of play time by working mothers.

Conceptualizing time as a discrete entity, divisible into segmented units to be allotted to work, family or other uses, most studies suggest that negative outcomes for families derive from work time's standard rigidity: A block of uniform work hours creates a preserve of time, energy, and space inaccessible to family needs. Even investigations of work schedule flexibility (e.g., flex-time) assume the use of time as a finite tool of analysis, readily quantifiable, a scarce resource to be allocated. Scant attention is given to the possibility that time is not always discrete, measurable, and apportionable.

But what about alternative conceptions of time? The implicit assumption that "work time" is a discrete block, a preserve unavailable to family, permeates most of the literature. Intrinsically, a dichotomy exists between "work time" and "family time." Accordingly, researchers look at how families allot their time to one or the other sphere, an approach which may indeed represent reality for urban working families whose lives must be structured around fairly uniform work patterns dictated by industrial or institutional employers.

Rural families, however, participate in an economy quite distinct from that of their urban counterparts. Urban economies present a diverse range of employment opportunities, while "rural economies are generally simple, characterized by one or two major industries, either natural-resource based nondurable manufacturing, or tourism," a restricted range of work opportunities at the unskilled or semi-skilled level further limited by "seasonal production and the economic cycles which these industries experience" (Teal, 1981, p. 28). Rural families, lacking the range of choices available to urban families, experience a different work context. Rather than automatically entering the workplace,

*Betty A. Beach is Assistant Professor in the Department of Elementary, Secondary and Early Childhood Education at the University of Maine, Farmington, ME 04938.

Reprinted from *Family Relations*, 1987, **36**, 412–416.

rural families often patch together an array of diverse work options; in parts of rural Maine, occasional factory jobs supplemented by seasonal part-time work as blueberry pickers, woods workers, Christmas wreath makers, and clam diggers are common examples. Also typical of such alternative arrangements are "microbusinesses":

> The economies of many rural areas are still made up of thousands of micro-businesses: cottage industries; one- or two-person service firms; low-volume and seasonal shops; labor-intensive manufacturing operations out of kitchens, barns and sheds; small specialized mail-order outfits; artisans and crafters; and small-scale agriculture. (Teal, 1981, p. 28)

Information on these small-scale enterprises so familiar to rural residents is sketchy, particularly compared with the wealth of data examining work and family relationships among employees of large corporations and institutions more representative of urban areas. Many potential distinctions between these two work settings can be explored, including the fundamental issue of time use. Do rural families in these home-based enterprises experience work time as a discrete entity, a bundle of minutes to be allocated exclusively to either work or family? Data from farm families suggest that time is not so readily divisible; Vanek's (1980) examination of time budget data from several earlier studies of rural families indicated that work, family, and leisure time and roles were indeed integrated rather than compartmentalized throughout the day for men and women, that work time was not always distinct from family time, or segregated from other uses. Boulding's (1980) examination of the labor of farm women emphasized variability in time use, suggesting that seasonal cycles and life-cycle rhythms markedly affect labor patterns among these women, resulting in diversity rather than uniformity of work time.

Historical studies, lending perspective, also caution against the presumption of a "standard" experience of work time. Before industrialization, "pre-modern" concepts of time prevailed rather than contemporary standardized notions; work time was dictated by the task at hand rather than an artificial structure of time. As men entered the modernizing public workplace, however, time was redefined; no longer irregular, seasonal, subject to personal or natural rhythms, it became routinized, standardized, and allocated into work units governed by mechanical timepieces. This transformation of time from pre-modern "task" orientation to modern, disciplined "time" orientation was described by E. P. Thompson (1967) who noted one of its outcomes—"a clear demarcation between 'work' and 'life' " (p. 93). Undoubtedly, industrialization has transformed Western culture—change in the concept of time is but one example—but the pervasiveness of such change may be uneven. In rural areas without a history of extensive industrialization, lacking a large number of industrial employers or centralized workplaces, might some families experience "work time" in alternate ways? If so, what would these "different" experiences imply for family life, vocational education, and the application of work/family research findings to rural families?

This study explores one thread of those potential differences: rural families' experiences of work time. Specifically, it investigates how home-working families engaged in the "microbusinesses" common to rural areas allocate time. It employs qualitative methods to investigate families generally ignored in the literature on work and family, and to explore a potential area of diversity. It then suggests implications for family and education professionals resulting from its findings.

## Method

### Participants

Fifteen home workers and their families participated in this study (a total of 30 adults and 27 children). To meet the criteria for participation, all workers were members of intact families in which there was at least one child under age 18 residing at home. All were residents of two rural counties in Maine.

Identifying and contacting potential participants presented special problems. Families working at home are usually self-selected and independent of membership in associations relating to their employment; they cannot be easily contacted through any group membership. (The dearth of studies on this group may reflect their inaccessibility to investigators.) At the time of the study, the

Bureau of Economic Analysis and Research of the Maine Department of Labor reported no statistics on home work, and no knowledge of home workers' gender, number, occupations, and so forth, due to their individuality. The U.S. Census Bureau does offer rough parameters on numbers through a long form 1980 census question on work commuting patterns in which 555 home workers were projected in one of the Maine counties under study out of a total labor force of 12,108. There is no further information available on actual number of hours worked, sex of home workers, income, nature of employment, and so forth.

To work around the accessibility issue, a snowball sample was used. Snowball sampling (Herriott & Firestone, 1983) can be utilized effectively when there is no claim to representativeness or randomness, and the sample can be checked against demographic data for comparison with the general population. It may also be an especially appropriate technique in small rural communities where personalized knowledge of residents is common. Using a snowball method, a total of 17 families were contacted by phone or mail to ask their willingness to participate. Two families were unable to do so, principally because not all family members could agree to be interviewed and/or observed. The 15 families who initially agreed to participate remained with the study throughout the 6 months of data collection; there were no drop-outs.

Participants included nine female and six male home workers representing the following occupations: day care provider, machine knitter (4), mechanic, chef, seamstress, flytier, hairdresser, translator, cabinetmaker, veterinarian, fine art dealer, and secretary. One third of the group held a baccalaureate degree or higher, while two thirds ranged from 9 years of high school to some postsecondary (usually vocational) training. Ages ranged from 27 to 50, with most home workers being in their 30s.

## Procedure

This study employed a combination of methods in an exploratory effort dealing both with subjects and work patterns without substantial precedent in family literature. Time use data reported here were part of a larger study on the work and family lives of home-working families. Data were gathered and input sought from *all* family members. While the identified "prime" participant was the home worker ($n = 15$), the full N of the study was 57 adults and children from whom data were gathered. The following methodology was employed:

1. Semistructured interviews with adults. A semistructured interview was held jointly with both adult family members, or individually where required by other constraints. It consisted of two parts: (a) a Demographic Data Sheet and (b) Family Work Interview. Questions dealt with how homeworking families organize their work day. Interviews were tape recorded and transcribed.

2. Naturalistic observation of the work/family process. Each family was observed twice, 2 hours per day, on a typical work day designated by the worker. Field notes (literal observational accounts) were taken during observation to increase reliability. Qualitative analysis (Schatzman & Strauss, 1973) of these field notes was undertaken to determine important themes and to triangulate data (Guba, 1981).

3. Structured interviews with verbal children. Two forms were employed, depending on age of child. Both forms were aimed at determining the child's understanding of the parent's work. Interviews were tape recorded and transcribed.

4. Daily time logs (two per family) were requested from each family. Each home worker received instructions and forms for reporting incidents of work/family interaction during an entire day. These logs were quantified for number of such interactions, amount of time, and nature. Such log keeping provided a quantifiable check on information regarding time use obtained through interview and observational data.

## Analysis

Qualitative research frequently employs "triangulation" (Guba, 1981) in an effort to cross check data; that is, data obtained from several sources or methods are cross checked to confirm, extend or question findings. Analysis in this study triangulated data regarding time use among homeworking families in the following manner:

1. Interviews were coded for reports of time use (i.e., daily work schedules reported, typical patterns of work, etc.).

2. Observations—Observational notes, taken during the home worker's self-designated "work time" were coded for specific

Table 1.
*Mean Number, Duration, and Nature of Interruptions to Workday by Sex: Log Analysis*

| Sex of Worker | Number | Interruptions Duration (in minutes) | Nature | |
|---|---|---|---|---|
| Men (*n* = 4)    8 logs | 4 | 45.5 | 2.1 | Household |
| | | | .7 | Tend to Child |
| | | | .5 | Errand |
| | | | .5 | Leisure |
| Women (*n* = 7) 14 logs | 7 | 32 | 4.8 | Household |
| | | | 1.3 | Tend to Child |
| | | | .6 | Leisure |
| | | | .1 | Errand |

number and nature of interruptions to that work time.

3. Logs—26 daily logs were returned, of which 22 were analyzable. Logs were quantified for hours worked, interruptions to work, and individual variability in work schedule.

## Results

### Logs

Analysis of the logs produced two striking characteristics of home workers' work day:

1. *Lack of a standard work day:* The reported total work day ranged from a low of 2 hours 50 minutes to 11 hours 50 minutes. (These figures are the reported parameters of the work day, that is, everything encompassed between the "start work for the day" time and the "stop work for the day" time.) This inconsistency in hours also applied to individuals as well as to the group: No individual reported the same work schedule on 2 days.

Also varying were the starting and stopping times; the earliest reported "start work" time was 6:00 a.m.; the latest reported "stop work" time was 11:00 p.m. Starting and stopping times for the group ranged within those figures, with most people finishing anywhere between 2:30 and the evening hours.

Actual number of hours spent on the work task within these parameters were more difficult to determine since every worker reported interruptions to his/her work day. Subtracting reported "nonwork" activities occurring within the work day from "work" activities resulted in a range of actual hours worked from a low of 170 minutes (2.8 hours) to a high of 810 minutes (13.5 hours). The average reported work time was 404 minutes (6.73 hours) per person. Though this reported

work time is less than the proverbial 8-hour day, several cautions must be employed in interpreting such results: (a) These logs are based on precise individual reports which naturally vary with the individual's dutifulness (one log delineated a 10-minute visit to the outhouse). (b) Most data on work day length results from aggregate, estimated time rather than accurate individual timekeeping; such large scale surveys mask variability in individual interpretation and accuracy of work time data. (c) Several participants in this sample reported doing additional work in the evening, simultaneously watching TV, visiting with friends, talking with children, and so forth, but do not report this as "work time." One respondent reported her work day as extending from 7:30 a.m. to 4:00 p.m. but added the comment: "I generally work during the evening starting around 7:30 p.m. ending anywhere from 10:00 p.m. to 11:00 p.m. I find that this is more of a 'jumping jack' period than during the days."

2. *Work days punctuated by interruptions:* In interviews, all workers reported interruptions to their work days, whether for personal or family chores. Logs were analyzed for the number of interruptions to the reported work day, length, and nature of such interruptions (see Table 1).

Initial working conclusions reached from analysis of logs indicate great variability among participants in work time use, evidenced across number of hours worked, daily work schedule, and interruptions to work day. For these participants, there was no approximation of a prototypical work day, with the concept of a straightforward, uninterrupted 8-hour work block irrelevant to their experience. Thus, strictly quantitative findings from logs suggest that time use among these families may indeed differ from the more common experiences of conventionally employed workers. However satisfactory such quantitative findings appear, a real deficiency exists in the log method's inability to capture what one female home worker characterized as the "real" work of women: the constant, ongoing interaction with children who are present while their parents work. One woman acknowledged this difficulty in comments on her log: "None of this (reported work day) includes 'dogs and cats' duty as well as 'little calls for help' from Darcy." The difficulty of measuring ongoing simultaneous activities has been acknowledged by other researchers, particularly in the study of housework (Berk & Berk, 1979). To provide a check against findings about time use from the logs, observational data were compared for insights.

## Observations

A critical function of the observations was to penetrate the facade of "work time" reported by participants in logs. All observations occurred during the worker's self-defined work time and thus might be expected to portray exclusively work activities. While all log reporters had been able to ascribe certain amounts of time to work activities in a straightforwardly measurable manner, observations of their self-designated work times revealed that this allocation was not nearly as monolithic or discrete as numerical reports might promise. Of 30 observations, only one displayed no interruptions to work activity during the 2-hour period. Interruptions fell readily into 6 categories, the distribution of which is listed as follows (30 observations/15 participants):

Tend to child: 127 occurrences
Household chore: 34 occurrences
Break/relax: 21 occurrences
Phone conversation (nonbusiness): 8 occurrences
Shortened work time (e.g., stopping early to greet visitors or children arriving home from school): 6 occurrences
Spouse business (messages or phone calls in support of spouse's work): 6 occurrences

Clearly, indications are that "work time" encompasses significant amounts of non-work activities which do not appear in log form. The bulk of interruptions are for child tending, an excerpted example of which follows (an example of one coded tending):

(Mother, a seamstress, is stuffing a crib mattress at the table)
2:20 p.m. Darcy (age 4 female) comes to table, "Is my Uncle James a cowboy?"
Mother: "Cowboys don't just ride horses. They also take care of cows. Your daddy's a cowboy."
Darcy scrapes her carrot on the table, mother asks her to stop.
"NO!"—Darcy drops some paper on the floor, needs to be coerced into picking it up, and then wants some hugging. She sits in her mother's lap, hugs, they make up. Darcy looks at the mattress fabric, "Those are pretty flowers. What are they?"
Mother: "Rosebuds"—they look at leaves and flowers together, talk about colors. Mother says: "If you go find a short book, I'll read it to you. A *short* one." (They read for the ensuing 20 minutes).

Such vignettes provide a flavor of how a work-at-home parent might interrupt his/her work time to tend to a child. Naturally, these interruptions (what one parent labelled "little calls for help") went unrecorded in logs since they occurred during work time. Observations proved to be a necessary tool for digging behind a self-defined work time which already had indicated variability in log reports. Counts during observation periods indicated that men performed 5.28 child tendings per each 2-hour period and women 6.92.

Although child tendings represented the bulk of interruptions to "work time" in observations, household chores were also performed. A total of 34 chores were noted over 30 observations, in the following breakdown: food preparation (11), stoke fires (7), laundry (3), pet care (3), yard work (1), dishes (1), plant seeds (1), sort mail (1), wash car (1), miscellaneous (3). The overall average of household chores performed by men and women was fairly similar, with men averaging 2 chores performed and women 2.44.

## Interviews

Interview data had initially suggested the importance to home workers of control over work time, a control subsequently evidenced in variable work days and interrupted work times. *All* home workers (15/15) expressed a positive sense of control over their work schedules:

"It's almost—you might as well say complete freedom . . . I mean now if I was in the shoeshop or in a mill doing this, I wouldn't be able to sit here and talk with you. When I want a cup of coffee, I can have a cup of coffee . . . And if right in the middle of (knitting) a sweater I feel like up and going to town to buy something, I can get up and go."

And:

" . . . it is a wonderful sense of having the time completely at your disposal and the advantage of being at home is that when you feel like you need a break, very often there is something that needs to be done anyway—like I take water down to the animals or something like that. So there is a kind of back and forth that can take place . . . "

Autonomy to control work schedule was valued by all home workers and empirically expressed in logs and observations. Crucially linked with this sense of personal autonomy to control work time was the accompanying power to restructure work time to meet family needs, an opportunity not afforded by conventional work schedules. In interviews, women particularly voiced the desirability of control over work time in order to accommodate family needs—attendance at a school pageant, helping a spouse or family member with a special task, caring for a sick child in a nondisruptive manner. For these home workers, the interspersing of work with nonwork chores and the opportunity to restructure the work schedule, was preferable to the conflict engendered by work time demands in the conventional work world. Correspondingly, logs and observations demonstrated frequent examples of such family accommodations.

## Conclusions

Emerging from the data on time use (interviews, observations, and logs) was not the importance of *allocation* of time but its *flexibility*. While most studies conceive of time as a resource to be allocated among competing demands, more impressive here was its use as a responsive medium. Rather than representing a finite resource to be distributed in segments (e.g., 8 hours to work, 2 hours to commuting, 1 hour to quality child interaction), time for work-at-home families was not uniform but flexible and in-

tegrated with daily functions. Participants reported variable work days of nonuniform hours, punctuated by breaks for specific needs—a child's violin lesson, decorating a birthday cake, doing laundry, or reading to a child. In their nonroutinized work days and schedules, these families display a distinctive concept of "work time." As such, it may more closely approximate the older premodern task rhythm described by Thompson (1967) than the time discipline imposed by the industrial structure. Such a potential distinction between rural and urban families (perhaps a creation more of the economic context in which they dwell than a mind-set) has not been explored; most literature on work and family relies on common basic assumptions of a standardized work world. If experiences of work time are different, might other work/family related experiences also differ? Some critics, deploring research reliance on large corporate and institutional employers, urge more attention to work/family experiences in the small-and family-business sectors (Bell, 1982) such as home-working families represent. Failure to consider these alternate work experiences, more familiar to rural than to urban families, masks the diversity that may exist.

Results found here also suggest a special complexity about time as a resource to be managed in home-based enterprises. Family economists and resource management specialists, incorporating home-based work in their analyses, have noted time use to be a critical and complex variable in such a venture (Beutler & Owen, 1980; Carsky, Dolan & McCabe, 1985). However, the specific implications for family interaction of work/family time integration have not as yet been spelled out, and the linkage of home-based work to the quality of family life not widely explored. Families in this study, working successfully at home, valued this integrated pattern of time use, perceiving it as a concrete indicator of family responsiveness. We know less about families who attempt home-based work and quit in frustration, about workers who can function only in compartmentalized time, and about the personal and family qualities encouraging the integrated time model. These are all areas for further consideration by family resource management specialists undertaking studies of the work/family interface in such home-based settings.

Findings in this study may also be

useful to families considering home-based work as an employment option. The economic trade-offs of such a choice were apparent to these families who cited the loss of fringe benefits, a stable salary, and job security as principal drawbacks. The appeal of undertaking home-based work lay in increased work autonomy and responsiveness to family needs. How they used time was not just a quantitative measurement but also a metaphor for family responsiveness. Individuals considering home-based work would benefit by paying particular attention to how work and family interact through time use in situations like these prior to deciding whether such a format fits their needs.

Cooperative extension programs, recognizing and responding to home-based businesses as a work alternative in rural areas, have made a concerted effort to provide families with education and information about this option. As rural families in declining economies seek new income sources, many state extension services are actively promoting home-based work as one possible solution. Informational meetings, training sessions and publications sponsored by cooperative extension are educating families about the economic and family life implications of home work, including the very particular concerns of sharing work and family space. Two such state extension publications focus on "Combining Work with Family" (Owen & Gray, 1986) and "The Family Environment" (Rowe, no date), both pinpointing "time" as an issue of special complexity for families to consider prior to undertaking work in the home. Extension workers, aware of the interactive nature of work and family time, can more accurately and helpfully inform potential home workers of the pros and cons of the setting. For some families, such time interplay may be enriching and responsive, while for others the inability to compartmentalize may lead to unproductivity and economic failure. Helping these families to examine anticipated time use realistically, to evaluate its suitability for them, and to establish sensible daily schedules are important contributions extension workers can offer potential home workers.

The work choices of rural women also deserve special attention, limited as those options may be. Traditional rural, low-income economies offer few attractive, upwardly mobile and/or gender-free job opportunities for women. One participant described this limited selection and the consequent appeal of home work very well:

"If you were working in Detroit making $12-$15 an hour, you could make a good argument for going and doing it. But when you're making the kind of money a lot of people make around here and you're living quite literally hand-to-mouth, you never actually get one foot ahead of the other, you say to yourself: Well, there is one thing I can do for myself. If there is some way I can make a few bucks and stay home at the same time, then hang up the factory job because you're not going to get ahead anyway. So you may as well stay home and not get ahead."

Precisely because those choices are so limited and unglamorous in a rural economy, women have opted for alternatives; the work-at-home microbusiness is one of those familiar alternatives in a rural area. Yet, critics of vocational education have noted that such programs usually disregard this option, and have

traditionally focused their efforts on preparing students for outside employment rather than self-employment or job-creation.... The absence of a self-employment orientation in vocational education is particularly evident in the programs available to most females: consumer and homemaking education, office and health occupations. (Teal, 1981, p. 54)

Female entrepreneurs have represented one of the fastest growing categories of employment for women over the recent decade, undertaking endeavors which are frequently home-based. Vocational education needs to consider the home-based microbusiness as a realistic option for women, particularly in rural areas, and design programs suited for such women. Ideally, such an education would include not just the business and marketing information necessary for success as a microbusiness proprietor, but also careful attention to the special characteristics of work and family interaction in home work settings.

Family life educators might stop to consider the experiences of students and parents in home-working families and the future experience of work for men and women who might choose this option. Plainly, the opportunity to integrate work and family through home work might appeal to individuals seeking to combine career and home; it is particularly attractive to those holding traditional values. Nonetheless, some care should be given to the implications of home work for family life. Interspersing family and work chores might appear attractive but could result in negative consequences. The constant demands from both arenas, the inability to focus for sustained periods on just one activity, the nonuniform work patterns could be frustrating for individuals who function better in more conventional, separate settings. Too much family time togetherness may intensify existing problems. At the very least, the dynamics of working at home merit more careful exploration, beyond the simple aspect of time, prior to being trumpeted as a cure which heals the division between family and work life.

### REFERENCES

Bell, C. (1982). Small employers, work and community. In S. Kamerman & C. Hayes (Eds.), *Families that work: Children in a changing world* (pp. 209-228). Washington, DC: National Academy Press.

Berk, R., & Berk, S. (1979). *Labor and leisure at home: Content and organization of the household day.* Beverly Hills, CA: Sage Publications.

Beutler, I. F., & Owen, A. A. (1980). A home productivity model. *Home Economics Research Journal, 9,* 16-26.

Bohen, H., & Viveros-Long, A. (1981). *Balancing jobs and family life.* Philadelphia: Temple University Press.

Boulding, E. (1980). The labor of U.S. farm women—a knowledge gap. *Sociology of Work and Occupations, 7,* 261-290.

Carsky, M. L., Dolan, E., & McCabe, E. (1985). *The development of a typology on home-based work.* Unpublished working paper for NEC-59 Committee on Managerial and Productive Activities of Rural Families.

General Mills, Inc. (1981). *General Mills American family report 1980-81: Families at work: Strengths and strains.* Minneapolis: Author.

Guba, E. (1981). Criteria for assessing the trustworthiness of naturalistic inquiries. *Educational Communication and Technology Journal, 29* (2), 75-91.

Herriott, R., & Firestone, W. (1983). Multistate qualitative policy research: Optimising description and generalizability. *Educational Researcher, 12* (2), 14-19.

Kamerman, S. (1980). *Parenting in an unresponsive society.* New York: Free Press.

Owen, A., & Gray, M. (1986). *Combining work with family.* Missouri Co-operative Extension Service, University of Missouri and Lincoln University.

Rowe, B. (no date). *Home-based business: The family environment.* Utah Cooperative Extension Service, Utah State University.

Schatzman, L., & Strauss, A. (1973). *Field research.* Englewood Cliffs, NJ: Prentice-Hall.

Staines, G., & Pleck, J. (1983). *The impact of work schedules on the family.* Ann Arbor: University of Michigan.

Teal, P. (1981). Women in the rural economy: Employment and self-employment. In S. Rosenfeld (Ed.), *Brakeshoes, backhoes and balance sheets: The changing vocational education of rural women* (pp. 27-65). Washington, DC: Rural American Women, Inc.

Thompson, E. P. (1967, December). Time, work-discipline and industrial capitalism. *Past and Present,* pp. 56-97.

Vanek, J. (1980). Work, family and leisure roles: Farm households in the United States, 1920-1955. *Journal of Family History, 5,* 422-431.

# Correlates of Inter-Role Conflict in Young Rural and Urban Parents*

Carol Mertensmeyer and Marilyn Coleman**

The study of role conflict increases in popularity as researchers explore how to help men and women manage their multiple and often conflicting familial and work roles. Family policymakers need to be aware of role conflict, specifically inter-role conflict and what can be done to reduce it. Dual-career and dual-worker families are becoming more commonplace today with nearly 60% of married men in the work force having wives working full- or part-time (Friedman, 1985). This is true for rural families as well as urban (Walters & McKenry, 1985). As individuals and families are confronted with multiple role expectations, inter-role conflict often results (Kahn, Wolfe, Quinn, Snoek, & Rosenthal, 1964). Anxiety, low self-esteem, unhappiness, or depression may accompany this conflict (Hinchcliffe, Hooper, & Roberts, 1978; Sharpley & Khan, 1980), and for many the tensions are sufficiently severe to impose heavy costs for the person (Khan et al., 1964).

It is well documented that the presence of young children relates to more inter-role conflict. In a study by Voydanoff (1982) the presence of children was strongly related to work/family interference. Keith and

Schafer's (1980) study of 135 two-job families indicated that age and number of children at home are major sources of work/family role strain among husbands and wives. Results of a study by Nevill and Damico (1975a) indicated that women's role conflict was greatest at two points: after birth of the first child and upon attainment of a large family (four or more children). Kelly and Voydanoff (1985) found that time shortage was related to the presence of preschool and school-age children.

Other variables leading to role conflict have been examined as well, but comprehensive studies are limited. Further research is needed to identify personal and familial variables which breed inter-role conflict. These variables need to be viewed in a more comprehensive fashion to more completely understand inter-role conflict.

The dynamics of role conflict in rural families as well as urban families need to be explored. Due to differences in the life styles and values of urban and rural families (England, Gibbons, & Johnson, 1979; Imig, 1983), factors contributing to role conflict may be different depending on rural or urban residence. Are there unique correlates of role conflict in rural families, or are role conflict correlates similar to those in urban families? Family policymakers need to be aware of variables contributing to role conflict in all American families. Identification of the contributing factors or correlates in rural and urban families is a first step in alleviating role conflict.

The present study of parents with infant and preschool children is conceptualized

*This chapter is a contribution from the Missouri Agricultural Experiment Station, Journal paper number 10229.

**Carol Mertensmeyer is a doctoral student in Child and Family Development, University of Missouri, Columbia, MO 65211. Marilyn Coleman is Professor and Department Chair in Child and Family Development, University of Missouri, Columbia, MO 65211.

Reprinted from *Family Relations*, 1987, **36**, 425-429.

within a theory of role dynamics where role conflict, specifically inter-role conflict, results from competing sets of expectations that are aroused by organizational, inter-personal, and personal factors (Kahn et al., 1964). Variables in each of these three categories are examined and their relationship to inter-role conflict is explored.

The first category examined is organizational. According to Kahn et al. (1964) conflicting role expectations are framed by the organizational context in which they occur. Organizational factors considered in this present study are employment status, residence (rural and urban), and sex.

Employment may create additional roles for parents, thus increasing role management problems. A working parent performs three roles simultaneously: worker, parent, and spouse (in most cases). A rural parent may have to perform farm-related roles as well. Because the time, energy, and commitment needed to carry out these roles are interdependent, considerable role conflict over competing expectations can result (Strong & DeVault, 1986). For example, lower conflict in both sexes generally tends to be correlated with fewer working hours (Holahan & Gilbert, 1979), and role conflict may be experienced differently by married working mothers based on work commitment and the nature of the job (Holahan et al., 1979).

Another organizational consideration is the location in which individuals live, specifically rural or urban communities. Value systems differ in rural and urban communities. For example, urbanites are less conservative than rural persons (Fischer, 1978) and have been reported to value economic and cultural aspects of community life, whereas ruralists value family and community interaction (Imig, 1983). Role expectations may vary due to different community value systems, and thus role conflict is experienced differently based on whether one lives in urban or rural communities.

Employment participation rates of rural wives/mothers almost parallel their urban counterparts (Walters & McKenry, 1985); but because of more traditional values, employment of rural wives and mothers is perhaps more conflictive and problematic than it is for urban women (Bescher-Donnelly & Smith, 1981; Stokes & Willits, 1974; Sweet, 1972). Traditional values of the husband, other family members, and various significant others would suggest that rural women

employed outside the home add labor force participation to their household and child care duties; and though they expect it, they get little emotional support in return (Feldman & Feldman, 1974).

Attempting to meet the demands of family and employer may cause more inter-role conflict in women than men. In addition, many married women who are employed assume primary responsibility for running the family (Scanzoni & Fox, 1980) and are often expected to be a full-time mother and wife (Strong & DeVault, 1986). Recent studies show fathers see their roles as "helping" their partner, and they spend only a few hours a week doing housework even if their wives work equally as long and hard as they do (Nichols & Metzen, 1982).

The second component of Kahn's et al. (1964) theory of role dynamics is "interpersonal relationships." This refers to those patterns of interaction among members of an organization (e.g., family). Dimensions of particular importance within this component include affective bonds and dependence of one on the other (Kahn et al., 1964). A variable that exemplifies these dimensions is family cohesion. It has been reported that family cohesion is related to role conflict (Berkowitz, 1981; Holahan & Gilbert, 1979). More specifically, it has been shown that higher spouse support generally tends to be correlated with lower conflict in both sexes (Holahan & Gilbert, 1979) and that husbands' support reduces negative consequences of role conflict in women (Berkowitz, 1981). Spending time in family activities is another indicator of family cohesion, and it has been suggested that the ability to do this reduces the amount of conflict felt (Voydanoff & Kelly, 1984).

The third component of the theory of role dynamics is "personality" or personal factors. Kahn et al. (1964) uses the term personality to describe a person's propensity to behave in certain ways (i.e., motives and values, sensitivities and fears, habits and the like). Such traits as positive self-esteem seem highly relevant to the successful management of the demands of several roles. Low self-esteem appears to afflict individuals with poor ability to cope and with low tolerance for differences and difficulties (Strong & DeVault, 1986). Holahan and Gilbert (1979) indicate that lower conflict in both sexes generally tends to be correlated with high self-esteem.

Psychological masculinity and feminini- ty are two other personality variables to con- sider in understanding role conflict. Bem and Lenney (1976) found that androgynous per- sons, those high in both masculine and feminine personality traits, showed less avoidance of cross sex-role behaviors. It may be less distressing for an androgynous per- son to juggle the multitude of roles that re- quire both sorts of behaviors. For example, an androgynous male is more likely to en- gage in nurturing behavior than a sex-typed male, and an androgynous woman is more likely to be independent and decisive than a sex-typed female. Findings from a study by Cooper, Chassin, and Zeiss (1985) indicate that for both men and women in dual-worker couples it was more adaptive to be androgy- nous. In executing these multiple roles both traditional and cross sex-type behaviors may be necessary (Cooper et al., 1985).

The purpose of this study is to identify organizational, interpersonal, and personali- ty variables that are correlates of inter-role conflict. It is hypothesized that employment status, sex, family cohesion, self-esteem, and sex-typing will be predictive of inter-role conflict in both rural and urban young parents.

# Method
## Subjects

Subjects in this study comprise a sub- sample of parents from a large regional in- vestigation of parenting beliefs. Subjects consisted of 231 individuals, 121 females and 110 males. These individual respondents were parents of target children who were either within a few months of 1 year of age or within a few months of 4 years of age. The target child, for purposes of this study, was always the firstborn child. Approximately 60% of the families had one child, 37% had two children, and the remaining families had three children. No families had more than three children or any children over the age of four. Forty-five percent of the subjects were from 13 rural Missouri counties, and 55% were from a Midwestern city of approximate- ly 70,000 population. A rural family was de- fined as one residing in a community area outside a 25-mile radius of a Standard Metro- politan Statistical Area (Bureau of the Cen- sus, 1970). Average age of fathers was 29.6 years; of mothers, 27.5 years. Socio-econom- ic status of subjects was mainly middle class; 42% of the subjects' occupations were classified into occupational categories as semi-professionals, farm owners, techni- cians, and small business owners; 29% were administrators and professionals; 29% ranged from clerical, sales workers, small farm and business owners to unskilled and menial service workers (Hollingshead & Red- lich, 1958). Ninety percent of all fathers and 78% of all mothers were employed. Ninety- four percent of the rural fathers, 87% of ur- ban fathers, 64% of rural mothers, and 68% of urban mothers were employed.

## Procedure

Subjects were located from birth an- nouncements in 1978 and 1981 newspapers. Both parents were administered the Family Adaptability and Cohesion Environment Scale (Faces II; Olson, Portner, & Bell, 1982), Rosenberg Self-Esteem Scale (Rosenberg, 1965), Role Conflict Scale (Nevill & Damico, 1974), and the Bem Sex-Role Inventory (Bem, 1974). Instruments were mailed (62%) or per- sonally administered in the parents' home (38%). Mothers and fathers were instructed to individually complete the instruments and, in the case of the mailed sample, to return them in the separate envelopes pro- vided.

## Instruments

The Family Adaptability and Cohesion Environment Scale (Faces II) is a 30-item self-report inventory designed to measure family dynamics. Faces II contains two subscales of cohesion and adaptability. High scores on the subscales are indicative of high family cohesion and adaptability. Due to the high correlation of adaptability and cohesion ($r = .63$ for rural and $r = .56$ for ur- ban individuals), only one of the subscales was used. Nunnally (1967) reports that the problem of multicollinearity reduces the $R^2$ value in a multiple regression analysis and therefore advises against using highly cor- related variables. When the two subscales were compared, cohesion appeared more reliable with a reported test-retest reliability of $r = .83$ and a Chronbach Alpha of $r = .87$. The test-retest reliability for adaptability was $r = .80$; the Chronbach Alpha was $r = .78$ (Olson et al., 1982). Cohesion may also be more valid. Olson et al. (1982) reported con- struct validity through factor analysis with the cohesion items loading scores ranging from .34 to .61 and the adaptability items loading from .10 to .55. Since cohesion seemed to be a more reliable and valid subscale, it was chosen over adaptability for inclusion in the regression analysis. Family cohesion measures the degree to which family members are separated from or connected to their family and is defined as "the emotional bonding that family members have toward one another" (Olson et al., 1982). It measures the cohesion dimensions of emotional bonding, boundaries, coalitions, time, space, friends, decision making, interests, and recreation.

The Rosenberg Self-Esteem Instrument measures the overall attitude that a person maintains with regard to his/her own worth and importance (Rosenberg, 1965). This instrument has 10 items, and individuals respond on a 4-point Likert scale from "strongly agree" to "strongly disagree." The range of scores is from 10 to 40. Low scores indicate a high self-esteem, and high scores indicate a low self-esteem. Studies support its validity (Rosenberg, 1965), and a test-retest reliability of r = .85 has been reported (Silber & Tippett, 1965).

Nevill and Damico (1974) developed a questionnaire (Role Conflict Scale) to assess inter-role conflict. This instrument has been validated and used extensively in researching women (Nevill & Damico, 1975a, 1975b, 1978). The questionnaire is designed to assess how often one feels conflict over the following categories: neglecting social obligations, housework, work, personal concerns; wanting to give more time to home or family, spouse; and not fulfilling expectations of self, spouse, or children. The questionnaire was slightly adapted for this study. The instrument is an 11-item, 6-point Likert scale. The range of possible scores is from 11 (never feel conflict) to 66 (always feel conflict).

The Bem Sex Role inventory (BSRI) is a 60-item instrument designed to measure sex role self-concept. The BSRI includes a masculinity and femininity scale (20 items each) consisting of attributes perceived as more desirable for one sex than the other (Bem, 1974). The remaining 20 items are neutral or non-sex-specific. Individuals respond on a 7-point Likert scale from "like-me" to "not-like-me." A dichotomous sex-type variable is derived by using the median split method. Males who obtained masculine scores above and feminine scores below the

sample's median scores were classified as sex-typed. The opposite was true for females. If their feminine scores were above and their masculine scores were below the median score, they were classified as sex-typed. Those defined as not sex-typed included those individuals whose masculine and feminine scores were above the median score (androgynous) and those individuals whose scores were below the median scores (undifferentiated). Twenty percent of the individuals in the present study were sex-typed; 80% were not sex-typed.

## Results

A Multiple Regression Analysis was used with five independent (predictor) variables and one dependent variable. Two continuous independent variables (family cohesion and self-esteem) were obtained respectively from Faces II and the Rosenberg Self-Esteem Scale. Three dichotomous independent variables, sex (male or female), mother's employment status (employed or unemployed), and sex-typing (sex-typed or not sex-typed as derived from the BSRI) were entered as dummy variables. The dependent variable was an inter-role conflict score derived from the Role Conflict Scale (Nevill & Damico, 1974).

Table 1.
*Mean Scores and Standard Deviations for the Variables*

| Variables | Urban (n = 126) | | Rural (n = 105) | |
|---|---|---|---|---|
| | M | SD | M | SD |
| Self-Esteem | 16.81 | 3.91 | 17.97 | 3.69 |
| Cohesion | 66.71 | 7.16 | 66.41 | 6.32 |
| Sex-Type | .26 | .44 | .27 | .45 |
| Mother's Employment Status | .32 | .47 | .36 | .48 |
| Gender | 1.48 | .50 | 1.47 | .50 |
| Role Conflict | 34.84 | 8.09 | 35.19 | 7.37 |

Mean scores and standard deviations for the variables can be seen in Table 1. Separate multiple regression analyses were conducted for urban (n = 126) and rural (n = 105) individuals (see Table 2). The linear combinations of independent variables were predictive of inter-role conflict for both urban ($R^2$ = .12, F = 2.386, p = .045) and rural ($R^2$ = .16, F = 3.20, p = .011) individuals. The variance explained was 12% and 16% re-

Table 2.
*Summary of Multiple Regressions for Urban and Rural Individuals*

| Variable | Urban (n = 126) | | | | Rural (n = 105) | | | |
|---|---|---|---|---|---|---|---|---|
| | b | Se | t | p | b | Se | t | p |
| Intercept | 45.605 | 10.235 | 4.456 | .000 | 41.780 | 10.358 | 4.034 | .000 |
| Self-esteem | .505 | .227 | 2.230 | .028 | .610 | .204 | 2.994 | .004 |
| Cohesion | -.294 | .129 | -2.275 | .026 | -.230 | .124 | -1.856 | .067 |
| Sex-type[a] | -.822 | 1.991 | -0.413 | .681 | .036 | 1.665 | .021 | .983 |
| Mother's employment status[a] | .344 | 2.003 | .172 | .864 | -1.466 | 1.564 | -0.937 | .351 |
| Sex[a] | -.233 | 1.750 | -0.133 | .894 | -1.015 | 1.548 | -0.656 | .514 |

Urban $R^2$ = .12    Rural $R^2$ = .16
Urban Adjusted $R^2$ = .07    Rural Adjusted $R^2$ = .12

[a]Dummy variables.

spectively for urban and rural models, although the adjusted variance constituted a small effect size with 7% of the variance explained for urban individuals and 12% explained for rural individuals (Cohen, 1977). Self-esteem was significant in predicting inter-role conflict for both urban ($p$ = .028) and rural ($p$ = .004) individuals. Cohesion scores were also significant in predicting inter-role conflict for urban individuals ($p$ = .026) but not rural ($p$ = .067).

## Discussion

It appears that employment status, sex-typing, and sex are unrelated to the inter-role conflict experienced by the young parents in this study. What is important is how they feel about themselves and, in the case of urban parents, the degree to which the family provides support and functions as a "tight-knit" unit. Specifically, as families with young children assume new roles, new responsibilities, and for many, incur financial strain, they are vulnerable to excessive inter-role conflict and lowered self-esteem.

Employment may have various meanings to different people in this study, especially to women. To some it may be seen as a necessity, obligation, and even a burden, for others a pleasurable experience and an opportunity to fulfill one's potential. Inter-role conflict may be a result of how people feel about their employment status rather than whether or not they are employed. Specifically, if unemployed people feel unsatisfied, guilty, and worried about their financial instability, or if employed and not able to meet traditional expectations, they may experience negative feelings. For example, women who choose to be employed, and whose husbands support that choice, are probably less concerned about neglecting housework and not fulfilling expectations than those who would rather not be working and whose husbands would prefer they not work. Either way the conflicting expectations may lead to low self-esteem and inter-role conflict. Therefore, it may not be additional roles associated with employment per se that create the inter-role conflict.

As with employment status, sex-typing is not a significant predictor in determining inter-role conflict. Perhaps it is not how traditionally feminine or masculine (i.e., sex-typed) individuals are but whether the actual roles played and role expectations (from self and others) are congruent. For example, a stereotypical feminine mother (sex-typed) who is a full-time housewife may feel conflict if her husband expects her to be employed full-time. On the other hand, a stereotypical masculine father (sex-typed) may feel conflict if he is expected to share household responsibilities with his employed wife.

The present findings indicate no significant relationship of sex to inter-role conflict. An increasing number of studies indicate minimal differences in inter-role conflict among men and women. Herman and Gyllstrom (1977) found no differences between men and women with children in their conflict between job and family. Staines and Pleck (1983) also found sex to make no differences in overall level of work/family conflict.

## Application

Findings from the present study indicate that a strong relationship exists between self-esteem and inter-role conflict. This supports Holahan and Gilbert's (1979) findings that lower conflict generally tends to be correlated with high self-esteem. With this in mind, attention should focus on increasing parents' self-esteem. Our competitive society is not conducive to supporting individual well-being, nor is there evidence that society views parenting as a highly esteemed role. Family policymakers should encourage employers to be more responsive in providing parents with alternatives that alleviate forced choices that are incongruent with parents' values. For example, corporate sponsored child care may offset the conflict a mother feels because she is not at home with her child. Flextime and paid maternal and paternal leaves are additional benefits that employers could provide employees. These benefits would help parents fulfill self and family expectations and would give parents evidence that our nation views parenting as a valuable role. After school day care programs for the children of working parents would help alleviate inter-role conflict and further enable families to meet expectations of self, spouse, and child.

Although self-esteem is a significant predictor of inter-role conflict for both rural and urban families, family cohesion is significant for only urban families. This suggests that high cohesion plays a less important role in reducing inter-role conflict for rural than for urban families. Perhaps urban individuals depend solely on their nuclear family's support, whereas rural individuals turn to extended family or community members for additional support. Close bonds with community members or with extended family would be indicative of low family cohesion as measured by Faces II.

The present study underscores the importance for policymakers to promote family cohesion in families with young children. Demands are great and inter-role conflict is high at this stage (Olson et al., 1983) especially in dual-career and dual-worker families. The fastest growing segment of the work force consists of mothers of preschool children, 52% of whom were in the labor force in 1984 (Friedman, 1985). The 1981 White House Conference on Families included as one of its major policy recommendations that employers institute more family-oriented personnel policies (Staines & Pleck, 1983). Recognizing that family well-being has a direct relationship to employee productivity, a growing number of employers have adopted programs to improve the quality of family life (Friedman, 1985). Just as maternity and paternity leave and flextime may increase individual self-esteem, these same policies may also increase family cohesion. Other policies, such as leave for children's sickness, job relocation, vacation time, and holidays, should receive special consideration. Policies such as these give individuals the opportunity to spend time with family members and the flexibility to meet family members' needs.

## Future Research

Future research should examine additional predictor variables. A larger effect size might be obtained if multiple regression analyses utilized more interpersonal and personality variables as opposed to the number or types of roles played. It may be more fruitful to study the effects of employer and government policies (e.g., employer sponsored day care, sick leave for child's illness as well as employee illness, paid maternity and paternity leave, flextime, etc.) on inter-role conflict rather than the more global maternal employment variables.

Rural and urban parents were quite similar on the variables studied, although rural parents were slightly lower in self-esteem and higher in role conflict (as seen in Table 1). This may be partially attributed to the farm crisis. The additional financial strain may affect rural parents in a number of ways. For example, financial insecurity may decrease rural parents' self-esteem. Specifically, it is often essential that rural mothers of young children be employed even though it is incongruent with their values. This not only adds additional and different roles to family members' existing roles, it may lower the self-esteem of men who are failing at the traditional role expectation of being the breadwinner and of women who are unable to meet their self-expectations as wife and mother. As these families reassign roles, take on new roles, and attempt to manage competing role expectations, the potential for role conflict increases. Continued study of young urban and rural parents through these stressful and rapidly changing times will help family policymakers assess the impact of new policies on family interaction over time and provide insight into the differential needs of rural and urban parents.

## REFERENCES

Bem, S. (1974). The measurement of psychological androgyny. *Journal of Consulting and Clinical Psychology, 42*, 155–162.

Bem, S. L., & Lenney, E. (1976). Sex typing and the avoidance of cross-sex behavior. *Journal of Personality and Social Psychology, 33*, 48–54.

Berkowitz, A. D. (1981). Role conflict in farm women. *Dissertation Abstracts International, 42*, 65–B. (University Microfilms No. 8119524).

Bescher-Donnelly, L., & Smith, L. W. (1981). The changing roles and status of rural women. In R. T. Coward & W. T. Smith (Eds.), *The family in rural society* (pp. 167–185). Boulder, CO: Westview Press.

Bureau of the Census. (1970). *Census of population.* United States Department of Commerce Publications.

Cohen, J. (1977). *Statistical power analysis for the behavioral sciences* (rev. ed.). New York: Academic Press.

Cooper, K., Chassin, L., & Zeiss, A. (1985). The relation of sex-role self-concept and sex-role attitudes to the marital satisfaction and personal adjustment of dual-worker couples with preschool children. *Sex Roles, 12*, 227–241.

England, J. L., Gibbons, W. E., & Johnson, B. L. (1979). The impact of a rural environment on values. *Rural Sociology, 44*, 119–136.

Feldman, H., & Feldman, M. (1974). The relationship between family and occupational functioning of a sample of urban welfare women. *The Cornell Journal of Social Relations, 9*, 35–52.

Fischer, C. (1978). Urban-to-rural diffusion of opinions in contemporary America. *American Journal of Sociology, 84*, 151–159.

Friedman, D. (1985). *Corporate financial assistance for child care.* New York: The Conference Board, Inc.

Herman, J. B., & Gyllstrom, K. (1977). Working men and women: Inter- and intra-role conflict. *Psychology of Women Quarterly, 4*, 319–332.

Hinchcliffe, M., Hooper, D., & Roberts, F. (1978). *The melancholy marriage: Depression in marriage and psychosocial approaches to therapy.* New York: John Wiley.

Holahan, C. K., & Gilbert, L. A. (1979). Conflict between major life roles: Women and men in dual-career couples. *Human Relations, 32*, 451–467.

Hollingshead, A., & Redlich, R. (1958). *Social class in mental illness.* New York: Wiley.

Imig, D. R. (1983). Urban and rural families: A comparative study of the impact on family interaction. *Rural Education, 1*(2), 79–82.

Kahn, R. L., Wolfe, D. M., Quinn, R. P., Snoek, J. D., & Rosenthal, R. A. (1964). *Organizational stress: Studies in role conflict and ambiguity.* New York: Wiley.

Keith, P. M., & Schafer, R. B. (1980). Role strain and depression in two-job families. *Family Relations, 29*, 483–488.

Kelly, R. F., & Voydanoff, P. (1985). Work/family role strain among employed parents. *Family Relations, 34*, 367–374.

Nevill, D., & Damico, S. (1974). The development of a role conflict questionnaire for women: Some preliminary findings. *Journal of Consulting and Clinical Psychology, 42*, 743.

Nevill, D., & Damico, S. (1975a). Family size and role conflict in women. *Journal of Psychology, 89*, 267–270.

Nevill, D., & Damico, S. (1975b). Role conflict in women as a function of marital status. *Human Relations, 28*, 487–498.

Nevill, D., & Damico, S. (1978). The influence of occupational status on role conflict in women. *Journal of Employment Counseling, 15*, 55–61.

Nichols, S., & Metzen, E. (1982). Impact of wife's employment upon husband's housework. *Journal of Family Issues, 3*, 199–216.

Nunnally, J. (1967). *Psychometric theory.* New York: McGraw-Hill.

Olson, D. H., McCubbin, H. I., Barnes, H., Larsen, A., Muxen, M., & Wilson, M. (1983). *Families: What makes them work.* Beverly Hills, CA: Sage Publications.

Olson, D. H., Portner, J., & Bell, R. (1982). Faces II: Family adaptability and cohesion evaluation scales. In D. H. Olson, H. I. McCubbin, H. Barnes, A. Larsen, M. Muxen, & M. Wilson (Eds.), *Family inventories: Inventories used in a national survey of families across the family life cycle* (pp. 5–24). St. Paul, MN: Family Social Science, University of Minnesota.

Rosenberg, M. (1965). *Society and the adolescent self-image.* Princeton: University Press.

Scanzoni, J., & Fox, G. L. (1980). Sex roles, family and society: The seventies and beyond. *Journal of Marriage and the Family, 42*, 743–756.

Sharpley, C., & Khan, J. (1980). Self-concept, values-systems, and marital adjustment: Some implications for marriage counselors. *International Journal for the Advancement of Counseling, 3*, 137–145.

Silber, E., & Tippett, J. S. (1965). Self-esteem: Clinical assessment and measurement validation. *Psychological Reports, 16*, 1017–1071.

Staines, G. L., & Pleck, J. H. (1983). *The impact of work schedules on the family.* Ann Arbor: Institute for Social Research, University of Michigan.

Stokes, C. S., & Willits, F. K. (1974). *A preliminary analysis of factors related to sex role ideology among rural-origin females.* Paper presented at the meeting of the Rural Sociological Association, Montreal, Canada.

Strong, B., & DeVault, C. (1986). *The marriage and family experience.* New York: West.

Sweet, J. A. (1972). The employment of rural farm wives. *Rural Sociology, 37*, 553–557.

Voydanoff, P. (1982). Work roles and quality of family life among professionals and managers. In B. M. Hirschlein & W. J. Braun (Eds.), *Families and work* (pp. 118–124). Stillwater: Oklahoma State University Press.

Voydanoff, P., & Kelly, R. F. (1984). Determinants of work-related family problems among employed parents. *Journal of Marriage and the Family, 46*, 881–892.

Walters, C., & McKenry, P. (1985). Predictors of life satisfaction among rural and urban employed mothers: A research note. *Journal of Marriage and the Family, 47*, 1067–1071.

**17**

# Normative Loss in Mid-Life Families: Rural, Urban, and Gender Differences*

Pauline Boss, Debra Pearce-McCall, and Jan Greenberg**

Adapting to loss is one of the most important developmental tasks of family systems. Previous research about boundary ambiguity focused on *unexpected* and ambiguous loss in families of disaster (e.g., families with a member missing-in-action; Boss, 1977, 1980a). This study is the first of a series to investigate loss that is normative and *expected* but still ambiguous. Since the adolescent leaving home does not represent a clear-cut and final exit from the family, the potential for boundary ambiguity is high.

Boundary ambiguity is defined as a state in which family members are uncertain in their perception about who is in or out of the family, and who is performing what roles and tasks within the family system (Boss, 1977, 1980a, 1980b, 1987). Events such as leaving home, death, separation, divorce, or chronic illness may be dysfunctional if they result in a high degree of boundary ambiguity; however, if family members can alter their perceptions of family boundaries, the same events may result in little or no dysfunction.

*Research funded by the University of Minnesota Agricultural Experiment Station Projects No. MIN-52-048 and MIN-52-049. Appreciation is expressed to Richard Sauer, Keith McFarland, and M. Janice Hogan for this support.

**Pauline Boss is Professor in the Department of Family Social Science, University of Minnesota, St. Paul, MN 55108. Debra Pearce-McCall is a doctoral student in the Department of Family Social Science, University of Minnesota, St. Paul, MN 55108. Jan Greenberg is Assistant Professor in the School of Social Work, University of Wisconsin, Madison, WI 53705.

Reprinted from *Family Relations*, 1987, **36**, 437–443.

Another way of understanding boundary ambiguity is as an incongruence between physical and psychological presence or absence. Family members may perceive a physically present member as psychologically absent (e.g., the situation where parents see a teenager at home but psychologically distant and removed from family life) *or* family members may perceive a physically absent member as psychologically present (e.g., parents are preoccupied with the adolescent who has left home). (For a detailed discussion, see Boss, 1987, and Boss & Greenberg, 1984.)

The concept of boundary ambiguity has been useful for researchers and clinicians in explaining how and why some families remain strong after a loss occurs whereas others do not. The concept is also therapeutically and educationally useful because it allows family members to structurally label their experience. *Family boundaries are ambiguous when adolescents leave home.* Families do not know whether adolescents are in or out if just as soon as they are gone, they come home again. Labeling the family boundary as ambiguous during this normative transition may in itself decrease some of the ambiguity for families. At least then counseling and educational goals become clear: to increase the ability of families to tolerate ambiguity by (a) enabling them to clarify when and on what basis the adolescent is "in or out," and (b) increasing flexibility so they can adapt to the entries and exits of the adolescent.

In this study, the ambiguity about who is in and who is out of the family (rather than the event of loss itself) is hypothesized to be the strongest predictor of family dysfunction after loss. A preliminary test of this premise is presented using a normative and primarily rural sample.

## Hypotheses and Research Questions

The purpose of this study was to investigate parental responses to the normative stressor event of an adolescent leaving home. The major hypothesis is that the more parents perceive their adolescent as psychologically present in spite of physical absence, the more parents will experience dysfunction. In other words, the higher the degree of boundary ambiguity as perceived by the father and/or mother, the higher the degree of individual and family dysfunction. Level of dysfunction was operationalized as felt level of stress resulting from these events, level of somatization, and an index of subjects' general emotional attitude toward their life (henceforth labeled "general affect").

In preparation for a larger study, the data collected provided an opportunity to gain a descriptive understanding and formulate more precise hypotheses about rural and urban mid-life families. These questions guided the analysis: Are there differences between rural and urban parents? Are there gender differences in the parents' perceptions of their absent offspring? Are there differences between those families having difficulty negotiating this transition and those who are not experiencing problems? Preliminary answers to these questions are reported.

## Methods and Procedures

### Sampling Method

The sample used in this study is part of a larger regional study of Minnesota couples.[1] The data set is based on a stratified random sample in Minnesota of 100 urban couples, 100 rural farm couples, and 100 rural nonfarm couples. The criteria for selection of an urban county were a representative urban Standard Metropolitan Statistical Area (SMSA) of 200,000 or more, not sharing contiguous population with any other state. Representative rural counties selected met the criteria of matching both

mean income and mean years of education for the state and of being over 50 miles from population centers of 50,000 or more. Data from the 1980 Census of the Population (U.S. Department of Commerce Census Bureau, 1982) were used to obtain this information.

The Minnesota rural/urban sample was selected using mailing lists purchased from a marketing company. Over-sampling was necessary to compensate for couples who did not meet sampling criteria and persons who did not return questionnaires. A 3:1 over-sampling ratio was used, and questionnaires were mailed to 918 households in the spring of 1984.

Following survey procedures outlined by Dillman (1978), reminder postcards were sent to all households 2 weeks after the questionnaires were mailed. People who did not return the first questionnaire after one month were sent another survey, along with a letter reiterating the importance of their participation. When analyses indicated no differences in responses to the first and second wave of surveys, responses to both surveys were pooled. A response rate of 29% was obtained, which, considering the use of a commercial sample (which had considerable errors in addressing) and the length of the questionnaire (28 pages per person), seems sufficiently high. Mail surveys are of course prone to self-selection bias; information is not available about differences between respondents and nonrespondents, but it is assumed that those who took the time to respond were less stressed than those who did not. Thus, the sample may be biased toward well-functioning families.

The final data set consisted of 70 rural and urban mid-life couples for whom *both* mother and father completed questionnaires, *both* reported having an adolescent who had left home, and *both* answered questions about the same child (N = 70).[2]

### Sample Description

The couples in this sample had been married for an average of 28 years, with the lengths of the marriages ranging from 10 to 41 years. The number of children ranged from 2 to 9, with a mean of 3.7. Slightly over half the sample consisted of rural nonfarm families, with the rest evenly divided between rural farm and urban families (23.2% each). Thus, nearly 75% of this sample was rural. Respondents had lived in their communities for an average of 29 years. The median family income before taxes was $36,000. All the participants were white and the majority were Protestant (over 70%).

The fathers ranged in age from 33 to 65 (mean = 51.7). Most had a high school education, with only 24 reporting some post high school studies (1 to 9 years). Eighty percent were employed full-time, primarily in precision products, executive and managerial occupations, or farming; only three fathers considered themselves unemployed.

The mothers ranged in age from 37 to 62 (mean = 49). Their amount of schooling ranged from 8 to 17 years, with a median of 12.2 Twenty-two mothers had completed post high school education and six had not completed high school. The highest percentage of mothers were either employed full-time outside the home (27.5%) or were full-time homemakers (29.0%). Fewer reported part-time employment (20%) or some combination of outside employment and home-making (11%). The remaining 7.2% were either self-employed or unemployed.

Respondents' scores on FACES II (a measure of family cohesion and adaptability developed by Olson, Bell, & Portner, 1979) were compared with national norms (Olson et al., 1982). The ranges of the respondents' scores were slightly more restricted than those of Olson et al.'s national sample, but the means were similar. In addition, this national sample and the Minnesota sample show very similar distributions across the three general regions into which scores can fall, termed balanced, midrange, and extreme (Olson et al., 1982). Overall, the similarities between the present sample and the national sample of 1,000 families on which FACES II was normed suggest that the self-selection bias inherent in the methodology has not produced an unusual or noncomparable sample, at least with regard to the family characteristics measured by FACES II.[3]

# Instrumentation

## Description of Mid-Life Questionnaire

Each respondent completed a 28-page questionnaire which included demographic data and a number of instruments. The focus of this study is on responses to a family stress scale, a somatization scale, a measure of general affect, and the boundary ambiguity scale. These scales will be described briefly.

## Family Stress Scale

The family stress scale used was an adaptation of the Family Inventory of Life Events and Changes (FILE) developed by Mc-Cubbin, Patterson, and Wilson (1981). Based on an analysis of data from the National Survey of Families conducted by Olson et al. (1982), events *not* frequently cited as stressful for mid-life families were identified by Mederer and Hill (1983). These items were dropped from the stress scale used in the mid-life questionnaire. Another change adopted in the present study was that respondents were asked to remember back only 3 years instead of 5 years, a change based on pretesting and on the research experience of Mederer and Hill (1983). They indicated that subjects in their study had difficulty remembering what had happened 5 years earlier, but could remember what had happened 3 years before.

The stress scale as adapted was designed to determine (a) whether mid-life respondents had experienced any of 48 commonly identified stressful life events in the past 12 months and the past 3 years, (b) the respondents' perceptions of the degree of stress connected with the events they experienced, and (c) the extent of pileup of stressful events they experienced. Respondents were asked to indicate how disturbing a past or present stressful event was by circling the appropriate number on a 5-point scale, ranging from not disturbing to extremely disturbing. For this analysis, a summary stress score was obtained by summing respondents' reported felt level of stress over all 48 items.

## Family Health and Somatization

The somatization scale is part of the *Inventory of Family Health*, a family health checklist developed by Rosalie Norem at Iowa State University. The scale directs respondents to comment on the extent to which they or other family members are affected by 12 physical symptoms which, according to the literature, are related to stress. These are: (a) had trouble sleeping, (b) had accidents, (c) had been irritable, (d) had been depressed, (e) smoked cigarettes, cigars, or pipe, (f) used prescription drugs, (g) had a weight problem, (h) used alcohol, (i) found it difficult to relax, (j) had headaches, (k) had muscle tension, nervous indigestion, or anxiety, (l) had colds or flu.

Respondents were instructed to indicate the frequency with which they had experienced each of these symptoms. In another study, the symptomology scale had an alpha reliability of .79 for wives and .77 for husbands (Norem & Brown, 1983). A simple additive procedure was used to score the scale in the present study and alpha reliabilities were .71 for wives and .72 for husbands.

## Measuring Boundary Ambiguity

The original boundary ambiguity scale was developed by Boss (1977) with a military sample of families in which the fathers were declared missing-in-action. Validity and reliability of the instrument were established for this unique sample experiencing ambiguous loss. The content validity of the boundary ambiguity scale as adapted for this normative study was determined with a panel of 20 family therapists who reviewed the scale and judged that the items "made sense" in indicating "psychological presence" of a physically absent adolescent, the dimension which Boss believes is critical in defining boundary ambiguity (Boss, 1980a). (See Tables 1 and 2 for the instrument as adapted for this study and the original factor.) Boundary ambiguity is operationalized as high scores on this psychological presence scale. A high score on the Psychological Presence Scale essentially means there is a high degree of preoccupation with the absent person.

## Index of General Affect

This variable provided a measure of the

Table 1.
*Boundary Ambiguity Items for Adolescents Leaving Home*

1. I feel that it will be difficult for me now that ___ has left home.
2. I feel that I prepared myself for ___ leaving home.
3. I have difficulty accepting that ___ has grown up.
4. I continue to keep alive my hope that ___ will return home to live.
5. I plan to use ___'s room for other purposes now that he/she has left home.
6. Our family talks about ___ quite often.
7. I think about ___ a lot.
8. I find myself thinking about where ___ is and what he/she is doing.
9. ___ still comes home to sleep.
10. I am bothered because I miss my son/daughter.
11. Since ___ left, I am bothered by feelings of loneliness.

Table 2.
*Items Contained in the Psychological Father Presence Factor*

| Loading | |
|---|---|
| −.8926 | I no longer consider myself an "MIA" wife. |
| −.6572 | I feel I have prepared myself for a change in status. |
| −.6023 | My children are able to talk about their father without becoming emotionally upset. |
| −.5894 | My children are aware of all "the facts" and have reconciled their father's loss. |
| −.4998 | I feel I am able to plan my future without feeling guilty for not continuing to wait for my husband. |
| −.4680 | I hope to remarry. |
| −.4570 | The Armed Services have done everything reasonably possible to account for my husband. |
| .8164 | I find myself still wondering if my husband is alive. |
| .8162 | I continue to keep alive my deepest hope that my husband will return. |
| .7722 | I feel guilty about dating (or wanting to date). |
| .7094 | My children still believe that their father is alive. |
| .5791 | I will never be satisfied until I have positive proof of my husband's death. |
| .4705 | My children and I talk about their father seemingly quite often. |
| .4368 | I think about my husband a lot. |
| .4255 | I feel it will be difficult, if not impossible, to carve out a new life for myself without my husband. |
| .3490 | I feel incapable of establishing meaningful relationships with another man. |
| .2623 | Conflicts with my own parents over my husband's change of status have presented a problem for me. |
| .2873 | My in-laws do not or would not approve of my plans to develop a life for myself. |

Note: Eigenvalue = 6.25. Total observed variance accounted for = 33%. Total explained variance accounted for = 39%.

respondents' affective and attitudinal states regarding their present life. Respondents were presented with a set of questions pairing affective adjectives (e.g., interesting/boring, rewarding/disappointing). For each pairing, they were asked to circle the number on a 7-point scale that best described how they felt about their present life. The measure consists of eight of these semantic differential items, and the variable "Index of General Affect" is calculated by taking the mean of each respondent's scores across the eight items (Campbell, Converse, & Rodgers, 1976).

## Results

### Information on Boundary Ambiguity Scale

The reliability of the boundary ambiguity scale was tested separately for mid-life fathers and mothers. With the mothers' data, a Cronbach's alpha of .75 was obtained; with the fathers' data, a Cronbach's alpha of .71 was obtained. As a check on the construct validity of the boundary ambiguity scale, scores were compared with respondents' ratings of two items. The first was a rating of how stressful it was when their child moved out of the household. For fathers and mothers, boundary ambiguity scores and responses to this one item were significantly correlated (fathers: $r = .29$, $p = .014$; mothers: $r = .37$, $p = .003$). Boundary ambiguity scores were also significantly correlated with how respondents felt about the child leaving home. For both fathers and mothers, the higher the boundary ambiguity score, the *worse* they felt about the child leaving home (fathers: $r = -.33$, $p = .003$; mothers: $r = -.22$, $p = .035$). This was measured by a single item reading, "Overall, how do you feel about your adolescent leaving home?" The five possible answers ranged from "very bad" to "very good." These results indicate adequate reliability and validity of the scale for the present sample.

In short, the members of each couple were similar in their perceptions regarding the degree of boundary ambiguity in their family; their boundary ambiguity scores were positively correlated ($r = .47$, $p = .001$). This indicates a significant amount of congruence between mothers' and fathers' perceptions, and similar degrees to which pairs of parents were continuing to keep the absent adolescent psychologically present.

Fathers' scores on the boundary ambiguity scale ranged from 16 to 38, with a mean of 26.57. Mothers' scores ranged from 16 to 42, with a mean of 27.84. A two-tailed t-tests between these means did not reach significance. However, item by item t-test did yield two significant differences between fathers and mothers: Women agreed more strongly with the statements that they think a lot about the child who left home ($t = 3.51$, $p = .001$) and that they feel lonely since the child left ($t = 2.01$, $p = .048$). So, while mothers and fathers did not differ with regard to total scores, there were two specific ways in which mothers were more preoccupied with the absent adolescent.

### Rural/Urban Comparisons

Interestingly, rural and urban mothers scored virtually identically on the boundary ambiguity scale. Fathers also showed no significant total score difference. However, on individual item comparisons, rural fathers reported thinking about their child significantly more than urban fathers ($t = -2.27$, $p = .026$), and rural fathers more strongly disagreed with the statement that they had prepared themselves for their child's leaving home ($t = -2.07$, $p = .042$).

Further comparisons of rural and urban families yielded very few additional differences. One significant difference which did emerge concerns the number of years since the adolescent had left home. Rural parents were responding about adolescents who had left an average of 2.7 years ago; urban parents reported their adolescents had left an average of 1.5 years ago ($t = -3.17$, $p = .003$). An interpretation of this finding is not possible with the presently available data but will be investigated further. As no significant differences emerged on the major variables of boundary ambiguity, somatization, or general affect, further rural/urban comparisons were not performed. It must be remembered that approximately 75% of the parents in the sample were from rural areas, so the findings of this investigation are more descriptive of rural than urban families.

### Correlational Analyses

As stated earlier, mothers and fathers were usually similar in their scores on the boundary ambiguity scale. When there was a

Table 3.
*Level of Boundary Ambiguity*

|  |  | Fathers | Mothers |
|---|---|---|---|
| SOMATIZATION | Fathers | .29 (.01) | .31 (.005) |
|  | Mothers | NS | NS |
| GENERAL AFFECT | Fathers | NS | -.27 (.01) |
|  | Mothers | NS | -.22 (.036) |
| STRESS | Fathers | NS | NS |
|  | Mothers | NS | NS |

Note: Correlations between boundary ambiguity scores and measures of individual and family functioning. Number in parentheses is *p* value.

discrepancy between father's and mother's boundary ambiguity scores, it appeared to decrease over time; that is, a significant and negative correlation was found between the number of years that had passed since the adolescent left home and the discrepancy between spouses' scores ($r = -.29$, $p = .006$). In other words, the more time that had elapsed since the adolescent left home, the less discrepancy existed between the spouses' perceptions regarding the psychological presence of their physically absent offspring.

The main hypothesis tested was that boundary ambiguity scores would be significantly correlated with measures of individual and family functioning. That is, higher boundary ambiguity scores would be associated with higher levels of dysfunction. Measures of functioning in this study included felt level of stress scores, somatization levels, and levels of general affect. These correlations are presented in Table 3.

Although boundary ambiguity scores were not significantly related to family stress scores, both fathers' and mothers' boundary ambiguity scores were significantly and positively related to fathers' somatization scores (fathers: $r = .29$, $p = .01$; mothers: $r = .31$, $p = .005$). This means that higher levels of preoccupation with the absent adolescent by *both* parents were associated with higher levels of somatic symptoms in the fathers. For mothers, boundary ambiguity scores were also significantly and inversely correlated with their general affect ($r = -.22$, $p = .036$), and with their husbands' general affect ($r = -.27$, $p = .01$). That is, the more the mothers kept the launched child psychologically present, the lower the general affect about life as reported by *both* parents.

## Regression Analyses

To further investigate the relationship between boundary ambiguity and measures of dysfunction, stepwise regression analyses were performed. Because rural/urban comparisons showed few or no differences, this categorical variable (urban versus rural) was not included in the regression analysis.

A small number of independent variables, including age, income, number of children, number of years married, stress scores, cohesion and adaptability scores, and the boundary ambiguity score, were regressed on the dependent variables. Regressions were performed with four different dependent variables: fathers' and mothers' well-being scores and fathers' and mothers' somatization scores. The independent variable was boundary ambiguity and, as hypothesized, boundary ambiguity was found to be predictive of fathers' somatization scores. However, boundary ambiguity did not predict mothers' somatization scores or either parent's well-being scores, and these analyses will not be discussed further.

Results of this multiple regression analysis showed the father's boundary ambiguity score to be the strongest predictor of his somatization score, accounting for 14% of the variance ($F = 8.5$, $p = .005$) (see Table

Table 4.
*Regression on Father's Somatization Score*

|  | F | P | $R^2$ Change |
|---|---|---|---|
| Father's boundary ambiguity score | 8.47 | .005 | .138 |
| Father's level of felt stress, past 3 years | 4.72 | .034 | .070 |
| Other variables | | not significant | |

4). The only other significant predictor variable of the father's amount of somatization was his total score on felt level of stress (F = 4.7, p = .034), accounting for an additional 7% of the variance. It should be noted that these two variables together accounted for only 21% of the variance, indicating that these results should be interpreted cautiously.

## Additional Analyses: Comparisons Between High and Low Boundary Ambiguity Families

Those couples in which *both* partners scored either in the *upper* third or the *lower* third of the distribution of scores for their sex were identified in order to explore whether any particular characteristics differentiated families scoring high on the boundary ambiguity scales from families scoring low on the scale. This procedure resulted in two subsamples: 7 couples with *both* spouses scoring in the upper third on the boundary ambiguity scale, and 15 couples with *both* spouses scoring in the lower third on the boundary ambiguity scale.

Due to the small size of this subsample and the exploratory nature of this comparison, no significance tests were performed. Results are reported in a descriptive manner, using means, frequencies, and percentages. A summary is given in Table 5.

*Demographic differences.* Demographic variables of potential importance in discriminating between high and low boundary ambiguity couples included age, length of marriage, number of children, income,

years of schooling, and years since the adolescent had left. Couples with *higher* boundary ambiguity scores were slightly younger (fathers: 53 vs 54.3; mothers: 49.7 vs. 52.2) and had been married for fewer years (26.8 vs. 30.7), yet they tended to have more children (4.3 vs. 3.5). About 80% of both subsamples were rural (12 of 15 low boundary ambiguity couples and 6 of 7 high boundary ambiguity couples). Although the percentage of rural couples varies slightly (80% versus 86%), these subsamples are too small to decipher whether there is a meaningful difference in place of residence between high and low boundary ambiguity couples.

In the couples with low boundary ambiguity, both fathers and mothers had more education than in high boundary ambiguity couples. All but one person in the low-scoring dyads had finished high school, with 16 individuals continuing their education beyond this level. For *high* boundary ambiguity couples, six of the seven women had finished high school, but only two of the seven men had done so. Corresponding to this pattern of difference in education is a large difference in average income, with high boundary ambiguity couples averaging $25,286 and low boundary ambiguity couples averaging $41,214.

Although exploratory, these findings suggest a need for further research to determine whether place of residence (urban/rural), income, education, and number of children separately predict levels of boundary ambiguity. Rural/urban differences, for example, may only be artifacts of income and educational differences. The present sample is too small to draw conclusions, but the findings do suggest hypotheses that need to be tested.

Table 5.
*Comparison of Low and High Boundary Ambiguity Couples*

|  | Low Boundary Ambiguity | High Boundary Ambiguity |
|---|---|---|
|  | N = 30 (15 couples) | N = 14 (7 couples) |
| Age | Mothers = 52.2, Fathers = 54.3 | Mothers = 49.7, Fathers = 53.0 |
| Number of years married | 30.7 | 26.8 |
| Number of children | 3.5 | 4.3 |
| Number completing high school | N = 29 | N = 8 |
| Income | 41,214 | 25,286 |
| Rural/Total | 12/15 (80%) | 6/7 (86%) |
| Fathers' somatic symptoms | 26.8 | 32.9 |
| Fathers' level of stress | 12.6 | 15.9 |
| Fathers' general affect | 5.6 | 4.9 |
| Mothers' general affect | 5.3 | 4.9 |

Note: Unless otherwise noted, numbers are means.

*Other variables.* Consistent with the results of already discussed analyses which suggest associations between boundary ambiguity, stress, and somatization in fathers, the men in the high boundary ambiguity group reported more incidence of somatic symptoms (32.9 vs. 26.8) and a higher level of stress accumulating over the last 3 years (15.9 vs. 12.6) relative to men in the low boundary ambiguity group. This pattern was *not* seen for women. In addition, high boundary ambiguity couples tended to be more negative in their affective evaluations of their own lives (fathers: 4.9 vs. 5.6; mothers: 4.9 vs. 5.3).

## Discussion

The differences between rural and urban mid-life couples were strikingly few. Although rural fathers scored higher on some items in the boundary scale, no other statistical differences emerged. In sum, although mothers, rural and urban, tended to score higher overall and rural fathers tended to report more boundary ambiguity (as compared to urban fathers), none of these differences were significant. Future studies on large samples will need to test the hypotheses that there are more gender than rural/urban differences in level of boundary ambiguity in mid-life couples after an adolescent leaves home.

In general, most fathers and mothers responded similarly to items about the psychological presence of their physically absent child. Discrepancies between scores (within couples) were predominantly due to the mothers reporting a higher level of boundary ambiguity. This difference decreased across the sample as the time increased since the adolescent left home. This finding corresponds to the temporal nature of the process of resolving loss: As the family members change their perceptions regarding who is in and who is out of the family, the level of boundary ambiguity decreases. Family counselors also observe that the parents' psychological preoccupation experienced when a child leaves home does for the most part decrease over time.

## Conclusion

Predictions concerning relationships between high boundary ambiguity scores, family health, and individual well-being were partially supported. For fathers, high boundary ambiguity scores were associated with higher incidence of various somatic symptoms. Fathers' scores on the boundary ambiguity scale were also significant predictors of their levels of somatization (dysfunction). The relationship between fathers' preoccupation with an adolescent who has left home and proclivity to somatic problems needs further investigation. It may be that mid-life fathers are less healthy than mid-life mothers, or it may be that "the empty nest syndrome" affects fathers in a more deleterious way than it does mothers. Another possible explanation may be that fathers, due to socialization, are less able to express the loss verbally and affectively. Their grieving may instead be expressed through somatization. Given longitudinal data, these speculations can be tested.

Results for mothers showed that their preoccupation with the launched child (higher boundary ambiguity scores) was associated with (a) being married to a man who reported higher levels of somatic symptoms, and (b) *both* husband and wife rating their lives more negatively on bipolar adjective scales (level of general affect). Mothers, as compared with fathers, tended to be slightly more preoccupied with the adolescent who left home. In particular, mothers reported that they thought about the adolescent who had left and felt lonely more often than fathers did.

At this time, the temporal relationships among somatization, affect, and boundary ambiguity are unknown. Attending to somatic symptoms may be an important factor in working with such couples, perhaps a way of joining with the father and his experiences. In a clinical setting, directing interventions to issues of general affect and satisfaction with life may provide a path into the *meaning* parents attach to this normative loss when they are having difficulty with children leaving home. Boundary ambiguity is a *perceptual* variable, thus changing perceptions regarding the event of loss may be the most efficient way to influence the level of individual and family dysfunction associated with the ambiguity.

For men, boundary ambiguity was associated with somatic symptoms; for women, it was associated with their general affect (attitude toward present life). Research is needed to determine *why* mid-life fathers react differently from mid-life mothers and whether this difference remains stable in samples with other demographic characteristics. A larger sample will be used to test the hypothesis that there is a significant difference in how mothers and fathers react to an adolescent leaving home.

The exploratory analysis of high and low boundary ambiguity couples suggests other considerations for future research. In this sample, high boundary ambiguity families tended to be larger, less educated, and less financially stable. In these high boundary ambiguity families, fathers reported more somatic symptoms, more stress, and less positive evaluations of their lives. This pattern across variables paints a picture of the rural family and especially fathers as being vulnerable psychologically as well as economically. When these preliminary data suggest rural/urban differences, rural families appear even more vulnerable. More research is needed to test and verify these relationships in larger samples, to determine cause and effect, and to answer the questions about gender versus rural/urban differences.

On the basis of these descriptive findings, the authors believe this more social/psychological approach to investigating the vulnerability of rural families would be useful to clinicians and researchers. In particular, for rural families, if high boundary ambiguity families have trouble dealing with the transitions of their adolescent leaving home, they may also have trouble making other transitions now needed for survival in rural families. The present study has produced and clarified hypotheses for further testing regarding differences between rural and urban families *and* gender differences within those families.

## What Does This Mean for Family Therapists and Educators?

Most mothers and fathers in this primarily rural sample had little difficulty negotiating the transition of launching an adolescent. However, when dysfunction was experienced, boundary ambiguity proved to be a stronger predictor of somatization for fathers than did felt level of stress or demographics (i.e., rural or urban).

These preliminary findings point to the need for asking more questions when working with families as counselors or educators.

A major question to ask is whether there are gender differences in how the launching of an adolescent is viewed and experienced in rural and urban families. Perhaps family therapists and educators have too easily accepted the Freudian assumption that "the empty nest syndrome" belongs to mothers. Professionals may too easily accept the assumption that fathers are not bothered when their children leave home. Trained in an era that prescribed mothers to be child-centered and fathers to be breadwinners, professionals may not pay enough attention to how fathers are affected by the "empty nest."

Another question is whether counselors and educators have paid enough attention to the fact that many mothers are delighted when their children grow up and leave home, showing no deleterious effects whatsoever. This was a finding in this study, but further research is needed before the old assumptions about "empty nest syndrome" can be laid to rest.

No generalizations can be made from this preliminary study, but findings do suggest new questions and hypotheses for clinical work, for family life education programs, and for future research. Rather than continuing to focus on rural/urban differences, professionals may need to ask about gender differences (even within the same family) before better knowing how a family works, how it negotiates life transitions, and how it deals with loss. Family professionals who work in rural communities can, through their observation of individual families faced with normative but ambiguous loss, make valuable contributions by sharing their observations with researchers who can then test their hypotheses deductively with larger samples. This teamwork between family counselors, educators, and researchers is necessary if family professionals are to be of help to rural families as they negotiate normative life transitions. The authors of this chapter, as they prepare for further analysis with a larger sample, invite responses from rural family educators, counselors, and clergy. Your hunches, ideas, and observational hypotheses are welcome.

END NOTES

1. University of Minnesota Agricultural Experiment Station, North Central Project, "Stress, Coping, and Adaptation in the Middle Years of the Family Life Cycle." Participant states include: Il-

linois, Indiana, Iowa, Kansas, Kentucky, Louisiana, Michigan, Minnesota, and Nebraska.

2. In research conducted on the larger sample from which this sample was drawn, Hadd (1984) found that there are varying degrees of spousal agreement, even on dichotomous items. He reported the finding that the more subjective the questionnaire item was, the lower the level of spousal agreement.

3. This similarity may also be partially attributed to similarities in sample characteristics. Olson's national sample (Olson et al., 1982) was Lutheran, white, and of above average income (over half the sample reported an annual family income of between $20,000 and $39,999), and the present sample was primarily Protestant, white, and at a similar financial level (median income = $36,000).

## REFERENCES

Boss, P. (1977). A clarification of the concept of psychological father presence in families experiencing ambiguity of boundary. *Journal of Marriage and the Family, 39*, 141–151.

Boss, P. (1980a, August). The relationship of wife's sex role perceptions, psychological father presence, and functioning in the ambiguous father-absent MIA family. *Journal of Marriage and the Family, 42*, 541–549.

Boss, P. (1980b, October). Normative family stress: Family boundary changes across the lifespan. *Family Relations, 29*, 445–450.

Boss, P. (1987). Family stress: Perception and context. In M. B. Sussman & S. Steinmetz (Eds.), *Handbook on marriage and the family* (pp. 695–723). New York: Plenum Press.

Boss, P., & Greenberg, J. (1984). Family boundary ambiguity: A new variable in family stress theory. *Family Process, 23*, 535–546.

Campbell, A., Converse, P. E., & Rodgers, W. L. (1976). *The quality of American life: Perceptions, evaluations, and satisfactions.* New York: Russell Sage Foundation.

Dillman, D. A. (1978). *Mail and telephone surveys.* New York: John Wiley and Sons, Inc.

Hadd, G. (1984). *A study of agreement and convergence in spouses' responses to survey items in family research.* Unpublished doctoral dissertation, University of Minnesota, St. Paul.

McCubbin, H., Patterson, J., & Wilson, L. (1981). *Family inventory of life events scale (FILE).* St. Paul, MN: University of Minnesota, Department of Family Social Science Publication.

Mederer, H., & Hill, R. (1983). Critical transitions over the family life span: Theory and research. In H. McCubbin, M. Sussman, & J. Patterson (Eds.), *Social stress and the family: Advances and developments in family stress theory and research* (pp. 39–60). New York: Haworth Press.

Norem, R. H., & Brown, W. C. (1983, October). *Family health indicators.* Paper presented at the annual meeting of the National Council on Family Relations, St. Paul, MN.

Olson, D., Bell, R., & Portner, J. (1979). *Family adaptability and cohesion evaluation scale (FACES).* University of Minnesota, unpublished manual.

Olson, D., McCubbin, H., Barnes, H., Larsen, A., Muxen, M., & Wilson, M. (1982). *Family inventories: Inventories used in a national survey of families across the family life span.* St. Paul, MN: University of Minnesota Department of Family Social Science Publication.

U.S. Department of Commerce Census Burea. (1982). *1980 Census of Population, Vol. 1. Characteristics of the Population, Part 25: Minnesota.* Washington, DC: U.S. Government Printing Office.

# 18

# Mothers-in-Law and Daughters-in-Law: The Effects of Proximity on Conflict and Stress*

**Ramona Marotz-Baden and Deane Cowan\*\***

Stories about problematic mothers-in-law abound, yet little research attention has been focused on their interaction with other family members. This is surprising given the prevalence of in-laws, the recent interest in work and the family, the fact that over 90% of American businesses are family owned (Rosenblatt, 1985), and that most will be passed on to adult children (Bratton & Berkowitz, 1976; Hedlund & Berkowitz, 1979).

A smoothly running family contributes to a successful family business (Prokesch, 1986), and mothers and daughters-in-law hold critical positions. For example, the daughter-in-law's feelings of acceptance, her perception of how well she, her husband, and her children are treated, their future economic security, and her enjoyment of farm/ranch life may contribute not only to the smooth running of the enterprise, but to the eventual success of an intergenerational transfer. Her unhappiness can disrupt the family and subsequently the enterprise. For example, she could convince her husband to move off the farm which would disrupt the transfer process; or, she may divorce him. A divorce can seriously disrupt or even bankrupt the enterprise depending upon the daughter-in-law's extent of ownership.

Very little research has focused on conflict between mothers and their daughters-in-law and the stress such unresolved conflict may produce in family businesses. This research reports on the mother/daughter-in-law dyad in two-generation farm and ranch families. It will attempt to identify sources of conflict between mothers-in-law and daughters-in-law and strategies used to cope with this conflict. In addition, the chapter will explore whether or not living in close proximity increases their conflict and stress. This information should be especially useful for counselors who work with members of farm and ranch families and for extension and other applied professionals who base programs and projects on research.

## Review of the Literature

A review of the literature revealed more concern than data about potential mother/daughter-in-law conflict in intergenerational situations arising from living in close proximity, shared labor, and constant interaction between families. Thus, the following review draws heavily upon the few relevant research studies found.

*This research was supported by the Montana Agricultural Experiment Station Grant No. MONB00266 and is part of the SAES Western Regional Research Project W-167. Appreciation is expressed to Jeff Larson, Wayne Larson, and Stephan Wilson for their comments on an earlier version of this chapter.

**Ramona Marotz-Baden is a Professor in the Department of Health and Human Development, Montana State University, Bozeman, MT 59717. Deane Cowan is a marriage and family therapist in Bozeman, MT.

Reprinted from *Family Relations*, 1987, **36**, 385-390.

## In-Law Relationships

On the basis of her national study of 5,020 American women and men, Duvall (1954) developed a model to explain kin conflict. She suggests that every married couple belongs to three different families. The first affiliation is with the new family that the couple begins together (i.e., their family of procreation). At the same time the couple also belong to both his and her families of origin. Unless a beginning family can form a cohesive family unit that is stronger than the one which ties either of the couple to his or her family of origin, the new family will feel threatened. In order to establish a strong family unit, a newly married couple must realign its loyalties such that their family comes before either his or hers.

According to Duvall (1954), the young couple requires autonomy in order to develop as an independent family unit. Any conflicting force emanating from either parental home that imperils the independence of the new pair may be construed as in-law difficulty. Duvall's model suggests that the greater the autonomy of the married adult children and the fewer the conflicts between the parents and the adult children, the more cohesive the marriage of the adult children.

According to Kieren, Henton, and Marotz's (1975) review of the literature, in most cases of marital conflict both husbands and wives believe that the husband's kin are more frequently the source of the conflict than are the wife's kin. In addition, more women than men report difficulty, and more female in-laws are found troublesome than male in-laws both among distant and close relatives (Duvall, 1954; Kirkpatrick, 1963; Komarovsky, 1964; Leslie, 1976).

In-laws, according to Duvall's (1954) respondents, were meddlesome, interfering, and dominating. Adult children criticized members of the parental generation more often than they were criticized by the older generation. Parents-in-law were often viewed as old-fashioned, resistant to change, uncongenial, and maintaining different traditions. Perhaps adult children were more critical as they were struggling for autonomy. Parents-in-law did not complain that their children were too modern; rather, they wished that their adult children would accept them as they were without negatively labeling them.

In sum, according to Duvall's (1954) model, good in-law relationships are problematic for young couples until they have developed their own autonomy. This may be more difficult to do if the young couple live in close proximity to their in-laws. Beavers (1977) found that family members with different values or needs experienced frequent conflict. Thus, establishing autonomy may be especially hard for young couples who work with and live near the older generation as is often the case for adult children of farmers and ranchers. The new wife will probably have more in-law problems because the more meddlesome in-laws are likely to be the husband's and because she is probably living closer to them than she is to her own parents and other relatives. The young couple will be struggling to obtain autonomy by psychologically distancing themselves equally from both her and his families when it may not be possible to change the physical parameters of their daily interaction with his parents with whom they work and perhaps live.

## Mother-In-law/Daughter-In-Law Relationships

In-law studies in Western societies consistently indicate that mother-in-law is the most difficult in-law (Duvall, 1954; Schlien, 1985). The intimate bond that mothers-in-law and daughters-in-law share with the son/husband is often the only tie between them. There may even be competition between them for his affection if the mother senses she is losing her special place to the daughter-in-law, and the daughter-in-law, who probably is not as experienced as her mother-in-law in cooking and cleaning, strives to please her husband (see, for example, the review in Kieren, Henton, & Marotz, 1975, pp. 204-217).

Fischer's (1983) case study of 33 daughters, 30 mothers, and 24 mothers-in-law indicates that the daughter-in-law tends to turn to her own mother for help after the birth of a child rather than to her mother-in-law, who may see herself as the primary maternal figure in her daughter-in-law's life. The daughter-in-law's discrimination in favor of her own mother and the orientation of both generations around the child brings more strain to the relationship of the mother-in-law and the daughter-in-law. Living near one's mother-in-law when one has children is associated with greater conflict than when one does not have children (Fischer, 1983).

Like Duvall, Fischer also found that daughters-in-law were irritated more often by the behavior of their mothers-in-law than were mothers-in-law with the behavior of their daughters-in-law. The greatest source of irritation for daughters-in-law was a result of differences over issues involving children. Complaints of mothers-in-law about the mothering practices of their daughters-in-law were often viewed by the daughter-in-law as attempts to subvert her child management practices (Fischer, 1983).

## Purpose of Study

Two-generation farm and ranch families share a common economic unit, and in addition to working together to effectively manage that unit, they often live in close proximity. Duvall's (1954) in-law theory suggests that, at least until a new husband and wife have established a cohesive family unit of their own which is stronger than the ties to either's family of origin, a mother-in-law's interference will negatively affect her daughter-in-law's marital satisfaction and stress level.

Since there has been so little empirical research on mothers-in-law and daughters-in-law, the research reported below is exploratory. Because this relationship has been stereotyped as one of conflict, descriptive data about typical problems in the relationship between these two generations of women and how they attempted to resolve them were collected to provide background data for this and future research. The correlation between residential proximity and stress levels of the two groups of women was tested. In addition, the relationship between daughter-in-law's stress and marital satisfaction and her perception of her mother-in-law's interference in her and her husband's lives was explored. Since mother/daughter-in-law interaction has been portrayed as rife with potential conflict, the results of this study should be important for counselors and mental health personnel who work with members of farm and ranch families as well as for extension agents, the clergy, and other professionals who present stress management workshops.

## Methodology

The sample was obtained with the help of the Montana Agricultural Stabilization and Conservation Service (ASCS) which provided a 10% random sample of Montana farms and ranches over 200 acres that their records indicated were being operated by more than one household. ASCS records did not distinguish between lineal and collateral kin. Therefore, operations of brothers and sisters were included in the list as well as those of parents and children. Two hundred acres was chosen as the minimum size in order to eliminate hobby ranches. Certain intensive units such as feed lots and poultry operations may have been eliminated by this decision.

Each of the 400 multifamily operations identified by the ASCS was sent a letter explaining the study and requesting the names and addresses of the mother and father in the older generation and at least one married son and his wife who worked on the operation. Of the 253 operations (63% of original sample) who responded after two follow-ups, only 7 or 2.8% were unwilling to participate. One hundred seventy-eight or 70.3% of the operations were not eligible, however, because they were not lineal kin or did not meet the criterion of an intact older generation with at least one married son.

Pretested questionnaires were sent to each adult member of the 68 intact, two-generation families (i.e., father, mother, married son, and daughter-in-law engaged in a farm or ranch operation). After two follow-up letters, 175 people responded. Of these, 44 were mothers-in-law and 55 were daughters-in-law. Although the sample is small, it represents almost all of the eligible daughters-in-law and most of the eligible mothers-in-law identified by the sampling procedure as living in two-generation family farm operations.

## Sample

The mean age of the 44 mothers-in-law was 60.1 years and of the 55 daughters-in-law 31.6 years. The mothers-in-law had been married an average of 35.8 years and averaged 4.1 children. The daughters-in-law had been married an average of 10.5 years and averaged 2.5 children.

Fifty-nine percent of the mothers-in-law had a high school education or less compared with 34% of the daughters-in-law. While approximately the same proportion (29%) had some college, more daughters-in-law had a college degree (20.8% vs. 2.6%).

Before tax income for both groups of women ranged from below $5,000 to over $80,000 in 1985. The mean income reported by mothers-in-law was in the $30,000 to $39,000 range; by daughters-in-law in the $20,000 to $29,000 range.

## Measures

Conflict and conflict resolution strategies were obtained by the following open-ended questions: "When we have problems getting along together, it is usually because . . . ; What strategies have you used that were effective when you were having problems getting along with your daughter-in-law (mother-in-law)?" Respondents frequently listed two or three problems and strategies. All responses were categorized and coded.

Proximity was measured with a forced choice question asking mothers-in-law and daughters-in-law how close they lived to each other in miles and fractions of miles. Differences in child-rearing practices between the generations were measured by a question asking about the occurrence of such differences in the last 2 years. The daughter-in-law's perception of her mother-in-law's interference in her family was measured by seven forced-choice questions. These questions were about jealousy, resentment, bossiness, husband's loyalty to his mother rather than to his wife, whether the mother-in-law tried to run her daughter-in-law's life, if she respected the daughter-in-law's privacy, and if the mother-in-law saw things differently from the daughter-in-law. The forced choice answers were never, sometimes, often, and all of the time.

Stress, defined as tension resulting from lack of adequate accommodation to occupational and general stressors, was ascertained by two measures. The Farm Family Stress Scale (FFSS) (Weigel, Blundall, & Weigel, 1984; Weigel, Weigel, & Blundall, 1987) was used to measure stress between the two generations. The FFSS measures stressors emanating from situations involving several families farming together. Respondents are asked how often 22 situations occurred in the last 2 years and how disturbing each situation was. The authors report the FFSS reliability as .90 for the older generation and .91 for the younger generation using Chronbach's alpha. Validity has not been established.

A factor analysis of the Family Farm Stress Scale yielded five underlying dimensions or factors (Marotz-Baden, 1986). They are Lack of Equal Status, reflecting a lack of equality between the two generations and among family members generally; Family vs. Farm, indicating that the demands of the farm are in conflict with time demands of the family; Financial Concerns; Independence/Dependence, which taps a desire for more independence; and Extended Family Conflict, reflecting concern over time spent together and differing childrearing practices.

The Perceived Stress Scale (PSS) devised by Cohen, Kamarck, and Mermelstein (1983) was used to measure general stress. This 14-item scale is a more general measure of stress than the Farm Family Stress Scale and is purported to measure the degree to which situations in one's life are appraised as stressful. Coefficient alpha reliability for the PSS ranges from .84 to .86 but falls off rapidly after 4-6 weeks, indicating that stress levels vary as daily hassles, major events, and coping resources change. This suggests that the PSS reliably measures current stress level.

The Locke-Wallace Short Marital Adjustment and Prediction Test was used to measure marital satisfaction. According to Locke and Wallace (1959), the reliability coefficient for the marital adjustment (accommodation of husband and wife to each other at a given time) component was .90 and .84 for the marital prediction (forecasting the likelihood of marital adjustment at a future time) component. Locke and Wallace tested their scale on known maladjusted and well adjusted couples and found it to be a valid measure of marital adjustment.

## Results

The data describing the kinds of problems between mothers-in-law and daughters-in-law and strategies for dealing with them are presented followed by a discussion of the effects on stress and marital satisfaction of proximity, differences in child rearing, and perceived interference.

## Conflict and Conflict Resolution Strategies

Because of the lack of research documenting conflict between mothers-in-law and daughters-in-law in two-generation farm and ranch families, the mothers and daughters-in-law in this study were asked what caused problems in their relationship, what strategies they used to cope with these problems, and to whom they turned for advice and support when they were having problems with each other. These questions were open-ended. Respondents could give as many answers as they wished. The three most frequent responses for both groups of women in each of these areas are reported below, as are responses that were given by at least 10% of either group.

*Conflict.* Of those women reporting conflicts, differences in values and opinions and lack of communication tied for first place (28% apiece) by the mothers-in-law as the most frequent problem-causing conflict. Neglect of the farm (17%) and outside stressors (14%) were their next most frequent complaints. The most frequent source of conflict for daughters-in-law was differences in values and opinions (50%). The second most frequently mentioned source of conflict for daughters-in-law was lack of family time (11%). There were two problems that tied for third place with 9% apiece: mother-in-law's critical remarks and outside stressors.

Of note is the high proportion of these women, especially mothers-in-law, who said they had no problems with each other. Twice as many mothers-in-law (34%) as daughters-in-law (17%) responded that there were no problems between the two generations of women. These data are consistent with those of Fischer (1983) and Duvall (1954).

*Strategies.* Both mothers-in-law and daughters-in-law were asked what strategies they used in getting along with each other. The strategy most frequently used by mothers-in-law (36%) was communication, compared with 19% of daughters-in-law who used this strategy. Ignoring the problem was the most commonly used strategy of daughters-in-law (33%). This was the second most frequently used strategy of mothers-in-law (17%). The second most frequently mentioned strategy by daughters-in-law was to take time out (27%). Only 11% of the mothers-in-law stated that they used this strategy for conflict reduction. Twenty-seven percent of the mothers-in-law and 13% of the daughters-in-law did not list any strategies because they said they had no problems.

*Getting Along Together.* The most frequently listed reasons mothers-in-law (23%) and daughters-in-law (26%) gave for getting along well together were that the other showed respect and was fair. For mothers-in-

law, not having any problems with daughter-in-law, having the same values and goals, and working and living apart were tied for second at 14% apiece. The second most frequent reason stated by daughters-in-law (18%) was having the same values and goals. Not having any problems with their mother-in-law was third (15%). Non-interference was stated as a reason by 12% of the mothers-in-law and 10% of the daughters-in-law.

*Advice.* When asked, "To whom do you turn for advice when you are having problems getting along with your mother-/daughter-in-law?" the most frequently listed person by mothers-in-law (32%) and daughters-in-law (39%) was husband. The second and third most frequently listed entities to whom the mothers-in-law turned for advice were their daughters and God, each with 12%. The second most frequently listed person to whom daughters-in-law turned for advice was mother (18%) and the third was friends (16%). Others were also listed as sources of advice by 12% of the daughters-in-law. Twenty-five percent of the mothers-in-law compared to 9% of the daughters-in-law said there was no one to whom they turned.

*Support.* Husbands were the most frequently listed source of support for conflict with one's mother-in-law or daughter-in-law. About one half (48%) of the mothers-in-law and daughters-in-law stated they turned to their husbands for such support. Mothers were the second most frequent source of support for daughters-in-law (15%), friends (13%) third, and others (11%) fourth. Daughters-in-law (15%) were almost the only other person besides husbands that mothers-in-law turned to for support.

Interestingly, almost one quarter (22%) of the mothers-in-law compared to 7% of the daughters-in-law said they did not seek support from anyone. These data and the high percentage (25%) of mothers who said they had no one to whom to turn for advice may mean that mothers-in-law are less willing to talk about such conflict and/or that their social network is smaller than that of their daughters-in-law.

## Effects of Proximity, Child-Rearing Differences, and Interference

Twenty-six percent of both groups of women said they lived within 1/8 mile of each other and an additional 13% between 1/8 and

Table 1.
*Pearson Correlations Between Proximity and the Stress Measures: The Five Factors and Total Scores of Family Farm Stress Scale (FFSS) and the Perceived Stress Scale (PSS)*

|  | FFSS Factors | | | | | Total Scores | |
|  | 1 | 2 | 3 | 4 | 5 | FFSS | PSS |
|---|---|---|---|---|---|---|---|
| Mother-in-law | .17 | .13 | .03 | .05 | .17 | .15 | .15 |
| Daughter-in-law | .20 | .17 | .18 | .06 | .03 | .06 | .27* |

*$p < .05$.

1/4 mile. Sixteen percent lived between 1/4 mile and 5 miles from each other, 16% between 5 and 10 miles, 19% between 10 and 50 miles, and only 10% over 50 miles. Clearly, close proximity was a fact of life for many of these women. Duvall's (1954) theory suggests that close proximity might decrease the young couple's autonomy. This could increase stress between the two women. Measures of stress from two types of stressors were used. To test for the effect of proximity on occupationally related stressors, Pearson product moment correlations were run for daughters-in-law and mothers-in-law between proximity and the Family Farm Stress Scale scores. As can be seen in Table 1, there were no significant correlations for mothers-in-law or daughters-in-law between proximity and the five factors and the total score of the Family Farm Stress Scale which measured stress between the two generations.

To test the effect of proximity on general stress, Pearson product moment correlations were run between proximity and the Perceived Stress Scale for mothers-in-law and daughters-in-law. The correlation for mothers-in-law was low ($r = .15$) and not significant (see Table 1). The correlation for daughters-in-law, while low and positive ($r = .27$), was significant ($p = .05$). Thus, as distance from her mother-in-law increased, the daughter-in-law's stress level went up. This finding is contrary to expectations. It should be pointed out, however, that proximity accounts for only .07 of the variance of the daughter-in-law's overall perceived stress score. Thus, these data suggest that proximity has little effect on the stress levels of these farm and ranch women. What effect it has appears to increase with distance. An alternative explanation based on conventional wisdom is that these sons and daughters-in-law chose to locate as close to his parents (and the farm job) as they thought they could satisfactorily tolerate. To the ex-

tent that this was true for this sample, if they erred, it was by living too far away.

A couple's identity formation, however, may be more dependent on time than proximity. If this is the case, the longer the couple had been married, the more likely they would be to establish a cohesive family unit separate from both sets of in-laws. All of the young couples except one (who had been married only one year) had been married for at least 2 years and had children. (The mean number of years married was 10.5). To test the effect of length of marriage on stress for daughters-in-law, analysis of variance was used. Length of marriage was arbitrarily divided into the following four categories: 1-3 years, 4-9 years, 10-14 years, and 15 years or more. There were no significant differences on any of the FFS scales or PSS scores by length of time married.

The literature review suggested that differences in child-rearing practices between the two generations would increase the daughter-in-law's stress level. One-way analysis of variance was run on the occurrence of differences in child-rearing practices between the generations and daughter-in-law's general stress level as measured by her PPS score. There were no statistically significant differences in child-rearing practices and stress levels.

Since this result was unexpected, the item measuring the frequency of occurrence of differences in child-rearing practices between the women and the extent to which such differences were disturbing was examined. The majority of mothers-in-law (67%) and daughters-in-law (54%) stated that differences in childrearing practices seldom occurred. A third (33%) of the mothers-in-law and 32% of the daughters-in-law said they occurred sometimes. Only 14% of the daughters-in-law, but no mothers-in-law, said they were frequent.

Not many of these women viewed differences in child-rearing practices as very disturbing. Forty-six percent of the mothers-in-law and 41% of the daughters-in-law said they were not disturbing, and 48% of the older and 44% of the younger women said they were either slightly or moderately disturbing. Only 6% of the mothers-in-law and 16% of the daughters-in-law said they were either quite or extremely disturbing. Controlling for proximity and length of time married did not alter these results. Thus, while some daughters-in-law are upset by child-rearing differences, for most, differences that exist are not very disturbing.

Duvall's (1954) in-law theory suggests that the daughter-in-law's perception of her mother-in-law's interference in her and her husband's lives will negatively influence her marital satisfaction. Seven questions measured different aspects of the daughter-in-law's perception of her mother-in-law's interference. One-way analyses of variance tests were run for each question and the daughter-in-law's score on the Locke-Wallace Short Marital Adjustment and Prediction Test. There were no significant differences.

One-way analysis of variance was also run for questions measuring interference and intergenerational farm-related stress as measured by each of the five factors and the total score of the Family Farm Stress Scale. Because these findings were contrary to expectations, the items measuring interference were examined. In brief, about a third of the daughters-in-law reported that their mothers-in-law interfered in their lives at least some of the time. Most did not report much interference. Sixty percent, for example, said that their mothers-in-law never tried to run their lives and that they were never jealous of their mothers-in-law. While seventy-five percent said that the mother-in-law was seldom or never bossy, 72% reported they were very satisfied with her respect for their privacy, and 70% said the mother-in-law sometimes saw things differently from themselves; only 28% said they were never resentful of their mothers-in-law.

Controlling for proximity and length of time married only altered the findings on the issue of privacy. Daughters-in-law who had been married 10-14 years and who lived 1/4 to 10 miles away from their mothers-in-law, were more satisfied with her respect for their privacy than were those who lived closer or farther away or who had been married a shorter or longer period of time (Chi-square = 7.95; df = 2; $p$ = .019). Nevertheless, it does not appear that the mother-in-law's interference significantly affected the daughter-in-law's satisfaction or intergenerational stress levels.

## Interpretation

Previous research suggests that relationships of mothers-in-law and daughters-in-law could be marked by conflict, especially if they lived in close proximity and the daughter-in-law had children. Further, this conflict could affect the stress levels and marital satisfaction of the daughters-in-law. The data from this study of farm and ranch women did not support this contention.

The majority of mothers-in-law and daughters-in-law in this study seemed to have good relationships with each other, although more daughters-in-law (83%) reported problems than mothers-in-law (66%). In fact, 34% of the mothers-in-law said they had no problems getting along with their daughters-in-law compared with 17% of the daughters-in-law. That daughters-in-law perceived more problems was expected. Previous research suggests that the mother-in-law is the most troublesome in-law. In addition, it was the daughter-in-law who most recently became a part of the farm/ranch operation and who was probably expected by everyone to do more adjusting.

Less than one third of the daughters-in-law reported that they had serious arguments with their mothers-in-law, that they were jealous or resentful of the older woman, that their mother-in-law tried to run their lives, or that their husband was more loyal to his mother than to his wife. Furthermore, 72% of the daughters-in-law were satisfied with their mothers-in-law's respect for their privacy. Only about 30% of the daughters-in-law stated that their mothers-in-law "often or always" saw things differently than they did.

Responses to another question in the study reaffirmed these findings. Sixty-two percent of the daughters-in-law reported that they got along well most of the time with their mothers-in-law. Thirty percent said they had some problems getting along. Only 8% said they got along poorly.

Values and goals were important to both mothers-in-law and daughters-in-law. Differences in values and goals were the primary sources of conflict for both. Similarity of values and goals was the second most frequently cited reason for getting along together. Thus, practitioners and researchers working with two-generation families should be alert for perceived differences in values and goals which could provide potential conflict.

Communication also played a critical role in the relations between these two groups of women. Thirty-six percent of the mothers-in-law said that communication was their most effective strategy in resolving conflict with their daughters-in-law. Lack of communication was tied with differences in values as the most frequently cited reason mothers-in-law gave for not getting along with their daughters-in-law. Programs designed to aid such families should, therefore, include a communications component.

The focus of this research was on identifying common sources of conflict between mothers-in-law and daughters-in-law in two-generation farm/ranch families. Large amounts of unresolved conflict were not discovered. Approximately two thirds of the mothers-in-law and daughters-in-law were effectively working out their problems. The remaining one third were experiencing problems they have yet to resolve. These problems did not seem to be appreciably related to either how close they lived to their mothers-in-law or to the length of time daughters-in-law had been married.

## Conclusions and Implications

Mothers-in-law have been viewed as problematic at least since the days of Hansel and Gretel. The purpose of this exploratory research on mother-in-law and daughter-in-law relationships in two-generation farm and ranch families was to identify sources of conflict between these two generations of women, to determine the impact of such conflict on stress levels and marital satisfaction, and to identify strategies these women used to cope with their conflict.

The relationships between mothers-in-law and daughters-in-law living in two-generation farm/ranch families were not as problematic as expected. The majority of mothers-in-law and daughters-in-law reported that they got along well together. One third of the women, however, were having problems. This figure is consistent with other data. Tension and strain between fami-

ly members, for example, was the second largest source of stressors reported in a 1981 study of Montana farm/ranch families (Marotz-Baden, 1985). In that study 29% of the couples surveyed reported increased conflict with in-laws or relatives during the last year.

These data have important implications for counselors, clergy, physicians, mental health personnel, and extension agents. It is important for these professionals to be aware that a significant minority of farm/ranch families are experiencing problems with their in-laws and other relatives. Such information should be useful as they prescribe treatment and plan programs to alleviate stress in rural families. Important factors to consider are differences in values, goals, and communication patterns.

Because this study was of *intact*, two-generation farm and ranch families, it is not known how many of the younger generation are no longer farming with their parents because they could not get along. Anecdotal data from one of the daughters-in-law in this study (in her second marriage) and from several sons, who did not qualify for the study, suggest that serious problems do exist in some families and that these can lead to a breakup of the two-generation family or divorce. In addition to the suggestions offered to applied professionals in the preceding section of this chapter, it seems appropriate to suggest that a critical time for preventative intervention may be when the son(s) marry and/or begin to farm with/for their parents.

This research also provides some baseline information for further research. Why do some multigeneration families get along so well and others poorly? If in-law conflict and proximity are not strongly related to stress and marital satisfaction, what factors in two-generation families are? These are but a few of the questions to be answered by further research.

REFERENCES

Beavers, W. (1977). *Psychotherapy and growth.* New York: Brunner Mazel.
Bratton, A., & Berkowitz, A. (1976, April-June). Intergenerational transfer of the farm business. *New York Food and Life Sciences Quarterly,* **9**(2), 7-9.
Cohen, S., Kamarck, T., & Mermelstein, R. (1983). A global measure

of perceived stress. *Journal of Health and Social Behavior,* **24,** 385-395.

Duvall, E. (1954). *In-laws: Pro and con.* New York: Associated Press.

Fischer, L. (1983). Mothers and mothers-in-law. *Journal of Marriage and the Family,* **45,** 187-192.

Hedlund, D., & Berkowitz, A. (1979). The incidence of social-psychological stress in farm families. *International Journal of Sociology and the Family,* **9,** 233-243.

Kieren, D., Henton, J., & Marotz, R. (1975). *Hers and his.* Hinsdale, IL: Dryden Press.

Kirkpatrick, C. (1963). *The family as process and institution.* New York: Ronald Press.

Komarovsky, M. (1964). *Blue collar marriage.* New York: Vintage Books.

Leslie, G. (1976) *The family in social context.* New York: Oxford University Press.

Locke, H., & Wallace, K. (1959). Short marital adjustment and prediction tests: Their reliability and validity. *Marriage and Family Living,* **21,** 251-255.

Marotz-Baden, R. (1985, May). Stress and the two-generation ranch family. In    J. Powell (Ed.), *Holistic Ranch Management Workshop Proceedings* (pp. 11-15). Casper, WY: Wyoming Agricultural Extension Service.

Marotz-Baden, R. (1986, November). *Two generation politics: Transferring the family farm.* Paper presented at the annual meeting of the National Council on Family Relations, Dearborn, MI.

Prokesch, S. (1986, June 11). When the relatives fall out. *The New York Times,* pp. 31, 43.

Rosenblatt, P. (1985). Family, Inc. *Psychology Today,* **19**(7), 55-59.

Schlien, J. (1985). *Structure-function, kinship terminology, and the mother-in-law.* Paper presented at the Annual Symposium on the Committee of Human Development.

Weigel, R., Blundall, J., & Weigel, D. (1984). *Research and education project.* Ames, IA: Cooperative Extension Service, Iowa State University.

Weigel, R., Weigel, D., & Blundall, J. (1987). Stress, coping, and satisfaction: Generational differences in farm families. *Family Relations,* **36,** 45-48.

# Rural and Urban Elderly: Differences in the Quality of the Parent-Child Relationship*

Joyce McDonough Mercier, Lori Paulson, and Earl W. Morris**

The idea that contemporary families are alienated from their elderly is not consistent with research. Studies have documented strong intergenerational ties, responsible filial behavior, and the prominence of families in the networks of aging people (Brody, 1981; Mercier & Powers, 1984). The family, whether in a rural or an urban setting, has consistently offered strong support to its aging members (Mercier & Powers, 1984). What has not been as clearly defined by research, however, is an understanding of the affective quality of the relationship between aging parents and their adult children. Nor is it clear whether there are differences in the quality of the relationship or its determinants in rural or urban settings.

The purpose of this study was to examine rural/urban differences in the quality of the relationship between older people and their children. The study developed from a concern with the way in which supportive interaction occurs between generations of family members. The quality of the interpersonal relationship was examined from the point of view of the parent. Because this relationship is so vital in the support systems of the elderly, a clearer understanding will enable family counselors, family life educators, and family policy specialists to develop more appropriate and effective helping techniques in support of elderly people.

Differences exist between the informal support systems of the rural and urban elderly residents (Mercier & Powers, 1984). More rural elderly people tend to live with a spouse than do urban elderly people. Even though more rural persons are married than widowed, the widowed make up a large proportion of the rural elderly population, and the rural widowed rely more on relatives for aid than do rural married individuals. Children of rural widows provide emotional support, advice, and transportation (Mercier & Powers, 1984; Solomon, 1975), yet fewer children are readily accessible in rural as contrasted to urban areas. In general, the rural aged have greater transportation, housing, and health problems than do the urban aged. Rural aged people are more vulnerable because of fewer support systems than urban aged people and, as a result, the rural aged may require more assistance from their children.

Studies of the general population have agreed that most adult children feel very close to their elderly parents and vice versa (Cicirelli, 1981). Parents are inclined to feel even closer to their children than their children do to them because of a generational stake in the relationship (Bengtson, 1979; Cicirelli, 1983), that is, the parents have more

*This research was funded by the Iowa Department of Elder Affairs. A version of this chapter was presented at the Midwestern Sociological Meeting, Chicago, IL, April 1987. Journal Paper No. 404, Home Economics Research Institute, College of Home Economics, Iowa State University.

**Joyce McDonough Mercier is Associate Professor, Department of Family Environment, Iowa State University, Ames, IA 50011. Lori Paulson is a doctoral candidate, Department of Family Environment, Iowa State University, Ames, IA 50011. Earl W. Morris is Professor, Department of Family Environment, Iowa State University, Ames, IA 50011.

Reprinted from Family Relations, 1988, 37, 68-72.

to lose in the relationship than do the children. Other studies reported similar findings (Johnson & Bursk, 1977; Streib, 1965).

Considering the importance of children to their aging parents in either a rural or an urban setting, it seems clear that the quality of the relationship that parents have with their children has been affected by the expectations a parent has of a child in providing care and support for the aging parent in later years. In an early study by Kerckhoff (1966) investigating parental expectations of children, low expectations were associated with high morale. No connection was made between parental expectations and the quality of the parent-child relationship, but it is logical that the level of parental morale will affect parents' relationships with their children (Johnson & Bursk, 1977).

Another factor receiving a great deal of attention in aging studies is locus of control (Lefcourt, 1976; Phares, 1976; Ziegler & Reid, 1983). Individuals with an internal locus of control have a generalized expectancy that the outcome of events is based on their own behavior. Those with an external locus of control view what happens to them as the result of fate or due to powerful others (Cicirelli, 1980; Molinari & Niederehe, 1984–85). A sense of control over desired outcomes is clearly meaningful for older people (Cicirelli, 1980; Ziegler & Reid, 1983). Further, Molinari and Niederehe (1984–85) reported that older people who live in a community were more internally controlled than younger people. They also found that there was a positive relationship between internality and adjustment to aging by noninstitutionalized elderly.

Locus of control appears to be a central construct that is related to the earlier experiences of an individual and not easily changed by aging (Cicirelli, 1980; Rotter, 1966). The relationship of family variables to locus of control is important within this context. Family life represents a long and continuous history for the individual, and family relationships are maintained in old age. The family helps to develop and maintain an internal locus of control. Those individuals who are more dependent on others are more externally controlled and less likely to be motivated to improve conditions for themselves (Cicirelli, 1980). Individuals with internal locus of control have made better use of information and of support systems than have individuals with external locus of control (Lefcourt, Martin, & Saleh, 1984; Sandler & Lakey, 1982). Those who seemed to be more autonomous appeared to benefit the most from social supports. Thus, locus of control has had an effect on the use of social support systems. It seems reasonable that locus of control affects the relationship between parent and child.

It is hypothesized that the locus of control a parent experiences and the expectations that parent has for his or her adult child affects the relationship with that child. It is believed that an older parent with an internal locus of control and low filial expectations will develop a higher quality relationship with the adult child than will an older parent with an external locus of control and high filial expectations. It is further expected that there will be rural and urban differences in predicting the quality of the parent-child relationship.

# Methodology

## Sample

The data used for this chapter were collected by personal interview as part of a study of elderly residents of a Midwestern state. A random stratified sample was drawn selecting respondents by age—60 to 74 years, and 75 years or older—and residence—rural or urban. Rural residence was defined as living in open areas or in towns with populations of less than 20,000; urban residence was defined as living in towns or cities with populations of 20,000 or more. The original sample included 277 men and women; but due to missing data and the fact that 38 respondents had no children, the sample sizes for the analyses were 111 rural and 112 urban residents; the combined subsample was 223.

No significant differences existed at the significance level of $p < .01$ between rural and urban groups in terms of their sociodemographic characteristics (Table 1). The rural group was slightly older, had less education and income, and had fewer children than the urban group. The number of children ranged from 1 to 12 for both groups. The rural sample was slightly healthier than the urban sample; 78% of the rural group described themselves as being in good or excellent health compared to 74% of the urban group. Sixty-four percent of the rural and urban groups were married. The rural group

Table 1.
*Means and t-scores for Selected Sociodemographic Variables.*

| Variables | Rural (n = 111) | | Urban (n = 112) | | |
| | Mean | Standard Deviation | Mean | Standard Deviation | T-Score |
| --- | --- | --- | --- | --- | --- |
| Health | 2.89 | 0.67 | 2.86 | 1.73 | −0.35 |
| Number of children | 3.00 | 1.73 | 3.23 | 2.07 | 0.87 |
| Education | 11.79 | 2.65 | 11.86 | 3.13 | 0.17 |
| Marital status | 0.64 | 0.48 | 0.64 | 0.48 | 0.04 |
| Sex | 0.48 | 0.50 | 0.43 | 0.50 | −0.73 |
| Age | 70.43 | 7.71 | 69.92 | 7.33 | −0.51 |
| Income | 22,010.01 | 23,533.95 | 24,686.86 | 21,813.74 | 0.88 |

was comprised of 53 (48%) men and 58 (52%) women; the urban sample included 48 (43%) men and 64 (57%) women.

When the parents were interviewed, they were asked to list the names of all their children. The parents were then questioned about the quality of the relationship and the amount and type of interaction that they have had with one of their children. This selected child was either the only child, or in the case of two or more children, a child randomly selected by the interviewer. This was done to ensure representation of all types of relationships between older parents and their adult children. Other studies (Cicirelli, 1981; Johnson & Bursk, 1977) have often used a child selected by the respondent or the geographically nearest child. These methods, however, limit generalizations that may be made from the studies.

In this study, some of the parents were emotionally and/or physically close to the selected children; some were not. For 44% of the rural parents, the selected children lived within 60 miles but not within the same community or household; 24% of the selected children of rural parents lived either in the same household or the same community as their parent. For 10% of the urban group, the selected child lived within 60 miles or less of the parent but not in the same community or household; another 49% of the selected children lived within the same community or household.

For the rural and urban groups, 52% and 46% respectively of the randomly selected children were daughters. Only 31% of both samples, however, reported that the randomly selected child was the child that they were most likely to turn to in an emergency.

## Measuring Variables

The dependent variable, quality of rela-tionship with the selected child, was measured by adding together the parents' responses to four questions about how much they cared about and trusted the selected child and how much the selected child cared about and trusted them. These questions were taken from a scale developed by Bengtson (Bengtson & Schrader, 1982). The response on the 5-point scale ranged from "not at all" to "a great deal." The alpha coefficients of reliability for the scale were .77 and .69 for the rural and urban samples respectively. Seventy-seven percent of both the rural and urban samples reported high levels of trust and care in the relationship with the selected child.

The variable, filial expectations, was measured by summing the responses to four statements to which the parents agreed or disagreed on a 5-point scale. The four statements were: "Adult children should take care of their parents, in whatever way necessary, when they are sick; Adult children should give their parents financial help if the parents need it; Parents are entitled to some return for the sacrifices they have made for their children; and No matter what, adult children should bring their parents into their home if the parents need help." The alpha coefficient of reliability for the rural sample was .74; for the urban sample it was .76.

Locus of control was measured by three questions regarding the amount of control that the parents have over their lives right now, how much control they would like, and how much they expect to have 2 years from now. The possible responses for each item ranged from 1 (low) to 7 (high) on a continuum. The responses from the three items were then scaled to form an index of control. The alpha coefficient of reliability was .77 for the rural sample and was .85 for the urban sample. The urban sample had a larger percentage of people who perceived themselves as having complete control or an internal locus of control (55%) compared to the rural sample (47%).

Geographic proximity was calculated by figuring the actual geographic distance between children and their respective parents. The scale ranged from one to seven; living in the same household was scored as seven or high, and living over 800 miles away was scored as one or low.

## Analysis

The quality of relationship with the selected child was predicted while controlling for the effects of number of children, health, age, income, education, marital status, sex of parent, identification of selected child as the significant child or the child to whom the parent was most likely to turn in an emergency, sex of the child, geographic proximity of the child, filial expectations, and locus of control of the parent. Separate analyses were run for rural and urban samples.

Because of the nonlinear distribution of the dependent variable, logistic regression was the appropriate method of analysis. The LOGIST procedure fits a model to a categorical dependent variable; the independent variables may be either categorical or interval data (Harrell, 1983). The LOGIST procedure also has the option of backward elimination. This allowed the researchers to enter all variables of interest into the equation. Maximum likelihood statistics were then computed on variables that were significant at a designated level; all variables that did not meet the significance requirement were dropped from the model. Any of the variables that were eliminated may be re-entered into the model one by one; whether that variable remained in the model depended on the significance level of that variable when it was included with the variables already in the model.

## Results

The results of the analyses for the rural and urban samples are presented in Table 2. The LOGIST regression eliminated variables that were not significant at $p < .15$ from both samples. In the analysis of the rural sample, the backward elimination procedure dropped six of the independent variables from the model. The model chi-square was 18.40 with 6 degrees of freedom and was significant at the $p < .01$ level; a high, significant chi-square in a LOGIST procedure indicates that the variables in the model are useful in prediction (Afifi & Clark, 1984).

The strongest predictor of quality of relationship with children in the rural sample was geographic proximity of the selected child. The chi-square for proximity was significant ($p < .01$). The individual R, a measure of the relative contribution of each

Table 2.
*Logistic Regression Coefficients of Quality of Relationship on Selected Demographic and Attitudinal Variables*

| Variables Entered | Rural | | | | Urban | | | |
|---|---|---|---|---|---|---|---|---|
| | Beta | Chi-Square | p | R | Beta | Chi-Square | p | R |
| Health | — | — | — | — | — | — | — | — |
| Number of children | -0.26 | 2.42 | 0.12 | -0.06 | — | — | — | — |
| Education | 0.91 | 2.95 | 0.09 | 0.09 | — | — | — | — |
| Marital status | — | — | — | — | — | — | — | — |
| Sex | — | — | — | — | — | — | — | — |
| Age | — | — | — | — | 0.07 | 3.57 | 0.06 | 0.11 |
| Income | — | — | — | — | — | — | — | — |
| Proximity | 0.49 | 7.82 | 0.01 | 0.22 | -0.21 | 2.86 | 0.09 | -0.84 |
| Sex of child | — | — | — | — | — | — | — | — |
| Significant Child | -1.08 | 2.90 | 0.09 | -0.09 | — | — | — | — |
| Filial Expectations | -0.17 | 2.92 | 0.09 | -0.09 | — | — | — | — |
| Control | 0.16 | 2.82 | 0.09 | 0.09 | 0.25 | 10.05 | 0.01 | 0.26 |

Rural: Constant = -1.08, Chi-Square = 18.40, df = 6, Model R = 0.23, n = 111

Urban: Constant = -7.36, Chi-Square = 17.17, df = 3, Model R = 0.30, n = 112 variable to the fit of the model, independent of sample size, was .22. The positive relationship suggests that the closer a child lived to a parent, the higher the quality of the relationship. Number of children remained in the model at this step but was not significant. Other variables that approached significance at the $p < .05$ level were identification of selected child as the significant child, education, filial expectations, and locus of control. This suggests that, for the rural sample, an older parent was more likely to have a higher quality of relationship with the randomly selected child if the parent was educated, lived close to the child, had an internal locus of control and low filial expectations, and if the child was not the one to whom the parent was most likely to turn in an emergency.

Different variables contributed to quality of relationship in the logistic regression equation for the urban sample. Only three variables, age, proximity, and locus of control, remained in the model. Locus of control was the strongest predictor of the quality of the relationship ($p < .01$). Its R was .26, demonstrating a moderate relationship between level of control and quality of relationship with children. Age and proximity approached significance at the $p < .05$ level. The model chi-square of 17.17 indicated that the three variables, particularly locus of control, were useful in explaining the quality of relationship. Urban parents who had a higher quality relationship with their children were older, lived farther away from their children, and had higher levels of control (i.e., internal locus of control) than did parents with a lower level quality of relationship with their children.

## Discussion and Conclusion

Differences do exist between rural and urban parents and the quality of the relationships that they have with their adult children. For rural parents, proximity of the child was the most important predictor; other variables that indicated quality of relationship were education, filial expectations, identification as the significant child, and locus of control. In contrast, locus of control was the most important predictor for urban parents. Age of the parent and proximity of the child also contributed to the prediction of the quality of the relationship.

Geographic proximity of the selected child to the parent was important in both locales. It was, however, a very strong predictor for the rural elderly. Since fewer of the selected children lived nearer their parents in the rural areas, it appeared that having a child nearby to help out if needed was important for the older parents. It may be that the lack of transportation and the lesser density of the population have increased dependence on children as a means of support for these elderly. The rural elderly depend more on the children for emotional support and assistance than do the urban elderly (Mercier & Powers, 1984; Solomon, 1975). Yet many rural elderly have children who have moved a considerable distance away for economic reasons.

In contrast, for the urban elderly whose children actually lived closer than did the children of the rural elderly, geographic proximity was not a statistically significant predictor at $p < .05$ of quality of relationship. This may be due to the fact that elderly people who live in urban areas have more services and a larger pool of support systems upon which to draw than do people who live in rural areas (Mercier & Powers, 1984).

Locus of control was the strongest predictor of the quality of the relationship for the urban elderly. The urban elderly with an internalized sense of control had higher quality relationships with their children. They believed more strongly that the outcome of events was based on their own behavior. For the urban elderly, it is important to be in control of their lives with as little outside influence on their decisions as possible (Cicirelli, 1980; Zeigler & Reid, 1983). For this group, the parent-child relationship is of a higher quality when the parents perceive that they have control over their own lives. Having a high level of internalized control means that the elderly person is independent, and the independence of the older individual contributes to a stronger relationship with adult children (Johnson & Bursk, 1977).

Locus of control, though still indicating internality, is not as important for the rural elderly as for the urban. Since the rural elderly scored somewhat lower on the control measure, it seems reasonable to expect residents of rural areas to be slightly more accepting of life's uncertainty. Living in a rural environment, they have been unable to control some of life's chances such as the weather and crop prices and may be more likely than urban elderly to view much of what happens to them to be the result of fate (Cicirelli, 1980; Molinari & Niederehe, 1984–85). It must be remembered that even though a lack of resources and services may contribute to rural elderly people not learning to access these systems, they want to have control of their lives, and control is still a factor in quality of the parent-child relationship.

For the rural parent, low filial expectations contribute to the quality of the relationship between parent and child. As hypothesized, expecting less duty and obligation from their children positively affects the quality of the relationship for the rural elderly parents. It may be that expectations are lower because few children live in the same community or household and are not there to be called upon for help with daily tasks.

Filial expectations do not contribute to the quality of the parent-child relationship for the urban elderly, however. The urban elderly have a higher level of internalized control than do the rural elderly and may be presumed to make better use of information and support systems than do elderly individuals with lower levels of internalized control (Lefcourt et al., 1984; Sandler & Lakey, 1982). Perhaps because of wider availability of resources and services, the urban elderly have developed a support system based more on formal supports than have the rural elderly. The formal supports allow them to be less dependent on their children than are the rural elderly. As a result, the level of the urban elderly's expectations of their children has no effect on the quality of the parent-child relationship. Thus, it may be surmised that locus of control neutralizes the impact of filial expectations on the quality of the relationship between urban parents and their adult children.

Interestingly, for the rural sample, being identified as the child to whom the parent was most likely to turn first in an emergency, the significant child, did not positively affect the quality of relationship with that child. The relationship with a child who is not the significant child may be more free from the stresses and concerns about the care and support of the parent than the relationship with the significant child. No association was observed between being identified as the significant child and the quality of relationship for the urban sample.

For the urban elderly, age was a relatively strong predictor of quality of relationship. The older they were, the higher was the quality of the urban parents' relationship with their children. This supported Bengtson's (1979) theory of generational stake. The older the person is, the more they have invested in the relationship and the more they have at risk. Older people have more to lose and, thus, see the relationship on a different level than do the children. Age did not remain in the model for the rural elderly and did not contribute to the quality of the parent-child relationship.

## Implications for Family Practitioners

In general, more and different variables were significantly related to the quality of the relationship for the rural elderly than for the urban elderly. These results have implications for family practitioners. The family counselor, family life educator, and the policymaker who are family advocates have interrelated roles in assisting families to maintain and increase the quality of the parent-child relationship.

A family counselor in the rural area who knows which older residents have children living nearby can work to reinforce and support those relationships. For example, in working with the family, the counselor may identify ways in which the adult child can aid the older parent (i.e., being available for shopping and to perform heavy tasks) without that child appearing to usurp the responsibilities of the older person. For those children who live farther away, it may be even more important for a counselor to suggest ways the more distant child can support the parent. That child may not be in a position to participate in shopping or with heavy tasks, but may be supportive in other ways such as interacting with the parent by telephone and the mail. Such actions will strengthen the relationship and enable it to endure.

A key focus for the counselor in working with any of the older adults should be in the area of communication between generations. Both the adult child and the parent require help in expressing their reactions to the aging of the parent. Learning to articulate their feelings about giving and receiving aid and the expectations each has for the other is important in reducing potential sources of conflict.

The family life educator has a major role

in bolstering the relationship of aging parents and their adult children. The educator is in a position to offer assistance to both generations in developing their decision-making skills. Both generations must learn to respect the situation of the other and to work together in making major decisions. For the child of the urban parent in particular, the knowledge of the importance of control to the parent may prevent the child from attempting to do too much for the parent or taking too great a role in decision making. The parents, in turn, must recognize that giving up their role in decision making may ultimately lead to greater dependence. Yet, both generations should recognize the importance of being able to accept help. The educator can teach them how to develop and use these skills.

For both the rural and urban elderly, the educator may be especially valuable in providing information about the variety of resources and services that are available and how they may best be utilized. When health becomes a problem for older people, they are more likely to depend upon their family for assistance; hence, the family will need support. This, coupled with a lack of knowledge and resources, may impose a strain on even the most supportive of family relationships. The family practitioner can ease the stress by providing information and referral services and suggesting ways that family members can utilize those services to assist the aging family member.

Availability of services and resources is obviously greater in an urban than a rural setting. It behooves the family policy advocate to strive to maintain the services and resources that already exist and are utilized in both areas. For example, in the rural area a major factor in resource availability and use of current resources is transportation. Transportation services in rural areas enable the resources to be utilized by the rural elderly and will also affect the relationship between parents and children. The parents will be able to perform certain tasks for themselves that they may formerly have relied on their children to do. Filial expectations that often create strain between generations may be reduced and the relationship improved. Besides helping the parent directly, the policymaker can have a positive impact on the lives of elderly people through economic means, such as tax incentives that benefit children who help their parents or creating new job opportunities that reduce the migration of the younger generation away from their parents.

For the rural elderly whose children have already migrated, it is necessary to remember that independence is important to the older parents, and allowing that individual to remain in control will help maintain his/her independence. Improving access to and availability of resources and services increases that independence.

Even though independence is a crucial value to older people, interdependence with other generations is normal and healthy. Developing appropriate and effective helping techniques that enable the family to have realistic expectations of each other is primary to the goal of a high quality relationship between older parents and their children. Because children are important components in the support systems of aging parents, their relationship with their parents requires as much support and nurture as possible from family practitioners.

## REFERENCES

Afifi, A. A., & Clark, V. (1984). *Computer-aided multivariate analysis.* Belmont, CA: Lifetime Learning Publications.

Bengtson, V. (1979). Research perspectives on intergenerational interaction. In P. K. Ragan (Ed.), *Aging parents* (pp. 37–57). Los Angeles: University of California Press.

Bengtson, V., & Schrader, S. (1982). Parent-child relations. In D. Mangen & W. Peterson (Eds.), *Research instruments in social gerontology: Vol. 2. Social roles and social participation* (pp. 115–185). Minneapolis: University of Minnesota.

Brody, E. M. (1981). "Women in the middle" and family help to older people. *The Gerontologist, 21,* 471–479.

Cicirelli, V. G. (1980). Relationship of family background variables to locus of control in the elderly. *Journal of Gerontology, 35,* 108–114.

Cicirelli, V. G. (1981). *Helping elderly parents: The role of adult children.* Boston: Auburn House.

Cicirelli, V. G. (1983). Adult children and their elderly parents. In T. H. Brubaker (Ed.), *Family relationships in later life* (pp. 31–46). Beverly Hills, CA: Sage Publications.

Harrell, F. E., Jr. (1983). The LOGIST procedure. In Stephenie P. Joyner (Ed.), *SAS Institute Inc. SUGI supplemental library user's guide* (pp. 181–202). Cary, NC: SAS Institute, Inc.

Johnson, E. S., & Bursk, B. J. (1977). Relationships between the elderly and their adult children. *The Gerontologist, 17,* 90–96.

Kerckhoff, A. C. (1966). Family patterns and morale in retirement. in I. H. Simpson & J. C. McKinney (Eds.), *Social aspects of aging* (pp. 173–192). Durham, NC: Duke University Press.

Lefcourt, H. M. (1976). *Locus of control: Current trends in theory and research.* Hillsdale, NJ: Lawrence Erlbaum Associates.

Lefcourt, H. M., Martin, R. A., & Saleh, W. E. (1984). Locus of control and social support: Interactive moderators of stress. *Journal of Personality and Social Psychology, 47,* 378–389.

Mercier, J. M., & Powers, E. A. (1984). The family and friends of rural aged as a natural support system. *Journal of Community Psychology, 12,* 334–346.

Molinari, V., & Niederehe, G. (1984–85). Locus of control, depression, and anxiety in young and old adults: A comparison study. *International Journal of Aging and Human Development, 20,* 41–52.

Phares, E. J. (1976). *Locus of control in personality.* Morristown, NJ: General Learning Press.

Rotter, J. B. (1966). Generalized expectancies for internal versus external control of reinforcement. *Psychological Monographs, 80*, (Whole No. 609).

Sandler, I. N., & Lakey, B. (1982). Locus of control as a stress moderator: The role of control perceptions and social support. *American Journal of Community Psychology, 10*, 65–80.

Solomon, G. (1975). *Patterns of social interaction among rural elderly widows and their adult children.* Unpublished master's thesis, Iowa State University, Ames, IA.

Streib, G. (1965). Intergenerational relations: Perspectives of the two generations on the older parent. *Journal of Marriage and the Family, 27*, 469–476.

Ziegler, M., & Reid, D. W. (1983). Correlates of changes in desired control scores and in life satisfaction scores among elderly persons. *International Journal of Aging and Human Development, 16*, 135–146.

# 20

# Kinship Ties Among Older People: The Residence Factor

## Gary R. Lee*

Over the years, sociological theory has provided a great deal of support for the popular stereotype that kinship ties are alive and well in rural areas, but decimated by urban residence. Louis Wirth (1938) and other urban sociologists in the first half of the twentieth century argued that city life is antithetical to primary relations of all types, including kinship, leading to alienation and anomie. Talcott Parsons (1943) theorized that the process of industrialization, along with urbanization, operated to produce the "isolated nuclear family" characteristic of modern urban society, in which households consist of only parents and their dependent children with minimal ties to extended kin.

The ensuing debate over whether the American nuclear family is "really" isolated from kin has finally and mercifully dissipated, due in large part to the impossibility of formulating and achieving consensus on any objective, absolute criteria of isolation (see Adams, 1970; Lee, 1980). Interestingly, very little of the voluminous research addressing this issue during the 1950s and '60s involved rural-urban comparisons, even though urbanization was accorded a major share of the blame for any apparent or presumed decline in the viability of kinship. Instead, many studies analyzed data from exclusively urban samples. These studies generally reported surprisingly high rates of interaction among kin, exchange of goods and services, and other forms of social bonds—surprising, at least, to those few who subscribed to the isolation hypothesis (see Sussman, 1965, and Adams, 1970, for reviews of these studies). One implication of this line of research is that, if kinship is such an important part of the lives of urban Americans, it must be even more so among rural residents.

Studies involving direct rural-urban comparisons have offered very little supporting for this position, however (see Lee and Cassidy, 1981, 1985, for reviews). Two studies from the 1960s conducted on samples of older persons (Bultena, 1969; Youmans, 1963) actually found higher rates of interaction with adult children among urban than rural residents. Other, more recent studies (for example, Lee and Whitbeck, 1987) have found very small negative effects of urban residence on interaction with close kin among elderly persons.

There are, however, several complicating factors that must be considered. Many studies, including most of those cited above, have either dealt with rather homogeneous samples of rural residents or have treated rural residents as a homogeneous category. The fact of the matter, of course, is that rural residents are very heterogeneous, and many of the differences within the rural category may be related to certain aspects of kinship bonds. Two major axes of differentiation involve occupation and region of the country.

While many people identify rural life with farm life, only a small proportion of rural residents are directly engaged in farming. However, farmers may be different than rural nonfarm residents in terms of their kinship

---

*Gary R. Lee is Professor, Department of Sociology, University of Florida, Gainesville, FL 32611.

176

relations. Klatzky (1972) found that rates of interaction between married men and their fathers are significantly higher for farmers than any other occupational or residential category. She also found that this difference is attributable primarily to the greater residential proximity of the generations among farm than nonfarm families, suggesting the importance of inherited or jointly owned land for farmers. Clearly, farm and rural nonfarm residents must be distinguished in any analysis of the effects of residence on kinship, since the processes operative in the respective categories may be quite different.

Region of the country also appears to be an important factor. Heller and Quesada (1977) compared samples of rural residents of Virginia and Nevada, and found the Virginians to be much more strongly oriented towared extended family ties. Subsequent analyses (Heller, Quesade, Harvey and Warner, 1981a, 1981b) added a sample of urban Ohio residents to the comparison, who turned out to be quite similar to the Nevadans. Heller et al. also attribute many of the differences they observed to differential proximity to kin, noting particularly that their rural Nevada residents were fairly recent migrants to the area and did not have extensive kin networks in the vicinity. Their findings suggest that higher levels of "extended familism" among rural residents may be restricted to the eastern portion of the United States. However, their data contain no urban westerners, who may, of course, be even less involved with their kin than their rural counterparts.

This study addresses both of the issues noted above by examining frequency of interaction with kin according to residential location among a sample of elderly residents of a western state. Unfortunately the sample does not contain residents of other regions of the country. However, the data permit a relatively precise identification of residential location, including a distinction between farm and rural nonfarm residents, within a state that is highly diverse in terms of its population distribution. This gives us an opportunity to determine whether residential location has any effect on kinship interaction in the western region of the country.

## Methods

The data were obtained from a sample of residents of Washington state aged 55 and older in 1980. Eligible respondents were located by means of random digit dialing. Those who agreed to participate (81.5% of those contacted) were mailed a questionnaire, of which 83.8% were returned in usable form. This analysis is restricted to respondents who have children who do not reside in the respondents' households, and who answered all items relevant to this analysis. This leaves us with 1,414 males and 1,726 females, for a total of 3,140 respondents. Some analyses were conducted only on the subsample of individuals (1,202 males and 1,526 females) who also had grandchildren.

Residential location is classified into five categories, including (1) rural farm; (2) rural nonfarm; (3) a town of less than 5,000 population; (4) a small city of 5,000 to 100,000 population; and (5) a large city of more than 100,000 population. While more refined categories are possible with these data, these are sufficient to show the important patterns that emerge.

Respondents who had children who did not live with them were asked three questions regarding their relations with these children (and grandchildren, if any). First, they were asked how frequently they see or visit with the child seen most frequently, on a seven-point continuum ranging from "less than once a year" to "almost every day." Second, they were asked how frequently they spend holidays with these children, with five response categories ranging from "never" to "almost always." Third, respondents with grandchildren were asked how often they visit with the grandchildren, on a five-point continuum ranging from "once a year or less" to "once a week or more."

## Findings

Table 1 shows the cross-classification of residential location and the frequency of visiting with the (non-coresident) child the respondent sees most often. The latter variable is collapsed into three categories for this analysis: once a month or less, more than monthly to weekly, and more than once per week. Differences across residential categories are not particularly striking, but the farm category does stand out, at least for men.

Slightly more than 30 percent of all male farm residents see a child more than once a

Table 1.
*Frequency of Visits with Most Frequently Seen Child, by Residence and Gender (in percent)*

| | Residence | | | | | |
| Frequency | Rural Farm | Rural Nonfarm | Small Town | Small City | Large City | Total |
|---|---|---|---|---|---|---|
| **Males** | | | | | | |
| 1/month or less | 32.8 | 48.8 | 41.7 | 45.8 | 39.5 | 43.1 |
| Monthly to weekly | 36.8 | 35.6 | 31.7 | 36.5 | 42.2 | 37.2 |
| More than 1/week | 30.4 | 15.6 | 26.7 | 17.7 | 18.3 | 19.7 |
| Total | 100.0 | 100.0 | 100.1 | 100.0 | 100.0 | 100.0 |
| *n* | 125 | 326 | 180 | 406 | 327 | 1,414 |
| | | Chi-square $= 27.31$   df $= 8$   $p < .001$ | | | | |
| **Females** | | | | | | |
| 1/month or less | 34.6 | 40.5 | 37.3 | 35.1 | 34.3 | 36.3 |
| Monthly to weekly | 36.8 | 39.7 | 33.9 | 36.9 | 45.9 | 39.5 |
| More than 1/week | 28.7 | 19.7 | 28.8 | 28.0 | 19.8 | 24.2 |
| Total | 100.1 | 99.9 | 100.0 | 100.0 | 100.0 | 100.0 |
| *n* | 136 | 380 | 236 | 510 | 464 | 1,726 |
| | | Chi-square $= 23.75$   df $= 8$   $p < .01$ | | | | |

week. This is the highest percentage of frequent visiting for any category in the table, male or female, and the only case in which the rate of frequent visiting among males exceeds that among residentially comparable females. For females, farm residents are not materially different from residents of small towns or small cities, but frequent visiting is more common among these categories than among rural nonfarm or large city residents. For both genders, rates of visiting with children are highest among farm residents and lowest among rural nonfarm residents. This is a strong demonstration of the need to differentiate rural populations according to this distinction.

Table 2 presents the relationships of residence to our other indicators of kinship interaction, in abbreviated form. Farm residents are once again most likely to visit grandchildren at least weekly. However, the highest proportion of respondents who report that they "almost always" spend holidays with children is found among residents of large cities. Rural nonfarm residents rank fairly low on both measures.

The bottom two rows of each panel of Table 2 provide some very important informa-

Table 2.
*Visiting Grandchildren, Spending Holidays with Children, and Proximity to Nearest Child by Residence and Gender (in percent)*

| | Residence | | | | | |
| Variable | Rural Farm | Rural Nonfarm | Small Town | Small City | Large City | Total |
|---|---|---|---|---|---|---|
| **Males** | | | | | | |
| Visits grandchildren 1/week or more | 27.6 | 21.7 | 22.5 | 24.3 | 25.4 | 24.0 |
| Almost always spends holidays w/children | 35.2 | 33.8 | 35.2 | 33.2 | 43.7 | 36.6 |
| Nearest child within 1 mile | 22.8 | 10.7 | 20.2 | 15.3 | 14.4 | 15.3 |
| Nearest child within 10 miles | 45.6 | 38.9 | 47.0 | 51.5 | 57.2 | 49.1 |
| **Females** | | | | | | |
| Visits grandchildren 1/week or more | 36.5 | 27.4 | 29.9 | 25.4 | 27.7 | 27.9 |
| Almost always spends holidays w/children | 49.3 | 49.3 | 45.8 | 49.6 | 53.3 | 50.0 |
| Nearest child within 1 mile | 35.3 | 14.1 | 24.9 | 20.3 | 17.0 | 19.9 |
| Nearest child within 10 miles | 47.1 | 45.8 | 53.7 | 54.7 | 59.7 | 53.4 |

tion about proximity to adult children. The third row shows the proportions of respondents who live within one mile of their nearest child; the fourth row shows the proportion who live within ten miles (inclusive of the previous row). Farm residents, especially women, are most likely to have a child living within a mile, while rural nonfarm residents are least likely. When we expand the range to ten miles, however, the farm advantage disappears entirely but the rural nonfarm disadvantage remains. Although residents of large cities are almost as unlikely as rural nonfarm residents to have a child within a mile, they are the most likely of any category (nearly six out of ten) to have a child within ten miles.

It is apparently the case that farmers have higher levels of interaction with adult children than others in large part because at least one child is likely to remain near the parental home after adulthood, perhaps because that child continues to work on the farm and will eventually inherit it. This is supported by other data (not shown here) indicating that 55 percent of the children seen most frequently by farmers are sons; the average for the remaining four residential categories is 44 percent. This supports Klatzky's (1972) observation of higher rates of interaction among male farmers and their fathers than for other occupational/residential categories, which she attributed to the unique characteristics of farming as an occupation, and particularly to the need for land. The argument that these patterns stem from occupational rather than residential factors is buttressed by the fact that rural nonfarm residents generally fall at the opposite ends of the interaction and proximity continua from farmers.

As noted, rural nonfarm residents are less likely than any other category to have

children living nearby. This may reflect minimal economic opportunities for young adults in these areas, or it may mean that the older rural nonfarm residents had themselves recently moved to these areas and thus moved away from children. The latter explanation is unlikely, however, since the same patterns obtain among those who have resided at the current address for at least 15 years (the median in the sample). At any rate, rural nonfarm residents appear to have low levels of face-to-face interaction with grown children because of their lack of proximity.

Residents of cities, on the other hand, are most likely to have a child living within ten miles, although it is rarely the case that the child lives in the same neighborhood. In fact, the larger the city the greater the odds of proximity (using the ten-mile criterion). However, residents of large cities are only marginally more likely than rural nonfarm residents to see a child frequently. This suggests that they may be less motivated than rural residents to take advantage of proximity, at least in terms of face-to-face interaction with children.

To examine this possibility, a multiple classification analysis was performed, which is shown in Table 3. In this table, the mean value of frequency of interaction with the child seen most often (on the original 7-point continuum) is given, separately for males and females. The values in the two "unadjusted" columns represent average deviations from the grand mean for each residential category. The values in the columns labeled "adjusted" show these same deviations from the mean after removing the effects of residential proximity. Eta, the correlation ratio, represents the bivariate relationship between residence and interaction frequency, while beta reflects the corre-

Table 3.
Visits with Most Frequently Seen Child by Residence and Gender, Controlling for Proximity (Multiple Classification Analysis)

| Residence | Males ($\overline{X}$ = 3.89) | | Females ($\overline{X}$ = 4.16) | |
| --- | --- | --- | --- | --- |
|  | Unadjusted | Adjusted* | Unadjusted | Adjusted* |
| Rural farm | 0.61 | 0.43 | 0.18 | 0.05 |
| Rural nonfarm | -0.15 | 0.05 | -0.16 | -0.06 |
| Small town | 0.09 | 0.07 | 0.06 | 0.09 |
| Small city | -0.14 | -0.11 | 0.07 | 0.07 |
| Large city | 0.04 | -0.10 | -0.03 | -0.09 |
| Eta/Beta | .13 | .09 | .06 | .04 |
| $R^2$ | .016 | .520 | .004 | .540 |

*Adjusted for proximity to nearest child.

sponding effect in the multivariate analysis; both statistics capture the nonlinear as well as the linear component of the relationship. The explained variance ($R^2$) totals indicate the variance accounted for by residence in the "unadjusted" columns, and the variance due to both residence and proximity in the "adjusted" columns.

The first and third columns show similar patterns to those presented in Table 1, as they should. Rates of interaction are highest in the farm category and lowest in the rural nonfarm, with residents of large cities closest to the overall averages. Residence accounts for little of the variation in interaction frequency, but the pattern is nonetheless clear, especially for men.

When proximity is controlled, the positive effect of farm residence virtually disappears for women, but is diminished only slightly for men. Residents of large cities become less likely than average to interact with their children. Rural nonfarm residents move closer to the mean. The pattern for small-city residents is somewhat puzzling, since men are slightly less likely than average to interact with children and women slightly more likely, regardless of the adjustment for proximity; however, these deviations are small.

This table suggests that the greater propensity of farm males to interact with children is due only partially to their greater proximity. However, rural nonfarm residents have low rates of interaction because of low proximity. Residents of large cities (and small cities for males) take relatively little advantage of their proximity to children for interaction. This supports Hendrix's (1976) conclusion that urban residence may decrease the motivation for kinship interaction even when the opportunity for such interaction exists.

We must also recognize, however, that the differences in kinship interaction according to residential location are really quite small. The similarities across residential categories are more impressive than the differences. While more than 50 percent of the variation in interaction with children is due to proximity, neither proximity nor interaction itself is strongly related to residence.

On the other hand, this may not be true for all segments of the older population. We know, for example, that elderly farm residents who are widowed are likely to move away from the farm (Clifford, Heaton, Voss, and Fuguitt, 1985), presumably in part because of the isolation factor. However, some widows remain on the farm, as well as in rural nonfarm areas. In these data, 30 of the 136 farm women and 68 of the 380 rural nonfarm women are widows. (The number of widowers is too small for analysis; only one widower in the sample is a farm resident.) Are widowed women who remain in rural areas able to do so because of stronger relations with more proximate kin? In other words, is the kinship network more important to rural widows than to their married counterparts?

Table 4 compares married and widowed women in terms of the dimensions of kinship we have examined. The most important result of this analysis is that, across all residential categories, the widowed and the married are virtually indistinguishable on interaction with children or grandchildren or

Table 4.
*Kinship Relations of Older Women, by Residence and Marital Status (in percent)*

| Variable | Marital Status | Residence | | | | | Total |
| --- | --- | --- | --- | --- | --- | --- | --- |
| | | Rural Farm | Rural Nonfarm | Small Town | Small City | Large City | |
| Visits children | M | 28.3 | 21.3 | 28.9 | 26.7 | 21.7 | 24.5 |
| more than 1/week | W | 31.0 | 17.6 | 29.9 | 31.4 | 18.9 | 25.5 |
| Visits grandchildren | M | 35.5 | 28.7 | 31.1 | 25.3 | 27.7 | 28.3 |
| 1/week or more | W | 39.4 | 25.8 | 25.6 | 27.0 | 29.7 | 28.2 |
| Almost always spends | M | 51.4 | 49.1 | 42.6 | 49.4 | 53.7 | 49.9 |
| holidays w/children | W | 41.3 | 55.2 | 52.3 | 53.6 | 54.5 | 53.1 |
| Nearest child within | M | 31.4 | 14.0 | 24.1 | 19.2 | 18.2 | 19.3 |
| 1 mile | W | 50.0 | 16.2 | 26.7 | 24.2 | 11.6 | 21.9 |
| Nearest child within | M | 42.8 | 46.4 | 52.7 | 53.6 | 59.6 | 52.3 |
| 10 miles | W | 60.0 | 42.7 | 56.9 | 59.7 | 63.4 | 57.4 |

proximity to children. Apparently the death of one's husband does not automatically result in higher levels of interaction with children or grandchildren.

The most notable difference between married and widowed women observable in this table occurs among farm residents and involves proximity to children. Fully one-half (fifteen out of thirty) farm widows in the sample live within a mile of their nearest child, compared to only 31 percent of their married counterparts. The difference is also evident when the 10-mile criterion is employed (60% vs. 43%). Interestingly, the greater proximity of farm widows to their children is not translated into higher levels of interaction; differences in interaction frequency are minimal, and farm widows are actually less likely than the married to spend holidays with their children. However, apparently proximity to children allows farm widows to remain on the farm, even though rates of interaction don't seem to increase after widowhood. The security of having a nearby child may be important.

The proximity advantage of farm widows is definitely not shared by their rural nonfarm counterparts. They are also less likely than farm widows to see children or grandchildren frequently, although they spend holidays with them more often. Less than half of the rural nonfarm widows live within ten miles of a child; this is the only residential category of widows for which this is true. However, rural nonfarm widows differ little from widowed residents of large cities in terms of the interaction indicators. This shows, once again, that a simple distinction between rural and urban obscures more than it illuminates.

## Conclusions

The data reported here do not reveal major rural-urban differences in the kinship relations of older persons. They do indicate, however, that the farm/nonfarm distinction is very important; farm residents typically rank at or near the top in terms of both interaction with and proximity to children and grandchildren, while rural nonfarm residents appear at or near the bottom of the same dimensions. The farm advantage is particularly evident among men, indicating that instrumental ties, probably involving access to land, frequently link the male members of adjacent generations of farm families. On the other hand, the children of rural nonfarm residents are most likely to have moved some distance away from their parents, minimizing opportunities for interaction.

Somewhat surprisingly, it is residents of large cities who are most likely to have at least one child residing within a ten-mile radius. This probably reflects the greater availability of occupational and other opportunities for young and middle-aged adults in urban centers, and thus the lesser need to relocate in pursuit of such opportunities. Residents of large urban areas rank relatively low on frequency of interaction with children in spite of this proximity, but high on frequency of interaction with grandchildren. This suggests either that much of the intergenerational interaction in urban areas is expressive and sociable, or that urban grandparents do a lot of babysitting.

One interesting aspect of these findings, upon which we have not yet commented, involves the simple univariate distribution of our primary dependent variable. Shanas (1979) has estimated that about 50 percent of all older Americans with children see at least one child at least once a day, and that about 75 percent live within a half hour's travel time of at least one child. These estimates are by no means replicated in this sample. As Table 1 shows, only about 20 percent of the men and 24 percent of the women see the child they see most frequently more often than once a week. We must recognize that these estimates are not precisely comparable, since this study investigated only interaction with the most frequently seen child; adding other children to the estimate would necessarily increase these percentages somewhat, as would the inclusion of children still living with the respondent. However, it is very doubtful that the resulting figures would approach Shanas's estimate.

It may be that kinship interaction is less frequent in the west than in other regions of the country, as Heller et al. (1981a, 1981b; Heller and Quesada, 1977) suggest. However, Heller and his colleagues attribute the difference they observed to the recency of migration to the west, a factor that is not likely to affect relations between elderly westerners and their descendants. Further careful, systematic comparisons of older persons from different regions of the country are needed to ascertain whether regional differences do indeed exist, and if so what factors account for them.

Based on this study and others noted earlier, it is increasingly clear that the rural elderly are not disproportionately embedded in extensive networks of supportive kin. Even though farm residents do interact with their grown children somewhat more often than urbanites, their advantage is by no means large. And older rural nonfarm residents come the closest of any residential category to being "isolated." Policies or programs based on the assumption that the rural elderly have greater access than others to the support of their children or other kin are clearly misguided.

## REFERENCES

Adams, B. N. (1970). Isolation, function, and beyond: American kinship in the 1960s. *Journal of Marriage and the Family, 32,* 403-410.

Bultena, G. L. (1969). Rural-urban differences in the familial interaction of the aged. *Rural Sociology, 34,* 5-15.

Clifford, W. B., Heaton, T. B., Voss, P. R., & Fuguitt, G. V. (1985). The rural elderly in demographic perspective. In R. T. Coward & G. R. Lee (Eds.), *The elderly in rural society: Every fourth elder* (pp. 25-55). New York: Springer.

Heller, P. L., & Quesada, G. M. (1977). Rural familism: An interregional analysis. *Rural Sociology, 42,* 220-240.

Heller, P. L., Quesada, G. M., Harvey, D. L., & Warner, L. G. (1981a). Familism in rural and urban America: Critique and reconceptualization of a construct. *Rural Sociology, 46,* 446-464.

Heller, P. L., Quesada, G. M., Harvey, D. L., & Warner, L. G. (1981b). Rural familism: Interregional analysis. In R. T. Coward & W. M. Smith, Jr. (Eds), *The family in rural society* (pp. 73-85). Boulder, CO: Westview Press.

Hendrix, L. (1976). Kinship, social networks, and integration among Ozark residents and out-migrants. *Journal of Marriage and the Family, 38,* 97-104.

Klatzky, S. R. (1972). *Patterns of contact with relatives.* Washington, DC: American Sociological Association.

Lee, G. R. (1980). Kinship in the seventies: A decade review of research and theory. *Journal of Marriage and the Family, 42,* 923-934.

Lee, G. R., & Cassidy, M. L. (1981). Kinship systems and extended family ties. In R. T. Coward & W. M. Smith, Jr. (Eds), *The family in rural society* (pp. 57-71). Boulder, CO: Westview Press.

Lee, G. R., & Cassidy, M. L. (1985). Family and kin relations of the rural elderly. In R. T. Coward & G. R. Lee (Eds.), *The elderly in rural society: Every fourth elder* (pp. 151-169). New York: Springer.

Lee, G. R., & Whitbeck, L. B. (1987). Residential location and social relations among older persons. *Rural Sociology, 52,* 89-97.

Parsons, T. (1943). The kinship system of the contemporary United States. *American Anthropologist, 45,* 22-38.

Shanas, E. (1979). Social myth as hypothesis: The case of the family relations of old people. *The Gerontologist, 19,* 3-9.

Sussman, M. B. (1965). Relationships of adult children with their parents in the United States. In E. Shanas & G. F. Streib (Eds.), *Social structure and the family: Generational relations* (pp. 62-92). Englewood Cliffs, NJ: Prentice-Hall.

Wirth, L. (1938). Urbanism as a way of life. *American Journal of Sociology, 44,* 3-24.

Youmans, E. G. (1963). *Aging patterns in a rural and an urban area of Kentucky.* Lexington, KY: Agricultural Experiment Station Bulletin No. 681, University of Kentucky.

# Informal Supports of Older Adults:
# A Rural-Urban Comparison*

**Jean Pearson Scott and Karen A. Roberto****

The family practitioner engaged in programming and service delivery to older
family members must be guided by accurate knowledge regarding special
characteristics and needs of their clientele.
An often voiced concern is that policy and
services should undergird and strengthen
existing informal support networks rather
than duplicating or detracting from the support structure (Coward, 1980). Knowledge of
the differential influence of environment, for
example, on family and friend networks
would be useful to practitioners who work
with rural and urban clientele.

The literature suggests that family and
friend relationships of older, rural adults are
unique in several respects. A number of
studies report that rural elderly interact more
frequently with kin than urban older adults
(Lee & Cassidy, 1985). There is a tendency for
a greater proportion of rural elderly to be
married and for fewer of them to be widowed
or divorced than urban elderly (Lee &
Cassidy, 1985; Schooler, 1975). Also, rural
older couples report more marital role
segregation than do urban couples (Lee &
Cassidy, 1985). Furthermore, older rural
adults perceive themselves as being more

conveniently situated to friends and family
than their urban counterparts. A consistent
finding is that rural elderly report greater
contact with friends and exhibit greater
neighboring behavior than urban older adults
(Kivett, 1985; McKain, 1967; Schooler, 1975).
Indeed, the data would suggest that the informal networks of older rural adults are a
more salient source of support than those of
older adults in urban settings.

On the other hand, some researchers
have concluded that more similarities than
differences exist between rural and urban informal support networks (Lee & Cassidy,
1985; Schooler, 1975). Few differences have
been observed in the frequency of contact
with children (Schooler, 1975) or in adjustment to widowhood (Lee & Cassidy, 1985).
Also, a few studies report that urban rather
than rural elderly have more frequent contact
with family (Bultena, 1969; Youmans, 1963).

Unfortunately, the literature regarding
family life of rural, older adults is sparse and
comparative studies are needed. When rural
elderly family and friend relationships have
been investigated, assessments of these
relationships are often limited to measures
of frequency of interaction. Another limita-
tion is the failure of many studies to control
for several important variables that have
been found to influence family and friend
networks. Findings indicate that family and
friend interaction is affected by respondent
characteristics including socioeconomic
level, gender, marital status, and availability
of network members and by contextual factors including region of the country, type of
comparison (i.e., farm/nonfarm, rural/small
town), and occupational structure. Kin in-

*Data reported in this chapter were collected in projects funded
by the AARP Andrus Foundation, Washington, DC, and The
Research Institute, Texas Tech University, Lubbock.
**Jean Pearson Scott is Associate Professor, Department of
Human Development and Family Studies, Texas Tech University,
Lubbock, TX 79409. Karen A. Roberto is Assistant Professor and
Coordinator, Gerontology Program, Department of Human Serv-
ices, University of Northern Colorado, Greeley, CO 80639.

Reprinted from *Family Relations*, 1987, **36**, 444-449.

teraction, for example, is largely conditioned by geographic distance (Lee & Lassey, 1980). Women are more invested in kin relations than men. Likewise, friendships are more extensive and meaningful for older women in comparison to older men (Arth, 1980; Booth & Hess, 1974; Roberto & Scott, 1986).

The primary purpose of the study reported here was to conduct a rural-urban comparison of family and friend support networks of older adults. Specifically, the following question was addressed: Are there rural-urban differences in patterns of family and friend interaction among older adults? And, if so, what is the nature of these differences? The study was designed to address shortcomings of previous research by comparing rural and urban samples, using measures of network helping behaviors and social activities, and controlling for several important background variables. A second purpose was to explore the influence of network support on morale of older adults *within* urban and rural groups.

# Method

## Sample

Two data sets collected in the same location of the Southwest were used in the study.[1] The urban sample, consisting of 180 white adults 65 to 90 years of age, was taken from a larger study and was randomly selected through a proportionate area sampling technique. Collection of the data took place during the spring and summer of 1980. The rural sample, consisting of 145 white adults age 65 to 89, was collected in the spring and summer of 1981 using a compact cluster sampling technique. This sample was drawn from a larger study that dealt with the characteristics and needs of the older rural adult.

## Procedure

The interview schedule used in both samples contained identical questions regarding family and friend relations. The questions were selected from interview schedules that had been used in other studies with elderly respondents. A pilot test and revision of the interview schedule was completed with a subsample of older adults prior to data collection. Questions regarding helping behavior, social activities, and demographic characteristics of the samples were used in this study. All respondents were interviewed in their own homes by a trained interviewer.

## Measures

*Helping Behavior.* Respondents were asked if they had received help from their children during the preceding year with transportation, household repairs, housekeeping, shopping, yard work, car care, illness, important decisions, legal aid, financial aid, and other types of help. The respondents were asked also if they had given help to their children with any of the items described above during the past year. Responses were coded either Yes or No. For purposes of examining the combined effect of these behaviors, responses across items were added together for a total help received from children score (HRC) and a total help given to children score (HGC). Reliability using Cronbach's Alpha was .85 and .83 for the rural and urban samples respectively on HRC. For HGC, Cronbach's Alpha coefficients were .83 and .87 for the rural and urban sample respectively.

The same helping behaviors listed above were used to ask respondents about the help received and the help given to their friends within the past year. One additional item, providing comfort during bereavement, depression, or when lonely, was included. Responses across items were summed for a total help received from friend score (HRF) and a total help given to friend score (HGF). Cronbach's Alpha coefficients for HRF were .77 and .86 respectively for rural and urban samples. For HGF, the coefficients were .72 and .82 for the rural and urban samples respectively.

*Social Activity.* Respondents were asked if they had participated with their children in any of the following activities during the past year: commercial recreation (movies, sports, plays, etc.), home recreation (picnics, card playing, watching TV, etc.), outdoor recreation (fishing, hunting or camping, gardening, etc.), brief drop-in visits for conversation, vacation visits, working at same location or at same occupation, happy occasions such as birthdays or holidays, attending the same church or religious participation together, shopping together, and other activities not mentioned above. Responses were coded Yes or No. The 12 items were added together for a total activities with children score (ACC). Reliability using

Cronbach's Alpha was .52 and .74 for the rural and urban samples respectively.

The same procedures described above were used to assess the participation of the respondents with their friends during the preceding year. The individual items were added together for a total activities with friend score (ACF). Reliability using Cronbach's Alpha was .55 and .71 for the rural and urban samples respectively.

*Income.* Monthly income was assessed by asking respondents to indicate the letter of the category that most nearly described their gross income. An annual income was computed from this information. Because many rural residents receive income for crops or rental property on a yearly schedule, rural respondents were asked to report their income received on an annual basis. Since respondents in the urban sample ranged from lower-middle to upper-middle incomes, only respondents with comparable incomes were drawn from the rural sample. In other words, persons below or hovering above the poverty threshold were excluded from the study (based on the 1979 Poverty Index level of a nonfarm two-person family head age 65 or older, $4,200; Schulz, 1980).

*Background Variables.* A set of background variables was used in the examination of factors influencing morale. These included marital status, coded as (1) single and (2) married; degree to which health troubles stood in the way of doing things you want to do, coded as (1) a great deal, (2) a little, and (3) not at all; and perceived income. Perceived income was measured with a 3-item index consisting of responses to the following: satisfaction with present standard of living, coded (1) very dissatisfied to (4) very satisfied; comparison of income to that of others, coded (1) far below average to (5) far above average; and change in financial situation during the last 5 years, coded from (1) worse to (3) better. Scores for the three items were weighted equally and summed for a total score. Inter-item consistency was .61 using Cronbach's Alpha. An additional residence variable, coded (1) open country or (2) small town, was included for the rural respondents.

*Morale.* Morale was assessed with the revised version of the Philadelphia Geriatric Center Morale Scale (Lawton, 1975). The scale is a 17-item multidimensional scale designed specifically for older respondents. The scale includes three factors that have been consistently reproduced—Agitation, Attitude Toward Own Aging, and Lonely Dissatisfaction. The scale has been shown to be reliably and structurally invariant across several dimensions in other samples of elderly persons (Morris & Sherwood, 1975). High scores reflect high morale.

## Data Analysis

Due to the categorical nature of the data, the major research question regarding rural-urban differences was addressed with chi-square statistical tests. Controls for gender, marital status, and proximity of children were employed.

The second research question relating to factors influencing morale was addressed with multiple regression. A multiple regression analysis was performed with each sample to determine the relative importance of background and informal network interaction variables to the morale of respondents. Variables entered first in the regression analysis included marital status, health, and perceived income. Residence was entered also for the rural analysis. The second set of variables to enter were the network variables: HRC, HGC, ACC, HRF, HGF, and ACF. Only those that showed some initial correlation with morale were included in each analysis.

## Results
### Descriptive Characteristics

The urban sample was composed of 135 females and 45 males ranging in age from 65 to 90 (mean age = 72.6). The rural sample consisted of 66 females and 79 males aged 65 to 89 with a mean age of 72.9 years. Of the urban sample 72% were married, 22% widowed, 1.5% never married, and 4.5% divorced or separated. For the rural sample 57.9% were married, 38.6% were widowed, 2.1% were never married, and 1.4% were divorced or separated. Due to the small numbers of never married, divorced, separated, and widowed males, only widowed females and married respondents were included in the data analysis.

The rural sample had a mean educational level of 10.2 years. The urban sample had completed an average of 11.6 years of school. The mean monthly income for the rural respondents was between $600 and $699. The urban respondents had a mean monthly income of between $700 and $799.

When asked how much their health troubles stood in the way of doing things they wanted to do, 44.4% of the rural sample said not at all, 33.9% said a little, and 21.8% said a great deal. In response to the same question, 49.2% of the urban sample reported that health problems did not stand in their way of doing things, 31.1% said a little, and 19.7% said health problems stood in their way a great deal.

Approximately 9 out of 10 respondents in both samples had children. The number of living children ranged from 1 to 8 with a mean of 2.5 for the rural respondents. For the urban respondents, the number of children ranged from 1 to 12 with a mean of 2.5 children. For rural parents, contact with children who lived in the same town or neighborhood was frequent with 47.6% of the respondents seeing at least one child daily; 34.1% saw children weekly, and 8.3% saw children monthly or less frequently. Data from the urban sample on frequency of contact with the oldest child indicated that 48.0% of the sample had a visit within the week of the interview.

In regard to friendships, 92.9% of the rural participants and 84.8% of the urban sample named at least one close friend. Only 7.1% of the rural and 11.5% of the urban sample reported not having a close friend at the present time. When respondents were asked how frequently they had contact with their close friend, 26.1% of the urban sample said several times a week, 55.0% said weekly, and 18.9% said monthly. For the rural adults, 19.0% said they had daily contact with their close friend, 27.6% said several times a week, 21.6% said weekly, and 28.1% said monthly.

## Help Received From Children

As shown in Table 1, there were relatively few significant rural-urban differences in the types of help received from children when proximity, gender, and marital status were controlled. Several significant differences were observed, however, with respect to household repairs, shopping, yard work, assistance when ill, important decisions, legal aid, financial aid, and the other category. Most notable was the significantly greater proportion of rural females receiving assistance when ill in comparison to urban females. Rural widows reported greater as-

Table 1.
Percentage of Respondents Receiving Help From a Child By Rural-Urban Residence (controlling proximity, gender, and marital status)

| | Married Males | | | | Married Females | | | | Widowed Females | | | |
|---|---|---|---|---|---|---|---|---|---|---|---|---|
| | Close[c] | | Distant[c] | | Close | | Distant | | Close | | Distant | |
| Helping Behavior[a] | Urban (n = 25) | Rural (n = 23) | Urban (n = 13) | Rural (n = 18) | Urban (n = 38) | Rural (n = 17) | Urban (n = 22) | Rural (n = 8) | Urban (n = 59) | Rural (n = 14) | Urban (n = 16) | Rural (n = 13) |
| Transportation | 20.0 | 26.1 | 23.1 | 5.6 | 47.4 | 41.2 | 40.9 | 37.5 | 74.6 | 78.6 | 18.8 | 23.1 |
| Household repairs | 44.0 | 17.4* | 15.4 | 11.1 | 34.2 | 47.1 | 18.2 | 37.5 | 57.6 | 71.4 | 18.8 | 53.8* |
| Housekeeping | 16.0 | 17.4 | 15.4 | 5.6 | 21.1 | 17.6 | 13.6 | 12.5 | 32.2 | 42.9 | 12.5 | 15.4 |
| Shopping | 16.0 | 21.7 | 23.1 | 0.0* | 34.2 | 35.3 | 22.7 | 25.0 | 49.2 | 57.1 | 12.5 | 30.8 |
| Yard work | 24.0 | 4.3* | 15.4 | 11.1 | 18.4 | 29.4 | 4.5 | 12.5 | 32.2 | 57.1 | 6.3 | 38.5* |
| Car care | 12.0 | 8.7 | 7.7 | 5.6 | 15.8 | 35.3 | 4.5 | 12.5 | 15.3 | 35.7 | 12.5 | 38.5 |
| Assist when ill | 44.0 | 60.9 | 15.4 | 27.8 | 47.4 | 94.1*** | 22.7 | 85.7** | 57.6 | 85.7* | 25.0 | 53.8 |
| Important decisions | 52.0 | 21.7* | 15.4 | 11.1 | 42.1 | 35.3 | 40.9 | 25.0 | 64.4 | 78.6 | 50.0 | 76.9 |
| Legal aid | 12.0 | 4.3 | 7.7 | 0.0 | 10.5 | 11.8 | 4.5 | 12.5 | 8.5 | 35.7** | 6.3 | 30.8 |
| Financial aid | 4.0 | 4.3 | 7.7 | 0.0 | 15.8 | 11.8 | 0.0 | 25.0* | 23.7 | 21.4 | 6.3 | 7.7 |
| Other[b] | 4.0 | 8.7 | 7.7 | 5.6 | 10.5 | 23.5 | 0.0 | 25.0* | 5.1 | 21.4* | 6.3 | 0.0 |

[a]Multiple responses.
[b]Other included such behaviors as sharing garden produce and household items.
[c]Close = within 49 miles; Distant = 50 miles or greater.
*p $<$ .05.
**p $<$ .01.
***p $<$ .001.

Table 2.
Percentage of Respondents Giving Help To a Child By Rural-Urban Residence (controlling proximity, gender, and marital status)

| | Married Males | | | | Married Females | | | | Widowed Females | | | |
| | Close[c] | | Distant[c] | | Close | | Distant | | Close | | Distant | |
| Helping Behavior[a] | Urban (n = 25) | Rural (n = 23) | Urban (n = 13) | Rural (n = 18) | Urban (n = 38) | Rural (n = 17) | Urban (n = 22) | Rural (n = 8) | Urban (n = 59) | Rural (n = 14) | Urban (n = 16) | Rural (n = 13) |
|---|---|---|---|---|---|---|---|---|---|---|---|---|
| Transportation | 24.0 | 21.7 | 15.4 | 11.1 | 23.7 | 29.4 | 22.7 | 0.0 | 16.9 | 14.3 | 6.3 | 23.1 |
| Household repairs | 24.0 | 13.0 | 23.1 | 5.6 | 18.4 | 11.8 | 0.0 | 0.0 | 11.9 | 28.6 | 12.5 | 7.7 |
| Housekeeping | 8.0 | 0.0 | 7.7 | 0.0 | 15.8 | 17.6 | 4.5 | 0.0 | 22.0 | 21.4 | 6.3 | 23.1 |
| Shopping | 4.0 | 13.0 | 7.7 | 0.0 | 21.1 | 17.6 | 4.5 | 0.0 | 18.6 | 21.4 | 6.3 | 15.4 |
| Yard work | 8.0 | 8.7 | 15.4 | 0.0 | 15.8 | 11.8 | 4.5 | 0.0 | 11.9 | 14.3 | 12.5 | 7.7 |
| Assist when ill | 16.0 | 47.8* | 15.4 | 33.3 | 23.7 | 82.4*** | 9.1 | 62.5** | 28.8 | 64.3** | 37.5 | 46.2* |
| Important decisions | 40.0 | 39.1 | 30.8 | 22.2 | 23.7 | 29.4 | 22.7 | 12.5 | 37.3 | 57.1 | 12.5 | 61.5 |
| Legal aid | 4.0 | 13.0 | 7.7 | 5.6 | 10.5 | 5.9 | 0.0 | 0.0 | 6.8 | 21.4 | 25.0 | 15.4 |
| Financial aid | 12.0 | 47.8** | 23.1 | 33.3 | 18.4 | 23.5 | 13.6 | 0.0 | 18.6 | 28.6 | 6.3 | 46.2 |
| Other[b] | 4.0 | 8.7 | 15.4 | 11.1 | 13.2 | 17.6 | 4.5 | 25.0 | 5.1 | 28.6** | | 23.1 |

aMultiple responses.
bOther included such behaviors as sharing garden produce and household items.
cClose = within 49 miles; Distant = 50 miles or greater.
*p < .05.
**p < .01.
***p < .001.

sistance from children in comparison to urban widows for household repairs, yard work, illness, legal aid, and other behaviors; however, this finding was not consistent across proximity of child levels. Also, rural married females with children living at a distance received a greater amount of financial aid from children than urban females.

Urban male respondents reported receiving greater assistance than rural male respondents. Specifically, urban males with children living in close proximity reported a higher rate of receiving assistance than their rural counterparts with respect to household repairs, yard work, and important decisions. Urban males with children living at a distance also reported significantly greater assistance with shopping in comparison to rural males.

## Help Given to Children

As shown in Table 2, rural older respondents reported a significantly higher percentage of giving assistance to their children when ill in comparison to urban respondents. Also, rural men whose children lived close by gave significantly more financial aid to children than their urban counterparts.

## Activities with Children

The results reported in Table 3 reflect several differences with respect to interaction with children. Rural respondents reported a significantly lower percentage engaging in commercial recreation with children in comparison to urban respondents. However, in some instances, a significantly greater percentage of rural respondents reported engaging in outdoor recreation, vacation visits, reunions, and working in the same location than urban participants.

## Help Received From Friends

When gender and marital status were controlled, rural female respondents reported a significantly greater percentage of help from friends than urban females in the areas of shopping, assistance when ill, important decisions, and financial aid (Table 4). Also, the data suggest that rural widows received more help from friends than their married counterparts with household repairs, yard work, car care, making important decisions, and comfort when bereaved, lonely, or depressed.

## Help Given To Friends

As shown in Table 5, the findings demonstrate significantly greater involvement in giving help to a friend on the part of rural widows. Rural widowed respondents reported giving more assistance to friends for housekeeping, shopping, illness, and important decisions than their urban counterparts. Similarly, rural males gave significantly more help to friends with illness. Help with yard work, on the other hand, was given by a higher proportion of urban men in comparison to rural males.

## Activities With Friends

As indicated in Table 6, significant differences were found between rural and urban respondents with regard to commercial recreation and happy occasions. Both activities were reported more frequently by urban rather than rural respondents. Females reported shopping with their friends more so than males.

## Influence on Morale

The multiple regression analysis using the rural sample was significant ($F = 8.3$, $p < .001$) and resulted in 38% of the variance in morale being explained by health ($B = .41$), perceived income ($B = .25$), and residence ($B = -.19$). Rural respondents reporting good health, higher perceived income, and living in the country as opposed to small towns had higher morale scores. None of the informal network variables were a significant predictor of morale.

The urban multiple regression analysis was significant ($F = 8.7$, $p < .001$) and accounted for 20% of the variance in morale scores. Urban respondents participating in more activities with friends ($B = .27$), having good health ($B = .21$), and being married as opposed to single ($B = .21$) reported significantly higher morale scores. None of the other network variables predicted morale.

## Discussion and Implications

The findings of the present study reveal differences as well as similarities in the helping and social interaction patterns of rural and urban samples of older adults. When proximity, gender, and marital status were controlled: (a) rural respondents both gave and received more help with illness with children and friends; (b) rural males gave more

Table 3.
Percentage of Respondents Participating in Social Activities with Children By Rural-Urban Residence (controlling proximity, gender, and marital status)

| Activity[a] | Married Males | | | | Married Females | | | | Widowed Females | | | |
|---|---|---|---|---|---|---|---|---|---|---|---|---|
| | Close[b] | | Distant[b] | | Close | | Distant | | Close | | Distant | |
| | Urban (n = 25) | Rural (n = 23) | Urban (n = 13) | Rural (n = 18) | Urban (n = 38) | Rural (n = 17) | Urban (n = 22) | Rural (n = 8) | Urban (n = 59) | Rural (n = 14) | Urban (n = 16) | Rural (n = 13) |
| Commercial recreation | 64.0 | 26.1** | 61.5 | 27.8* | 57.9 | 11.8*** | 68.2 | 25.8* | 72.9 | 28.6** | 62.5 | 23.1* |
| Home recreation | 64.0 | 82.6 | 53.8 | 72.2 | 55.3 | 70.6 | 50.0 | 75.0 | 50.8 | 64.3 | 62.5 | 69.2 |
| Outdoor recreation | 28.0 | 34.8 | 15.4 | 50.0* | 21.1 | 23.5 | 31.8 | 37.5 | 16.9 | 14.3 | 6.3 | 15.4 |
| Drop-in visits | 80.0 | 91.3 | 30.8 | 22.2 | 86.8 | 94.1 | 18.2 | 12.5 | 71.2 | 85.7 | 12.5 | 38.5 |
| Vacation visits | 32.0 | 69.6** | 46.2 | 72.2 | 34.2 | 58.8 | 59.1 | 100.0* | 42.4 | 85.7** | 75.0 | 84.6 |
| Reunions | 32.0 | 52.2 | 23.1 | 44.4 | 34.2 | 64.7* | 36.4 | 25.0 | 30.5 | 78.6*** | 25.0 | 46.2 |
| Work same location | 8.0 | 30.4* | 7.7 | 5.6 | 5.3 | 23.5* | 0.0 | 0.0 | 5.1 | 14.3 | 6.3 | 0.0 |
| Happy occasions | 80.0 | 91.3 | 61.5 | 72.2 | 94.7 | 88.2 | 86.4 | 75.0 | 94.9 | 92.9 | 68.8 | 84.6 |
| Attend church together | 16.0 | 39.1 | 15.4 | 11.1 | 39.5 | 29.4 | 9.1 | 0.0 | 40.7 | 42.9 | 12.5 | 23.1 |
| Shop together | 28.0 | 39.1 | 46.2 | 16.7 | 47.4 | 64.7 | 72.7 | 25.0* | 57.6 | 71.4 | 43.8 | 38.5 |
| Other | 4.0 | 4.3 | 7.7 | 5.6 | 5.3 | 0.0 | 12.5 | 11.1 | 5.1 | 7.1 | 6.3 | 23.1 |

[a]Multiple responses.
[b]Close = within 49 miles; Distant = 50 miles or greater.
*p < .05. **p < .01. ***p < .001.

Table 4.
*Percentage of Rural and Urban Respondents Receiving Help From a Friend (controlling for gender and marital status)*

| Helping Behaviors[a] | Married Males | | Married Females | | Widowed Females | |
|---|---|---|---|---|---|---|
| | Urban (n = 38) | Rural (n = 42) | Urban (n = 60) | Rural (n = 27) | Urban (n = 75) | Rural (n = 29) |
| Transportation | 21.1 | 21.4 | 38.3 | 37.0 | 53.3 | 44.8 |
| Household repairs | 15.8 | 4.8 | 11.7 | 7.4 | 24.0 | 20.7 |
| Housekeeping | 7.9 | 0.0 | 6.7 | 11.1 | 5.3 | 10.3 |
| Shopping | 7.9 | 4.8 | 10.0 | 29.6* | 14.7 | 27.6 |
| Yard work | 15.8 | 11.9 | 16.7 | 3.7 | 17.3 | 17.2 |
| Car care | 13.2 | 14.3 | 8.3 | 0.0 | 8.0 | 10.3 |
| Assist when ill | 21.1 | 35.7 | 26.7 | 63.0*** | 28.0 | 58.6** |
| Important decisions | 10.5 | 16.7 | 15.0 | 7.4 | 17.3 | 34.5* |
| Legal aid | 7.9 | 2.4 | 6.7 | 3.7 | 6.7 | 3.4 |
| Financial aid | 7.9 | 21.4 | 6.7 | 37.0*** | 6.7 | 44.8*** |
| Comfort | 52.6 | 59.5 | 60.0 | 63.0 | 65.3 | 79.3 |
| Other | 5.3 | 14.3 | 1.7 | 0.0 | 0.0 | 10.3 |

[a]Multiple responses.
*p < .05.
**p < .01.
***p < .001.

Table 5.
*Percentage of Rural and Urban Respondents Giving Help To a Friend (controlling for gender and marital status)*

| Helping Behaviors[a] | Married Males | | Married Females | | Widowed Females | |
|---|---|---|---|---|---|---|
| | Urban (n = 38) | Rural (n = 42) | Urban (n = 60) | Rural (n = 27) | Urban (n = 75) | Rural (n = 29) |
| Transportation | 28.9 | 31.0 | 40.0 | 29.6 | 33.3 | 48.3 |
| Household repairs | 23.7 | 9.5 | 11.7 | 3.7 | 5.3 | 13.8 |
| Housekeeping | 7.9 | 0.0 | 11.7 | 0.0 | 4.0 | 17.2* |
| Shopping | 5.3 | 7.1 | 15.0 | 29.6 | 13.3 | 34.5** |
| Yard work | 18.4 | 4.8* | 11.7 | 3.7 | 2.7 | 10.3 |
| Car care | 7.9 | 14.3 | 10.0 | 0.0 | 2.7 | 6.9 |
| Assist when ill | 21.1 | 42.9* | 48.3 | 59.3 | 38.7 | 65.5** |
| Important decisions | 7.9 | 16.7 | 13.3 | 3.7 | 12.0 | 37.9** |
| Legal aid | 5.3 | 2.4 | 8.3 | 3.7 | 4.0 | 0.0 |
| Financial aid | 5.3 | 4.8 | 8.3 | 3.7 | 5.3 | 3.4 |
| Comfort | 52.6 | 50.0 | 75.0 | 74.1 | 77.3 | 79.3 |
| Other | 0.0 | 5.6 | 0.0 | 6.9 | 2.6 | 2.4 |

[a]Multiple responses.
*p < .05.
**p < .01.

Table 6.
*Percentage of Rural and Urban Respondents Participating in Social Activities with Friends (controlling for gender and marital status)*

| Activity[a] | Married Males | | Married Females | | Widowed Females | |
|---|---|---|---|---|---|---|
| | Urban (n = 38) | Rural (n = 42) | Urban (n = 53) | Rural (n = 28) | Urban (n = 75) | Rural (n = 29) |
| Commercial recreation | 55.3 | 19.0*** | 56.7 | 7.4*** | 53.3 | 24.1** |
| Home recreation | 55.3 | 69.0 | 51.7 | 66.7 | 41.3 | 58.6 |
| Outdoor recreation | 23.7 | 33.3 | 18.3 | 22.2 | 8.0 | 0.0 |
| Drop-in visits | 89.5 | 78.6 | 81.7 | 85.2 | 88.0 | 79.3 |
| Vacation visits | 15.8 | 28.6 | 21.7 | 11.1 | 18.7 | 24.1 |
| Work together | 10.5 | 19.0 | 6.7 | 11.1 | 6.7 | 10.3 |
| Happy occasions | 52.6 | 26.2* | 53.3 | 25.9* | 54.7 | 44.8 |
| Attend church together | 31.6 | 38.1 | 43.3 | 55.6 | 40.0 | 41.4 |
| Shopping together | 10.5 | 7.1 | 41.7 | 37.0 | 46.7 | 55.2 |
| Other | 2.6 | 14.3 | 0.0 | 14.8 | 2.7 | 10.3 |

[a]Multiple responses.
*p < .05.
**p < .01.
***p < .001.

financial aid to children; (c) rural widows gave more help to friends than urban widows; (d) rural respondents engaged in more vacation visits and reunions with children and in less commercial recreation with them than did their urban counterparts; and (e) rural respondents also engaged in less commercial recreation and happy occasions with friends.

With one exception, that being urban older adults' social activities with friends, support network variables had no significant influence on the morale of older adults in the sample. These findings are consistent with other studies indicating virtually no relationship between kin interaction and morale (Lee & Ellithorpe, 1982; Mancini, 1979). The significance of social activities with friends to morale is supported by previous studies (Edwards & Klemmack, 1973; Kivett, 1985; Lemon, Bengtson, & Peterson, 1972). Since friendships appear to be a more salient feature of rural rather than urban support networks (Bultena, Powers, Falkman, & Frederick, 1971; Donnenworth, Guy, & Norvell, 1978), one might have expected that social activities with friends would have significantly influenced the morale of rural older adults as well. One speculation is that rural friendships take on greater instrumental functions than urban friendships, thereby having a leveling effect on morale. Urban friendships, on the other hand, possess less instrumental qualities and more leisure/ social qualities than rural friendships, thus giving a boost to morale.

The finding that among rural respondents, residing in open country as opposed to small towns was beneficial to morale, underscores the importance of examining differences *within* various "rural" locales rather than using one broad category (Lee & Lassey, 1980; Rowles, 1986). The differential effect of small town and open country residence on morale warrants further examination. Also, policymakers might want to give attention to the diversity that exists between and within rural areas.

Health was important to the morale of both rural and urban adults; however, it figured more prominently in predicting the morale of rural adults. A well-documented and consistent finding is the lack of available medical care in rural areas (Lassey & Lassey, 1985). This was true of the rural sample used in this study as well. Of particular importance to practitioners is the finding that informal supports (i.e., children, friends) in rural areas compensate for lack of health care by providing more assistance when illness strikes. This assistance may take the form of transporting the family member to the nearest doctor, sitting or providing respite care, seeking medical care or equipment, preparing meals, and providing actual health care. It is important to note that these older adults were not only on the receiving end with respect to help with illness. When adult children were ill, for example, help was provided by their elderly parents. Practitioners involved in service delivery should take the needs of older caregivers into consideration as their needs may differ considerably from younger caregivers. In addition, the relatively greater involvement of friends in providing care should be recognized as an asset to health care efforts and be utilized.

Despite the fact that the samples were fairly comparable with respect to income, rural males were giving more financial aid to their children. One explanation is that in rural areas, children are often tied economically to the family farm. Parental aid to children may reflect the greater stake of multigenerational rural families in maintaining the family farm or ranch. Parental efforts to protect the farm may come at a cost to the wellbeing of older rural family members. Financial assistance programs that are responsive to the particular needs of farm families may be a means to ensure a secure financial future.

In summary, practitioners must (a) continue to target health care services to rural areas, (b) involve family caregivers in the planning and delivery of health care, (c) acknowledge and encourage friends' assistance with health care, (d) recognize diversity within rural settings, (e) provide services that undergird the support system of the widowed, and (f) assist families in financial planning and in utilizing programs that can provide financial security.

The findings reported in the present study are limited to one geographical area, to married-widowed comparisons, to a white, predominately middle class sample, and to limited aspects of the support network (i.e., children, friends, helping, and social behavior). Therefore, further research is warranted before more definitive conclusions can be drawn. Findings from the present study highlight the importance of examining the differential involvements of older rural and urban adults with their informal support networks as a preliminary step in any intervention effort.

## END NOTE

1. The rural sample was selected from two rural counties located within the same 15-county planning and service area as the urban sample. The rural area included farming, ranching, and small towns of less than 2,500 persons. Both rural counties were sparsely populated with densities of 4 and 36 persons per square mile. The urban sample was drawn from selected census tracts in a city of approximately 175,000 population.

## REFERENCES

Arth, M. (1980). American culture and the phenomenon of friendship in the aged. In C. Tibbitts & W. Donahue (Eds.), *Social and psychological aspects of aging* (pp. 529–546). New York: Arno Press.

Booth, A., & Hess, E. (1974). Cross-sex friendship. *Journal of Marriage and the Family, 36,* 38–47.

Bultena, G. (1969). Rural-urban differences in the familial interaction of the aged. *Rural Sociology, 34,* 5–15.

Bultena, G., Powers, E., Falkman, P., & Frederick, D. (1971). *Life after 70 in Iowa* (Sociology Report No. 95). Ames, IA: Iowa State University.

Coward, R. T. (1980). Research-based programs for the rural elderly. In W. R. Lassey, M. L. Lassey, & G. R. Lee (Eds.), *Research and public service with the rural elderly* (pp. 39–56). Corvallis, OR: Western Rural Development Center, Oregon State University.

Donnenworth, C., Guy, R., & Norvell, M. (1978). Life satisfaction among older persons: Rural-urban and racial comparison. *Social Science Quarterly, 57,* 578–583.

Edwards, J. N., & Klemmack, D. L. (1973). Correlates of life satisfaction: A reexamination. *Journal of Gerontology, 28,* 497–502.

Kivett, V. R. (1985). Aging in rural society. Non-kin community relations and participation. In R. T. Coward & G. R. Lee (Eds.), *The elderly in rural society* (pp. 171–191). New York: Springer.

Lassey, W. R., & Lassey, M. L. (1985). The physical health status of the rural elderly. In R. T. Coward & G. R. Lee (Eds.), *The elderly in rural society* (pp. 79–104). New York: Springer.

Lawton, M. (1975). The Philadelphia Geriatric Center Morale Scale: A revision. *Journal of Gerontology, 30,* 85-89.

Lee, G. R., & Cassidy, M. L. (1985). Family and kin relations of the rural elderly. In R. T. Coward & G. R. Lee (Eds.), *The elderly in rural society* (pp. 151–169). New York: Springer.

Lee, G. R., Ellithorpe, E. (1982). Intergenerational exchange and subjective well-being among the elderly. *Journal of Marriage and the Family, 44,* 217–224.

Lee, G. R., & Lassey, M. L. (1980). Rural-urban differences among the elderly: Economic, social, and subjective factors. *Journal of Social Issues, 36,* 62–74.

Lemon, B. W., Bengtson, V. L., & Peterson, J. A. (1972). An exploration of the activity theory of aging: Activity types and life satisfaction among inmovers to a retirement community. *Journal of Gerontology, 27,* 511–523.

Mancini, J. A. (1979). Family relationships and morale among people 65 years of age and older. *American Journal of Orthopsychiatry, 49,* 292–300.

McKain, W. C. (1967). Community roles and activities of older rural persons. In E. G. Youmans (Ed.), *Older rural Americans* (pp. 75–96). Lexington, KY: University of Kentucky Press.

Morris, J. N., & Sherwood, S. (1975). A retesting and modification of the Philadelphia Geriatric Center Morale Scale. *Journal of Gerontology, 30,* 77–84.

Roberto, K. A., & Scott, J. P. (1986). Friendships of older men and women: Exchange patterns and satisfaction. *Psychology and Aging, 1,* 103–109.

Rowles, G. D. (1986). *What's rural about rural aging? An Appalachian perspective.* Paper presented at the meeting of the Gerontological Society of America, Chicago, IL.

Schooler, K. K. (1975). A comparison of rural and nonelderly on selected variables. In R. C. Atchley (Ed.), *Rural environments and aging* (pp. 27–42). Washington, DC: Gerontological Society of America.

Schulz, J. (1980). *The economics of aging.* Belmont, CA: Wadsworth.

Youmans, E. G. (1963). *Aging patterns in a rural and urban area of Kentucky.* (Agricultural Experiment Station, Bulletin No. 681). Lexington, KY: University of Kentucky Press.

# Older Rural Fathers and Sons:
# Patterns of Association and Helping*

Vira R. Kivett**

Most elderly adults, though relatively self-sufficient until late old age, require assistance at some time from adult children, other kin, or nonfamily supports. Of these resources, children are the most frequent and perferred source (Cicirelli, 1981; Lee, 1980). Daughters, or female kin, traditionally have been found to provide the majority of assistance (Kivett, 1985; Lee, 1980; Troll, 1971). Dwindling national and local funds, as well as the gradual loss of peers and generational kin, require that family support systems be reinforced and expanded beyond the "female level."

The significance of daughters as a resource to older parents is well documented (Adams, 1968; Cicirelli, 1981; Powers & Brubaker, 1985; Streib & Beck, 1980; Troll, 1971). The importance of sons to the support network of older men, however, is unclear. Information on male kin interaction in the main must be generalized from studies of female kinship which imply the relative unimportance of male relationships (Lee, 1980; Schorr, 1980; Streib & Beck, 1980; Troll, 1971). Women, reportedly, live closer to significant kin, interact to a greater extent with relatives, engage more frequently in patterns of mutual aid, and show greater levels of affect toward kin than men. As a result, women are viewed as having broader support networks in old age.

Further impacting the paucity of information on the older father-son relationship is the lack of studies on rural male kin, individuals thought to be traditionally bound through strong agrarian ties (Powers & Brubaker, 1985). Extensive out-migration of the young from rural areas over the past four decades has important implications for interaction among male kin. Information on intergenerational relationships is of particular interest to practitioners and service providers addressing the support needs of older rural adults.

The overall purposes of this study were to investigate the extent to which adult sons were incorporated into the support network of older rural men and to determine the components of their interaction. More specifically, this study determined (a) the levels of association and helping between older fathers and sons (compared to those of other rural parent-child dyads) and (b) the factors contributing to the frequency of their association and helping. The first hypothesis stated that fathers and sons would have significantly lower levels of association and helping than other parent-child dyads. Secondly, it was hypothesized that several social structural factors empirically found to create the opportunity for or to limit intergenerational interaction and the subjective importance assigned to the son would ex-

*Project NCARS 13822. The Cooperative State Research Service, United States Department of Agriculture, Washington, DC (data collected in 1980-81). Chapter presented at the 38th Annual Scientific Meeting of the Gerontological Society, New Orleans, LA, November, 1985.

**Vira R. Kivett is Professor, Department of Child Development and Family Relations, University of North Carolina, Greensboro, NC 27412-5001 and is associated with the North Carolina Agricultural Research Service, North Carolina State University, Raleigh, NC 27650-7601.

Reprinted from *Family Relations*, 1988, **37**, 62-67.

plain a significant amount of variance in association and helping behaviors between older fathers and sons.

## Conceptual Framework

The conceptual framework for the present study is based upon a review of the literature suggesting the greater relative strength of the mother/daughter tie to that of other parent-child dyads (Atkinson, Kivett, & Campbell, 1986; Lee, 1980; Streib & Beck, 1980) and an adaptation of a theoretical perspective of intergenerational interaction by Mutran and Reitzes (1984), which integrates exchange principles and symbolic interaction tenets. Mutran and Reitzes' convergence of perspectives is based upon the premise that social background and related roles, subjective meaning and self-feelings, as well as exchange processes influence the interaction of adult children and their elderly parents. Although divergent in their approaches, exchange theory and symbolic interaction theory both seek to explain social interaction and subsequently are seen as having concurring themes. The convergence perspective as projected by Mutran and Reitzes (1984) suggests three aspects of development in the study of intergenerational family roles: (a) the impact of social structure on family interaction, (b) the impact of subjective and self-motives on interaction, and (c) the relationship of exchange and interaction to feelings among the elderly. Because the main objectives of the current study were to determine factors contributing to intergenerational interaction and not the impact of balance of exchanges on the subjective well-being of fathers, this latter posit was not incorporated into the design of the study.

## Methodology

### The Sample

The data used in this research were from a larger study of the kin network system of 321 adults 65 years or older living in a rural-transitional county in the Southeastern United States. The county contained two towns with populations of 3,000 and 25,000. Both towns and the outlying areas displayed distinctively rural characteristics relative to population density, education and income levels, and institutions. The county is adjacent to several urban counties, and the major

industry in the area is textiles. As a result of its proximity to a large urban area, it was described best as being in a rural to urban transition at the time of the study. Subjects were selected based upon a sampling ratio using an area cluster sampling strategy. Information was gathered from the subjects in their homes. The data included information on demographic characteristics, income, health, morale, and interaction with children, grandchildren, in-laws, and collateral kin. Subjects were asked to respond to questions with regard to kin of most contact at each of seven levels. For purposes of this study, the major respondents of interest were men who indicated that their child of most contact was a son ($N = 56$). The instruments designed for the larger study from which this secondary analysis was conducted simulated those used in an original theoretical paper by Bengtson, Haddad, and Olander (1976) but were not piloted prior to the present analyses. Internal reliability was established, however, on the dependent measures.

### Measures

The dependent variables in the study were association, help received, and help given. *Association* was determined by asking the father to indicate the extent to which he had gotten together with the son of most contact during the past year. The listing consisted of 12 activities (Table 1). Also added to this scale was the extent to which the father had received telephone calls and letters from the son. A 9-point response scale was used ranging from *daily* to *never*. Cronbach's Alpha for reliability for the association scale was .69. *Help received* was measured by asking the fathers the extent to which they had received help in 10 areas of assistance from their sons during the last year. The same response schedule as that used with the association measure was employed. The reliability coefficient for the scale was .80. *Help given* was determined by rephrasing the helping question in terms of the amount of help that fathers had given to sons. Cronbach's Alpha of reliability was .76.

Five independent variables, each empirically linked to intergenerational interaction, were included in the analyses. The first four of these variables—proximity to son (Bengtson et al., 1976; Kivett, 1985; Marshall & Rosenthal, 1985), self-perceived health

(Bengtson et al., 1976; Kivett, 1985), perceived adequacy of income (Bengtson et al., 1976), and number of children (Kivett, 1985; Powers & Brubaker, 1985)—were social structural factors which, according to Mutran and Reitzes (1984), either create an opportunity for, or limit the interaction of, elderly parents. Briefly, close proximity to parents has been found to increase interaction, poor health of older parent to stimulate association and helping on the part of children, higher income of older parents to increase the likelihood of association, and a larger number of children to contribute to more association and helping.

*Proximity to son* was a functional measure of distance between the residence of father and son. Responses were on a scale of 1–6, ranging from *live in the same house* to *one day or more away*. *Health* was a self-report measure in which the respondent was asked how he would rate his health on a scale of 0–9. The *best of health* was represented by the top of the scale, and the *poorest of health* was represented by the bottom. *Perceived adequacy of income* was measured through responses to the question, "How adequate is your income? —always adequate, adequate most of the time, adequate if careful, and never adequate." *Number of children* was the total number of living children including natural, foster, and adoptive offspring. The final variable, *confidant*, represented a subjective factor. According to Mutran and Reitzes (1984), in line with symbolic interaction tenets, positive subjective meanings attached to a kinsperson (such as that of confidant) will increase intergenerational interaction. Thus the meaning attached to a child is seen to influence the receptiveness of an older parent to give or receive aid or to associate with a child. The confidant variable was measured by asking the respondents if they had a confidant and who that person was in terms of their relationship to them. The confidant variable was dichotomized into a dummy variable, son vs. other, with the son category serving as the referent.

## Statistical Analyses

The first hypothesis, which stated that fathers and sons would have lower levels of association and helping than other parent-child dyads, was tested by one-way analysis of variance. The Scheffe test was used for multiple comparison of means, and a conservative level of .01 was used to confirm significance. The second hypothesis, that social structural factors and subjective and self-motives would explain a significant amount of variance in association and helping behaviors between fathers and sons, was analyzed through three hierarchial multiple regression analyses (the alpha level used to confirm significance was .05). The social structural variables of proximity to son, health, perceived adequacy of income, and number of children were included as a block in the first step of the analysis.

The subjective measure of confidant was entered on the second and final step. Association, help received, and help given served as dependent measures in each of the three multiple regression models. Other variables descriptively analyzed in the study were fathers' perceptions of feelings of closeness toward sons, their perception of how well they "got along," and the extent to which they and their sons had similar life views.

## Findings

The mean age of the 56 fathers in this analysis was 72.76 years ($SD = 5.59$), and they had an average of 2.07 daughters and 1.94 sons. Slightly more fathers, 54%, reported a son as a child of most contact than a daughter, 46%. The majority, 91%, were white and married, 88%. Most fathers were retired, 86%, and had been either craftsmen or operatives, 61% (blue-collar workers). Less than 3% had been farmers. Older subjects had a mean educational level of 8.65 years ($SD = 3.51$) and a self-rated health mean of 6.13 ($SD = 2.52$). Fathers, 84%, most frequently said that they usually or always had enough money to meet their needs. The majority, 91%, reported that they had a confidant. Of those reporting a confidant, approximately 80% named their spouse and 5% mentioned a son. The mean age of sons of most contact was 41.35 years ($SD = 9.24$), and they had a mean educational level of 12.70 years ($SD = 3.41$). Approximately 7% of the sons of most contact lived in the household with the father, and an additional 47% lived within 60 minutes of the older subjects' homes. Daughters of most contact, 56%, usually lived more than 60 minutes from older fathers.

Three items measured affect between fathers and sons. The first two questions related to extent to which fathers "got along with" or "felt close to" sons, and each had four Likert-type responses. Fathers, 96%, usually indicated that they got along very well with their son of most contact, and the same percentage reported feeling very close. The third item of affect related to common life views. Fathers were asked to indicate on a scale of 0–9 the extent to which they and their sons had similar views regarding life. The overall mean was 8.32 ($SD = 0.86$).

## Inferential Results

*Dyad comparisons.* Table 1 shows that in only one comparison of association, mothers and daughters, did fathers and sons show lower levels of contact. Fathers and sons were most likely to have been associated during the past year through visiting, telephoning, family reunions, and happy occasions such as birthdays and other special events. Similarly, differences in help received were found between father-son and mother-daughter dyads, yet in no other parent-child comparisons. Fathers showed significantly lower levels of help received from sons than mothers from daughters (Table 2). Only moderate to low help was received by fathers from sons and assistance was most likely to have been with transportation, household repairs, car care, yard work, help in illness, and help in decision making. Both fathers and mothers were most likely to have received help with transportation from their son or daughter. Mothers, however, received considerably more help from daughters than fathers received from sons. The type of assistance in other areas differed.

Largest discrepancies appeared to be in traditionally male or female role-related areas; for example, help with shopping, housekeeping, and health care was more likely to have been received by mothers from daughters than fathers from sons. A notable discrepancy was also seen in the larger extent to which mothers received help in decision making from daughters.

No significant differences were found in the amount of help given by fathers to sons and other parent-child dyads (Table 3). However, mothers reported giving more assistance to daughters than to sons. Fathers, approximately one third, were most likely to have provided transportation to sons than other services. Overall, amount of assistance given to sons was low and less than that received from sons with the possible exception of transportation. On the basis of these observations, hypothesis one was rejected since fathers and sons did not show lower levels of association and helping than all other parent-child dyads. Only in the case of association (mothers and daughters) and help given by children (mothers and daughters) were differences observed between father-son dyads and other father-child comparisons.

*Variance explained in association and helping behaviors.* Examination of the results of the first regression analysis showed the model to explain a significant amount of variance in father-son association [$R^2 = .13$, $F(5,47) = 2.55$, $p < .05$] (Table 4). Proximity to son, a social structural variable, was the only factor contributing to the frequency with which fathers and sons associ-

Table 1.
*Association Between Older Parent and Child of Most Contact According to Sex of Parent and Child*

| Association | Fathers/ sons[a] | | | Fathers/ daughters[b] | | | Mothers/ daughters[c] | | | Mothers/ sons[d] | | |
|---|---|---|---|---|---|---|---|---|---|---|---|---|
| | Percent | M | SD | Percent | M | SD | Percent | M | SD | Percent | M | SD |
| Commercial recreation | 21 | 1.6 | 1.3 | 33 | 1.6 | 1.1 | 23 | 1.6 | 1.3 | 9 | 1.3 | 0.9 |
| Home recreation | 36 | 2.4 | 2.1 | 46 | 2.5 | 1.8 | 51 | 3.0 | 2.3 | 37 | 2.4 | 2.0 |
| Outdoor recreation | 25 | 1.9 | 2.0 | 25 | 1.8 | 1.5 | 22 | 1.7 | 1.6 | 17 | 1.6 | 1.6 |
| Visiting | 89 | 5.5 | 2.9 | 85 | 5.8 | 2.6 | 83 | 6.1 | 2.8 | 83 | 6.0 | 2.8 |
| Vacation | 27 | 1.6 | 1.0 | 27 | 1.7 | 1.2 | 32 | 1.8 | 1.3 | 23 | 1.5 | 1.2 |
| Family reunion | 45 | 1.9 | 1.2 | 54 | 2.3 | 1.3 | 55 | 2.3 | 1.3 | 50 | 2.1 | 1.2 |
| Emergency | 36 | 2.0 | 1.8 | 38 | 1.8 | 1.1 | 57 | 2.1 | 1.3 | 35 | 2.0 | 1.9 |
| Working together | 5 | 1.1 | 0.6 | 4 | 1.2 | 1.2 | 5 | 1.3 | 1.3 | 4 | 1.1 | 0.5 |
| Baby-sitting | 5 | 1.2 | 0.9 | 13 | 1.6 | 1.8 | 18 | 1.8 | 2.0 | 8 | 1.4 | 1.3 |
| Happy occasions | 82 | 3.3 | 1.2 | 75 | 3.2 | 1.4 | 94 | 3.8 | 1.1 | 83 | 3.8 | 1.4 |
| Church | 52 | 3.2 | 2.6 | 43 | 3.1 | 2.6 | 62 | 3.7 | 2.5 | 51 | 3.5 | 2.8 |
| Shopping | 27 | 1.9 | 1.8 | 35 | 2.3 | 2.0 | 75 | 4.1 | 2.2 | 31 | 2.3 | 2.1 |
| Writing | 58 | 3.2 | 2.3 | 60 | 3.1 | 2.1 | 62 | 3.4 | 2.4 | 46 | 2.8 | 2.3 |
| Telephoning | 85 | 6.0 | 2.6 | 92 | 7.1 | 2.5 | 90 | 7.0 | 2.5 | 87 | 6.5 | 2.6 |
| Range (Summed score) | 16–73 | | | 17–63 | | | 17–83 | | | 18–73 | | |
| Means (Summed score) | 37.73 | | | 40.00 | | | 44.23[e] | | | 38.42 | | |

[a]$n = 56$. [b]$n = 98$. [c]$n = 94$. [d]$n = 79$. [e]Significantly higher than fathers/sons, mothers/sons ($p < .01$).

ated. Contact with fathers increased with sons' proximity to fathers. The subjective factor, confidant, was of no relative importance to how often fathers and sons got together. The results from the two remaining regression analyses were non-significant, that is, the variables examined did not explain a significant amount of variance in either help received by fathers [$R^2$ = .10, $F(5,47)$ = 2.12, $p$ > .05] or help given to sons [$R^2$ = -.02, $F(5,46)$ = .76, $p$ > .05]. As a result, the findings only supported in part the hypothesis that social factors provide or limit opportunities for interaction and that subjective importance accorded the son explains a significant amount of interaction between fathers and sons. Only in the case of association was this observed. Consequently, the second hypothesis was also rejected.

## Discussion

The results of this study represent older father-son relations in a geographical area of rural change stimulated by encroaching industry and urban sprawl. This rural type is increasingly frequent on the continuum of rural communities and may pose unique problems for service providers.

The data show that adult sons are incorporated only marginally into the support network of older rural-transitional fathers as viewed through frequency of association (other than obligatory contact) and mutual helping. Furthermore, sense of obligation appears to play a significant role in association. For example, most contact appears to be prescribed by birthdays, family reunions, other family ceremonies, and by emergencies. These data support earlier observations of the obligatory nature of older parent-son relations (Troll, 1971).

Contrary to most research findings (Adams, 1968; Cicirelli, 1981; Troll, 1971), sons were found to be a more frequent child of contact to fathers than daughters and to live nearer to older fathers. Furthermore, in contrast to current concerns of migration effects, most older rural fathers in the current study had at least one son living within 60 minutes distance. The distant proximity of a number of sons of most contact, however, suggested constraints on certain types of support such as those requiring quick or regular access to the older father. The results showed, for example, that extent of association with older fathers was dependent upon father-son proximity.

Despite the finding of no relative instrumental importance of adult sons to the support system of older fathers, the high levels of affect held for sons by fathers suggested sons' psychological importance. Bengtson, Mangen, and Landry (1984) pointed out the important "stake" that older parents have in intergenerational consensus and regard and its subsequent positive effects on the strength of family ties.

Adult sons in this study showed evidence of moderate "kin tending" through the frequency of their telephoning and visiting older fathers. Some of these behaviors may have been initiated by daughters-in-law. Nevertheless, they occurred and with some frequency. These behaviors, too, have been identified as important to intergenerational solidarity (Bengtson et al., 1976).

Father-son interaction was seen to be less salient than mother-daughter interaction in relation to association and parent to child help but, otherwise, of similar saliency to other older rural parent-child dyad ties (father-daughter, mother-son). Mothers and daughters had higher overall frequencies of

Table 2.
*Help Received by Older Fathers and Mothers According to Sex of Child of Most Contact*

| Help Received | Fathers/ sons[a] | | | Fathers/ daughters[b] | | | Mothers/ daughters[c] | | | Mothers/ sons[d] | | |
|---|---|---|---|---|---|---|---|---|---|---|---|---|
| | Percent | M | SD | Percent | M | SD | Percent | M | SD | Percent | M | SD |
| Transportation | 39 | 2.5 | 2.0 | 60 | 3.6 | 2.5 | 80 | 5.0 | 2.5 | 58 | 3.6 | 2.6 |
| Household repairs | 30 | 2.0 | 1.6 | 28 | 2.0 | 1.9 | 40 | 2.4 | 2.1 | 47 | 2.9 | 2.4 |
| Housekeeping | 11 | 1.4 | 1.1 | 44 | 3.0 | 2.6 | 53 | 3.2 | 2.6 | 17 | 1.9 | 2.2 |
| Shopping | 16 | 1.7 | 1.7 | 45 | 3.0 | 2.5 | 71 | 4.3 | 2.6 | 23 | 2.2 | 2.3 |
| Yard work | 27 | 2.1 | 2.0 | 19 | 1.7 | 1.7 | 30 | 2.2 | 2.1 | 41 | 2.8 | 2.4 |
| Car care | 25 | 1.8 | 1.6 | 11 | 1.3 | 0.9 | 11 | 1.4 | 1.1 | 29 | 2.1 | 2.0 |
| Illness | 32 | 2.3 | 2.3 | 60 | 3.5 | 2.8 | 61 | 3.6 | 2.8 | 37 | 2.7 | 2.5 |
| Decision making | 30 | 1.8 | 1.3 | 32 | 2.2 | 2.1 | 65 | 3.7 | 2.5 | 47 | 2.9 | 2.4 |
| Legal aid | 5 | 1.2 | 0.7 | 11 | 1.5 | 1.6 | 18 | 1.5 | 1.2 | 12 | 1.4 | 1.4 |
| Financial aid | 2 | 1.0 | 0.3 | 7 | 1.2 | 1.0 | 16 | 1.6 | 1.5 | 13 | 1.5 | 1.6 |
| Range | 10–46 | | | 10–52 | | | 10–74 | | | 10–90 | | |
| Means | 18.75 | | | 23.81 | | | 29.38[e] | | | 24.68 | | |

[a]$n$ = 56. [b]$n$ = 48. [c]$n$ = 94. [d]$n$ = 79. [e]Significantly higher than fathers/sons ($p$ < .01).

Table 3.
*Help Given by Older Fathers and Mothers According to Sex of Child of Most Contact*

| Help Given | Fathers/ sons[a] | | | Fathers/ daughters[b] | | | Mothers/ daughters[c] | | | Mothers/ sons[d] | | |
|---|---|---|---|---|---|---|---|---|---|---|---|---|
| | Percent | M | SD | Percent | M | SD | Percent | M | SD | Percent | M | SD |
| Transportation | 31 | 2.0 | 1.8 | 40 | 2.4 | 2.0 | 25 | 2.0 | 1.9 | 12 | 1.4 | 1.2 |
| Household repairs | 18 | 1.5 | 1.2 | 19 | 1.5 | 1.2 | 5 | 1.2 | 0.9 | 47 | 2.9 | 2.4 |
| Housekeeping | 2 | 1.0 | 0.3 | 8 | 1.4 | 1.6 | 22 | 2.0 | 2.3 | 17 | 1.9 | 2.2 |
| Shopping | 11 | 1.4 | 1.3 | 15 | 1.6 | 1.6 | 30 | 2.2 | 2.0 | 23 | 2.2 | 2.3 |
| Yard work | 13 | 1.4 | 1.0 | 6 | 1.2 | 0.7 | 4 | 1.2 | 1.0 | 41 | 2.8 | 2.4 |
| Car care | 11 | 1.3 | 0.8 | 4 | 1.1 | 0.6 | 2 | 1.1 | 0.4 | 29 | 2.1 | 2.0 |
| Illness | 15 | 1.4 | 1.2 | 19 | 1.6 | 1.5 | 33 | 2.1 | 2.1 | 37 | 2.7 | 2.5 |
| Decision making | 22 | 1.6 | 1.5 | 19 | 1.5 | 1.1 | 29 | 1.9 | 1.5 | 47 | 2.9 | 2.4 |
| Legal aid[e] | — | 1.0 | 0.0 | — | — | — | 6 | 1.1 | 0.4 | 12 | 1.4 | 1.4 |
| Financial aid | 6 | 1.2 | 1.2 | 10 | 1.4 | 1.4 | 15 | 1.3 | 1.1 | 13 | 1.5 | 1.6 |
| Range | 10–45 | | | 10–33 | | | 10–43 | | | 10–50 | | |
| Means | 14.93 | | | 15.77 | | | 17.07[f] | | | 13.28 | | |

[a]$n = 56$. [b]$n = 48$. [c]$n = 94$. [d]$n = 79$. [e]Blanks denote less than .01 percent. [f]Significantly higher than mothers/sons ($p < .01$).

association and helping than fathers and sons. This finding was probably related in part to the generally higher levels of expectation (norms of familism) held by women than by men (Hagestad, 1977, 1984). Daughters and mothers were more likely to engage in discretionary activities such as shopping, attending church together, and sharing recreational activities than were fathers and sons. Similarly, daughters were a much more frequent resource to mothers than sons to fathers in illness and in special areas such as transportation, decision making, and household assistance. The data support earlier observations that women are more likely to interact with relatives and to engage more frequently in mutual aid than are men (Adams, 1968; Lee, 1980; Streib & Beck, 1980).

Examination of the types of association and helping between older parent-child dyads in the present study suggests greater potential for mutual interests between rural mothers and daughters based upon traditionally sex-related interests, as well as

Table 4.
*Regression of Association upon Proximity to Son, Health, Perceived Adequacy of Income, Number of Children, and Child as a Confidant*

| Independent Variables | B | t |
|---|---|---|
| Social structural | | |
|   Number of children | .02 | .14 |
|   Perceived adequacy of income | -.11 | -.76 |
|   Self-reported health | .23 | 1.60 |
|   Proximity to son | .34* | 2.48* |
| Subjective | | |
|   Confidant | -.14 | -.99 |

$R^2$ (adjusted) = .13.
[$F(5,47) = 2.55$ ($p < .05$).]

*$p < .05$.

greater opportunity for reciprocal exchanges. Examples were seen in areas in which large sex-linked discrepancies occurred such as shopping, health care, home recreation, and transportation. Also helping behaviors showed greater potential for reciprocity for mothers and daughters than for other groups. Reciprocity, a basic component of exchange theory, has been identified as an important factor in intergenerational helping behaviors (Adams, 1968). The observation of stronger mother-daughter than father-son ties could also be related to the socioeconomic characteristics of the sample. That is, important sex-linked relationships have been observed among working-class families (Streib & Beck, 1980). Based upon their educational levels, sons of most contact appeared to have remained at a similar social class level as their fathers, most of whom had been blue-collar workers.

Adult sons were relatively unimportant to the helping network of older rural fathers. When help was provided by sons, it usually was infrequent and of the essential type such as transportation and health care. As in the case of association, help that was more discretionary in type was less likely to occur. Unlike association, geographical proximity of the son was not important to help received or given by older rural fathers. Possibly contributing to the paucity of help received from sons was the observation that most older men were relatively independent. They were in moderately good health, usually perceived their income as adequate to meet their needs, and were married. In other words, their dependency needs did not appear to be large and most had a wife who served as their major support (wives were men's most frequently mentioned resource in a crisis and confidant). As a result, sons may have perceived fathers' needs to be adequately addressed through mothers' roles. Cicirelli (1981) found levels of help given to older parents to correspond with children's perceptions of parental needs.

The characteristics of the sons, too, may have contributed to low levels of helping and to discretionary association. Most sons were in early middle age which suggests that they were highly involved in the work role and perhaps in child launching. Also contributing to the infrequent contact (except for special events) was the fact that approximately 45% of sons lived 60 minutes or more away from fathers.

The data indicated the difficulty in identifying variables contributing to the rural father-son relationship in later life. Only a small but significant amount of variance could be explained in the interaction between fathers and sons and only in the area of association, not helping. Social structural factors such as the dependency needs (health) or resources (income and number of children) of fathers, previously theorized to influence generational interaction, were unimportant to father-son interaction (with the exception of proximity) to association and helping.

In summary, the results of the present study show that adult sons play a relatively minor role in the support network of older rural-transitional fathers as seen through helping. They appear to play a moderately active role through their participation in family ceremonies and in emergencies, behaviors which serve to strengthen family bonds. Older fathers view their sons as having life views similar to their own, to be psychologically close, and to be highly compatible, all factors important to intergenerational solidarity. In terms of support networks, older rural men would appear to be mainly dependent upon wives, with sons as well as daughters being of only marginal instrumental importance.

## Implications for Practitioners

Practitioners should be aware that the potential role of sons in the support system of older fathers may be obscured by the presence of the older mother. The data underscore the vulnerability of the support network of older rural men in the event of widowhood, separation, or divorce. For ex-

ample, most men were married and showed considerable psychological and crisis-based dependency upon wives. As a result, persons working with the rural elderly should seek ways to maintain interaction between older men and adult children that perpetuates or creates strong family ties, especially over geographical distances. One such way might be through the development or expansion of attachment behaviors between older fathers and sons. Cicirelli (1981) found attachment behaviors (an important factor in family cohesion) to be more important to adult children's present helping behaviors and future commitment to help older parents than filial obligation. He suggested that practitioners, rather than appeal to adult children's sense of duty, attempt to induce attachment behaviors such as visiting and telephoning. Thus, increased communication is seen as an indirect means of stimulating help to parents. Strengthening older father-son ties may involve the creation of more special family occasions such as the revitalization or initiation of family reunions or other opportunities for intergenerational contact or rituals.

Older men should also be encouraged to develop interaction which incorporates mutuality of interests between themselves and sons (as seen between mothers and daughters) and behaviors promoting reciprocity. Consistent with exchange theory, it has been observed that many middle-aged children develop "filial anxiety" at the anticipation of providing more help than the rewards received upon helping dependent parents or at the anticipation of providing larger amounts of help in the future (Cicirelli, 1981). Practitioners may intervene in this process by assisting adult children, in this case sons, to become more knowledgeable of the aging process and the outside supports available to reduce the sacrifice that they may be required to make in order to meet their parents' changing needs. Older sons may also become more sensitized to older parents' needs through more frequent communication (e.g., telephone calls, writing, and visiting).

The development of other local informal support systems should also be encouraged among older rural men, given the geographical distance of many of their children of most contact. This process is increasingly difficult as rural areas become more transitional and relationships more transitory. As more formal support systems develop or are accessible through encroaching urbanization, older adults will need to be educated to their acceptance, function, and use. Although it is not reasonable to expect friends and neighbors to be long-term supports, short-term, emergency, and "reprieve" supports should be fostered among this "readily" available group. Other relatives living in close proximity can also be considered as part of the potential support system of older men. As the support system moves out to more secondary kin, however, it is imperative that behaviors be cultivated that encourage mutual exchanges because of their important implication for reciprocity. Behaviors found to strengthen friend and family bonds include telephoning, writing, nonessential and reciprocal exchanges. Most importantly, practitioners must be ever cognizant of the large continuum of rural communities, their changing nature, and the subsequent implications for older adults and their support systems.

Several limitations on the generalizability of this study should be acknowledged: First, the reader is reminded that respondents reported on interaction with sons of most contact. As a result, relationships with sons of moderate or no contact were excluded and observations represented maximal levels of father/son interaction. Second, also not measured by this study is the amount of contact or assistance that may occur within the father/son dyad via the daughter-in-law. Third, the unusually low percentage of blacks in the sample, although proportional to the number of older blacks in this rural-transitional area, did not allow for the testing of possible racial differences.

With regard to future intergenerational research, studies should include the adult child and not depend upon the older parent as proxy. Attention also needs to be given to instruments used in the measurement of affect between generations. The instruments

used in the current study, for example, did not allow for variability between subjects. This observation suggests the need for more "unobtrusive" measures of affection and consensus between generations.

## REFERENCES

Adams, B. N. (1968). *Kinship in an urban setting.* Chicago: Markham.

Atkinson, M., Kivett, V. R., & Campbell, R. T. (1986). Intergenerational solidarity: An examination of a theoretical model. *Journal of Gerontology,* **41**, 408–416.

Bengtson, V. L., Haddad, E. B., & Olander, A. A. (1976). The "generation gap" and aging family members: Toward a conceptual model. In J. F. Gubrium (Ed.), *Times, roles, and self in old age* (pp. 66–72). New York: Human Sciences Press.

Bengtson, V. L., Mangen, D. J., & Landry, P. H. (1984). The multigenerational family: Concepts and findings. In V. Garms-Homolova, E. M. Hoerning, & D. Schaeffer (Eds.), *Intergenerational relationships* (pp. 63–73). Lewiston, NY: C. J. Hogrefe, Inc.

Cicirelli, V. G. (1981). *Helping elderly parents: The role of adult children.* Boston, MA: Auburn House Publishing Company.

Hagestad, G. O. (1977). *Role change in adulthood: The transition to the empty nest.* Unpublished manuscript, University of Chicago, Committee on Human Development.

Hagestad, G. O. (1984). Multi-generational families: Socialization, support, and strain. In V. Garms-Homolova, E. M. Hoerning, & D. Schaeffer (Eds.), *Intergenerational relationships* (pp. 105–114). Lewiston, NY: C. J. Hogrefe, Inc.

Kivett, V. R. (1985). Consanguinity and kin level: Their relative importance to the helping network of older adults. *Journal of Gerontology,* **40**, 228–234.

Lee, G. R. (1980). Kinship in the seventies: A decade review of research and theory. *Journal of Marriage and the Family,* **42**, 923–934.

Marshall, V. W., & Rosenthal, C. J. (1985). The relevance of geographical proximity in intergenerational relations. *Gerontology,* **25** [Special issue], 15.

Mutran, E., & Reitzes, D. C. (1984). Intergenerational support activities and well-being among the elderly: A convergence of exchange and symbolic interaction perspectives. *American Sociological Review,* **49**, 117–130.

Powers, E., & Brubaker, T. (1985). Family networks and helping patterns. In E. A. Powers, W. J. Goudy, & P. M. Keith (Eds.), *Later life transitions: Older males in rural America* (pp. 97–110). Boston: Kluwer-Nijhoff.

Schorr, A. (1980). *Thy father and thy mother: A second look at filial responsibility and policy* (SSA Publication No. 13-/1953). Washington, DC: U.S. Government Printing Office.

Streib, G., & Beck, R. W. (1980). Older families: A decade review. *Journal of Marriage and the Family,* **42**, 937–956.

Troll, L. E. (1971). The family of later life: A decade review. *Journal of Marriage and the Family,* **33**, 263–290.

# 23

# Old and Single in the City and in the Country: Activities of the Unmarried

**Pat M. Keith and André Nauta***

This research provides information on the groups and activities in which older, widowed, divorced, and never-married persons were most frequently involved in rural and urban settings, the importance of various activities to well-being, and gender differences in involvement by size of place. The research assists practitioners in determining whether to differentiate the activities and programs they provide for rural and urban residents, and it identifies barriers to participation of the unmarried aged in both large and small communities. By specifying conditions under which participation of the unmarried aged is impeded, it is possible to suggest educational and program efforts to address some of the barriers. Identification of gender-linked patterns of activity that most often promote well-being makes it possible to determine whether cross-sex leisure pursuits may warrant encouragement by those who design programs.

This research then highlights some significant issues for those who plan programs for older persons: (a) Is there a difference between rural and urban elderly in the amount and type of activities in which they engage? If differences exist, they should be taken into account in planning intervention efforts. (b) Are certain activities more impor-

tant than others to well-being of participants? If such activities are identified, practitioners will likely want to facilitate involvement in those which seem most beneficial. (c) To what extent do the activities and affiliation of the unmarried elderly differ from what is known about the patterns of involvement of the general aged population which is largely based on samples of married persons? Findings from this research should aid in planning for the unmarried so that their interests are not overlooked. Until recently, affiliation and activities of both the rural and unmarried aged have been neglected.

In assessing social involvement of older persons, Kivett (1985) observed that "A significant void in the literature is the relative lack of research comparing the social activity of the rural to that of urban populations" (p. 188). Even less is known about comparative patterns of activities of the unmarried in rural and urban places. Research on affiliation and activities of the unmarried should provide useful information for practice for several reasons: (a) The unmarried are a substantial and growing proportion of the aged population; (b) the older unmarried depend more on both formal and informal services than the married and therefore might be expected to benefit especially from programs designed with their social needs in mind; and (c) the unmarried are generally regarded as more vulnerable to isolation and presumably could benefit from efforts to provide opportunities for social integration (Keith, 1986).

Since clients of practitioners increas-

*Pat M. Keith is Professor, Department of Sociology, Iowa State University, Ames, IA 50011. Andre Nauta is a graduate student, Department of Sociology, Iowa State University, Ames, IA 50011.

Reprinted from *Family Relations*, 1988, **37**, 79-83.

ingly will be unmarried, knowledge of activities that contribute most to their well-being should be useful in deciding which programs to foster. In assessing needs and developing new programs, planners will want to take into account the extent to which activities of the unmarried and those that have positive outcomes for well-being vary by size of place.

## Affiliation and Activities of Rural/Urban Aged

Comparisons of affiliation and activities of the aged in rural and urban areas often have not focused on marital status, but both the findings and some of the theories are informative. Theoretical perspectives indicating that social networks are responsive to structural opportunities and constraints suggest rival hypotheses about differences in activities of the rural and urban aged. Fischer (1982) theorized that urbanism affects the social context in which people establish their relationships with others by expanding opportunities for building ties outside the family and neighborhood. Other data, however, suggest the effects of urbanism on activities may be mitigated somewhat by density of the aged. Rates of interaction may be higher in communities in which the aged represent a greater proportion of the population, thus favoring their involvement in smaller communities.

The distribution of the aged by marital status and gender in urban and rural communities may also affect their ties with others. Blau (1973) observed the adverse effect of marital status on social participation when it placed individuals in an atypical position relative to age and sex peers. In the United States, unmarried older men are not disproportionately located in either rural (22%) or urban areas (24%). Older women in urban areas, however, are somewhat more likely (65%) to be unmarried than their rural age peers (55%). Unmarried women regardless of community size will have more same sex, unmarried age peers with whom to affiliate.

The more varied opportunities associated with urbanism argue for greater involvement in these areas, while concentration of the aged may increase options for interpersonal relations in rural areas. More available same sex and age peers would favor the in-

volvement of unmarried women over that of men regardless of location.

Although research is limited, there is some evidence that older persons in rural areas may participate less in most formal organizations than their urban counterparts (Kivett, 1985). Reasons offered for this apparent difference have included more limited personal resources of the rural aged (i.e., lower incomes, poorer health, less available transportation), fewer available options for membership, and perhaps less inclination to adopt newer opportunities for affiliation such as senior citizens' programs (Kivett, 1985). Although it might be expected that participation would thrive where there is greater density of older persons, data on this relationship have been contradictory.

Kivett (1985) concluded that in contrast to their lesser involvement in formal organizations, rural people may engage in more formal interaction with nonkin. However, some of the samples on which this generalization was based were limited to a particular geographical area. Homogeneity in age and social class (Kivett, 1985) may favor greater informal participation in rural areas, but these may be offset by more limited income and poorer transportation which may constrain the nonkin activities of the rural aged.

Typically kin, especially adult children, are a major source of social contact for the aged. Early research found that the urban aged more than their rural peers interacted with kin (most often children). More recent research showing greater interaction between rural families and their kin probably reflects higher rates of interaction by farmers and not of rural residents generally (Lee & Cassidy, 1985). More interaction between farmers and their children is probably due to residential proximity or joint farming operations. There is little consistent evidence that nonfarm rural families see children and other kin any more often than the aged living in larger places.

It was expected that factors connected to position in the social structure (education, income, employment status) and the personal resource of health would provide opportunities for formal/informal involvement whereas deficits in these areas would constrain participation. Good health promotes social involvement, and aspects of socioeconomic status prompt participation especially in formal organizations (Palmore, 1981).

## Methodology

### Sample

Data were analyzed from the 1979 wave of the Longitudinal Retirement History Study conducted by the U.S. Bureau of the Census for the Social Security Administration. From a national sample of 11,153 persons aged 58 to 63 in 1969, a subsample of unmarried men (n = 375) and women (n = 1,674) interviewed in both 1969 and 1979 were studied. Of these respondents, 1,245 women and 251 men resided in areas with populations of 2,500 or greater; 429 women and 124 men lived in communities of less than 2,500 or in the open country. Of the rural sample, 16% (n = 87) lived on farms. Since initial analyses of variables of interest indicated that farm and rural nonfarm respondents were quite similar, these groups were combined.

## Measures

### Income

Income was coded into 23 categories ranging from under $1,000 to $30,000 or over. Median incomes of men were in the $4,000 to $4,999 range and were higher than those of women ($3,500-$3,999; $t = 3.63$, $p < .001$).

### Employment Status

Employment status was coded 0 (retired), 1 (employed). Fourteen percent of the men and 12% of the women were employed.

### Health

Functional capacity was assessed by summing responses to two questions: "Do you have any health condition, physical handicap, or disability that limits how well you get around?" and "Does your health limit the kind or amount of work or housework you can do?" (yes, no). A higher score indicated better health.

### Well-Being

Global happiness was measured by an item often used in surveys: "Taking things altogether, would you say you are happy, pretty happy, or not too happy these days?" Responses were coded as follows: happy = 3, pretty happy = 2, not too happy = 1. Respondents also indicated how satisfied they were with their level of activity (from very unsatisfactory coded as zero, to more than satisfactory coded as 4).

### Formal Participation

Respondents noted the number of formal organizations in which they maintained memberships. They also reported their frequency of involvement in (a) clubs and organizations, (b) church/temple activities, (c) volunteer work (not at all, daily), and (d) participation in a senior center (yes, no). Responses across the first three items were summed with a higher score reflecting greater participation in formal organizations.

### Informal Participation

Respondents indicated how often they had contact with siblings, relatives who were less close kin than siblings, and friends in person or by phone (daily coded as 4, to not at all coded as zero). Contacts in person and by phone were summed with higher scores indicating higher informal participation. Preliminary analyses indicated there were no differences in contact with children by place of residence; since affiliation with children did not contribute significantly to well-being of the formerly married, interaction with children was excluded from the multivariate analyses.

### Leisure Activities

Respondents reported how often they engaged in each of nine leisure activities: watch television; read (books, magazines, newspapers); work on hobbies; home maintenance or small repairs; take walks; participate in sports or exercise; go to restaurant, cafeteria, or snack bar; go to concerts, plays, movies, and so forth; take a trip away from home lasting longer than one day (not at all coded as zero, to daily coded as 4). Higher scores indicated greater involvement.

### Analyses

T-tests and multiple regression analyses were used to address questions about rural/urban differences in participation and in the outcomes of involvement. In separate multiple regression analyses of happiness and satisfaction with level of activity, education, income, employment status, and health were always considered as the first block. In the first analysis formal/informal activities were included as the second block; in a second analysis, other leisure activities formed the second block.

Table 1.
*Formal/Informal and Leisure Activities by Place of Residence and Sex*

| | Comparisons of Amount of Involvement | | | |
| --- | --- | --- | --- | --- |
| | Urban Men vs. Rural Men[a] | Urban Women vs. Rural Women | Urban Women vs. Urban Men | Rural Women vs. Rural Men |
| **Formal/Informal** | | | | |
| Total Number of Organizations | | + | + | |
| Clubs | + | + | + | + |
| Church Services | | + | + | + |
| Volunteer Work | | + | + | + |
| Senior Center | | + | + | + |
| Friends | + | + | + | + |
| Siblings | | | | |
| Relatives | | | + | + |
| **Leisure Activities** | | | | |
| Television Viewing | | | + | + |
| Reading | | + | + | + |
| Hobbies | | | + | + |
| Movies/Plays/Concerts | + | + | | |
| Maintenance | | | – | – |
| Walking | | | – | – |
| Sports/Exercise | + | + | – | |
| Restaurant | + | + | – | – |
| Trips | | + | + | |

[a]T-tests were used to assess differences in participation by size of place and sex except a chi-square analysis was used for senior center participation; signs (+, –) indicate activities on which there were significant differences. A plus (+) indicates the group mentioned first had significantly higher involvement than the second group; a minus (–) denotes significantly less involvement by the first group. (Detailed results available from author.)

# Results

## Rural/Urban Differences in Activities

It was anticipated that frequency of engagement in activities would vary since some were accessible on a daily or more frequent basis (e.g., reading) whereas others were less available or perhaps selected less often (e.g., movies, plays, concerts). Among all respondents, television viewing, reading, and taking walks were most frequent activities while attendance at movies/plays/concerts, sports events, and volunteer work least often occupied these older unmarried adults regardless of location.

When within-sex comparisons were made by size of place and significant differences in level of involvement were found, rural residents always participated less, regardless of gender (Table 1, columns 1 and 2). Activities of women were more differentiated by place of residence than those of men (Table 1). The personal communities of urban women differed from those of men and other women. For them, urbanism seemed to

have distinctive outcomes since they were more active in most types of activities— interpersonal, solitary, and in formal organizations. Their lives appeared to be fuller and more varied. Urban men and women maintained more contact with friends than their same sex counterparts in rural areas, although urban men and rural women differed little in their ties with nonkin.

Perhaps the most graphic findings were the fairly consistent gender differences in activities independent of place of residence. Both rural and urban men engaged in more traditionally gender-linked physical activities; they spent more time on home maintenance and small repairs, took more walks, and urban men were involved in exercise and sports more often. Taking walks and doing odd jobs are among the more commonly recognized masculine activities in old age (Rubinstein, 1986). These unmarried men ate more meals away from home in restaurants. Hobbies, volunteer work, church activities, and affiliation with relatives were more often the purview of women regardless of size of place.

Table 2.
*Multiple Regressions of Happiness and Formal/Informal and Leisure Activities of the Unmarried in Rural/Urban Communities[a]*

| Personal Characteristics | Urban Men | | Rural Men | | Urban Women | | Rural Women | |
|---|---|---|---|---|---|---|---|---|
| | r | Beta | r | Beta | r | Beta | r | Beta |
| Income[b] | .18 | .14* | .19 | .04 | .23 | .12** | .17 | .04 |
| Education | -.03 | -.06 | .24 | .06 | .18 | .06 | .22 | .13** |
| Employment | .04 | .08 | .08 | -.02 | .07 | .01 | .12 | .07 |
| Health | .34 | .30** | .43 | .37** | .23 | .17** | .20 | .15** |
| $R^2$ | | .135 | | .220 | | .095 | | .085 |
| **Formal/Informal Activities** | | | | | | | | |
| Volunteer Work | .14 | .16** | | | | | | |
| Church Services | .20 | .12* | | | | | | |
| Friends | | | | | .18 | .06* | | |
| Siblings | | | | | .11 | .08** | | |
| Total $R^8$ | | .192 | | .272 | | .121 | | .108[c] |
| **Leisure Activities** | | | | | | | | |
| Hobbies | .14 | .14** | | | .14 | .06** | .14 | .09* |
| Trips | | | | | .19 | .08** | | |
| Restaurants | | | | | .19 | .08** | | |
| Sports/Exercise | | | | | | | -.04 | -.10** |
| Total $R^2$ | | .171 | | .248[c] | | .118 | | .114 |

[a]Only formal/informal and leisure activities that contributed to happiness are listed.
[b]In analysis of formal/informal and leisure activities, income, education, employment, and health were included as the first block. They are shown only once.
[c]No single activitiy was significant at $p < .10$.
*$p < .10$.
**$p < .05$.

## Happiness

After taking personal characteristics into account, which activities were important to happiness and were comparable activities salient among rural and urban unmarried older people? Health contributed most to happiness regardless of residence or gender, although it was most important to rural men (Table 2). Lower income did not diminish the happiness of rural people as it did for urban men and women. When rural women had more education, they were advantaged by having greater happiness.

For the most part, few of the specific formal or informal activities contributed to happiness. Involvement in volunteer work was especially important to happiness of urban men. Only urban women derived greater happiness from ties with friends and siblings. Of the leisure activities, hobbies were important to happiness among most of the respondents except for rural men. In general, the two models (formal/informal and leisure activities) were both better predictors of happiness of men, especially rural men, than of women.

## Satisfaction with Level of Activity

Across gender and place of residence, persons in good health were most satisfied with their level of activity. Of the background characteristics, employment was important to satisfaction of rural women and income to urban men (Table 3).

No formal and informal social ties consistently contributed to satisfaction with level of activity. Urban women were more satisfied when they worked as volunteers, participated in a senior center, and belonged to a larger number of organizations. Rural men derived satisfaction from volunteer work, while rural and urban women obtained some benefit from involvement in church activities. Urban men were more satisfied with their level of activity when they had greater involvement in activities in which women most often participated (e.g., hobbies, reading, television).

## Formal/Informal Participation

Income constrained the involvement of

Table 3.
*Multiple Regressions of Satisfaction with Level of Activity and Formal/Informal and Leisure Activities of the Unmarried in Rural/Urban Communities[a]*

| Personal Characteristics | Urban Men | | Rural Men | | Urban Women | | Rural Women | |
|---|---|---|---|---|---|---|---|---|
| | r | Beta | r | Beta | r | Beta | r | Beta |
| Income[b] | .24 | .19** | .07 | .00 | .17 | .04 | .10 | .02 |
| Education | -.06 | -.12 | .19 | .02 | .09 | -.04 | .09 | .00 |
| Employment | .18 | .08 | .14 | .06 | .10 | .05 | .15 | .09* |
| Health | .36 | .28** | .35 | .32** | .33 | .28** | .25 | .21** |
| $R^2$ | .188 | | .150 | | .122 | | .077 | |
| *Formal/Informal Activities* | | | | | | | | |
| Volunteer Work | | | .25 | .19* | .19 | .08** | | |
| Number of Organizations | | | | | .17 | .08** | | |
| Senior Center | | | | | .15 | .07* | | |
| Church Services | | | | | .17 | .05* | .14 | .09* |
| $R^2$ | .228 | | .212 | | .169 | | .100 | |
| *Leisure Activities* | | | | | | | | |
| Reading | .25 | .16** | | | | | .16 | .10* |
| Hobbies | .22 | .15** | | | .16 | .11** | | |
| TV Viewing | .19 | .14** | | | | | | |
| Walking | | | | | | | .12 | .10** |
| Restaurants | | | | | .15 | .07** | | |
| Trips | | | | | .16 | .05* | | |
| $R^2$ | .300 | | .200[c] | | .147 | | .104 | |

[a]Only formal/informal and leisure activities that contributed to happiness are listed.
[b]In analysis of formal/informal and leisure activities, income, education, employment, and health were included as the first block. They are shown only once.
[c]No single activity was significant at $p < .10$.
*$p < .10$.
**$p < .05$.

all men and women in formal organizations, but it had a less consistent influence on informal ties (Table 4). Education facilitated all women's involvement in formal organizations and the informal ties of rural women as well. Although the models generally explained little variance, they tended to be somewhat more efficient predictors of formal than informal activities, especially those of rural men for whom both income and employment increased their opportunities to participate in formal organizations. Thus, some of the resources in which rural residents tended to be disadvantaged (e.g., income, education) were important to their integration into the community. As observed above, however, formal and informal activities were less salient to happiness and satisfaction of rural than urban people. For example, except for volunteer work for rural men and church activities for rural women, formal/informal participation had little significance for satisfaction of these rural residents.

# Summary and Implications for Practice

Do these data suggest that practitioners may want to distinguish between rural and urban aged as they plan programs and activities? In general, urban women manifested the most diverse participation and rural men the least. Assuming that frequent associations and contacts would translate into social support when needed, then urban women were indeed the most favored and rural men the least. Urban women capitalized on the diversity of an urban environment in ways that urban men did not although their comparatively more peripatetic involvement was not reflected in greater satisfaction with level of activity.

Health was especially critical to well-being of unmarried rural men who may have relied more on physical labor to sustain themselves, particularly those living on farms. These men had comparatively tenuous connections with their communities,

Table 4.
*Multiple Regressions of Formal/Informal Activities and Personal Characteristics of the Unmarried in Rural/Urban Communities*[a]

| Personal Characteristics | Urban Men | | Rural Men | | Urban Women | | Rural Women | |
|---|---|---|---|---|---|---|---|---|
| | r | Beta | r | Beta | r | Beta | r | Beta |
| | | | | Formal Activities | | | | |
| Income | .20 | .20** | .35 | .28** | .26 | .15** | .28 | .17** |
| Education | .08 | —a | .24 | .09 | .26 | .16** | .28 | .18** |
| Employment | .02 | — | .26 | .21** | .02 | -.04 | .15 | .09* |
| Health | .04 | .01 | .18 | .12 | .20 | .16** | .17 | .10** |
| $R^2$ | .040 | | .197 | | .112 | | .128 | |
| | | | | Informal Activities | | | | |
| Income | .14 | .16** | .24 | .21** | .19 | .16** | .16 | .09 |
| Education | -.01 | -.04 | .14 | .04 | .12 | .03 | .17 | .12** |
| Employment | — | — | .06 | .02 | .04 | -.01 | .10 | .08 |
| Health | .22 | .20** | .18 | .15* | .11 | .08** | .08 | .04 |
| $R^2$ | .066 | | .085 | | .042 | | .046 | |

[a]Variables (—) did not enter the equation.
*$p < .10$.
**$p < .05$.

and should their health become precarious they would seem even more vulnerable. Frail, unmarried rural men especially may warrant the attention of practitioners.

Effects of size of place of residence and gender tended to blur for urban men and rural women. Urban men probably benefited some from the greater offerings of their communities whereas perhaps gender-linked interests and sociability more characteristic of females enabled women in rural areas to compensate for some of the limitations of their environment. Other research points to the need for educational and intervention programs to take into account differences in resources among categories of the unmarried (e.g., widowed, divorced) (Hennon, 1986).

Were activities in which persons participated less than their peers those which contributed to well-being? Volunteer work, for example, was an activity which brought urban men happiness and provided satisfaction for rural men. Indeed, volunteer work seemed to perform a function for men that it did not for rural women. But earlier analysis showed that men were also less likely to participate. In some instances, volunteering may be a meaningful extension of a former work environment for men. Furthermore, it is an activity which practitioners may want to encourage and for which a need exists. Although volunteer work was particularly satisfying to rural men, structured opportunities to volunteer may be less prevalent in these areas. Such activities might help men, especially if they capitalized on their interests and skills in maintenance and small repairs. Practitioners may want to ensure that opportunities to volunteer are available and are especially extended to men.

Participation in cross gender activities by men were important to their happiness or satisfaction. For example, urban men who participated more in hobbies, reading, and television viewing were more satisfied with their level of activities. Except for health, hobbies were the most consistent source of well-being across gender and size of place. Increased encouragement of hobbies may be especially useful for older urban men.

Although eating out was not associated with well-being for men, it was a frequent activity and may, in part, have reflected the limited cooking skills of single men. Neighborhood and small town restaurants are also places for socializing on a fairly regular basis. The frequency with which single men ate away from home suggests that nutrition education should be a component of programming for older singles. It may be especially difficult for older people to adhere to prescribed diets when eating in restaurants.

Senior centers are often among the most visible organizations for the aged, although involvement in them per se was not directly important to happiness or satisfaction of these single men and women. Yet, they would seem to be ideal places to foster some of the activities and skills that contribute to well-being.

Were rural men and women disadvantaged by having less income and education? When rural people had lower incomes, their happiness was not diminished as it was for urban residents. Rural men were the only group for whom income consistently constrained involvement in both formal and informal activities. Rural women were advantaged when they had more education by enjoying greater happiness. Education may have provided rural women with competencies and skills that gave them a boost to overcome some of the other barriers to participation in smaller communities.

Education may have also enhanced the employment opportunities of older women. Continued employment, perhaps reflecting their less adequate incomes, was important to rural men and women in ways it was not for urban residents. Employment facilitated participation of rural men and women in formal activities, and it contributed to satisfaction of rural women as well. Although opportunities for employment in small communities are dwindling, this research indicated its importance to older unmarried rural men and women.

To what extent did these findings for older singles mirror other conclusions on rural/urban differences in participation by the aged? Perhaps most importantly the findings underscored that the influence of size of place was tempered primarily by gender. All urban people were not more involved in formal organizations, as suggested by some research; for example, urban men were not usually more active than rural women. Women embraced the diversity of urbanism more than men. In contrast to some findings (Kivett, 1985), rural life did not result in greater abundance of ties with nonkin. And affiliation with family (siblings, other relatives) reflected gender more than place.

Variation in patterns of participation by gender may reflect differential socialization of men and women in which females may manifest greater sensitivity and interest in other people; in turn, this might predispose them to reach out for more opportunities to affiliate with others. Women with more social skills also may have a greater tendency to locate in larger communities and this, combined with urban structural characteristics which include numerous outlets for participation, may even heighten involvement of females in these settings. It was not possible to ferret out how much of the difference in affiliation and activities of rural and urban people was due to structural effects of similarity (e.g., sex, marital status, age) of available peers versus that attributable to greater opportunities for participation in larger places. Even so, these data suggested that educational and intervention efforts should not ignore place of residence and gender.

Finally, on meager measures of well-being, quality of life did not seem to vary much by size of place. But variation in the style of life and the content of the days of these older unmarried people suggested that much of importance was probably left uncaptured.

## REFERENCES

Blau, Z. (1973). Old age in a changing society. New York: Franklin Watts.

Fischer, C. (1982). To dwell among friends. Chicago: University of Chicago Press.

Hennon, C. (1983). Divorce and the elderly: A neglected area of research. In T. Brubaker (Ed.), Family relationships in later life (pp. 149-172). Beverly Hills, CA: Sage Publications.

Keith, P. (1986). The social context and resources of the unmarried in old age. International Journal of Aging and Human Development, 23, 81-96.

Kivett, V. (1985). Aging in rural society: Non-kin community relations and participation. In R. Coward & G. Lee (Eds.), The elderly in rural society (pp. 171-191). New York: Springer.

Lee, G., & Cassidy, M. (1985). Family and kin relations of the rural elderly. In R. Coward & G. Lee (Eds.), The elderly in rural society (pp. 151-169). New York: Springer.

Palmore, E. (1981). Social patterns in normal aging: Findings from the Duke longitudinal study. Durham, NC: Duke University Press.

Rubinstein, R. (1986). Singular paths: Old men living alone. New York: Columbia University Press.

# 24

# Isolation and Farm Loss:
# Why Neighbors May Not Be Supportive*

**Sara E. Wright and Paul C. Rosenblatt\*\***

Thousands of families have left farming in recent years because they could not afford to stay. Hundreds of thousands more are in serious economic trouble. The reasons for these difficulties are complex and vary from region to region and from farm to farm. A simplified summary of what has happened would include the following. Farming is always financially risky as a result of bad weather, plant and animal diseases and pests, farm accidents, and economic factors. Currently, the costs of farm operation are quite high relative to the prices received for farm products. Many farm families bought land at record high prices, borrowing money at high interest rates. They assumed that land prices would not drop. Now many of these families cannot even pay the interest on their loans. With land prices having deflated as much as 70%, many of these farm families cannot borrow money, with their land as collateral, to finance another few months of farm operation, nor can they refinance their loans at a lower interest rate. Lenders are inclined to terminate loans on which payments are delinquent or on which the loan amount exceeds the value of the

farm which serves as the collateral for the loan. The families who bought land at now-deflated values cannot sell their land at a price high enough to pay off their debts.

The loss of a farm can be a disaster. It is not merely that the economic loss threatens health, well-being, and comfort, but that a valued way of life, one's occupation, and one's home may be lost. The farm that is being lost may have been passed down across generations, and it may have been intended as a heritage to pass to one's own offspring. Issues of self-worth, competence, adequacy as a spouse, parent, and adult offspring are involved. One may not seem to oneself or to others to have the job skills to earn a decent living at anything other than farming, and there may not seem to be alternative ways to earn a living in the community, county, or region in which one has been living. So it is not even clear that the farm family losing a farm can continue to live near relatives and friends, in an area that may have been home all of their lives.

It might be assumed that when people lose their farm or are in serious danger of doing so, neighbors would rally in support of them emotionally, spiritually, and materially. In urban areas neighbors can be a powerful source of support (Unger & Wandersman, 1985), and there is evidence that neighbors in rural areas are even more supportive (Oxley, Barrera, & Sadalla, 1981). Yet there are stories of people who while losing the family farm felt that they had also lost some or all of their neighbors (Graham, 1986, pp. 135-138).

From a systems theory perspective, both a family in trouble and their neighbors

*Work on this chapter was supported by the University of Minnesota Agricultural Experiment Station. For comments on an earlier draft, the authors are indebted to Carol Elde, M. Janice Hogan, and Cynthia J. Meyer.
**Sara E. Wright is a Psychologist at Dakota Mental Health Center, 744 19th Ave. N., South St. Paul, MN 55075. Paul C. Rosenblatt is a Professor in the Department of Family Social Science, University of Minnesota, St. Paul, MN 55108.

Reprinted from *Family Relations*, 1987, **36**, 391-395.

may do things that block ordinary support processes. This chapter offers an analysis of the systems factors that could lead a family in trouble and their neighbors to do things that would isolate the family and provide it with what appears to be little or no support. As with other aspects of farming (Salamon, 1980), there may be ethnic differences in individual, family, and community reactions to farm loss, but the factors discussed in this chapter may be applicable to many communities.

## Nonsupport as Help

An apparently nonsupportive neighbor may feel that the apparent nonsupport is helpful. That is, what looks to an outsider as nonsupport and what may be experienced by the family in economic trouble as nonsupport may be intended to be supportive.

Neighbors who draw away from a farm family in trouble may believe that their distance is polite and respectful and a way to minimize the discomfort of the distressed family. By not interacting with the family in trouble, people do not embarrass them by witnessing their shame, sorrow, confusion, and feelings of failure and do not risk saying things that will in some way cause the people in trouble to feel grief, shame, anger, or other difficult emotions. People may also be aware that well-meaning help may be a burden to people in trouble (Rosenblatt, 1983, pp. 145–149).

At the extreme, there may be fear that saying or doing the wrong thing could produce disaster. Particularly when there are reports in the news that some people who have lost a farm have committed suicide or killed a loan officer, there may be concern that saying or doing the wrong thing could lead to a tragedy.

Neighbors may believe that their own well-being may be a source of pain to a family in serious economic trouble. Contact by that family with people who are doing comparatively well may be perceived as potentially painful for the family—they may feel greater pain if they see how well others are doing. In that sense, the neighbors are trying "not to rub it in," not to make it more evident than it already is that they are doing well. One hears stories, in this regard, of neighbors driving new tractors who go miles out of their way in order to avoid going past the house of a family who is losing a farm.

In the relationships of neighboring farm families there is often a kind of half-playful, half-serious competition. People are aware, for example, of whose livestock looks better, who has built a new farmhouse, who started and finished planting and harvesting first, whose crop yielded better, who received a better price, who has a bigger farm operation. The competition may at times be a source of entertainment and an incentive to do better. But when one of the competitors "loses" in the sense of losing the farm, the history of competition may make competitors whose farm operation is still viable fear that offering support would seem like gloating. Thus, not to offer support may be an attempt to minimize the discomfort of the distressed family.

If not offering help to a family in trouble is intended as a kind of help for them and as a way of being respectful to them, it is also possible that actions that do not at first glance seem like support are intended as and felt as support. For example, asking a neighbor who is in trouble for advice or assistance may be a way of saying, "You are still a member of my community," and that may be perceived as helpful by somebody who has to leave farming. It also may be supportive to attend an auction of equipment and livestock of a family who has lost the farm, a form of support like attending a funeral. Neighbors attending such an auction may show their respect by witnessing the events of the auction and by not bidding. Bidding ordinarily will not change the circumstances of the family and could be seen by the family as an attempt to gain from their loss. However, at some auctions bidding can be done in a way that supports the family in trouble. At some auctions, neighbors are able to buy machinery or other possessions of the family in trouble at extremely low prices and then to sell or donate those assets back to the family in trouble.

Another way that what looks like nonsupport may be intended as a form of help is that it may seem helpful not to acknowledge the loss. It may be seen as helpful to those in trouble to avoid treating them as in trouble, in effect to say that nothing has changed and that we still see you as okay. In this regard, people may have concerns that any attempt to offer direct help will alter the ongoing relationship and perhaps be an inappropriate invasion of privacy (Chesler & Barbarin, 1984). Neighbors may decide that it is better to try to keep things as they have been.

## Breakdown of the Basis of Community

People may be committed to providing support to members of their community, but at some point they may decide that somebody is no longer a member of that community. Particularly when it is only one or a small number of families in trouble, the family or families in trouble may become excluded from the community. How and when people make a decision to treat a family as much less in the community or no longer there is a matter for further theory and research, but equity theory can lead one to speculate that one point at which such a decision may be made is when the family in trouble seems unlikely ever to be able to reciprocate. To the extent that community is based in part on exchange, a relationship future that seems entirely one-sided may not be acceptable to some people. There may be a kind of "lame duck neighbor" phenomenon such that somebody who does not seem able to maintain an exchange relationship is treated as having left the community.

The family in trouble may itself not want help for similar reasons, being concerned that if they cannot reciprocate assistance, it is inappropriate to burden their neighbors. Although the family in trouble has resources such as their time and sociability that could be used in an exchange relationship, economic troubles may make these resources less available in exchange relationships. Sociability, for example, may be in short supply from people who are depressed and preoccupied. They may not be fun to be with, may not be appropriately gracious, and may not even be particularly civil.

Community can break down also because the neighbors of a family in trouble may have experienced an economic loss as a result of actions by the farm family in trouble. Some neighbors of a farm family in trouble may be creditors who have not been paid. Many others may be friends and relatives of those unpaid creditors. Neighbors may feel that they are indirectly supporting a family in trouble by continuing to pay taxes that support schools, roads, police, and other services the family in trouble uses. Neighbors may also feel that they are supporting a family in trouble by patronizing main street stores and agricultural suppliers to which the farm family in trouble is indebted.

The continuing neediness of a member of a community can be a threat, particularly when that neediness is very great. There can be a fear that they will ask for "too much"—too much emotional support, for example, or too much time. Neighbors may even feel that without being asked for anything, they may find themselves volunteering to give or to do too much for the family in trouble. These fears may be intensified by an awareness that the family in trouble has vast needs, that they need, among other things, tens of thousands of dollars and help with deep emotional depression. The fearsome needs of a family in trouble may seem particularly great to a neighbor if other neighbors have backed away from the family in trouble. If there are fewer people to whom the family in trouble can turn, there is more concern that any one helper may be overburdened. The prospect of helping may be particularly frightening if the neighbors are themselves on the margin economically. People can fear giving help that would jeopardize their own economic situation.

Community is also based on a certain amount of sharing of common experience. People who are leaving farming may no longer be good partners for discussing what to plant, when to plant, when to sell, commodity prices, national agricultural policy, and other topics commonly discussed in rural meeting places. People who do not share life circumstances have trouble finding shared interests to discuss. Community may also be undermined when a farm family is in economic difficulty because the sustaining of common experience may require a certain amount of money. If the farm family in trouble cannot afford to bring a dessert to the covered dish supper, cannot afford to keep a child in a community organization, and cannot afford to go bowling or city shopping with their neighbors, it may be harder for the neighbors to remain connected with them.

## Contagious Misfortune

Misfortune may seem contagious, and there may be both nonrational and rational bases for such a perception. It may seem irrational to fear that bad luck rubs off, yet people may feel that way. Any misfortune, a car vandalized, a serious noncontagious illness, a problem with infertility, or a death in the family may lead others to want to avoid those experiencing the misfortune lest the misfortune somehow rub off on them. The family in trouble may itself feel that in a sense its difficulties are contagious, particularly when they are in the depths of self-blame, and may give signals to their neighbors that say "keep away."

There may be something rational about fearing contagion from a farm family in trouble. If one's reputation in the community and one's credit arise in part from the company one keeps, it might be sensible to stay away from people who no longer have credit. In some communities, being seen with a farm family in trouble may affect how a loan officer, veterinarian, or feed dealer will perceive one and how likely they will be to extend credit to one. It may be a matter of their perceptions of people or of their theories of human nature—a kind of "birds of a feather flock together" phenomenon. It also may be a kind of exchange phenomenon—if the banker, veterinarian, or feed dealer are owed a great deal of money by a family, one way for the banker, veterinarian, or seed dealer to bring the exchange relationship back into some sort of psychological balance is to charge more or give less credit to people who are associated with that family.

Another way in which it might be in some sense rational to avoid people who are leaving farming is that they may be so desperate as to want help with acts that border on being illegal or immoral. For example, a family about to enter into bankruptcy proceedings may want help from friends and neighbors in hiding assets. They may, for example, want to conceal livestock among those of neighbors or to sell their motor home or lake lot to a friend who would agree to sell it back to them after the bankruptcy proceedings have ended. People may fear that to help the family in trouble may be illegal or immoral, may offend creditors in the area, and may be financially risky.

## Distancing Emotions and Personal Threats

Neighbors may avoid a family in trouble in order to avoid their own discomfort and anxiety. People might not want to face the personal distress, depression, emotionality, disorganization, or strong words of families losing a farm. For example, as stated earlier, they may feel anxious over the possibility

that their presence could cause others to feel greater pain than they otherwise might (Chesler & Barbarin, 1984) or could cause a grown man to cry and perhaps feel embarrassment or shame at being seen crying.

Even if one does not know what the feelings of the people in trouble might be, one can fear that they will express feelings that are difficult to handle, for example, envy, jealousy, or a desire to commit violence. Neighbors who are uncertain about what to expect may fear that they might not be very competent to deal with unfamiliar, powerful, and possibly even destructive emotions.

Neighbors might also want to avoid feelings of fear about their own future that might be set off in the presence of a family in serious economic trouble. The disaster may be too close to what might happen to one's own family. The disaster of the family losing their farm may confront one with one's own deteriorating financial situation, with one's own powerlessness and vulnerability in the face of vast economic forces, and with one's existential aloneness in times of difficulty (Wright, 1985). Neighbors may not want to be reminded that good people behaving rationally and working hard can lose a farm.

One may also feel survivor's guilt about staying in farming when somebody else is not. Such guilt can be experienced by anyone but might be especially powerful if one can afford luxuries while those in trouble are not even able to afford necessities. A competitive neighbor still in farming may fear that in some way the competition caused the economic disaster, for example, drawing the insolvent family into taking chances by expanding the farm when land prices and interest rates had reached new heights. One may distance guilt feelings, just as one may distance other unpleasant feelings, by avoiding whatever sets off those feelings, in this case a farm family in serious economic trouble.

## Lack of Tradition and Ceremony

For deaths, Americans have funerals. For the loss of a farm, there are no societal rituals. A funeral helps neighbors to bridge the abyss that was formed between them and somebody bereaved by a death. Without comparable ritual for people losing their farm, the abyss remains. People who have lost a farm may feel too powerless to ask for help and too undeserving or needy to accept it (Chesler & Barbarin, 1984). Their neighbors may feel too unsure of what to say or do in order to reestablish a relationship.

A second reason why ritual would be desirable is that often the point at which loss has occurred is so ambiguous, it may be difficult for months or even years for anybody to know what the status of the farm is. When a person dies, ordinarily the exact moment of death is known. A farm loss is usually a much more ambiguous loss. There are many moments of loss, each of which may be experienced as the absolute end by some people but not by others. For example, people may have lost the farm in the sense of no longer being able to pay debts or to finance further operation, yet they may still own the farm on paper. They may have lost the farm on paper but still be living on it and even farming it. They may have lost the farm in every sense and yet still be living on the farm, and by state law they may have first claim to the land when it comes back on the market. The ambiguity about whether the farm has actually been lost makes it even harder for neighbors to know how to act toward a family in economic difficulty.

## Blaming the Victim

Victims are often blamed for their misfortune (Wortman & Dunkel-Schetter, 1979). Just as people tend to blame crime victims for their misfortune, they may blame people who have to leave farming. Poor farming practices and laziness may drive any farm into bankruptcy. But many of the farm operations that are going under are operated by hard working, knowledgeable people who were following the best advice available when they borrowed to establish or to expand the farm operation or to mechanize it further. Blaming the victim makes it easier to distance the victim ("You have to be incompetent to lose a farm, and I don't like hanging out with incompetents") and to feel safe from whatever has harmed the victim ("It won't happen to me because I haven't been greedy about expansion the way they were"). But blaming is a disservice to the victim and blinds those doing the blaming to a situational reality that they are trying to ignore.

Realities are negotiated in close relationships (Berger & Kellner, 1964). They involve selective perception and interpretation and a good deal of effort to maintain them in the face of the inevitable evidence that things are more complicated and may even be quite different from the socially negotiated reality. To maintain that negotiated reality, much that is threatening and much that is inconsistent with it must be pushed into the shadows, out of sight, and perhaps out of awareness (Rosenblatt & Wright, 1984). Any crisis, any major change may illuminate what is in the shadows. For a farm family, all the reasons why farming is a less than ideal way of life may be in the shadows (Rosenblatt & Anderson, 1981). That would include information on the high rate of work-related injury and illness for people in farming, the low rate of return on dollars invested, the ways in which people in farming have less freedom than people with regular 9:00 to 5:00 jobs, and the very serious risks of losing one's farm and most or all of one's financial assets. In order to distance such uncomfortable, alternative realities, people may want to avoid families who remind them of those realities.

## Nonsupport and Farm Values

Nonsupport of people who are leaving farming for economic reasons may be inconsistent with the values of farm communities, values such as community concern and caring for people you know who are in trouble. Yet the nonsupport also may reflect other values in that community, particularly the valuing of individualism and independence. The values of individualism and independence imply that everyone must live with the decisions they make as individuals, taking the consequences, whatever they may be. From that perspective, the nonsupport by neighbors of a farm family in serious economic trouble may arise from values that say, "If they got themselves into it, it's their job to get themselves out of it or they should live with the consequences." These values may also be expressed by a family in trouble, who may evidence a strong desire to solve their problems by themselves.

## Self-Isolation When in Trouble

This chapter emphasizes how the neighbors of a family in trouble may do things that isolate that family. This emphasis is important because, just as farm families may be blamed for their economic trouble, they may be blamed for their isolation. However, the emphasis on what neighbors do should not blind us to what the family in trouble may do to isolate itself. Among factors not yet discussed here that are involved in the dynamics of self-isolation for farm families in trouble, four stand out: impression management by a family in trouble, emotional control through avoidance of whatever sets off the emotion being controlled, anger at neighbors, and the cost of putting all time and energy into trying to save the farm or to make ends meet.

People who fear that their reputation will be tarnished in the community when others learn that their farm is about to be lost or has been lost may keep the information from others. That, of course, makes it impossible for others to be supportive. If they believe that others know about their economic problems, they may try to avoid them. By avoiding others, they cannot learn how much their reputation has fallen and will not have to answer humiliating questions they fear will be asked. By avoiding others, they may also maintain a profile low enough so that there will be less gossiping about them. They may also need to stay off stage because they have not yet come to new self-presentations; they may not be sure who they now are or how to present the new self, let alone to have the new performance polished and persuasive.

People in economic difficulty may be working hard at controlling "difficult" emotions that can accompany a loss as great and as comprehensive as the loss of a farm, emotions such as grief, anxiety, and depression. The control of emotions seems to rely in part on the avoidance of things that set off those emotions (Rosenblatt, 1983, chap. 9). To the extent that neighbors set off those emotions, members of farm families in economic difficulty may avoid their neighbors.

People who are losing a farm may be strongly inclined to blame (Rosenblatt & Keller, 1983) and may feel enormous anger—anger at each other and at themselves, anger at lenders, government officials, lawyers, city people, and others. They may also be angry with their neighbors. The neighbors may be seen as having encouraged heavy indebtedness, as gloating over the misfortune of others, as being unhelpful or nonsupportive, or as being potential bidders on the land the family in trouble may lose. Members of the farm family in trouble

may be generally irritable and prone to angry attack of others, without any particular instigation to attack. Feeling so prone to be angry, they may avoid their neighbors in order not to do something that would be regretted someday, because they find their anger embarrassing and inappropriate, or because in their anger they have written off their neighbors as people worth talking to. They may also be expressing their anger by not communicating, a passive aggressive attack.

Finally, farm families in trouble may be putting so much of their time and energy into trying to save the farm or into trying to keep food on the table that they may be unable to take the time to maintain contact with neighbors. They may still value their neighbors but feel that they have to put subsistence and saving the farm at a higher priority.

## Educating Farm-Leavers and Their Neighbors

A major challenge of family life education is to support the growth, development, and maintenance of community. No family can exist alone or deal alone with all its own neediness. Death, sickness, economic trouble, accidents, and the other problems of family life require support, material assistance, help at understanding, and much more. Community agencies and private therapy will not be contacted by most families in need (Rosenblatt & Burns, 1986) and cannot meet all the needs of any family. All families in trouble need the help of people outside the immediate family, and most of that help will come from relatives, neighbors, and friends. How can family life education support families in seeking and providing necessary community? How can family life education counteract the systems phenomena discussed in this article that may isolate farm families in economic trouble or families in any kind of trouble?

The first step may be to emphasize the importance of community. Being linked well to friends, relatives, neighbors, church, community organizations, and the crowd at the local cafe is a first step to coping with family problems.

A second step is to help people be aware of the factors that work against community when a family is experiencing a disaster. People need to be aware when they are being distanced by one in need, and they need to think through how to deal with it. They need to have a sense of how to deal with their own blaming—for example, to realize that the people they are blaming still hurt and still need; and if they cannot completely quash their own blaming, they need to be able to recognize that not all members of the family in trouble are to blame for what has happened to that family. Neighbors in farm communities need to have a good sense of how everybody is in the same boat, that helping a farm family to pull through toward some sort of economic viability may make it more likely that there will be tax revenues to pay for schools, road maintenance, and other basic community services and that the community stores, banks, churches, and voluntary organizations may be longer lived.

People also need to devise ways to deal with their distancing of other people's emotions. Certainly one approach is to realize that one may be wrong about the emotions others are feeling. Members of a farm family in trouble may not be feeling great anger or depression. They may even feel relief that a long, drawn-out process of uncertainty and economic failure is drawing to a conclusion, freeing them to move on to a different place in life.

Another family life education message that can support community is to emphasize that often people can be helped by small deeds (Rosenblatt, Anderson, & Johnson, 1984; Rosenblatt & Burns, 1986). A family may need tens of thousands of dollars in order to keep a farm, but the task of the neighbors is not to raise that money. It is to support the family, if they want it, in their difficult feelings and relationships and in their confusion about the future. It may not take much—a chat, a caring phone call, a dish of cookies—to provide support that can make a big difference in what happens to that family. A casual visit may be helpful simply by pushing the family members to deal with one another and to some extent focus on something other than their problems. Community members need to know that small acts are important and meaningful.

Ideally families in trouble should not wait passively for help to arrive. It is important for family life education to encourage people to find support when they need it. People need to recognize when they are distancing support and to understand what they

lose by doing so. They need to be open to the help that is offered, and to remain in contact with the people who have been in their lives. Family life education can help people realize that it is okay to ask for help; in fact, asking for help can be a way of easing the discomfort of caring neighbors.

Effective growth, development, and maintenance of community require widespread support. Family life educators must see to it that clergy, newspaper editors, the local librarian, school board members, and other community leaders understand the macroeconomic factors leading to the current farm crisis and are alert to the importance of community. There are, however, limits to the effectiveness of education for community, even when many voices speak in support of it. Family life education may be ineffective in helping people who feel intense shame about losing a farm or needing help. Such people may need stronger intervention than can be provided by a typical adult education program.

Referral to professional help is always a possible need. The amount and types of professional help available vary enormously from one rural community to another. A key source of professional help may be a community mental health agency, a counselor at the county social service agency, a psychiatrist at the county clinic, a financial specialist who travels a circuit for a religious or fraternal organization, an extension agent with financial planning expertise, or a member of the clergy with good counseling skills. Family life education can help by providing the basics for being referred and for referring. Family life education should legitimate the use of professional services. Family life education should also teach people how to refer others to professional services. Referral requires knowledge of the services available and a mixture of directness, tact, and caring that must be sensitive to each person's unique situation.

A final way in which family life education may help to counteract the neighbors problem discussed in this chapter is to emphasize that the people in our lives are resources. A large monetary loss need not rob one of relationship resources nor prevent one from being a relationship resource for other members of the community. Family life education can encourage people to invest their time and energy in maintaining themselves as part of a community (a winning battle) rather than saving a farm that cannot be saved (a losing battle).

## REFERENCES

Berger, P. L., & Kellner, H. (1964). Marriage and the construction of reality. *Diogenes, 46,* 1–24.

Chesler, M. A., & Barbarin, O. A. (1984). Difficulties of providing help in a crisis: Relationships between parents of children with cancer and their friends. *Journal of Social Issues, 40* (4), 113–134.

Graham, K. H. (1986). *A description of the transition experiences of 28 New York state farm families forced from their farms: 1982-1985. Unpublished master's thesis, Cornell University, Ithaca, NY.*

Oxley, D., Barrera, M., Jr., & Sadalla, E. K. (1981). *Relationships among community size, mediators, and social support: A path analytic approach. American Journal of Community Psychology, 9,* 637–651.

Rosenblatt, P. C. (1983). *Bitter, bitter tears: Nineteenth century diarists and twentieth century grief theories.* Minneapolis: University of Minnesota Press.

Rosenblatt, P. C., & Anderson, R. M. (1981). Interaction in farm families: Tension and stress. In R. T. Coward & M. W. Smith (Eds.), *The family in rural society* (pp. 147-166). Boulder, CO: Westview Press.

Rosenblatt, P. C., Anderson, R. M., & Johnson, P. A. (1984). The meaning of cabin fever. *Journal of Social Psychology, 123,* 42–53.

Rosenblatt, P. C., & Burns, L. H. (1986). Long term effects of perinatal loss. *Journal of Family Issues, 7,* 237–253.

Rosenblatt, P. C., & Keller, L. O. (1983). Economic vulnerability and economic distress in farm couples. *Family Relations, 32,* 567–573.

Rosenblatt, P. C., & Wright, S. E. (1984). Shadow realities in close relationships. *American Journal of Family Therapy, 12* (2), 45–54.

Salamon, S. (1980). Ethnic differences in farm family land transfers. *Rural Sociology, 45,* 290–308.

Unger, D. G., & Wandersman, A. (1985). The importance of neighbors: The social, cognitive, and affective components of neighboring. *American Journal of Community Psychology, 13,* 139–169.

Wortman, C. B., & Dunkel-Schetter, C. (1979). Interpersonal relationships and cancer: A theoretical analysis. *Journal of Social Issues, 35* (1), 120–155.

Wright, S. E. (1985). An existential perspective on differentiation/fusion: Theoretical issues and clinical applications. *Journal of Marital and Family Therapy, 11,* 35–46.

# 25

# Identifying Stressors and Coping Strategies
# In Two-Generation Farm Families*

**Randy R. Weigel and Daniel J. Weigel***

Studies investigating the occurrence of stressors on the farm have dealt primarily with weather and income variation, accident rate, work load, and transfer of property (Rosenblatt & Anderson, 1981; Rosenblatt, deMik, Anderson, & Johnson, 1985). A handful of studies have focused on relationship issues within the farm family, such as marital tension, farm-wife role conflict, and sibling rivalry (Berkowitz & Hedlund, 1979). Relatively few studies, however, have researched the stressors and coping of two-generation farm families.

Unlike most families, work and family roles are intertwined in two-generation farm families. Both generations receive their livelihood from the same source, and they must interact on an almost daily basis. Boundaries between work and family, parent and child, male and female are often unclear. This blurring of expectations and roles can create stress for farm families as well as challenge professionals working with two-generation farm families.

The study reported here identifies differences in stressors experienced and coping strategies used by members of two-generation farm families in the normal course of farm family life. The results of this study may lead to a better understanding of the interpersonal dynamics as well as give guidance to family life educators as they work in this field.

## Background

One of the first attempts to understand how stress affects families was undertaken by Hill (1949). To explain how families respond to crisis, he developed the ABCX crisis model which states that how a family experiences crisis (X) depends upon the interaction of the stressful event, or stressor (A), the family's crisis-meeting resources (B), and the perception the family has of the stressor (C). McCubbin et al. (1981) expanded upon Hill's original model and developed the double ABCX model which proposes that families are rarely dealing with a single stressor, but a "pileup" of several stressors simultaneously.

Much research during the past two decades has tried to identify the specific stressors impinging upon families. In a landmark study, Holmes and Rahe (1967) examined the stressors, which they called life events, of hospital patients. From their research, the social readjustment rating scale was developed to quantify emotional stress. Research efforts then began comparing populations and conditions on the social readjustment rating scale: Italian-Americans

*This chapter was supported by an Iowa State University Cooperative Extension grant. An earlier version of this chapter was presented at the annual meeting of the National Council on Family Relations, San Francisco, CA, October 1984.

**Randy R. Weigel is Home Economics Program Leader and Assistant Professor, Department of Home Economics, University of Wyoming, Laramie, WY 82071. Daniel J. Weigel is Extension Human Development Specialist, Iowa State University Cooperative Extension Service, Storm Lake, IA 50588.

*Reprinted from Family Relations, 1987, **36**, 379–384.*

(Bruhn, Phillips, & Wolf, 1972), Swedes and Americans (Rahe, Lundberg, Bennett, & Thenell, 1971), and clinical depression (Paykel, 1974).

Brown (1972), however, instead of comparing populations on the social readjustment rating scale, believed that research would be more valuable if it focused on identifying the stressors of different populations. Coddington (1972), for example, documented stressors faced by preschool, elementary, and secondary-aged children; French and Caplan (1973) identified stressors in the work environment; and Marx, Garrity, and Bowers (1975) studied stressors experienced by college students. McCubbin et al. (1981) broadened the usefulness of stressor inventories by developing an inventory of stressful events experienced by families and suggesting its utility for education and clinical work, in addition to research.

Weigel (1981) identified stressors faced by adult farmers. Included in the scale were events such as machinery breakdown, disease outbreak, accidents, and government regulations. From this scale, educational efforts were undertaken to help farm families cope with stressors they experienced on the farm. Weigel (1982) pointed out that farm stress came not only from crisis events such as disease outbreaks or accidents, but also from interacting with other members of the farm family.

## Coping in Two-Generation Farm Families

There is a growing conviction that it is not enough just to identify stressors. Family specialists should try to understand how families cope with those stressors. The double ABCX model proposes that the family does not passively react to stressors, but actively employs cognitive and behavioral strategies to cope with the situation. Pearlin and Schooler (1978) identified three broad categories of active coping responses: (a) responses to modify the situation, (b) responses that help individuals manage tension, and (c) responses that are used to reappraise the meaning of the problem. Coping thereby becomes a process in which the family tries to maintain a balance between normal family functioning and the demands placed upon it (McCubbin et al., 1981).

Several studies have focused on the strategies farm family members use to cope with specific farm stress events. When ex-

amining specific strategies, Rosenblatt and Keller (1983) reported that "remaining objective" was a major coping mechanism for farm couples facing economic hardship. Berkowitz and Perkins (1985) found that husband and wife relationships were crucial in differentiating negative and positive health factors. The greater the agreement between husband and wife about farm roles, the greater the support from the husband; and the greater the marital satisfaction, the less likely were farm wives to report stress-related health symptoms. In comparing rural and urban adults, Marotz-Baden and Colvin (1986) found that reframing was most often used as a coping strategy for rural husbands and wives. In issues regarding the stressor of decision making between father and son, Coughenour and Kowalski (1977) found that the more status a son was given in the farm operation, the more decision-making power he had and consequently, the more important he perceived his role to be in the farm operation.

Less study has been given to the coping strategies of the four main actors in two-generation farm families—fathers, mothers, sons (usually), and daughters-in-law. Russell, Griffin, Flinchbaugh, Martin, and Atilano (1985) studied the strategies used by two-generation farm families in coping with the stress of intergenerational farm transfer. In their study, the coping strategies reported to be used most were self-management and discussion skills. This was true regardless of family position. Expression of anger, advice of professionals, and involvement in farm organizations were less frequently reported as coping strategies.

Up to this point, however, no research has been published which identified the strategies farm members use to handle the regular challenges of two-generation farm family living. The present study was designed to identify the stressors encountered and coping strategies used by family members in two-generation farm families. It builds upon the literature reviewed above by studying differences between the generations and among family members.

## Methodology

### Sample

Subjects in this study were adult members of two-generation farm families. Two-generation farm families were defined as an older generation, which consisted of fathers and mothers actively involved in the management or operation of the farm together with a younger generation consisting of sons and daughters-in-law.[1]

County extension agents throughout the state of Iowa provided names of two-generation farm families. An initial letter was sent to 533 older generation couples requesting their participation in the study. If a couple agreed to participate, they were also asked to provide the name of one adult married child who was actively involved in the farm operation. The older generation was then sent two questionnaires, while their married child was sent a letter describing the project along with two questionnaires. A total of 800 questionnaires were sent to the four members of the two-generation farm families. Thus 200, or 38%, of the initially contacted families were sent questionnaires. Questionnaires were coded to distinguish among family members and for follow-up. Reminders were sent at 2 weeks and at 4 weeks to those who had not yet responded. To reduce the chance of collusion, respondents were instructed to complete the questionnaire without discussing it with others and to answer questions based on their personal perception of their family farm situation. Questionnaires were returned in separate, postage-paid envelopes.

Completed questionnaires were returned by 481 adults, a response rate of 60.1%. There were 128 fathers, 114 mothers, 136 sons, and 103 daughters-in-law. Most (72.1%) came from multi-purpose grain and livestock farms. Also, 77.3% of the farm operations fully supported four or more individuals. The older generation was typically 57 years of age and had been farming for an average of 35 years. Fifty-six percent had completed high school only and 31% had a college degree. The younger generation averaged 29 years of age and 9 years of farming, with 25% having only a high school degree and 63% a college degree. In only 71 cases were complete sets of four questionnaires returned from one family. Consequently, the reader should keep in mind that analysis is on data reported from individuals who are not necessarily members of the same families.

## Measures of Stressors and Coping

A 22-item "Family Farm Stressor Scale" was developed to measure the pileup of stressors experienced by two-generation farm families. An initial pool of 51 stressors was identified from personal interviews with 15 two-generation farm families. A panel of judges consisting of farm family members and farm and family extension specialists reduced the pool to the final 22 items. The criteria for final inclusion of stressor items was their frequency of occurrence in two-generation farm families. Those items that were rated by the judges as potentially occurring often in the families were included. Participant responses were recorded on a 5-point Likert scale from "never" to "always" with regard to the frequency of stressor occurrence over the past 2 years. Reliability for the scale was .93 using Chronbach's alpha.

To measure coping, a 15-item "Farm Family Coping Scale" was developed using a similar procedure. From an original pool of 26 items, the same panel of judges ranked the final 15 coping behaviors based on the frequency of their use in two-generation farm families. A 5-point Likert scale from "never" to "more than once a week" was also used to record frequency. A reliability of .69 was obtained using Chronbach's alpha.

## Results

### Stressors

Living with "tight money" was the most frequently occurring stressor among all family members. Ratings of stressors were fairly similar for all members except not being on one's own, which rated much higher for sons and daughters-in-law. Taking responsibility for risks and disagreements over spending appear to be more frequent stressors for fathers and mothers, while not being a part of the operation was more frequently reported for mothers and daughters-in-law.[2]

Factor analysis using a principal components solution with an orthogonol varimax rotation was used on all responses to obtain the underlying dimensions, identified as factors of the pileup of stressors in two-generation farm families. Table 1 presents the factor structure. Four independent factors accounted for 54.2% of the total variance of the factor solution.

Factor I, labeled "Equality and Influence" (Equality), is the most prevalent cluster with 37.5% of the explained variance. This factor captures the dimension of equali-

Table 1.
*Factor Structure: Two-Generation Farm Family Stressors*

|  | Factor I | Factor II | Factor III | Factor IV |
|---|---|---|---|---|
| **FACTOR I: EQUALITY** | | | | |
| No influence over farm | .676 | | | |
| Labor rather than management | .551 | | | |
| No family decision making | .721 | | | |
| Not part of operation | .795 | | | |
| Not on own | .449 | | | |
| **FACTOR II. TEAMWORK** | | | | |
| Difficulty working as team | | .495 | | |
| Fear of economic clout | | .683 | | |
| Disagree over expenditures | | .752 | | |
| Influence of other generation | | .613 | | |
| Negative criticism | | .570 | | |
| Not able to talk | | .356 | | |
| Taking more risks | | .560 | | |
| **FACTOR III: VALUES** | | | | |
| No written agreement | | | .366 | |
| Child-rearing differences | | | .534 | |
| Differing time commitments | | | .477 | |
| Too much family contact | | | .684 | |
| Favoritism | | | .572 | |
| Displaced anger at spouse | | | .685 | |
| **FACTOR IV: COMPETITION** | | | | |
| Farm over family | | | | .548 |
| Living with tight money | | | | .463 |
| No time for grand/children | | | | .756 |
| Neighbors doing better | | | | .630 |

|  | Eigenvalue | Percentage of explained variance |
|---|---|---|
| Factor I | 8.248 | 37.5 |
| Factor II | 1.348 | 6.1 |
| Factor III | 1.199 | 5.4 |
| Factor IV | 1.149 | 5.2 |

ty and having an important role in the farm operation. Stressors such as feeling like labor rather than management, having no involvement in making decisions, and not feeling like part of the operation highlight this dimension of influence and involvement.

Factor II, "Teamwork Difficulties" (Teamwork), addresses the interactional nature of the farm family. This second factor contains stressors describing the difficulties family members can have in communicating and working as a team. Such stressors are manifested in disagreements over expenditures, negative criticism, fear of the other generation using its economic clout, and not being able to talk to other family members.

Factor III, "Value and Generational Conflict" (Values), highlights the intergenerational dimension of the two-generation farm family. Items such as favoritism, child-rearing differences, and varying amounts of time invested are stressors which underlie many types of generational relations. Also

included in this factor is the stressor of too much contact, a situation which the very nature of the two-generation farm operation only intensifies.

The final factor, labeled "Competition Between Farm and Family" (Competition), relates to the complications created by combining work and family roles on the farm. These stressors indicate the tension members experience in having the farm take priority over their children and family.

A two-way analysis of variance was used to test for significant generation and gender effects in the frequency of stressors reported (Table 2). Means for each dependent variable, which were the four factors identified through the factor analysis, were obtained from the items making up each factor. The total stressor score mean was the mean of all items.

As the F-scores indicate, there were generational and gender effects and one interaction effect. The younger generation reported a significantly greater frequency of ssors by Family Position and ANOVA Results

| Stressc. | Fathers (N = 107) | Mothers (N = 99) | Sons (N = 120) | Daughters In-Law (N = 94)[a] | Effects of Generation F | Effects of Gender F | Interaction F |
|---|---|---|---|---|---|---|---|
| Total stressor | 1.895 | 2.017 | 2.224 | 2.537 | 46.097* | 15.089* | 2.284 |
| Equality | 1.179 | 1.980 | 2.123 | 2.739 | 37.177* | 23.308* | 5.022* |
| Teamwork | 1.854 | 1.967 | 2.215 | 2.424 | 33.076* | 6.000* | .311 |
| Values | 1.703 | 1.882 | 2.063 | 2.407 | 41.240* | 19.072* | 2.785 |
| Competition | 2.216 | 2.241 | 2.496 | 2.577 | 15.363* | .638 | .249 |

[a]Because of missing data, 420 cases were used in this analysis.
[b]df Generation = 1, Gender = 1, Interaction = 1, Error = 416.
*$p < .05$.

overall stressors. Similar effects were found when examining the Equality, Teamwork, Values, and Competition variables. Women likewise reported more frequency of stressors in all variables except Competition. The gender and generation interaction effect was in the Equality factor. Daughters-in-law recorded the most frequency of stressors in this factor.

## Coping

Having faith in God was the most frequently used coping strategy. Ratings of other coping strategies were similar among members with encouraging each other, being flexible, analyzing problems, and visiting friends most often used as coping skills.

Factor analysis, using a principal components solution with an orthogonal varimax rotation, was also used to identify the underlying factors of coping for all family members. Table 3 presents the factor structure. Four independent factors accounted for 49% of the total variance of the factor structure.

Factor I, termed "Faith and Attitude" (Faith), pertains to the strategies two-generation farm family members use to mentally reframe the stressors. Coping strategies in this dimension include acceptance of what can not be changed, maintaining flexibility, having faith in God, encouraging each other, and analyzing the problem. This factor highlights family members' attempts at a more positive, realistic attitude toward stress.

"Fun and Physical Activity" (Fun) is the second factor. It refers to partaking in leisure and physical activities. Such activities relieve stressful tension and allow family members to recuperate and recharge energy levels.

Factor III, "Talking with Others" (Talking), addresses the importance members

place on talking about problems and stress. This factor includes talking with immediate family, as well as relatives, other farm families, and professionals.

Sometimes coping with stress involves avoiding the situation. Factor IV, "Avoidance of Problem" (Avoidance), contains the coping strategies of leaving the problem, waiting until the problem goes away, and venting. These strategies may be helpful, providing family members eventually address the situation.

A two-way analysis of variance was used to test for significant generation and gender effects in the reported frequency of coping skills. Table 4 shows that women, regardless of generation, reported using more total coping strategies of Faith and Fun, while the F-score for gender on Talking almost reached significance ($p = .058$), suggesting women also frequently employ Talking as a coping skill. A significant generation effect was seen with the younger generation reporting using Avoidance as a coping strategy more often than the older generation.

## Discussion

This research was intended to extend the knowledge of specific stressors faced by members of two-generation farm families and the strategies they used to cope with them. The four stressor factors identified in this study—Equality, Teamwork, Values, Competition—highlight some key interactional dimensions in the farm family system. For example, in order for the younger generation to be seen as an integral part of the farm operation, the issue of equality may need to be resolved.

A second issue, addressed by the Teamwork factor, is that family members must be

Table 3.
*Factor Structure: Two-Generation Coping Strategies*

|  | Factor I | Factor II | Factor III | Factor IV |
|---|---|---|---|---|
| FACTOR I: FAITH |  |  |  |  |
| Acceptance | .543 |  |  |  |
| Faith in God | .681 |  |  |  |
| Problem analysis | .543 |  |  |  |
| Being flexible | .603 |  |  |  |
| Encouraging each other | .593 |  |  |  |
| FACTOR II. FUN |  |  |  |  |
| Outside interests |  | .526 |  |  |
| Visiting friends |  | .744 |  |  |
| Physical activity |  | .699 |  |  |
| FACTOR III: TALKING |  |  |  |  |
| Family meeting |  |  | .649 |  |
| Talk to other families |  |  | .567 |  |
| Talk to relatives |  |  | .298 |  |
| Help from professionals |  |  | .640 |  |
| FACTOR IV: AVOIDANCE |  |  |  |  |
| Leave problem |  |  |  | .686 |
| Venting |  |  |  | .625 |
| Procrastinate |  |  |  | .645 |

|  | Eigenvalue | Percentage of explained variance |
|---|---|---|
| Factor I | 3.131 | 20.9 |
| Factor II | 1.594 | 10.6 |
| Factor III | 1.381 | 9.2 |
| Factor IV | 1.242 | 8.3 |

able to work together as a team. There are many details to attend to and decisions to make in farming and the better the unit can do this, the less stress they may experience.

The Values factor accentuates differences in two-generation farm families. While the younger generation grew up and began farming in the more prosperous years of the 1960s and 1970s, the older generation's values were often molded during the Dust Bowl years. There can be vast differences in the work ethic and expectations for standard of living. Without understanding and acceptance of these differences, tension and conflict are likely.

The final factor, Competition, highlights the conflict between work and family which

is common not just for two-generation farm families, but for all families. By examining these factors in detail, a clearer picture of the differences between generations and among family members may emerge.

Studying the means of family members (Table 2) indicates that the younger generation reported experiencing more stressors. The means for both sons and daughters-in-law on all factors and total stressors were higher than the means for fathers and mothers. Daughters-in-law recorded the highest mean on all factors. Part of the explanation may be found in the means on individual factors. Fathers, mothers, and sons recorded the highest means for the Competition factor. Items under this factor included the farm

Table 4.
*Mean Scores of Coping Strategies by Family Position and ANOVA Results*

|  | Fathers (N = 107) | Mothers (N = 99) | Sons (N = 120) | Daughters In-Law (N = 94)[a] | Effects of Generation F | Effects of Gender F | Interaction F |
|---|---|---|---|---|---|---|---|
| Coping[b] |  |  |  |  |  |  |  |
| Total coping | 2.788 | 2.957 | 2.791 | 2.971 | .023 | 12.429* | .010 |
| Faith | 3.439 | 3.939 | 3.629 | 3.815 | .037 | 14.248* | 2.140 |
| Fun | 3.242 | 3.438 | 3.093 | 3.344 | .407 | 5.346* | .262 |
| Talking | 2.027 | 2.160 | 2.179 | 2.186 | 2.476 | 3.607 | 2.072 |
| Avoidance | 1.919 | 1.889 | 2.187 | 2.237 | 12.859* | .000 | .010 |

[a]Because of missing data, 420 cases were used in this analysis.
[b]df Generation = 1, Gender = 1, Interaction = 1, Error = 416.
*$p < .05$.

taking priority over family, living with tight money, no time for children or grandchildren, and neighbors doing better. However, the daughters-in-law reported the highest mean in the Equality factor. Items in this factor included no influence on the farm, feeling like labor, no say in decisions, not being on my own, and not feeling like part of the operation. This finding corroborates other studies (Russell et al., 1985) in which daughters-in-law were less likely to report themselves as having influence in the farm transfer decision. Younger women, because they have married into the family more recently, may hold the least involved family position. Also, they may be the outsider coming into a family system with a long history.

Sons recorded the second highest means on all factors and total stressors indicating that the younger members appear to experience more frequency of stressors, perhaps because they have less control and feeling of power on the farm. The reports of more stressful events might occur because as Kohl (1976) suggested, a paradox exists where farm offspring are socialized toward independence and the control of their own enterprise while still being more or less controlled in the two-generation farm operation. Weigel, Weigel, and Blundall (1987) believed it might also be due to the developmental stage of the younger members. They are at a point in their lives of building their careers and may feel more stressful with how far they must go; whereas the older members are well established and perhaps satisfied with where they have been.

The fact that the farm women in this study reported a higher frequency of stressors is not surprising. Hanson (1982) pointed out that farm women often assume the peacekeeping role on the farm. Since many of the stressor events in this study involved relationship issues, the potential for experiencing stressors may be greater for the women. In addition, farm women may have greater awareness of the stress involved in the farm operation or more openness to acknowledge the stress than do farm men.

The study also identified four dimensions that encompass coping strategies—Faith, Fun, Talking, and Avoidance. In general, these factors relate to Pearlin and Schooler's (1978) categories of coping responses: modifying the situation (Talking), managing tension (Fun, Avoidance), and

reappraising the meaning of the problem (Faith). Of the four factors, Faith was the most frequently used. Having a positive attitude and belief in the two-generation farm family appears crucial for success in these families. This supports Hill's ABCX model in that perception may directly influence a family's vulnerability to crisis and subsequent adaptation.

The means of the family members regarding coping strategies (Table 4) reflect what might be considered basic values of rural America. The highest recorded means by every family member was on the Faith factor. Items in this factor reflect the willingness to accept a rural way of life and desire to meet the problem head-on. Since the reported means of all family members indicate less desire to talk to outsiders (relatives, other families, or professionals), the value of self-reliance is evidenced. Apparently, these people use coping strategies that are part of the rural culture and way of life. This also supports the work of Marotz-Baden and Colvin (1986) in which the rural respondents in their study tended to view problems in a positive fashion and were confident of their ability to solve problems.

An analysis of Table 4 revealed fewer differences in coping strategies than stressors among family members. It is interesting that the farm women, though reporting more stressors, also reported a significantly greater frequency of total coping strategies. They may perceive two-generation farm families as stressful but are attempting to cope with the situation. However, one cannot assume that just because they use more coping strategies, the women were more highly stressed. Their more frequent use of coping strategies may be as effective in minimizing stress as other family members who use fewer strategies but report fewer stressors. Future research is needed to clarify this question.

Finally, the younger generation reported using Avoidance strategies significantly more often than did the older generation. It is plausible that the younger members, because of perceptions of less power and authority in the two-generation farm family, use venting and leaving the problem as coping mechanisms to the stressors they face.

## Implications

The results of this study have implications for researchers, practitioners, and educators. While this study focused on differences among members of two-generation farm families in two components of the double ABCX model—stressors and coping—further research is required to understand how these components interact with a family's resources and perceptions of the stressors to affect the family's adaptation to the two-generation farm situation. A second issue is that even though a coping strategy is frequently mentioned, it does not mean it is necessarily effective. Research that clarifies which coping strategies are most successful would be helpful. Finally, the results of this study identified daughters-in-law as vulnerable family members. They are often the key to how well the two-generation farm family survives (Hanson, 1982; Weigel, Blundall, & Weigel, 1986). Future researchers might want to focus their efforts upon the role daughters-in-law play in the adjustment and long-term success of the family farm.

Even though the results of the study describe members of two-generation farm families, it would be interesting to compare these findings to members of other families in which both generations work together on a regular basis. However, one should be cautious about generalizing the results of this study. First, the sample of two-generation farm families was not a random one. Second, the lower reliability (.69) of the coping scale is a concern. An explanation might be found in responses to the items in the scale. Many individuals responded only to the coping behaviors they relied on most often and disregarded the other behaviors. This might have skewed the measure and reduced its reliability.

The data also hold several implications for practitioners. Practitioners should remember that the two-generation farm family is a system. The needs and expectations of each family member are intertwined and dependent upon the other. Directing services and efforts toward just one member may have limited success. Whether the assistance provided is of a financial, legal, or emotional nature, systems theory would dictate that practitioners should work with the entire unit and not only with individual members.

Practitioners might find the stressors and coping strategies helpful as a diagnostic tool for identifying pileup of stressors or limitations in coping strategies for two-generation farm families. However, one must be cautious in approaching these families using a deficit or dysfunctional model. The research of Stinnett (1979) has reinforced the need to build upon strengths currently existing in the family. The respondents in this study already use a variety of strategies to cope with their stressors. Professionals should build upon those existing strengths.

Finally, this study may be particularly useful to educators of two-generation farm families. The majority of stressors mentioned by family members in this study pointed out the complex nature of the two-generation farm family. For example, work-related issues appear to be areas of concern more often than family-related issues. Not feeling like part of the operation, less say in decision making, and difficulty working as a team are reported to occur more often than childrearing differences and lack of time for family and children. There appears to be greater confusion regarding roles in the work sphere than in the family sphere. In the family sphere, members relate to each other in more familiar parent/child, husband/wife, mother/father roles. However, in the work sphere these roles change to ones of co-worker, partner, equal. These work roles are newer and less common for most members and may account for the greater frequency of work-related stressors. Also, by its very nature the work sphere calls for frequent, face-to-face interaction. These conditions are not easily addressed in traditional one-time workshops. Rather, a great deal of processing, discussing, and communicating is probably necessary to successfully handle these issues.

It should also be remembered that the stressors studied are not "crisis-oriented" (i.e., disease outbreak, farm foreclosure, drought). In coping with crisis, specific, short-term skills are needed until the crisis subsides (Aquilera & Messick, 1974). To cope with the types of stressors listed in this study, more long-range, generalizable coping skills are required—the type reported by family members in this research. But these coping behaviors also take time to develop. They must be incorporated into the personality and behavioral patterns of the farmer.

Therefore, the approach in developing stress management programs for two-generation farm families should be longitudinal. Rather than trying to cover all aspects of farm family stress and coping in one meeting, several sequential efforts are suggested. Examples of longitudinal programming might be adult night school short courses, farmer-led study groups, weekend farm family retreats, and ag-preparatory or family living classes in high school and junior high.

In carrying out such efforts, educators might wish to consider an in-depth approach, focusing on a few topics. The stressor and coping factors could provide guidelines for education—for example: Equality (self-esteem, leadership, power); Teamwork (communication skills, conflict resolution, problem solving, and decision making); Values (understanding the developmental needs of both generations, values clarification); and Competition (balancing work/family demands, goal setting, consequences of farm operation decisions on personal and family functioning). The coping factors could provide similar guidance in deciding which strategies to emphasize. Educational efforts should not be limited to just two-generation farm families; other professionals who work with farm families—lenders, attorneys, clergy, clinicians—would benefit from a deeper understanding of the uniqueness of these rural families.

Educators, however, must be cautious. In some cases, educational approaches to dealing with farm family stress may be inadequate in addressing the complex dynamics which are often extremely resistant to change. In such cases, referrals to clinicians may be necessary.

## END NOTES

1. While there was no attempt to focus solely on married sons and daughters-in-law actively involved in the farm operation, only six daughters responded; therefore, a separate analysis of them would be meaningless.

2. Contact the authors to obtain the complete rankings of the "Farm Family Stressor Scale" and "Farm Family Coping Scale." Items included in both scales can be found in Tables 1 and 3.

## REFERENCES

Aquilera, D., & Messick, J. (1974). Crisis intervention. Theory and methodology. Saint Louis: C. V. Mosby.

Berkowitz, A., & Hedlund, D. (1979). Psychological stress and role congruence in farm families. Cornell Journal of Social Relations, 14(1), 47-58.

Berkowitz, A., & Perkins, H. (1985). Correlates of psychosomatic stress symptoms among farm women: A research note on farm and family functioning. Journal of Human Stress, 11, 76-81.

Brown, G. (1972). Life events and psychiatric illness: Some thoughts on methodology and causality. Journal of Psychosomatic Research, 16, 311-320.

Bruhn, J., Phillips, B., & Wolf, S. (1972). Social readjustment and illness patterns: Comparisons between first, second, and third generation Italian-Americans living in the same community. Journal of Psychosomatic Research, 16, 465-471.

Coddington, R. (1972). The significance of life events as etiologic factors in the diseases of children. A study of a normal population. Journal of Psychosomatic Research, 16, 205-213.

Coughenour, C., & Kowalski, G. (1977). Status and role of fathers and sons on partnership farms. Rural Sociology, 42, 180-205.

French, J., & Caplan, R. (1973). Organizational stress and individual strain. In A. Marrow (Ed.), The failure of success (pp. 30-66). New York: AMACOM.

Hanson, R. (1982). Family members on friendly terms while farming together. Lincoln, NE: University of Nebraska, Department of Agricultural Economics.

Hill, R. (1949). Families under stress. New York: Harper and Row.

Holmes, T., & Rahe, R. (1967). The social readjustment rating scale. Journal of Psychosomatic Research, 11, 213-218.

Kohl, S. (1976). Working together: Women and family in Southwestern Saskatchewan. Toronto, Ontario, Canada: Holt, Rinehart & Winston of Canada.

Marotz-Baden, R., & Colvin, P. (1986). Coping strategies: A rural-urban comparison. Family Relations, 35, 281-288.

Marx, M., Garrity, T., & Bowers, F. (1975). The influence of recent life experiences on the health of college freshmen. Journal of Psychosomatic Research, 19, 87-98.

McCubbin, H., Patterson, J., Cauble, A., Larson, A., Comeau, J., & Skinner, D. (1981). Systematic assessment of family stress, resources and coping: Tools for research, education and clinical intervention. St. Paul: University of Minnesota, Department of Family Social Science.

Paykel, E. (1974). Recent life events and clinical depression. In E. Gunderson & R. Rahe (Eds.), Life stress and illness (pp. 134-163). Springfield, IL: C. C. Thomas.

Pearlin, L., & Schooler, C. (1978). The structure of coping. Journal of Health and Social Behavior, 19, 2-21.

Rahe, Lundberg, U., Bennett, L., & Thenell, T. (1971). The social readjustment rating scale: A comparative study of Swedes and Americans. Journal of Psychosomatic Research, 15, 241-249.

Rosenblatt, P., & Anderson, R. (1981). Interaction in farm families: Tension and stress. In R. Coward & W. Smith, Jr. (Eds.), The family in rural society (pp. 147-166). Boulder, CO: Westview Press.

Rosenblatt, P., deMik, L., Anderson, R., & Johnson, P. (1985). The family in business. San Francisco: Jossey-Bass.

Rosenblatt, P., & Keller, L. (1983). Economic vulnerability and economic stress in farm couples. Family Relations, 32, 567-573.

Russell, C., Griffin, C., Flinchbaugh, C., Martin, M., & Atilano, R. (1985). Coping strategies associated with intergenerational transfer of the family farm. Rural Sociology, 50, 361-376.

Stinnett, N. (1979). In search of strong families. In N. Stinnett, B. Chesser, & J. DeFrain (Eds.), Building family strengths: Blueprints for action. Lincoln, NE: University of Nebraska Press.

Weigel, D., Blundall, J., & Weigel, R. (1986). Keeping peace on the farm. Journal of Extension, 14,(Summer), 4-6.

Weigel, R. (1981). Stress on the farm—an overview. Ames, IA: Iowa State University, Cooperative Extension Service.

Weigel, R. (1982). Supporting today's farm family: An opportunity for family life educators. In N. Stinnett, J. DeFrain, K. King, H. Lingren, G. Rowe, S. VanZandt, & R. Williams (Eds.), Family strengths 4. Positive support systems (pp. 409-422). Lincoln, NE: University of Nebraska Press.

Weigel, R., Weigel, D., & Blundall, J. (1987). Stress, coping and satisfaction: Generational differences in farm families. Family Relations, 36, 45-48.

# 26

# Understanding the Health Care
# Needs of Rural Families*

**Clarann Weinert and Kathleen Ann Long\*\***

Health is an aspect of life which affects not only the individual, but families and social networks as well. The abilities to work, to adapt, to change, and to relate socially and within a family are greatly influenced by health status. An increasing amount of literature addresses the health needs and problems of rural people (Bisbee, 1982; Rosenblatt & Moscovice, 1982; Whiting & Hassinger, 1976). The health perceptions and health care preferences of rural people themselves, however, have not been adequately determined. Stein (1982; Stein & Pontious, 1985) has done pioneering work focused on how the culture of a given rural area affects the health care behaviors of those rural people. Stein (1982) further emphasized that health care providers must understand the life constraints, belief systems, and environmental context of rural people if they are to be effective in meeting rural health needs.

A comprehensive survey of health risk prevalence in rural Montana (Moon & Gray-

bird, 1982) revealed that these people believed strongly in self-responsibility for health. Major risk factors for both men and women were identified as stress and high-risk driving; smoking was also identified for men. In each risk area the significance of cultural and environmental variables is evident. Further, the emphasis on self-responsibility for health speaks to the need for those providing services to understand and work *with* rural people, rather than provide directives or advice based solely on professional knowledge.

The purpose of this chapter is to present and discuss the perceptions of residents of Montana, as one rural subgroup, with regards to health, health needs, and health services. The chapter draws selectively from descriptive data collected during 6 years of qualitative and quantitative study in Montana in order to identify and examine important health-related trends. This information should have relevance for health care planners and providers involved with rural populations, particularly those characterized by ranching and farming economies similar to those in Montana. The data presented and discussed in this chapter provide baseline information which can assist policy specialists and planners at the programmatic level, as well as counselors and other health care providers at the individual level. Health care programs, services, and practitioners will not be acceptable to, nor well utilized by, rural people unless they address relevant needs through methods congruent with rural life styles (Flax, Wagenfeld, Ivens, & Weiss, 1978; Scheidt, 1985).

*The authors wish to acknowledge the work of Montana State University, College of Nursing graduate students and faculty. Qualitative data collected and analyzed by them form the basis for a substantial portion of this chapter. Ethnographic data collection and analysis were supported in part by a U.S. Dept. HHS, Division of Nursing, Advanced Training Grant to the Montana State University, College of Nursing (#1816001649A1). The project which provided the survey data was funded by a Montana State University Faculty Research/Creativity grant.
**Clarann Weinert and Kathleen Ann Long are Associate Professors, College of Nursing, Montana State University, Bozeman, MT 59717.

Reprinted from *Family Relations*, 1987, **36**, 450-455.

## Method

The approach used in generating the data for this chapter was derived from two distinct research methods. Broad descriptions were derived from an ethnographic data production method, while specific measurements were acquired through the use of a survey method. The authors contend that concurrent examination of data generated by each of the two methods contributes to a better understanding of the phenomenon of interest, in this case, rural health. Reynolds (1976) identified individual observations, as in ethnography, and survey approaches as two of the primary research methodologies in the social sciences. Further he emphasized the value of examining phenomena with more than a single type of research strategy. Kleinman (1983) stated: "Qualitative description, taken together with various quantitative measures, can be a standardized research method for assessing validity. It is especially valuable in studying social and cultural significance, e.g., illness beliefs, interaction norms, social gain, ethnic help seeking, and treatment responses" (p. 543).

The population of interest for this research was the people of Montana. Montana is the fourth largest state in the United States with a land area three times that of the state of Pennsylvania. It is an extremely sparsely populated state with less than 800,000 people and an average population density of less than five persons per square mile. Fifty-five percent of Montana's counties have three or fewer persons per square mile, with six of those counties having less than one person per square mile. There is only one metropolitan center in the state; it is a city of nearly 70,000 people with a surrounding area that constitutes a center of approximately 100,000 (Population profiles, 1985).

### Qualitative Data Production

*Background.* Data collection was initiated in the late 1970s. At this time little literature addressed the health care needs and health service preferences of rural persons from the perspective of the rural consumer. No formal literature addressed these issues for persons in Montana. Research in the rural health field was focused primarily on the assessment of health care needs by organizations and agencies outside the rural

setting and on the examination of problems related to retaining health care providers in rural areas (Coward, 1977; Flax, Ivens, Wagenfeld, Weiss, 1979; Weaver, 1976).

Data collection occurred initially as part of course work designed to assist graduate nursing students to understand health and health care from the rural client's perspective. An ethnographic approach was selected because this technique allows for the development of grounded theory built on data provided by informants. Spradley (1979) indicated that the goal of ethnographic study is to " . . . build a systematic understanding of all human cultures from the perspective of those who have learned them" (p. 10). Specifically, the goal for the students was to learn about the culture of rural Montanans from rural Montanans; the particular aspects of cultural learning emphasized were health beliefs and practices. Although the initial purpose of data collection was student learning, a rich data base for theory development was also acquired.

*Sample and Techniques.* Students used Spradley's (1979) ethnographic techniques to gather information from individuals, families, and health service providers. Interview sites were selected by students on the basis of specific interest and convenience. During the 6-year period, data were gathered from approximately 25 locations. In general each student worked in depth in one community, collecting data over a period of at least one year. Data were gathered primarily from persons in ranching and farming areas and towns of less than 2,500 persons. In some instances, student interest led to extensive interviews with specific rural subgroups, such as men in the logging industry or elderly residents in a rural town.

The graduate students, as part of their course work, received a thorough preparation as ethnographic interviewers. The students selected key informants, lay persons as well as health service providers, using Spradley's (1979) criteria. In general these criteria emphasize the thorough enculturation and current involvement of informants. The open-ended questions used for the ethnographic interviews were also developed using Spradley's (1979) guidelines. Essentially the questions emphasized seeking the informants' views without superimposing the cultural biases of the interviewer. For example, the opening question was, "What is health (to you, from your viewpoint, your definition)?" All interviewers used the same format and initial series of questions.

*Analysis.* Domain analysis was used to categorize the qualitative data (Spradley, 1979). This aspect of the analysis involved a group process in which three to five nursing faculty members, each with expertise in health assessment and health service delivery, worked toward consensus about specific ethnographic material. Each group was led by a faculty member familiar with the domain analysis of ethnographic material. Within the framework of domain analysis, the following components were identified: cover terms, systematic relationships, included terms, and boundaries. The criteria for the inclusion of any term was that the term occur repeatedly in numerous different ethnographic interviews. This repeated occurrence was taken as an indicator that the term had relevance and importance for the rural informants in relation to their view of health. Terms were categorized under the major dimensions of person, health, environment, and nursing (Fawcett, 1984) and were ordered from the more general to the more specific. After data were organized in this fashion, indicators of relationships between terms were considered, again emphasizing the informant's view, and key concepts were identified. Throughout the analysis the focus was on the identification of concepts significant to understanding health and health care needs from the perspective of those living in sparsely populated areas.

## Quantitative Data Production

*Technique.* In 1983 a study was initiated to further the psychometric evaluation of the Personal Resource Questionnaire (Brandt & Weinert, 1981), a social support measure. A second purpose of the study was to begin to validate some of the concepts related to the health of rural people which had emerged from the ethnographic research endeavors. Therefore, survey instruments with established psychometric properties were selected to measure the specific concepts of interest. These concepts were physical and mental health status, health perceptions, personal and community demographic variables, and sources of help and support. Participants completed a mailed questionnaire packet containing the Personal Resource Questionnaire (Brandt & Weinert, 1981), Beck Depression Inventory (Beck, 1967), Trait

Anxiety Scale (Spielberger, Gorsuch, & Lushene, 1970), General Health Perception Scale (Davies & Ware, 1981), and a comprehensive background information form.

The General Health Perception Scale (Davies & Ware, 1981) is a 35-item measure designed to provide a comprehensive definition of health based on the underlying constructs of both mental and physical health. This scale was part of an extensive, large-sample study conducted by the Rand Corporation. Comprehensive psychometric evaluation has indicated that it is a valid and reliable measure (Davies & Ware, 1981). In the Montana study the reliability estimates closely paralleled those reported in the literature with an alpha reliability coefficient of .87 for the "General Health Rating Index."

The Beck Depression Inventory (Beck, 1967) is a 21-item scale which can be used to detect depression in non-clinical populations and to assess the level of depression in persons with psychiatric diagnoses. The measure has been used extensively for nearly 25 years, and psychometric evaluation has established that it is a valid and reliable instrument (Beck, Steer, & Garbin, in press). For the Montana rural sample an internal consistency estimate of alpha .71 was obtained.

The Trait Anxiety Scale is a 20-item measure of the relatively stable individual differences in anxiety proneness. Adequate validity has been established and an internal consistency coefficient of .92 was reported in the literature (Spielberger et al., 1970). In the current study the reliability coefficient was alpha .89.

*Sample.* The survey sample was generated using a variety of strategies in order to reach adults ages 50 to 70 living in both urban and more rural portions of Montana. Sources for identifying participants included the Extension Service, professional nurses working throughout the state, and church groups. This sample was composed of 128 women and 53 men who were white, middle class, with an average age of 61.4 years. Since the qualitative data discussed in this chapter were generated through ethnographic interviews with persons living in the more rural areas of the state, only the survey data from persons living in similar settings are included in this discussion. The rural survey sample consisted of 40 women and 22 men residing in 13 counties. Of these 13, Richland County (14,700) is the most populated with a population density of 5.9 persons per square mile and with the largest town having a population of nearly 6,000 persons. Carter County (1,700), with a population density of 0.5 persons per square mile and the largest town having a population of 600 persons, is the least populated. The 62 survey participants, whose data are used in this report, were white, middle class, with an average of 13.5 years of education, and with a range in age from 50 to 78 years and a mean age of 61.3 years.

## Results and Implications

The ethnographic data yielded several concepts which reoccurred in material from numerous communities and thus were deemed to be important in understanding rural health. These concepts are presented individually with the inclusion of illustrative quotes from the ethnographic data, as well as relevant complementary survey data. Implications are discussed in relation to each concept.

### Concept of Health

*Qualitative: Health Description.* The ethnographic data repeatedly indicated that Montana people define health as the ability to work or to be productive in one's role. Ranchers and farmers stated that pain would be tolerated for extended periods so long as it did not interfere with the ability to function, specifically to perform necessary occupational tasks. Similarly, women informants who worked as housewives and mothers said that one was healthy when one was able "to do what needs to be done," that is, function in one's role. The cosmetic, comfort, and life-prolonging aspects of health were rarely viewed as important.

*Quantitative: Health Measurement.* Analysis of the scores from the health perception scale provided valuable insight into the perception of health by rural people

and augmented the data gained from ethnographic research. The rural survey participants reported experiencing less pain with a mean score of 2.74 (higher score indicating less pain) as compared to 1.99 for an age-comparable urban sample as reported by Davies and Ware (1981). However, the rural people's overall perception of their health status, as measured by the "General Health Rating Index," was significantly less healthy than that reported (Davies & Ware, 1981) for other age-comparable samples (see Table 1). This is in keeping with the findings of Paringer, Bluck, Feder, and Holahan (1980) related to the elderly in rural areas. They found that the rural elderly are more likely than their urban counterparts to rate their health as "poor" or "fair" rather than "good."

*Mental Health.* When queried regarding mental health status via the Beck Inventory and the Trait Anxiety Scale, the rural sample demonstrated less depression and anxiety than persons in urban settings as reported by Beck (1967) and Spielberger et al. (1970) (see Table 1). Likewise, mental health problems were rarely mentioned by respondents in the ethnographic interviews. It may be possible that rural people experience less depression and anxiety. With regard to elderly populations, Coward and Lee (1985) summarized studies which indicated that while those in rural areas experience more isolation than urban dwellers, they do not score higher on indices of depression.

Consideration must be given, however, to the view that rural people simply report fewer mental health symptoms, either because they do not define symptoms as a "mental health" problem or they are reticent to admit to the symptoms. The ethnographic data, emphasizing health as the ability to work, would indicate that symptoms of mild to moderate depression or anxiety might be ignored or discounted. Flax et al. (1979) emphasized that rural dwellers often do not use mental health services because they do not

Table 1.
*Summary of Health Measures*

| Measure | Literature | | Montana Study | |
|---|---|---|---|---|
| | Mean | SD | Mean | SD |
| Pain | 1.99 | .76 | 2.74* | .92 |
| General Health Index | 80.82 | 13.56 | 74.08* | 13.27 |
| Beck Depression Inventory | 10.90 | 8.10 | 5.77* | 3.81 |
| Trait Anxiety Inventory | 42.68 | 13.76 | 34.55* | 8.47 |

*$p < .001$.

define their symptoms as indicating a mental health problem.

*Social Support.* A major variable assessed through the quantitative method and one which is repeatedly cited in the literature as being related to the promotion of both mental and physical health is social support. As Wortman (1984) noted in a comprehensive review of the literature, social support has been claimed to have positive effects on a wide variety of outcomes including physical health, mental well-being, and social functioning.

The level of perceived social support for the rural sample was assessed by the Personal Resource Questionnaire (PRQ) (Brandt & Weinert, 1981). This measure of social support was developed with principal reliance on Weiss's (1969, 1974) model of relational functions. Part 2 of the PRQ is a 25-item Likert-type scale which measures the respondent's *perceived level* of social support. The authors of the tool have reported that psychometric evaluation has indicated sound construct and content validity estimates and reliability coefficients ranging from .85 to .93 (Weinert, 1984; Weinert & Brandt, in press). An alpha of .88 was obtained for the current study.

The level of perceived social support was consistently higher for this rural sample than for age-comparable samples living in urban settings (Austin, 1985; Iverson, 1981; Muhlenkamp, 1985; Weinert, 1983b). Social support has been found to be associated with positive mental health, and thus one possible explanation for less depression and anxiety in this sample is the effect of the perceived high level of social support. Sources of perceived support are not directly tapped by the PRQ, but based on the fact that these people were living in sparsely populated areas, it can be hypothesized that their family members serve as major sources of support.

The small rural community may also provide a sense of support and belonging. Twenty-nine of the respondents lived in small towns; of the 33 who lived outside of a town, 97% had a neighbor who lived less than 3 miles away. Previous research indicated that distance orientation for rural people is quite unique, for example, 3 miles to the nearest neighbor may be perceived as close. In a study by Snyder (1981a) she found that rural people receiving home kidney dialysis, a complex health care procedure,

perceived distances of 200 to 900 miles from their dialysis training center as being "close." From these observations it is apparent that the perception of social support by rural people is not directly related to the proximity of neighbors or health care centers.

*Concept of Health: Summary.* Research and service implications are apparent from both the qualitative and quantitative findings. It seems clear that the definition of health as expressed by rural people varies from that of urban dwellers. The rural people studied in Montana placed less emphasis on pain and on mental health symptoms but greater emphasis on the ability to function and work. The surveyed population reported a perception of lower overall health while reporting significantly less pain, depression, and anxiety than several other age-comparable samples. The perception of lower overall health, however, was not substantiated by Lee (1986) who tested 162 farmers and ranchers in Montana using the General Health Perception Scale. Her respondents, a sample with a mean age of 56 years, indicated a level of general health that closely approximated the health status reported by Davies and Ware (1981) for comparable urban samples.

Pain was rarely mentioned by Montanans in discussing health; rather the focus was on the ability to function. Perhaps pain does not serve as a strong cue to ill health for rural dwellers. It appears that other signals, such as the inability to work, may be considerably more significant in the rural person's perception of health status and decision making regarding the need to seek health care. It should be noted that many rural persons are self-employed farmers and ranchers who do not have paid sick days or health insurance. These considerations provide a basis for understanding the high rate of chronic illness coupled with low or sporadic utilization of health services often found among rural populations (Rosenblatt & Moscovice, 1982). The significance of the work ethic among these rural families may have an impact on their use of social service and recreational programs, as well as those related to health.

Health care providers attempting to deliver services to rural families must be aware of how health is defined and how that definition may impact on health-related and health care-seeking behaviors. In the Montana population it appears that being restored to a state where one is able to work or function in one's role is more important than being helped to be pain free, attractive, or in better overall health. In addition, the role of social support in health maintenance and the perception of distance among rural people need further study. Research efforts are also needed to refine health status measures so that they are more sensitive to the definition of health which is relevant to rural populations.

*Self-Help Concept: Qualitative.* An additional concept which became evident from the ethnographic data is that of family and/or community "self-help." This underlying theme was displayed clearly in a preference for self-care or family care in relation to health needs as expressed in ethnographic interviews. Professional providers and formal health care services were not the resource of choice for most rural families. A rancher's wife stated: "Our Women's Club provides health education, and we raise money so that our volunteer service has equipment for stabilizing and transporting people hurt in accidents." A farmer from another area of the state noted, "We use our own judgment and knowledge regarding home treatment. We decide for ourselves how we're progressing with a health problem." The mythical self-reliance of rural people appears quite real in relation to their strategies for coping with health problems.

*Self-Help Concept: Quantitative.* To further evaluate the self-help concept which emerged in the ethnographic data, the availability of resources among rural people was assessed using data from the Personal Resource Questionnaire, Part 1. This portion of the PRQ consists of 10 life situations in which one might be expected to need some assistance; it includes questions related to physical and emotional problems. For both the physical and emotional questions, the rural sample indicated that they had fewer resources than were available to persons in the urban samples.

Both rural and urban groups relied on informal resources such as family, relatives, and friends. However, urban samples frequently reported relying on health care professionals and formal human service agencies in addition to family and friends (Weinert, 1983a). This was not so for the rural sample. This smaller network of resources for rural people may make them more vulner-

able to health-related problems if changes occur in their network of family and friends.

One explanation for the low reliance on formal sources of support by the rural sample may be that these sources of help are simply less available. When asked the distance to emergency medical care and to routine health care, the 29 respondents who lived in small towns indicated that both types of care were available in their town. However, the 33 who lived outside of town indicated that they traveled an average of nearly 23 miles for emergency care and an average of 57 miles for routine health care. Road and weather conditions, as well as work demands such as harvesting, may be major deterrents to the actual use of formal health and human service agencies by those living in more remote rural areas. These factors offer one explanation for the delay in seeking health care that is frequently attributed to rural people.

Snyder's research (1981b) indicated that rural kidney dialysis families developed independent and innovative coping strategies to compensate for their long distances from formal health care agencies. The rural people in her study developed a network of linkages with other dialysis families living in Montana and used this for support and the exchange of information and equipment. These characteristics of self-reliance and interdependence within an informal support system are key factors to be taken into consideration when planning human services for families living in rural areas. Rural people may desire more indirect services, such as consultation and health education, which enhance their ability to care for a sick or needy family member *on their own.* Frequent and direct contacts by human services professionals may be both unnecessary and undesirable in many instances.

*Old Timer/Newcomer Concept: Qualitative.* The related concepts of "old timer-newcomer" and "outsider-insider" were evident in the ethnographic data. Length of residence, as well as family history and type of occupation, seemed to be important variables in determining a person's placement in one of the opposing categories. A rancher stated, "Around here, a 'newcomer' is someone who's lived here from about 3 months to 4 years; an 'old timer' is someone who's ranched here at least one generation." The implications of this categorization on the acceptance of health care providers is evident in the following quote from another rancher, "The nurse at the ranger station just doesn't 'stack up' to the 'old RN' we used to have. Many of us call on Sam, the general store manager, now for everything including health advice. He's been here all his life and knows us and what we need." It would appear that this set of attitudes could well influence the willingness of rural dwellers to utilize outside experts in fields such as education and family life as well as health.

*Old Timer/Newcomer Concept: Quantitative:* The concepts of self-identity and ascribed identity by the community were directly pursued in the survey. Respondents were asked to describe themselves as: "Native," "Old timer," "Newcomer," or "Outsider" and then to indicate how those in their community perceived them using the same four categories. If their grandparents or parents settled in Montana, they most generally described themselves as "a native." If they did not have these types of roots in the state but had lived in Montana for 20 years or more, there was a 50-50 split between describing themselves as "a native" or "an old timer." Those who had lived in Montana *over 10 years* but less than 20 still considered themselves to be "newcomers." A nearly identical pattern was evident when respondents described how they believed others saw them.

The respondents to the survey had lived in Montana an average of 44 years with a range of one year to 78 years of residence in the state. As a group they would be well aware of how family history and the amount of time lived in the state affect one's acceptance by, and role in, the community. Old timer-newcomer concepts may significantly influence how rural people deal with health and human service providers who enter their community. One would hardly expect these rural people to establish close ties with, or rely upon, professionals who have recently entered the community. These providers would be categorized as "outsiders" and "newcomers." In addition, agencies which rotate personnel so that rural clients see a different professional each time they seek service would tend to further alienate clients. Continuity of providers, a thorough understanding of informal help systems, and the involvement of indigenous persons as both workers and consultants appear to be factors of paramount concern when dealing with rural families.

## Summary

Ethnographic and survey data have revealed a number of concepts that are particularly important in understanding how rural people in Montana view health and health care needs. Health is defined in relation to the ability to function and work; pain appears to be less important in determining the rural person's notion of health. Self-reliance and self-help are significant strategies which these rural people use to cope with illness, both their own and that of family members. Family and close friends are relied upon for support much more often than are formal agencies or professional care providers. An extensive period of residence, over 10 years, is needed for full integration into some rural communities. The rural people studied seem accustomed to persons staying on their land and in their community for a long time.

These findings have important implications for policy specialists, health care planners, and health care providers in rural areas. Since work is of major importance to many rural groups, health care delivery must fit within work schedules. Offering health care programs or clinics during peak times in the rural economic cycle, such as haying or calving, is self-defeating. Rural dwellers will put off health care until the activities required for economic survival are addressed. This point is reiterated by Stein (1982) in his study of Oklahoma wheat farmers. Also, since health is defined as the ability to work, health care promotion must address the work issue. For example, a health education campaign related to hypertension should emphasize the potential danger of stroke and long-term disability, rather than the opportunity for a more comfortable, longer life.

Health care services must be tailored to suit the preferences of rural persons for family and community help during periods of illness. Health care professionals can provide instruction, support, and relief to family members and neighbors who are often the primary care providers for sick and disabled persons. The formal health care system needs to fit into the informal helping system in rural areas. The volunteer ambulance service, for instance, can be augmented with new equipment and instruction for attendants, rather than simply replaced by a professional service. The community drug store proprietor can be assisted in providing accurate advice to residents through the provision of reference materials and a telephone backup system. In each instance, one can anticipate greater acceptance and use by rural residents of an upgraded, but old and trusted health care resource rather than a new, professional, but "outsider" service.

Health care and other human service professionals cannot successfully superimpose models based on urban experiences or professional traditions when dealing with rural populations. The environmental realities of rural living, including distances and work demands, as well as the worldview and values of rural people, must be carefully assessed. The unique aspects of each rural population must be included in any equation which is to yield a relevant, effective human service program for them.

## REFERENCES

Austin, A. (1985). The relationship of social support and creative potential to loneliness in older women. *Dissertation Abstracts International,* **45,** DA8421424. (University Microfilms No. AAD84-21424).

Beck, A. (1967). *Depression: Causes and treatment.* Philadelphia: University of Pennsylvania Press.

Beck, A., Steer, R., & Garbin, M. (in press). Psychometric properties of the Beck Depression Inventory: Twenty-five years of evaluation. *Clinical Psychology.*

Bisbee, G. (Ed.). (1982). *Management of rural primary care—concepts and cases.* Chicago: Hospital Research and Educational Trust.

Brandt, P., & Weinert, C. (1981). The PRQ: A social support measure. *Nursing Research,* **30,** 277-280.

Coward, R. (1977). Delivering social services in small towns and rural communities. In R. Coward (Ed.), *Rural families across the life span: Implications for community programming* (pp. 1-17). West Lafayette, IN: Indiana Cooperative Extension Services.

Coward, R., & Lee, G. (1985). *The elderly in rural society.* New York: Springer.

Davies, A., & Ware, J. (1981). *Measuring health perceptions in the health insurance experiment.* Santa Monica, CA: Rand.

Fawcett, J. (1984). *Analysis and evaluation of conceptual models of nursing.* Philadelphia: F. A. Davis.

Flax, J., Ivens, R., Wagenfeld, M., & Weiss, R. (1979). Mental health and rural America: An overview. *Community Mental Health Review,* **3,** 3-15.

Flax, J., Wagenfeld, M., Ivens, R., & Weiss, R. (1978). *Mental health and rural America: An overview and annotated bibliography.* Rockville, MD: U.S. Government Printing Office.

Iverson, C. (1981). *An exploratory study of the relationships among presence and perception of life change, social support, and illness in an aging population.* Unpublished master's thesis, University of Washington, Seattle, WA.

Kleinman, A. (1983). The cultural meanings and social uses of illness: A role for medical anthropology and clinically oriented social science in the development of primary care theory and research. *The Journal of Family Practice,* **16,** 539-545.

Lee, H. (1986). *Relationship of ecological rurality to current life events, hardiness, and perceived health status in rural adults.* Unpublished doctoral dissertation, University of Texas, Austin.

Moon, R., & Graybird, D. (1982). *High risk prevalence: A report card for Montana.* Helena, MT: Montana Department of Health and Environmental Sciences.

Muhlenkamp, A. (1985). [Social support: Elderly participants in a senior center]. Unpublished raw data.

Paringer, L., Bluck, J., Feder, J., & Holahan, J. (1980). *Health status and use of medical services: Evidence on the poor, the black, and the rural elderly.* Washington, DC: The Urban Institute.

*Population profiles of Montana counties: 1980.* (1985). Bozeman, MT: Montana State University, Center for Data Systems and Analysis.

Reynolds, P. (1976). *A primer in theory construction.* Indianapolis: Bobbs-Merrill.

Rosenblatt, R., & Moscovice, I. (1982). *Rural health care.* New York: John Wiley.

Scheidt, R. (1985). The mental health of the aged in rural environments. In R. Coward & G. Lee (Eds.), *The elderly in rural society* (pp. 105-127). New York: Springer.

Snyder, T. (1981a, September). Home care, role of distance to the home training center. Part I. *Contemporary Dialysis,* pp. 42-52.

Snyder, T. (1981b, October). Home care, role of distance to the home training center. Part II. *Contemporary Dialysis,* pp. 44-47.

Spielberger, C., Gorsuch, R., & Lushene, R. (1970). *STAI Manual for the State-Trait Anxiety Questionnaire.* Palo Alto, CA: Consulting Psychologist.

Spradley, J. (1979). *The ethnographic interview.* New York: Holt, Rinehart, and Winston.

Stein, H. (1982). The annual cycle and the cultural nexus of health care behavior among Oklahoma wheat farming families. *Culture, Medicine, and Psychiatry,* **6,** 81-99.

Stein, H., & Pontious, J. (1985). The family and beyond: The larger context of noncompliance. *Family Systems Medicine,* **3,** 179-189.

Weaver, J. (1976). *National health policy and the underserved.* St. Louis: C. V. Mosby.

Weinert, C. (1983a). [Psychometric evaluation of the PRQ]. Unpublished raw data.

Weinert, C. (1983b). [Social support: Rural people in their "new middle years"]. Unpublished raw data.

Weinert, C. (1984). Evaluation of the PRQ: A social support measure. In K. Barnard, P. Brandt, and B. Raff (Eds.), *Social support and families of vulnerable infants* (pp. 59-97). Birth Defects, Original Article Series, 20. White Plains, NY: March of Dimes Defects Foundation.

Weinert, C., & Brandt, P. (in press). Measuring social support with the PRQ. *Western Journal of Nursing Research.*

Weiss, R. (1969). The fund of sociability. *Trans-Action,* **6,** 36-43.

Weiss, R. (1974). The provisions of social relationships. In Z. Rubin (Ed.), *Doing unto others* (pp. 17-26). Englewood Cliffs, NJ: Prentice-Hall.

Whiting, L., & Hassinger, E. (Eds.). (1976). *Rural health services organization, delivery, and services.* Ames, IA: Iowa State University Press.

Wortman, C. (1984). Social support and the cancer patient. *Cancer,* **53,** (May 15 Supplement), 2339-2360.

# Use of Informal In-Home Care by Rural Elders

**Janette K. Newhouse and William J. McAuley***

With the increased longevity experienced by Americans comes the tendency toward functional impairment that may require long-term care. The high cost of institutional care and the federal mandate to shift the responsibility of caring for older persons away from the public sector are two important factors accounting for the interest in community-based long-term care as an alternative to institutionalization.

This study explores one aspect of community-based long-term care as it examines the utilization of selected in-home care services from informal sources (family members, friends, and neighbors) among older rural adults. Specifically, this investigation deals with the use of a core of six generic in-home services that, when taken collectively, have the potential to delay or avoid institutional long-term care. The services under consideration are telephone and visiting reassurance, continuous supervision, homemaker/household assistance, meal preparation, nursing care, and personal care. This examination of the predictors of in-home care utilization in rural environments should be useful to both policymakers and practitioners in establishing and implementing programs that will complement, rather than interfere with, the existing informal caregiving system.

## Review of the Literature

One reason for the rural elderly population being of particular interest is the turnaround in rural to urban migration that has caused older people to live disproportionately in rural areas (Beale, 1982; Longino, Wiseman, Biggar, & Flynn, 1984; Wardwell, 1982). Furthermore, the comparative literature indicates that older rural residents are in a disadvantaged position with regard to housing, income, education, transportation, and access to medical care (Coward & Lee, 1985). Thus, the needs of rural older people seem great while the resources to address these needs including funding, gerontological research, and appropriate service delivery models are limited (Ambrosius, 1981; Steinhauer, 1980).

The focus on informal care provision seems appropriate since the current shift in emphasis from institutional to community-based long-term care has generated increased interest in the role of the informal caregiving network of impaired elderly people (Crossman, London, & Barry, 1981). It is generally accepted among social gerontologists that the availability and use of informal, mainly familial, support is a key element in preventing or delaying institutionalization (Palmore, 1983; Scott & Roberto, 1985). Older people perceive the informal network of kin, friends, and neighbors as the appropriate social support in most situations of need (Arling, 1981; Shook, 1980). The literature further points out that only when assistance from the informal system is unavailable or

*Janette K. Newhouse is Assistant Professor, Department of Family and Child Development, and Extension Specialist in Adult Development and Aging at Virginia Polytechnic Institute and State University, Blacksburg, VA 24061. William J. McAuley is Associate Professor, Department of Family and Child Development, and Director of the Center for Gerontology at Virginia Polytechnic Institute and State University, Blacksburg, VA 24061

Reprinted from *Family Relations*, 1987, **36**, 456-460.

exhausted do older people and their families turn to formal organizations (Cantor, 1980).

Despite evidence that the informal family network usually is strong and responsive to most of the needs of its older members, many people continue to believe the myth of abandonment of elderly family members. Research during the past several decades has systematically refuted the idea that contemporary families are alienated from their older members and do not take care of them (Brody, 1981). Shanas (1979) documented, through national survey research, the frequent contact of elderly persons with family members and the high incidence of family support to disabled elderly members. It is also well documented that most elders living in the community receive the bulk of their supportive personal care from family and friends (Brody, Poulshock, & Masciocchi, 1978; Krout, 1986; McAuley, Arling, Nutty, & Bowling, 1980). Although the myth of abandonment lacks empirical support, it is persistent and pervasive among the general population and policymakers as well. The tenacity of this belief is evident in the current legislative concern that the provision of formal community-based services will reduce family participation in caregiving by undermining family responsibility and encouraging families to withdraw support from their elderly members (Masciocchi, Thomas, & Moeller, 1984). Previous studies, however, have shown that formal services do not necessarily substitute for family efforts (Greene, 1983; Horowitz & Dobrof, 1982; Shanas, 1979). That is, families continue to provide care even when formal services are being utilized.

The political issue then becomes one of supplantation versus supplementation of informal sources of care by formal sources of care. From a bureaucratic perspective the demand for fiscal restraint in government spending has shifted the focus of long-term care for elderly people back to the family (Sivley & Feigener, 1984). Thus, the care provided by family members, friends, and neighbors will become even more critical in helping older family members to maintain their optimal quality of life. This study endeavors to gain a clearer understanding of what variables predict different patterns of in-home care use from informal caregivers. The specific intent of this investigation is to generate and translate information about service use into practical knowledge to en-

hance policy-making, educational programming, and service delivery for rural elders and their informal caregivers.

## Methodology

Information from this study was extracted from the Statewide Survey of Older Virginians (McAuley et al., 1980) which used an instrument based on the Older Americans Resources and Services (OARS) multidimensional functional assessment questionnaire (Duke University Center for the Study of Aging and Human Development, 1978). The Statewide Survey was a face-to-face interview of 2,146 people 60 years of age or older who were selected by means of a multistage area probability technique designed to produce a representative sample of noninstitutionalized older people. In order to insure representativeness with regard to health status, informants were consulted to facilitate the completion of the survey for 8% of the sample whose physical or mental limitations precluded their participation. To further enhance representativeness, the sample was weighted to more closely reflect the state's noninstitutionalized population. The sample size represents an 87% response rate of the sample initially identified.

The OARS instrument has been found to have content, consensual, and criterion validity as well as interrater reliability (Fillenbaum, 1978; Fillenbaum & Smyer, 1981). Further, when the survey instrument was pretested, it was determined to be appropriate for the intended audience (McAuley et al., 1980).

The 20 independent variables in this investigation represent the combination of a group of sociodemographic variables suggested by the literature and the five dimensions of functional impairment extracted from the OARS instrument. These summary ratings from OARS allow researchers to assess the individual's functional impairment in terms of social resources, economic resources, mental health, physical health, and performance of activities of daily living (ADL). Each of the five OARS ratings is coded as follows: 1 = excellent resources, 2 = good resources, 3 = mildly impaired, 4 = moderately impaired, 5 = severely impaired, and 6 = totally impaired. The other independent variables and their coding are: marital status (1 = married, 0 = not married); living arrangement (1 = alone, 0 = not alone); age (60–99 as a continuous variable); race (1 = white, 0 = nonwhite); education (values of 1 = 0 to 4 years of schooling to 8 = post college graduate); sex (1 = male, 0 = female); income (values from 1 = less than $5,000 to 6 = more than $40,000); having a car, having a telephone, having a confidant (all coded 1 = yes, 0 = no); network satisfaction (Do you see significant others as often as you would like?) (1 = satisfied, 0 = dissatisfied); frequency of visits to family, frequency of visits to friends (values of 1 = not at all to 4 = every day); distance to family and distance to a friend (values of 1 = no relative/friend to 6 = within 1 mile).

The sociodemographic and functional impairment variables have been categorized as predisposing (e.g., race and sex), enabling (e.g., income and distance to family), or need (e.g., physical health and ADL performance) variables to reflect Andersen's paradigm for conceptualizing service use (Andersen & Aday, 1978; Andersen & Newman, 1973). The Andersen model was conceived in order to relate individual characteristics to utilization patterns in a logical manner. The model was designed to serve as a guide to select relevant variables for inclusion in an analysis. Andersen and his associates assumed that a sequence of conditions contributes to the volume of health services that an individual uses. Use is dependent on the predisposition of the person to use services, the ability of the individual to secure services, and the illness level of the person (Andersen & Newman, 1973).

Service use, the dependent variable, is based on use of a designated service within the 6 months prior to the survey. Six generic in-home care services from the OARS instrument are considered in this study: telephone and visiting reassurance (to check with an individual via telephone or in person); continuous supervision (to have a caregiver for 24 hours a day); homemaker/household assistance (to perform chores such as cleaning and laundry); meal preparation (to assist with meal management activities); nursing care (to administer prescribed treatments and medication); and personal care (to facilitate activities of daily living such as bathing, dressing, and toileting). Service use is formulated by assigning the code "one" to each of the six in-home care services that a respondent received from a family member, a friend, or a neighbor; assigning the code "zero" to each of the services not received and then summing across all six services.

Formal service use is measured in the same manner; however, a formal service is conceptualized as one provided by an agency or organization. This produces a variable with a range of seven categories from *used no services* to *used six services*.

The final construct to be operationalized here is rural. Persons were defined as rural residents and included in this study if they resided on a farm or ranch; in the country, but not on a farm or ranch; or in a small town or city of less than 25,000 people. Because of the geographic configuration of Virginia where small towns and rural areas are typically located immediately adjacent to metropolitan areas, this technique for conceptualizing "rural" seems reasonable. According to this conceptualization of "rural," 1,196 persons in the Statewide Survey of Older Virginians were categorized as rural. For further information concerning the statewide survey of older Virginians, please see McAuley et al. (1980).

## Results

### Level of Service Use and Source of Service

By merging the six in-home care services into one variable, the number of services each respondent used can be examined (see Table 1). More than half (53.4%) of the sample used no services. The overwhelming majority (92.2%) of noninstitutionalized rural older people used zero, one, or two of the services. When only the rural older persons who receive services are considered, most of them receive in-home care exclusively from

Table 1.
*Frequencies and Percentage Distributions of Use of In-Home Services by Rural Elders*

|  | n | Percent |
|---|---|---|
| Level of Service Use |  |  |
| No services | 617 | 53.4 |
| One service | 358 | 31.0 |
| Two services | 90 | 7.8 |
| Three services | 32 | 2.7 |
| Four services | 27 | 2.3 |
| Five services | 18 | 1.5 |
| Six services | 14 | 1.2 |
| TOTAL | 1,156 | 99.9 |

Note: Frequency total differs from sample size because of missing values, and percentage distribution total does not equal exactly 100% because of rounding.

family members, friends, and neighbors. Thus, Table 1 indicates that community-based rural older people are most likely to use no in-home care services; however, when they do use these services, they are likely to receive only one or two types of assistance. That assistance is most frequently (91.7%) provided by members of the elder's informal network rather than from the public sector. Next in order of frequency, although at a much lower rate (5.5%), is simultaneous help from informal and formal sources, followed by help exclusively from formal sources (2.8%).

## Results of the Multiple Regression Analysis

Table 2 provides the results of the multiple regression analysis of rural elders who receive assistance with in-home care exclusively from informal sources. Five significant predictors of service use emerge. Two of these variables, having a car and distance to a friend, are categorized as enabling variables. Rural elders without a car and those who live closest to their nearest friend use

more in-home services from informal sources. The three other significant variables—economic resources, physical health, and ADL performance—are all classified as need variables. Elders with better economic resources, limited ADL performance, and impaired physical health receive more informal in-home services. Because of the number and level of obtained significance for need variables in the regression analysis, need seems to be the best indicator of informal service utilization among rural older people. This study reinforces the consistent finding in the service use literature that the use of services in older populations is more closely related to a person's level of functional impairment than to sociodemographic status (Krout, 1983). It is also important to note that the 20 independent variables in this study account for nearly one third (32.6%) of the variance in informal service use among rural elders.

## Discussion and Implications

The dramatic changes in the age structure of the American population make planning and providing services for the elderly

Table 2.
*Multiple Regression of Level of Use of In-Home Care Services from Informal Sources on Independent Variables*

| | Beta | Standard Error | F |
|---|---|---|---|
| Variables | | | |
| Enabling Variables | | | |
| Having a telephone | -.008 | .106 | 0.09 |
| Having a confidant | .011 | .143 | 0.06 |
| Having a car | -.079 | .075 | 5.87* |
| Visits to family | .029 | .030 | 0.85 |
| Visits to friends | .006 | .029 | 0.04 |
| Distance to family | .058 | .025 | 3.43 |
| Distance to a friend | -.059 | .045 | 4.82* |
| Network satisfaction | .041 | .063 | 2.25 |
| Income | -.038 | .013 | 1.21 |
| Predisposing Variables | | | |
| Age | -.006 | .004 | 0.04 |
| Sex | -.003 | .065 | 0.01 |
| Race | .050 | .085 | 3.19 |
| Education | .024 | .019 | 0.51 |
| Marital status | -.071 | .087 | 3.06 |
| Need Variables | | | |
| Social resources | -.058 | .036 | 3.03 |
| Economic resources | -.102 | .036 | 7.75** |
| Mental health | .019 | .047 | 0.33 |
| Physical health | .071 | .036 | 4.77** |
| ADL performance | .050 | .043 | 192.31** |

Model statistics: $df = 20, p = .000, R^2 = .326, n = 1,114.$

*Note:* Frequency total differs from sample size because of missing values.
*$p < .05.$
**$p < .01.$

segment of society one of the major challenges of the decade. An often neglected participant in this planning process is the informal caregiver who provides in-home assistance. The results of this study emphasize the importance of informal caregivers to those rural elders who receive at least one of the six in-home services examined in this research; over 90% receive such care only from informal sources, whereas formal providers are the sole source of in-home care in less than 3% of the cases. Clearly, the value of the informal support system to rural elders should be more fully appreciated and recognized. Public officials could begin by providing opportunities to celebrate the significance of informal caregivers. One step in this direction is President Reagan's proclamation of National Family Caregivers Week. However, given the substantial involvement of rural informal caregivers in the provision of in-home services, it is particularly important that current and potential informal providers be a major focus of policy initiatives and formal service delivery plans in rural areas. Below are some specific suggestions for application.

First, some of the in-home care being provided by informal sources (e.g., personal care and nursing care) can require special skills, and the physical well-being of the elder receiving care could be jeopardized if the individuals providing such assistance do not have adequate knowledge of the techniques. By offering training in the basic skills necessary to successfully manage the care of rural elders receiving in-home care, public agencies can help ensure that the best possible care is being provided. This type of program would likely have the added benefit of increasing the efficiency of the informal provider, thus offering more time for noncaregiving activities. Such training could also serve to limit the stress associated with attempting procedures that are not fully understood.

A second method of making informal caregivers the focus of policies and services is to address the physical and emotional strain and, particularly in the rural environment, the potential social isolation that in-home caregiving might cause. Among the ways to address these concerns are to provide occasional direct relief from the caregiving responsibility and to make available counseling and emotional support to the caregiver. Occasional relief from caregiving can be provided through respite programs that might operate most effectively in rural areas if made available in the home. Emotional support can be offered through counseling and support groups. Programs of relief and emotional support may need to be carefully coordinated, since availability of respite care might influence the utilization of counseling and support groups.

A third approach may be to consider direct financial compensation for informal caregiving. Financial compensation may be of value because it could give informal providers the flexibility to purchase some services as needed and to reduce economic hardships caused by the circumstances of caregiving. However, there may be some disadvantages to offering direct financial support for informal caregiving, including the potential of formalizing the informal care relationship (Arling & McAuley, 1986). Only by designing and evaluating demonstration projects will professionals determine the actual impact of this strategy. Such demonstrations should be completed in both rural and urban areas so that any possible differential effects of these types of environments and life styles on the impact of direct financial support can be revealed.

A fourth approach involves the development of lines of communication between formal organizations and agencies and informal caregivers. To operate effectively, communication must be in both directions. Rural informal caregivers should be given information on how to effectively utilize the formal service system and when it is appropriate to do so. Such efforts could be particularly important in rural areas where there may be less familiarity with the formal service system, considerable geographic distance and dispersion of potential service agencies, and a resistance to using the formal service system. If rural informal caregivers are more familiar with available programs including when and how to effectively use them, they may be more prone to seek assistance before the burden of care becomes so great that they are no longer able to cope or the physical well-being of the elder is threatened. Improved communication should also enhance the opportunities the formal service delivery system will have to draw upon the insights, experience, and special knowledge rural informal caregivers accumulate as a result of their intimate involvement in the lives of the elders they assist. Their knowledge could be valuable in gaining the acceptance of the elders, as well as in determining service content, format, and delivery strategies that are consistent with the life styles of the caregivers and the special needs and concerns of the older care recipients.

The results of this study also suggest which elderly groups in rural areas might be appropriate audiences for services and programs. First of all, the significant independent effects of ADL and physical health upon receipt of in-home care only from informal sources indicate that the more frail and impaired are the ones receiving help from their family members and friends. This was expected due to the logical connection between the types of care examined in this study and health status and impairment. If the condition of those frail, impaired elders who are receiving more types of care solely from informal sources worsens, these older people and their caregivers may become appropriate targets for service programs.

The multiple regression also makes it possible to consider which characteristics of rural elders have an effect on informal service use independent of ADL and physical health. The results indicate that the isolated and less mobile older rural population might be targeted for services, since those who live greater distances from friends and those without automobiles use fewer services from informal sources and thus may be in need of help from the formal system. This conclusion is supported by additional analysis under the same set of controls (not reported here) showing that neither formal service use nor combined formal and informal use by rural elders is significantly associated with having a car or distance from friends.

The findings reported here also suggest that the financially disadvantaged receive fewer services from informal sources when other factors are controlled. Additional analysis (not reported here) indicates that this group may be currently targeted for assistance from formal sources. This additional analysis found a significant independent effect of income upon formal service use, with those at lower income levels receiving more services from formal sources only. Further research is called for to determine whether low income elders receive all the services they require from formal sources and to examine why rural elders who are more financially disadvantaged receive less assistance from informal sources under con-

trols for health and ADL impairment.

One caveat to the analysis is in order. Although OARS is a useful general assessment of the characteristics of older people, the variables addressing the nature, extent, and composition of the informal support network (e.g., network satisfaction, distance to family and friends, and frequency of visits with family and friends) are, at best, imprecise and incomplete. Future research should incorporate such measures as level of intimacy and commitment of potential informal caregivers, as well as their capacity to provide assistance.

In summary, this study suggests that the informal caregiver functions in an essential role of providing in-home care to community elders in rural areas. The results imply that the informal caregiver ought to be a major focus of efforts to support and enhance caregiving activities. Among the strategies that can be considered are approaches that enhance the skills of the caregivers; direct relief, emotional support, and financial compensation; and strengthen the lines of communication between formal organizations and agencies and rural informal caregivers. The results also suggest that services should be targeted to frail and impaired elders who are more isolated and less mobile and have limited financial resources.

## REFERENCES

Ambrosius, G. R. (1981). To dream the impossible dream—delivering coordinated services to the rural elderly. In P. K. H. Kim & C. P. Wilson (Eds.), *Toward mental health of the rural elderly* (pp. 289–316). Washington, DC: University Press of America.

Andersen, R., & Aday, L. A. (1978). Access to medical care in the U.S.: Realized and potential. *Medical Care, 16*, 533–546.

Andersen, R., & Newman, J. F. (1973). Societal and individual determinants of medical care utilization in the United States. *The Milbank Memorial Fund Quarterly, 51*, 95–124.

Arling, G. (1981, July). *Public policy and informal caregiving: Findings from the Statewide Survey of Older Virginians.* Report prepared for delegates to the 1981 White House Conference on Aging, Richmond, VA.

Arling, G., & McAuley, W. J. (1986). The feasibility of public payments for family caregivers. In L. E. Troll (Ed.), *Family issues in current gerontology* (pp. 162–177). New York: Springer.

Beale, C. L. (1982). *Older rural Americans: Demographic situations and trends.* Statement presented before Senate Special Committee on Aging, Washington, DC.

Brody, E. M. (1981). Women in the middle and family help to older people. *The Gerontologist, 21*, 471–480.

Brody, S. J., Poulshock, W., & Masciocchi, C. F. (1978). The family caring unit: A major consideration in the long-term support system. *The Gerontologist, 18*, 556–561.

Cantor, M. H. (1980). The informal support system: Its relevance to the lives of the elderly. In E. F. Borgatta & N. G. McCluskey (Eds.), *Aging and society: Current research and policy perspectives* (pp. 133–144). Beverly Hills, CA: Sage Publications.

Coward, R. T., & Lee, G. R. (Eds.). (1985). *The elderly in rural society.* New York: Springer.

Crossman, L., London, C., & Barry, C. (1981). Older women caring for disabled spouses: A model for supportive services. *The Gerontologist, 21,* 464–470.

Duke University Center for the Study of Aging and Human Development. (1978). *Multidimensional functional assessment: The OARS methodology* (2nd ed.). Durham, NC: Author.

Fillenbaum, G. G. (1978). Validity and reliability of the multidimensional functional assessment questionnaire. In *Multidimensional functional assessment: The OARS methodology* (2nd ed.) (pp. 25–35). Durham, NC: Duke University for the Study of Aging and Human Development.

Fillenbaum, G. G., & Smyer, M. A. (1981). The development, validity, and reliability of the OARS multidimensional functional assessment questionnaire. *Journal of Gerontology, 36,* 428–434.

Greene, V. L. (1983). Substitution between formally and informally provided care for the impaired elderly in the community. *Medical Care, 21,* 609–619.

Horowitz, A., & Dobrof, R. (1982). *The role of families in providing care to the frail and chronically ill elderly living in the community.* New York: Brookdale Center on Aging of Hunter College.

Krout, J. A. (1983). Knowledge and use of services by the elderly: A critical review of the literature. *International Journal of Aging and Human Development, 17,* 153–167.

Krout, J. A. (1986). *The aged in rural America.* Westport, CT: Greenwood Press.

Longino, C. F., Jr., Wiseman, R. F., Biggar, J. C., & Flynn, C. B. (1984). Aged metropolitan-nonmetropolitan migration streams over three census decades. *Journal of Gerontology, 39,* 721–729.

Masciocchi, C., Thomas, A., & Moeller, T. (1984). Support for the impaired elderly: A challenge for family caregivers. In W. H. Quinn & G. A. Hughston (Eds.), *Independent aging* (pp. 115-132). Rockville, MD: Aspen.

McAuley, W. J., Arling, G., Nutty, C., & Bowling, C. (1980). *Final report of the Statewide Survey of Older Virginians* (Research Series No. 8). Richmond, VA: Virginia Commonwealth University, Virginia Center on Aging.

Palmore, E. (1983). Health care needs of the rural elderly. *International Journal of Aging and Human Development, 18,* 39–45.

Scott, J. P., & Roberto, K. A. (1985). Use of informal and formal support networks by rural elderly poor. *The Gerontologist, 25,* 624–630.

Shanas, E. (1979). The family as a social support system in old age. *The Gerontologist, 19,* 169–174.

Shook, W. M. (1980, November). *Urban and rural older people: Their well-being and needs.* Paper presented at 33rd annual meeting of the Gerontological Society of America, San Diego, CA.

Silvey, J. P., & Fiegener, J. J. (1984). Family caregivers of the elderly: Assistance provided after termination of chore services. *Journal of Gerontological Social Work, 8,* 23–24.

Steinhauer, M. B. (1980). Obstacles to the mobilization and provision of services to the rural elderly. *Educational Gerontology, 5,* 399–407.

Wardwell, J. M. (1982). The reversal of nonmetropolitan migration loss. In D. A. Dillman & D. J. Hobbs (Eds.), *Rural society in the U.S.: Issues for the 1980s* (pp. 23-33). Boulder, CO: Westview Press.

# PART IV: REVITALIZATION: TAKING ACTION

The revitalization of rural families involves the taking of action in several areas. Family specialists who apply their expertise as family life educators, policy specialists or family therapists can contribute to the revitalization of the rural family.

First, the family life educator can provide information which enables families to deal with their changing situations. The development of family management programs has been one way in which family life specialists have attempted to assist rural families. Nora Keating's chapter examines development of stress management programs and provides data from a sample of 753 men and women farmers. The findings of this study suggest that family life specialists need to encourage the development of personal resources. The chapter by Elizabeth Thompson and Hamilton McCubbin provides an overview of resource materials available to family life educators, social workers, counselors, and county extension agents. A selection of programs, publications, and media productions are discussed to enable the family life specialists to develop presentations about rural families.

The second practitioner addressed in this section is the family policy specialist. Robert Hughes examines the economic changes within rural America during the 1980's and discusses several empowerment strategies for use within a community setting. Supports for rural families and communities are presented. John Scanzoni and Cynthia Arnett compare a sample of rural husbands and wives with a sample of urban husbands and wives. The primary differences are education and gender role preferences. Implication for program planning and policy development are presented. The third chapter in this section, written by Stephen Wilson and Gary Peterson, addresses the life satisfaction of rural, young adults. The chapter reports findings from a study of 322 low-income youth from rural Appalachia. A number of positive and negative predictors of life satisfaction are identified. Implications for policymakers and practitioners are discussed.

Family therapists can assist rural families in taking action to deal with the changing situation. Anthony P. Jurich and Candyce S. Russell examine the data from 15 farm families who have sought therapy to deal with farm crises. A description of who seeks therapy, the therapy process and outcomes of therapy are presented.

The key to this section is the variety of ways in which family practitioners can assist rural families. Family life educators, policy specialists, and therapists can each contribute to the revitalization of rural families. Family practitioners can provide support to rural families in their stressful times, as they adapt to changes and as they seek to revitalize their family situation.

# 28

# Reducing Stress of Farm Men and Women*

**Norah C. Keating\*\***

"How can you plan your life when you don't know if you'll be farming next year? I work hard, but it's all out of my hands. It's the bank, the weather, the price of wheat ... it's sad" (male, age 50, wheat farmer).

Farm men and women have been identified by therapists and educators as a group which is vulnerable to personal stress. They are subject to the vagaries of weather, interest rates, markets, and changing consumer demands; and they have multiple work roles with farm, household, and off-farm jobs competing for limited amounts of time and energy (Keating, Doherty, & Munro, 1987). In the difficult economic climate of the 1980s, many such people are at risk of losing their businesses. Nearly one quarter of all farms in western Canada are under severe financial stress as measured by at least one of the following: debt load exceeding 40% of farm sales; total borrowing in a year exceeding 110% of new investment in that year; or net worth less than 15% of total assets (Klein & Barichello, 1985). The situation may be even worse in the United States where it is estimated that 9% of farms (as compared to 4.8% of Canadian farms) are either insolvent or in severe financial stress (Brinkman, 1985). Those who do continue to farm may find that there are pressures on them to work

longer and harder and to expect more involvement and commitment of other family members. As well, they are often required to subsidize their own businesses with income from other sources, especially off-farm employment (Bokemeier, Sachs, & Keith, 1983).

Extension specialists have begun to use the term "farm crisis" to describe the negative experiences of farm families with the economic exigencies of farming in the 1980s. Because the farm crisis places extra demands on farm families (high debt loads, long work days, and the need to work at both on- and off-farm jobs), professionals who work with these families are concerned about their high levels of stress (Walker, Walker, & MacLennan, 1986). According to Berkowitz (1984), stress in the farm setting is defined as a set of physical or mental reactions to anything that places demands upon a person which exceed his or her ability to cope.

One response to the farm crisis has been the development of intervention programs on stress management (Fetsch, no date; Lencucha, 1986; Light & Thorndal, no date). Several different program models have been used. Some are general stress management programs which do not specifically focus on farm families. This type of program, as exemplified by Light and Thorndal, is based on four steps toward managing stressful situations: recognizing feelings, noting sources of feelings, understanding emotional reactions to situations, and planning to alleviate or cope with sources of stress. Although the program is called "Strengthening *family life* in tough times" (author's emphasis), exercises are oriented toward individual adults. Other programs are more ex-

*This research was supported by the Agricultural Research Council of Alberta, Farming for the Future.
**Norah C. Keating is Professor, Department of Family Studies, University of Alberta, Edmonton, Alberta, Canada T6G 2E2.

Reprinted from *Family Relations* , 1987, 36, 358-363.

243

plicitly oriented to farm families. Fetsch's program, for example, is based on helping farm families develop strategies to manage farm stress. These strategies include time management, goal setting, and stress management techniques such as relaxation and exercise. Farm couples are the intended audience for this program. Other stress management approaches for farm families simply comprise collections of information and exercises on farm stress and stress management from which the family life educator can develop appropriate intervention programs. The Lencucha package is an example of this type of approach.

Fetsch's program is noteworthy in that it is a family life education program explicitly based on empirical findings about the successful coping strategies of farm men and women. He argues that the skilled educator should become informed about research on stress symptoms and stress management techniques of farm families and then use this information to both inform farm families and elicit from them the healthy coping strategies they already use (Fetsch, 1985).

The belief that there should be a close connection between research and practice has many proponents (Burr, Mead, & Rollins, 1973; Luckey, 1974). In the case of farm families and stress, this connection is made difficult because of the paucity of research on the human elements of farming (Berkowitz, 1984; Fetsch, 1985). The purpose of this chapter is to provide further empirical support for the development of stress management programs for farm families. Findings from a study of factors associated with stress in farm men and women will be summarized, and the implications of these findings for family life education practitioners will be presented. Before discussing these findings and implications, however, it is useful to review the conceptual foundations for the study.

## Conceptual Foundation of the Study

Demands placed on farmers by the farm crisis are often obvious and dramatic. In particular, high debt load and heavy work demands are seen as stressful (Ekstrom, Leholm, Leistritz, & Vreugdenhil, 1985). However, the work of stress theorists (McCubbin & Patterson, 1982; Wheaton, 1980) suggests that these demands represent only part of the stress equation and that resources or family strengths will also affect the amount of stress experienced. Of the latter, social resources (e.g., a supportive spouse) and personal resources (e.g., a sense of control over one's life) are especially important (Pearlin & Schooler, 1978). Since farm families are known to be resilient and self-reliant and to live in stable communities which place high value on mutual supportiveness, an understanding of the resource side of the stress equation can be particularly useful to family life educators whose mission is to help families build upon strengths rather than focus on deficits.

### Financial Demands

Debt load has been seen as one of the major contributors to psychosomatic stress, with many eloquent testimonials from farm men and women about the devastating effects of heavy debt loads (Ireland, 1981; Women of Unifarm, 1978). Some farm families seem to manage under heavy debt loads, perhaps because they have very modest expectations of the financial returns from farming (Rosenblatt & Keller, 1983), but others resent the expectation that their standard of living should be low (Ireland, 1981). Those who see farming as a way of life rather than a profit-making business may be willing to accept a satisfying life style as compensation for meager financial returns (Wilkening, 1981).

### Work Demands

Long hours of work at several different work tasks are part of the lives of farm women and men. Farming has been called a "greedy occupation" (Kanter, 1977) requiring more than full-time commitment of farm family members. Yet long hours may be more or less demanding depending upon the type of work done (Sieber, 1974). For example, since farm men see their dominant identities as farmers (Symes & Marsden, 1981), doing farm work may actually keep stress levels low. The same number of hours at an off-farm job may produce stress since off-farm work is generally done to support the farm operation and may symbolize hours away from real work (Wilkening, 1981).

Many farm women see their primary domain as the household (Heffring Research Group Ltd., 1983). For them, hard work in the household may be demanding but satisfying.

Their attitudes toward off-farm employment are less clear. While some (Bescher-Donnelly & Smith, 1981) have argued that rural women traditionally have a negative attitude toward employment outside the home, others believe that economic contributions from women's off-farm employment may reduce stress by giving them more power in decision making in the farm business (Coughenour & Swanson, 1983).

It is not clear how farm work hours are related to stress in farm women. A heavy work load in a farm role that is unrecognized (Kohl & Bennett, 1982) and perhaps not part of her identity (Scholl, 1982) might well cause stress reactions. Farm women who are able to reach agreement with their husbands about their farm roles are less likely to report stress-related health symptoms than their counterparts who disagree with their husbands about farm roles (Berkowitz & Perkins, 1985).

## Personal Resources

Several authors (Lefcourt, 1983; Pearlin & Schooler, 1978; Wheaton, 1980) argue that a sense of being in control of one's life helps to keep stress levels low, particularly where individuals have a fair amount of discretion or freedom of movement. Thus, for farmers who feel self-confident and expect to solve problems successfully, stress may not be as severe as for those who feel as if their own efforts make little difference (Weigel, 1981). The latter group is vulnerable to stress because problems are attributed to external causes: to the banks, the weather, the wheat board (Rosenblatt & Keller, 1983).

## Social Resources

As with personal resources, it has been argued that social or interpersonal resources can reduce the impact of the many demands of farm life. Because of the interdependence of the work and family lives of farm couples, support from one's spouse has been considered one of the most important social resources for farmers (Berkowitz & Perkins, 1985). Much of the work of farm women is invisible to those outside their families, but acknowledgement by their husbands of their physical work has been shown to help reduce stress-related health symptoms (Hedlund & Berkowitz, 1979; Jensen, 1982). Although there are few studies of the importance of spousal support in reducing stress

levels of rural men, farm women's role by definition includes providing "support and back-up to the primary farm operator" (Heffring, 1983, p. 8).

While this literature provides evidence that financial and work demands are likely to result in stress reactions for farm men and women, the evidence concerning the importance of human resources is less clear. Concern about the farm crisis and its focus on the problems and deficits of farm families implies that the resources of these farm families are inadequate to withstand the demands imposed by this crisis. This implication needs further examination if programs to assist farm families are to be based on their real needs and experiences.

## Methodology and Findings of the Study

The data reported in this chapter come from a larger study of work patterns, resources, and stress of farm men and women. A random sample of grain farm owners in Alberta was drawn by Statistics Canada, and identical questionnaires for the farm man and farm woman were mailed to each farm. There were 753 individuals from 414 farms in the sample.

As noted earlier, the findings reported in this chapter focus on the identification of factors associated with stress in farm men and women. Data were analysed using stepwise multiple regression analyses with stress as the dependent variable and demands (finances and work) and resources (personal and social) as independent variables. Separate analyses were run for men and for women. The measure of stress in this study is an adaptation of a 22-item scale developed by Langner (1962) and adapted by Berkowitz and Perkins (1985) for use with farm families. Financial demand was measured by debt load, a ratio of debt to gross sales of agricultural products. Work demands included two measures: total yearly hours spent in each of farm, off-farm, and household work; and a mean score of felt conflict over home, farm, and off-farm employment work roles. Personal resources were measured by a mastery scale developed by Pearlin and Schooler (1978). Social resources were a measure of satisfaction with spousal support for one's work involvement and in coping with tensions. The stress scale and measures of work conflict and social resources were taken from Berkowitz and Perkins (1985).

Results of the analyses indicated that, for both men and women, the personal resource of mastery was the strongest predictor of stress. For men, all remaining significant predictors of stress were work-related demands. In contrast, the second most important predictor for women was the social resource of husband's support, followed by work demands. Notably absent for both men and women in this analysis were financial demands. These findings do not support contemporary assumptions about the sources of the farm crisis. For these subjects, resources were stronger predictors of stress than were demands, with some differences between men and women in the demands and resources affecting their stress levels.

The personal resource of mastery was the most important predictor of stress for both men and women. High stress farmers felt that their fate and consequently their livelihood was out of their control. "Your hours are so great and then your return is a gamble. Last year when we got hailed out we were totally devastated. We couldn't see the light at the end of the tunnel. Everything we had was gone" (female, age 45, married, 4 children, grain and livestock farm). This finding supports the contention of many that perception of control is a significant determinant of how people respond to aversive demands in their environment. Such demands are part of the lives of all farm men and women, yet high mastery men and women are confident that they will manage these problems. "You do the best you can and if it doesn't work out you have to be brave enough to face the consequences. It is a good life. We've had it difficult but we wouldn't trade it."

The only significant social support which was a predictor of stress was that of husband's support for women's farm work. Although most women in the study did farm work, they were not considered to be farmers. Women are dependent for recognition upon those people who know about their farm work, notably their husbands. For high stress women, this acknowledgement was absent. As one husband said, "No, she doesn't do farm work. She just picks rocks and roots and drives the other tractor" (male, age 56, married, 4 children, grain and livestock farm). Low stress women felt much

more support. "I work side-by-side with my husband in our farm operation and enjoy every minute of farm life" (female, age 37, married, 3 children, grain and livestock farm). In this study, spouse support was not related to stress for men, possibly because men's identities are so clearly focused on farm work with general community support for their farm role.

Of the demands examined, the most important for men was off-farm employment hours, with low off-farm hours associated with high stress. Having an off-farm job may be an indicator to the farm man of his lack of success at the farm operation. He is reminded of his inability to be a success at full-time farming and yet he earns a low income at that job because he is working only a few hours. The farm man who works full-time at his off-farm job at least has something other than farming on which to fall back.

Although it was expected that farm women would suffer from role overload because of their many work roles, women's work hours were not related to stress. A strong work ethic and a strong attachment to the land may be one reason why long work days and irregular hours do not result in stress symptoms. "Sure I work hard. If there is no hired man, my role in the farm increases dramatically. If the children are involved scholastically or in extracurricular things, they are unable to help in the farm duties. Then I do field work, chores, etc. Even though it is unpredictable and busy, there is no place I'd rather live though it is really true that you have to want to be there or you really wouldn't" (female, age 40, married, 3 children, grain and livestock farm).

Although work loads did not affect stress levels, role conflict was a predictor of stress for both men and women. "Why should I have to work at two jobs just to do the one I want to do?" (male, age 44, married, 4 children, grain farmer). For men, conflict came primarily from the competition of off-farm work with that of the farm and from not meeting personal standards regarding the success of the farm operation. A major concern of these farm men was the neglect of their farm duties. For women, conflict came from feelings of not meeting the expectations of either themselves or others. Women in this study felt that their lack of knowledge and skill about the farm operation prevented them from doing more. "I'd like to help him more but I just don't know enough to help with the big decisions. Well, I suppose some-one has to be the go-for" (female, age 52, married, 3 children, grain farm).

Contrary to expectations, debt load was not a significant predictor of stress. This may be in part because those whose debt loads were so high that they had lost their farms were not a part of the study. It may also be because debt had different meanings for different people. For some the way of life is worth the costs. "If I won a million, I would farm until I was broke" (male, age 30, married, 2 children, wheat farmer).

The assessment of farming as a good way to make a living was associated with lower levels of stress for men. This personal evaluation of the adequacy of income was more important than actual income variables. Some were discouraged about farming as a way to make a living—"We will have little to pass along to our children; not a way or means to make a decent living; only a place to live" (female, age 37, married, 2 children, grain farm), while others appeared more accepting—"Basically our indoctrination was to use what we could afford, not what we would like" (male, age 63, married, 3 children, wheat farmer).

In sum, the findings of this study suggest that high mastery provides the best buffer against stress for both farm men and women. For women, the additional resource of husband's support for their farm work was also important. Of the demands considered, work conflict was important for both, although probably for different reasons. Low hours of off-farm employment and the evaluation of farming as a poor way to make a living were associated with stress for farm men.

## Implications for Practitioners

Several implications for practitioners emerge from this study of factors related to stress in farm men and women. These include implications for content and strategies in interventions designed for farm families, implications for potential audiences for these interventions, and implications for the kinds of interventions to be made by those who work with farm families.

### Content and Strategies

The findings of this study suggest that although interventions by educators and therapists to reduce demands are important,

too much emphasis may have been placed on financial concerns with insufficient attention given to helping farm families augment personal and social resources. Attention to personal resources is particularly important since high mastery individuals tend to see life as more controllable and most life events as less catastrophic than do low mastery individuals. Educators can assist farmers attending intervention programs to augment their personal resources and thus increase their sense of mastery by focusing attention on three goals:

1. *Changing one's perspectives about demands.* Since families which are more resistant to stress tend to be solution- rather than catastrophe-oriented, educators need to assist farmers to see demands as solvable. Farm men and women can be encouraged to evaluate their emotional reactions and to reduce their negative thinking about these demands. The work of Albert Ellis (1973) is particularly relevant to this goal. Ellis' premise is that people can learn to see high demands as unfortunate rather than as unbearable and thus free themselves to face the future with hope rather than with despair. This perspective encourages individuals to concentrate on what can be accomplished rather than to focus on what is out of one's hands.

2. *Increasing one's knowledge about demands.* Educators can help farm men and women to gain as much knowledge as possible about the various demands in their lives. The premise here is that the more one knows about these demands, the more these will be seen as manageable. Although some educators caution against an emphasis on the didactic (Mace, 1974), information on farm matters (i.e., changes in taxation legislation, commodity prices, farm incorporation, marketing strategies) may not only provide a sound basis for making decisions but may also contribute to a sense of mastery over one's life and livelihood. In order to be seen as credible in helping farmers obtain this information, practitioners may need to draw upon a network of rural specialists for current information on the particular demands which face farm families in their area.

3. *Encouraging farm families to take action.* Engaging farm men and women in specific actions related to the major demands in their lives may also help to augment personal resources and increase mastery. The development of skills in deci-

sion making, goal setting, and time management will be more meaningful and more likely to make a difference when these are presented in a context which emphasizes taking actions to minimize real constraints and to optimize the returns from one's own work.

In addition to helping augment personal resources, those who work with farm families may also need to help them augment social resources. While the support of one's spouse may help to minimize stress, many farm men and women do not take advantage of this resource. To say that more open communication between spouses would be useful is one of the truisms of family life education. The more difficult challenge, however, is to effect that increased openness, since that may require some renegotiation of both the personal and the business relationships of these spouses. Nevertheless, this is one aspect of augmenting social resources which might help to reduce stress, particularly for farm women.

Social support also comes from others, both friends and professionals. One of the best buffers against stress is a network of people who understand one's situation because they are or have been in similar circumstances. Yet many farm families seem to be caught between two conflicting norms: (a) Rural communities pull together, with members helping one another in difficult times, and (b) family difficulties are private ones, with their solution the responsibility of family members. Educators can encourage participants in intervention programs to examine these norms in the light of their own preferred methods for dealing with problems and in the light of their own particular needs for social support outside the family.

Since many farm families have negative perceptions of the professionals with whom they have contact, there may be less potential to use professionals as resources. One study in rural Canada illustrates the problem (McGhee, no date). In this study, physicians were seen as creating hazards by prescribing mood-altering drugs to people who had to operate heavy equipment and to look after large animals; loan officers at banks frowned upon vacations or any other personal expenditures, especially if one's debt load was high; and staff at rural mental health centers were perceived as having little understanding of the nature of rural life and its problems. These perceptions of professionals by farm families may not have been accurate, but they did limit the willingness of these families to seek professional help.

Although the findings of this study indicate the importance of helping families to augment personal and social resources, the demand side of the stress equation should not be ignored in interventions with farm families. Currently, much is already being done in farm communities by provincial, state, and federal governments to reduce the impact of financial problems on farm families. But the findings reported here suggest that some attention also needs to be given to reducing the stressful nature of farm work demands. Farm men, for example, might be assisted to examine both the emotional and the financial advantages and the disadvantages of off-farm employment since such work is likely to be stressful, particularly if wages are low. Farm women might be encouraged to attend farm business courses on topics ranging from financial management to the servicing of farm equipment. Knowledge about farm operations would not only help women to become more competent partners but might also help to reduce their stress levels, since the lack of such knowledge appears to contribute to the role conflicts of farm women.

Farm men and women might also be encouraged to challenge their personal concepts of success. Boss (1986) argues that many farm men come from a tradition which says that a successful farmer does not have to work off the farm, that his wife also does not have to work off the farm, and that the burden of responsibility for the farm business rests on his shoulders. Such attitudes are likely to be stressful for farm men, but farm women may also find them stressful as they may see themselves as supportive but not an equal partner in the business operation. One challenge for educators in these intervention programs may be to help farm men to redefine success as a farmer and to help both farm men and farm women redefine the place of women in the farm operation.

## Potential Audiences

According to the findings of this study, arguments could be made for farm family intervention programs which focus on individuals, on couples, or on families as the target audience. Since the sources of stress are somewhat different for farm men and women, separate programs could allow individuals to gain information, develop skills, explore issues, and establish networks which are pertinent to their own situations. During informal conversations with this author, some farm women stated that when a program was designed especially for farm women, they felt free to attend and to leave farm chores and child care to their husbands. When the audience for the intervention was not defined, these wives felt that they should allow their husbands to attend.

However, the fact that the stress experience may be different for farm men and women is also a good argument for developing intervention programs for couples rather than for individuals. Such programs may help husbands and wives to understand each other's experience and to work together to resolve specific farm problems. Intervention programs for farm couples also have the potential to contribute to the development of one's partner as a source of social support.

Since farming is generally a family operation, practitioners might also consider the development of intervention programs for whole families. Although there is little information on the sources of stress of young farm children, recent findings show that adult farm children have high stress levels (Weigel, Weigel, & Blundall, 1987).

## Kinds of Practitioner Interventions

Findings from this study suggest that family life educators may assist farm families in several different ways. One of the most obvious ways is through the development of intervention programs at the personal or family level to assist farm families in augmenting resources and coping with demands. The need for such interventions is apparent, and family life practitioners possess many of the skills and abilities required for such programming. Some suggestions for fulfilling this task have been presented in this chapter.

This study also suggests that there is a need for family life practitioners to mediate between the farm family and other community professionals with whom they may interact. Knowledgeable family life educators might help these professionals to develop strategies to deal with the negative reactions of farm families and to acquire the understanding of rural life experience that is

necessary in order to more effectively serve as resources for farm families. Since this mediation task occurs on the societal rather than the personal level, this family life education effort has the potential to serve all farm families in a community, not just those who attend intervention programs. (In fulfilling this mediation role, however, practitioners might want to include in their intervention programs ways in which farm families might identify and communicate their needs and concerns more effectively to community professionals.)

Implied in this study is the need for family life practitioners to conduct or participate in research on farm families. While such research is needed to ensure that intervention programs are addressing the real needs and experiences of farm families, it is also important as one basis for the development of sound social policies and legislation affecting these families.

## Conclusions

As with any research, this study was limited by the context in which it was conducted. Farmers in the study were grain farmers, all in the province of Alberta. Since the sample was drawn from census data of farm owners, those who have lost their farms were not a part of the sample pool. Thus, United States dairy farmers facing bankruptcy, for example, might not have the same experiences of stress.

Nevertheless, the findings reported here and the discussion of their implications should help to augment the knowledge base of practitioners working with farm families and ensure that a variety of interventions are developed. Practitioners are challenged to expand, not only the content and strategies of their programming, but also the kinds of interventions which may be most helpful to farm families.

REFERENCES

Berkowitz, A. D. (1984). *Coping with stress on the farm.* Paper presented at the Annual Finger Lakes Grape Growers Convention, Keuka Park, NY.
Berkowitz, A. D., & Perkins, H. W. (1985). Correlates of psychosomatic stress symptoms among farm women: A research note on farm and family functioning. *Journal of Human Stress,* **11**(2), 76-81.
Bescher-Donnelly, L., & Smith, L. W. (1981). The changing roles and status of rural women. In R. T. Coward & W. M. Smith (Eds.), *The family in rural society* (pp. 167-186). Boulder, CO: Westview Press.

Bokemeier, J., Sachs, S., & Keith, V. (1983). Labor force participation of metropolitan, nonmetropolitan and farm women: A comparative study. *Rural Sociology, 48,* 515-539.

Boss, P. (1986). Farm family displacement and stress. In *Increasing understanding of public problems and policies—1985* (pp. 61-78). Oakbrook, IL: Farm Foundation.

Brinkman, G. L. (1985). *The agricultural finance problem in perspective.* Report presented at the Agricultural Credit Conference, Saskatoon, Saskatchewan, Canada.

Burr, W., Mead, D. E., & Rollins, B. C. (1973). A model for the application of research findings by the educator and counselor: Research to theory to practice. *The Family Coordinator, 22,* 285-290.

Coughenour, C. M., & Swanson, L. (1983). Work statuses and occupations of men and women in farm families and the structure of farms. *Rural Sociology, 48,* 23-43.

Ekstrom, B. L., Leholm, A. G., Leistritz, F. L., & Vreugdenhil, H. (1985). Farm financial stress in North Dakota: Selected characteristics of farm and ranch operations. *North Dakota Farm Research, 42*(6), 23-27.

Ellis, A. (1973). *Humanistic psychotherapy.* New York: McGraw-Hill.

Fetsch, R. J. (1985, November). *Stress and coping on the farm: A comparison of farmers with nonfarmers.* Paper presented at the annual meeting of the National Council on Family Relations, Dallas, TX.

Fetsch, R. (no date). *Stress management for couples.* Lexington: University of Kentucky, College of Agriculture, Cooperative Extension Service.

Hedlund, D., & Berkowitz, A. D. (1979). The incidence of social-psychological stress in farm families. *International Journal of Sociology of the Family, 2,* 233-243.

Heffring Research Group Ltd. (1983). *Information needs of Alberta farmers and farm families: Focus group report.* A brief presented to the Planning Secretariat, Alberta Agriculture.

Ireland, G. (1981). *The psychological effects of financial stress on farm families.* A brief presented to the Ontario Federation of Agriculture Task Force on the Financial Crisis. Hanover, Ontario, Canada.

Jensen, L. (1982). Stress in the farm family unit. *Resources for Feminist Research, 11*(1), 11-12.

Kanter, R. (1977). *Work and family in the United States: A critical review and agenda for research and policy.* New York: Russell Sage Foundation.

Keating, N., Doherty, M., & Munro, B. (1987). The whole economy: Resource allocation of Alberta farm women and men. *Canadian Journal of Home Economics, 37,* 135-139.

Klein, K. K., & Barichello, R. (1985). *Farm finances in Western Canada.* Calgary, Alberta: Canada West Foundation.

Kohl, S. B., & Bennett, J. W. (1982). The agrifamily household. In J. W. Bennett (Ed.), *Of time and the enterprise* (pp. 148-171). Minneapolis: University of Minnesota Press.

Langner, T. S. (1962). A twenty-two item screening score of psychiatric symptoms indicating impairment. *Journal of Health and Human Behavior, 3,* 269-276.

Lefcourt, H. M. (1983). *Research with the locus of control construct: Vol. 2.* New York: Academic Press, Inc.

Lencucha, J. (1986). *Alberta farm families and stress.* Background paper for the Alberta Agriculture Development Corporation Review Committee.

Light, H., & Thorndal, N. (no date). *Strengthening family life during tough times.* Fargo: North Dakota State University, Division of Continuing Studies.

Luckey, E. (1974). What I have learned about family life. *The Family Coordinator, 23,* 307-313.

Mace, D. (1974). What I have learned about family life. *The Family Coordinator, 23,* 189-195.

McCubbin, H. I., & Patterson, J. M. (1982). Family adaptation to crisis. In H. I. McCubbin, A. E. Cauble, & J. M. Patterson (Eds.), *Family stress, coping and social support* (pp. 26-47). Springfield, IL: Charles Thomas.

McGhee, M. (no date). *Women in rural life: The changing scene.* Ontario Ministry of Agriculture and Food.

Pearlin, L., & Schooler, C. (1978). The structure of coping. *Journal of Health and Social Behavior, 19,* 2-21.

Rosenblatt, P. C., & Keller, L. O. (1983). Economic vulnerability and economic stress in farm couples. *Family Relations, 32,* 567-573.

Scholl, K. (1982). Household and farm task participation of women. *Family Economics Review, 3,* 3-9.

Sieber, S. D. (1974). Toward a theory of role accumulation. *American Sociological Review, 39,* 567-578.

Symes, D. G., & Marsden, T. K. (1981). Complementary roles and asymmetrical lives. *Sociologia Ruralis, 23*(3/4), 229-241.

Walker, J. L., Walker, L. S., & MacLennan, P. M. (1986). An informal look at farm stress. *Psychological Reports, 59,* 427-430.

Weigel, R. (1981). *Stress on the farm.* Pamphlet available from Alberta Agriculture, Edmonton, Alberta, Canada, #884-00-19.

Weigel, R. R., Weigel, D. J., & Blundall, J. (1987). Stress, coping and satisfaction: Generational differences in farm families. *Family Relations, 36,* 45-48.

Wheaton, B. (1980). The sociogenesis of psychological disorder: An attributional theory. *Journal of Health and Social Behavior, 21,* 111-124.

Wilkening, E. A. (1981). Farm families and family farming. In R. T. Coward & W. M. Smith (Eds.), *The family in rural society* (pp. 27-38). Boulder, CO: Westview Press.

Women of Unifarm. (1978). *Stresses in the farm family unit.* Report available from Women of Unifarm, Box 186, Hussar, Alberta, Canada T0J 1S0.

# Farm Families in Crisis:
# An Overview of Resources*

**Elizabeth A. Thompson and Hamilton I. McCubbin****

The unstable economy of the United States has had a profound, if not devastating, impact upon the agricultural community and its economic base. While most farmers remain in relatively sound financial condition, in 1985 the Farm Cost and Returns Survey indicated approximately 10 to 12% (approximately 214,000 farm operations) were adversely affected by the deteriorating condition of the United States economy. In that survey, (Agricultural and Rural Economics Division, 1986), a debt-asset ratio of more than 40% and negative net cash flow were used to identify which farm operations and particularly which farm families were experiencing financial difficulty and vulnerability. Most vulnerable were approximately 38,000 to 40,000 farm operators with a negative net cash flow who were already technically insolvent. The report from the 1985 survey also indicated that many other farm operations would also fail. These farm operations and farm families were not able to fully service their existing debts nor were they sufficiently solvent to

achieve adequate equity to justify increasing or rolling over debt.

This financial condition affecting many farm families stemmed from their inability to respond to their existing interest repayment and debt load. For example, a recent report by the Agricultural and Rural Economics Division (1986) pointed out that the problems had been exacerbated by the sharp decline since 1981 in farm family asset values which has reduced the farmers' ability to borrow to offset their negative cash flow. This same report also noted that nearly $220 billion in owners' equity had been lost through land value depreciation between December 1981 and December 1985; farm value surveys indicated that the value of farm land declined approximately 13% nationwide within a one-year period, 1984 through 1985; and that this depreciation followed a national average decline of 7.0% for the period of 1981 through 1983; as of April 1985, land value declines of as much as 49% from the 1981 peaks were registered for parts of the Corn Belt, with the state of Iowa suffering the most severe decline, followed by Nebraska, the other low Corn Belt states, and Great Lakes states.

It was also reported that dairy farms, which are predominately located in the Great Lakes states, appeared to be the most seriously affected by financial stress. Even though milk prices have fallen less than prices of other commodities, dairy farmers were more highly leveraged than other farmers and had traditionally operated on narrow profit margins. Additionally, recent declines in farm level milk prices were start-

*This project was funded by the Agricultural Experiment Station, Project 3021, University of Wisconsin, Madison, WI. The authors thank Assistant Dean Anne K. Thompson and Director Neal Jorgensen for their support of this project and effort.

**Elizabeth A. Thompson is a Project Assistant for the Family Stress, Coping and Health Project at the University of Wisconsin, Madison, WI 53706, and a senior at St. Olaf College in Northfield, MN. Hamilton I. McCubbin is Dean and Professor of the School of Family Resources and Consumer Sciences at the University of Wisconsin, Madison, WI 53706.

Reprinted from *Family Relations*, 1987, **36**, 461-467.

ing to create adjustment problems for dairy farmers who were highly leveraged. Thus, these families had suffered serious asset value declines and concomitantly a serious cash flow shortfall.

Crisis among farm families is not new. During the 1950s and 1960s, the reduction in the number of farms and farm families was related to mechanization and labor-saving innovations, reduction of profit margins which required farmers to increase volume of output per farm, and the attraction of superior income earning opportunities in urban areas. This shift impacted upon the southern tenant system of field-crop farming and a greater majority of ethnic minority families (Agricultural and Rural Economics Division, 1986).

The farm family crisis resulting from farm failure or displacement in the 1980s is far different from those experienced two to three decades ago. The major shifts in today's economic crisis are related to macro and agricultural economic conditions, affecting the regions of the Great Northern, Great Plains, and the Corn Belt states, and involving those with substantial human capital who operated family-sized commercial enterprises. The families and individuals leaving agriculture today appear to be overwhelmingly from the middle and upper middle sector of commercial agriculture (Agricultural and Rural Economics Division, 1986). During the past agricultural crises it was quite common in farm communities for half of all persons reaching adulthood during the decade to move away to other areas. To add to the complexity of the recent problem, many of the families and individuals from farm families currently being displaced from agriculture have attempted to remain in their home community and retain that valued aspect of their rural lives. In recent times the majority of employed farm women work in nonfarm jobs. Such employment supplements the family income and makes a decision to move away more difficult as both spouses would then have to find new jobs. Ties to home community and local employment of spouses (who are usually wives) make many ex-farmers more willing to accept local work that is below their abilities and their former income level.

## Innovative Strategies for an Emerging and Persistent Problem

It is not uncommon for farmers and farm families to believe that the crisis will disappear and that things will return to what they were (Agricultural and Rural Economics Division, 1986). However, a review of current national and international issues would encourage people to be more cautious about their optimism for the farm crisis. Land values have not risen, interest rates remain relatively high, and prospects of government intervention in the form of subsidies to support farm families appear bleak (Agricultural and Rural Economics Division, 1986). At both the national and international levels there is a deliberate effort to unify on a policy that would eliminate all agriculture subsidies by the year 2000. The kinds of policies, programs, and resources needed to support farm families in this current crisis are a major challenge for both policymakers and human resource specialists, particularly the Agriculture Extension Service. The Agricultural and Rural Economics Division of the United States Department of Agriculture recommended three types of public policies: (a) human capital development programs to enhance the employability, mobility, and labor market skills of displaced farmers and their families; (b) programs to encourage economic development in impacted regions so that displaced farmers and their families can work locally; and (c) income transfer programs for low income and older farmers and those who derive little capital from agriculture (Agricultural and Rural Economics Division, 1986).

Concomitantly, the Cooperative Extension Service (CES) has chosen to emphasize the development of programs designed to assist farm families in dealing with psychological and interpersonal stress. Additionally, the CES programs emphasized problem solving and decision making in an effort to facilitate family analyses of the situation and identification of options. Publications designed to foster problem solving and decision making for these families were also developed and distributed.

In this review of resources designed to support farm families in crisis, the authors have chosen to underscore the deliberate efforts of those state and federal agencies responsible for the delivery of human resource programs. Particular attention was paid to innovative and important efforts designed by the Cooperative Extension Service, as well as related resource articles, books, videotapes, films, and programs designed to shed light upon the problem and to offer assistance.

## Overview of Farm Family Efforts

The leadership for developing programs to aid farm families has come from the Cooperative Extension Service. Through Cooperative Extension, many programs have been organized at the local and national level. The strength of extension programs comes from their connection to each individual state. The programs are developed in direct response to the needs of the agricultural community. Each state program has been created with aspects judged to best benefit that particular state. These individualized programs (shown in Figure 1) have offered important resources to farmers experiencing financial crisis.

Many different strategies have been instigated by Cooperative Extension to aid farm families. The following discussion looks at a few of the most common ways that state programs attempt to help the agricultural community. An overview of programs organized and categorized by states is presented in Table 1.

The number of programs offered by individual states is increasing in response to the need of the rural community. In several states farm families have been directly involved in Cooperative Extension programming decisions through surveys and polls. This direct contact between programs and families is a positive step toward best serving the needs of the people.

### One-on-One Counseling

A popular tool for helping farmers is one-on-one counseling. Financial and emotional needs can be dealt with through individualized counseling with professionals or trained peers. Many states use one-on-one counseling to help farmers set up individualized financial programs for their farms. These financial plans help farmers deal with present problems as well as set up long-term goals and strategies for dealing with financial crisis.

### Small Group Counseling

Not all individuals affected by the farm crisis need intensive one-on-one counseling.

*Figure 1:* Percentage of States Using Selected Methods for Helping Farm Families Meet the Financial Crisis.

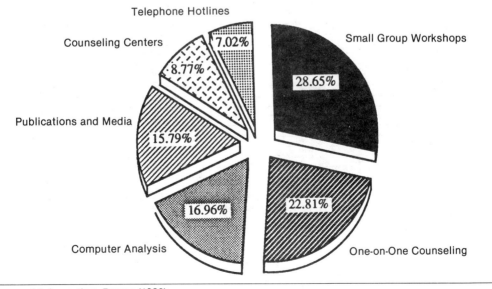

Source of Information: Brown (1986)

Table 1.
*Delivery Methods/Procedures Used to Assist Financially Distressed Farm Families, by State and Territory, Fiscal Year 1986*

| State and Territory | One-on-One Consultation | Small Group/ Workshops | Computerized Decision Aids | Farm Management Associations | Support for Stress Problems | Publications and Media[1] |
|---|---|---|---|---|---|---|
| Alabama | • | • | • | • | • | • |
| Alaska |  |  |  |  |  |  |
| Arizona | • | • | • |  | • | • |
| Arkansas | • | • | • | • | • | • |
| California |  | • | • | • | • | • |
| Colorado | • | • | • | • | • | • |
| Connecticut | • | • | • |  | • | • |
| Delaware | • | • | • | • | • | • |
| Florida | • | • | • | • | • | • |
| Georgia | • | • | • | • | • |  |
| Guam | • |  |  |  |  |  |
| Hawaii |  | • | • |  | • | • |
| Idaho | • | • |  | • | • | • |
| Illinois | • | • | • | • | • | • |
| Indiana | • | • | • | (3) | • | • |
| Iowa | • | • | • | • | • |  |
| Kansas | • | • | • | • | • | • |
| Kentucky | • | • | • | (3) | • | • |
| Maine | • | • | • | • | • | • |
| Maryland | • | • | • |  | • | • |
| Massachusetts | • | • | • |  | • | • |
| Michigan | • | • | • | • | • | • |
| Micronesia | • |  |  |  |  |  |
| Minnesota | • | • | • | • | • | • |
| Mississippi | • | • | • |  | NA | • |
| Missouri | • | • | • | • | • |  |
| Montana | • | • | • |  | • | • |
| Nebraska | • | • | • | • | • | • |
| Nevada | • | (3) | • | (3) | • |  |
| New Hampshire | • | • | • |  | • | • |
| New Jersey | • | (3) | • | (3) | • | • |
| New Mexico | • | • | • |  | • | • |
| New York | • | • | • |  | • | • |
| North Carolina | • | • | • |  | • | • |
| North Dakota | • | • | • |  | • | • |
| Ohio | • | • | • |  | • | • |
| Oklahoma | • | • | • | • | • | • |
| Oregon | • | • | • |  | • | • |
| Pennsylvania | • | • | • |  | • | • |
| Puerto Rico | • | • | • | • | • | • |
| Rhode Island | • |  | • |  | NA | (3) |
| South Carolina | • | • | • | (3) | • | • |
| South Dakota | • | • | • | • | • | • |
| Tennessee | • | • | • |  | • | • |
| Texas | • | • | • |  | • | • |
| Utah | • | • | • |  | • | • |
| Vermont | • | • | • | • | • | • |
| Virginia | • | • | • | • | • | • |
| Washington | • | • | • |  | • | • |
| West Virginia | • | • | • |  | • | • |
| Wisconsin | • | • | • | • | • | • |
| Wyoming | • | • | • |  | • | • |

[1]Include publications, radio, TV, video, and press activities.
[2]Other delivery methods/procedures include working through lenders and other organizations, home study courses, referrals, and personal correspondence.
[3]Planned.
Source: *Cooperative extension* (1987).

An effective way to reach a greater number of people is through small group counseling. Cooperative Extension Agents and professional counselors in many states have trained volunteers to lead these small counseling groups. These volunteers are often themselves members of the rural community. The support group gives financially and emotionally stressed farmers a place to express their feelings. Because these groups are made up of the farm families' peers, they appear to be an excellent source of support in an often alienating time.

## Workshops

Workshops are another useful resource which seem to benefit a great number of people. Many Cooperative Extension programs employ professionals to present relevant workshops to rural communities. Workshops exist on a wide range of topics including issues of family stress and coping in the rural crisis, reducing personal stress, and financial and legal strategies for farmers. The workshops have reached thousands of people who otherwise would not have access to this important information.

## Computerized Decision Aids

One of the newer technological aids for farmers are financial computer programs. These programs are designed to help farmers evaluate their present financial conditions and to predict future conditions. Programs allow the farmer exploration of different financial planning alternatives and help the farmer look to the future. Because the computer programs focus on the future, they are likely to create an optimistic outlook for farm families and to help reduce their financial and emotional stress.

## Other Support for Stress Problems

In addition to one-on-one counseling and counseling groups, several other programs have been developed to aid with emotional stress. One method of giving support for stress has been the establishment of Rural Concern Hotlines. Telephone hotlines provide an information source for farmers, as well as a place for farmers to voice their emotional responses to stress. Some states have added legal and financial counseling on their hotlines in addition to emotional counseling. The stress of the financial crisis does affect the whole family, and these programs have made a concerted effort to involve all members of the farm family.

## Publications

Many states have produced magazines, newspapers, television shows, or videotapes which help to publicize the resources available through their programs. Although many excellent programs have been developed, it is crucial to alert farm families to the resources that are available to them. Through agricultural publications this is made possible.

Mass media coverage of the farm crisis is also important. Through general media coverage farmers and nonfarmers can be informed of the availability and goals of these programs. The scope of the farm crisis is not fully realized by many urban Americans, and their ignorance of the crisis hinders public support for farm programs.

# Resources

## Programs

Many states have responded to the need for rural stress assistance by making programs available to farm families. The resources available to farmers vary from state to state. The majority of states are involved in developing programs through the Cooperative Extension Service. The following list does not represent all the programs (i.e., group meetings, television shows, counseling sessions, hotlines, etc.) that exist, but rather it explores several different states' approaches to rural family stress.

• *Colorado*: The "Agricultural Resources in Colorado" Program (ARC) provides support systems for farmers facing crisis. Cooperative Extension offers counseling services for farmers and seminars on strengthening family relationships in crisis. ARC also provides legal advice for farmers. The community colleges and vocational schools of Colorado are also involved by offering farmers year-round technical assistance.

• *Illinois:* In 1986, Illinois expanded the number of state counseling centers for rural concerns. In addition, many counseling and peer support programs are in effect on the local level. "Your Financial Condition," a teaching program on financial planning developed by the state, is used at the local level to teach farmers financial planning. A 12-hour TeleNet Course entitled "Analyzing the Financial Strength of Your Farm Business" has also been used to help farmers.

• *Iowa*: Iowa's Cooperative Extension program to aid farmers, called ASSIST, has three main objectives: to help individuals and families deal positively with uncertainty and loss by building family strength and stability; to enhance the abilities of organizations at state and local levels to train professionals to work with families; and to assist farmers to make life style transitions as a response to forced change. Iowa has worked toward achieving these objectives through many services provided by ASSIST. A Rural Concerns Hotline is one way Iowa has employed to reach farm families in crisis. The ASSIST program has also trained many professionals and volunteers to help farm families analyze their financial and emotional situations.

• *Kansas*: The State Board of Agriculture, in cooperation with Kansas Extension, has developed a program called FACTS to provide farmers with pertinent information. The telephone hotline provides emotional counseling and financial counseling, but the main thrust of the program is legal counseling. An attorney works with the FACTS staff to answer legal questions posed by farmers.

• *Minnesota*: "Project Support," Minnesota's Cooperative Extension Farm Program, involves many different aspects of rural aid. A computer program, called FINPACK, is available to help farmers with business management techniques. Counseling and information are available on the issues of farm financial management, family resource and stress management, and community resource development.

• *Missouri*: The central project of Missouri's Cooperative Extension, entitled MOFARMS, is a project in cooperation with Missouri's State Department of Agriculture. MOFARMS provides a farm crisis hotline which refers farmers to the appropriate information. Counselors for MOFARMS help families to deal with the short- and long-term aspects of their individual situations.

• *Nebraska:* Nebraska's Cooperative Extension Program, "Managing for Tomorrow,"

has advised thousands of rural families on farm financial planning. Several counseling services have also been organized to aid farm families. In addition to a special state counseling center, support groups have been created at the county level. The leaders for the county support groups are usually people from the rural community. These groups, called Support Teams Acting on Rural Stress (STARS), seem to be effective because they provide peer support for crisis victims.

• *Wisconsin:* Wisconsin's Cooperative Extension Program, "Strategies on Survival" (SOS), has also helped farmers with financial and personal aspects of the farm crisis. One-on-one counseling is available for farmers, as well as small group counseling and special interest workshops. One interesting facet of the SOS program is the computer programs that have been set up to quickly analyze a farmer's financial situation. Legal help is also available through the Wisconsin Attorney General's Office. SOS tries to help farmers look beyond the present crisis to see an overall picture of the future.

## Articles

• Berkowitz, A. D., & Perkins, H. W. (1984). Stress among farm women: Work and family as interacting systems. *Journal of Marriage and the Family,* **46,** 161-166.

Berkowitz and Perkins' study of the stress of farm women is presented along with several factors that influence women's stress. Husband's support, farm and home task load, and women's feelings of role conflict between home and farm responsibilities are presented as possible indicators of stress. The findings are well displayed in graphics suitable for teaching aids.

• Coghenour, C. M., & Swanson, L. (1983). Work status and occupations of men and women in farm families and the structure of farms. *Rural Sociology,* **48,** 23-43.

This article discusses the stress of off-farm employment on the farm family itself and includes several interesting graphs which compare the off-farm occupations of men and women. In addition to an important evaluation of how off-farm employment affects the family, it also shows the transition that rural women have had to make due to the farm crisis.

• Lyson, T. A. (1985). Husband and wife work roles and the organization and operation of family farms. *Journal of Marriage and the Family, 47,* 759-764.

The author evaluates how off-farm employment, of either the husband or the wife, affects the farm structure and the decision-making process on the farm. A pertinent issue for families facing forced change in their farming operations is presented.

• Rosenblatt, P. C., & Keller, L. O. (1983). Economic vulnerability and economic stress in farm couples. *Family Relations, 32,* 567-573.

The correlation between economic vulnerability and family stress is highlighted. An important concept presented is the idea that economic stress often leads to blaming, which increases family stress.

• Salamon, S. (1984). Incorporation and the farm family. *Journal of Marriage and the Family, 46,* 167-178.

This article discusses how incorporation of family farms affects the competitiveness of the farm as a business. It also looks at how family relationships are affected by farm incorporation. This is an excellent source for studying the changes that modern business has made on farming structures, farm family relationships, and farm family stress.

Since 1978, *Successful Farming* has been committed to helping farmers by presenting articles dealing with the topic of stress. Numerous articles on rural stress and coping have appeared in the magazine. These articles present a different perception of farm stress in that they were written especially for a farming audience.

• Tevis, C. (1982). Fortify your life with resources which resist stress. *Successful Farming, 80,* 26-27.

The author explores different methods to reduce stress in rural families. The importance of having hobbies and activities separate from the farm is a key concept. The forced transition to a nonfarming life is more easily accepted if some activities of the family are not farm related.

• Tevis, C. (1982). Stress. *Successful Farming, 80,* 27-42.

This article presents case histories of farmers who have experienced rural stress, as well as practical tips for avoiding unnecessary stress. The article, which received the Oscar for Agriculture Award of journalism presented by the DeKalb Agricultural Research Association, includes a stress questionnaire for farmers prepared by Stanford's Heart Disease Prevention Program.

• Tevis, C. (1984). Role reversal creates new women farmers. *Successful Farming, 82,* 26.

Role reversal due to the farm crisis is a fairly common theme of the rural stress literature, but this article addresses the idea of women becoming private farmers or the primary farm worker of the family. Tevis presents several case studies of female farmers.

• Tevis, C. (1985). There's more help for rural stress. *Successful Farming, 83,* 15.

Lists of organizations designed to help rural families are included in this article. Emotional counseling, financial counseling, and farm crisis hotlines are all pinpointed.

• Tevis, C. (1986). How off-farm work alters family life. *Successful Farming, 84,* 19-20.

The off-farm work of women and the changes in the farm system because of their absence are explored here. Several case studies of farm women who have had to seek employment off the farm are presented.

• Bosc, M. (1987, February 2). Learning to survive on the land. *U.S. News and World Report, 102* (4), 30.

This article focuses on farmwives and their attempts to help their families and other farm families to cope more successfully with stress. It addresses the issue of low self-esteem which often occurs in farm families after bankruptcy or forced life style transition.

• Dentzer, S., McCormick, J., Thomas R., Weathers, D., Abramson, P., Shapiro, D., & Wang, P. (1985, February 18). Bitter harvest. *Newsweek, 105,* 52-60.

A look is offered at farmers' attempts to fight foreclosure on farms and to change government policy. Also, the article focuses on the fear and anger of farm families as they face losing their farms.

• Dreifus, C. (1987, January). If anything good comes of the farm crisis, it will be a new respect for the skills of rural women. *Glamour, 85*, (1), pp. 190-191, 229-231, 236.

The change in rural women's roles is shown through three case studies which are all representative of women who have made drastic changes in their life styles in order to keep their family farms. The article highlights farm women's strengths and adaptability to forced life style changes.

• Financial stress on the farm: How serious is it? (1985, November). *Farmline, 6* (10), 4-6.

*Farmline* is a magazine published by the United States Department of Agriculture. This article presents economic factors of the farm crisis and breaks them down regionally. Several excellent graphics and maps showing the economic side of the farm crisis are included.

• Flint, J. (1986, September 22). Some problems won't go away. *Forbes, 138* (6), 74-78.

The author uses some excellent graphics to explain why the present farm crisis cannot be solved quickly and provides an excellent overview of the financial aspects threatening family farm organizations.

## Books

• Coward, R. T., & Smith, W. M., Jr. (Eds.). (1981). *The Family in Rural Society*. Boulder, CO: Westview Press, 238 pages.

*The Family in Rural Society* is a resource for studying the farm crisis. The book has four sections: Current Trends in the Family in Rural Society, Patterns and Forms of Rural Families, Family Dynamics and Family Stress, and Prospects and Perspectives on Rural Families. This would be an excellent book for classroom use, as each section is relevant to the current topic of rural family stress.

• Figley, C. R, & McCubbin, H. I. (Eds.). (1983). *Stress and the Family*. New York: Brunnel & Mazel, Vol. I 266 pages, Vol. II 246 pages.

This work is an overview of different issues of family stress. The second volume is devoted entirely to coping with catastrophe, which is very applicable to the present farm crisis.

• Fite, G. C. (1981). *American Farmers—The New Minority*. Bloomington: Indiana University Press, 265 pages.

This is an excellent book for obtaining a better historical perspective of the farm crisis. The central point is to provide a historical perspective on the declining numbers of American farmers. The author gives a good overview of past and present federal agricultural policy, as well as discussing the numerous problems that face the modern farmer.

• Loomis, C. P., & Beegle, J. A. (1975). *A Strategy for Rural Change*. New York: John Wiley & Sons, Inc., 525 pages.

The goal of this book is to interpret rural life and farm families in terms of the discipline of rural sociology. The authors carefully discuss the problems of maintaining rural life in the shadow of a highly industrialized world.

• McCubbin, H. I., Cauble, A. E., & Patterson, J. M. (Eds.). (1982). *Family Stress, Coping and Social Support*. Springfield, IL: Charles Thomas, 272 pages.

To understand the reactions of rural families to the farm crisis, one should first look at how families in general deal with crisis. Several chapters in this volume are relevant to farm crisis issues, especially the works on Family Stress and Unemployment, and Family Coping.

• Vogeler, I. (1981). *The Myth of the Family Farm*. Boulder, CO: Westview Press, 352 pages.

This book shows the small family farm in contrast to the large agribusiness. Vogeler discusses the use of the "family farm ideal" to pass legislation that, in reality, profits the large agribusiness and hurts the family farm operation.

• Waterfield, L. W. (1986). *Conflicts and Crisis in Rural America*. New York: Praeger Publishers, 235 pages.

The author analyzes the culture of rural America and how that society deals with conflict and crisis. By examining aspects of the culture such as religion and music, the differences between rural and urban America are shown. The urban and rural cultural differences that exist often lead to a misinterpretation of rural life. Because this work is written from the cultural standpoint of rural America, it provides a different perception of rural concerns.

## Videotapes and Films

• *Crisis in Yankee Agriculture.* Massachusetts Department of Food and Agriculture. Color, 28 minutes, 16mm, rental $35.00.

Made by the Massachusetts Department of Food and Agriculture, this film portrays the loss of farms in urban areas through beautifully photographed stories of the lives of farmers. Available from Cambridge Media Resources, 36 Shepard Street, Cambridge, MA 02138.

• *Down on the Farm.* (1984). Time Life, Nova Series. Color, 57 minutes, ½" VHS, $15.00.

This videotape looks at the dilemma of American agriculture, examining why farmers, agricultural scientists, and policymakers are all caught in a system that pits short-term need for profit against the long-term needs of the land. This videotape explores reasons why farmers, faced with soaring interest rates and falling farm profits, are forced to work their land harder, thus accelerating soil erosion and pumping ground water for irrigation at rates that cannot be replenished. This is a relevant look at the natural aspects of farming in contrast with the financial aspects that often control farm decisions. Available from the University of Wisconsin, Bureau of Audiovisual Instruction, 1327 University Avenue, Madison, WI 53715.

• *Farmwife.* Ohio University TeleCommunications Center. Color, 60 minutes, VHS, rental $60.00 for one week, purchase price $350.00.

A documentary, taped at various farming operations in nine states across the country, the film portrays woman's expanded role in farming. This is a good film for discussing the feminist issues of the farm crisis. Available from ITV Coordinator, Telecommunications Center, Ohio University, Athens, OH 45701.

• *Portrait of Agriculture.* (1983). Rural Images, Keith Krohn and Wanda Sanders. Color, videotape, 20 minutes.

This film tells of daily life on a typical dairy farm, exploring changing responsibilities of modern farm families and problems facing farmers in the farm-to-market process. Curriculum packets are available for students. Also appropriate for adults. For rental price write Rural Images, Box 315, Brandon, WI 53919.

• *Surviving the Crisis.* (1986). Oklahoma State University. Color, 90 minutes, VHS.

*Surviving the Crisis* is a teleconference sponsored by the Oklahoma State University Cooperative Extension Service in the fall of 1986. Issues of stress and coping for farm families are discussed by a panel of experts. Information for ordering the videotape can be obtained by writing to: Gene Allen, Cooperative Extension Service, Oklahoma State University, Department of Agricultural Information, 102 Public Information Building, Stillwater, OK 74078.

• *The Wisconsin Farm Woman.* (1982). Wisconsin Educational Network. Color, 60 minutes, 16 mm, $17.00.

Portraits of farm women, past and present; with commentaries and controversies about their roles on and off the farm, their perceptions of farm life and city life, and the perceptions others have of them. This film would be a good choice for studying the changes the present farm crisis has made on rural women's roles. Write: Wisconsin Humanities Committee, 716 Langdon Street, Madison, WI 53706.

• *Business Management in Agriculture Videotape Series.*

A series of 10 videotapes on the financial aspects of farming were produced by the Cooperative Extension Service to be used in its educational programs. The videotapes are available at each state's Cooperative Extension office.

• *Iowa State University Farm Crisis Videotapes.* (1986). Iowa Cooperative Extension Service. Color, ½" VHS ($25.00), ¾" VHS ($35.00). Rental, $12.00 + shipping.

This series, developed by the Iowa Cooperative Extension Service to aid farm families, provides practical ideas for crisis management. The 10-tape series explores such issues as stress management and facing transitions in family life. The tapes can be ordered by calling Media Resources (515-294-1540), or writing to Media Resources, 112B Pearson, Iowa State University, Ames, IA 50011.

1. *Dealing With Blame: Helping Farm Families in Crisis.* This film helps rural people to understand the blaming that occurs as a result of farm family stress. Interviews with farm families who have experienced this blaming process are included. (Video #75385)

2. *The Rural Crisis Comes to School.* This videotape is designed as a guide for school teachers and other members of the rural community to understand the stress of farm children. The videotape presents talks with teachers and students and suggests some activities that can aid youth in dealing with their stress. (Video #75379)

3. *Farm Neighbors: A Guide for Self-Help Groups.* This videotape explores the role of peer support groups in the farm crisis. In this video, advice on how to start a self-help group is given. Also, two self-help groups that have been very productive are shown and interviewed. (Video #75417)

4. *Farmers and Lenders: Working Through Crisis.* This videotape helps teach lenders how to deal with stressful situations. The tape deals with stress in the farmer and lender relationship, as well as the stress that lenders themselves experience. The central idea of the tape is that by developing better communication skills, the stress of farmers and of lenders can be reduced. (Video #75400)

5. *Landing a Job: Strategies for Women.* The goal of this videotape is to provide practical information for rural women who need to enter the work force. The tape gives information to help rural women make themselves more employable in the modern job market. (Video #75438)

6. *Rebuilding Self-Esteem for Farm Women.* This videotape emphasizes the importance of a positive self-image in a time of crisis. Several farm women are interviewed about how they view their own situations. They discuss ways in which they can deal positively with their own feelings as well as help other farm family members deal with the crisis. (Video #75451)

7. *Changes on Main Street.* The impact of the farm crisis on rural businesses is the focus of this tape. Rural business people discuss how the farm crisis has affected small towns and businesses. The importance of community togetherness during the farm crisis is stressed. (Video #75452)

8. *Farm Families in Transition.* This videotape explores options for farm families who are facing forced life style changes. The tape shows several men and women who have successfully made the transition from farming to off-farm employment. Methods for dealing with the emotions of such a major life style change are presented. (Video #75453)

9. *Never the Same Again.* This video reviews the programs of the Extension Service, specifically in Iowa. The tape includes interviews with families who have been affected by the Extension Service Programs. (Video #75427)

10. *Teens Dealing with Stress.* The tape presents a more general look at teen stress, both rural and urban. Teens discuss general stress they experience and how they deal with it. (Video #75441)

REFERENCES

Agricultural and Rural Economics Division. (1986). *Public policies for displaced farmers and their families.* Unpublished report, Economic Research Service, United States Department of Agriculture, Washington, DC.

Brown, Thomas. (1986). *Cooperative extension: Helping farm families survive today and build for tomorrow.* Columbia, MO: University of Missouri, Department of Agricultural Economics.

*Cooperative extension—agricultural profitability and competitiveness: Intensive assistance for financially distressed farm families and communities.* (1987, May). Annual Survey Report, 1986, United States Department of Agriculture, Washington, DC.

# Empowering Rural Families
# and Communities*

**Robert Hughes, Jr.\*\***

Since the early 1980s there have been severe financial problems in American agriculture. In 1985 a survey of financial conditions among farmers indicated that 46% of Midwest farmers had substantial debt problems and 20% to 27% of the rest of the country's farmers reported economic problems (Schotsch, 1985). While explanations about the causes of the financial crisis abound, awareness of the human costs are just beginning to emerge.

Heffernan and Heffernan (1986) studied the impact of the farm crisis on a group of Missouri farm families. They found that members of farm families who had left farming due to economic problems experienced depression, restlessness, loss of a sense of worthiness, eating and sleeping difficulties, and other symptoms. Additionally, families reported increased substance abuse and physical aggressiveness. In a study of rural adolescents, Hoberman (1985) found that 3% had attempted suicide in the last month and that levels of depression were twice the national average.

Mermelstein and Sundet (1986) surveyed community mental health centers in the Midwest and noted that there had been significant increases in psychological distress among rural residents including depression, withdrawal/denial, substance abuse, and spouse abuse. One mental health center in rural Minnesota reported 200% to 300% increases in service utilization in the last 3 years (Ashley, 1986).

In addition to the effects of the agricultural crisis on the family, there is evidence that communities have also been impacted. Economists estimated that rural businesses and services will bear much of the farm debt (Heffernan & Heffernan, 1986). The Advisory Commission on Intergovernmental Relations (1986) reported that many counties throughout the United States are having difficulty with local taxes due to the farm recession. The Commission noted that there will be a significant deterioration in the property tax base in farm-dependent communities. They also projected that there will be reduced state aid for rural community services such as health and education.

In response to these problems there have been numerous programs developed by the Cooperative Extension Service, community mental health centers, and a variety of other community and religious organizations. These responses have been modelled on clinical, educational, self-help, and advocacy helping strategies evolving out of the particular orientation of the implementing organization. For example, the Cooperative Extension Service has taken primarily an educational approach by teaching families skills in budgeting and management

*The author wishes to convey special thanks to Cheryl Bielema, Stan Eden, Curt Eisenmayer, Bob Hayward, Deborah Pflasterer, Donna Mann, Evelyn Prasse, Harry Wright, and all of the other Illinois county advisors whose work with farm families forms the basis of this chapter. Appreciation also goes to Karen Davis-Brown, Sonya Salamon, and Karen Zotz for their comments on an earlier draft of this chapter.

**Robert Hughes, Jr. is an Assistant Professor and Extension Specialist of Family Relations in the School of Human Resources and Family Studies at the University of Illinois, 905 S. Goodwin, Urbana, IL 61801.

Reprinted from *Family Relations*, 1987, **36**, 396-401.

(Crawford, 1986). Community mental health agencies have focused on the emotional crises experienced by these families (Blundall, 1986), and farmers' organizations have addressed legislative approaches to the problem (Herrick, 1986). Recent examinations of the helping process have suggested that the method through which help is provided may be as significant as the help itself (Brickman et al., 1982). Researchers have begun to document the adverse consequences of helping efforts finding that in some cases receiving help may be more detrimental than no help at all (Brickman et al., 1982).

At present there are little evaluative data regarding the effectiveness of intervention attempts with rural families and communities. This chapter considers empowerment as a helping strategy and examines efforts to implement this strategy in Illinois. Additionally, several rural development initiatives based on empowerment principles will be proposed.

## Models of Helping

In their review of helping models, Brickman and his colleagues (1982) identify a typology which distinguishes between attributions of responsibility for a problem (who is to blame for a past event) and attribution of responsibility for a solution (who is to control future events). Four types are derived: (a) the *moral* model holds persons responsible for both problems and solutions and suggests that persons need proper motivation to improve the situation; (b) the *enlightenment* model holds persons responsible for the problem but not the solution; people are viewed as unable or unwilling to provide solutions and need discipline; (c) the *medical* model holds persons neither responsible for the problem nor the solution, but as needing treatment; and (d) the *compensatory* model does not hold persons responsible for the problems, but does hold them responsible for the solutions for which they need to be empowered. Brickman and his colleagues (1982) assert that the failure to choose the appropriate model of helping may undermine effectiveness and that different models may be more useful in specific situations. Thus, it is important to carefully consider the most appropriate approach to helping rural families and communities in crisis.

## Selecting a Helping Model for the Rural Crisis

There is little basis on which to select appropriate helping models for situations. Two central questions may begin to identify an appropriate strategy. First, what model fits the situation; that is, who is responsible for the problem and/or the solution? Second, what are the possible negative consequences of choosing a model and how do these compare to other choices?

A careful study of the agriculture crisis suggests that while farmers may have made some contribution to the economic situation, fiscal policies and other economic trends beyond an individual farmer's control were the primary cause of the problem (Bullock, 1986). Thus, it would seem inappropriate to blame farmers for the problem as the moral and enlightenment models propose.

While neither the medical nor compensatory models blame people for the problem, they make different assumptions about who should be responsible for the solution. The medical model assumes that experts are best suited to provide treatment and solutions to the rural situation, while the compensatory model allows families and communities to be responsible for the solutions. Both models have potentially adverse consequences. The compensatory model may result in alienation as people become hostile and bitter from having to solve problems that are not of their own making. On the other hand, the negative outcome of the medical model is dependency, relying on others to deal with problems.

In comparing these two consequences, the risk of alienation is preferable to dependency. In studies of helplessness, persons who believe they can control their outcomes are more likely to persist in the face of difficulties (Seligman, 1975). Additionally, the evidence indicates that dependency created by the medical model can foster increased helplessness and even result in people losing the ability to do something they once did well (Langer & Benevento, 1978).

There are some additional reasons for selecting the compensatory model. The strength of the model is that "it allows people to direct their energies outward, working on trying to solve problems or transform the environment without berating themselves for their role in creating these problems, or permitting others to create them, in the first place" (Brickman, et al., 1982, p. 372). Also, with this model persons are not blamed for their problems but are given credit for finding solutions. Indeed the help that is provided is not offered because of personal deficiencies, but rather to assist in obtaining a solution.

Despite strong reasons for selecting the compensatory model as the most appropriate strategy to assist rural families and communities, it should be noted that no approach can guarantee success or appropriateness in all cases. This is especially true since our understanding of the helping models is limited and there is little empirical data to provide direction. Nevertheless, the compensatory model fits the situation, appears less likely to undermine current functioning of families and communities, and offers potential long-range benefits.

## Empowerment Strategies

The compensatory model suggests empowerment as the strategy for providing help; therefore, it is important to examine the empowerment process in more detail. The term "empowerment" has been used by many authors to capture ideas about helping. Empowerment is generally agreed to be the attempt to "enhance the possibilities for people to control their own lives" (Rappaport, 1981, p. 15). Vanderslice (1984) broadens this idea to include the ability to "influence those people and organizations that affect their lives and the lives of those they care about" (p. 2).

The empowerment strategy rests on several assumptions. Both Rappaport (1981) and Cochran (1986b) note that empowerment is based on a non-deficit model; that is, the assumption that all individuals, families, and communities have some strengths and/or competencies and as recipients of help are not totally dysfunctional. One way in which services can provide help that implies an assumption of strengths is by not having eligibility requirements that necessitate persons demonstrate they have some type of weakness or problem in order to get help.

A second related assumption expressed by both authors is that people have valid and valuable knowledge of their own needs, values, and goals that can be put into action. This assumption suggests that "experts" are not the only source of ideas for changing or improving a situation and that helpers should respect this knowledge by assuming the role of collaborators rather than experts. For example, the collaborative helper asks, "What can we do together to address this problem?" or "How can I help?" The helper promotes mutual respect and creates opportunities for others to develop their capabilities (Cochran, 1986b; Rappaport, 1981).

A third assumption of the empowerment strategy is that diversity is useful and adaptive. Berger and Neuhaus (1977) argue that public policy should "sustain as many particularities as possible, in the hope that most people will accept, discover, or devise one that fits" (p. 44). Rappaport asserts that since situations and problems are diverse, diverse solutions will be necessary. He writes,

> Empowerment needs to be based on divergent reasoning that encourages diversity through support of many different local groups rather than the large centralized social agencies and institutions which control resources, use convergent reasoning, and attempt to standardize the ways in which people live their lives. (Rappaport, 1981, p. 19)

A fourth assumption offered by Berger and Neuhaus (1977) is that help will be most effective when provided by small, intimate social institutions. They assert that most people find meaning in their lives through their families, neighborhoods, churches, and voluntary associations and that these social institutions will be best at providing the appropriate assistance. Cochran (1986b) suggests that a critical strategy within the empowerment process is facilitating informal resource exchange among individuals and families. This strategy could be achieved by the development of support groups, helping individuals develop personal support systems, and other means of facilitating social connections. Empowerment will include efforts to strengthen social networks, neighborhoods, churches, and voluntary associations.

An additional assumption proposed by Cochran (1986a) is that empowerment can take place at several levels ranging from an individual's sense of well-being to community action. This assumption suggests that empowerment strategies may be directed towards various outcomes. Some efforts may assist people to achieve positive self-perceptions, while other efforts may focus on facilitating change-oriented community action. These strategies would at least in part depend on the current stage of the participants. Cochran and Henderson (1985) have conducted the most extensive attempt to empower parents at all of these levels.

In summary, the empowerment process is based on four assumptions that suggest criterion for examining efforts aimed at helping rural families and communities. These are: (a) recognizing and fostering strengths and competencies, (b) acknowledging and utilizing the wisdom of everyday experience, (c) promoting diversity of ideas and approaches, and (d) strengthening social networks and community institutions. Additionally, the focus of the program on individual or community change can be examined.

## Rural Programming Utilizing Empowerment

The rural crisis has prompted a variety of programs and services to address family and community issues. This section will review some Illinois programs that utilize empowerment strategies. It should be noted that some of these programs were designed using the empowerment principles as guidelines, while others arose naturally in response to concerns and issues. By studying these examples, it is possible to examine the degree to which they fit the empowerment approach, their degree of success, and the limits of these efforts.

### Families in Transition

The primary challenge of the rural crisis has been assisting families with financial difficulties that have resulted in changes in the family/business enterprise. These financial problems range from minor difficulties in meeting a few bills to major problems that are only resolved by bankruptcy and/or foreclosure. The difficulties these families face include not just economic problems, but legal, family, and personal concerns (Heffernan & Heffernan, 1986).

Rural Route, a University of Illinois Cooperative Extension program, was designed to help rural families facing transitions due to financial problems. The program included a toll-free telephone service to Extension professionals who were familiar with financial and family issues. Advising centers

were also founded and staffed by Extension staff. In setting up the program, Extension staff were encouraged to work with families in an advisory capacity. Staff were to help families understand their current situation and to consider alternative courses of action. To fulfill this advising role, the program allowed families to remain anonymous if they wished. While families were encouraged to come to the Centers, staff were willing to meet in the home if the family desired. Staff were encouraged to be supportive, but not to provide specific solutions. When the families presented legal, medical, or psychological problems that were beyond the advisor's ability, referrals to appropriate services were offered.

To what extent does Rural Route embody empowerment assumptions? First, the program makes no mention of focusing on strengths of the families. However, the program did not have deficit eligibility requirements; that is, families did not have to fit a predetermined criteria of need in order to get assistance. Any family requesting information was allowed to participate. J. C. Eisenmayer (personal communication, September 29, 1986) noted that families who merely were interested in better financial management sought advice as well as persons with serious financial difficulties. Also, the program did not offer itself solely as a crisis-oriented program; the subtitle, "Helping farm families make difficult decisions" implies a wide range of concerns. By not using need as a criteria, the program does not automatically assume that participants are devoid of strengths and abilities.

There is some evidence that the program fostered utilization of everyday knowledge and experience. Commenting on her work with families, D. J. Phflaster (personal communication, September 29, 1986) noted, "I think if you can walk them through some of their interests and capabilities and some of what they do well, then you can help them see they have qualifications to do many things besides farming." Other staff (D. M. Mann, personal communication, September 30, 1986; E. Prasse, personal communication, September 29, 1986) reported similar efforts to help families examine their own knowledge about how to address their situation.

The problem-solving approach used by advisers encourages a diversity of ideas and solutions. In the brochure describing the program, participants are repeatedly reminded that they determine the issues to be discussed and the final actions taken. For example, in answer to the question, "What will you talk about?" the answer is, "That depends on you." Also, the brochure reminds participants that the advisers "won't make your decisions and they won't sign you up for anything," suggesting that the advisers be supportive and help generate alternatives in a collaborative rather than an expert role. This aspect also suggests that diverse solutions would be acceptable. In general, the program conforms to many of the empowerment assumptions.

## Support Services for Families

In addition to financial advising, other informal helping programs for rural families in crisis have been established. Two of these efforts will be examined. The first support system program focuses on helping communities understand the rural crisis and how they can respond. After viewing a videotape of one farm family's experience of losing their farm called, "Beyond the Sale" (Hughes, 1986), community members are provided with a brief description of several types of support activities: neighboring, support groups, and peer listeners. The participants then brainstorm what, if any, type of support system might be developed in their community.

This program incorporates several empowerment principles. First, it assumes that communities have the capacity to develop effective support systems. The program presents alternatives and ideas for action as possibilities rather than as specific solutions. Rather than prescribing that all communities create a specific support response, the program encourages participants to design the most appropriate support system for their community. Thus, the program facilitator adopts a collaborative stance and demonstrates a willingness to accept diverse solutions. Lastly, the program encourages the inclusion of clergy, social service providers, and other community groups that may be able to respond to rural families in crisis, thus seeking to work with community institutions.

Another community support program for rural families is called Rural Caring, begun by farmers for farmers in response to growing concerns about their neighbors in crisis. The program organizers state, "We listen, refer people to special services, and we answer questions about assistance programs available to farmers" (About rural caring, 1986, p. 13). The program consists of volunteers trained in basic listening skills who are available via a telephone hotline. In describing the program the volunteers note, "We got started over a cup of coffee one morning. Nobody was doing anything about the problem . . . so we called a meeting and Bureau County Rural Caring grew out of that meeting" (About rural caring, 1986, p. 13). The methods used are described in such terms as "We like to be positive, to solve prob lems, not to pin blame; . . . We're going to work together . . . " (About rural caring, 1986, p. 13).

Many empowerment assumptions are evident in the description of this peer support program. There is an emphasis placed on problem solving and positive approaches to problems. Also, the development of this program by lay people suggests the recognition of the valid and valuable knowledge of individuals' experience. Volunteers were trained by clergy, counselors, and farmers and the organization of the program included Extension, Farm Bureau, a hospital, and a community mental health agency suggesting the degree to which the program is embedded in the community and reflects diverse local values.

## Communities in Transition

The decline in the agricultural economy has also affected rural America at the community level. Heffernan and Heffernan (1986) have discussed the ripple effect as agricultural suppliers and other rural businesses are impacted by farm losses. Local governments have also experienced declining revenues and there is the potential of a reduction in health and human services (Advisory Commission on Intergovernmental Relations, 1986). These changes have suggested a variety of community development needs.

One effort at community revitalization is taking place in Pike County, Illinois (C. Bielema, personal communication, September 25, 1986; Wright, 1986). A task force on rural development has been created which includes agribusiness leaders, clergy, attorneys, realtors, Extension, community college leaders, and various other business and agricultural representatives. The purpose of this group is to develop ideas for diversifying the local economy, attracting businesses, and sponsoring community development. Initial efforts have included a business showcase where local businesses displayed their products and services in an attempt to generate and share ideas about business opportunities. In discussing this initiative Wright (1986) suggested the importance of personal involvement, the development of mutual understanding, and constructive public and private partnerships. Also, this group identified and prepared citizens in the community to testify at hearings sponsored by the Governor's Task Force on Rural Illinois.

This community development strategy also embodies many empowerment assumptions. There is an emphasis on both the strengths of individuals and on those of the community. The diverse membership of the task force suggests an openness to diverse ideas and solutions. Also, proposals for partnerships and mutual understanding suggest that the community development effort needs to be a collaborative enterprise. This program is designed to empower people to create community change and influence policymakers.

## Dependent Care

Another major dilemma confronting rural families and communities is the care of young children and the elderly. Traditionally, women have cared for both the young and old. However, one of the primary ways in which rural families have recently begun to cope with lower incomes is for both husbands and wives to be employed. Current estimates suggest that about 46.7% of farm women and 51.5% of nonfarm women in rural communities are working outside the home (U.S. Department of Labor, 1984). Problems with child care are readily apparent. Shoffner (1986) reports that of those who had worked since their children were born, one third left jobs because of problems related to child care. Similarly, she notes 40% indicated that if suitable care were available, they would seek employment.

Another demographic trend in rural communities is the increasing number of elderly, with about one fourth of the nation's elderly living in rural areas (Clifford, Heaton, Voss, & Fuguitt, 1985). Townsend (1967) has reported that women provide most of the care for elderly in rural areas. Thus, the movement of farm and rural women into the paid labor force will increase the need for alternative dependent care arrangements for both the young and the elderly in rural areas.

One community's response to this problem has been to establish church-based child care (S. Salamon, personal communication, May 17, 1986). The church provided space for a day care center and subsidized utility costs so that care could be provided to rural families for a moderate fee. A significant aspect of this community-wide solution to the need for child care is the church's ability to set aside the traditional value of women as homemakers and caretakers. By compromising this tradition, the church was able to meet a critical need of families with young children and provide a place where parents could feel that other important community and religious values would be fostered.

The important empowerment principles evident in this example are the utilization of local resources and problem solving. The development of a day care center in a community that traditionally values home-based care suggests an openness to diverse ideas and solutions.

## Summary

The empowerment strategies presented illustrate some of the ways that concerns of families and communities can be addressed. It is important to note that there is currently no evaluation data to document the effectiveness of these efforts. Evaluations will not only help to determine the effects of these efforts, but may also provide information about the limits of these strategies. At present it seems unlikely that an empowerment approach would be useful for severely dysfunctional families or incapacitated communities. In these cases a medical model may be more appropriate. Finally, most of these empowerment efforts are aimed at fostering individuals' sense of well-being rather than encouraging them to engage in community or public policy change.

## An Empowerment Approach to Rural Development

Strategies for rural development have been widely discussed at the state and national level. For example, a statewide task force has been established to examine future policies and strategies that will affect rural Illinois communities (Office of the Governor, 1986). Minnesota Senator Durenberger (1986) has called for a similar task force at the federal level.

It is important to understand the recent farm crisis within the context of 20th century rural America and recent rural development efforts. Services to rural families have long been either unavailable or severely limited; the lack of health care, child care, and child abuse prevention services in rural communities has been well documented (Herwig, 1983). Difficulties faced by rural families in the 1980s only serve as a reminder of the continuing disadvantages of living in rural America.

The current need for rural development is not new. Rasmussen (1985), in a historical account of rural development, documents the many efforts to build roads, improve housing, and to provide adequate water, sewage treatment, and electricity in rural communities. While there has been much progress in developing an adequate rural infrastructure and fostering economic development, the current crisis illustrates the need for human service and human resource development. In order to overcome many of the current family and community problems, attention must be paid to the human as well as economic enterprise. Human services such as education, job training, health (including mental health), and child welfare (child care and child safety) must be targeted in development efforts. Additionally, there is a need for leadership development if human resources are going to be adequately tapped.

The empowerment strategy can provide some direction to policy-makers considering how to bring about this development. Program developers and policymakers could begin by carefully examining already existing empowerment strategies such as those described in this chapter. In some cases perhaps dissemination of strategies is all that is needed. Additionally, there are other examples of empowerment strategies that may be useful to adapt to rural families and communities. Cochran, Dean, Dill, and Woolever (1984) describe a model of home visits and family clustering that is aimed at empowering families to foster children's development. Also, Carlson (1985) developed a program to assist families in the decision-making process.

Clearly there will continue to be issues and concerns that need attention. One way to address continuing needs would be the identification and training of facilitators to enable families and communities in the utilization of empowerment principles. These facilitators would work with people to identify competencies, invite ideas, and develop plans for action. Facilitators could also work closely with community organizations to foster effective partnerships. Vanderslice (1984) provides numerous additional ideas for how facilitators can empower people.

To address more family and community development issues, more extensive efforts will be needed. A critical issue for families is education and/or job training. Perhaps what is needed is legislation similar to the GI Bill where direct cash payments would be made available to all rural families. Making this available to all families would address needs not only of those recently displaced from jobs, but of other families in rural areas. The family would be able to use the money not only for schooling, but for child care, transportation, and other family needs. This corrects some of the difficulties with current job training programs that can provide tuition-free training, but cannot provide transportation to and from the training site. Also, by enabling the family to decide how to allocate the funds, recipients are able to develop an individualized solution to their unique situation.

In order to effect rural human resource development, there must also be a strategy directed at the community level. In an analysis of the difficulties that prevent community development, Wilkinson (1986) identified "dependence" as a major problem. He noted two types of dependence that inhibit the rural community—that of small communities on larger communities for services and that of local service providers on larger centralized institutions that limit the ability to focus on local concerns.

An empowerment approach can help overcome this dependency problem. Assuming that local communities are competent and that local residents can provide valid and valuable input, greater flexibility in the design and use of resources could be a first step toward the development of appropriate services in rural communities. It will be difficult, if not impossible, to design programs to fill the gap created by the loss of businesses and services, inadequate transportation, and the numerous other needs confronting rural communities. Rather than attempt to create a universal community development program, it may be more useful to develop a rural opportunities program designed to allow all rural communities to receive financial assistance for improving their communities. Thus, rather than designing separate programs to address employment, dependent care, health and human services, general funds would be available to communities for revitalization. The community itself would decide how to allocate its resources to various community needs.

## Conclusion

This chapter has reviewed the moral, enlightenment, medical, and compensatory helping models in order to understand how help can best be provided to rural families and communities. The importance of understanding the method through which assistance is provided as well as the content was also stressed, since failure to choose an effective helping strategy may do more harm than good. With all of the attention focused on rural families in distress, it is especially important to examine existing rural services and programs to determine whether more appropriate efforts are needed.

In examining programs and services addressing concerns of rural Illinois families and communities, many were found to embody empowerment principles. This should not lead one to conclude that most attempts to address the rural crisis assume an empowerment approach. This survey was not exhaustive, and it is easy to imagine how efforts could fail to empower participants. Shortcomings such as failing to understand strengths and competencies, treating all families and communities as if they are alike, assuming families or communities are dysfunctional, or prescribing solutions without providing for participant input, are very possible. Undoubtedly, some programs have some or all of these problems.

Also, despite the fact that the empowerment strategy was the focus of this chapter, it is not the only approach to helping rural families. Some families and communities with severe problems may need to be treated utilizing the medical model. This discussion does not mean to imply that the empowerment model will solve all rural problems.

Clearly, a variety of strategies will be required.

Empowerment provides important roles for family educators and community developers. In communities there is a need for someone who understands and could teach others about the process of empowerment. No approach is going to quickly eliminate longstanding rural problems; however, the empowerment strategy provides one basis for designing potentially useful programs, services, and policies.

REFERENCES

About rural caring. (1986, July 31). *Bureau County Republican*, p.13.
Advisory Commission on Intergovernmental Relations. (1986). *The agricultural recession: Its impact on the finances of state and local governments*. Report to the United States Senate Subcommittee on Intergovernmental Relations, Washington, DC.
Ashley, A. (1986, April). *From the frontline: Perspectives on rural stress*. Paper presented at the Policy Forum on Rural Stress, Chicago.
Berger, P. L., & Neuhaus, R. J. (1977). *To empower people: The role of mediating structures in public policy*. Washington, DC: American Enterprise Institute for Public Policy Research.
Blundall, J. (1986). The initial response from a community mental health center. *Human Services in the Rural Environment*, 10, 30–31.
Brickman, P., Rabinowitz, V. C., Karuza, J., Jr., Coates, D., Cohn, E., & Kidder, L. (1982). Models of helping and coping. *American Psychologist*, 37, 368–384.
Bullock, J. B. (1986). The farm credit situation: Implications for agricultural policy. *Human Services in the Rural Environment*, 10, 12–20.
Carlson, G. (1985). *Up the road to change*. Jefferson City, MO: Missouri Cooperative Extension Service, Lincoln University.
Clifford, W. B., Heaton, T. B., Voss, P. R., & Fuguitt, G. V. (1985). The rural elderly in demographic perspective. In R. T. Coward & G. R. Lee (Eds.), *The elderly in rural society* (pp. 25–55). New York: Springer.
Cochran, M. (1986a, April). *Family matters: Evaluation of a parental empowerment process*. Paper presented at the National Extension Family Life Specialists' Workshop, Purdue University, West Lafayette, IN.
Cochran, M. (1986b). The parental empowerment process: Building on family strengths. In J. Harris (Ed.), *Child psychology in action* (pp. 12–33). Cambridge, MA: Brookline Books.
Cochran, M., Dean, C., Dill, M. S., & Woolever, S. (1984). *Empowering families: Home visiting and building clusters*. Ithaca, NY: Family Matters Project, Cornell University.
Cochran, M., & Henderson, C. R., Jr. (1985, January). *Family matters: Evaluation of the parental empowerment program*. A final report to the National Institute of Education, Ithaca, NY: Cornell University.
Crawford, C. (1986). Response to the rural crisis: Missouri Cooperative Extension Service. *Human Services in the Rural Environment*, 10, 33–35.
Durenberger, D. (1986, April). *Strategies for rural revitalization*. Paper presented at the Policy Forum on Rural Stress, Chicago.
Heffernan, W. D., & Heffernan, J. B. (1986). Impact of the farm crisis on rural families and communities. *The Rural Sociologist*, 6, 160–170.
Herrick, J. M. (1986). Farmers revolt! Contemporary farmers' protests in historical perspective: Implications for social work practice. *Human Services in the Rural Environment*, 10, 6–11.
Herwig, J. E. (1983). Young children and their families: Rural community needs and expectations. In R. T. Coward & W. M. Smith, Jr. (Eds.), *Family services: Issues and opportunities in contemporary rural America* (pp. 135–149). Lincoln, NE: University of Nebraska Press.

Hoberman, H. (1986, April). *Depression and suicide among rural adolescents.* Paper presented at the Policy Forum for Rural Stress, Chicago.

Hughes, R., Jr. (1986). *Beyond the sale: Farm family stress and coping.* Urbana, IL: Cooperative Extension Service, University of Illinois.

Langer, E. J., & Benevento, A. (1978). Self-induced dependence. *Journal of Personality and Social Psychology, 36,* 886–893.

Mermelstein, J., & Sundet, P. A. (1986). Rural community mental health centers' responses to the farm crisis. *Human Services in the Rural Environment, 10,* 21–26.

Office of the Governor. (1986, March). *Task force on the future of rural Illinois.* Springfield, IL.

Rappaport, J. (1981). In praise of paradox: A social policy of empowerment over prevention. *American Journal of Community Psychology, 9,* 1–25.

Rasmussen, W. D. (1985). 90 years of rural development programs. *Rural Development Perspectives, 12,* 2–9.

Schotsch, L. (1985). Who will farm in five years? *Farm Journal,* **109,** 13–15.

Seligman, M.E.P. (1975). *Helplessness.* San Francisco: Freeman Press.

Shoffner, S. M. (1986). Child care in rural areas: Needs, attitudes, and preferences. *American Journal of Community Psychology,* **14,** 521–539.

Townsend, P. (1967). *The family life of old people.* Glencoe, IL: Free Press.

U.S. Department of Labor, Bureau of Labor Statistics. (1984, April). *Employment and earnings.* Washington, DC: U.S. Government Printing Office.

Vanderslice, V. (1984). *Communication for empowerment.* Ithaca, NY: Family Matters Project, Cornell University.

Wilkinson, K. P. (1986). In search of community in the changing countryside. *Rural Sociology, 51,* 1–17.

Wright, H. (1986, September 24). Take a look at "local dinosaurs." *The Pike Press,* p. B-6.

# Policy Implications Derived from a Study of Rural and Urban Marriages*

**John Scanzoni and Cynthia Arnett\*\***

Based on an extensive literature review, as well as on their own empirical research, Schumm and Bollman (1981) conclude:

> Policy makers and human service professionals responsible for the delivery of rural family programs do not have the benefit of adequate research findings. However, it remains to be demonstrated that primary family relationships differ in any consistent, substantial manner from rural to urban areas. (p. 140)

Schumm and Bollman are arguing that rural family professionals have no firm empirical basis on which to plan services and programs that would be uniquely different from programs and services addressed to urban families. Nonetheless, some observers contend that rural farm families "have, when compared to nonfarm families, some unusual but potentially powerful relationship stressors" (Rosenblatt & Anderson, 1981, p. 163). The unique stresses facing farm families appear to stem chiefly from the fact that because family members work together, they may actually experience "too much" togetherness (Rosenblatt & Anderson, 1981;

Rosenfeld, 1985). Thus work-related conflicts among those family members may spill over on to socioemotional matters.

However, given the well-known demographic data showing that the proportion of farm families (i.e., both adults working solely on the farm and having no other employment) facing such work-related issues is declining (Brown, 1981), professionals increasingly tend to deal largely with rural nonfarm families (i.e., one or both partners drawing significant levels of total family income from the paid labor force) for which the Schumm and Bollman (1981) proposition may have some relevance. Thus the research question posed by Schumm and Bollman is, "How different/similar are rural (nonfarm) families as compared to urban families?" As Bescher-Donnelly and Smith (1981) put it, " 'Farm wife' is not synonymous with 'rural woman,' and the roles and responsibilities of women in rural areas today are . . . complex and diversified" (p. 167). Consequently, one objective of this chapter is to contribute information to the broad question of actual rural/urban family differences in order to enhance the work of family professionals.

In addition, a second and inherently related objective of this chapter is to address the issues raised by Bescher-Donnelly and Smith (1981). They indicate that in spite of voluminous literature on sex role changes in the United States, as well as a growing literature on rural families, "comparatively little attention has been given to the rural woman and her changing roles and status in society" (p. 167). The literature that is available suggests that "rural women appear to be maintaining a more [compared to urban

*This research was supported by NCARS Project 13838. Paper No. 10728 of the Journal Series of the North Carolina Agricultural Research Service, Raleigh, NC 27695-7601. The authors wish to thank Deborah Godwin for statistical consultation in the preparation of this chapter.

**John Scanzoni is Professor of Sociology, University of Florida, Gainesville, FL 32611. Cynthia Arnett is Vice President of Working Family, Inc., Greensboro, NC 27412.

Reprinted from *Family Relations*, 1987, **36**, 430-436.

women] traditional sex-role ideology" (p. 169). Based on that conclusion, they indicate that

> Social policy designed to improve the social and economic conditions of rural women should be directed toward changing both the structural conditions and the traditional sex-role ideology that restrict both males and females in their life situations. Resocialization techniques and institutional restructuring procedures must be developed to permit both [rural] men and women to choose role options most appropriate to their needs, preferences, and ability, without inhibitions based on sex-role stereotypes. (pp. 180–181)

Rural family professionals not only need information regarding how rural and urban families diverge/converge in general, they also need information on the related question that has become so pervasive within the literatures of family studies, sociology, and marriage and family therapy: "In what ways are women and men similar or different whether residing in rural or urban areas?" These two objectives overlap. First, to consider relevant differences between rural/urban families inevitably means examining differences between men and women. It is those normative and behavioral differences between the sexes, whether in rural or urban areas, that tend to place most United States women at substantial socioeconomic disadvantages compared to most men (Bescher-Donnelly & Smith, 1981). Second, to consider relevant differences between women and men inevitably means considering rural/urban residence in order to determine if rural women are potentially liable to even greater disadvantages than are United States women in general.

The final objective of this chapter is to derive specific policy implications from the results reported. These implications consist of suggested programs and services, as well as potential clinical strategies.

## Procedures

### Sampling and Data Collection

Respondents for the study were obtained by means of stratified random sampling techniques from a county located in a Standard Metropolitan Statistical Area (SMSA) and also from a county bordering the SMSA and defined as rural by the Census Bureau. Table 1 describes selected characteristics of the samples by sex. Respondents from both samples are clustered in their mid-30s and have been married approximately 11 years. Both samples (especially the rural) are overwhelmingly white. The samples diverge in terms of education with rural persons having fewer years of schooling. Urban males also have higher annual incomes than rural males. There is a somewhat higher percentage of rural wives who are employed, and they also work more hours per week. However, rural employed wives receive relatively less for their efforts than do urban employed wives (the ratio of hours worked per week to mean annual income is 650 for urban wives and only 572 for rural wives; the range of incomes for rural wives extends from $2,760 to $30,732, and among urban wives the upper figure is $41,652). Moreover, 8% of rural men are unemployed, as compared with only 2% of urban men. These economic realities, along with the finding that employed rural men earn fewer dollars, probably creates greater economic pressure on rural women to seek employment and to pursue it somewhat more extensively. Furthermore, the mean number of children is larger in rural households, indicating that whatever dollars are earned must be stretched to care for greater numbers of persons.

Initial contact with potential respondents was made by letter asking them to participate in a broad-based research project. They were then contacted by phone to screen for sample eligibility. The wife had to be under age 40, the spouses had to be residing together, and both had to agree to participate. Upon meeting these criteria, an appointment was made for an interviewer to go to the couple's home. Husbands and wives completed identical questionnaires in separate rooms while being monitored to ensure noncollusion.

Since no economic incentives were offered, it was not an easy task to obtain cooperation simultaneously from both spouses. When one spouse was willing the other often was not, thus making it impossible to gather data from either one. Even when willing, coordination of times when both spouses could be together simultaneously always proved difficult to manage.

Table 1.
*Selected Characteristics of Rural and Urban Samples, by Spouse*

| | Husbands | | Wives | |
|---|---|---|---|---|
| | Urban | Rural | Urban | Rural |
| Age[a] | 36.3 | 35.1 | 33.8 | 33.0 |
| Years of education[a] | 15.3 | 14.6 | 14.5 | 13.9 |
| Years married[a] | 11.2 | 10.9 | 11.2 | 10.9 |
| Percent white | 88 | 95 | 88 | 95 |
| Annual income[a] | $33,008[b] | $30,614[b] | $14,361[b] | $15,616[b] |
| Hours worked per week[a] | 46.4[b] | 42.0[b] | 22.1[b] | 27.3[b] |
| Children in household[a] | 1.5 | 1.8 | 1.5 | 1.8 |
| Percent employed | 98 | 92 | 64 | 72 |
| *n* | (164) | (61) | (164) | (61) |

[a]Mean scores.
[b]Among those employed.

Couples in the rural county were particularly suspicious and hesitant to cooperate. In spite of these difficulties an overall 43% response rate among eligible couples was obtained (55% for the urban county; 17% for the rural county). Based on their exhaustive review of studies utilizing both husbands and wives, Hiller and Philliber (1985) conclude that whenever the simultaneous cooperation of two persons from the same household is required, it is always more difficult to obtain as high a response rate as compared to samples requiring cooperation from only one person.

Demographically, these two samples are more alike than they are different. Their ages and years married are quite comparable. They are different where expected—in terms of education and husbands' earnings. In addition, the differences for women's labor force activity are also predictable given greater rural male unemployment and lower earnings for both sexes. The somewhat higher fertility of rural couples is also expected. The finding that the mean levels of education for both samples are higher than those found in the general population suggests that in this study, as in most studies where no economic incentives are offered, the less well-educated are more likely to refuse to participate (Hiller & Philliber, 1985). Had more persons with less education been included in both samples, the findings reported in this chapter would likely be stronger than they are at present. This speculation is particularly salient given the positive association between education and gender role modernity (Scanzoni & Fox, 1980). The less well-educated are more gender role traditional, and since rural persons tend to be less well-

educated, they are likely to be more role traditional. Consequently, more representative samples would very likely include less educated persons, hence adding increased validity both to this study's conclusions and its policy suggestions.

## Measures

The present authors, following Scanzoni and Fox (1980), assume the existence of an underlying construct called gender role modernity/traditionalism. This construct lies on a continuum, one pole of which represents preferences for strict role *specialization* according to traditional patterns, while the other pole represents preferences for comprehensive role *interchangeability* according to *contemporary* or modern patterns. Measures of gender role preferences were borrowed from Scanzoni and Szinovacz (1980). This broad construct may be assessed by four measures of each of the roles found in dual-adult households—wife, husband, mother, father. Items were measured in Likert fashion. Measures of three dimensions of locus of control of one's marriage were adapted from Levenson (1974) and from Walkey (1979). The three dimensions are: perceiving the control of one's marriage to be in *self*; perceiving locus of marital control to reside in luck, fate, or chance; perceiving marital control to lie with spouse. Each item on these three scales was measured by asking respondents "how true" each item was on a scale of zero to six. The measure of conflict resolution was taken from Rands, Levinson, and Mellinger (1981) and was based on the respondent's perceptions of spouse's behaviors during conflict/negotiation. Each item was measured on a scale from zero to six—describes spouse "very well" to "not at all." The measure of love/caring was taken from Rubin (1970) and further adapted by Steck, Levinson, and Kelley (1982). Each item was assessed by the respondent on a scale from zero to six—"very true" to "not true at all." Religious devoutness was measured by a Guttman-type scale borrowed from Pollock and Finn (1984). Respondents were asked "how often" they did a "certain activity" or had a particular "religious feeling." Authors of the Pollock and Finn (1984) study (a national probability sample including rural women and men) report that the measure of devoutness was the single strongest predictor in terms of accounting for variation over a wide range of values, norms, and behaviors pertaining to marriage and family. The measure of marital commitment was a single item from Spanier's (1976) Dyadic Adjustment Scale. Although the item was taken from the dyadic satisfaction subscale and although satisfaction and commitment are not equivalent, the use of this single item is justified to measure commitment if one defines commitment in Becker's (1960) terms as a *bet* on the future. According to Becker, if one perceives that the rewards of pursuing a course of action outweigh the costs, one will determine to follow that course vigorously and indefinitely on into the future. In effect, that is commitment. Spanier's item is well-suited to measure that formal definition. Respondents were asked to make a single choice from an array of op-

tions regarding how they felt about the future of their "relationship" with their spouse. The item measured if respondents perceived enough rewards in their relationships to keep working at them. Table 2 displays descriptions of this array of measures.

## Results

Following McCall (1970), Tables 3 and 4 present the results of two multiple analyses of variance.[1] In Table 3 urban/rural residence is the criterion variable. Sex of respondent is included in the calculations as a type of control variable to discover if being male or female moderates or influences the consequences of rural/urban residence. Children present and length of marriage are added for the same reason. The significance levels for the series of one-way ANOVAs in row 1 reveal that rural persons have significantly fewer years of education than urban persons. Significant differences also appear on the father gender role and the husband gender role—urban persons are more modern than rural persons. Conflict resolution is perceived more positively by rural than by urban persons, and rural persons are more devout than urban persons.

The results of the MANOVA presented in Table 3 answer the question, "How different are rural from urban persons taking into account as a whole all of the dimensions in Table 3?"[2] The first criterion answering that question is the Wilks test reported in

Table 2.
*Reliability Coefficients (alpha), Means, and Standard Deviations for All Persons in Rural and Urban Samples*

| | Alpha | Mean | | Standard Deviation | |
| | | Males | Females | | |
| | (n = 450) | (n = 225) | (n = 225) | Males | Females |
|---|---|---|---|---|---|
| Gender Role Preferences | | | | | |
| Role of Mother | 77 | 14.21 | 15.47 | 4.84 | 4.81 |
| Role of Husband | 57 | 13.23 | 13.94 | 2.74 | 2.92 |
| Role of Wife | 73 | 14.48 | 14.45 | 3.19 | 3.65 |
| Role of Father | 81 | 14.21 | 16.84 | 4.80 | 5.19 |
| Locus of Marital Control | | | | | |
| In Spouse | 71 | 10.32 | 9.13 | 5.71 | 5.85 |
| In Self | 68 | 17.41 | 19.23 | 5.32 | 4.68 |
| In Fate | 70 | 4.37 | 4.84 | 4.25 | 4.26 |
| Marital Conflict Resolution | 85 | 35.95 | 38.00 | 10.59 | 11.01 |
| Love/Caring | 89 | 63.47 | 62.33 | 9.00 | 10.62 |
| Religious Devoutness | 89 | 14.52 | 15.84 | 6.61 | 6.67 |
| Marital Commitment | a | 0.75 | 1.04 | 0.66 | 0.72 |

[a]*Alpha not calculable; see text.*

Table 3.
*Univariate and MANOVA Comparisons Between Urban and Rural Residents on Selected Family Variables.*
(mean scores)[a]

| | URBAN | | RURAL | | Signifi-cance Level | Standardized Discriminant Function Coefficient |
|---|---|---|---|---|---|---|
| | N = 328 | Standard Deviation | N = 122 | Standard Deviation | | |
| Education | 14.9 | (2.0) | 14.2 | (1.9) | .01 | .43 |
| Wife Role | 14.5 | (3.6) | 14.3 | (3.0) | ns | -.13 |
| Father Role | 15.9 | (5.3) | 14.5 | (4.7) | .02 | .27 |
| Mother Role | 14.9 | (5.0) | 14.7 | (4.4) | ns | -.42 |
| Husband Role | 13.8 | (2.9) | 13.0 | (2.7) | .01 | .27 |
| Locus Self | 18.4 | (4.9) | 18.1 | (5.5) | ns | .08 |
| Locus Luck | 4.5 | (4.0) | 5.0 | (4.8) | ns | -.27 |
| Locus Spouse | 9.8 | (5.8) | 9.7 | (5.9) | ns | .04 |
| Love/Caring | 62.6 | (9.4) | 63.8 | (10.9) | ns | -.33 |
| Conflict Resolution | 36.3 | (10.9) | 38.7 | (10.6) | .04 | -.36 |
| Marital Commitment | 0.87 | (.69) | 0.95 | (.74) | ns | -.44 |
| Religious Devoutness | 14.6 | (6.8) | 16.5 | (6.0) | .01 | -.42 |
| Length of Marriage | 11.2 | (5.1) | 11.0 | (5.3) | ns | .20 |
| Children Present | 0.17 | (0.38) | 0.15 | (0.36) | ns | .18 |
| Sex of Respondent | 0.5 | (0.5) | 0.5 | (0.5) | ns | .19 |

Wilks test = .93.
*$p < .001$.
[a]The higher the score, the greater the: education; degree of modernity on the roles of wife, father, mother, husband; locus of marital control in self, luck, or spouse; love/caring; positive conflict resolution; marital commitment; religious devoutness; years married. High score means children present and female respondents.

Table 3; rural and urban persons regardless of sex are indeed significantly different from each other.

Having established that rural/urban persons are distinctive considering the array of variables as a whole, the next issue is, "What are the specific ways in which they are the most different?" "What variables in Table 3 are more powerful than any of the others as far as their capabilities of discriminating between rural/urban persons are concerned?" In the last column of Table 3 the strongest *positive* standardized coefficients are with education, the father role, and the husband role.

Based on these three coefficients, the conclusion is that rural/urban persons are distinguished from each other most strongly in terms of education, with urban persons having significantly higher mean levels of schooling. Second, rural/urban persons are substantially different in terms of preferences for both the husband and father roles. From the reported mean differences, it appears that rural persons are more traditional than urban persons on these two roles. Finally, based on McCall (1970), the variables with negative coefficients in Table 3 contribute little if anything to rural/urban dif-

ferences. Instead they actually add strength to the conclusion that the three positive coefficients do discriminate importantly between rural/urban persons.[3]

Table 4 asks the question, "How different are women from men?" In Table 4 sex of respondent becomes the criterion variable, but county is included in the calculation to discover if being rural or urban moderates or influences the consequences of sex. The Table 4 ANOVAs for the four gender roles reveal that women are significantly more modern than men on three of the four dimensions, the wife role being sole exception. Significant one-way differences also appear on the locus of marital control in spouse variable, on perceptions of degree of positive conflict resolution, on marital commitment, on religious devoutness, and strongly on education. The Wilks test reveals that taking all of the variables in Table 4 into account as a whole, women do indeed differ significantly from men, regardless of county.

The strength of two of the positive standardized coefficients reveals that education (men are better educated) and the wife role are both powerful discriminators between women and men. According to McCall (1970), that is the proper conclusion even though

Table 4.
*Univariate and MANOVA Comparisons Between Women and Men on Selected Family Variables.* (mean scores)[a]

| | MEN | | WOMEN | | Signifi-cance Level | Standardized Discriminant Function Coefficient |
| | N = 225 | Standard Deviation | N = 225 | Standard Deviation | | |
|---|---|---|---|---|---|---|
| Education | 15.1 | (1.8) | 14.3 | (2.2) | .001 | .52 |
| Wife Role | 14.5 | (3.2) | 14.4 | (3.7) | ns | .40 |
| Father Role | 14.2 | (4.8) | 16.8 | (5.2) | .001 | -.67 |
| Mother Role | 14.2 | (4.8) | 15.5 | (4.8) | .01 | -.22 |
| Husband Role | 13.2 | (2.7) | 13.9 | (2.9) | .01 | -.21 |
| Locus Self | 17.4 | (5.3) | 19.2 | (4.7) | .001 | -.42 |
| Locus Luck | 4.4 | (4.2) | 4.8 | (4.3) | ns | -.21 |
| Locus Spouse | 10.3 | (5.7) | 9.1 | (5.8) | .03 | .12 |
| Love/Caring | 63.5 | (9.0) | 62.3 | (10.6) | ns | .12 |
| Conflict Resolution | 35.9 | (10.6) | 38.0 | (11.0) | .04 | -.22 |
| Marital Commitment | 0.75 | (.66) | 1.03 | (.72) | .001 | -.32 |
| Religious Devoutness | 14.5 | (6.6) | 15.8 | (6.7) | .04 | -.50 |
| Length of Marriage | 11.1 | (5.1) | 11.2 | (5.1) | ns | .03 |
| Children Present | 0.17 | (0.38) | 0.16 | (0.36) | ns | .15 |
| County of Residence | 0.27 | (0.45) | 0.27 | (0.45) | ns | .09 |

Wilks test = .75.
*$p < .001$.
[a]The higher the score, the greater the: education; degree of modernity on the roles of wife, father, mother, husband; locus of marital control in self, luck, or spouse; love/caring; positive conflict resolution; marital commitment; religious devoutness; years married. High score means children present and rural resident.

the one-way ANOVA difference on the wife role was not significant.[4] In effect the four highly intercorrelated gender role dimensions are all tapping the same underlying construct—how egalitarian does the respondent prefer women and men to be?[5] The MANOVA picks out of the four role dimensions the one variable that in the presence of the remaining three gender roles best discriminates between women and men. Hence, it may safely be concluded that the sexes are substantially different—women prefer egalitarianism more strongly than men. The remaining positive coefficients in Table 4 (love/caring, locus of control in spouse) lag in strength far behind education and the wife role, while the series of negative coefficients in Table 4 suggest that education and the wife role have even more powerful effects than their positive Table 4 coefficients suggest.

## Conclusions and Applications

Application of these findings begins with the proposition that rural (nonfarm) men and women do differ in what Schumm and Bollman (1981) call a "substantial manner" from urban men and women. At the same time, it is equally clear that women and men also differ from each other in a substantial manner regardless of residence. Urban

women differ from their men, and rural women differ from their men. Connecting these two conclusions is a third, namely that the "substantial manner" differentiating between these two categories of persons is quite similar and comparable. Years of education, for instance, has a major effect in distinguishing between rural and urban persons, as well as between women and men: Urban persons are better educated than rural persons, and men are better educated than women. Bescher-Donnelly and Smith (1981) concur with these findings by suggesting that not only do rural people "lag behind their urban counterparts in virtually all areas of educational attainment . . . rural women are more educationally disadvantaged than their urban counterparts" (p. 175). They go on to state that limited education hinders the opportunities of rural women to participate effectively in the paid labor force, thus also limiting the levels of economic inputs they are able to make to their families. These limitations, disadvantages, and inequities can be seen in the findings that even though rural wives work a few more hours per week than urban wives, they actually earn fewer dollars than do urban wives in spite of their increased efforts. Since rural wives are less well-educated, they very likely work at lower status, lower-paying jobs than urban wives.

The related issue, differences in

preferences for gender role traditionalism, raised by Bescher-Donnelly and Smith (1981) is virtually equal in power and significance with education. Rural persons emerge as more traditional than urban persons on both dimensions of male behaviors, the father and husband roles. These same kinds of conclusions are reported by Fink (1986) in her recent study of Iowa rural nonfarm and farm families. Concomitantly, in this study men emerge as more traditional than women, with the wife role dimension being representative of males' gender traditionalism in general.

These differences in education and gender role traditionalism occur while taking into account other vital matters such as marital love/caring, marital commitment, conflict resolution evaluation, locus of marital control, and religious devoutness. In short, while there are several kinds of univariate differences between rural/urban persons (e.g., religious devoutness) and also between women and men (e.g., devoutness again, but also marital commitment, conflict resolution evaluation, locus of marital control in self and in spouse), given the MANOVA procedure, these kinds of dimensions do not seem to matter as greatly (their relative importance is less) as do education and degree of gender role traditionalism in distinguishing between rural and urban persons and between women and men.

## General Policy and Specific Programs and Services

The issue of "relative importance" becomes the basis for guiding the family professional in planning programs and services. First, it seems that in several basic respects (locus of control measures, marital commitment, love/caring) rural and urban persons are quite comparable. Moreover, rural persons report a more positive score than urban persons on the conflict resolution measures. Thus while educational and clinical programs focusing on marital communication and enrichment are vital for rural couples, those dimensions are not what primarily distinguish them from urban couples. And while rural persons are more religiously devout than urban persons, the standardized coefficients in Tables 3 and 4 reveal that in conjunction with other variables, religion is not a major distinguishing characteristic. To be sure, the literature (D'Antonio, 1983) reports that religious

devoutness and role traditionalism are positively associated, but given the emotionally charged character of contemporary United States religion, the family professional would be hard-pressed to design programs minimizing gender role stereotyping by seeking to critique traditional religious values. Instead a general policy aimed at overcoming rural women's disadvantages can be pursued which by comparison is emotionally much less controversial and much more effective. Notions of educational opportunity, as well as greater economic equality for all persons, are after all *conservative* values in the classic American sense.

According to Naisbitt (1984), effective specific programs are derived from a broad-based general policy, a policy that identifies a vision of what are desirable ends. Hence the family professional might adopt what could be called the education/gender role policy for rural persons. This general policy is based on a resolution passed by a national conference stating, "The President and Congress should establish a federal rural education policy designed to overcome inequalities in opportunities available to rural women and girls" (Bescher-Donnelly & Smith, 1981, p. 181). For purposes of this education/gender role policy, rural women's education is defined very broadly to include information on "a wide variety of social issues, including personal growth and development" (Bescher-Donnelly & Smith, 1981, p. 176). Given the high empirical correlation between years of formal education and gender role modernity (Scanzoni & Fox, 1980), it would appear that in planning programs, as well as clinical strategies, the family professional needs simultaneously to stress increased formal education as well as less stereotypical role preferences. These two objective and subjective dimensions appear to "feed forward" on each other over time. If one or the other is missing from specific programs aimed at rural (or urban) persons, then conditions exist which are less than necessary and sufficient to achieve general policy goals aimed at overcoming the social and economic inequalities to which Bescher-Donnelly and Smith refer.

Specific programs to assist rural persons in developing less traditional gender roles and more positive views towards formal education could be age-graded. A life span approach takes into account differing specific emphases stemming from the more general education/gender role policy. For example, commencing with preschoolers specific programs would be developed by family professionals to assist parents, churches, day care workers, and others to value and use nonsexist toys, play, and clothing. Picture books and reading materials would emphasize that, both at their current ages and as adults, boys and girls need not be excluded from important realms just because of sex: Boys can perceive that being nurturant and caring are highly desirable characteristics. In fact, observations of preschool boys reveal that they do appear naturally to be quite nurturant (Pitcher & Schultz, 1983). Building on that base, specific programs can develop the theme further to make the point that boys can look forward to being meaningfully involved in parenting. Concomitantly, boys and girls can learn to accept the desirability of girls and women becoming involved in meaningful employment. The point of seeking to influence male as well as female attitudes even at this early age is that (based on Table 4 results) to the degree that males shift their orientations and behaviors, to that extent will it be less difficult for girls and women to attain the benefits of increased education and gender role equality.

Those same premises and strategies carry over into program planning and services for grade school and preteen children. During these years children are becoming involved in numerous organizations in rural (as well as urban) areas, and in some of these at least (e.g., 4-H, extension, churches, scouts, etc.) family professionals have a certain degree of influence. This influence can be exercised to promote endorsement of the above general policy and to plan specific programs accordingly. For example, it is during this period when boys tend to suppress the nurturing characteristics of preschool years and begin to assume certain stereotypical masculine (macho) traits, many of which are negative in terms of achieving the larger policy goals stated above. Clinicians, educators, and program planners can devise delivery services to assist parents, teachers, and others to help both boys and girls maintain nurturant and expressive characteristics, while at the same time developing positive strength-type characteristics. In that same vein, family professionals (teachers, professionals who are also citizens) can make their influence felt by helping to shape

public school curricula. While the schools and the organizations cited above have moved away to some degree from pervasive traditional gender stereotyping, there has been little effort by most family professionals and clinicians to endorse and adopt a broad-based education/gender role policy from which might flow innovative programs both outside and inside the schools encouraging less traditional gender stereotyping and concomitantly increased years of formal schooling.

Endorsing such a general policy not only for children, but also for adolescents and adults (discussed below), raises an important issue. Specifically, Bescher-Donnelly and Smith (1981) caution that such a policy could not ignore the reality that "many rural women may choose to follow the traditional 'feminine' behavior patterns and will be content in their roles as wives and mother" (p. 181). While the family professional, they say, should affirm the validity of that traditional option, the professional might couch the above education/gender role policy in terms of the needs of many other rural women who "may wish to choose additional options or alternatives in some or all of the life sectors now limited almost exclusively to males" (p. 181). In short, it is not that the family professional wishes to transform rural into urban persons or women into men merely for the sake of doing so or for purely ideological reasons. Instead, the basic issues are exposing persons to a greater range of options and providing access to those options so that rural women, men, and children have greater opportunities from which to choose among the varieties of life styles currently more readily available to urban persons.

Programs for rural adolescents would benefit particularly from an explicit education/gender role policy. For example, programs designed to teach sexuality currently tend to be focused on the problem of avoiding pregnancy. Family life education programs now tend to focus more on the sorts of variables identified above such as love/caring, commitment, conflict resolution—that is, marital communication and enrichment. If both sexuality programs and family life programs could be placed into a broader policy context, specific program decisions might be weighted somewhat differently. Recent studies for instance (Herzog & Bachman, 1982; Leuptow, 1984) show that

United States adolescents remain quite traditional (especially rural adolescents who are not college bound) regarding male/female roles in spite of all the larger societal changes around them. Paid employment for married women/mothers still tends to be viewed by adolescents in contingency terms—as an option—in spite of evidence supplied by Weitzman (1985) and others that high rates of marital instability severely undermine the economic well-being of mothers and their children. Based on the above general policy, it would be quite reasonable for professionals to plan specific programs for rural adolescents as well as provide them with counseling built on the premise that *women no longer have the option not to be economically self-sufficient.* Simultaneously, that particular program emphasis would help strengthen the implementation of adolescent sexuality programs in which the premises are no longer merely *negative* (avoid pregnancy) but which instead are *positive*—take control of one's sexual and reproductive life so that one is able to fully explore all possible options (e.g., increased formal education) thus furthering personal autonomy and economic self-sufficiency. Based on that same general policy, concrete programs/counseling aimed at adolescents and single young adults would be designed around the notion that if one considers romantic involvement/partnership/marriage, one should explicitly probe for the other person's gender role preferences, including views on women's employment and child care matters.

In that same vein, national policymakers are now wondering how to deal with the welfare dependence of young women with children living in rural (as well as urban) areas. The solutions proposed tend, in the main, to be economically and materially based. Frequently mentioned, for instance, are programs encouraging these women's immediate employment and job training. Less stress is placed on generating opportunities for increased formal education and none on the gender role issue. Such programs operate largely without benefit of an overall guiding vision or policy. However, if family professionals endorse the above general policy, then it follows that matters of rural women's poverty cannot solely be a material question. Their current poverty flows in part from a set of traditional gender arrangements that effectively blocks their full participation in the economic opportunity structure (Fink, 1986). Thus while designing programs and while providing counseling addressing rural women in poverty, the family professional would broach the fundamental question of how to alter gender role stereotypes so that women are encouraged to pursue their own development and men are encouraged to participate with them in that pursuit.

Given the traditionalism with which many rural (and urban) couples commence their marriage, it is clear that when family professionals/counselors shift their attention to currently married persons, the stakes become high indeed. Quite apart from program intervention, the literature (Gerson, 1985; Scanzoni, 1978) shows that over time many women who began their marriages in traditional fashion tend to change towards a less traditional direction. Women, for example, may wish to become employed and/or return to school. Concomitantly, they implicitly or explicitly request that their husbands become more involved in routine household tasks and/or child care. As women change, their husbands may become threatened, and thus the love/caring aspects of the relationship may be undermined. Consequently, derived from the above policy, professionals/counselors need to design specific "resocialization techniques ... [aimed at] both men and women" (Bescher-Donnelly & Smith, 1981, p. 181). The techniques might include, for instance, specific focus on the ways and means of carrying out effective joint decision making (Scanzoni & Szinovacz, 1980). Gerson (1985) shows that working wives and their husbands spend large amounts of time throughout their marriages struggling together over numerous issues related to wives' employment. The rationale for involving couples (younger, as well as mid-life) in programs/counseling aimed at their becoming effective joint decision makers is derived from the general policy. Apart from this policy men and women who are caught up in these employment-related changes may fail to grasp that there is no alternative for them but to maintain what Raush (1977) calls a continuing "commitment to negotiation" (p. 182). Failing to grasp that point may lead men especially to want to fall back on traditional practical solutions based on male headship.

The issue of rural married couples struggling over gender roles and economic production behaviors has become especially salient of late owing to numerous farm mortgage foreclosures. The traumatic shift from farm to rural nonfarm family status has been accompanied by these mostly white wives/mothers often having to assume unfamiliar (either co- or sole) provider roles. Similarly, husbands have been forced to take on unfamiliar responsibilities for housework and child care. Not only do clinicians and professionals contemplating delivery services and programs for these stressed families face difficult challenges, they also have a historically unique opportunity to devise specific programs and therapies based on the above general policy. Family professionals are working with a particular population that has been economically devastated by a system that essentially provided no independent and autonomous economic activity for wives (Fink, 1986; Rosenfeld, 1985). Wives have been forced into an unwanted behavioral egalitarianism for which they do not possess the requisite supporting subjective orientations. Consequently, based on the general policy, one task of the professional is to gently guide them into adapting egalitarian orientations so that the stress caused by the dissonance between their behaviors and beliefs diminishes. Moreover, changes within this adult population can function as a vivid case study for their own children and for other rural persons in general. The point being made keenly is that the greater the opportunities for rural women to participate independently in the opportunity system, the less likely it is for rural families to become economically devastated and the greater their overall economic and social well-being.

## Summary

Reported data reveal substantial differences between rural/urban persons and between women and men within both locales both in terms of formal education and also gender role preferences. Evidence was also found for strong similarities between rural/urban persons in terms of marital commitment and love/caring. Assuming that reported differences directly penalize women, and that failing to fulfill their potential is ultimately harmful to men and children as well, a broad-based policy is suggested endorsing both formal education and gender role equality and role interchangeability. From this general policy or "vision" family profes-sionals/educators/counselors/clergy and so forth can derive specific programs addressing particular needs of rural persons at various points throughout the life span. While acknowledging the preferences of some rural persons to maintain traditional arrangements, rapidly shifting agricultural and economic conditions suggest that programs and delivery systems explicitly spell out to rural (and urban) persons the risks inherent in maintaining those traditional arrangements. Concomitantly, the potential benefits to adults, children, and to society as a whole of adopting a fresh gender and education policy would also be programmatically addressed.

### END NOTES

1. A *two-way* or *two-factor MANOVA* was calculated prior to examining the effects of county and the effects of sex. This procedure tests for any possible interaction effects between the predictor variables of county and sex. The result of this test produced a nonsignificant ($p < .501$) Wilks score indicating no interaction effects between county and sex. One predictor variable is not dependent on, or interacting with, the other predictor variable. Thus it becomes valid to examine the consequences of each predictor separately.

2. One could stop with the results of those *one-way ANOVAs* but McCall (1970) cautions that "separate univariate analyses must be interpreted with the tacit assumption that each response occurs independently of every other response" (p. 1367). In the case of Table 3, the "unspoken assumption" is that every one of the row variables is actually separate from every other one (i.e., locus of marital control does not affect gender role, love/caring is not affected by education, conflict resolution does not affect marital commitment, and so forth). However, in the "real world" of families, all of these types of elements become activated together, each affecting the other continually over time. As McCall (1970) puts it, the assumption that those elements are actually separate is "untenable because responses cannot usually be extricated from their behavioral context without denuding them of much of their meaning" (p. 1367).

3. According to McCall (1970) negative coefficients are "suppressor" variables which reduce the capability of the positive coefficients to predict rural/urban differences. If the effects of those suppressor variables are "subtracted out by weighing [them] ... negatively, then the predictive power of ... [the positive coefficients] is sharpened" (p. 1369). In effect what each of the negative coefficients in Table 3 tells is, first, that they actually contribute little if anything to rural/urban differences, and second, they actually underscore the strength of the variables that do discriminate. The suppressor variables in the equation detract from the strength of the positive coefficients. If the suppressor variables were not present, the positive coefficients would presumably be stronger than they now appear.

4. McCall (1970) warns that "it would [be] misleading to conclude on the basis of ... [nonsignificant] univariate analyses alone" that the measure of the wife role is not related to "sex of respondent" (p. 1372).

5. Correlations for all cases combined of *father* role with: *wife* role = .48; with *mother* role = .52; with *husband* role = .66. Correlation of *mother* role with: *wife* role = .55; with *husband* role = .45. Correlation of *husband* role with *wife* role = .55.

## REFERENCES

Becker, H. S. (1960). Notes on the concept of commitment. *American Journal of Sociology, 60,* 32–40.

Bescher-Donnelly, L., & Smith, L. W. (1981). The changing roles and status of rural women. In R. T. Coward & W. M. Smith, Jr. (Eds.), *The family in rural society* (pp. 167–186). Boulder, CO: Westview Press.

Brown, D. L. (1981). A quarter century of trends and changes in the demographic structure of American families. In R. T. Coward & W. M. Smith, Jr. (Eds.), *The family in rural society* (pp. 9–26). Boulder, CO: Westview Press.

D'Antonio, W. V. (1983). Family life, religion, and societal values and structures. In W. V. D'Antonio & J. Aldous (Eds.), *Families and religions: Conflict and change in modern society* (pp. 81–108). Beverly Hills, CA: Sage Publications.

Fink, D. (1986). *Open country Iowa: Rural women, tradition and change.* Albany: State University of New York Press.

Gerson, K. (1985). *Hard choices: How women decide about work, career and motherhood.* Berkeley: University of California Press.

Herzog, A. R., & Bachman, J. G. (1982). *Sex role attitudes among high school seniors.* Ann Arbor, MI: Institute for Social Research.

Hiller, D., & Philliber, W. W. (1985). Maximizing confidence in married couple samples. *Journal of Marriage and the Family, 47,* 729–732.

Levenson, H. (1974). Activism and powerful others: Distinctions within the concept of internal-external control. *Journal of Personality Assessment, 38,* 377–383.

Lueptow, L. B. (1984). *Adolescent sex roles and social change.* New York: Columbia University Press.

McCall, R. B. (1970). Addendum. The use of multivariate procedures in developmental psychology. In P. H. Mussen (Ed.), *Carmichael's manual of child psychology* (3rd ed.) (pp. 1366–1377). New York: Wiley.

Naisbitt, J. (1984). *Megatrends.* New York: Warner Books.

Pitcher, E. G., & Schultz, L. H. (1983). *Boys and girls at play: The development of sex roles.* New York: Praeger.

Pollock, J. C., & Finn, P. (Eds.). (1984). *The Connecticut Mutual Life report on American values in the '80s: The impact of belief.* Hartford, CT: University Press of America.

Rands, M., Levinson, G., & Mellinger, G. D. (1981). Patterns of conflict resolution and marital satisfaction. *Journal of Family Issues, 2,* 297–321.

Raush, H. L. (1977). Orientations to the close relationships. In G. Levinger & H. L. Raush (Eds.), *Close relationships: Perspectives on the meaning of intimacy* (pp. 163–188). Amherst: University of Massachusetts Press.

Rosenblatt, P. C., & Anderson, R. M. (1981). Interaction in farm families: Tension and stress. In R. T. Coward & W. M. Smith, Jr. (Eds.), *The family in rural society* (pp. 147–166). Boulder, CO: Westview Press.

Rosenfeld, R. A. (1985). *Farm women: Work and family in the U.S.* Chapel Hill: University of North Carolina.

Rubin, Z. (1970). Measurement of romantic love. *Journal of Personality and Social Psychology, 16,* 265–273.

Scanzoni, J. (1978). *Sex roles, women's work and marital conflict.* Lexington, MA: D.C. Heath.

Scanzoni, J., & Fox, G. L. (1980). Sex roles, family and society: The seventies and beyond. *Journal of Marriage and the Family, 42,* 743–756.

Scanzoni, J., & Szinovacz, M. (1980). *Family decision-making: A developmental sex role model.* Beverly Hills, CA: Sage Publications.

Schumm, W. R., & Bollman, S. R. (1981). Interpersonal processes in rural families. In R. T. Coward & W. M. Smith, Jr. (Eds.), *The family in rural society* (pp. 129–146). Boulder, CO: Westview Press.

Spanier, G. B. (1976). Measuring dyadic adjustment: New scales for assessing the quality of marriage and similar dyads. *Journal of Marriage and the Family, 38,* 15–30.

Steck, L., Levinson, D. M., & Kelley, H. H. (1982). Care, need and conditions of love. *Journal of Personality and Social Psychology, 43,* 481–491.

Walkey, F. H. (1979). Internal control, powerful others, and chance: A confirmation of Levinson's factor structure. *Journal of Personality Assessment, 43,* 532–535.

Weitzman, L. J. (1985). *The divorce revolution: The unexpected consequences for women and children in America.* New York: Free Press.

# Life Satisfaction Among Young Adults From Rural Families*

### Stephan M. Wilson and Gary W. Peterson**

The "quality of a person's life" has been an important topic of social commentary by popular and scientific writers for a number of years (Dalkey, 1972). Despite substantial interest in this topic, the diverse definitions assigned to "life quality" have been obstacles to a thorough analysis of this concept (Bunge, 1975). In some cases, life quality has referred to (a) objective conditions of the human environment such as finances, health, and work (Liu, 1976); (b) specific attributes of people such as fatalism, ambition, and optimism (Andrews & Withey, 1976); or, (c) comparisons about a person's present circumstances versus those which a person hopes for in the future (Campbell, 1972).

A central issue in conceptualizing the quality of life is concerned with the relationship between *objective* indicators (e.g., health standards, environment, salary, and occupational attainment) and *subjective* indicators of a person's life circumstances (e.g., the self-reported satisfactions with job, marriage, housing, family life, or the perceptions of overall well-being) (Allardt, 1978; Andrews & Withey, 1976; Campbell, Converse, & Rogers, 1976; Schneider, 1976; Stipak, 1979). Critics of objective indicators as determinants of overall life circumstances argue that deeper examinations of "quality" in life experiences require knowledge of a person's subjective assessments (Campbell & Converse, 1972; Dalkey, 1972).

The distinction between objective and subjective indicators as a basis for intervention programs for rural individuals and families may determine their success. Over the last 25 years many public and private efforts addressing "objective problems" have failed to change some of the basic economic and material realities in rural areas (Dillman & Tremblay, 1977; Ross, Bluestone, & Hines, 1979). Many of the decisions, programs, and policies designed for rural America were developed by urban professionals with good intentions who confused their own worldviews with those of the rural populations they intended to serve (Gaventa, 1980). Unfortunately good intentions, "outsider" value judgments, or interventions that are incongruent with the goals of target audiences are unlikely to bring about local acceptance and long-term success (Peters, Wilson, & Peterson, 1986). The purpose of this study was to compare the relative ability of *objective* indicators of life conditions (i.e., measures of status attainment and characteristics of residence) and *subjective* measures of life circumstances (i.e., individual self-esteem and frustrations about educational requirements and limited job opportunities) to predict overall life satisfaction in a sample of low-income youth from rural Appalachia.

*Support for this research was provided by the Agricultural Experiment Station, Knoxville, TN, Projects S126 and TN682.
**Stephan M. Wilson is Assistant Professor of Family Science and Human Development, and Director of the Unit of Human Development and Counseling, Department of Health and Human Development, Montana State University, Bozeman, MT 59717. Gary W. Peterson is Professor and Chair in the Department of Family Resources and Human Development, Arizona State University, Tempe, AZ 85287.

Reprinted from *Family Relations*, 1988, **37**, 84-91.

## Issues About the Quality of Life in Rural Areas

In addition to extensive definitional confusion, nostalgic and romantic images of nonmetropolitan living are obstacles to the accumulation of scientific knowledge about the quality of life in rural areas (Melton, 1983). Persisting as a central theme in American culture is the popular belief that life is better in the pastoral atmosphere of rural areas (Korte, 1983; Photiadis & Simoni, 1983). Contrary to these idealized images of bucolic settings, however, several deficiencies exist in the objective indicators of life quality beyond the boundaries of cities and suburbs. Rural areas, for example, have lower incomes, higher levels of unemployment or underemployment, and greater proportions of citizens who live below the poverty line (Chadwick & Bahr, 1978; Nilsen, 1979). Despite these economic deficiencies, investigators have reported that rural inhabitants report greater satisfaction with their places of residence, standards of living, and family circumstances than do urban residents (Johnson & Knop, 1970; Korte, 1983; Rodgers, 1979). According to this literature, a person's "quality of life" is conceptualized as an individual's subjective perception and evaluation of various aspects of his/her physical, personal, and social conditions of living.

## Objective Predictors of Life Satisfaction

Some of the most important objective criteria of life quality in American society have been linked to upward mobility or status attainment. Consistent with mainstream American values, a person's income level, occupational prestige, and educational attainment are viewed as keys to fulfillment in life (Jencks et al., 1979; Otto, 1986; Sewell, Haller, & Portes, 1969). The assumption that progress up the social ladder will translate into greater satisfaction with life has rarely been questioned in either the popular or social science literatures on American culture. A related supposition is that various subgroups in American society (e.g., rural Appalachia) are equally committed to the values and traditions of mainstream, urban America (Brown & Schwarzweller, 1970). These assumptions about cultural homogeneity increasingly have been called into

question as the adaptive qualities of extensive regional, ethnic, and socioeconomic differences have become more apparent to observers of subcultural variations in American society (Laosa, 1984; Peterson & Ellis, in press).

Many intervention programs were designed to improve the educational, occupational, and financial circumstances of individuals and families in rural Appalachia (Southern Regional Technical Committee for Family Life, 1974). An important feature of these programs is the belief that upward mobility is a worthy goal for most (if not all) Americans and that achievements in educational and occupational settings are the primary means of accomplishing this end (Jencks et al., 1979). It appears, however, that opportunities for educational and occupational attainment are more limited in rural Appalachia than in other regions (Peters, 1983; Turner, 1982). The contradictions between these "mainstream" beliefs and the economic realities of Appalachia provided justification for examining the use of objective indicators of life circumstances as predictors of overall life satisfaction. *It was hypothesized that educational attainment, occupational attainment, and financial resources would demonstrate little if any relationships with the life satisfaction of low-income youth from rural Appalachia.*

Other investigators have suggested that rural Americans' perceptions of life quality might be predicted upon a different set of variables (Melton, 1983; Rodgers, 1979). These might include the size of one's residential community and the degree of proximity to one's childhood home. The first of these variables, community size, encapsulates a variety of issues relating to the accessibility of the social, political, and economic systems that have substantial significance for individuals and families from rural areas (Rodgers, 1979). Closely related is the special emphasis of Appalachian families on maintaining proximity to their homes of origin (Ball, 1970; Beaver, 1982; Peters et al., 1986). Consequently, both the size of residential environments and continued proximity to childhood homes may function as indirect measures of the emotional, material, and social support from extended families and communities to which individuals from rural backgrounds are accustomed. *It was hypothesized, therefore, that life satisfaction would increase as youth from Ap-*

*palachia lived closer to their homes of origin and decrease as they resided in more urbanized areas. In short, proximity to one's childhood home was expected to be a positive predictor and community size a negative predictor of overall satisfaction with life among these low-income youth.*

## Subjective Predictors of Life Satisfaction

Other observers have argued that subjective assessments of life circumstances might be the foremost predictors of life satisfaction (Korte, 1983). Self-esteem may have important implications for assessments by individuals of their overall sense of well-being. In the case of rural Appalachians, for example, one study found that their average self-esteem scores were comparatively high. This suggests that acceptance of individual circumstances is common in Appalachia and raises the possibility of positive carryover into other dimensions of life (Reed & Kuipers, 1976). Furthermore, previous investigators have reported that higher levels of self-esteem were associated with positive feelings of overall life satisfaction (Andrews & Withey, 1976; Campbell et al., 1976). *It was hypothesized, therefore, that self-esteem would be a positive predictor of overall life satisfaction among low-income youth from rural Appalachia.*

Other subjective experiences include frustrations that result from specific discrepancies between goals that individuals *aspire* to attain, and more pragmatic *expectations* rooted in the realistic circumstances of everyday life. Such discrepancies and consequent frustrations, in turn, may have important implications for the perceived well-being of individuals (Campbell et al., 1976; Mason & Faulkenberry, 1978). In short, it is the degree of incongruence between aspirations and expectations that gives rise to a person's frustration which, in turn, predicts the extent to which dissatisfaction with life will result.

Occupational attainment is a dimension of life in which subjective discrepancies may have consequences for a person's overall sense of well-being. Specifically, when job aspirations exceed job expectations, frustrations and discontent may arise to the extent that individual goals are perceived as incongruent with the limited opportunities of a

person's environment. Correspondingly, as this "opportunity gap" diminishes, and as frustration declines, increases in life satisfaction are expected to result. *Thus, it was hypothesized that discrepancies between occupational aspirations and expectations would be negative predictors of overall life satisfaction among low-income youth from rural families in Appalachia.*

Educational attainment is another aspect of life in which subjective discrepancies may have consequences for overall well-being. It is common for Appalachian youth from low-income backgrounds to have educational expectations that exceed their aspirations for schooling. Part of this is due to feelings of ambivalence of low-income parents and their youth about the usefulness of advanced education, questions about the fit between urban values of schools and those of rural Appalachia, and substantial alienation from educational settings (Photiadis, 1980; Reck & Reck, 1980). A possible result, therefore, is that frustrations and dissatisfactions will arise as educational expectations exceed aspirations and individuals feel pressured to meet higher than desirable standards for "success." *Consequently, it was hypothesized that discrepancies between educational expectations and aspirations would be negative predictors of overall life satisfaction among low-income youth from rural Appalachia.*

## Control Variables

Previous investigators have found that individuals who are brought up in families of higher socioeconomic standing (SES) often have easier access to "attainment resources" (e.g., financial resources for higher education) and are more likely to experience higher levels of overall well-being than persons from more modest circumstances (Andrews & Withey, 1976; Campbell et al., 1976; Jencks et al., 1979; Wilcox, 1981). Furthermore, the influence of gender has been identified through findings indicating that males have higher life satisfaction levels than females (Andrews & Withey, 1976; Campbell et al., 1976; Wilcox, 1981). *Therefore, the respondents' gender and the SES of their families of origin were included as control variables in relation to life satisfaction.*

## Method

### Sample

Data for this study were acquired as part of the Southern Regional Projects S-63, S-176, and S-171, a longitudinal investigation of low-income rural youth sponsored by co-operating Agricultural Experiment Stations in seven southeastern states (Southern Regional Technical Committee for Family Life, 1974). This study is part of the larger project; it is based on surveys of a purposive sample of youth who were contacted during the respondents' grade school, high school, and early adult years within economically depressed areas of Kentucky, North Carolina, and Tennessee. The baseline sample consisted of 579 mother-child pairs (287 with a male and 292 with a female child) from rural Appalachian counties of the participating states.

The original phase of the sampling design involved the selection of elementary schools in areas characterized by high levels of unemployment and poverty. Elementary schools were selected from rural areas containing nearby towns of 2,500 or fewer residents. All of the fifth and sixth graders (88%) who attended the selected schools on the day of assessment were administered the Otis-Lennon Mental Ability Test to screen out children who could not respond effectively to the project questionnaires.

Because the project objectives concerned the acquisition of a low-income sample, mother-child pairs from families of higher socioeconomic levels were excluded from the sample based on the occupational status and educational attainment of parents. The mothers and fathers of the participating youth were employed in the lower categories of the United States Census classifications (i.e., craftsmen, operatives in factories, laborers, miners, clerical workers, service workers, and agricultural workers). The mean education for these parents was 9.1 years for mothers and 8.5 years for fathers.

The present study was concerned with the subsample of 322 youth (140 males and 182 females) who responded to project questionnaires during all three phases of data collection. In the initial phase of the study, project questionnaires were administered to respondents (mean age = 11.2 years) in their fifth and sixth grade classrooms by members of the research team. The second panel of data was acquired during the respondents' late teen years (mean age = 17.1 years) with survey questionnaires administered either in high school classrooms or in the homes of those who were high school dropouts. A third panel of data was acquired during the respondents' youth or early adulthood years (mean age = 21.1 years) by mailing questionnaires to the sample members and requesting that they complete and return these instruments by mail. All of the data for the present study were acquired during the third data collection period.

The original sample size decreased from 579 to 322. Some subjects did not respond to all questions and some dropped out. Analyses for the effects of sample dropout were conducted; these indicated that those youth who participated in all three phases of data collection did not differ significantly in terms of family background and SES variables from those who were not reassessed.

### Measurement

Life satisfaction was assessed by summing scores for responses to nine Likert-type items measuring a respondent's degree of satisfaction with: (a) job, (b) income, (c) high school, (d) oneself in terms of how well he/she took advantage of high school, (e) marriage, (f) closeness to one's home, (g) size of residential community, (h) living arrangements, and (i) housing. These areas of overall satisfaction (scored on a 4-point scale where 1 was "very dissatisfied" and 4 was "very satisfied") were included because of their availability in the existing data set and use in previous studies of overall well-being (Andrews & Withey, 1976; Campbell et al., 1976). Subjects were included in the present sample only if they responded to seven or more of the satisfaction domains because some of the respondents were neither married nor were they high school graduates. Life satisfaction scores were standardized by summing the Likert-type responses for the specific domains and then by dividing these total scores by the number of domains to which an individual provided responses. The Cronbach's Alpha reliability was .73.

An initial group of predictor variables measuring objective indicators of life conditions consisted of educational attainment, occupational attainment, financial resources, proximity to one's childhood home, and community size. Occupational attainment was assessed by asking, "Now what is your present job?" Responses were classified and scored according to the prestige levels of the National Opinion Research Center (NORC) Occupational Prestige Scale (Reiss, 1961).

Educational attainment was assessed by asking, "How far have you gone in school?" Possible responses to this item designated 10 successively higher levels of education. For example, a score of 1 represented "left before finishing the eighth grade," while 10 indicated that a person "went beyond college (graduate or professional school)." Financial resources were assessed by asking respondents to check "the category that best describes the amount of money you are making (before taxes and other deductions)." The seven categories ranged from none to $1,500 or more per month.

Proximity to one's childhood home was assessed by asking, "How close are you living now to where you were living when you were growing up and going to school?" Responses to this item were scored from 1 to 4: 1 = In a different part of the USA, 2 = In a nearby state, 3 = In the same state, but a different community, and 4 = In the same community or very near.

Community size was assessed by the question, "Do you now live in the country, in a town, or a city?" Responses were scored from 1 to 4: 1 = In open country or a small town (under 10,000 people), 2 = In a big town or small city (10,000-49,000 people), 3 = In the country near a big city or its suburbs (50,000 people and up), and 4 = In a big city or its suburbs (50,000 people and up).

A second group of predictor variables measuring subjective indicators of life conditions consisted of self-esteem, frustrations about the job opportunity gap, and frustrations about educational demands. Self-esteem was measured by a scale of four Likert-type items (scored on a 4-point "disagree strongly" to "strongly agree" scale) asking respondents to indicate whether they (a) took a positive attitude toward themselves, (b) felt they were persons of worth, (c) were able to do things as well as most other people, and (d) on the whole, were satisfied with themselves. The Cronbach's Alpha reliability was .72.

Frustrations about the job opportunity

gap and educational demands were measured by the degree of congruence between the respondents' aspirations and expectations. The extent of congruence for the job opportunity gap was calculated by subtracting the subjects' occupational expectations scores from their occupational aspirations scores. Degree of congruence for educational demands was determined by subtracting the subjects' educational aspirations scores from their educational expectations scores. Absolute values for the differences between aspirations and expectations were used as the discrepancy scores for frustrations about the job opportunity gap and educational demands.

Occupational aspirations and expectations, the components of the job opportunity gap variable, were each assessed by a single questionnaire item. In the case of occupational aspirations, the item asked respondents to specify a job title that they "really would *like* to have in the future (i.e., what is *hoped* for)." For occupational expectations, an item requested that respondents specify a job title that they "*really would* have in the future (i.e., what actually is believed to be their likely outcome)." The subjects' responses to these items were classified and scored according to the occupational prestige levels of the NORC (Reiss, 1961).

Educational aspirations and expectations, the components of the educational demands variable, were each assessed by a single questionnaire item. The educational aspirations item asked respondents to specify "how much additional education or training they would *like* to have in the future (i.e., what is *hoped* for)." The educational expectations items requested that respondents specify "how much additional education or training they thought they *really would* get in the future (i.e., what actually is believed to be their likely outcome)." Subjects' responses to these items were classified according to six categories representing successively higher levels of education or training.

Socioeconomic status of the respondents' families of origin was measured by their fathers' occupational prestige. Specifically, mothers were asked to provide their husbands' job description or their own in response to an item on the project questionnaire during the initial (or grade school) phase of data collection. Mothers' responses were classified and coded according to Duncan's Socioeconomic Index (Duncan, 1961).

## Results

Research questions required that life satisfaction, a continuous criterion variable, be predicted by nine continuous and one categorical (dummy) variables; therefore, multiple regression was used. This analytical procedure determines the overall variance explained in the criterion variable and assesses the relative contribution and direction of each predictor. Specifically, occupational attainment, educational attainment, financial resources, self-esteem, frustrations about the job opportunity gap, frustrations about educational demands, community size, proximity to one's childhood home, the SES of respondents' families of origin, and the subjects' gender were entered into a regression equation as predictors of life satisfaction. To test each hypothesis, standardized (betas) and unstandardized regression coefficients were examined for statistical significance ($p < .05$). The combined predictive capacity of the 10 predictor variables in relation to life satisfaction was evaluated with the Multiple R and $R^2$ (Cohen & Cohen, 1983).

Because important gender differences have been documented in the worldviews of Appalachian men and women (Hennon & Photiadis, 1979), a dummy variable was included in the regression equation to test for gender differences in life satisfaction (males coded 0, females coded 1). Also, it was included to create terms in the model (used as

predictor variables) involving interaction between the gender-of-respondent variable and each principal predictor variable (e.g., the interaction between respondent's gender and self-esteem) to test for gender effects between each of the principal predictor variables and life satisfaction (Cohen & Cohen, 1983). Although the present sample was intentionally limited to low-income youth and families, there was sufficient variability in the SES composition of the participants (standard deviation = 9.96 on a 100-point occupational prestige scale; mean = 56.18) to warrant the inclusion of an SES control variable.

Partial support was provided for the first hypothesis, which proposed that educational attainment, occupational attainment, and financial resources would demonstrate little, if any, relationship with life satisfaction (see Table 1). Specifically, the nonsignificant betas for educational and occupational attainment as predictors of life satisfaction were consistent with the first hypothesis, whereas the positive beta (.11) for financial resources and life satisfaction did not support the research expectation.

The second hypothesis, which proposed that proximity to one's childhood home would be a positive predictor and community size a negative predictor of life satisfaction, was supported (see Table 1). The beta for proximity to one's childhood home was .14 and the beta for community size in relation to life satisfaction was –.18.

Substantial support was provided for the third hypothesis which posited that self-esteem would be a positive predictor of life

Table 1.
*Multiple Regression Results for Predictor Variables with Life Satisfaction Among Low-Income, Rural Appalachian Young Adults*

| Variables | Correlation Coefficients | Unstandardized Beta | Standardized Beta |
|---|---|---|---|
| Occupational Attainment | .14* | .00 | .02 |
| Educational Attainment | –.01 | –.02 | –.06 |
| Financial Resources | .11* | .04 | .11* |
| Job Opportunity Gap | –.23*** | –.01 | –.16** |
| Educational Demands | .11* | .03 | .09 |
| Community Size | –.25*** | –.11 | –.18** |
| Proximity to Childhood Home | .17** | .10 | .14* |
| Self-esteem | .35*** | .08 | .32*** |
| SES of Family of Origin | .04 | .00 | .10 |
| Gender | .07 | .09 | .11 |

| | | | |
|---|---|---|---|
| Multiple Correlation (R) | 0.4803 | *$p < .05$. | |
| Multiple Correlation Squared ($R^2$) | 0.2307 | **$p < .01$. | |
| F-value | 9.3243 | ***$p < .001$. | |
| Significant F | 0.0001 | | |

satisfaction. The positive beta of .32 was highly significant and the strongest predictor of life satisfaction in the regression model (see Table 1).

The fourth hypothesis proposed that frustrations with the job opportunity gap were expected to be a negative predictor of life satisfaction. This hypothesis was supported. A beta of -.16 supported the research expectation for the relationship between the job opportunity gap and life satisfaction. In contrast, the nonsignificant beta for educational demands as a predictor of overall well-being was not consistent with the fifth hypothesis (see Table 1).

While the respondents' gender and their families' socioeconomic background came close to being significant (i.e., $p = .053$ and $p = .051$ respectively), neither the respondents' gender nor their family socioeconomic backgrounds demonstrated significant betas in relation to life satisfaction. Since there was no evidence that the relationships between these two variables differed for males and females, all of the interaction terms were dropped from the final model and are not shown in Table 1. In contrast, the combined model of 10 predictors was strongly significant and accounted for 23% of the variation in life satisfaction ($R^2 = .23$).

## Conclusions and Discussion

The results of this study did not provide much support for the work of previous investigators indicating that "objective" attainment (i.e., educational and occupational attainment) leads to higher levels of life satisfaction (Andrews & Withey, 1976; Campbell et al., 1976). The subjective evaluations of life conditions of perceived job opportunity gap and self-esteem were better predictors of overall well-being than some of the most commonly used attainment variables (i.e., educational and occupational attainment). These data are consistent with research that suggests that, compared to urban populations, low-income youth from rural Appalachia seemed to place less emphasis on "objective" attainment as determinants of life satisfaction (Hennon & Photiadis, 1979; Peters et al., 1986; Photiadis, 1980; Photiadis & Schwarzweller, 1970).

Although *objective* occupational attainment was not a predictor, a diminished overall quality of life became evident to the extent that *subjective* frustrations about the job opportunity gap were increasing. Based on these results, it seems evident that rural youth from low-income backgrounds "aspire" to higher occupational levels but are frustrated by the limited economic possibilities in their environments and do not "expect" to attain their career goals. A realistic response to this dilemma is to de-emphasize attainment as a means of increasing life satisfaction and to develop other means of gaining status and improving one's quality of life.

Both the objective and subjective indicators of educational pursuits failed to predict feelings of overall well-being. One possible explanation for this is that low-income Appalachians value schooling more for its instrumental than for its intrinsic worth. That is, higher education is pursued primarily because individuals believe that further schooling provides access to material goals, rather than being an end in itself (Photiadis & Simoni, 1983; Reck & Reck, 1980; Schwarzweller & Brown, 1969). Because of the limited job opportunities, the links between educational attainment, job opportunities, and a better standard of living are not as clear in rural Appalachia as in other regions of the larger society. Compared to youth from the urban middle class, a realistic assessment of the likely (or expected) outcomes from additional schooling might conclude that educational pursuits create fewer opportunities for rural Appalachians and have fewer implications for the quality of their lives.

Self-esteem was the strongest predictor of overall life satisfaction, supporting previous research (Andrews & Withey, 1976; Campbell et al., 1976). These results suggested that individuals who accept themselves in a positive manner and believe that a similar viewpoint is shared by others will develop a more positive evaluation of their overall conditions of life.

It is important to recognize that feelings of self-worth have greater implications for the overall well-being of individuals than such indicators of life conditions as objective achievement (i.e., financial resources, occupational attainment, and educational attainment), subjective evaluations of attainment (i.e., the job opportunity gap and educational demands), and a person's place of residence (i.e., proximity to one's childhood home and community size). In addition, this finding for self-esteem supports the symbolic interactionist argument that the meanings we assign to ourselves have substantial implications for our conceptions of social reality (including personal evaluations of our overall life circumstances) and are inextricably linked to the ongoing processes of everyday life (Rosenberg, 1986).

## Alternative Avenues and Obstacles to Attainment

The availability of alternative avenues for gaining status in rural Appalachia might explain the tendency to place less emphasis on educational and occupational attainment. These alternative means of assigning status include such mechanisms as kinship ties, family name and reputation, social standing in one's church, and recognition of special talents and abilities (Peters et al., 1986).

In the area of family traditions, for example, family name has functioned in rural Appalachia for generations as an alternative means of defining a person's ascribed status or prestige. Because kin groups have acquired notoriety for certain traits that kinsmen are believed to share, having a particular family name provides youth with a kind of moral and social reputation within their communities. In other words, being industrious, shiftless, ruthless, good-natured, dishonest, or trustworthy are some of the qualities that become part of a family's reputation and provide members with a legacy for them to affirm or endure (Batteau, 1982).

Another reason youth seek attainment through alternative avenues is the limited economic opportunities of rural areas which serve as obstacles to upward mobility (Chadwick & Bahr, 1978; Nilsen, 1979). They must deal with such economic liabilities as low-income family backgrounds, residence in areas with few employment opportunities, and inadequate educational backgrounds for many of the jobs that do become available. Social mobility through occupational attainment, therefore, may neither be a realistic alternative for many low-income Appalachians nor a useful predictor of life satisfaction to the same extent as it is for youth in the urban mainstream.

The existence of obstacles to attainment and alternative means of gaining status highlight the importance of examining the

extent to which traditional measures of occupational prestige are accurate in assessing status or attainment in rural Appalachia. Additional research is necessary to determine if newer forms of measurement are required to account for the high influence of family reputations, rates of underemployment, seasonal employment, involuntary part-time employment, and relatively low salaries. Such assessment tools would more accurately portray the extent to which work settings have important implications for life satisfaction within economically depressed areas of rural America.

## Other Objective Conditions

Although occupational and educational attainment failed to be predictive, another group of "objective" conditions (i.e., financial resources, proximity to one's childhood home, and community size) fared more favorably in relationships with life satisfaction. Financial resources demonstrated a positive relationship with life satisfaction that was contrary to the first hypothesis but supportive of previous research on life satisfaction with samples from the urban middle class (Andrews & Withey, 1976; Campbell et al., 1976).

A basic error in underestimating the meaning and significance of financial resources might explain the lack of support for the research hypothesis concerned with this variable. Although initially conceptualized as more central to the values of urban populations outside Appalachia, other studies have indicated that financial resources have greater applicability to life conditions and are better predictors of life satisfaction than were originally proposed (Katona, 1972). In a study by Campbell et al. (1976), for example, income was found to be one of the strongest predictors of life satisfaction, with the most significant effects being reported for those with lower incomes. Consequently, it seems that at least a minimum or threshold level of financial security may be a "necessary but not sufficient" condition for the attainment of higher levels of life satisfaction.

The present study also confirmed earlier evidence that community size was a negative predictor and proximity to one's childhood home a positive correlate of life satisfaction. This suggests that young adults from rural areas are more likely to feel comfortable in either their childhood communities or environments with many similarities to the "home place." The respondents of this study were socialized within and seemed to be psychologically prepared for rural communities—either their "home place" or living environments with similar characteristics. The relative comfort and well-being expressed by residents of small communities reflect the belief that the personal atmosphere of rural areas has advantages over the impersonality of metropolitan areas. Compared to urban contexts, rural areas are supposed to be characterized by more frequent and positive contacts among family members and neighbors, less criminal activity, more civility, and greater frequency of helping gestures (Korte, 1983).

The importance of proximity to one's childhood home as a predictor of life satisfaction, in turn, seems to underscore the importance of family bonds as important sources of overall well-being. Because rural Appalachia has an unusually long history of extended family ties, obligations to kin, and strong familistic bonds (Beaver, 1982; Peters et al., 1986), adults who remain close to their childhood homes may benefit in terms of overall well-being from a deep and abiding sense of loyalty to one's "home place." Furthermore, close proximity to one's childhood home and family may enhance the quality of a person's life by providing psychological and material support in response to everyday stressors (e.g., alternative child care) as well as more serious crises (e.g., divorce, death, and unemployment).

## Implications for Intervention

A principal conclusion of this study is that professionals who work with low-income youth and families from this region should recognize that life satisfaction is a product of both objective conditions as defined by others and subjective definitions that a person imposes on his/her circumstances. It is both fascinating and perplexing that different individuals view and evaluate the same "objective" circumstances in very different ways. Although people may tolerate "minimum levels" of objective circumstances as an appropriate range of disparity, intense debates are waged about the exact definition of "acceptable baselines" and the consequences of conditions beyond these thresholds. Because the quality of life results from this mixture of subjective and objective conditions, professionals who work with youth and families should develop intervention strategies that target both. Specifically, unequal access to objective conditions and subjective interpretations of limited opportunities should be the focus of comprehensive intervention programs.

Policymakers should not use the importance of subjective circumstances as the basis for neglecting some obvious deficiencies in the objective conditions of rural life. Instead, reports of high satisfaction in the face of adversity might simply reflect the fact that coping mechanisms have been developed and expectations lowered in response to insurmountable obstacles. Support for this possibility was provided by results indicating that Appalachian youth from low-income backgrounds seemed capable of translating self-acceptance (i.e., self-esteem) into higher satisfaction with their overall life conditions. It would appear, therefore, that self-acceptance functioned as a coping mechanism by providing young people with the personal strength to redefine their deficient circumstances in a more positive light.

Despite the fact that subjective variables predicted life satisfaction, results from this study also indicated that financial resources played an important role in a person's quality of life. Thus, some form of income maintenance programs for low-income families might be helpful. An experimental program in New Jersey, for example, found that youth from low-income families who received income maintenance had higher levels of school enrollment, while the heads of these households were motivated to seek higher-paying jobs. Furthermore, the recipient families tended to gain rather than lose their incentives because they now had the necessary financial base to escape the vicious cycle of poverty and the realistic opportunity to seek better conditions of life in the future (Watts & Rees, 1977). Related to this is the need for economic development, though not necessarily industrial development, in rural Appalachia so that youthful aspirations for higher-paying jobs can have realistic opportunities for attainment.

On the basis of the data, politicians and practitioners would find their efforts more fruitful if they developed public policy and intervention programs that fit the distinctive qualities of their intended populations. Interventions should fit the value systems of the targeted group, be realistic, arise from local concerns, and provide meaningful opportunities for involvement and control by community leaders. Since groups may differ in the specific criteria that lead to life satisfaction, it is important that program development for rural Appalachia not be dominated by urban professionals whose world-views fail to coincide with perspectives of the targeted population. Current work on subcultural differences, for example, suggests that family life educators and other professionals who seek to improve the quality of life for low-income youth and families should refrain from using deficit models (Laosa, 1984). Instead, professionals who seek to improve the circumstances of these populations must identify and capitalize on existing family strengths as they empower families with new information and skills (Cochran & Woolever, 1983). To be successful, intervention must utilize ongoing socialization processes and provide family members with accurate information about career issues upon which youth and other family members can draw.

A fundamental strength of rural Appalachia and a source of life satisfaction is the important role that strong family bonds (i.e., measured by proximity to one's childhood home) play in the lives of those who reside in this region. Across generations, kinship has been the central organizing principle of life through which the young are taught to place family interests above individual concerns (Peters et al., 1986). Educators and school personnel can build on this source of life satisfaction by developing and implementing effective family life education programs in the schools to provide youth with greater knowledge and skills. This will enable young people to assess alternative family situations, enhance their self-awareness, develop realistic expectations, and enhance the quality of family relationships.

An important implication of the finding that life satisfaction among Appalachian youth declines to the extent that "job opportunity gaps" are perceived to exist is the development of career education programs to encourage more realistic attainment goals and minimize discrepancies between occupational aspirations and expectations. Furthermore, these programs should balance the goal of raising the occupational

aspirations of youth, with the recognition that goals may become unrealistic when adult offspring remain close to their families in areas in which economic opportunities are limited. Objectives of this kind are accomplished by providing knowledge and skills in career education programs that enhance (a) self-awareness, (b) basic academic/vocational skills, (c) awareness of work values, (d) knowledge about work, (e) work habits, (f) involvement in work roles outside the school, (g) job seeking and application skills, (h) job placement opportunities, (i) awareness of the required programs for each position, (j) knowledge about the interface between work and family roles, and (k) an understanding how the work-family interface may increase or inhibit the quality of a person's life (Haertel, 1978; Rheinhart, 1979).

Career education programs are more effective if they involve the entire school and consist of planned experiences throughout the formal education of youth. Career education should not be packaged as a separate course or as a specific experience. Instead it should be woven throughout the entire educational program of a student. Because they have frequent contact with rural families, agricultural extension agents and family life specialists from the State Cooperative Extension Service (CES) can be especially helpful in providing family life and career information to parents of low-income rural youth. Recently, representatives of CES and the profession of home economics have indicated in a national report that the development of family support systems for low-income families should be given high priority (United States Department of Agriculture, 1981).

## REFERENCES

Allardt, E. (1978). The relationship between objective and subjective indicators in light of a comparative study. In Richard F. Tomasson (Ed.), *Comparative studies in sociology* (pp. 203-216). Greenwich, CT: J.A.I. Press.

Andrews, F. M., & Withey, S. B. (1976). *Social indicators of well-being: Americans' perception of life quality.* New York: Plenum Press.

Ball, R. (1970). Social change and power structure: An Appalachian case. In J. D. Photiadis & H. K. Schwarzweller (Eds.), *Change in rural Appalachia* (pp. 147-166). Philadelphia: Pennsylvania University Press.

Batteau, A. (1982). Mosbys and Broomseldge: The semantics of class in an Appalachian kinship system. *American Ethnologist,* 9, 445-466.

Beaver, P. D. (1982). Appalachian families land ownership and public policy. In R. L. Hall & C. B. Stack (Eds.), *Holding on to the land and the Lord: Kinships, ritual, land tenure, and social policy in the rural South* (pp. 146-154). Athens, GA: University of Georgia.

Brown, J. S., & Schwarzweller, H. K. (1970). The Appalachian family. In J. D. Photiadis & H. K. Schwarzweller (Eds.), *Change in rural Appalachia: Implications for action programs* (pp. 85-98). Philadelphia: University of Pennsylvania Press.

Bunge, M. (1975). What is a quality of life indicator? *Social Indicators Research, 2,* 65-79.

Campbell, A. (1972). Aspirations, satisfaction, and fulfillment. In A. Campbell & P. E. Converse (Eds.), *The human meaning of social change* (pp. 441-466). New York: Russell Sage Foundation.

Campbell, A., & Converse, P. E. (1972). Social change and human change. In A. Campbell & P. E. Converse (Eds.), *The human meaning of social change* (pp. 1-16). New York: Russell Sage Foundation.

Campbell, A., Converse, P. E., & Rogers, W. L. (1976). *The quality of American life: Perceptions, evaluations, and satisfaction.* New York: Russell Sage Foundation.

Chadwick, B. A., & Bahr, H. M. (1978). Rural poverty. In T. R. Ford (Ed.), *Rural USA: Persistence and change* (pp. 182-188). Ames: Iowa State University Press.

Cochran, M., & Woolever, F. (1983). Beyond the deficit model: The empowerment of parent with information and informal supports. In I. E. Sigel & L. M. Laosa (Eds.), *Changing families* (pp. 225-245). New York: Plenum Publishing Co.

Cohen, B. E., & Cohen, P. (1983). *Applied multiple regression/correlation analysis for the behavioral sciences* (2nd ed.). Hillsdale, NJ: Lawrence Erlbaum Associates.

Dalkey, N. C. (1972). *Studies in the quality of life: Delphi and decision making.* Lexington, MA: Lexington Books.

Dillman, D., & Tremblay, K., Jr. (1977). The quality of life in rural America. *Annals of the American Academy of Political and Social Science, 429,* 115-129.

Duncan, O. D. (1961). A socioeconomic index for all occupations. In A. J. Reiss (Ed.), *Occupations and social status* (pp. 109-138). Glencoe: Free Press.

Gaventa, J. (1980). *Power and powerlessness: Quiescence and rebellion in an Appalachian valley.* Urbana: University of Illinois Press.

Haertel, G. D. (1978). Literature review of early adolescence and implications for programming. In National Science Foundation, *Early Adolescence: Perspectives and recommendations* (pp. 93-183). Washington, DC: U.S. Government Printing Office.

Hennon, C. B., & Photiadis, J. (1979). The rural Appalachian low-income male: Changing role in a changing family. *The Family Coordinator, 28,* 608-615.

Jencks, C., Bartlett, S., Corcoran, M., Crouse, J., Eaglesfield, D., Jackson, G., McClelland, K., Muesser, P., Oleneck, M., Schwartz, J., Ward, S., & Williams, J. (1979). *Who gets ahead: The determinants of economic success in America.* New York: Basic Books.

Johnson, R., & Knop, E. (1970). Rural-urban differentials in community satisfaction. *Rural Sociology, 35,* 544-548.

Katona, G. (1972). The human factor in economic affairs. In A. Campbell & P. E. Converse (Eds.), *The human meaning of social change* (pp. 229-262). New York: Russell Sage Foundation.

Korte, C. D. (1983). The quality of life in rural and urban America. In A. W. Childs & G. B. Melton (Eds.), *Rural psychology,* (pp. 199-216). New York: Plenum Press.

Laosa, L. M. (1984). Social policies toward children of diverse ethnic, racial, and language groups in the United States. In H. W. Stevenson & A. E. Siegel (Eds.), *Child development research and social policy* (pp. 1-109). Chicago: University of Chicago.

Liu, B. C. (1976). *Quality of life indicators in U.S. metropolitan areas: A statistical analysis.* New York: Praeger Publishers.

Mason, R., & Faulkenberry, G. D. (1978). Aspirations, achievements and life satisfaction. *Social Indicators Research, 5,* 133-150.

Melton, G. B. (1983). Ruralness as a psychological construct. In A. W. Childs & G. B. Melton (Eds.), *Rural psychology* (pp. 1-13). New York: Plenum Press.

Nilsen, S. (1979). *Assessment of employment and unemployment*

status for non-metropolitan areas. Washington, DC: United States Department of Agriculture.

Otto, L. B. (1986). Family influences on youth's occupational aspirations and achievements. In G. K. Leigh & G. W. Peterson (Eds.), *Adolescents in families* (pp. 226-255). Cincinnati: South-Western.

Peters, D. (1983). *The status attainment process in Appalachian youth.* Unpublished doctoral dissertation, University of Tennessee, Knoxville.

Peters, D. F., Wilson, S. M., & Peterson, G. W. (1986). Adolescents and rural Appalachian families. In G. K. Leigh & G. W. Peterson (Eds.), *Adolescents in families* (pp. 456-472). Cincinnati: South-Western.

Peterson, G. W., & Ellis, G. J. (in press). Countering ethnic and cultural myopia in the study of families. *Family Perspectives.*

Photiadis, J. D. (1980). *The changing rural Appalachian community and low-income family: Implications for community development.* Morgantown, WV: Center for Extension and Continuing Education.

Photiadis, J. D., & Schwarzweller, H. K. (1970). *Change in rural Appalachia: Implications for action programs.* Philadelphia: University of Pennsylvania Press.

Photiadis, J. D., & Simoni, J. J. (1983). Characteristics of rural America. In A. W. Childs & G. B. Melton (Eds.), *Rural psychology* (pp. 15-32). New York: Plenum Press.

Reck, V. M., & Reck, G. G. (1980). Living is more important than schooling: Schools and self concept in Appalachia. *Appalachian Journal, 8,* 19-25.

Reed, H. M., & Kuipers, J. L. (1976). *Rural family functioning.* Knoxville: University of Tennessee, Agricultural Experiment Station, Bulletin 562.

Reiss, A. J., Jr. (1961). *Occupations and social status.* New York: Free Press.

Rheinhart, B. (1979). *Career education: From concept to reality.* New York: McGraw-Hill.

Rodgers, W. (1979). *Residential satisfaction in relationship to size of place.* Ann Arbor, MI: Institute for Social Research.

Rosenberg, M. (1986). *Conceiving the self.* Melbourne, FL: Krieger.

Ross, P., Bluestone, H., & Hines, F. (1979). *Indicators of social well-being in U.S. counties.* Washington, DC: United States Department of Agriculture.

Schneider, M. (1976). The "quality of life" and social indicators research. *Public Administration Review, 36,* 297-305.

Schwarzweller, H. K., & Brown, J. S. (1969). *Social structure of the contact situation: Rural Appalachia and urban America* (Report 1). Morgantown, WV: Appalachian Center.

Sewell, W. H., Haller, A. O., & Portes, A. (1969). The educational and early occupational attainment process. *American Sociological Review, 34,* 82-92.

Southern Regional Technical Committee for Family Life. (1974). *Research report—baseline and experimental phases: Influences on occupational goals of young people in three Southern subcultures.* Greensboro, NC: Agricultural Experiment Station, School of Home Economics, University of North Carolina, Information Series 1.

Stipak, B. (1979). Citizens satisfaction with urban services: Potential misuse as a performance indicator. *Public Administration Review, 39,* 46-52.

Turner, E. J. (1982). *An investigation of the factors influencing the occupational aspirations of low-income Southern youth: A longitudinal study.* Unpublished doctoral dissertation, University of North Carolina at Greensboro.

United States Department of Agriculture. (1981). *A comprehensive national plan for new initiatives in home economics research, extension, and higher education.* Miscellaneous Publication No. 1405, Science and Education Administration, USDA, Washington, DC 20250.

Watts, H. W., & Rees, A. (Eds.) (1977). *New Jersey income maintenance experiment.* New York: Academic Press.

Wilcox, A. R. (1981). Dissatisfaction with satisfaction: Subjective social indicators and the quality of life. In D. F. Johnston (Ed.), *Measurement of subjective phenomena* (pp. 1-20). Washington, DC: Department of Commerce. Special Demographic Analysis CDS-80-3.

# 33

# Family Therapy with Rural Families in a Time of Farm Crisis*

**Anthony P. Jurich and Candyce S. Russell\*\***

The peaceful bucolic scene that once portrayed rural America has turned into a panorama of financial crisis, interpersonal stress, and despair with the advent of the farm crisis. Although few studies have focused specifically upon the effect of the farm crisis on rural families and communities, there has been ample mounting evidence to support the contention that rural America is undergoing a great deal of stress.

The rural family is caught between two key financial stressors. Prices for crops and livestock are in a downward spiral, while land values continue to plummet. For example, Kansas farmland values fell 20% from 1984 to 1985 (Sicilian, 1985). This situation has forced an estimated 5.55% of Kansas' 72,000 farmers into foreclosure during 1986 (Ward, 1986). Another 12.5% are in critical financial difficulty with debt-to-asset ratios of over 70%. For every five farmers who go out of business, one rural business also goes under. If this trend continues in the state of Kansas, over 200,000 rural residents (25% of the Kansas rural population) will be displaced by 1991. Nationally, this translates into 100,000 farmers per year going broke with the potential to displace as many as two and a half million people within the next 6 years (Ehrbar, 1985). The "ripple effect" of this throughout the banking industry, the farm credit system, and rural communities has the potential to destroy much of rural America.

## The Nature of Farm Family Stress

These ramifications of the farm crisis cannot help but greatly escalate the stress levels of rural farm families and their members. Farmers find themselves unable to solve the problems of rural families and feel personally distressed about the rural crisis (Braun, 1985). According to Holmes and Rahe (1967), three of the most stressful crises which people experience are death, divorce, and the loss of a job. To the farmer, losing the farm is obviously the loss of a job and source of livelihood. Jurich has been reported by Denton (1986) as making the point that displaced farmers may be under more stress than the typical worker who loses his or her job for several reasons. First, farming is quite different from other jobs "in the market." Although the farmer has many skills which may be useful in other occupations, he lacks the formal experience required by many labor unions and businesses to compete with workers who have been working full-time in those jobs. Second, the loss of the farm often requires the farmer to move geographically because of the lack of

---

*Support for this study was provided by the Kansas Agricultural Experiment Station Projects 448 and 555. Contribution No. 87-249-J from the KAES.

**Anthony P. Jurich and Candyce S. Russell are both Professors in the Department of Human Development and Family Studies, Justin Hall, Kansas State University, Manhattan, KS 66506.

Reprinted from *Family Relations*, 1987, **36**, 364-367.

jobs in his rural community. Therefore, the farmer is further displaced, often to an urban environment, from his whole life style and familiar base of operation. Lastly, the loss of a farm often means the loss of the farmer's home also. Therefore, the loss of a job spells severe displacement for the farmer. The loss of the farm is also a "death" to the farm family. A farm is a living, breathing entity. The farm has been nurtured by the farm family and they have watched it grow and produce. Losing it is like experiencing the death of a family member. As mentioned above, it is often also the death of a rural life style and a family's way of life. Finally, the loss of a farm is also a divorce. It is a divorce from previous generations in that the farmer feels that he has betrayed the previous generations who established and paid for the farm, and a divorce from future generations, to whom the farmer was expecting to leave a legacy. How do you ask forgiveness from a great-grandfather who is in his grave or from an unborn child of your daughter? These are monumental stressors whose effects ripple throughout the entire rural family.

In their Double ABCX Model of family adaptation to stress, McCubbin and Patterson (1983) predict that a pileup of stressors, such as these presently being experienced by farmers, can lead to either bonadaptation or maladaptation, depending upon the family's access to new or existing resources and their perception of the pileup of stressors. Rural areas do not have a ready access to psychosocial services as resources the way that urban environments do (Jurich, Smith, & Polson, 1983). Resources such as clinics are more distant and service is more sporadic. In addition, the deliverers of services to rural families may attempt to transplant "urban models of counseling and therapy" to rural settings, without taking into account the differences between the urban and rural settings (Coward & Smith, 1982). This tends to alienate rural families from utilizing these resources. The value characteristics of the farm family itself also serve to isolate the family from its professional resources (Jackson, 1983). Some farm families tend to see psychosocial problems as private matters which should be shared with friends and not discussed with strangers, even if they are professionals. Problems may be viewed as being created by the individual and, consequently, there is a philosophy that the individual should try to "tough it out" by

himself or herself. Because of the lack of anonymity in small rural towns, there is a greater social stigma attached to seeking services from a professional because simply parking the family car in front of the clinic can call attention to the whole town that "that farm family has problems which they can't handle themselves." This philosophy of self-sufficiency makes the farmer overtake responsibility for his farm financial difficulties, despite the fact that he or she may have little or no control over such key factors as United States bank lending policies or foreign markets. Without help in gaining perspective on the farm crisis and without access to professional resources, many rural residents find themselves sliding toward the maladaptive end of the coping continuum and turning to more destructive coping mechanisms (Fetsch, 1985).

As stress rises in a family, the appearance of social, emotional, and physical symptoms is likely to increase (Bowen, 1978; Hill, 1958; McCubbin, Cauble, Comeau, Patterson, & Needle, 1980). Any family, given enough stress, is vulnerable to the development of symptoms. However, families whose resources are low, who have a perception of stress which immobilizes them, and whose stress "piles up" onto preexisting stress are especially susceptible to the symptom development associated with maladaptive coping strategies. Twelve to 18% of the farm families who were disenfranchised reported an increase in the use of alcohol (Heffernan & Heffernan, 1986). Forty-nine percent reported becoming more physically violent (Bosc, 1985), and much of that violence was being turned toward family members (Heffernan & Heffernan, 1986). Children are beginning to show more signs of hypersensitivity, tension, and depression (Lindholm, 1986; Wall, 1985). Divorce is on the upswing (Lane, 1985). Often, maladaptive attempts at coping end fatally. Newspaper articles have well documented the trail of bloodshed staining rural America, from L. D. Hill's attempt to stop the sale of his farm by committing suicide in Georgia to Dale Burr's murder of his wife, a neighbor, and a banker, and his subsequent suicide in Iowa. In addition, since suicide is notoriously underreported, especially in rural areas (Pollard, 1985), we may be witnessing only the tip of the iceberg.

With the mounting stress of the families in rural America, new methods of coping and problem solving must be incorporated into the fabric of American rural life. The best resource to rural America is the farm family itself. If we are to cultivate this resource, families must be given access to professional resources which they can approach and utilize. Family therapy is a key professional intervention when symptoms develop, following times of high stress, pileup, and low family resources (Gurman & Kniskern, 1981). Therefore, an ongoing research project was instituted at the Kansas State University Family Center to study the rural families who came to the Center for family therapy and compare them to their nonfarm counterparts.

## Farm Families Who Seek Marriage and Family Therapy

Our preliminary data allowed us to focus on 15 rural families who came to the Kansas State University Family Center, agreed to take part in the research project, and filled out the appropriate forms at intake, at the conclusion of therapy, and at a 3-month phone follow-up. These 15 families consisted of eight intact families, five remarried families, and two single parents. The years married ranged from 2 to 19 with a mean of 5.1 years. The mean number of children was 2.2 with the range being from none to five.

Although all of these families expressed difficulties with the farm crisis, the most frequent symptom presented by these rural families requesting marriage and family therapy service at the Center was marital conflict (60% of the families). Couples reported being depressed and withdrawn, feeling confused, minimizing communication, and reporting mood swings of unusual intensity. This was disruptive of typical marital patterns and prevented the couple from coordinating their adaptations to the farm stress. Frequently one partner's solution to the economic difficulties on the farm was a unilateral suggestion which conflicted with the other spouse's feelings and goals. For example, it was very typical for one spouse (most typically but not exclusively the wife) to suggest either drastically changing the nature of the farm or the business operation or moving to the city as a solution to the farm financial stress. Rather than helping the adaptation process, such solutions most often severely raised the level of anxiety for the other partner who was trying to

cope with competing loyalties to an intergenerational family tradition that values independence and closeness to the land. These competing loyalties and heightened anxiety in both spouses increased emotional reactivity between partners and severely interfered with effective problem solving.

The children in the family also seemed to fall victim to the economic crisis in rural America. In one case, the child was a direct victim of parental maladaptive coping since the presenting problem was child abuse. However, in most cases the child was not typically directly involved in the family's monetary crisis but still felt extremely vulnerable to the mounting stress and tension within the family. The children voiced that the security of their rural life style had been threatened and, in some cases, shattered. Because of their level of cognitive development, most of these children and adolescents were so "egocentric" that they placed the blame for the farm crisis on themselves, thereby developing an overresponsibility for anything bad that happened to the family. This was exacerbated by the fact that most rural parents tried to "protect" their children by not discussing their financial crisis with their children. While the motive for this strategy of cutting off communication was understandable, it only served to increase the child's uncertainty and feelings of lack of control. Therefore, the children and adolescents either punished themselves with guilt or they manipulated others to punish them by "acting out" in a socially disapproved way (e.g., bedwetting or delinquent acts). This led to child behavior problems being listed as the presenting problem in 20% of the cases and adolescent adjustment problems as the presenting problem in 13% of the cases. In the general sample, although children and adolescents had similar presenting problems, they did not seem to take on the same type of burden of responsibility nor did they feel as "left in the dark" as their rural counterparts. Although these problems were not always the presenting problem which brought the family into therapy, almost all the children and adolescents in therapy from rural families presented a similar pattern of maladjustment.

## The Process of Therapy

The first step in therapy is always "joining." This was more important and more crucial in therapy with rural families than with their nonrural counterparts. Rural families demonstrated a greater reluctance to come into therapy. During the time 15 rural families came to the Family Center, 105 nonrural families were seen at the Center. Among those rural families who did come in for therapy, there was a greater reluctance to initially join with the therapist and open up about their family problems. During the initial sessions, 86% of the interventions were either attempts to join with the family or probe as to the nature of their difficulties. However, once this initial phase of caution was completed, most therapists found the rural families to be more open than their nonrural counterparts. Rural families seem to act cautious at first, testing to see if this professional is safe enough to be allowed to pierce the boundary of the family. However, if the therapist passes this initial test of caution, the rural family seems to open up to the therapist with less defensiveness than the nonrural family.

The therapeutic intervention used most often in the subsequent sessions with rural families was "reframing." In this type of intervention, the therapist reconceptualizes a symptom, a behavior, or a viewpoint to one which is less negative, more helpful, and more acceptable. Examples of reframing include identifying the positive function of the presenting problem or normalizing a problematic issue so as to detoxify it. This type of technique seeks to change the perception element of the crisis, utilizing McCubbin and Patterson's Double ABCX Model (1983), so as to redefine the situation in a less destructive and more useful way. By reframing the marital conflict, the rural couple can stop the pattern of mutual blame for the farm crisis and can work together as a team to cope with the farm stress. Reframing a child's or an adolescent's antisocial or delinquent acts as an attempt to remove guilt from the family and place it on the delinquent child helps the family understand the positive motivation for the child's negative acting out. The child is literally trying to "save" the family from the farm crisis. Similarly, "broadening the symptom," so as to expand the family's definition of the problem from one in which it is one person's problem to include other family members, and "identifying family myths," such as the infallibility of the mother or the children's ability to bring about a heart failure in their father if they misbehave, both

serve to give the rural family members new insight as to the existing patterns of interaction within the family. These interventions were used a greater proportion of the time with rural families than they were with nonrural families. Understanding these dynamics seemed to greatly benefit the rural families who came to the Family Center for therapy. They needed to change their "perception" of the stress and their coping strategies, and these techniques were utilized to accomplish that goal.

The other therapeutic interventions, which were used more with rural than nonrural families, fell under the category of giving the rural families more resources to utilize in coping with their farm stress. "Actualizing the family's transactional patterns" (Minuchin, 1974, pp. 140-143) allowed the family to act out their conflicts and maladaptive coping patterns in the therapy session. Not only does this allow the family and therapist to watch the family "in action" but it also encourages the family to tap their own resources for change. Because the family is allowed to interact with each other "on their own terms," they often become aware of alternative patterns of interaction upon which they can tap. The rural families at the Family Center were much more likely to receive specific training in communication techniques and problem-solving skills than their nonrural counterparts. The rural families needed to broaden their repertoire of resources in the form of exploring their own coping skills and creating new resources through communication and problem-solving skills training. The rural families seemed to appreciate the concreteness of these tasks and the relatively quick, tangible results. This seemed to fit the motif of farming in which results are tangible and concrete. To aid in the learning of these new skills, the families were asked to complete in-session tasks, such as practicing communication skills, and performing homework tasks, such as behaviorally contracting to solve specific problems. These interventions fulfilled the need of the family to expand its repertoire of resources upon which to draw when dealing with farm stress.

The therapist tended to use more straightforward and less indirect approaches with rural families than with nonrural families. The rural families seemed less inclined to metacommunicate about family structural patterns than their nonrural counterparts. While intergenerational themes were often explored with rural families in order to discuss family loyalties, a full-blown Bowen-type of therapeutic structure tended not to be the main goal of therapy. After the initial difficulty of the primary joining process, the rural families were quite open, lessening the necessity for overcoming resistance through the use of strategic techniques. Furthermore, strategic interventions in some cases served to make the rural family distrustful of the therapist.

Rural families felt very ill at ease when confronted with "teams" behind the two-way mirror. This lack of trust recreated the initial lack of trust, necessitating an energy and time-consuming effort to rejoin with the family again. Therefore, most therapists preferred to work with the rural families in direct, open, and concrete ways in which the family could receive a relatively immediate payoff. Because of this, therapy tended to be relatively short (the mean number of sessions was 9.6), especially considering the seriousness of the problems presented. Furthermore, 73% of the rural family cases were terminated by the family before the therapist felt that the family should terminate. The rural families were impatient to use their new insight and skills and be "on their own" again.

## The Outcome of Therapy

To assess the outcome of therapy with rural families, each family was asked to fill out a battery of tests at the time of the intake interview and after the last therapy session. Since the size of the rural sample was so small in comparison with the nonrural sample, no tests of significance could legiti-

mately be run. However, Table 1 contains the mean scores on the various instruments for both the husband and the wife for the rural population and the total population on the pretest and posttest.

All of the measures were in the predicted direction for both the rural sample and the total sample. Keeping in mind the small sample size, rural families showed a slightly better increase in well-being over the course of therapy than did the total sample; but their stress levels, while reduced, showed less reduction than nonrural families, with the exception of the wife's marital stress which was reduced greatly. The Spanier (1976) Dyadic Adjustment Scale Marital Satisfaction Score showed similar increases for both the rural and total populations. These scores, while indicating a therapeutic gain for both groups on all four measures, demonstrate that rural families felt very good as a result of therapy but were still experiencing higher levels of stress when compared to the general population. This may be indicative of the release of having someone to help them with their problems after the rural family's having held them in for so long. However, these scores may also indicate that, despite being helped by therapy, the stress of these rural families continued unabated in the form of the increasing level of farm stress in rural communities.

This finding is underscored by the results of the 3-month phone call follow-up. Although the rural families reported being only slightly less satisfied with their quality of life than the total sample (3.25 to 3.415 on a 4-point scale with 3 = satisfactory and 4 = excellent), their life satisfaction was far lower than the total group of therapy families

Table 1.
*Mean Scores of Husbands and Wives in the Rural and Total Samples During Pretest and Posttest on Several Outcome Measures*

| Measure | Pretest | | Posttest | |
|---|---|---|---|---|
| | Rural Sample | Total Sample | Rural Sample | Total Sample |
| Husband's Well-Being | 9.7 | 9.0 | 11.0 | 10.8 |
| Wife's Well-Being | 8.3 | 8.3 | 11.5 | 10.8 |
| Husband's Parental Stress* | 19.4 | 17.3 | 20.7 | 20.7 |
| Wife's Parental Stress* | 14.4 | 14.6 | 20.2 | 21.3 |
| Husband's Marital Stress* | 24.2 | 21.9 | 28.7 | 27.3 |
| Wife's Marital Stress* | 19.9 | 20.5 | 30.0 | 27.2 |
| Husband's Dyadic Adjustment Scale | 35.2 | 33.4 | 41.7 | 38.6 |
| Wife's Dyadic Adjustment Scale | 31.0 | 31.5 | 36.0 | 37.0 |

*These are inverse scales. The higher the number, the lower the stress.

(3.71 to 5.02). This indicated that, regardless of being satisfied with therapy, the farm stress was so overpowering that it continued to damage the family despite their newly learned perceptions and resources. The rural families reported themselves as adapting better, but the farm stress continued to eat away at their life satisfaction. In contrast to the gains in life satisfaction by the general sample, this slippage back to almost pretherapy life satisfaction is indeed disheartening. It shows the power of the farm crisis upon rural families. It also makes us shudder at the thought of how satisfied with life the rural families would have been if they hadn't come in for family therapy! Family therapy can't solve all problems. It is not a panacea. In the case of rural farm families, it may be very necessary to make an intolerable situation livable.

## REFERENCES

Bosc, M. (1985, November 18). Family life takes a beating in farm crisis. *U.S. News and World Report*, p. 62.

Bowen, M. (1978). *Family therapy in clinical practice*. New York: Aronson.

Braun, D. (1985). What distressed farmers need most. *Farm Journal*, **109** (11), 32-33.

Coward, R. T., & Smith, W. M., Jr. (1982). Families in rural society. In D. A. Dillman & D. J. Hobbs (Eds.), *Rural society in the U.S.: Issues for the 1980's* (pp. 77-84). Boulder, CO: Westview Press.

Denton, B. C. (1986). When you're losing the farm, get help for farm stress. *Kansas Farmer*, **123** (19), 29-31.

Ehrbar, A. (1985, November 11). Facts vs. the furor over farm policy. *Fortune*, **112**, pp. 114-120.

Fetsch, R. J. (1985, November). *Stress and coping on the farm: A comparison of farmers and nonfarmers*. A paper presented at the annual meeting of the National Council on Family Relations, Dallas, TX.

Gurman, A. S., & Kniskern, D. P. (1981). Family therapy outcome research: Knowns and unknowns. In A. S. Gurman & D. P. Kniskern (Eds.), *Handbook of family therapy* (pp. 742-775). New York: Brunner/Mazel.

Heffernan, W. D., & Heffernan, J. B. (1986). Impact of the farm crisis on rural families and communities. *The Rural Sociologist*, **6**, 160-170.

Hill, R. (1958). Generic features of families under stress. *Social Casework*, **49**, 139-150.

Holmes, T. H., & Rahe, R. H. (1967). The social readjustment scale. *Journal of Psychosomatic Research*, **11**, 213-218.

Jackson, R. W. (1983). Delivering services to families in rural America: An analysis of the logistics and uniquenesses. In R. T. Coward & W. M. Smith, Jr. (Eds.), *Family services: Issues and opportunities in contemporary rural America* (pp. 69-86). Lincoln, NE: University of Nebraska Press.

Jurich, A. P., Smith, W. M., Jr., & Polson, C. J. (1983). Families and social problems: Uncovering reality in rural America. In R. T. Coward & W. M. Smith, Jr. (Eds.), *Family services: Issues and opportunities in contemporary rural America* (pp. 41-66). Lincoln, NE: University of Nebraska Press.

Lane, L. (1985). The disaster nobody prepares for. *Farm Journal*, **109** (8), 32-33.

Lindholm, L. (1986, October 16). Farm children require more understanding, survey reveals. *Kansas State Collegian*, p. 3.

McCubbin, H. I., Cauble, A. E., Comeau, J. K., Patterson, J. M., & Needle, R. (1980). Family stress and coping: A decade review. *Journal of Marriage and the Family*, **42**, 855-871.

McCubbin, H. I., & Patterson, J. M. (1983). Family transitions: Adaptation to stress. In H. I. McCubbin & C. R. Figley (Eds.), *Stress and the family: Vol. I. Coping with normative transitions* (pp. 5-25). New York: Brunner/Mazel.

Minuchin, S. (1974). *Families and family therapy*. Cambridge, MA: Harvard University Press.

Pollard, B. (1985). Resume from suicide. *Farm Journal*, **109** (9), 35-37.

Sicilian, S. K. (1985). Farm crisis affects other sectors of the Kansas economy. *Kansas Business Review*, **9** (1), 27.

Spanier, G. B. (1976). Measuring dyadic adjustment: New scales for assessing the quality of marriage and similar dyads. *Journal of Marriage and the Family*, **38**, 15-28.

Wall, W. L. (1985, November 7). Growing up afraid: Farm crisis is taking subtle toll on children in distressed families. *The Wall Street Journal*, p. 1.

Ward, S. L. (1986). Rural isolation: The need for information. *Educational Considerations*, **13** (2), 32-34.